MW01234237

The Writer's Craft

WKWK

254 Elmton Street Middleton, Wisconsin 53562 phone: 608-555-

Ms. Sheri Douglas
329 Prospect Ave.
Middleton, Wisconsin 53562

Dear Ms. Douglas,

Thank you for your letter regarding the
internship program at WKWK radio station.
Please complete and return the enclosed
application as soon as possible.

Sincerely,

Rita Gomez

Rita Gomez
Director of Personnel

The Writer's Craft

SENIOR AUTHOR

SHERIDAN BLAU

University of California at Santa Barbara

CONSULTING AUTHOR

PETER ELBOW

University of Massachusetts at Amherst

SPECIAL CONTRIBUTING AUTHOR

DON KILLGALLON

Baltimore County Public Schools

SENIOR CONSULTANTS

Arthur Applebee

State University of New York at Albany

Judith Langer

State University of New York at Albany

McDougal Littell
A HOUGHTON MIFFLIN COMPANY
Evanston, Illinois • Boston • Dallas

SENIOR AUTHOR

Sheridan Blau, Senior Lecturer in English and Education and former Director of Composition, University of California at Santa Barbara; Director, South Coast Writing Project; Director, Literature Institute for Teachers

The Senior Author, in collaboration with the Consulting Author, helped establish the theoretical framework of the program and the pedagogical design of the Workshop prototypes. In addition, he guided the development of the spiral of writing assignments, served as author of the Literary Workshops, and directed the Contributing Authors in the completion of Guided Assignments.

CONSULTING AUTHOR

Peter Elbow, Professor of English, University of Massachusetts at Amherst; Fellow, Bard Center for Writing and Thinking

The Consulting Author, in collaboration with the Senior Author, helped establish the theoretical framework for the series and the pedagogical design of the Writer's Workshops. He also provided material for use in the Writing Handbooks and reviewed selected units for consistency with current research and the philosophy of the series.

SENIOR CONSULTANTS

These consultants reviewed lesson prototypes to ensure consistency with current research. In addition, they reviewed and provided editorial advice on the completed Writer's Workshops.

Arthur N. Applebee, Professor of Education, State University of New York at Albany; Director, Center for the Learning and Teaching of Literature; Senior Fellow, Center for Writing and Literacy

Judith A. Langer, Professor of Education, State University of New York at Albany; Co-director, Center for the Learning and Teaching of Literature; Senior Fellow, Center for Writing and Literacy

SPECIAL CONTRIBUTING AUTHOR

Don Killgallon, English Chairman, Educational Consultant, Baltimore County Public Schools. Mr. Killgallon conceptualized, designed, and wrote all of the features on sentence composing.

ACADEMIC CONSULTANTS

In collaboration with the Consulting Author and Senior Author, the Academic Consultants helped shape the design of the Workshops. They also reviewed selected Workshops and mini-lessons to ensure appropriateness for the writing classroom.

Linda Lewis, Writing Specialist, Fort Worth Independent School District

John Parker, Professor of English, Vancouver Community College

CONTRIBUTING AUTHORS

C. Beth Burch, Visiting Assistant Professor in English Education, Purdue University, Indiana, formerly English Teacher with Lafayette High School

Sandra Robertson, English Teacher, Santa Barbara Junior High School in California; Fellow and teacher-consultant of the South Coast Writing Project and the Literature Institute for Teachers, both at the University of California, Santa Barbara

Linda Smoucha, formerly English Teacher, Mother Theodore Guerin High School, River Grove, IL

Robert and Marilyn Shepherd, education consultants and writers, Rockport, MA

Carol Toomer Boysen, English Teacher, Williams School, Oxnard, California; Fellow and teacher-consultant of the South Coast Writing Project and the Literature Institute for Teachers

Richard Barth-Johnson, English Teacher, Scattergood Friends School, West Branch, Iowa; National Writing Project Fellow

John Phreaner, formerly Chairman of the English Department at San Marcos High School, Santa Barbara; Co-director of the South Coast Writing Project and the Literature Institute for Teachers

Wayne Swanson, Educational Materials Specialist, Chicago, IL

Joan Worley, Assistant Professor of English and Director of the Writing Center at the University of Alaska, Fairbanks; National Writing Project Fellow

Cherryl Armstrong, Assistant Professor of English at California State University, Sacramento; National Writing Project Fellow

Valerie Hobbs, Co-director of the Program in Intensive English, University of California, Santa Barbara; Fellow of the South Coast Writing Project and the Literature Institute for Teachers

STUDENT CONTRIBUTORS

Brandy Barton, Cedar Rapids, IA; Ryan Fiel, San Marcos, CA; Jason Moneymaker, DeSoto, TX; Andy Ness, Seattle, WA; Kathy O'Brill, Northfield, IL; Victoria Reilly, Bethpage, NY; Adam Shoughnessy, Watertown, MA

TEACHER REVIEWERS

Dr. Joanne Bergman, English Teacher, Countryside High School, Clearwater, FL

Regina Dalicandro, English Department Chairperson, Mather High School, Chicago, IL

Sister Sheila Holly, S.S.J., M.A., English Department Chairperson, Saint Maria Goretti High School, Philadelphia, PA

Dr. William J. Hunter, Assistant Principal, English Department, John Jay High School, Brooklyn, NY

Margaret N. Miller, Language Arts Consultant (6-12); Library Coordinator (K-12), Birdville I.S.D., Fort Worth, TX

Janet Rodriguez, English Teacher, Clayton Valley High School, Concord, CA

Mark Rougeux, English and Journalism Teacher; Newspaper Advisor, Glenville High School, Cleveland, OH

Bennie Malroy Sheppard, English Teacher, High School for Law Enforcement and Criminal Justice, Houston, TX

Sue Wilson, English Department Chairperson, Wade Hampton High School, Greenville, SC

Printed in the United States of America.

ISBN 0-395-86383-X

1 2 3 4 5 6 7 8 9 10 — VJM — 01 00 99 98 97

Contents Overview

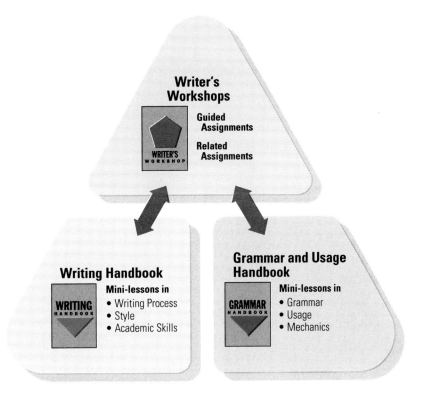

Writer's Workshops

Guided Assignments

Related Assignments

WRITER'S WORKSHOP

Writing Handbook

Mini-lessons in
• Writing Process
• Style
• Academic Skills

WRITING HANDBOOK

Grammar and Usage Handbook

Mini-lessons in
• Grammar
• Usage
• Mechanics

GRAMMAR HANDBOOK

You are an individual. You think and act in ways that are uniquely your own. This book recognizes that individuality. On every page you will be encouraged to discover techniques best suited to your own personal writing style. Just as important, you will learn to think your way through every writing task.

In each of the Writer's Workshops, you will experiment with ideas and approaches as you are guided through a complete piece of writing. Cross-references to the Handbooks will allow you to find additional help when you need it. Then, as you write, you will discover what you think about yourself—and about the world around you.

Table of Contents

For more in-depth treatment of each stage of the writing process, see the Writing Handbook, pages 324–360.

Writer's Workshops

Observation and Description

Narrative and Literary Writing

Informative Exposition: Classification

Informative Exposition: Analysis

Informative Exposition: Synthesis

Persuasion

Writing About Literature

Reports

Writing for Assessment

Writing Handbook Mini-lessons

WRITING PROCESS

Prewriting

Drafting

Revising and Publishing

Grammar and Usage Handbook Mini-lessons

Writer to Writer

DISCOVERING YOUR WRITING PURPOSE

Writing is an extraordinary application of ordinary skills. It offers you both power and knowledge in dealing with and understanding yourself and your world.

Writing as Power

▼

Writing can give you power, for we live in a complicated technological society, and those people who can collect information, order it into significant meaning, and then communicate it to others will influence the course of events within the town or nation, school or university, company or corporation.

Donald Murray, writer and educator

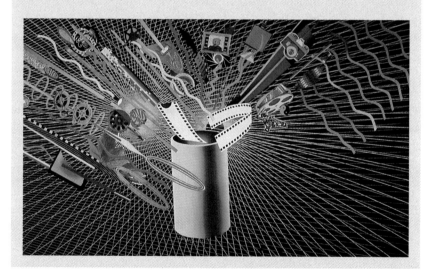

Writers, from the authors of the Magna Carta to the compilers of the NFL rule book, have shaped the world. Your writing, too, can give you power. If you have problems with a friend, school administrator, or car insurance company, you can write an explanation and effect a solution. When you enter the business world, your ideas for improvements (as well as your request for a raise) will be met with the suggestion that you "put it in writing." The more effectively you can communicate through writing, the more effective you will be in accomplishing your goals.

The Community of Writers Writing is a craft, and writers must practice it often to learn to do it well. Your progress as a writer, like the writing process itself, will be recursive rather than linear: that is, you will not always move smoothly and continuously forward in a step-by-step progression. Rather, you will sometimes jump forward, sometimes turn back to previous steps, as your writing skills evolve and you find a process that works best for you. As you establish and refine your writing process, you will receive help from your teacher, who functions as an editor and fellow writer, and from your classmates, who serve as peer planners and reviewers. In this way your classroom becomes a community of writers.

As you grow older, you begin to take your place within a larger community of writers as well. You may write an announcement for a company newsletter or an acceptance speech for an annual awards ceremony. You may write a fundraising appeal for your service group, to be mailed to business leaders within your town; you may write to an elected representative, voicing your concern and urging action. You may contribute an article to a nationally distributed periodical. Your writing reaches beyond you, broadening your sphere of communication and influence.

Collaborative Writing One of the benefits of being part of a community of writers is the opportunity to participate in **collaborative writing.** In your classroom, as your teacher directs, you may collaborate with classmates by brainstorming together, by sharing writing tasks on a project, or by working together to revise. Within the larger writing community, for example, you may collaborate with fellow members of an advisory committee to write a proposal for action. Such collaboration exposes you to a wealth of ideas and viewpoints, as well as providing you with helpful support as you write. In the business and academic worlds, in fact, much writing is produced by teams and committees.

This textbook itself is the product of a community of writers. One person could not have written it alone, nor could a group of people working individually. What you see is the result of many people functioning sometimes separately and sometimes collaboratively in a complex community. The skills you learn in this book will enable you to become a fully contributing member of that community.

Writing as Knowledge

We do not write in order to be understood; we write in order to understand.   **C. Day Lewis, essayist**

In addition to giving you power to affect the outside world, writing can give you insights into that world and, perhaps more important, into yourself as well. Many writers, both professionals and students, have observed that it isn't until they write about a topic that they discover what they think about it. Writing thoughts down is slower than simply thinking them, but writing also extends the range of complexities that the mind can deal with. For example, without writing, you could easily think up something to do on a Saturday, but you could not so easily clarify the links between Flannery O'Connor's life and the themes of her fiction. You would probably need to list events and trace connections in writing to formulate a causal analysis.

Learning logs, journals, and writing portfolios offer excellent opportunities to write for understanding. Recording what you are learning, both in and out of school, in a **learning log** enables you to clarify and reflect on what you have learned. As the number of entries in your log increases, you can watch your reflections broaden and deepen. You also will begin to see connections that enable you to integrate and use your knowledge most effectively.

In **journals,** you have a place to write whatever you like without necessarily showing it to anyone. You can explore your thoughts, clear your mind of problems by writing them out, or experiment creatively with the sounds and rhythms of language. (Some writers also keep a writer's file or sourcebook in their journals, assembling clippings, photos, bits of conversation, and interesting work by other authors.) In a **writing portfolio,** you can collect your finished pieces of writing. By reviewing the materials in your portfolio, you can track your progress as a writer, noting the development of your writing process and of your writing voice.

One thing that is always with the writer—no matter how long he has written or how good he is—is the continuing process of learning how to write. **Flannery O'Connor, novelist**

Professional writers and educators agree that the only way to learn to write is the way you learn any other skill—by doing it. In using this book, you will begin writing immediately, following the specific guidelines presented in the Writer's Workshops. While you write, you will be directed to the **Writing Handbook** and the **Grammar and Usage Handbook** for additional help as you need it.

Writer's Workshops

The **Writer's Workshops** are rich forums for writing. Each workshop focuses on a specific writing strategy or type and allows you to explore it in three different settings—a guided assignment and two related assignments.

Guided Assignments The guided assignments introduce the basic strategy or type and provide specific suggestions for completing the piece of writing. If you need additional explanation or practice as you write, you can consult the handbooks at the back of the book. These assignments encourage you to explore your own approaches.

Related Assignments Two related writing applications accompany each guided assignment. The related assignments allow you to extend the skills presented in the guided assignments with more opportunity to structure your own writing process.

Additional Writing Opportunities The book also offers many occasions to play with ideas and practice your style. The **Sketchbooks** give you the opportunity to do short, quick writings that you may or may not share or develop into a finished piece of writing. The **Sentence Composing** features provide numerous sentences from professional writers that you can use as models to improve and vary your own writing style and technique.

Handbooks

Everyone learns by different means and needs different help in the process. This text addresses individual differences by providing detailed information related to writing in handbooks that you can

consult at any point in your writing process and in any way you need—for quick reference or for thorough practice of a skill. The **Writing Handbook** covers aspects of the writing process, style, and academic skills; the **Grammar and Usage Handbook** covers grammar, usage, and mechanics.

Adapting the Book to Your Needs

Use this book in any way that works well for you as you complete a specific piece of writing. You will not necessarily use it the same way for every writing activity or the same way your classmates use it. That's appropriate, since every writing situation and every writer is different. This book provides you with the direction, background information, and flexibility you need to write well in any situation and to keep growing personally as a writer.

Discovering Your Writing Process

Whenever you write anything—a letter, a poem, an essay, or a postcard—you discover more about yourself and the world. Writing extends and enhances the familiar processes of thinking and speaking and helps you to discover new strategies for creating, communicating, and understanding ideas.

THE STAGES OF THE WRITING PROCESS

There are as many writing styles as there are writers, so your writing is bound to be highly personal—a unique expression of you and your experiences. Nonetheless, most writers work through four basic stages as they write:

- **prewriting**—getting your creative juices flowing by exploring ideas and collecting materials
- **drafting and discovery**—trying out your ideas on paper to see how they sound, how well they fit together, and where they lead
- **revising and proofreading**—reviewing your writing to evaluate how well you have achieved your goals
- **publishing and presenting**—sharing your completed writing with others

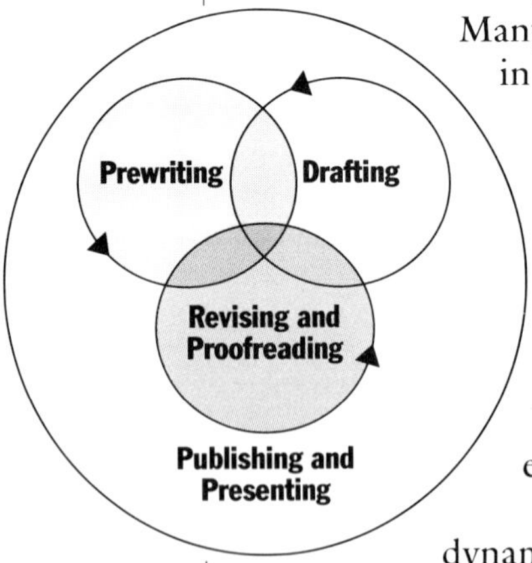

Many writers do not work through these four stages in chronological order. Some writers feel more comfortable bypassing the prewriting stage and beginning their first drafts immediately. Others revise one paragraph before writing another. Whatever process they choose, however, all writers share the same goal—to express their ideas and feelings as precisely and as eloquently as they can. So the writing process you should use is the one that works best for you and enables you to achieve that goal.

The diagram at the left illustrates the flexible, dynamic nature of the writing process.

Prewriting

Drafting

Revising and Proofreading

Publishing and Presenting

To understand the writing process in action, consider how one student, Steve, created a piece of writing for publication in a detective magazine. Notice the various writing techniques he used and how he adapted the writing process to suit his personal style.

Prewriting

At this stage of his development as a writer, Steve felt that he was ready to try to get published professionally and decided to write a piece for his favorite mystery magazine. First, he would have to choose a topic. At some point he also would have to establish a general purpose as well as his specific personal goals for writing. In addition, he needed to identify his audience, choose a form for his piece, and gather and develop information. As you analyze Steve's writing process, consider how you might approach the same activity.

Choosing a Topic Recently, Steve had watched a television program commemorating the one hundredth anniversary of Sir Arthur Conan Doyle's first story about the famous sleuth, Sherlock Holmes. The show reminded Steve of a movie adaptation of the Sherlock Holmes tale *Adventure of the Speckled Band,* which had fascinated him. Steve thought he might like to write about Doyle and his fictional detective. He began by doing some freewriting to help him recall his impressions of the Sherlock Holmes character.

ONE STUDENT'S PROCESS

Holmes is a great example of competence in action. Funny, but his pipe never seems to go out, and that cape gives him an aura of mystery and intrigue. I think it would be incredibly exciting to lead the life of an independent, respected detective. And he's always right! Always! He seems cool and distant, yet people are captivated by him. I wonder if Doyle modeled Holmes after himself or someone else he knew. If nothing else, Doyle must have shared Holmes's quick, deductive mind.

Steve then began searching for some facts about Holmes's creator. He found a biography of Sir Arthur Conan Doyle in the city library that explained how Doyle had actually modeled Sherlock Holmes after one of his medical school professors. Because Steve was very interested in movies, he also went to a local video store, where he found fourteen Sherlock Holmes titles. These included a 1939 version of *The Hound of the Baskervilles* and a 1985 adventure tale called *Young Sherlock Holmes.* As he watched these movies, Steve realized that he wanted to know why so many had been made and that he was actually more interested in the video adaptations of the Holmes literature than in Doyle himself. Steve thus decided to focus his writing on these adaptations.

Establishing a Purpose The most common purposes for writing are to **express yourself, to analyze, to inform, to entertain,** and **to persuade.** Sometimes your writing will combine several purposes. For example, if you wrote a humorous story about a bumbling detective, your primary purpose probably would be to entertain your audience. If you discussed your fondness for detective stories, you might have two purposes: to express your feelings and to persuade your audience to read and develop an appreciation for detective stories.

Writers not only establish a general purpose for writing, but they also determine specific, **personal goals** they want to accomplish. For example, you might want to analyze the appeal of an author's works, learn more about a literary character, or understand the historical context of a novel or play. Many writers determine their purpose and goals for writing by asking themselves questions such as the following:

- What do I want my writing to accomplish?
- How do I want my audience to respond to my writing?

As Steve considered these questions, he was able to bring the purpose and goals of his writing into sharper focus.

Almost everyone knows who Sherlock Holmes is, but most people probably have never thought about why so many movies are made about him. I'd like to explain why movies about Holmes are so popular. Since many of my readers might have seen <u>Young Sherlock Holmes</u> or maybe a TV version of a Sherlock Holmes story, I could start by discussing modern adaptations. Then I could describe some earlier films for comparison. This will give me a chance to talk about how filmmakers convey the drama and suspense created by good writers.

Identifying Your Audience Knowing your audience—the people who will read what you write—will enable you to determine not only what type of information you need to include, but also the best way to present that information. Sometimes your audience will be predetermined. For example, if you are writing a movie review for your school's film club, your audience is the club members. Other times you can choose who your audience will be or decide whether you even want to share your work with others.

Some writers choose to write for their own satisfaction and identify an appropriate audience later. Usually, however, you will want to identify your audience at some point during your writing process. Keeping an audience in mind will help you communicate effectively by tailoring your writing to meet your readers' needs. To help you understand your audience, ask yourself questions such as the following.

- What do my readers already know about the topic? What do they need to know to understand it?
- What aspects of my subject will my readers likely find most interesting?
- What approach and language will make my presentation most effective?

Because Steve planned all along to submit his work to the mystery magazine, he knew his audience would be readers of the magazine. He jotted down some notes about those readers to give him a clearer picture of their needs and expectations.

I can assume that my audience already knows many of Holmes's personality traits and his deductive method of solving crimes. But they will want to know how movies about him capture his personality so well—which actors played him best—and which directors succeeded in conveying Doyle's tone and mood.

Choosing a Form   Form is the type of writing in which you express your ideas. Stories, plays, essays, poems, articles, reports, speeches, letters, and journal entries are different forms for communicating ideas, feelings, opinions, and information. The best form for your writing might not be clear initially, but it may emerge as you focus your topic, consider your purpose and personal goals, and identify your audience. Since Steve already knew where he wanted to submit his piece of writing, he first considered the standards for submitting manuscripts set by the mystery magazine. These guidelines, which were listed in the magazine itself, were very broad, stating only that the material must be original work. Therefore, Steve was free to choose a form for his writing.

Suppose Steve had decided that his purpose was to entertain his readers by showing the humorous side of Sherlock Holmes. In that case, he might have written a comic play full of ridiculous clues for his hero to follow. On the other hand, if Steve had decided to write something for the community film society, he might have written a report explaining the techniques filmmakers used to showcase the mystery and suspense in Sherlock Holmes movies.

Steve had already decided that his general purpose was to analyze the screen popularity of Sherlock Holmes and his specific goal was to help his readers appreciate Holmes's character. He also knew that his audience consisted of readers of the magazine. After considering his purpose and audience, Steve decided that an article would be the most suitable form for his writing.

Gathering and Developing Information   Steve knew that to write a truly informative article, he had to do some research on his subject. He began by watching several videotapes of Sherlock Holmes movies and television presentations. He also consulted several books that included still photographs from Holmes movies. In addition, he read reviews of filmmakers' adaptations of Doyle's stories. Then he read several of the stories themselves.

The librarian who helped Steve find many of his source materials suggested that Steve interview the president of the Deerstalkers, a local club for Sherlock Holmes enthusiasts. Steve developed a list of questions and took notes during the interview. He used quotation marks to indicate the president's exact words.

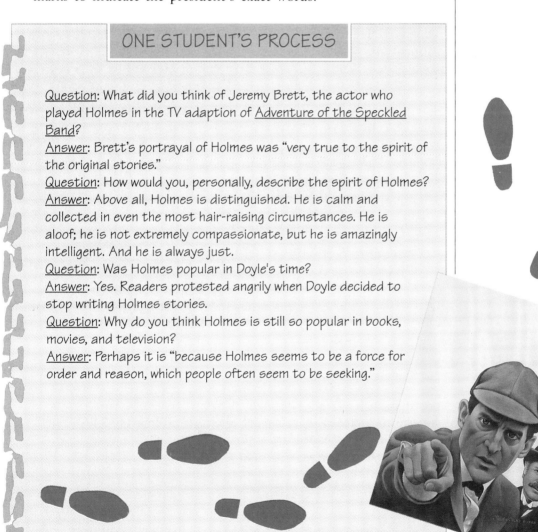

ONE STUDENT'S PROCESS

Question: What did you think of Jeremy Brett, the actor who played Holmes in the TV adaption of Adventure of the Speckled Band?

Answer: Brett's portrayal of Holmes was "very true to the spirit of the original stories."

Question: How would you, personally, describe the spirit of Holmes?

Answer: Above all, Holmes is distinguished. He is calm and collected in even the most hair-raising circumstances. He is aloof; he is not extremely compassionate, but he is amazingly intelligent. And he is always just.

Question: Was Holmes popular in Doyle's time?

Answer: Yes. Readers protested angrily when Doyle decided to stop writing Holmes stories.

Question: Why do you think Holmes is still so popular in books, movies, and television?

Answer: Perhaps it is "because Holmes seems to be a force for order and reason, which people often seem to be seeking."

Drafting and Discovery

Drafting is the discovery stage of writing—the time when you begin to create and organize your own meaning from the facts and ideas you have gathered. As you draft, follow your thoughts wherever they lead. This is the time to experiment with form and content, to change your opinions or your examples, or even to start over again with a new focus for your writing.

As Steve began drafting his article, he realized that he needed to discuss the character of Holmes in order to explain Holmes's popularity. He looked through his notes and found the following information, which he used to draft a paragraph about Holmes's personality.

ONE STUDENT'S PROCESS

o Holmes is an encyclopedia of knowledge on every subject.
o Holmes is an intellectual, not just another brawny superhero.
o Holmes is always cool and rational, even in the most terrifying situations.
o Everyone daydreams about being as brilliant, self-assured, and invincible as Holmes.

As he drafted, Steve also discovered that his notes contained some information about famous actors who have portrayed Sherlock Holmes. He decided to include a few paragraphs in his article about these actors because he felt they had helped make Sherlock Holmes a popular character. As he looked over the information in his notes, Steve realized he would need more details and anecdotes about the actors.

Like Steve, you can use the drafting stage to expand, alter, or refocus your topic. You may find that you want to backtrack, change your purpose, or broaden your personal goals for writing. Feel free to experiment as you draft. Don't worry about making mistakes in grammar, usage, or the mechanics of writing. You will have the opportunity to correct errors, consider effective word choice, and check your logic later in the writing process.

Because drafting is a discovery process, it usually involves some amount of revision. Some writers continually rework and reshape their writing as they draft. Others write first and revise later. You may find that your first draft needs very little revision; or you may need to write several drafts. You might want to reconsider your audience and purpose for writing. You may need to experiment with form, conduct additional research, or even rethink your topic. No matter how much you revise as you draft, pay attention to the direction your writing is taking, and keep the following questions in mind:

- **Content** Are you developing your initial ideas or focusing on just one or two details? Is a new idea emerging as the real focus of your work? If your writing is taking a new direction, do you want to pursue that or return to your original ideas? What questions might your readers ask?
- **Structure** What are the relationships among the ideas you are expressing—spatial, temporal, causal, comparative? How can you organize your ideas so that they will clearly express these relationships? If your ideas have changed since you began drafting, how should you restructure your writing?

Peer Response

One way to help solve a problem in your life, clarify an idea, or find a new way of doing something is to talk things over with friends. The same strategy can also work when you're writing. Discussion with your peers can help you at any stage of the writing process—to find new ideas, see your subject from a different perspective, or identify problems in logic, mechanics, or usage. Peer responses enable you to see your own writing more clearly and objectively.

After finishing his first draft, Steve set it aside for a few days. When he reread it, he wanted to change it but wasn't sure how. He had some friends read his draft and respond to these questions:

- What did you like best about my article? least?
- Were there any parts that seemed confusing or dull?
- What message am I trying to get across?
- What did you want to know more about?
- Was the beginning interesting?
- What did you think about the ending?

Here are some of the responses Steve received from his friends.

Your introduction really captured my interest.

How? What did he look like?

Who? How did their portrayals differ from Rathbone's?

"Elementary, my dear Watson." With those four words, Sherlock Holmes dismisses the most complex deductive processes as child's play. Playing that superhuman character, however, could hardly have been easy for the actors who portrayed Holmes. The actor most identified with Sherlock Holmes was Basil Rathbone. Rathbone looked the part. Movie audiences must have agreed, since Rathbone played Holmes many times. The first Rathbone film was <u>Hound of the Baskervilles.</u> This film is highly regarded. Later films, set in wartime London, are less popular. Many other notable actors besides Rathbone have portrayed Sherlock Holmes.

Revising

After rereading his draft and considering his friends' responses, Steve reevaluated his writing and was ready to revise his article.

Like Steve, you should set your draft aside for a few hours—or even days—before revising. When you reread what you have written, you will better be able to evaluate whether you have achieved your general purpose and your personal goals.

As you revise, consider your peer readers' comments carefully. However, make only those changes that you believe will improve your piece. If you do decide to make a change, determine what kind of revision it requires:

- Rethinking content
- Reworking structure
- Refining mechanics and usage

Content Your peer readers' comments, new information or perspective, or knowledge that you have reached a dead end in your writing may lead you to revise its content. You may find that you can improve your draft by reworking it; or you might want to try some different prewriting activities or perhaps even to change the subject of your writing.

When you consider the content of your writing, ask yourself whether you have expressed your main ideas clearly. Also make sure you have developed your ideas fully. The "Checklist for Rethinking Content" on page 392 includes additional questions to consider.

Structure When you are satisfied that your content is clear and fully developed, consider whether your writing is organized as effectively as possible. Look over your peer readers' comments to see if any of them had trouble following your ideas. If you decide to rework the structure of your writing, examine its overall organization. Make sure you have included all the necessary information and arranged it logically. Examine your transitions to make sure they effectively connect your ideas and show the relationships between them. Finally, eliminate any details that blur the focus of your writing. Refer to the "Checklist for Reworking Structure" on page 394 for additional suggestions.

Mechanics After you have revised your content and structure, you can refine and polish your writing by editing, or proofreading, your work. Review your work carefully to make your sentences clear and concise and to correct errors in punctuation, spelling, grammar, and usage. See the "Checklist for Refining Mechanics" and the standard revising and proofreading marks on pages 394–395.

Steve used these marks when he revised his first draft. Notice that he incorporated many of the changes suggested by his peer readers. He also corrected errors he found in the structure and mechanics of his writing.

These two sentences will read more smoothly if I combine them.

This sentence has nothing to do with Rathbone.

"Elementary, my dear Watson." With those four words, Sherlock Holmes dismisses the most complex deductive processes as child's play. Playing that superhuman character, however, could hardly have been easy for the actors who portrayed Holmes. The actor most identified with Sherlock Holmes was Basil Rathbone. Rathbone looked the part. Movie audiences must have agreed, since Rathbone played Holmes many times. The first Rathbone film was Hound of the Baskervilles. This film is highly regarded. Later films, set in wartime London, are less popular. Many other notable actors besides Rathbone have portrayed Sherlock Holmes.

Publishing and Presenting

For most writers, sharing their finished work is the final stage of the writing process. You may choose not to share journal writing or writing that you feel is incomplete or very personal. You may also continue revising your work even after sharing it. However you choose to handle the publishing and presenting process, you can find many exciting avenues for sharing your work.

Reader's circles Form a reader's circle with at least three other students. Take turns reading your writing to the group and discussing the ideas it conveys and the feelings it evokes.

Writing exchange groups As a class, share your writings with students from another class or school.

Collected works Publish an anthology of student work. The anthology might focus on a particular form or on writings about a particular subject.

Print media Submit your writing to your school or community newspaper or to a magazine.

Performances Dramatize your work and produce it for your class, school, or community.

Videos and multimedia presentations Create a video or multimedia expression of your work. Enhance your writing by using music, slides, pantomime, acting, dance, or a combination of these art forms to accompany it.

Portfolios Collect your work in a file and reread it occasionally. Choose the pieces you like best and mount them in a portfolio of your writing. Use the portfolio as a sample of your work or as a measure of your progress from month to month.

EXTENDING YOUR WRITING PROCESS

You can learn and grow as much from how you write as from what you write. Whenever you finish a piece of writing, reflect on your writing experience as well as your finished product. Ask yourself questions such as the following to help you better understand your process.

- Did I become involved in my topic and learn something important about it?
- Which stages of the writing process were easiest for me? Which were most difficult?
- What part of my writing process is getting easier?
- What was the biggest problem I encountered during my writing process? What solution did I find? How can I use this experience to improve my writing process next time?
- When I compare this piece of writing with others in my portfolio, do I see any changes in my writing style?
- What features of my peers' or professional writers' work would I like to experiment with in my own writing?
- How can I apply the skills I have learned?

Write the answers to these questions and attach them to your finished work before placing it in your portfolio. This record of your writing process will help you become more aware of your progress and goals as a writer and help you attain them.

Swinging, by Vasily Kandinsky, 1925

Writer's Workshops

Sketchbook

A writer's sketchbook, like an artist's, is a place to experiment with ideas. Use the words and images on the Sketchbook pages that appear throughout this book as invitations to sketch out ideas and have fun exploring them. You may find that you will want to refine some sketches later, but for now, just see where your thoughts take you.

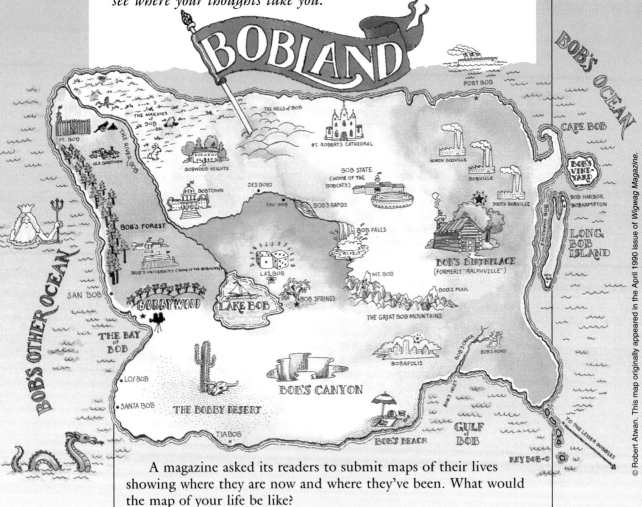

A magazine asked its readers to submit maps of their lives showing where they are now and where they've been. What would the map of your life be like?

Personal and Expressive Writing

Guided Assignment
REFLECTIVE ESSAY

Related Assignment
AUTOBIOGRAPHICAL INCIDENT

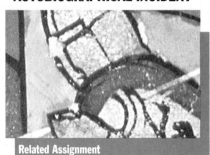

Related Assignment
MONOLOGUE

All your life you've been learning lessons from the world's best teacher—experience. This teacher has taught you how to manage in your daily life—how to be the best person you can be, how to cope with adversity, how to help yourself and others, how to share joy and sorrow. Much writing that illustrates basic truths about human nature draws on lessons taught by experience.

In the following guided assignment, you will consider some important personal experience and explain what it taught you about life. In the related assignments, you will investigate your past for help in writing an autobiographical narrative and a monologue.

21

Reflective Essay

HUNGER

— OF MEMORY —

BY RICHARD RODRIGUEZ

Reflective writing employs memories of a past event to make a statement about human experience. As a small boy Richard Rodriguez came to the United States from Mexico with his family. In this excerpt from his autobiography *Hunger of Memory*, Rodriguez uses his mother's reactions to his first published essay to reflect on the life and obligation of a writer.

I am writing about those very things my mother has asked me not to reveal. Shortly after I published my first autobiographical essay seven years ago, my mother wrote me a letter pleading with me never again to write about our family life. "Write about something else in the future. Our family life is private." And besides: "Why do you need to tell the *gringos* about how 'divided' you feel from the family?"

I sit at my desk now, surrounded by versions of paragraphs and pages of this book, considering that question.

When I decided to compose this intellectual autobiography, a New York editor told me that I would embark on a lonely journey. Over the noise of voices and dishes in an East Side restaurant, he said, "There will be times

when you will think the entire world has forgotten you. Some mornings you will yearn for a phone call or a letter to assure you that you still are connected to the world." There have been mornings when I've dreaded the isolation this writing requires. Mornings spent listless in silence and in fear of confronting the blank sheet of paper. There have been times I've rushed away from my papers to answer the phone; gladly gotten up from my chair, hearing the mailman outside. Times I have been frustrated by the slowness of words, the way even a single paragraph never seemed done.

I had known a writer's loneliness before, working on my dissertation in the British Museum. But that experience did not prepare me for the task of writing these pages where my own life is the subject. Many days I feared I had stopped living by committing myself to remember the past. I feared that my absorption with events in my past amounted to an immature refusal to live in the present. Adulthood seemed consumed by memory. I would tell myself otherwise. I would tell myself that the act of remembering is an act of the present. (In writing this autobiography, I am actually describing the man I have become—the man in the present.)

Times when the money ran out, I left writing for temporary jobs. Once I had a job for over six months. I resumed something like a conventional social life. But then I have turned away, come back to my San Francisco apartment to closet myself in the silence I both need and fear.

I stay away from late-night parties. (To be clear-headed in the morning.) I disconnect my phone for much of the day. I must avoid complex relationships—a troublesome lover or a troubled friend. The person who knows me best scolds me for escaping from life. (*Am* I evading adulthood?) People I know get promotions at jobs. Friends move away. Friends get married. Friends divorce. One friend tells me she is pregnant. Then she has a baby. Then the baby has the formed face of a child. Can walk. Talk. And still I sit at this desk laying my words like jigsaw pieces, a fellow with ladies in housecoats and old men in slippers who watch TV. Neighbors in my apartment house rush off to work about nine. I hear their steps on the stairs. (They will be back at six o'clock.) Somewhere planes are flying. The door slams behind them.

"Why?" My mother's question hangs in the still air of memory.

The loneliness I have felt many mornings, however, has not made me forget that I am engaged in highly public activity. I sit here in silence writing this small volume of words, and it seems to me the most public thing I have ever done. My mother's letter has served to remind me: I am making my personal life public. Probably I will never try to explain my motives to my mother and father. My mother's question will go unanswered to her face. Like everything else on these pages, my reasons for writing will be revealed instead to public readers I expect never to meet.

Think AND Respond

Richard Rodriguez uses this essay to reveal important truths about life as a writer. What kinds of details does he use to create a strong portrait of a writer's life? How does he vary his sentences to strengthen the impact of his essay? What incidents from your own life revealed important truths to you?

INVITATION
TO
Write

Writing *Hunger of Memory* taught Richard Rodriguez important lessons about life as a writer. Now write your own reflective essay based on an experience that taught you a lesson about life.

When you write a reflective essay, you do not simply narrate an important personal experience. You take that experience one step farther by showing its larger significance—how it reflected or underscored some important truth about life. Reflective writing enables you to share a part of your life with your readers and also prompts them to think about similar experiences in their own lives. Autobiographies, letters, and memoirs frequently contain reflective writing.

PREWRITE AND EXPLORE

FOR HELP & PRACTICE

Writing Variables, p. 329

Reflecting, pp. 331–332

Hypothesis Testing, p. 472

1. Look for ideas. Try some of the following activities to help you remember experiences in your life that have taught you important lessons about the world and your place in it.

Exploratory Activities

- **Experience inventory** Freewrite about some "first experiences" and some "most experiences." Use the following suggestions to get started, but feel free to add any others you wish: the first time I was left on my own, the first time an adult really listened to me, the first time I fell in love, the first time I knew I was grown up, the most foolhardy thing I ever did, the most embarrassing thing that ever happened to me, the most courageous moment of my life.
- **Photoplay** Look through an album of family photographs. Do the photos remind you of any special experiences from your past? Freewrite in your journal about any remembrances of people and places suggested by these photographs.

- **Heroes and heroines** A reflective essay can also be based on an incident from the life of someone you admire. Make a list of people who inspire you. What have these people done to earn your admiration? Jot down some notes about an incident from each person's life that best illustrates his or her heroic qualities.

Teacher Gloria de Souza developed a unique approach to education that has made her an important force for change and improvement in India's schools.

- **Reading literature** A line from a story, play, or poem can often spark memories of past experiences. What personal experiences do the following quotes from literature suggest to you? Add any of your favorite literary quotes to this list and respond to them as well.

"It was the best of times, it was the worst of times."

Charles Dickens

"I have always depended on the kindness of strangers."

Tennessee Williams

"He feared most of all the choices, that cried to be taken."

Gwendolyn Brooks

"Fame is a fickle food . . ." **Emily Dickinson**

2. Choose an idea. The prewriting activities you've engaged in should have yielded a long list of remembrances—both personal experiences and the experiences of others. If you are still searching for ideas, check your journal, look at the writing you did for the Sketchbook on page 20, or try the suggestions in "Apply Your Skills" on page 37. Then decide which of the experiences you've come up with would make the best subject for a reflective essay. To make an effective choice, keep in mind the purpose of reflective writing—to relate an incident from your past or from the life of another person and show how it illustrates some basic truth about human nature or experience.

Look through your list for experiences that will enable you to fulfill this purpose. You might want to talk over some possible choices with classmates. Which experience interests them most? Why? Which experience do they feel teaches an important lesson? Do any of their experiences remind you of incidents in your own life?

PROBLEM SOLVING

What experiences have had special meaning to me?

Reflective Essay **25**

3. Explore your idea. Reflecting on a subject means giving it complete and thoughtful consideration. As you reflect on the meaning of the experience you've chosen, don't settle for its most obvious significance. Your essay will be more meaningful if you dig a little deeper. In fact, *digging* is a good way to explore the significance of your experience.

Imagine you're an archaeologist exploring the remains of some ancient village. As you uncover one layer of artifacts—pottery fragments, tools, bits of jewelry—you learn something about the people who inhabited this village. If you stop at the first level, however, your information will be incomplete. So you uncover a second layer, and then a third, and so on until a complete picture of the village begins to emerge.

You can apply the same process to your idea. Write down the most obvious lesson you learned from your experience. That's the first level of meaning. Then think about what you've written. What else did your experience teach you? Write two sentences or phrases that extend the lesson you want to communicate. Now you have a second level of meaning. Continue in this manner until you've thoroughly considered your subject. Then use your reflections to write a sentence or two that state the true significance of your experience—the deepest level of meaning.

Shawn decided to write about a sports injury that helped him see his life from a different perspective. Throughout this guided assignment, you will follow Shawn's process as he completes his essay. Here's how he reflected on the significance of his experience. Notice how that significance evolved as he dug deeper and uncovered new levels of meaning.

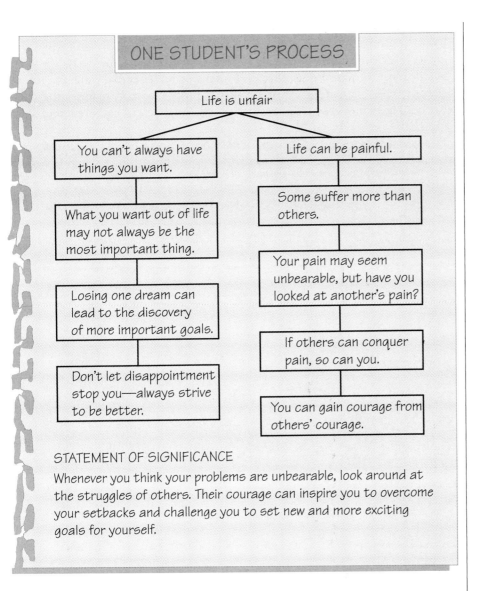

ONE STUDENT'S PROCESS

Life is unfair

You can't always have things you want.

What you want out of life may not always be the most important thing.

Losing one dream can lead to the discovery of more important goals.

Don't let disappointment stop you—always strive to be better.

Life can be painful.

Some suffer more than others.

Your pain may seem unbearable, but have you looked at another's pain?

If others can conquer pain, so can you.

You can gain courage from others' courage.

STATEMENT OF SIGNIFICANCE

Whenever you think your problems are unbearable, look around at the struggles of others. Their courage can inspire you to overcome your setbacks and challenge you to set new and more exciting goals for yourself.

4. Identify narrative elements. A reflective essay relates a personal experience. Sometimes that experience is mentioned only briefly, however, and the writer focuses the major part of the essay on his or her reflections about the experience. In his essay, for example, Richard Rodriguez included some narration of what life was like for him as he wrote his autobiography. Rodriguez, however, spent most of his time thinking about how the experience affected him.

PROBLEM

S O L V I N G

How will I convey my experience and its impact?

Reflective Essay   **27**

A good narrative has characters, a plot, some type of conflict, and a theme. It also creates a feeling of tension or suspense about the outcome. Think about the story that will be part of your essay. As you do, list the elements that will make it an effective narrative. Identify the characters. Write a brief plot summary. State the conflict. Explain what will create the tension. Describe the theme. The theme is likely to be the statement of significance you wrote after you reflected on your experience. Notice how Shawn planned the narrative section of his essay.

ONE STUDENT'S PROCESS

o <u>Characters</u>—me and Darren, my physical therapist
o <u>Plot</u>—I am injured in a baseball game. After surgery, I learn I won't be able to play baseball anymore. I enter rehabilitation with a bad attitude. Darren shows me the burn unit at the institute. I learn to look at life differently.
o <u>Conflict</u>—I feel if I can't play baseball, my life is just about over. I don't want to do well in rehabilitation—I fight it.
o <u>Tension</u>—Will I give up rehabilitation? Will I change my attitude? Can Darren help me to care?
o <u>Theme</u>—When your problems seem unbearable, look at the struggles of others who are less fortunate. Their courage can inspire you to set new and exciting goals for yourself.

 Writer's Choice   Your essay can be primarily narrative or mainly reflective, depending on the type of experience you have to relate.

What do I want my readers to come away with?

5. Try collaborative planning.   Discuss your plans for your reflective essay with a partner. Cover the following issues:

- Your goals—what your readers will learn, think, or feel
- Your audience—who your readers are likely to be and how difficult it may be for them to understand your point of view

1. Begin drafting. If you are writing your essay as a narrative, use your plot summary as a skeleton outline for your draft. Conflict should be apparent but does not need to be stated directly. If you focus on reflections about an incident, look for examples, anecdotes, and analogies you can use to clarify your reactions and make the significance of your experience clear to your readers.

2. Organize your essay. The following strategies can help you express your ideas clearly.

Strategies

- **Chronological order** The most common way to arrange narrative events is in the order in which they occurred.
- **Flashback** A flashback takes the reader to an event that happened prior to the present. Consider using a flashback to explain some past event that clarifies the actions in the present. Richard Rodriguez, for example, writes in the present but uses flashbacks to recall events from the past.
- ***In medias res*** This Latin phrase means "into the midst of things." A writer might begin a mystery story with a murder and then circle back to the events that led up to the murder. Consider beginning your essay in the middle or even at the end to emphasize the significance of an experience.

3. Elaborate on ideas. Precise, vivid words and images will enhance your narration and help you convey the significance of your reactions. Here are some descriptive strategies to try.

- **Simile** A **simile** is a comparison using such words as *like, as,* or *resembles.* Rodriguez used a simile to suggest the difficulty of writing: "I sit at this desk laying my words like jigsaw pieces."
- **Metaphor** A **metaphor** is a comparison between two unlike things that doesn't use such words as *like, as,* or *resembles.* Instead, a metaphor is *implied.* Rodriguez made an implied comparison between still air and memory when he wrote "My mother's question hangs in the still air of memory."
- **Personification** Humans and inanimate objects may be compared through the use of **personification**—endowing the objects with human qualities.

  The ancient DeSoto's engine **protested, coughed,** and **died.**

HANDBOOKS

FOR HELP & PRACTICE

Organizing Your Work, pp. 349–357

Drafting Styles, pp. 361–362

Elaborative Details, pp. 376–378

Figurative Language, pp. 435–436

PROBLEM

S O L V I N G

What are effective ways to present my ideas?

• **Analogy** An **analogy** is also a comparison, one that stresses how two different things are alike.

> Kelly approaches her schoolwork the same way a worker bee lives out its life—it's all work and no play day after day.

Shawn began his draft by using precise, vivid language to narrate the incident during which he was injured. Then he described in chronological order what happened during his recuperation and what happened to change his viewpoint about his experience. He concluded by explaining the significance of the experience to him. The following is the beginning of Shawn's unrevised first draft.

ONE STUDENT'S PROCESS

Three years ago this spring, I thought my life had come to an end. On a warm, breezy afternoon in May, I stood on first base during the final inning of a varsity baseball game between my team, the Summervale Panthers, and the team from Roosevelt High. As Roosevelt's pitcher leaned in for the sign, I took a long lead off first base, intending to break toward second with the pitch. As the ball sailed toward the plate, I took off. I slid into second, headfirst, my right arm reaching for the bag. Then the shortstop hurried over to take the throw from the catcher. He stumbled and fell. His knee landed hard on the elbow of my outstretched arm. I heard a loud crack and felt a sharp stab of pain. Then I passed out.

4. Set your essay aside. After you complete the first draft of your essay, take a break. Then go back to the essay, rereading it and sharing it with several peer readers. Use questions such as the following to help you recognize the strengths and weaknesses in what you have written.

Questions for Yourself

- Are the events in my essay presented in an orderly way?
- Have I used description effectively?
- Is the significance of my experience clear?
- Have I related my experience clearly to the lesson I believe I learned?

Questions for Your Peer Readers

- Did I make it clear why my experience holds such significance for me?
- Did my essay hold your interest? Where, if anywhere, did you feel your interest lagging?
- Is any part confusing? What makes that part unclear?
- When you finished reading my essay, what did you think, feel, or want to do?
- Do my reflections hold true in your life as well? How?

R EVISE   YOUR   WRITING

1. Evaluate your responses. Think about your own responses to your essay and the responses of your peer readers. Consider which ideas would improve the essay. Also consider that an effective reflective essay usually displays certain basic characteristics.

Standards for Evaluation

An effective reflective essay . . .

- is written from the first-person point of view.
- tells about an important experience in the writer's life or in the life of someone the writer admires.
- uses the writer's experience to make a general observation about life.
- encourages readers to think about the significance of the writer's experience in light of their own lives.
- uses precise, vivid descriptive language and images.

FOR HELP & PRACTICE

Unity and Coherence, pp. 382–391

Peer Response, pp. 397–400

Dialogue in Nonfiction, p. 455

2. Problem-solve. Carefully consider your draft in light of your own responses, your peer reader's comments, and the Standards for Evaluation. Think about which suggested revisions are in keeping with your goals and audience. Decide which changes you will make. Then rework your draft. Shawn made the following changes to one section of his reflective essay. Look at the suggestions of one peer reader and notice how Shawn responded to these suggestions.

ONE STUDENT'S PROCESS

After a worried, whispered consultation, the doctors called in a specialist to perform emergency reconstructive surgery.

I was rushed to the hospital emergency room. As I lay in bed following the operation, my arm encased in plastar, the surgeon delviered her verdict. The surgery, she said, had gone well. The bones in my arm would knit together again, and there would be almost no scarring, however, I had suffered no simple broken arm. I

The bones around the elbow joint had shattered, and

had a compound fracture of my elbow and forearm. I was going to need quite a bit of physical therapy to regain the normal use of my arm.

"And I'm afraid, she said, that your baseball playing

Your elbow will never withstand the stress of throwing a ball with any velocity.

days are over." She said some other things, too, but I was too stunned to listen.

Exciting but also confusing. You skip too fast to what happens after the operation.

I like the way tension builds here.

I could use more information. What's a compound fracture? Why can't you play baseball anymore?

3. Proofread your essay. After you've revised your essay, prepare a clean copy. Read this copy carefully, looking especially for errors in grammar, usage, punctuation, and spelling. Since it is often difficult to see your own mistakes, you might also want to have a friend read your essay to look for any mistakes you might have missed. Neatly correct any errors you find.

Quotation Marks

If your essay is narrative, you may be including dialogue. Review the following rules for using quotation marks.

1. Periods and commas appear inside the quotation marks.

   "Put these on," he said.

2. Question marks or exclamation points appear inside the quotation marks when they are part of the quoted material and outside when they are not.

   Bob wheeled around and shouted, "I don't believe it!" Did he really say, "I've never been more bored"?

3. When a quotation is divided, both parts appear in quotation marks. The first word of the second part of the quotation is capitalized only if it begins a new sentence.

   "I want to know," she said, "when the play begins."

4. Begin a new paragraph each time the speaker changes.

See Grammar Handbook 41 for additional help.

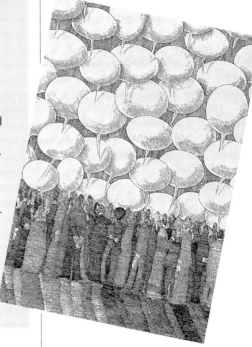

PUBLISH AND PRESENT

- **Publish a book.** With your classmates, turn your essays into a book. Decide on a way to organize the essays—in alphabetical order by author, for example, or by general topic. Create a table of contents. Then copy and bind the essays into book form.
- **Present the essay orally.** Form a small group with classmates and read your essays aloud. Share positive comments about one another's work, and talk about ways the essays reflect experiences that are universal.
- **Create a personal essay collection.** Begin collecting your writing about your experiences. Such a collection can help you probe your feelings and give other readers insights into who you are.
- **Save your reflective essay in your writing portfolio.**

FOR HELP & PRACTICE

Preparing Manuscript, pp. 414–415

Out at Second

Shawn O'Malley

Narrative begins with a strong description

Three years ago this spring, I thought my life had come to an end. On a breezy afternoon in May, I stood on first base during the final inning of a varsity baseball game between my team, the Summervale Panthers, and our rivals from Roosevelt high. As Roosevelt's pitcher leaned in for the sign, I took a long lead off first base, intending to break toward second with the pitch. As the ball sailed toward the plate, I took off, digging my spikes into the infield dirt. I slid into second, headfirst, my right arm reaching for the bag. As the shortstop hurried over to take the throw from the catcher, he stumbled and fell. His knee landed hard on the elbow of my outstretched arm. I heard a loud crack and felt a sharp stab of pain. Then I passed out.

I was rushed to the hospital emergency room. After a worried, whispered consultation, the doctors called in a specialist to perform emergency reconstructive surgery. As I lay in bed following the operation, my arm encased in plaster, the surgeon delivered her verdict. The surgery, she said, had gone well. The bones in my arm would knit together again, and there would be almost no scarring. However, I had suffered no simple broken arm. I had a compound fracture of my elbow and forearm. The bones around the elbow joint had shattered, and I was going to need quite a bit of physical therapy to regain the normal use of my arm.

"And I'm afraid," she said, "that your baseball-playing days are over. Your elbow will never withstand the stress of throwing a ball with any velocity.'' She said some other things, too, but I was too stunned to listen.

More than my elbow was shattered that afternoon. I had been playing baseball since I was able to walk—T-ball, Little League, junior varsity, varsity. I was counting on a baseball scholarship to pay my college expenses. My best friends—my only friends—were the guys on the team. Now it seemed as if everything had been taken away from me.

Suggests the conflict of the narrative

Six weeks later, the cast came off and physical therapy began. During those six weeks, I grew nearly impossible. I spoke to almost no one, and when I did I either lashed out in anger or whined in complaint. My family and friends stopped trying to deal with my mood swings. They left me alone, and I sulked.

Includes good transition to show chronology

My first week of therapy was a similar story. Darren, my therapist, would explain the exercises that would restore mobility to my arm, and I would complain that they were too hard, or hurt too much, and that I really didn't care. By the end of the week, I had become openly hostile with Darren. That's when he took matters into his hands.

When I showed up for my hour-long session on Monday, there was a note from Darren taped to the door. It said to meet him at the entrance to the Culver Wing. When I asked a passing nurse where the Culver Wing was located, he look puzzled. "It's on 3 South," he said. "It's the burn trauma ward."

Use of dialogue adds drama to narrative

I stepped off the elevator on 3 South to find Darren waiting for me near the nurse's station. "Put these on," he said, handing me a gown, surgical mask and cap, latex gloves, and slip-on shoe covers.

"What's this for?" I asked.

"Put them on, follow me, and keep quiet," he said.

We passed through two swinging doors and into another world. I will never forget what I saw and heard as we passed from room to room in that trauma unit.

There was a six-year-old girl whose legs had been burned in a car accident and who was learning to walk again. Darren explained to me that grafted skin doesn't grow or stretch like normal skin, so every step the girl tried to take was agony. She screamed and cried as she worked her way along two parallel bars. Somehow, she made it to the end.

In another room, a man about my father's age was lying on a draped gurney. Darren said he had suffered chemical burns when a tank at the chemical plant where he worked exploded. Doctors were stripping off the lifeless, burned skin from his chest, a process called "debridement." A nurse encouraged him to scream to distract him from the excruciating pain.

Description adds impact to narrative

For the next half hour, as we moved quietly through the trauma unit, I saw and heard much more of the same. Finally, I told Darren I was feeling sick. We left the Culver Wing and walked out into the institute's rooftop solarium. I sat down and dropped my head between my knees as Darren started talking.

"You might not believe it, Shawn," he said, "but just about all those people we saw today will walk out of here. They may never forget their pain, but they'll make it. It seems the worse they're hurt, the harder they try to recover. Sometimes I wonder if I would have that kind of courage."

He paused and then went on. "Think about what you saw today, Shawn. Tomorrow, either be ready to work—and work hard—or don't bother coming back to therapy. Those people we saw today need me. I don't have time to waste on someone with your bad attitude." When I looked up, he was gone.

Significance is made clear in closing paragraph

I went back the next day, and every day for four weeks after that. I continued to work on my arm at home and in the weight room at school. Today, my arm looks normal and is almost as strong as it once was. I still can't put stress on it—baseball and other sports are out except for cross-country. And I know when it's going to rain long before the forecasters do—the elbow stiffens up and aches. But whenever I start feeling sorry for myself, I think about that afternoon in the Culver Wing three years ago. I think about the courage I saw there, the incredible will to survive and go on. That's enough to remind me that my limitations aren't really limitations at all, and I'm grateful that I'm able to tackle whatever challenges life has in store for me.

WRITER TO WRITER

I write of one life only. My own. If my story is true, I trust it will resonate with significance for other lives.

Richard Rodriguez, Essayist

FOR YOUR **PORTFOLIO**

1. Reflect on your writing. Write a note that you can attach to your reflective essay as an introduction or place in your writing portfolio, reflecting on your writing process in producing your essay. As you reflect on your essay, consider the following questions:

- How has writing this essay influenced your thinking about the experience you tell about? Do you have a different or new sense of its significance?
- What has writing this essay taught you about yourself or about your past?
- What parts of your essay or stages in writing it did you find most difficult? How did you get through the difficulties?
- What have you learned, as a result of writing this essay, about yourself as a writer?

2. Apply your skills. Use what you have learned in this workshop about reflective writing to complete one or more of the following activities.

- **Cross-curricular** Make a list of four or five significant historical or scientific discoveries. Choose the one that interests you the most or about which you know the most. After thoughtful reflection, write a brief essay explaining how that event changed some aspect of the world.
- **Literature** Select a favorite poem. Write a brief essay reflecting on how the theme of the poem relates to your life and to life in general.
- **Related assignments** Follow the suggestions on pages 40–48 for writing an autobiographical incident and a monologue.

Autobiographical Incident

LITTLE THINGS ARE BIG

BY JESÚS COLÓN

How often do you find yourself in the center of a group of friends, telling a story about something that happened to you? Your friends listen intently because the story reminds them of a similar experience of their own.

A good autobiographical anecdote touches the emotions or the common experience of listeners and readers. As you read Jesús Colón's account of an experience on a subway platform, notice how he conveys the thoughts that ran through his mind as he tried to decide what he should do.

It was very late at night on the eve of Memorial Day. She came into the subway at the 34th Street Pennsylvania Station. I am still trying to remember how she managed to push herself in with a baby on her right arm, a valise in her left hand and two children, a boy and girl about three and five years old, trailing after her. She was a nice looking white lady in her early twenties.

At Nevins Street, Brooklyn, we saw her preparing to get off at the next station—Atlantic Avenue—which happened to be the place where I had to get off. Just as it was a problem for her to get on, it was going to be a problem for her to get off the subway with two small children to be taken care of, a baby on her right arm and a medium sized valise in her left hand.

And there I was, also preparing to get off at Atlantic Avenue, with no bundles to take care of—not even the customary book under my arm without which I feel that I am not completely dressed.

As the train was entering the Atlantic Avenue station, some white man stood up from his seat and helped her out, placing the children on the long, deserted platform. There were only two adult persons on the long platform some time after midnight on the eve of last Memorial Day.

I could perceive the steep, long concrete stairs going down to the Long Island Railroad or into the street. Should I offer my help as the American white man did at the subway car? Should I take care of the girl and the boy, take them by their hands until they reached the end of the steep, long concrete stairs of the Atlantic Avenue station.

Courtesy is a characteristic of the Puerto Rican. And here I was—a Puerto Rican—hours past midnight, a valise, two white children and a white lady with a baby on her arm palpably needing somebody to help her at least until she descended the long concrete stairs.

But how could I, a Negro and a Puerto Rican, approach this white lady who very likely might have preconceived prejudices against Negroes and everybody with foreign accents, in a deserted

subway station very late at night?

What would she say? What would be the first reaction of this white American woman, perhaps coming from a small town with a valise, two children and a baby on her right arm? Would she say: Yes, of course, you may help me. Or would she think worse than that perhaps? What would I do if she let out a scream as I went toward her to offer my help?

Was I misjudging her? So many slanders are written every day in the daily press against the Negroes and Puerto Ricans. I hesitated for a long, long minute. The ancestral manners that the most illiterate Puerto Rican passes on from father to son were struggling inside me. Here was I, way past midnight, face to face with a situation that could very well explode into an outburst of prejudices and chauvinistic conditioning of the "divide and rule" policy of present day society.

It was a long minute. I passed on by her as if I saw nothing. As if I was insensitive to her need. Like a rude animal walking on two legs, I just moved on, half running by the long subway platform, leaving the children and the valise and her with the baby on her arm. I took the steps of the long concrete stairs in twos until I reached the street above and the cold air slapped my warm face.

This is what racism and prejudice and chauvinism and official artificial divisions can do to people and to a nation!

Perhaps the lady was not prejudiced after all. Or not prejudiced enough to scream at the coming of a Negro toward her in a solitary subway station a few hours past midnight. If you were not that prejudiced, I failed you, dear lady. I know that there is a chance in a million that you will read these lines. I am willing to take that millionth chance. If you were not that prejudiced, I failed you, lady, I failed you, children. I failed myself to myself.

I buried my courtesy early on Memorial Day morning. But here is a promise that I make to myself here and now; if I am ever faced with an occasion like that again, I am going to offer my help regardless of how the offer is going to be received.

Then I will have my courtesy with me again.

Think AND Respond

Why do you think Jesús Colón chose to share this experience? How does his writing heighten the significance of this "little" incident? Think about "little" incidents that have been important to you. What feelings do these incidents evoke?

INVITATION ─TO─ *Write*

Jesús Colón's article demonstrates how a writer can use a simple story to reveal values that are important to him. Use the guidelines below to write about an incident in your life that had special significance for you.

Many events and experiences in your life have had a lasting impact on you. In at least some small way, they have changed you, your beliefs, or your entire outlook. By exploring such an incident in writing, you can more thoroughly examine its impact on you and the meaning that you drew from it. In this assignment you can explore and evaluate an important event in your past.

E XPLORING YOUR PAST

FOR HELP & PRACTICE

**Reflecting,
pp. 331–332**
**Informal Sharing,
p. 412**
Tone, pp. 424–425
**Dialogue in
Nonfiction,
p. 455**

1. Choose an event. What should you write about? The best ideas are frequently the ones you tend to overlook, the ones that are closest to you. You might spend some private time rummaging through your grade-school and high-school keepsakes, boxes of favorite childhood games, autograph books, and photo albums. Is there a picture, a souvenir from a summer at camp, or a ticket stub from a game or a concert that strikes an emotional chord or triggers powerful memories? Also, do not overlook the present. What has happened during the past few days—at home, with friends, or at work—that has affected you in some way?

As you list ideas, mark those that evoke the strongest personal response from you. When you are finished listing, freewrite on one or two of the most powerful memories, remembering the details of each experience and examining their significance to you.

2. Evaluate your ideas. Choose a subject that is more than just an interesting incident. Which event contained special meaning for you or had a special impact? Which event taught you something that would be meaningful to other readers?

3. Identify your goals. Once you have selected your topic, it is time to determine your specific goals. What do you want to accomplish by telling this autobiographical incident? Do you want to entertain, to teach a lesson, or to elicit a strong emotional response? For example, Colón wanted to encourage people to live up to what they really believe in. What will your narrative do? What kind of response do you want to elicit from your audience?

4. Choose a tone. Writing can be serious, humorous, formal, or informal. In his account, Colón used a simple, straightforward, almost reporter-like tone to convey the situation and his own dilemma. Decide what tone would be suitable for your narrative and your goals, as well as for your audience. Are you writing for adults? Are you entertaining a younger audience? Know your audience before you begin to draft your anecdote so that you can gauge your tone and style effectively.

Writing
—TIP—
Spend some time reading the Sunday newspaper. Look especially for human-interest stories that trigger a strong emotional response. Would you like to model your narrative on one of these stories?

DRAFTING YOUR NARRATIVE

1. Begin your narrative. Try freewriting for a while, playing with your story. Be relaxed about style, grammar rules, and punctuation. There will be time later to perfect your mechanics. At this point it is the story that is important.

2. Use dialogue to dramatize your story. Since Colón never approaches the woman, he cannot appropriately use dialogue. However, he does speculate about what the woman might say, thus giving us a more complete picture of her. Try to use dialogue to re-create a scene, to breathe life into your characters, or to change the pace of your narrative.

3. Vary your writing techniques. As you think about your story, consider some of the ways you can make your writing more vivid. For example, using descriptive details can enliven your narrative. Try to include graphic details that appeal to the five senses: sight, hearing, taste, touch, and smell. Describe the setting for the anecdote as concretely and colorfully as you can. Do not hesitate to describe your own feelings at various points as you unfold the incident. Colón clearly portrays his feelings when he says "like a rude animal walking on two legs, I just moved on. . . ."

Writer's Choice The elements of surprise and irony often work well in an autobiographical anecdote. Try to use these elements to appeal to your readers' interest and sense of humor, if they are appropriate to your story.

REVIEWING YOUR WRITING

1. Reread your narrative. Many writers find it helpful to let a piece of writing rest awhile before doing the final shaping. If you have time, put your work away for a while. After a few days, reread your narrative. You will probably gain a fresh perspective on your writing. Does it achieve the goals you set? Is the significance of the incident clear? If, in answering these questions, you discover any lapses in your narrative, now is the time to repair them.

2. Think about the story. An autobiographical incident is, in effect, a brief story. It should therefore contain similar elements. Are your characters well defined? Does the narrative flow smoothly? Have you focused on only those events that contribute to the incident? Ask a peer reader to respond to these questions, and to other points you want to check.

3. Rework material. If necessary, revise your material. Remember that your details should not only re-create the incident, they should also show the significance of what happened to you. Polish the dialogue and word choice so that each sentence conveys your message exactly.

PUBLISHING AND PRESENTING

- **Read your narrative to a small group.** Watch their reactions. Did your anecdote trigger the emotion you desired? Invite comments from your audience.
- **Take to the airwaves.** If your school has a radio station, consider establishing a weekly radio spot such as the kind popularized by Garrison Keillor, who wrote *Lake Wobegon Days*. Open the spot to anyone who has a story to share.
- **Become a columnist.** A weekly column in the school newspaper might be an alternative to a radio broadcast.
- **Seek a broader audience.** Submit your narrative to a local newspaper or to a teen or young adult magazine. Many publications are looking for fresh young talent.

On the Lightside

WORD SEPARATION

Imagine trying to read this book if there were no paragraphs, no spaces between words, no capitalization, and no punctuation. It is not a totally ridiculous notion. In fact, that is how books were written before the Middle Ages.

In antiquity, people generally read aloud, so the sound of a word was more important than how it looked on a page. When texts were transcribed, the scribes merely wrote the letters one after another, leaving it up to the readers to separate the words. Medieval readers, however, began to sense that texts were being corrupted. They felt their scribes sometimes made mistakes, particularly with proper names, by mixing together letters. As a result, the concept of dividing the unbroken script into distinct words came into use. But it was not until the eighth and ninth centuries that capital letters came to be used, and it wasn't until the eleventh century that paragraphs and other grammatical marks started finding their way into texts. Often, these marks were added by readers after books were transcribed. Even after printing came

Fifteenth century
painting of a scribe

into use, monks went through the books in their libraries word-for-word, adding punctuation, accents, and hyphens the printers did not provide.

If today's rules of grammar and mechanics at times seem overwhelming, imaginewhatitwouldbe likeiftherewerenorulesatall.

Monologue

Have you ever mentally replayed a disagreement with a classmate or imagined different ways to handle a conflict with a parent? Sometimes arguing with ourselves helps us resolve a troubling situation.

Playwrights often use internal arguments to reveal the personal struggles of characters. Through monologue, or solo conversations, characters tell us aloud of their inner conflicts. As you read this monologue from the musical *Camelot*, try to define the dilemma that King Arthur faces. What personal values and beliefs help him decide what to do?

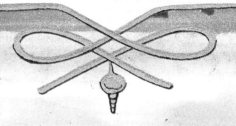

✦ FROM CAMELOT ✦

PROPOSITION ✦ *If I could choose, from every woman who breathes on this earth, the face I would most love, the smile, the touch, the voice, the heart, the laugh, the soul itself, every detail and feature to the smallest strand of hair they would all be Jenny's.*

PROPOSITION ✦ *If I could choose from every man who breathes on this earth a man for my brother and a man for my son, a man for my friend, they would all be Lance.* (His bitterness mounts.) *Yes, I love them. I love them, and they answer me with pain and torment. Be it sin or not sin, they betray me in their hearts, and that's far sin enough. I see it in their eyes and feel it when they speak, and they must pay for it and be punished. I shan't be wounded and not return it in kind. I'm done with feeble hoping. I demand a man's vengeance!* (He moves violently, then tries to control himself.)

✠ BY ALAN JAY LERNER ✠

PROPOSITION ✠ *I'm a king, not a man. And a civilized king. Could it possibly be civilized to destroy what I love? Could it possibly be civilized to love myself above all? What of their pain and their torment? Did they ask for this calamity? Can passion be selected?* (His voice rising.) *Is there any doubt of their devotion . . . to me, or to our Table?* (He raises high the sword in his hand.) *By God, Excalibur, I shall be a King! This is the time of King Arthur, and we reach for the stars! This is the time of King Arthur, and violence is not strength and compassion is not weakness. We are civilized!*

RESOLVED ✠ *We shall live through this together, Excalibur: They, you and I! And God have mercy on us all.* (The decision made, he becomes almost relaxed, almost at peace.) *They're waiting for us at the table.* (He starts to walk off.) *Let's not delay the celebration.*

Think AND Respond

What conflict does King Arthur face? How does he decide to resolve it? What do you learn about Arthur from this monologue? How did the writer convey these impressions to you? What kind of character or conflict can you imagine presenting in a monologue?

INVITATION TO Write

The monologue from *Camelot* helps the audience understand King Arthur's internal struggle. Now use the guidelines below to write a monologue of your own, presenting a conflict from a fictional character's point of view.

Like all reflective writing, a monologue involves the working out of ideas and inner struggles. However, a monologue, unlike a reflective essay, presents a fictional situation, not a real one. A monologue gives the audience a chance to see the inner workings of a character's mind.

PREPARING A MONOLOGUE

FOR HELP & PRACTICE

Choosing Different Voice, pp. 419–422

Emphasis/Tone/ Mood, pp. 423–428

Varieties of Language, pp. 429–434

Poetic Language, pp. 435–438

Point of View, pp. 446–449

1. Select a situation.   You may want to choose a conflict inspired by a piece of literature you have read. For example, the clashing of wills between Eliza Doolittle and Henry Higgins in George Bernard Shaw's *Pygmalion* might inspire a monologue by either character. Alternatively, you may want to create a situation from your own imagination: competition between classmates, temptation to cheat on an examination, or conflicts involving loyalty to a friend are possible situations from which a monologue might arise.

2. Choose a point of view.   Once you have chosen a situation, you must decide from whose point of view the conflict will be argued. Presumably Jenny or Lance in *Camelot* would have engaged in a much different monologue from Arthur's even though they would have been reacting to the same situation. You may want to experiment by talking into a tape recorder, recording the thoughts and ideas of various characters about the same conflict. Speak always in the first person as though you were actually acting the part of the character. As you listen to your tape, decide which point of view you are most comfortable with. Also, begin to think which ideas can shape the monologue.

CREATING A REALISTIC MONOLOGUE

1. Reveal character through word choice. The way a character speaks reveals a great deal about his or her personality. For example, Arthur uses formal and elegant language, suiting his position as a king as well as the nobility of his character. He also prefaces his thoughts with "Proposition" and "Resolved." These words, used in formal logic, help us to see that Arthur is a very rational person. Yet the beautiful images and tender phrases he uses to describe his wife and his friend reveal a romantic and poetic soul as well. What would very informal speech or violent language reveal about a character? How might you indicate through word choice that a character is highly emotional?

2. Show, don't tell about, a character. You can learn much about Arthur's character from the questions he asks himself. From these questions, you come to realize that Arthur values civilized behavior and compassion above vengeance. Because you see him struggle and doubt, you are more convinced of his values than you would be if he just declared them. Think of ways you can show your character's values other than just stating them.

 Writer's Choice Introducing your monologue with a few sentences of background information will save you from the awkwardness of having to include the needed information in the monologue itself.

3. Experiment with narrative techniques. Not all characters speak as coherently or logically as Arthur. Some might jump from one idea to another, in a stream of consciousness, because the author wants to communicate an insecure or agitated state of mind. For example, in Shakespeare's *Macbeth,* the agonized king argues with himself as he stands alone on stage. Then the tolling of a bell reminds Macbeth of a death knell and then his desire to kill King Duncan takes over. You may want to experiment with stream of consciousness in your monologue.

Tette de Femme,
Pablo Picasso

47

4. Consider adding stage directions. In Arthur's monologue, the stage directions serve as hints to the actor for appropriate movements, gestures, and tones of voice. As you draft your monologue, consider what your character should do as he or she speaks. If you want your character to perform movements such as pacing to and fro or wringing hands, add the necessary directions to your script.

REVIEWING YOUR WRITING

1. Perform your monologue for a small audience. As you read, check the monologue for clarity. Have you provided enough information for your listeners to understand the situation? Is the point of view clear and consistent throughout the monologue?

2. Check word choice and speech patterns. Remember that your goal is to reveal character through speech. Make sure that the vocabulary you chose and the sentence structures you created are appropriate for your character.

The Far Side Cartoons by Gary Larson are reprinted by permission of Chronicle Features, San Francisco, CA.

PUBLISHING AND PRESENTING

- **Conduct mock tryouts for actors.** Use your own monologue and those of your classmates as material for tryouts for an imaginary play. You will need a director who will decide who reads the part best, as well as a group of potential actors eager to land a part in the "play."
- **Present a staged reading of your monologue.** Complete your staging with costumes, stage props, lighting, and music.

Sentence

Analyzing Sentence Structures

In these Sentence Composing lessons, you will analyze and imitate the sentence structures used by professional writers. Then you will use those structures to add emphasis, clarity, and detail to your own writing.

Notice the differences in structure in the three sentences below.

MODELS

1. Along the roads around Goderville, the peasants and their wives were coming toward the little town, for it was market day.
2. The men walked with plodding steps, their bodies bent forward at each thrust of their long bowed legs.
3. They were deformed by hard work, by the pull of the heavy plow which raises the left shoulder and twists the torso, by the reaping of the wheat which forces the knees apart to get a firm stand, by all the slow and strenuous labors of life on the farm.

Guy de Maupassant, "The Piece of String"

A. Identifying Imitations   Identify the sentence that imitates the structure of the model.

Model: Along the roads around Goderville, the peasants and their wives were coming toward the little town, for it was market day.

1 a. When the computer beeped, Maria suddenly realized that the data was inaccurate, a fault of the information she had been given.
  b. Near the end zone by the flagpole, Coach Royden and his team were trotting toward the field, for it was time for the second half.

Model: The men walked with plodding steps, their bodies bent forward at each thrust of their long bowed legs.

2 a. Our car stalled at every intersection, its carburetor clogged with all manner of accumulated engine sludge.
  b. He stood ironing the shirt, and he felt his thoughts sweeping back and forth with the iron.

Model: They were deformed by hard work, by the pull of the heavy plow which raises the left shoulder and twists the torso, by the reaping of the wheat which forces the knees apart to get a firm stand, by all the slow and strenuous labors of life on the farm.

3 a. Since no one had believed Corky's wild story, she had retired to her room to sulk and brood over the incident, to write angry notes to all of us, and to fume about the injustices in her life.
   b. We felt proud of our school, of its standing in a competitive league that challenges the best teams and destroys the worst, of its reputation in a district that urges the teachers always to demand high academic performance, of its longstanding and thorough commitment to the best interests of the students.

B. Unscrambling Sentences Unscramble each group of sentence parts below to create a sentence that matches the model.

Model: Along the roads around Goderville, the peasants and their wives were coming toward the little town, for it was market day.

1 a. because there was road work
   b. near the exit to the stadium
   c. the cars and trucks were coming to a grinding halt

Model: The men walked with plodding steps, their bodies bent forward at each thrust of their long bowed legs.

2 a. their faces peering out
   b. through the windshields with angry, tired expressions
   c. the drivers sat with forced patience

Model: They were deformed by hard work, by the pull of the heavy plow which raises the left shoulder and twists the torso, by the reaping of the wheat which forces the knees apart to get a firm stand, by all the slow and strenuous labors of life on the farm.

3 a. by the length of the twisting detour
   b. by all the unexpected but inevitable problems of travel on highways
   c. that slowed commuter traffic and wrecked schedules
   d. they were upset by the delay
   e. by the noise of the jackhammer
   f. that broke the pavement up to expose the yellow topsoil

C. Imitating Sentences Now you will apply your skills to new sentences. Write a sentence that imitates the structure of each model sentence below. Major parts of each model are separated by slash marks (/). Punctuate your sentences as the models are punctuated.

Model	Sometimes in the night / the ranch people, / safe in their beds, / heard a roar of hoofs go by. **John Steinbeck, *The Red Pony***
Student Sentence	Often in the spring / the school children, / curious about the tulips, / saw a bunch of buds open up.

1. Time, / as we know it, / is a very recent invention.
   Aldous Huxley, "Time and the Machine"

2. Next morning I woke up / at my usual hour, / fizzling like a bottle of champagne.   **Frank O'Connor, "My Oedipus Complex"**

3. Hooking the window back, / he noticed that a little tree / in the Square Gardens / had come out in blossom, / and that the thermometer stood at sixty.   **John Galsworthy, "The Flowering Quince"**

4. He closed his eyes and swung wildly, / and Angel, / laughing, / belted the side of his headguard.   **Robert Lipsyte, *The Contender***

5. One day a big locust whirred drily past her head, / and she jumped up with a cry, / scattering her sewing things.
   Nadine Gordimer, "The Soft Voice of the Serpent"

6. The twins, / smeary in the face, / eating steadily from untidy paper sacks of sweets, / followed them in a detached way.
   Katherine Anne Porter, *Ship of Fools*

Application Write a paragraph describing a group activity (for example, a barbecue, a concert, or a sports event). In your paragraph, include imitations of at least two of the model sentences in this lesson.

Grammar Refresher In order to analyze a sentence, you must be able to identify its subject and predicate. For information on identifying subject and predicate, see Handbook 32.

Sketchbook

Bank Langmore, the Texas photographer who captured this shot of cowboys bathing, noticed that "the last things they take off are their hats, . . . even when they are taking a bath or crawling into their bedrolls."

What do you notice about the people and activities around you?

Additional Sketches

If you could meet any person in the world, whom would you choose? What would you talk about?

Watch someone doing a common, everyday task. See if you can write a description of the person's actions that includes details you've never noticed before.

Observation and Description

PERSONALITY PROFILE

JOURNALISTIC NARRATIVE

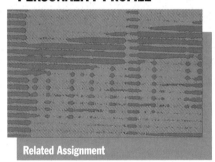

Related Assignment
VIDEO

How accurately could you describe everything you saw today? What was the weather like? With whom did you talk? What make was the car that screeched around the corner? In the routine of our lives, we look at many things without really seeing them. Yet when we concentrate, we can see an extraordinary amount of detail.

In this workshop, you will focus your powers of observation and description. In the guided assignment, you will write a narrative based on your close observation of an experience or event. In the related assignments, you will use your descriptive powers to write a profile of a person and to create a video that captures a scene.

53

Journalistic Narrative

Journalists often employ the techniques found in fiction to set scenes, reveal character, and tell a narrative story. Yet their stories are true, based on close observation of actual events.

Samuel G. Freedman spent a year observing life at an inner-city high school before writing a book-length journalistic narrative about his experiences. Notice how the prologue to his book uses specific details to set a scene and introduce the main character.

. . . FROM SMALL VICTORIES . . .

It is June 24, 1987, Graduation Day for Seward Park High School, and Jessica Siegel has a pocketbook full of bobby pins and tissues. The bobby pins are for her students. The tissues are for herself.

The high school sits empty and silent in the late afternoon, a breeze nudging litter down the streets outside, for the commencement is being held eighty blocks farther north in Manhattan, at Hunter College. Here the streets unfold with boutiques and diplomatic mansions and elegant apartment buildings, with awnings and doormen and gilt doors that glint in the summer sun. The college itself looms like a fortress castle, all turrets and archways, medieval grandeur reincarnated amid the metropolis.

With footsteps both urgent and tentative, the students and their families arrive. Six rise from the Lexington Avenue subway, palms shading their eyes. Five pile out of a Dodge Dart piloted by an uncle. Four emerge from the gypsy cab on which they have splurged, with its smoked windows and air freshener. All of them pause to gape, and the cabbie, too, waits an extra moment before driving on, leaning out the window to admire the promised land. Their world is the Lower East Side, its streets crammed with tenements and bodegas and second-story sweatshops, its belly bursting with immigrants, its class and tongues and customs so foreign here at Hunter, only twenty minutes from home.

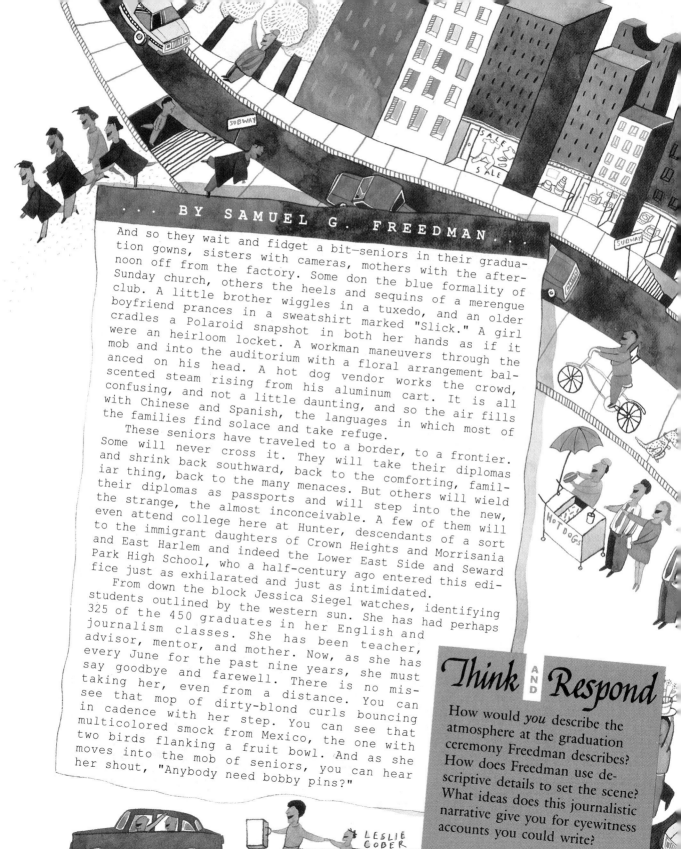

... BY SAMUEL G. FREEDMAN ...

And so they wait and fidget a bit—seniors in their graduation gowns, sisters with cameras, mothers with the afternoon off from the factory. Some don the blue formality of Sunday church, others the heels and sequins of a merengue club. A little brother wiggles in a tuxedo, and an older boyfriend prances in a sweatshirt marked "Slick." A girl cradles a Polaroid snapshot in both her hands as if it were an heirloom locket. A workman maneuvers through the mob and into the auditorium with a floral arrangement balanced on his head. A hot dog vendor works the crowd, scented steam rising from his aluminum cart. It is all confusing, and not a little daunting, and so the air fills with Chinese and Spanish, the languages in which most of the families find solace and take refuge.

These seniors have traveled to a border, to a frontier. Some will never cross it. They will take their diplomas and shrink back southward, back to the comforting, familiar thing, back to the many menaces. But others will wield their diplomas as passports and will step into the new, the strange, the almost inconceivable. A few of them will even attend college here at Hunter, descendants of a sort to the immigrant daughters of Crown Heights and Morrisania and East Harlem and indeed the Lower East Side and Seward Park High School, who a half-century ago entered this edifice just as exhilarated and just as intimidated.

From down the block Jessica Siegel watches, identifying students outlined by the western sun. She has had perhaps 325 of the 450 graduates in her English and journalism classes. She has been teacher, advisor, mentor, and mother. Now, as she has every June for the past nine years, she must say goodbye and farewell. There is no mistaking her, even from a distance. You can see that mop of dirty-blond curls bouncing in cadence with her step. You can see that multicolored smock from Mexico, the one with two birds flanking a fruit bowl. And as she moves into the mob of seniors, you can hear her shout, "Anybody need bobby pins?"

Think AND Respond

How would *you* describe the atmosphere at the graduation ceremony Freedman describes? How does Freedman use descriptive details to set the scene? What ideas does this journalistic narrative give you for eyewitness accounts you could write?

LESLIE COBER

Journalistic narratives combine the techniques of nonfiction and
fiction. The main purpose of journalism is to inform—to present
factual information about a subject. By closely observing a subject
and asking incisive questions, a journalist can gather the material
needed to develop a rich, accurate portrait. Then, by presenting the
information as a narrative, the journalist can also tell a story. The
journalistic narratives in magazines, newspaper feature sections, and
nonfiction books employ such elements as character, setting, mood,
and plot to tell compelling stories that often read like good fiction.

PREWRITE AND EXPLORE

HANDBOOKS

FOR HELP & PRACTICE

Observing,
p. 332
Interviewing,
p. 378

1. Look for ideas. What have you always wanted to do? Where
have you wanted to go? Is there someone or something you are
curious about? Writing a journalistic narrative is a way to investigate
firsthand subjects that intrigue you. Try one or more of the
following activities to look for subjects to explore.

Exploratory Activities

- **Listing**   What are your special interests? List them and then
  freewrite about aspects of them that you could explore
  through an eyewitness account.
- **Events**   With a group of classmates, brainstorm for ideas
  about events—everything from sports to concerts to public
  meetings—that you could witness and describe.
- **Places**   What places hold special meaning to you? What places
  would you like to know more about? List interesting and
  unusual places you could visit and describe.

Many events, such as this exciting rescue, make good subjects for journalistic narratives.

- **A day in the life**   If you could be a fly on the wall, observing everything that happens around you for a day, where would you want to be?
- **Reading literature**   Find examples of dramatic journalistic narratives, such as those written by Tom Wolfe, Norman Mailer, or Joan Didion, and examine the techniques that the writers used. What ideas do these narratives give you for ones you could write?

2. Choose a subject.   Look over your ideas, and freewrite about the ones you find most promising. Keep in mind that you will need to gather firsthand information about your subject, so choose one you will be able to research effectively. If you have trouble finding a subject, thumb through your journal, check your writing for the Sketchbook on page 52, and consider the suggestions under "Apply Your Skills" on page 65.

3. Gather background information.   First, acquaint yourself generally with the subject. Newspapers are a valuable resource, both for facts about subjects and for ideas on people to talk to. Check your library's newspaper indexes, magazine indexes, and books.

4. Identify your sources.   Your sources are people you can talk to, written information you can gather, and physical evidence—both objects and places—you can observe and describe. Brainstorm by yourself or with classmates to find ideas on what types of evidence you can gather and how you can go about your reporting.

5. Begin reporting.   Your main tools in reporting are your powers of observation and your ability to ask questions.

- **Observation**   Just noticing what goes on around you will provide some of your most important reporting. Record your observations of everything you see.

Writing ━**TIP**━
Pick a subject you really like and want to learn more about.

- **Interviews** Talk to the people involved in your subject. Come prepared with a list of questions you want answered, but keep yourself open to new information. As you talk to people, you may find your story moving in directions you hadn't anticipated. Also, ask the people you interview to suggest other people you should consult.

6. Record your information. Accurate reporting of information is essential in journalistic writing. As you explore your subject, take notes recording facts, details, your own reactions, and questions you want to follow up.

Fred had been intrigued by a gem mine in the mountains near his hometown ever since he and his friends had stumbled on it during a camping trip. He decided to contact the mine owners and ask if he could write a feature story on the mine for his local newspaper. Here are some of the notes he took on his tour of the mine.

ONE STUDENT'S PROCESS

Coming up to the mine. Day is foggy, drizzly. Bumpy road snakes around through the hills, ends abruptly. Oak trees all around. Simple whitewashed frame at steep slope. John McLean, foreman: sandy hair, full bushy beard.

Tim digs in soupy pocket, pulls out quartz, small tourmaline. Everyone oohs and ahs but McLean. McL: "There are no gems here. Those are too small to bother with."

Using ropes to pull us through zigzag passageways. Air smells. McL:"It's nitro from blasting yesterday."

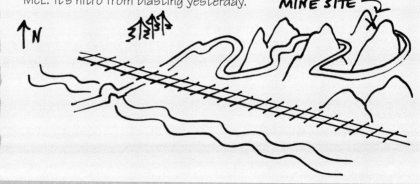

7. Share your notes. Go over your notes with a small group of writers. Look for ideas about what central idea, angle, or theme seems to be emerging from your notes. What details do you and your writing group feel are still missing? Try freewriting for ten minutes for ideas on how you might shape your narrative.

 Writer's Choice Do you want to make yourself a part of your narrative and tell it from the first-person point of view, or do you want to report what you see using the third-person point of view?

8. Determine your purpose and goals. In journalistic writing, your overall purpose is to inform. However, you may also have some personal goals. They may be as simple as satisfying your curiosity; or you may wish to learn more about a subject, share your enthusiasm for it, or draw attention to a problem.

9. Identify your audience. Keep in mind how much or little your readers know about your subject. You may need to define key terms or provide background information so they can easily follow your narrative.

DRAFT AND DISCOVER

1. Look for an angle. When journalists approach a story, they don't just gather facts and report them. They analyze their subject in order to find a dominant impression, or angle, that captures its significance.

As Fred thought about the gem mine, he first considered focusing on how it operates or on its history. However, as he reviewed his notes, what struck him most was the excitement of searching for gems. That would be his angle.

2. Organize your draft. Many journalistic narratives are presented chronologically, from start to finish. Some start in the middle, describing some attention-grabbing incident, and then use a flashback to fill in the reader about events that led up to it. Freedman uses the graduation-day scene to introduce the characters and issues he would discuss; then later he returns to the beginning of the school year and tells his story in chronological order. Another alternative is to present a series of loosely related scenes, each one revealing important points about your subject.

PROBLEM SOLVING

How can I decide what direction my writing should take?

FOR HELP & PRACTICE

Narrative Introductions, pp. 371–374

Elaborative Details, pp. 376–378

Mood, pp. 426–427

Point of View, pp. 446–447

Mastering Dialogue, pp. 452–455

3. Elaborate on ideas. The following strategies can be helpful in revealing the essential qualities of your subject.

Strategies

PROBLEM

S O L V I N G

How can I make my experience real for my readers?

- **Description** Look for the telling details that will make your subject real for the reader. For instance, Freedman described a girl who "cradles a Polaroid snapshot in both her hands as if it were an heirloom locket."
- **Narration** Think about ways of using narration to build suspense or create a mood. You can enhance your narrative by using techniques associated with fiction, such as creating a vivid character, setting a scene, and developing a plot.
- **Dialogue** Using direct quotations can reveal the character of the people you write about and convey the atmosphere of the event you are describing.

Fred decided to begin his narrative with a description of his group approaching the gem mine.

ONE STUDENT'S PROCESS

On a foggy, drizzly day not long ago, a small expedition made its way up the dirt road through the hills not too far from Lake Henshaw. The road ended halfway up a steep slope covered with oak trees. This spot was the entrance to the Himalaya Mine. It's not very impressive to look at, but in the past century a fortune in gems has come from this mine.

Writer's Choice Some journalistic narratives are written in the present tense to heighten the "you are there" quality. You can choose to use present or past tense, depending on the impression you want to make.

4. Reread and react. Once you have completed your draft, set it aside for a time. Then review it, and ask your peer readers to respond to it.

R E V I E W   Y O U R   W R I T I N G

Questions for Yourself

- Have I found a strong angle, or is my journalistic narrative a collection of random pieces of information?
- Have I used descriptive details to vividly re-create people, places, and events?
- Have I made clear why my subject is important to me?

Questions for Your Peer Readers

- What dominant impression did you get from my essay?
- What sentences or passages stand out as particularly vivid or memorable?
- Is anything unclear, irrelevant, or unnecessary?
- Is there anything I wrote about that you would like to know more or less about?

R E V I S E   Y O U R   W R I T I N G

1. Evaluate your responses. Look over the responses you have received and see what changes you want to make. Also keep in mind these guidelines for evaluating journalistic narratives.

Standards For Evaluation

An effective journalistic narrative . . .

- presents a dominant impression or angle on its subject.
- accurately presents information about the subject.
- uses facts and descriptive details to present a vivid picture of the subject.
- tells an engaging, easy-to-follow story.
- demonstrates a clear sense of audience.

2. Problem-solve. The draft on the next page shows changes that Fred made in response to suggestions from his peer readers. Rework your own draft, incorporating all the revisions you have decided to make.

FOR HELP & PRACTICE

**Unity/Coherence,
pp. 382–391**

**Peer Response,
pp. 397–400**

**Varieties of
Language,
pp. 429–433**

**Using Source
Materials,
pp. 482–489**

One of the novices knelt and ~~put~~ thrust his hand into the ~~hole~~ pocket which was ~~wet~~ soupy with water that had ~~come~~ seeped in

during the night. Soon he pulled out a few chunks of

quarts z and a few pale pink ~~crystals~~ tourmalines that fit in the palm

of his hand. Then a few larger crystals of a deeper

pink. Each discovery was greeted with wild enthusiasm

by the others, who were clamoring impatiently for a

chance to dig in the hole; but our foreman McLean was

not impressed. "There are no gems here," he said. "Those are too small to bother with."

More precise word choice would help.

Nice description! I feel like I'm there.

Why wasn't he impressed?

Grammar
TIP

Be sure to check that you have spelled proper names and other proper nouns correctly.

3. Proofread your work. Make a clean copy that incorporates all your changes, and look for errors in grammar and mechanics.

LINKING
GRAMMAR **AND** WRITING
Precise Nouns and Verbs

Using precise nouns and verbs will enhance your descriptions. For example, Samuel G. Freedman could have written, "Five [people] get out of a car driven by an uncle." Instead, he wrote, "Five *pile* out of a *Dodge Dart piloted* by an uncle."

4. Publish and present. Collect all the journalistic narratives written by classmates and publish them, with each article laid out with appropriate photographs or illustrations.

- **Submit your article to a newspaper.** Contact the editor of your school or community newspaper about printing your article.
- **Save your work in your writing portfolio.**

HANDBOOKS
FOR HELP & PRACTICE

Publishing Your Writing, pp. 413–415

The Search for Buried Treasure

Fred Dobbs

On a foggy, drizzly day not long ago, a small expedition made its way up the rutted dirt road that snaked through the hills not too far from Lake Henshaw. The road ended halfway up a steep slope covered with oak trees. There in front of us was only a simple, white-washed frame around an opening in a hill. This drab spot marked the entrance to the Himalaya Mine. It's not very impressive to look at, but in the past century a fortune in gems has come from within.

The Himalaya is a tourmaline mine. Tourmaline, a pencil-shaped crystal that comes in a variety of translucent colors, is gaining popularity among jewelry designers, gem carvers, and mineral specimen collectors. On this day, our small expedition of novice miners would have a chance to search for this rare gem.

Mine foreman John McLean, a sandy-haired man who looks the part of a miner with his full, bushy beard, outfitted us with hard hats and miners' lamps, and then led us into the cool, dank darkness of the mine. McLean directed us down a sloping tunnel toward a crater, about ten feet in diameter, that was the beginning of a new shaft. The previous day, he said, a pocket (a clay-filled opening in the stone) had

Uses descriptive details
to set the scene

Narrates the story
of the exploration
of the mine

been discovered that might contain tourmaline.

One of the novices knelt and thrust his hand into the pocket, which was soupy with water that had seeped in during the night. Soon he pulled out a few chunks of quartz and a few pale pink tourmalines that fit in the palm of his hand, then a few larger crystals of a deeper pink. Each discovery was greeted with wild enthusiasm by the others, who were clamoring impatiently for a chance to dig in the hole; but our foreman, McLean, was not impressed.

"There are no gems here," he said. "Those are too small to bother with."

Then another novice miner reached down and pulled out a giant specimen—a pointed crystal four inches tall and three inches in diameter, half pink and half green.

McLean was finally impressed. "If it looks as good outside in the daylight as it does here, it's probably a $3,000 piece," he said.

McLean next led us up a zigzag passageway to another shaft. The acrid smell of nitroglycerin from the previous day's blasting lingered in the air as we hoisted ourselves up the ropes that guided us. Again we dug for buried treasure. Here the clay was soft and gooey, but mixed in were shards of quartz and other materials that could easily slice open unsuspecting fingers. Two novice miners had to give up early when they opened deep gashes in their hands.

Meanwhile, McLean methodically cleaned out a pocket, hardly stopping to examine the crystals he found. "You get jaded," he said. To him, a fine crystal is a commodity that will buy another case of dynamite so he can continue his job. Still, he appreciates the wonderment of what the earth can create. He guided me to a pocket and coached me as I groped through the muck. Finally, I felt the outline of a crystal—a rich, pink, finger-sized shaft of tourmaline.

As the crystal was released from the clay, McLean said approvingly, "You're the first to touch this in eighty million years."

Presents a dominant impression, or angle—the excitement of a group searching for gems

Uses dialogue to present information

Uses precise, vivid words to describe the action

Reinforces the dominant impression in the conclusion

WRITER TO WRITER

Hating to ask questions and never trusting the answers has defined the type of reporting I do. What I do is hang around. Become part of the furniture. An end table in someone's life. It is the art of the scavenger: set a scene, establish a mood, get the speech patterns right.

John Gregory Dunne, journalist, novelist, and screenwriter

1. Reflect on your writing. As an end note for your journalistic narrative, write a brief narrative describing your experiences writing it. Tell how you reported your piece, explaining any difficulties you encountered and how you might avoid them in the future. Describe how you gathered details. Did you find enough to write rich descriptions? Consider what you would do differently if you were to write another journalistic narrative.

2. Apply your skills. Try completing one or more of the following activities.

- **Cross-curricular** Using the techniques of a journalistic narrative, re-create a moment in the history of science. This might be a moment of discovery or a visit to the laboratory of a famous scientist. Feel free to interview participants, create quotes, or even make yourself part of the scene. As an alternative, re-create an important event in history.
- **Literature** Select a scene from a well-known work of literature and re-create it in a journalistic narrative. Feel free to interview characters, quoting directly from the work and making up quotations of your own. Add yourself to the scene as a new character, if you want to.
- **General** Attend a sports event and write a journalistic narrative describing the occasion—the spectators, the setting, and the experience as a whole.
- **Related assignments** Follow the suggestions on pages 68–74 to create a personality profile or a video.

FOR YOUR **PORTFOLIO**

Personality Profile

Basketball player Michael Jordan—already a legend in the sports world! Obviously writer Sally Donnelly thinks so, as you will discover when you read this excerpt from a personality profile she wrote for *Time* a few years back.

While you are reading, notice how Donnelly interweaves descriptions of Jordan's physical characteristics and actions with his personality traits to convey her enthusiasm and admiration for Jordan, not only as an outstanding athlete but also as an exceptional human being.

Election night, 1988. In a darkened Madison Square Garden, a murmur of anticipation ripples through the standing-room-only crowd. On the floor below, the guest of honor stands, head bent, a bit overwhelmed and maybe a bit embarrassed by the spectacle. "Ladies and gentleman," booms a voice as the spotlight rakes the now cheering audience, "No. 23, Miiichaaael Jooordaaan!" As one, the 19,591 men, women, and children rise to pay thunderous tribute. . . .

So what's all the fuss about? Simply that this is the first time during the 1988-89 season that the world's most exciting basketball player is visiting New York. A JORDAN FOR PRESIDENT sign even appears in the stands, a semiserious calling to a higher order.

For now, Michael Jeffrey Jordan is high enough, thank you. . . . He is the hottest player in America's hottest sport. Only 25, Jordan has already won every major individual award the NBA has to offer. . . . Small wonder some sportscasters call Jordan "Superman in Shorts."

Such high-flying praise is all the more astounding given Jordan's size. At 6 ft. 6 in., he is a full inch shorter than the average NBA player, but he transcends his handicap by spending most of his time above the others. His perfectly proportioned frame. . . soars up, around and over the mere mortals he opposes. Most guards . . .prefer the quiet of the perimeter to the violent collisions of leviathans under the hoop. But Jordan is most dangerous around the basket, with his arsenal of double-clutch lay-ups and

GREAT **LEAPIN'** LIZARDS

hyperspace dunks over men very nearly a foot taller. . . .

For Jordan, the world of basketball is a world without bounds. He gyrates, levitates and often dominates. Certainly he fascinates. In arenas around the country, food and drink go unsold because fans refuse to leave their seats for fear of missing a spectacular Jordan move to tell their grandchildren about. . . .

Jordan is one of only a handful of NBA players who truly seem to enjoy themselves. [He] plays as if what he calls "the best job in the world" might be gone tomorrow. He even has a "love of the game" clause written into his contract, which allows him to play basketball anytime, and anywhere, the urge strikes, especially on the playgrounds back home in North Carolina. But Jordan's delight in the sport is not the main reason he plays basketball. Competition drives Michael Jordan. Incessantly.

INVITATION
TO
Write

Sally Donnelly's piece on Michael Jordan has given you a feel for Jordan as an individual. Now try your hand at writing a profile of a special individual of your choice.

The personality profile is a popular feature in most newspapers and magazines. Therefore, when you are writing your personality profile, you will use some of the same skills and techniques you employed in writing a newspaper story. You will need to make observations, do research, and conduct interviews to gather information on your subject.

PREPARING YOUR PROFILE

FOR HELP & PRACTICE

**Interviewing,
p. 378
Unity/Coherence,
pp. 382–390
Varieties of
Language,
pp. 429–434
Problem Solving,
pp. 472–473
Research Skills,
pp. 479–489**

1. Choose a subject. The person you decide to profile should be someone you admire. He or she doesn't have to be a contemporary celebrity such as Michael Jordan, or a historical figure such as Eleanor Roosevelt. You may prefer to write about a subject closer to home—a favorite relative, a neighbor, or a local government or business leader. Choose someone, though, whose story or particular qualities you consider special.

2. Research or interview to gather information. You can start researching a historical figure in encyclopedias or in the library card catalog. Sunday newspaper supplements and the *Readers' Guide to Periodical Literature* are useful sources of information about contemporary celebrities. If you decide to profile a lesser-known person, interviewing is the best method for getting information. Also think about interviewing other people who know your subject well. They may give you information that is not available anywhere else.

3. Set your goal for writing. To help decide on your goal, ask yourself questions like these: What makes this person special to me? What impression of him or her do I want to leave in the minds of my readers?

WRITING YOUR PROFILE

1. Choose a form. Your profile may take any of several forms. One possibility is a narrative describing a day in your subject's life; another is analysis that elaborates on certain characteristics, actions, and traits of your subject, one at a time. Choose one of these or any other form that works well for you.

2. Be selective. Review the information you've gathered, and select only those facts that will help you reach your writing goal. Notice how Sally Donnelly's profile emphasizes two main things about Michael Jordan: his physical traits as an athlete and his personal values.

3. Try out your ideas in a draft. Capture your readers' attention at once with a title and opening paragraph that make your subject come alive: you might begin with an interesting quotation from your subject, or show the person in action. Then develop your profile by presenting other special traits of your subject.

REVIEWING YOUR WRITING

1. Invite constructive criticism. Ask peer readers to go over your draft. Does it achieve your goal? Does it make readers feel they now know your subject?

2. Check for precise words and significant details. Have you used exact nouns, lively modifiers, and action-oriented verbs? Does each descriptive detail suggest something of the subject's traits and values?

PUBLISHING AND PRESENTING

- **Enter an oral reading lottery.** Have someone draw names of at least ten students who will read their profiles aloud. Discuss each one.
- **Collect the class's profiles in an "Unforgettable Individuals" booklet.** Include photographs of the subjects, if possible. Distribute copies to the school and local library and to senior citizen centers in your community.

Video

Related ASSIGNMENT

When you write, you carefully choose the words and phrases that will most effectively communicate your ideas. Words, however, needn't be the only resource you draw on. Think of speeches you have heard, movies you have seen, and news stories you have watched on TV. In all these instances, words and images combine to communicate a powerful message.

As you read this script for a high school news show, notice how the images and words work together to present the story of a school assembly to welcome a political candidate.

- A U D I O -		- V I D E O -
1 Tuesday morning Evergreen Hills High School became the latest battleground in our community's hard fought mayoral race when candidate and city supervisor Christine Rutherford addressed a special student assembly.	→	Reporter standing in front of school trophy case.
2 The supervisor received a warm greeting from Principal Jeffries and his staff, but it was nothing. . .	→	{Cut to} Supervisor Rutherford arriving in front of school and being greeted by principal and other school staff members.
3 . . .compared to the enthusiastic reception she was accorded by students and faculty in assembly hall.	→	{Cut to} assembly hall and cheering students.
4 The message Supervisor Rutherford brought to Evergreen Hills High was a simple one: the curriculum must get tougher if America intends to compete on an equal footing with foreign competitors.	→	{Cut to} long shot of supervisor addressing students.
5 {Excerpt of supervisor's speech synchronized to video track.}	→	{Cut to} close shot of supervisor speaking.

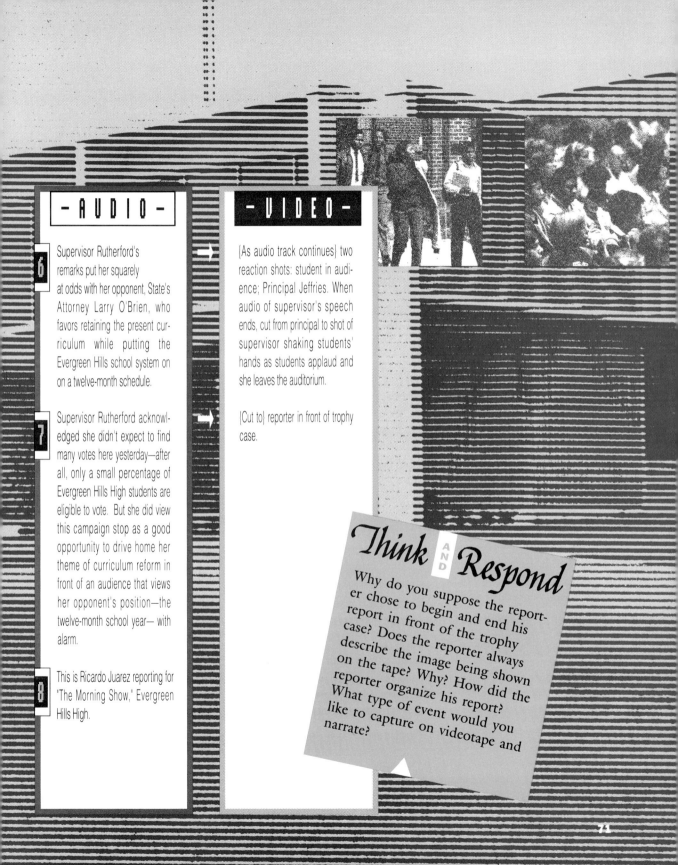

- A U D I O -

6 Supervisor Rutherford's remarks put her squarely at odds with her opponent, State's Attorney Larry O'Brien, who favors retaining the present curriculum while putting the Evergreen Hills school system on on a twelve-month schedule.

7 Supervisor Rutherford acknowledged she didn't expect to find many votes here yesterday—after all, only a small percentage of Evergreen Hills High students are eligible to vote. But she did view this campaign stop as a good opportunity to drive home her theme of curriculum reform in front of an audience that views her opponent's position—the twelve-month school year— with alarm.

8 This is Ricardo Juarez reporting for "The Morning Show," Evergreen Hills High.

- V I D E O -

→ {As audio track continues} two reaction shots: student in audience; Principal Jeffries. When audio of supervisor's speech ends, cut from principal to shot of supervisor shaking students' hands as students applaud and she leaves the auditorium.

→ {Cut to} reporter in front of trophy case.

Think AND Respond

Why do you suppose the reporter chose to begin and end his report in front of the trophy case? Does the reporter always describe the image being shown on the tape? Why? How did the reporter organize his report? What type of event would you like to capture on videotape and narrate?

INVITATION TO Write

News excerpts like the one you just read may appear for only one minute, but they can convey a great deal of information. Now plan a one-to-three-minute videotape of an event that you think will have an impact on your audience or community.

The skills of observation you employed to write your journalistic narrative become even more important when you take up a video camera. When your audience views your videotape, they will literally see the event through your eyes. As you prepare to tape, think of yourself as a member of your audience. Ask yourself what they would like to see and at what points they want to look more closely. Don't be intimidated by the video equipment—it's easy to use. All those hours of television watching have already taught you what makes a good video.

GETTING READY TO TAPE

HANDBOOKS

FOR HELP & PRACTICE

**Reflecting/
Observing,
pp. 331–332**

**Planning Your Work,
p. 348**

**Collaborative
Planning,
pp. 358–360**

**Introductions/
Conclusions,
pp. 365–375**

**Vantage Point,
pp. 450–451**

1. Decide what you want to tape. Your goal is to choose an event that can be covered within a one-to-three-minute period. Consider where you must go to tape your event. An individual sports competition, a public meeting, or a rally on a controversial topic might provide you with good footage. Perhaps you prefer to tape in a particular classroom, the school's lunchroom, on a street corner, or at a public park.

2. Think about your story line. If possible, decide on the story you want to tell, or the message or point you want to convey. Of course, these may not become completely clear until after you have taped quite a few scenes and details.

3. Practice camera shots and moves. Become familiar with some of the events available to you. In a **long shot,** you can portray a large canvas with many small details. Following such a shot, you might

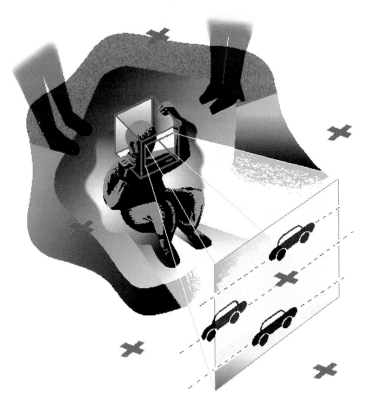

zoom in closer to your subject. You can also **pan,** moving the camera horizontally; **tilt,** moving the camera vertically; or **track,** moving at right angles to or parallel with your subject. Experiment with these different camera movements until you are familiar with the effects they achieve.

4. Select a focus for your tape.   A camera is like the voice that tells a story on a page. Decide if you want your camera to be an impartial witness to events—an omniscient third-person narrator like the television news camera—or if you prefer to take a subjective viewpoint in order to make a more personal statement.

TAPING YOUR STORY

1. Establish a background for your story.   Begin with a long shot that shows where you are and gives your audience a clear context for your story.

2. Balance long shots with detailed close-ups.   Every single shot should tell part of your story, and few shots should last longer than about six to ten seconds. You can cut away between shots by pressing the PAUSE button and then releasing it when you find your next shot.

Writing
—**TIP**—

A storyboard may help you clarify your video in your own mind before you do any actual cutting.

Writer's Choice   Sometimes you may need to take shots that last longer than ten seconds. If you have to focus on one shot for so long, keep your audience's interest by zooming, panning, or otherwise moving your camera.

3. End your story.   Make sure your tape comes to a natural conclusion. You may want to end with a long shot or by slowly moving your camera away from the subject and fading out.

4. Edit your tape.   If the equipment is available, cut and splice different portions of your tape to tighten your story or allow your focus to come through more clearly.

5. Add narration or music.   If your tape has no sound, you will need to add some narration or music to clarify the focus of your story.

REVIEWING YOUR VIDEO

1. View your tape by yourself or with an eyewitness to the event.   Decide whether your tape tells the story you intended to tell. Did your focus come through clearly? Did the narration or background music you added contribute effectively to your story?

2. Make another tape.   The wonderful thing about videotaping is that you can always tape over your mistakes. Now that you know more about how to create the effects you want, tape your story again, or follow the same steps to tape a different story.

PUBLISHING AND PRESENTING

- **Contact a local station.**   If your tape shows an event of local importance, send it to your local or cable television station.
- **Compare tapes.**   Compare your tape with that of a friend who taped the same event. How does your point of view differ from your friend's?
- **Consider a video yearbook.**   Explore the idea of a video yearbook, a concept many schools are using. A production team can decide the best arrangement for the tapes, and a design group can add graphics or narration between each tape. Decide whether you need an anchorperson or reporters to introduce the various segments.

Sentence

Imitating Sentence Structures

Effective writers often use phrases and clauses to elaborate on the main idea of a sentence. In the sentence below, notice the three present participles (verb forms ending in *-ing* and used as modifiers). Each begins a phrase, and the three participial phrases parallel each other, which gives the sentence detail and a rhythm that catches the reader's interest.

Model: Sometimes a gaggle of them came to the store, filling the room, chasing out the air, and changing the well-known scents.

Maya Angelou, *I Know Why the Caged Bird Sings*

A. Identifying Imitations Identify the sentences that imitate the model.

1. After lunch Lee returned to his research, pieces of which were spread all over the desk in the workroom above the garage, and picked up the slide that had so intrigued him.

2. Sometimes a pack of hunting dogs roamed through the field, circling the abandoned barn, sniffing constantly for the trail, and never stopping their frantic pursuit.

3. Often a horde of job applicants arrived at the office, completing the long application, sitting tensely in the waiting room, and repeatedly rearranging their nervous legs.

4. When the alarm clock rang, it jolted him, as if someone had opened up his head, located his brain, and flicked a finger against it.

5. Soon a more relaxed version of the young woman appeared in the room, commanding the attention of everyone, speaking confidently to the audience, and never losing her quiet poise.

B. Unscrambling Sentences Decide which sets of sentence parts can be made into sentences whose structure matches the model. Then, for the ones that match the model, unscramble the parts and write the sentences.

1 a. and occasionally calling to a passing friend
  b. watching the people go by
  c. often a group of us stood on the corner
  d. shifting from one foot to another

2 a. we always felt uneasy
  b. not knowing whether to worry about our pets
  c. whenever a coyote howled at night
  d. and wishing they were safe at home

3 a. chatting with each other
   b. every Monday morning the seniors sat at their desks
   c. comparing notes about their weekends
   d. and sometimes sharing whispered secrets

5 a. Beowulf dove into the murky depths
   b. with the warning still ringing in his ears
   c. and found the lair of the monster's hideous mother
   d. until his lungs were strained to bursting

4 a. but Bea did it without hesitation
   b. on the bulletin board in the math room
   c. no one had yet solved the problem
   d. and without even thinking hard

6 a. fumbling in his notebook
   b. dropping everything with a crash onto the floor
   c. nervously Ken rummaged around for the assignment
   d. and calling attention to what should have been unnoticed

C. Combining Sentences   Use the first sentence in each set as a foundation. Whenever necessary, change the verbs in the sentences following the foundation into present participles. Then insert the participial phrases into the foundation, forming a sentence that matches the model.

Model: Sometimes a gaggle of them came into the store, filling the room, chasing out the air, and changing the well-known scents.
                                    Maya Angelou, *I Know Why the Caged Bird Sings*

Example   Then he hit his stride. He *gripped the baton in his right hand.* He *watched the other runners fall away.* He *floated down the track as if he could fly.*

Combined   Then he hit his stride, gripping the baton in his right hand, watching the other runners fall away, and floating down the track as if he could fly.

1. Always a crowd of spectators filled the stands. They spread their nervous excitement. They hooted their cheers. They even tried to outshout the fans of the opposing team.

2. Frequently a gathering of senior citizens sat in the park. They enjoyed the weather and played checkers. They told favorite stories.

Model: That winter my mother and father came and we set up house-keeping, buying furniture on the installment plan, being cheated, and yet knowing no way to avoid it.

Richard Wright, *Black Boy*

3. That morning we brought out the arrowhead, and Renee examined it. She was eyeing it in a curious way. She was growing interested. And yet she was showing no sign of recognizing it.

4. Friday evening the breeze picked up, and a deep blush spread over the sky. It was changing the clouds to the color of ripe peaches. It was deepening to red. And then it was vanishing as quickly as it had come.

D. Expanding Sentences   Both model sentences above end in a series of three participial phrases. Expand each sentence below by adding a similar series of participial phrases.

> **Example**   At least once a week, the computer went crazy.
>
> **Student Sentence** At least once a week, the computer went crazy, throwing strange patterns on the screen, refusing to do what the keystroke asked it to do, acting like a stubborn electronic donkey that wouldn't budge.

1. Sometimes the class made the teacher proud to be a teacher.

2. Too often the car would suddenly break down.

3. Unexpectedly the music would make her forget all her troubles.

4. Suddenly the weather changed dramatically and drastically.

5. Now a group of ninth-grade students invaded the cafeteria.

E. Imitating Sentences   Now that you are familiar with the arrangement of sentence parts in the models, write three sentences that imitate the structure of the models.

Application   Write a short paragraph that includes one of the imitations you wrote for Exercise E.

Grammar Refresher   The sentences in this lesson contain present participial phrases. For more about phrases, see Handbook 33. For more about present participles and present participial phrases, see Handbook 33.

Sketchbook

"The Pasture"

I'm going out to clean the pasture spring;
I'll only stop to rake the leaves away
(And wait to watch the water clear, I may):
I sha'n't be gone long.—You come too.

I'm going out to fetch the little calf
That's standing by the mother. It's so young
It totters when she licks it with her tongue.
I sha'n't be gone long.—You come too.

Robert Frost

Write a poem or something somewhat poemlike that uses some of the elements Frost uses. For example, you may want to start each stanza with a phrase like "I'm going . . . ," then tell where you're going, and end each stanza with a recurring line or phrase.

Additional Sketches

Alone on stage, blinded by the spotlight, you say . . .

Set a scene from your latest blockbuster movie, or narrate an episode from a movie that you've seen and remember vividly.

Narrative and Literary Writing

Guided Assignment
DRAMATIC WRITING

Related Assignment
STORY

Related Assignment
CHORAL POEM

I n 1938, many thousands of people jumped into their automobiles to flee an invasion from Mars. They had been listening to a radio version of *The War of the Worlds.* The medium of radio demonstrated the extraordinary power of dramatic narrative to move the hearts and minds of audiences.

Film and video plays today are just the most recent manifestations of an ancient art form—the drama. In this workshop, you will explore ways you can combine dialogue and staging in a dramatic scene to convey situations and ideas. You will then use the techniques of the drama to create a story and a choral poem.

Dramatic Writing

FROM
THE ELEPHANT MAN
BY
BERNARD POMERANCE

The London Hospital.   MERRICK *in bathtub.*
TREVES *outside.*
Enter MISS SANDWICH.

TREVES: You are? Miss Sandwich?

SANDWICH: Sandwich. Yes.

TREVES: You have had experience in missionary hospitals in the Niger.

SANDWICH: And Ceylon.

TREVES: I may assume you've seen—

SANDWICH: The tropics. Oh those diseases. The many and the awful scourges our Lord sends, yes, sir.

TREVES: I need the help of an experienced nurse, you see.

SANDWICH: Someone to bring him food, take care of the room. Yes, I understand. But it is somehow difficult.

TREVES: Well, I have been let down so far. He really is—that is, the regular sisters—well, it is not part of their job and they will not do it. Be ordinarily kind to Mr. Merrick. Without—well—panicking. He is quite beyond ugly. You understand that? His appearance has terrified them.

SANDWICH: The photographs show a terrible disease.

TREVES: It is a disorder, not a disease; it is in no way contagious though we don't in fact know what it is. I have found however that there is a deep superstition in those I've tried, they actually believe he somehow brought it on himself, this thing, and of course it is not that at all.

SANDWICH: I am not one who believes it is ourselves who attain grace or bring chastisement to us, sir.

TREVES: Miss Sandwich, I am hoping not.

SANDWICH: Let me put your mind to rest. Care for lepers in the East, and you have cared, Mr. Treves. In Africa, I have seen dreadful scourges quite unknown to our more civilized climes. . . .   Appearances do not daunt me.

TREVES: It is really that that has sent me outside the confines of the London [Hospital] seeking help.

SANDWICH: "I look unto the hills whence cometh my help." I understand: I think I will be satisfactory.

> (*Enter* PORTER *with* tray.)

PORTER: His lunch.

> (*Exits*)

TREVES: Perhaps you would be so kind as to accompany me this time. I will introduce you.

SANDWICH: Allow me to carry the tray.

TREVES: I will this time. You are ready.

SANDWICH: I am.

TREVES: He is bathing to be rid of his odor.

> (*They enter to* MERRICK.)

> John, this is Miss Sandwich. She—

SANDWICH: I—(*Unable to control herself.*) Oh my good God in heaven.

> (*Bolts room.*)

TREVES: (*Puts* MERRICK'S *lunch down.*) I am sorry. I thought—

MERRICK: Thank you for saving the lunch this time.

TREVES: Excuse me. . .

> (*Exits to* MISS SANDWICH.)

SANDWICH: You didn't say.

TREVES: But I—

SANDWICH: Didn't! You said just—words!

TREVES: But the photographs.

SANDWICH: Just pictures. No one will do this. I am sorry.

> (*Exits.*)

TREVES: Yes. Well. This is not helping him.

Fadeout

Think AND Respond

Bernard Pomerance conveys a good deal about Merrick, Sandwich, and Treves without ever describing them directly. What traits do the characters' dialogue and actions reveal about them? What details of dialogue and stage direction convey the different traits? What ideas for a piece of dramatic writing does Pomerance's scene suggest to you?

INVITATION
—— TO ——
Write

Bernard Pomerance used his dramatic scene to convey what key characters in his play are like and to underscore his play's conflict. Now it is your turn to write a dramatic scene for stage, screen, or radio.

Some of the most popular stories nowadays are not stories that people read. They are stories dramatized and presented on stage, screen, television, or radio. Dramas have the same elements as stories: **plot, character,** and **setting.** Also, like stories, they revolve around a central conflict. This conflict may take place within a character's mind or between a character and some external force.

Dramas are meant to be acted out, using speech and movements. As a result, dramas differ from stories in important ways. Information about characters, plot, and conflict must be conveyed almost entirely through **dialogue,** or what the characters say. Additional information about setting, how characters move and speak, and sound effects, can be conveyed through stage or set directions.

Writing a full-fledged play your first time out is a large task. You should master the basics before trying an entire drama. In this assignment, you will write just one scene. You might introduce the characters, the setting, and a central conflict, or you might develop one key moment.

FOR HELP & PRACTICE

Reflecting,
pp. 331–332
Observation Charts,
p. 341
Plot Diagrams,
p. 346
Collaborative Planning,
pp. 358–360
Elaborative Details,
pp. 376–378

PREWRITE AND EXPLORE

1. Look for ideas. Drama and conflict are all around you. Try some of the following activities to look for dramatic ideas.

Exploratory Activities

• **Browsing** Many writers for stage, screen, and radio get their ideas from news headlines. Sometimes they actually buy the rights to true stories. At other times, they use a headline as a springboard for their own imaginations from which they develop completely different characters and settings. Look through newspapers and magazines, and you will probably find a great many ideas.

- **Recalling and freewriting** Think of a time in your own life when you felt a really strong emotion—whether positive or negative. Freewrite about this time and this emotion and see if you can come up with an idea for a character who is embroiled in a similarly emotion-producing situation.
- **Charting** Create a character with interesting traits and skills. Think of conflicts, internal and external, in which this character might be involved. List these in a chart with such headings as *Internal Conflicts, Conflicts with People, Conflicts with Institutions, Conflicts with Things in the Natural World,* and *Conflicts with Social or Political Forces.*
- **Asking "what if" questions** Ask yourself off-the-wall "what if" questions about ordinary things in your experience. For example, the makers of the movie *Who Framed Roger Rabbit?* probably asked themselves, "What if cartoon characters were real and treated like second-class citizens?" Ask yourself about the conflict potential of each situation you dream up.
- **Reading literature** A common source of dramatic ideas is material that already exists in another form. Dramas have been based on legends, biographies, comic books, comic strips, historical events, and events from the Bible. Bernard Pomerance based *The Elephant Man* on memoirs about John Merrick written by Sir Frederick Treves. Consider taking a real historical character and creating a dramatic version of a portion of that character's life or taking an existing story, such as a myth or fable, and retelling it in dramatic form.

2. Choose an idea. Look through your ideas. Choose one or more that look promising and freewrite about them, seeing which ones have the most potential. Share your freewriting with a small group of classmates. If you are having trouble finding an idea, you might also glance through your journal, look at the writing you did for the Sketchbook on page 78, or check the "Apply Your Skills" section on page 97.

Dale asked himself a series of "what if" questions. Then he did some freewriting and chose the idea that seemed most workable. Throughout this workshop, you will follow Dale's process as he develops his ideas into a dramatic scene.

PROBLEM SOLVING

How will I find ideas for a scene with a strong conflict, riveting characters, or an intriguing setting?

ONE STUDENT'S PROCESS

What if . . .

dolphins were tired of the way people were experimenting
with them and decided to capture people to experiment with?

✳ human minds were like computer files and one could make
copies of them, erase them, copy one program on top of
another, and so on?

a group of people traveled back in time and were able to change
the Constitution in some way?

a scientist developed a new strain of rice that grew without
moisture but didn't realize the rice would have some disastrous
effect twenty years later?

What if someone is going to be erased and doesn't want to be?

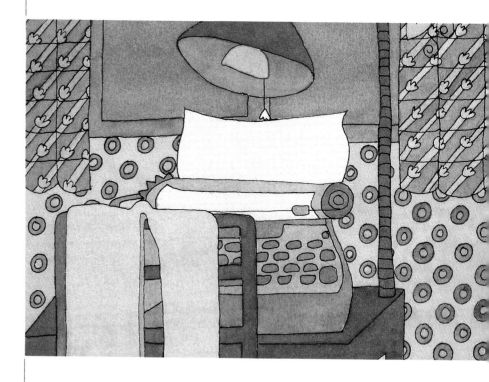

3. Explore your idea. Before you begin drafting, you will want to make decisions about your drama's basic elements—character, setting, plot, and conflict. You may wish to freewrite about each element, or use charts, clusters, or sketches to gather details.

- **Character** Identify your main characters and describe their physical characteristics and important attitudes and beliefs. Then flesh out these characters by writing minibiographies or résumés listing their education, work experience, and interests. You may also want to draw sketches of your characters and establish unique identities for them by giving them special habits, such as habitual turns of phrase or gestures.
- **Setting** Decide where and when your drama takes place. Establish both its physical setting and its time period. You may want to draw sketches of your settings and set designs and create floor plans. You can use these sketches to plan how your characters will move.
- **Plot** Make a rough plan of what will happen in the beginning, middle, and end of your drama. In many dramas, the beginning introduces the characters and establishes the conflict. The middle develops the conflict, adding complications and sometimes showing attempts at a resolution. The end resolves the conflict and presents the final outcome. You may want to make a time line of your plot, divided into appropriate units, such as minutes, hours, or days.
- **Conflict** Decide what the central conflict will be. You may wish to experiment by freewriting about a turning point or showdown that reveals the conflict that must be resolved.

 Writer's Choice Once you have looked over the notes you have developed, you can decide what type of scene you feel most comfortable writing. You can write an introductory scene, one that develops a key character, one that develops the central conflict, or any other scene.

4. Create a mood. Once you have established the basic elements of your drama, consider the general emotional quality, or atmosphere, you want to convey. All elements of a drama contribute to the mood, and a skillful writer manipulates elements consciously to change the mood as appropriate throughout the drama.

5. Use collaborative planning. With a partner discuss your potential audience by considering such questions as these: Are you writing for children? Do you want your work to be viewed primarily by teenagers? By parents? By adults in general?

PROBLEM SOLVING

Who will my characters be? What will happen in my drama? Where will my drama take place?

Writing **—TIP—**

One way to create realistic characters is to base them on people you know. This can help you give your characters natural-sounding speech.

Once you have decided what audience to appeal to, establish what you want to accomplish. Will you be introducing your characters? Will you be presenting your central conflict or developing it? Will you be dramatizing the climax? Also keep in mind the overall goal of your drama, which could include teaching a lesson or getting the audience to see something in an entirely new light.

6. Explore your scene. Before you begin writing your scene, develop a rough plan. You might write an outline or a synopsis. You might also take the roles of the characters in your scene and play the parts of each one, having them talk to each other. Your scene will grow out of what the characters say.

7. Playact. With your rough plan in place, explore your scene further with a partner. Take different parts and perform them. See how the characters interact and speak. Experiment with ways of moving your plot forward through dialogue and actions.

DRAFT AND DISCOVER

1. Begin your draft. If you have trouble starting, simply place your characters in a situation and have them start talking to one another. The scene will grow out of what they say. If you feel more comfortable with one part of your scene than you do with others, start with that part and build around it.

2. Organize the draft. You will want to organize your dialogue and stage and set directions in ways that *show* rather than *tell* your audience what is happening. Think of your scene as a series of moments, like the moments caught in photographs, being presented to the eyes of the audience. Here are some strategies you can use.

Strategies

- **Dialogue** Use your dialogue to move your story along. Do the characters see some danger? Advance the plot by having them describe the danger, express their reactions to it, and pursue an escape from it. Use your dialogue to show your characters' personalities as well. Bernard Pomerance used Treves's dialogue to portray him as a dedicated and devoted doctor. Try to create real people with natural-sounding voices and try to make each voice distinct. Experiment with different speech patterns and levels of language.

FOR HELP & PRACTICE

Drafting Styles, pp. 361–362

Emphasis/Tone/ Mood, pp. 423–428

Varieties of Language, pp. 429–434

Dialogue in Drama, pp. 452–453

PROBLEM

S O L V I N G

How can I *show* rather than *tell* in my scene?

- **Stage and set directions** Use your stage and set directions to establish setting; describe costumes; tell characters when, where, and how to move; describe the use of props; and detail sound effects. Directions for a screen or television play should also specify the point of view from which a shot should be seen and whether the shot is long, close, or panning.

You will need to put your dialogue and stage and set directions in a format that will make them easy to use for actors and directors. If you are writing for the stage or radio, use the format of the scene from *The Elephant Man* (page 80). If you are writing for the movies or television, follow that of *Replacement Parts* (page 92).

 Writer's Choice A narrator can move a drama forward by providing background information or raising important issues. Would a narrator be useful in your scene?

Dale decided to write his scene as a television play. He also decided to use a narrator and to develop an introductory scene in which he would present his setting and characters and establish his central conflict. Here is how he used dialogue and stage and set directions in the unrevised first draft of his scene.

Your word-processing program may be able to help you automatically format your dialogue and stage directions. In addition, computer programs are available for formatting screenplays.

ONE STUDENT'S PROCESS

INTERIOR. BREAKFAST TABLE AT BED AND BREAKFAST CLOSE-UP. CENTER TOP OF TABLE WITH FOOD.

NARRATOR (Voice over). It isn't often that a mother and daughter get to take a vacation together, to linger over coffee and Danish just to shoot the breeze.

MOTHER (v.o.). Just try a bite. Like this. (SOUND OF MOTHER EATING)
DAUGHTER (v.o.). I'm not putting that in my mouth.

PULL BACK TO REVEAL *MOTHER* AND *DAUGHTER* FROM ABOVE. EACH HAS A SHAVEN BALD HEAD AND WEARS A TOGALIKE GARMENT.

3. Reread and react.   Reread your draft aloud to make sure your dialogue sounds natural and believable. You may also want to share your draft with one or more peer readers by assigning the various roles and reading the scene aloud. Make sure your stage and set directions give information that will help actors and directors convey your meaning. The following are questions you can ask yourself and the readers or listeners who review your draft as you look for the strengths and weaknesses in your work.

R E V I E W   Y O U R   W R I T I N G

Questions for Yourself

- Is the conflict introduced, developed, or resolved in a powerful and interesting way? Is the part of the plot presented in my scene clearly understandable?

- Do I have a vivid sense of who my characters are? Of what they look and sound like? Do they have their own distinct habits, emotional states, or mannerisms?

- Is my setting clear? What details can I add to make it more vivid? Have I put to good use the appropriate methods for developing setting, including set pieces, costumes, sound effects, and characters' comments?

- Are there places where I can do more to *show* instead of *tell*?

Questions for Your Peer Readers

- Does the scene capture your attention from the very beginning? If not, how can I change the opening so that it really involves you?

- Do my characters seem like real people to you? Is their dialogue convincing and natural?

- Does this scene take place in a recognizable locale? Can you picture the time and place in your mind? Which details of my setting are most and least effective?

- How do my characters, conflict, and setting make you feel? How do your feelings change or develop as the scene progresses?

- Is there any part of the scene that is not clear to you? If so, what part?

1. Evaluate your response. Consider your own responses and those of your peers. Then, based on these responses, revise your draft. As you revise, also keep in mind that effective dramatic writing generally displays certain basic characteristics.

Standards for Evaluation

Effective dramatic writing . . .

- deals with an interesting conflict that is clearly conveyed by the plot.
- sustains the interest of the audience.
- uses the elements of character and setting to create a convincing world of its own.
- uses language appropriate to its characters.
- shows rather than tells what is occurring.
- includes complete stage directions as necessary.
- uses appropriate format for dramatic writing.

2. Problem-solve. Revise your draft, making changes based on your own review and the reviews of peer readers or listeners. Dale made changes in his draft in response to the comments of one peer listener. They are shown on the next page.

HANDBOOKS
FOR HELP & PRACTICE

Introductions/ Conclusions, pp. 365–375
Elaborative Details, pp. 376–378
Unity/Coherence, p. 388
Revising Effectively, pp. 392–396
Varieties of Language, pp. 429–433

I love this weird stuff—could you add details to make it even stranger?

REPORTER. Technicai͡ns at Brigham and Women's Rejuvenation center in the North American state of Boston are still trying to sort out how the three erasures could have occurred. Normally, before people go through rejuvenation, technicians copy the contents of their minds͜ into a nanotech storage unit, or NSU. (HOLDS UP , including all stored memories, habitual processing routines, and so on, PRISM-SHAPED INSTRUMENT LIKE THAT SEEN STICKING FROM *MOTHER͜S* HEAD.) During the copying process, backups are made and shipped to separate storage locations͡, , so that if anything goes wrong at one location, there will be a good, clean copy of the person on file elsewhere.

INT. ~~BRIGHAM AND WOMEN'S~~ REJUVENATION CENTER LABORATORY — MEDIUM CLOSE SHOT OF *TECHNICIAN* WITH INSET OF *REPORTER'S* TALKING HEAD.
REPORTER'S HEAD SWIVELS 120°TO SPEAK DIRECTLY TO *TECHNICIAN*. *TECHNICIAN* LOOKS AT HEAD AS THOUGH SPEAKING TO A PHYSICALLY PRESENT PERSON.

REPORTER. So how could this tragedy have happened͡.͡?

TECHNICIAN. We just don't know. When time came for these three rejuvs, we did standard grafts of the recently backed up NSUs. However, in these͜ cases, after operations, there ~~are~~ no readings for mental functions.
three
were
INT. OPERATING THEATER. A TEENAGER ON A STRETCHER IS BEING FITTED WITH A PRISM BY SURGEONS. *TECHNICIAN* (Cont., v. o.)

Gets better and better, but you could make this grabbier by cutting to the operating room and showing someone undergoing the operation.

3. Proofread your work. Once you are finished with your revisions, make a final copy and proofread it carefully for errors in grammar, usage, spelling, and mechanics.

LINKING
GRAMMAR [AND] WRITING
Formats for Dramatic Writing

The basic formats and the use of capitalization, punctuation, and abbreviations in dialogue and stage directions vary among the different forms of dramatic writing. For information on specific formats, see sources such as the following:

Cole, Hillis R., and Judith Haag. *The Complete Guide to Standard Script Formats.* Hollywood: CMC Publishing, 1980.

Field, Sid. *The Screenwriter's Workbook.* New York: Dell, 1988.

Goldman, William. *Adventures in the Screen Trade.* New York: Warner Books, 1983.

Hilliard, Robert L. *Writing for Television and Radio.* New York: Hastings House, 1976.

P UBLISH AND PRESENT

- **Present your scene as reader's theater.** In reader's theater, a play is read by actors who present the dialogue and the stage directions, either standing in position or sitting in chairs. To present your scene as reader's theater, assign the different parts to different readers. Choose a narrator to read the stage directions. Place someone in charge of sound effects.
- **Produce your scene.** Choose several scenes from your class to produce and present to other classes. Select students to direct the scenes; to play the parts; and to plan simple sets, costumes, and props. If possible, videotape your scenes.
- **Complete your play and have the drama teacher review it.** Develop additional scenes to complete your whole play. Ask your school's drama teacher to give you some suggestions for improving your work.
- **Save your work in your writing portfolio.**

HANDBOOKS

FOR HELP & PRACTICE

Preparing Manuscript, pp. 414–415

Replacement Parts

Dale Berger

ACT ONE

INT. BREAKFAST TABLE AT BED AND BREAKFAST

CLOSE-UP

CENTER TOP OF BREAKFAST TABLE WITH A PLATE OF CROISSANTS AND DANISH, A PITCHER OF ORANGE JUICE, ANOTHER OF COFFEE.

SFX: BIRDS TWITTER

NARRATOR (v.o.) It isn't often that a mother and daughter get a chance to talk—really to talk. That's why it's such a good idea to take a short vacation together, to linger over coffee and Danish just to shoot the breeze.

HANDS OF *MOTHER* AND *DAUGHTER* REACH INTO SHOT, GRABBING DANISH, POURING JUICE, ETC.

MOTHER (v.o.) Just try a bite. Like this. (SOUND OF MOTHER EATING)
DAUGHTER (v.o.) I'm not putting that in my mouth. It's too weird.

PULL BACK TO REVEAL *MOTHER* AND *DAUGHTER* FROM ABOVE. EACH HAS A SHAVEN BALD HEAD AND WEARS A TOGALIKE GARMENT. THE *DAUGHTER* HAS A TRIANGU-LAR PATCH ON THE TOP REAR CROWN OF HER HEAD. EM-BEDDED IN THE SAME POSITION ON THE *MOTHER'S* HEAD IS A PRISM-SHAPED MECHANICAL DEVICE, TRIANGULAR AT ITS BASE AND RAISED TWO TO THREE INCHES FROM THE *MOTHER'S* SKULL. *MOTHER* AND *DAUGHTER* ARE RE-MARKABLY SIMILAR IN APPEARANCE.

Uses screenplay format, including abbreviations for set directions such as INT for "interior," SFX for "special effects," and v.o. for "voice over"

Uses dialogue to present believable, engaging characters

Set directions provide descriptions for understanding characters.

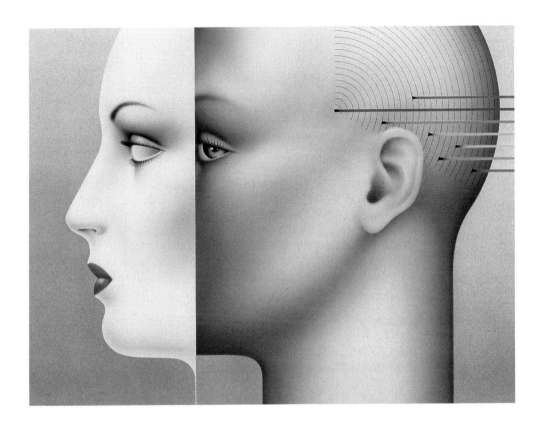

MOTHER (TO *DAUGHTER*) You know that I'm spending a great many credits on this vacation. The least you can do is to try and have the whole experience. Come on now. Just a nibble.

DAUGHTER It's *too* weird. I can't believe people actually used to nourish themselves this way.

MOTHER OK . . . I tell you what. Take a few bites while I watch the news, and then we'll go out to the feelioport.

DAUGHTER Great. Now you're talking.

ANGLE ON *MOTHER*, WHO SWIVELS IN CHAIR.

POINT OF VIEW SHOT—MOTHER'S VIEW OF A PASTORAL SCENE THROUGH WINDOW BY THE TABLE

MOTHER (v.o.) News on.

Develops characters to make them part of their own distinct world

TIGHT SHOT—PASTORAL SCENE THROUGH WINDOW.
IRIS OPEN SLOWLY TO WALL-SIZED COMPUTER SCREEN.
LOGO FOR "CONNECT PNN," A NEWS NETWORK, WITH
INSET TALKING HEAD OF *PERSONAL NEWS ANNOUNCER*.

PERSONAL NEWS ANNOUNCER Connect PNN, your Personal News Network. Good morning, Sarah 42. Today is Tuesday, August 14. Are you enjoying your vacation?
MOTHER (v.o.) Yes. Very much.
PERSONAL NEWS ANNOUNCER I'm glad to hear it. You have no appointments scheduled. There is a priority news bulletin from the office of Reproductive and Rejuvenatory Affairs. Do you wish to see it?

ANGLE ON *MOTHER*

MOTHER Sure. (ASIDE TO *DAUGHTER*) These things are getting chattier and chattier.

INT. DAY, UNITED NATIONS. INSET HEAD OF *REPORTER*.

REPORTER Officials here at the United Nations are stunned by reports from the North American Sector that three citizens have, to use an ancient word, *died*. Yes, died.

EXT. DAY, ENTRANCE TO FUTURISTIC HOSPITAL WITH SIGN READING "BRIGHAM AND WOMEN'S REJUVENATION CENTER." INSET TALKING HEAD OF *REPORTER*.

REPORTER Technicians at Brigham and Women's Rejuvenation Center in the North American state of Boston are still trying to sort out how the three erasures could have occurred. Normally, before people go through rejuvenation, technicians copy the contents of their minds, including all stored memories, habitual processing routines, and so on, into a nanotech storage unit, or NSU. (HOLDS UP PRISM-SHAPED INSTRUMENT LIKE THAT SEEN STICKING FROM *MOTHER'S* HEAD.) During the copying process, backups are made and shipped to separate storage locations, so that if anything goes wrong at one location, there will be a good, clean copy of the person on file elsewhere.

Uses language and situations appropriate for its intended audience—young adults and adults

INT. REJUVENATION CENTER LABORATORY—MEDIUM CLOSE SHOT OF *TECHNICIAN* WITH INSET OF *REPORTER'S* HEAD. *REPORTER'S* HEAD SWIVELS 120° TO SPEAK DIRECTLY TO *TECHNICIAN*. *TECHNICIAN* LOOKS AT HEAD AS THOUGH SPEAKING TO A PHYSICALLY PRESENT PERSON.

REPORTER So how could this tragedy have happened?
TECHNICIAN We just don't know. When time came for these three rejuvs, we did standard grafts of the recently backed up NSUs.

INT. OPERATING THEATER. A TEENAGER ON A STRETCHER IS BEING FITTED WITH A PRISM BY SURGEONS.

TECHNICIAN (cont., v.o.) However, in these three cases, after the operations, there were *no readings for mental functions.* Three NSUs failed, and we don't know why. This would not be a tragedy, except that *all the backup NSUs for these citizens also failed.*

INT. REJUVENATION CENTER, DATA PROCESSING LABORATORY. *TECHNICIAN* AND INSET OF *REPORTER'S* HEAD.

REPORTER So these three citizens are . . . dead. Is that a fair assessment?
TECHNICIAN (STRICKEN) Well, it appears that . . . yes . . . I guess you could say that they . . . that they no longer exist . . . that's correct.
REPORTER Thank you. That was technician Amahl 47 of Boston Rejuv.

INT. FAMILY AT BREAKFAST TABLE

MOTHER News hold.
DAUGHTER What does the telly mean, that these people have "died"?
MOTHER Well, back before the rejuv was invented, people didn't live forever. Then, in the twenty-first century scientists figured out how to grow perfect copies of people from genetically altered somatic, or body, cells—to make *clones.* However, try as they might, scientists could never figure out how to stop people from growing old and dying.

Dialogue moves plot along.

DAUGHTER What do you mean, "growing old"?

MOTHER Well, people used to wear out. Like disposable automobiles. That's when we hit on the idea of creating clone children, like you, and then doing a mind swap once the children became teen-agers.

DAUGHTER Sure, I understand that. You'll have your mind inserted in me, and then a new clone will be made and raised to be a teen-ager, and then the minds will be swapped again, and so on forever and forever. But what is this death? I don't understand that part.

MOTHER Let's see. (THINKS FOR A MOMENT) You know, of course, that when we do the rejuv, and my mind goes into your body, your mind will be erased because it's just a temporary.

DAUGHTER (NOT AN ASSENT, BUT WITH THE MEANING, "YES, GO ON TO THE IMPORTANT PART.") OK.

MOTHER Well, death is like being erased. Only it happens to immortals, like me.

DAUGHTER How very odd. You mean *erase an immortal*?

MOTHER Well, it *never* happens. At least not often, thank goodness.

DAUGHTER (AFTER A PAUSE) How weird!

MOTHER Are you OK?

DAUGHTER Oh, yeah. Sure. If you don't mind, though, I'd like to stay around the hotel for a bit. Why don't you just go on to the feelioport, and I'll catch up later.

MOTHER OK, but don't be long.

INT. *DAUGHTER'S* ROOM IN BED AND BREAKFAST. SHE LOOKS INTO A MIRROR AND TOUCHES THE PATCH ON THE BACK OF HER HEAD.

MUSIC. PULL BACK

NARRATOR (v.o.) Sarah 43, daughter of the immortal Sarah 42 of Boston State in the North American Sector of Planet Earth, year A.D. 2385. Genetically engineered to be, for her mother, a replacement part. It is a utopian world in which death does not exist and perfection has at last been attained. Or has it? This is the question that Sarah 43 is beginning to ask herself—in contradiction to her own biological programming.

Shows rather than tells what is occurring by describing character's actions

Uses narration to reveal the conflict

WRITER TO WRITER

[T]he rule of dramatic structure [is this]: **Every story, every plot, every subplot has to have a beginning, a middle, and an end.** This is a classic dramatic structure and is what makes a story a story. As simple as it seems, the lack of a complete story is one of the most common mistakes that writers make.

Carl Sautter, screenwriter

FOR YOUR
PORTFOLIO

1. Reflect on your writing. Write an introduction to your dramatic scene in which you share with the audience for your play some of the background on how this play came to be written and what it means to you. Tell about where you got your ideas for your characters or plot, what other plays or TV shows or fiction influenced your work, and what you hope your audience will understand or appreciate in your drama. Attach your introduction to your dramatic scene when you submit it to your teacher and when you place it in your portfolio.

2. Apply your skills. The following are some additional writing activities involving skills practiced in this workshop.

- **Cross-curricular** Imagine that you have been hired to write a 30-second public-service radio commercial for a cause related to public health, such as ending drug abuse or cigarette smoking or raising money for cancer research. Write the commercial, using the dramatic skills that you have acquired in this workshop.
- **Literature** Choose a short story by a classic American writer such as Nathaniel Hawthorne or Edgar Allan Poe. Write a dramatic adaptation of the story to be presented as reader's theater, as a film, or as a conventional play. Remember that you may have to add dialogue or even whole scenes to make an effective dramatization.
- **Related assignments** Follow the suggestions on pages 100–107 to write a story and present a choral poem.

Maud Martha ❧
Spares the Mouse

from *Maud Martha*
by Gwendolyn Brooks

Have you ever had a revelation—a moment of great personal discovery? You may find significance in life's grandest moments—in victories, confrontations, and achievements—or in simple moments of quiet reflection.

As you read Gwendolyn Brooks's short story, notice how she reveals a deeper personal significance in an everyday occurence.

There. She had it at last. The weeks it had devoted to eluding her, the tricks, the clever hide-and-go-seeks, the routes it had in all sobriety devised, together with the delicious moments it had, undoubtedly, laughed up its sleeve—all to no ultimate avail. She had that mouse.

It shook its little self, as best it could, in the trap. Its bright black eyes contained no appeal—the little creature seemed to understand that there was no

hope of mercy from the eternal enemy, no hope of
reprieve or postponement—but a fine small dignity.
It waited. It looked at Maud Martha.

She wondered what else it was thinking.
Perhaps that there was not enough food in its larder.
Perhaps that little Betty, a puny child from the start, would not, now, be
getting fed. Perhaps that, now, the family's seasonal house-cleaning, for
lack of expert direction, would be left undone. It might be regretting that
young Bobby's education was now at an end. It might be nursing personal
regrets. No more the mysterious shadows of the kitchenette, the uncharted
twists, the unguessed halls. No more the sweet delights of the chase, the
charms of being unsuccessfully hounded, thrown at.

Maud Martha could not bear the little look.

"Go home to your children," she urged. "To your wife or husband."
She opened the trap. The mouse vanished.

Suddenly, she was conscious of a new cleanness in her. A wide air
walked in her. A life had blundered its way into her power, and it
had been hers to preserve or destroy. She had not destroyed. In the center
of that simple restraint was—creation. She had creat-
ed a piece of life. It was wonderful.

"Why" she thought, as her height doubled,
"why, I'm good! I am *good*."

She ironed her aprons. Her back was straight.
Her eyes were mild, and soft with a godlike
loving-kindness. 🍂

Think AND Respond

What conflict does Maud Martha face, and how does she resolve it? How does the narrator
reveal the meaning of the incident for Maud Martha? What
point do you think Gwendolyn
Brooks was trying to make?
What incidents have you experienced that could be the starting
points for stories?

INVITATION
═ TO ═
Write

Gwendolyn Brooks built an engaging story around a simple
incident. Now write your own story, relating an experience
that happened to you, retelling a tale you have heard before,
or creating a completely new story.

Stories are all around you. Your everyday activities, the daily news,
and your private thoughts can all be sources of ideas you can turn
into stories. Your stories might be mostly true or entirely made up.
You are limited only by your own imagination. Yet no matter what
you write, from a simple anecdote to a complex drama, you will rely
on the same basic elements: characters, setting, plot, and a conflict,
or struggle, that must be resolved.

◢ INDING YOUR STORY

HANDBOOKS
FOR HELP & PRACTICE

Reflecting,
p. 331
Gathering
Information,
p. 332
Plot Diagram
p. 346
Narrative
Intros/Conclusions,
pp. 371–375
Elaborative Details,
pp. 376–381
Dialogue in Fiction,
pp. 452–453

1. Generate story ideas. Personal experiences are often the best
starting points for stories. Think about things you have experienced,
scenes you have witnessed, or unusual people you have observed.
What ideas for stories do these experiences and observations suggest? Also consider stories that you could "borrow" from happenings in the news, or set your mind free to consider the imaginary
and the improbable. As a short story writer, you are free to go
wherever your story takes you.

2. Explore the elements of your story. Consider elements of
stories—characters, setting, plot, and conflict. Who will appear in
your story? Where will your story take place? What happens in your
story? What conflict must be resolved? Freewrite about each of these
elements, or use charts, clusters, or time lines to gather the details
you can use to develop your story. Pay particular attention to
developing a meaningful conflict. For example, the conflict in
"Maud Martha Spares the Mouse" is seemingly simple, but the way
that Gwendolyn Brooks resolves the story's conflict reveals a deeper
significance.

3. Set goals for your story. You may want your readers to sympathize with a particular character, or to understand why a character acted as he or she did. Similarly, your goal may be to strike fear into your audience or to make a point or deliver a message. In any case, all the elements of your story should contribute to your specific goal or goals.

4. Choose a narrator. Who will tell your story? You can choose a first person narrator who participates in the story and relates his or her own experiences, or a third person narrator who stands outside the story and describes the action. You can even make a third person narrator omniscient—able to understand the thoughts and motivations of characters as well as their actions—like the narrator in "Maud Martha Spares the Mouse." Notice how the narrator reveals Maud Martha's reasons for sparing the mouse and the effect her action has on her mood.

 Writer's Choice Regardless of whether you use a first or third person narrator, you can choose to make your narrator an active participant in your story or someone who tells about the actions happening to others.

1. Begin drafting. By now, you should have a good idea about what you want to happen in your story, but keep yourself open to new ideas as you write. Start with any part of your story, and see where it takes you. You can rearrange the sections later.

2. Create a vivid world. Careful description can put your readers in the middle of the action and help them understand why events are taking place. Add details of sight, sound, touch, taste, and scent to draw your readers into the setting and mood of your tale.

3. Develop your characters. Rather than simply telling about your characters, show them in action. Put them in a situation and show how they think, act, and talk. Using dialogue to have characters speak in their own voices is an effective way to reveal what they are really like.

4. Organize your story. Many writers tell their stories in chronological order, starting with the first incident. Others begin in the middle or even at the end, using an attention-grabbing incident to capture their readers' attention. Then they use flashbacks to fill the readers in on the events that led up to the incident. Remember that whatever order you use, your story should show the development and eventual resolution of a conflict.

REVIEWING YOUR WRITING

1. Reread your story. Does your tale have a strong beginning that attracts the attention of readers? Do you establish a conflict and explore the conflict in the middle of the story? Does the ending resolve the conflict or reveal the outcome? Is the setting vividly described with sensory details? Do the characters ring true to life? Have you developed your characters by showing them in action, rather than by merely telling about them? Have you met the goals that you set for yourself?

2. Proofread your story. Check your writing for errors in spelling, punctuation, and grammar. If your story takes place in the past, have you been consistent in the tense of your verbs?

3. Ask a friend to read your story. After you have worked on a story for a long time, you probably can't be objective about it. For a fresh response, ask a friend or classmate to read your story and tell you which parts were confusing and which worked well.

4. Rewrite your story. Most authors write several drafts of their stories, improving them each time. Taking your reader's comments into consideration, redraft your story. Look for ways that you can make the story clearer, more suspenseful, or more compelling.

PUBLISHING AND PRESENTING

- **Tell your story aloud.** Decide whether you will use different voices for different characters and whether you want to mime the actions of the story. Don't forget to make eye contact with everyone in your audience.
- **Present your story as reader's theater.** If your story is largely dialogue, have members of your class act it out in a readers' theater. Take the role of the narrator, and assign your classmates to play the different characters of your story.
- **Submit your story for publication.** Send your story to a magazine that publishes young authors.
- **Enter your story in writing contests.** Your school or local library may sponsor competitions for young writers.
- **Hold a program for parents.** Present a selection of your class's stories in an evening program. Use several methods for presenting the stories.

Writing
—TIP—

As you redraft, use a synonym dictionary to find the precise word you want and to keep from repeating the same words. Also avoid using the passive voice, substituting active verbs wherever possible.

Choral Poem

The End of the World

based on a poem by Archibald MacLeish

[The sound of circus music, a calliope, perhaps, is heard very faintly in the background as the first speaker begins. The calliope music disappears after the first stanza. The first stanza is read excitedly, and there is in the background a general hubbub—crowd noise, clapping, random voices. For the first stanza, which evokes a circus scene, you may prefer to use small groups of speakers rather than individual speakers. The speakers should communicate an almost breathless excitement.]

SPEAKER 1: Quite unexpectedly

SPEAKER 2: (Interrupting)　　　as Vasserot
The armless ambidextrian was lighting
A match between his great and second toe

SPEAKER 3: (Continuing without pause)
And Ralph the lion was engaged in biting
The neck of Madame Sossman while the drum
Pointed,

[Here you hear a slight drum roll.]

SPEAKER 4: (Again, without pause)
and Teeny was about to cough
In waltz-time swinging Jocko by the thumb—

SPEAKER 1: (As if finally being allowed to finish his or her original sentence)
Quite unexpectedly (pause) the top blew off:

[At this point we hear a loud explosion-like noise, then the sound of wind whistling faintly in the background. This second stanza should be much quieter than the first one. Fewer speakers should read it, to give the audience a sense of the desolation and emptiness of the end of the world.]

SPEAKER 2: And there,

SPEAKER 3: (Forceful)
there overhead,

Long before poems were written down, ballads and verse narratives were recited aloud and passed from generation to generation. When you hear a choral, or group, presentation of a poem, you may feel a bit like those ancient listeners to poetry—as though you are seeing a very condensed and exciting play.

With your classmates, choose parts, rehearse, and read aloud this choral version of "The End of the World" by Archibald MacLeish. How does the script help you to interpret the poem for an audience?

[In the next lines, there should be an emphasis on *there*.]

SPEAKER 4:   there,

SPEAKER 1:   there, hung over
                         Those thousands of white faces, those dazed eyes,

SPEAKER 2:   There in the starless dark the poise, the hover,

SPEAKER 3:   There with vast wings across the canceled skies,

SPEAKER 4:   There in the sudden blackness the black pall

[Now all noises are increasingly softer, until the last *nothing* is almost a whisper. The wind also dies down to silence so that by the end of the poem there is an almost overwhelming stillness.]

                     Of nothing,

SPEAKER 3:   nothing,

SPEAKER 2:   nothing—

SPEAKER 1:   nothing at all.

Think AND Respond

Notice how the poem is broken into lines for different speakers. How are directions for reading provided? How are sound effects indicated? Do you think the reading directions create a valid interpretation of the poem? Can you think of other ways the poem can be interpreted, or other ways to present it orally?

INVITATION
TO
Write

You have just read or performed a choral interpretation of "The End of the World." Now write a poem on a subject you care about or choose a published one. Then prepare the text for a choral presentation.

When you listen to a choral reading of a poem, you experience drama; the speakers act out or dramatize the words of the poem. A choral interpretation also draws on the inherent qualities of poetry —rhythm, meter, and rhyme. Pay special attention to these elements in the poem you write or choose because they provide the music of the poem and make listening to it a rich experience.

CHOOSING A POEM

HANDBOOKS

FOR HELP & PRACTICE

**Peer Response,
pp. 400–401**

**Emphasis/Tone/
Mood,
pp. 423–428**

**Using Poetic
Language,
pp. 435–438**

**Using Dialogue
in Poetry,
p. 454**

1. Find a poem to interpret. Choose a poem that appeals to you or intrigues you, or write about a topic that is important to you. Look also for a poem (or write one) with interesting rhymes or rhythms that you can exploit in an oral reading. A ballad with a refrain or a poem with more than one speaker works well. Narrative poems, like the old Scottish ballad "Sir Patrick Spens" are good choices, as are many of the expansive poems of Walt Whitman and Carl Sandburg.

2. Choose a form. There are many ways to prepare a poem for a choral presentation. You may, for example, choose to have one primary speaker who tells a story or presents a situation, and a chorus or group of speakers who respond in unison. Other scripts may call for several speakers, small groups, or combinations of individuals and groups. The public library may have recordings of choral poetry that will give you ideas for preparing your poem.

Writer's Choice You may want to explore the possibility of presenting some of the choral poems or odes from ancient Greek tragedies, such as Sophocles' *Antigone* or *Oedipus Rex*.

3. Analyze the poem. As you prepare to assign parts to speakers, look for places where the poem naturally divides. These natural breaks occur between stanzas, before refrains, at punctuation marks, or preceding the introduction of a new speaker. Parenthetical material—text between a set of parentheses, dashes, or commas—can often be read by another voice. Sets of quotation marks also suggest spots to introduce a new speaker.

PREPARING THE POEM

1. Create a script. After you arrange the poem into several parts, transform it into a script. Begin by writing the names of the speakers in the left margin, beside their parts.

2. Consider the dynamics. How can the dynamics—the speed, volume, and intensity with which lines are spoken—add to your interpretation? Add directions for delivery in parentheses, as in the script for "The End of the World." Some lines may need to be whispered; others may need to be shouted. Your readers may sing or chant some lines slowly or spew out others rapidly. They can sound hesitant, joyful, fearful, arrogant, or sad.

3. Add sound effects. In between the individual speaking parts, note sound effects that you think may be effective.

PERFORMING A CHORAL POEM

1. Rehearse and revise. Practice until your performance is smooth and polished. As you practice, you may discover that you want to alter certain parts of the script to make the reading even more effective. If you can tape your rehearsals, do so. Sometimes it is easier to be objective about your work when you listen to it on tape.

2. Prepare an introduction. Before you perform, prepare an introduction so that one of your group can introduce the poem and the readers to the audience.

3. Perform the poem. For the public performance of your poem, choose an appropriate location such as the stage in a drama classroom. Be sure the lighting is appropriate and coordinate your sound effects and any props that may be required for the choral reading. After the performance, have a group member invite the audience to share their reactions and interpretations.

Writing
—TIP—
You can always tape the sounds and play the tape rather than creating the sound effects during the live reading.

On the Lightside

THE BULWER-LYTTON FICTION CONTEST

Every year the Bulwer-Lytton Fiction Contest awards prizes for atrocious opening sentences of imagined wretched novels. Based on the famous opening sentence, "It was a dark and stormy night . . ." from a badly written Victorian novel by Edward George Earle Bulwer-Lytton, the contest requires the winners to skillfully control their mixed metaphors, hilarious *non sequiturs*, outrageous imagery, and meandering narratives.

Here are some bold and disgraceful contest entries.

"It was a dark and stormy knight who stood rigidly at the cliff's edge, scowling out over the cruel sea, and ruggedly bracing himself against the fierce winds which howled in from the west, where a ship had appeared suddenly on the horizon, silhouetted sharply in the long, snaking claws of lightning that crackled in over the cliff to freeze Sir Richard's saturnine, chiseled patrician features . . ."

Peter S. Ford

Detective fiction is a favorite category of contestants:

"There are things a good detective can feel in his bones, and Dillon Shane knew Jesimine Kimberly Collinsworth did not drown in her sleep on New Year's Eve."

Frances H. Shaw

"With the radio squawking that a 4711 was in progress at 37th and 127th, Murphy knocked car 495 into 3rd and headed up 5th at 70, little reckoning as he thumbed his .38, that this would be the day when his number came up."

R.B. Nelson

Can a Western be far behind?

"Rex Spurr sat so tall in the saddle that the Mexicans didn't know if he was a god or a saguaro cactus, and who could say that they cared, given the torturous temperature which the fireball sun beat down on the frying-pan flat landscape, like pellets of fire raining from the mouth of a volcano, but this was not Hawaii, no, this was Texas!"

Jim Heiden

Sentence
COMPOSING

Adding Phrases and Clauses

Effective writers add detailed information to their sentences and variety to their writing by using phrases and clauses in different positions. In this lesson you will learn to add phrases and clauses to the beginning of sentences (openers), between the subject and the verb (s-v split), and at the end of sentences (closers).

Contrast the two sets of sentences below. The first set contains only the foundation of each sentence, the independent clause containing the main subject and predicate. The second set contains the original sentences. Notice their increased information, sophistication, and style.

MODELS

Foundations

    s   **v**
1. He seemed more than ever like a gnome.

       s   **v**   **v**
2. The park had already disappointed him.

  s   **v**
3. He hung around L.A.

Original Sentences

1. Opener added: With his yellowish stubbly low-growing hair, his stony unblinking eyes, his stoop, his feet planted apart and his knees bent, his clenched held-forward fists, he seemed more than ever like a gnome.
   Doris Lessing, *The Fifth Child*

2. S-v split added: The park, formal, unlovely, its amusements a mere glimmer of Palisades or Coney Island, had already disappointed him.
   Brian Moore, *The Lonely Passion of Judith Hearne*

3. Closer added: He hung around L.A., broke most of the time, working as an usher in movie theatres, getting an occasional part as an extra on the lots, or a bit on TV, dreaming and yearning and hungry, eating cold spaghetti out of the can.
   John Dos Passos, "The Sinister Adolescents"

Punctuation Note: Openers, s-v splits, and closers are generally set off by commas.

A. Imitating Sentences Imitate each model, one sentence part at a time. Openers, s-v splits, and closers are underlined and labeled.

Model
　　　　　Mr. Steffens,
　　　　　<u>borne upon the shoulders of four white rabbits,</u> (s-v split)
　　　　　was carried down a flight of stairs
　　　　　<u>which magically appeared in the floor</u>. (closer)
　　　　　Ray Bradbury, *The Martian Chronicles*

Student Sentence Louisa, secluded in the mountains of the Santa Lucia range, was camped in a meadow of wildflowers that rarely bloomed in the lowlands.

1. <u>Skirting the end of the willows,</u> (opener)
he stealthily approached the trail further on.
　　　　　Elliott Merrick, "Without Words"

2. <u>Cramped, cold, and worn out,</u> (opener)
she went to her room.
　　　　　Mary Lavin, "One Summer"

3. The shower curtain,
<u>a pallid pastel pink,</u> (s-v split)
was drawn protectively around the claw-footed tub.
　　　　　Stephen King, *The Shining*

4. There she had to creep and crawl,
<u>spreading her knees and stretching her fingers like a baby trying to climb the steps</u>. (closer)　　**Eudora Welty, "A Worn Path"**

B. Combining Sentences Use the first sentence in each set as the foundation. Insert the underlined parts of the other sentences into the foundation, using the positions indicated in parentheses. Punctuate correctly.

1. He built a small fire to boil the kettle. He built it <u>over a knoll in a thick clump of firs</u>. (opener)　　**Elliott Merrick, "Without Words"**

2. Manuel kicked at the bull's muzzle with his slippery feet. Manuel was <u>lying on the ground</u>. (s-v split)　　**Ernest Hemingway, "The Undefeated"**

3. Within a minute, it seemed, they were at the lakeside. That was <u>where they found her classmates gathered, timidly trying out the ice</u>. (closer)
　　　　　Mary Lavin, "One Summer"

4. Jody straightened as the ranch hand sauntered out of the barn. It was Jody <u>who was helping Doubletree Mutt, the big serious dog, to dig out a gopher</u>. (s-v split)   **John Steinbeck, The Red Pony**

C. Expanding Sentences   Expand each sentence foundation by adding parts that start with the words provided. Write the   complete sentence. Then compare your sentences with the originals on page 322.

Example	The old woman slid to the edge of her chair and leaned forward, shading . . . (closer)
Student Sentence	The old woman slid to the edge of her chair and leaned forward, shading herself with her faded pink parasol and fanning herself with her program.
Original	The old woman slid to the edge of her chair and leaned forward, shading her eyes from the piercing sunset with her hand.

**Flannery O'Connor,
"The Life You Save May Be Your Own"**

1. Wanting . . . , she turned and opened the door on her right and stepped into the dim crowded parlor. (opener)

Shirley Jackson, "The Little House"

2. Professor Kazan, wearing . . . , was the first ashore. (s-v split)

Arthur C. Clarke, Dolphin Island

3. He moved restlessly, looking round . . . (closer)

Richard Wright, Native Son

4. He had become part of the group of young unemployed, who . . . (closer)   **Doris Lessing, The Fifth Child**

Application   From something you have written recently, select five sentences to improve by adding information in the opener, s-v split, and closer positions. Use sentence parts similar to the ones in this lesson, and add at least one sentence part to each sentence. Notice how this elaboration increases the amount of detail in your sentences as well as the maturity of your writing style.

Grammar Refresher   Some of the sentences in this lesson contain subordinate clauses. For more on dependent clauses, see Handbook 33.

Sketchbook

*E*nglish, *n. A language so haughty and reserved that few writers succeed in getting on terms of familiarity with it.*

*H*appiness, *n. An agreeable sensation arising from contemplating the misery of others.*

*H*istory, *n. An account mostly false, of events mostly unimportant, which are brought about by rulers mostly knaves, and soldiers mostly fools.*

*L*awyer, *n. One skilled in the circumvention of the law.*

*Y*ear, *n. A period of three hundred and sixty-five disappointments.*

Ambrose Bierce,
THE ENLARGED DEVIL'S DICTIONARY

The nineteenth-century satirest Ambrose Bierce filled a dictionary with definitions showing how he felt words should be defined. We all attach personal meanings to certain words. Write definitions of words that have special meanings to you.

Additional Sketches

Describe the emotion you understand least.

A phobia is an extreme fear that often has no logical basis. Acrophobia is the fear of heights. Apiphobia is the fear of bees. Xenophobia is the fear of strangers. Describe any phobias that you have experienced.

Informative Exposition: Classification

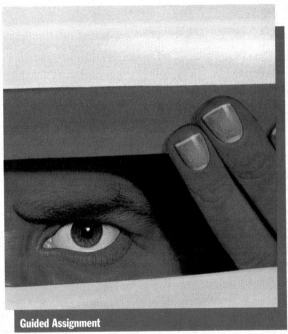

Guided Assignment
EXPLAINING CONCEPTS AND IDEAS

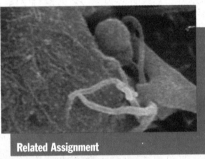

Related Assignment
SCIENCE REPORT

Related Assignment
COLLABORATIVE WRITING

Start reading a newspaper or magazine and you're likely to encounter a variety of complex ideas and concepts: an article about the policies of *glasnost* and *perestroika,* an editorial about the *conservative* shift on the Supreme Court, or news about *apartheid* in South Africa. If a subject is unfamiliar to you, your understanding will depend largely on the effectiveness of the writer's explanation.

In this workshop, you will consider various ways to explain a complex idea or concept to someone who doesn't understand it. You will continue to sharpen your explanatory skills as you write a science report and try collaborative writing.

113

Explaining Concepts and Ideas

What is a *majority?* According to the dictionary, a majority is "a number greater than half of a total." This dictionary definition is adequate for everyday use. Yet when the term *majority* is applied to a complex society like the United States, it takes on a more complex meaning that is not so easily explained. Writer James Baldwin explored the concept of majority in a speech to a college audience. As you read this excerpt, notice the techniques he used to clarify the meaning of this complex concept.

In Search of a Majority

By James Baldwin

AN ADDRESS

I am supposed to speak this evening on the goals of American society as they involve minority rights, but what I am really going to do is to invite you to join me in a series of speculations. Some of them are dangerous, some of them painful, all of them are reckless. It seems to me that before we can begin to speak of minority rights in this country, we've got to make some attempt to isolate or define the majority.

Presumably the society in which we live is an expression— in some way—of the majority will. But it is not so easy to locate this majority. The moment one attempts to define this majority one is faced with several conundrums. Majority is not an expression of numbers, of numerical strength, for example. You may far outnumber your opposition and not be able to impose your will on them or even to modify the rigor with which they impose their will on you, i.e., the Negroes in South Africa or in some counties, some sections, of the American South. You may have beneath your hand all the apparatus of power, political, military, state, and still be unable to use these things to achieve your ends. . . .

I suppose it can be said that there was a time in this country when an entity existed which could be called the majority, let's say a class, for the lack of a better word, which created the standards by which the country lived or which created the standards to which the country aspired. I am referring or have in mind, perhaps somewhat arbitrarily, the aristocracies of Virginia and New England. These were mainly of Anglo-Saxon stock, and they created what Henry James was to refer to, not very much later, as our Anglo-American heritage, or Anglo-American connections. Now at no time did these men ever form anything resembling a popular majority. Their importance was that they kept alive and they bore witness to two ele-

ments of a man's life which are not greatly respected among us now: (1) the social forms, called manners, which prevent us from rubbing too abrasively against one another and (2) the interior life, or the life of the mind. These things were important; these things were realities for them and no matter how rough-hewn or dark the country was then, it is important to remember that this was also the time when people sat up in log cabins studying very hard by lamplight or candlelight. That they were better educated than we are now can be proved by comparing the political speeches of that time with those of our own day.

Now, what I have been trying to suggest in all this is that the only useful definition of the word "majority" does not refer to numbers, and it does not refer to power. It refers to influence. Someone said, and said it very accurately, that what is honored in a country is cultivated there. If we apply this touchstone to American life we can scarcely fail to arrive at a very grim view of it. But I think we have to look grim facts in the face because if we don't, we can never hope to change them.

Think AND Respond

How would you summarize, in your own words, Baldwin's explanation of the concept of a majority? How is Baldwin's view of the concept different from the dictionary definition? What strategies does Baldwin use to support his personal concept of majority? What concepts and ideas in today's world do you think are important for people to understand?

115

INVITATION
━TO━
Write

James Baldwin's speech explained his concept of a majority. Now write your own explanation of a concept or idea so that its meaning and importance will be clear.

Concepts and ideas are usually abstract rather than concrete, and that makes them more challenging to explain. The Grand Canyon, for example, is a concrete thing. It has specific dimensions. It is made up of particular types of rock. You can show someone a picture of it. You can describe it down to its smallest detail. On the other hand, *perestroika* is an abstract concept. It has no dimensions, no physical substance. You can't take a picture of a concept or an idea. You can't touch it, smell it, taste it, hear it.

Nevertheless, as a writer you can use a wide variety of techniques to explain a complex concept or idea. You can construct a formal definition of it. You can describe its characteristics. You can give examples that show it in action. You can relate an anecdote that illustrates it. You can create an analogy that compares it to something more familiar. By doing so, you can increase your own understanding.

PREWRITE AND EXPLORE

FOR HELP & PRACTICE

**Reflecting,
pp. 331–332
Thinking
Techniques,
pp. 333–334
Collaborative
Planning,
pp. 358–360
Finding the Best
Source,
p. 493**

1. Look for ideas.   What concepts or ideas intrigue you? Try one or more of the following exploratory activities to find interesting concepts and ideas you might want to explain.

Exploratory Activities

• **Listening**   For the next several days, listen carefully to the evening news. Be alert for concepts and ideas that you'd like to learn more about, and write them down in your journal. Here are some you might hear. Add others you hear to this list.

socialism	liberalism	judicial restraint	diplomacy
due process	censorship	civil disobedience	monopoly

- **Reading** Your textbooks are a rich source of complex concepts and ideas. Look for such ideas as you read. For example, what is the *global village, homeostasis, plate tectonics, existentialism, superego*? List interesting terms as you come across them.
- **Reflecting and freewriting** Think about some area of the arts or humanities that you are especially interested in, and then do some freewriting about your interest. Look over your freewriting and highlight any concepts and ideas you would like to learn more about or would enjoy explaining to others.
- **Brainstorming and collaboration** Get together with some of your classmates and brainstorm a list of concepts and ideas that relate to moral or ethical matters. See how many terms you can add to this list: *honesty, tolerance, dignity, compassion, fairness, responsibility*.
- **Responding to literature** Use sayings that define concepts, such as these, as starting points for your own definitions.

PROBLEM SOLVING

How can I find a concept that intrigues me and would make a suitable paper?

''What does education often do? It makes a straight-cut ditch of a free meandering brook.''

Henry David Thoreau

''True love is like ghosts, which everyone talks about and few have seen.''

François de la Rochefoucauld

2. Select a writing topic. Review the list of concepts and ideas you've been generating to discover a topic to explain. Which topic interests you the most? Perhaps you think it is especially important to clarify one of these ideas for a particular audience. For example,

Bouquet with Flying Lovers, (detail), Marc Chagall

Explaining Concepts and Ideas **117**

you may want to educate a politically unaware group about apartheid. Perhaps you have always wanted to clarify in your own mind just what one of these concepts or ideas really means. If you are having trouble coming up with a topic, try reading several entries in your journal, look at the ideas you explored in the Sketchbook on page 112, or check the ideas listed under "Apply Your Skills" on page 131.

Writer's Choice Do you want to write a straightforward report on a concept with an objective, widely agreed upon meaning? Would you prefer to write a more personal essay on a concept such as beauty or friendship, which means different things to different people?

3. Try collaborative planning. Working with a partner, discuss your plans for your essay. Pay particular attention to the following issues.

- **Your purpose and goals** Your general purpose, of course, is to explain the meaning of the concept or idea you have chosen; however, do you want to take a serious approach, or write a humorous essay? Do you have specific goals as well? For example, do you want to clarify a term in preparation for an important presentation or debate? Do you want to suggest a new way of looking at an old idea, to break down a stereotype by examining a concept from a new perspective? Clarifying your goals will help you determine the focus and tone of your writing.

- **Your audience** Who are your readers and what do you want them to think or feel as a result of reading your essay? What do you have to do to make sure your readers understand you? How much background do you need to supply? What examples or comparisons would help them grasp your meaning?

As Susan began looking into careers she might pursue, she was struck by how widely pay scales seemed to vary. She was particularly concerned that some jobs requiring more training or experience paid less than simpler jobs. She had heard the term *comparable worth* used in discussions about this issue, so she decided to investigate what it really meant.

4. Identify sources of information. James Baldwin drew on his knowledge of American history and the civil rights movement for his speech on the idea of majority. There are many sources of information you can draw on as you plan your explanation. The following are a few possibilities.

- **Your own knowledge** Don't underestimate what you already know. Brainstorm or freewrite about your subject. Try to list everything you already know about it. You might try writing about it from different points of view.
- **Other people** Often you can gain interesting insights into the meaning of a term by comparing what different people have to say about it. For example, people have very different ideas and feelings about such concepts as *tradition, adventure, creativity,* and *solitude.*
- **Authorities** Sometimes you may wish to consult people who have a particular expertise in the area you are writing about. If you are explaining the idea of free markets, for instance, you might consult an economist. If your subject is Manifest Destiny, an American history professor might prove helpful. Also look for articles, studies, and books written by authorities.
- **Dictionary and thesaurus** These are logical places to look if you want to define a term. You might discover shades of meaning that hadn't occurred to you before. You'll also learn the history of a term, which can shed additional light on its meaning.
- **Other reference works** Don't overlook specialized reference works. There are many specialized dictionaries, for example, including dictionaries of science, philosophy, literary terms, music, arts, and so on. You'll find these in the reference section of your library.

5. Gather information. Once you know where to look, decide what type of information you are after. Remember, your purpose is to explain your concept or idea as clearly and precisely as possible. Look for concrete examples, step-by-step explanations, interesting anecdotes, revealing analogies, historical definitions—any information that adds to your knowledge of your subject and that will make your explanation informative and compelling. Also, don't ignore your own feelings about the subject.

To gather information for her essay, Susan first looked up the term *equal pay* in the subject catalog at her library. The catalog referred her to listings on *comparable worth* and *pay equity*. There she found books such as Steven Willborn's *A Comparable Worth Primer* and Joan Acker's *Doing Comparable Worth,* as well as a number of studies that had been published by the federal and state governments and by private institutes. Susan wrote the following notes from the information she gathered.

ONE STUDENT'S PROCESS

Comparable worth theory says . . .
—people doing equally difficult or valuable jobs deserve equal pay
—women and minority groups have been historically "crowded" into certain fields (e.g., nursing)
—pay rates in these fields have reflected the discrimination against women

Advocates of comparable worth . . .
—want to evaluate various types of work whose contents have very little in common (e.g., nurse and tree surgeon)
—this would be likely to upgrade certain traditionally "female" professions and close the earnings gap between men and women

Opponents say . . .
—it's impossible to compare different fields of work scientifically
—bureaucratic nightmare would result
—downgrading of certain jobs would hurt women and children (e.g., wives of male factory workers)
—best way to close earnings gap is to recruit and promote women for currently high-paying jobs

6. Synthesize your information. Simply put, *synthesize* means "combine various parts into a coherent whole." You've gathered a great deal of information about your topic, but what does that information suggest to you about the direction your explanation should take? Look over your information. Which details seem the most important or interesting? What theme seems to be emerging in your research, thoughts, and feelings about the subject? About what aspect of the subject have you gathered the most information? Think back to the goals you established. What information best supports those goals? Freewrite about what you know so far. As you synthesize, highlight the information you want to be sure to include in your explanation.

PROBLEM
S O L V I N G

How does all my information fit together? How can I draw generalizations about my information?

DRAFT AND DISCOVER

1. Consider the form. After thinking about your topic and synthesizing the information you've gathered, you are now ready to consider the form you want your explanation to take. Here are some possibilities.

- **Expository article** Write a straightforward, informative treatment of your concept or idea, the type of article that might appear in an encyclopedia.
- **Persuasive essay** Argue for or against a particular view of your topic. For example, you might argue that free expression must include tolerance for unpopular viewpoints as well as those in the mainstream.

HANDBOOKS
FOR HELP & PRACTICE

Graphics for Organizing,
pp. 343–347

Organizing Your Work,
pp. 349–357

Introducing Nonfiction,
pp. 365–367

Figurative Language,
pp. 435–436

- **Personal essay**   Write an essay that explains what a concept means to you personally. Such an essay usually includes a widely accepted definition of the concept as well.
- **Exploratory article**   Write an examination of an idea from several different points of view, without endorsing any particular explanation, or explore problems in understanding or analyzing the idea.

 Writer's Choice   Sometimes the best form for your explanation will be immediately apparent to you. At other times, you may want to begin drafting to discover which form is best suited to what you want to say.

2. Focus your explanation on a central idea or thesis.   Begin by identifying your **thesis,** the main idea or point you want to make. Try expressing your thesis in a sentence or two. This preliminary thesis statement can guide your draft, helping you to stick to your central idea as you develop and elaborate it in the body of your paper. You may or may not wish to include a version of this thesis statement in your final draft.

James Baldwin's thesis, for example, is that influence, not numbers, characterizes a majority. Although this thesis is not expressed in a thesis statement at the beginning of his speech, it is implied, and all of Baldwin's main points relate to it. Try one or more of the following strategies to help you explain your ideas to your readers.

Strategies

- **Examples**   Give specific examples that illustrate your main point. Examples are especially helpful to your readers when your subject is abstract.
- **Comparison and contrast**   Compare your subject with something familiar to your readers. How are the two alike? How are they different?
- **Figurative language**   Metaphors, similes, and personification can be especially striking forms of comparison that will help you explain an abstract subject in a way that appeals to your readers' imagination.

Susan decided to compare the situation of a woman with a low-paying job with that of a man with a higher-paying job. Notice that she put the comparison in the form of a narrative, with specific characters, in order to enhance reader interest.

PROBLEM

S O L V I N G

Which strategies can help me clarify my explanation?

Fran Katcavage is a nurse in the emergency room of a busy city hospital. Every day she uses her skills, education, and experience to save the lives of people who have been shot by strangers, injured by passing automobiles, or attacked by mysterious microorganisms. Doctors rely on her coolness and patients rely on her compassion. Fran, who makes twenty-one thousand dollars a year, lives in a two-bedroom house in an old, crowded surburb just across the city's border. Fran has called a local tree surgeon, Sam Robustelli, to prune the oak tree in her yard. With a few expert passes of the chain saw, Sam cuts off the sick branches in order to save the healthy ones. When Fran gets out her checkbook, however, she's embarrassed: she doesn't have enough money to pay Sam, who makes thirty-five thousand a year.

3. Consider ways to organize your information. In what order will you present the main ideas and details that explain your subject? Consider using one or more of the following strategies to organize your draft.

Writing
—TIP—

Making an outline can help you analyze and classify the information you have gathered.

Strategies

- **General to specific** After you have introduced your subject with a broad definition, begin discussing the specific details that will develop your explanation. James Baldwin began his speech by stating his general goals for the evening. Then he progressed to an abstract discussion of the term *majority*. Finally, Baldwin developed his explanation through the use of specific examples.
- **Analysis** Can your subject be divided into parts or subgroups? If so, devote a paragraph to each of these specific aspects. Begin each paragraph with a sentence that both introduces the part or subgroup you want to discuss and links it with the part or subgroup that came before it. Be sure these parts or subgroups are logically presented.

Explaining Concepts
and Ideas   **123**

- **Narration**   If you choose to use narration, use chronological order to tell the story of your subject. Where does your subject originate? What is its history? Why or how is your subject important today?
- **Classification**   Develop categories into which your subject can be placed and explain how it fits into each category.

4. Take a break.   When you have a draft that you are reasonably satisfied with, put your work aside for a day or two. When you come back to it, you will be able to read it with a fresh eye, seeing both its strengths and its weaknesses. You may also want to share your draft with one or more of your peer readers. Use the following questions to help you evaluate your draft.

REVIEW YOUR WRITING

Questions for Yourself

- Have I used concrete examples to illustrate my ideas?
- Is my explanation overly broad or overly specific? Is it clear enough to be readily understood by someone unfamiliar with my subject?
- Did I present a dominant impression?
- Is there anything in my explanation that I think might be unclear to my reader and that should be clarified with additional details, descriptions, definitions, or background information?

Questions for Your Peer Readers

- What ideas did you have about my subject before you began reading? Did my explanation clarify the subject for you or give you any new insights about it?
- Did you find my explanation interesting? What parts did you like best? What parts could be made more interesting, and how might I do this?
- Is there any part of the explanation that is not clear to you? Which part?
- Are you aware of any facts or points of view that I've overlooked? Would you change the central definition in any way? How?

REVISE YOUR WRITING

1. Evaluate your responses. Consider your own responses and those of your peer readers. Use the responses to guide the revision of your draft. As you revise, keep in mind that explanations of concepts and ideas generally display these characteristics.

Standards for Evaluation

An effective explanation of a concept . . .

- includes an interesting introduction that clearly states the subject to be explained and a reason for explaining it.
- conveys a dominant impression of its subject.
- uses examples, comparisons, and figurative language, as appropriate, to present the information in a lively manner.
- presents information logically and effectively through the use of an appropriate organizational strategy.
- demonstrates an awareness and clear sense of audience through the use of appropriate language and details.

2. Problem-solve. Revise your draft, making whatever changes you consider necessary. The next page shows revisions Susan made in response to comments from her peer readers.

FOR HELP & PRACTICE

Unity/Coherence, pp. 382–391
Avoiding Wordiness, pp. 406–408

Could you give examples?

Before reading your essay, I didn't really understand these implications.

This isn't clear to me. How do you "measure" these qualities?

Avocates of comparable worth claim that some
d   *the*   *theory*

occupational fields have been historically undervalued.
such as nursing, teaching, and secretarial work

People entering these occupations have earned less

money than people entering bussiness management or
, on the average,   *d*

skilled, unionized blue-collar jobs. Women have been
It's no coincidence that the lower-paid jobs are ones that have been predominantly filled by women.

"crowded" into certain fields, and the pay rates in those

fields reflect the discrimination against women in

society as a whole.

Avocates of comparable worth have tried in recent
d

years to establish new pay scales by measureing four
based on evaluations of jobs' worth. Such job evaluations usually involve the measurement of

qualities: Skill, responsibility, effort, and working

conditions. The higher the evaluation, the more pay
levels of the first three factors, and the more dangerous the conditions,

deserved. *under this theory*

3. Proofread your work. When you have finished revising your draft, make a final copy of your essay. Proofread it carefully for errors in grammar, spelling, usage, and mechanics. Neatly correct any errors you find.

LINKING
GRAMMAR AND WRITING

If a one-sentence definition is used to define a term or idea, the word to be defined and the definition should be a similar part of speech. For example, if the word to be defined is an adjective, the definition should be an adjective or an adjective phrase or clause.

Incorrect: *Supercilious* means "a haughty person."
Incorrect: *Supercilious* means "to be haughty."
Correct: *Supercilious* means "haughty."

If the word to be defined is a noun or another word acting as a noun, then the definition should also be a noun or a word, phrase, or clause acting as a noun.

Incorrect: A *foul* is "when you hit a ball outside the base lines."
Correct: A *foul* is "a ball hit outside the base lines."

Grammar
—**TIP**—
Remember to underline the word you are defining and to enclose the definition in quotation marks.

PUBLISH AND PRESENT

- **Make a speech.** Present your explanation to the class as a speech. Augment your speech with appropriate charts, graphs, or illustrations.
- **Submit your work in another class.** If your explanation relates to math, science, history, art, or some other school subject, you may wish to share it with your teacher and classmates in that class.
- **Save your work in your writing portfolio.** Look over your earlier work in your portfolio. How is your explanation different? Is it better? Think about all of the ways you have grown as a writer.

HANDBOOKS
FOR HELP & PRACTICE

Publishing, pp. 412–415

Equal Pay for Different Work?

Susan Miller

Fran Katcavage is a nurse in the emergency room of a busy city hospital. Every day she uses her skills, education, and experience to save the lives of people who have been shot by strangers, injured by passing automobiles, or attacked by mysterious microorganisms. Doctors rely on her coolness and patients rely on her compassion. Fran, who makes twenty-one thousand dollars a year, lives in a two-bedroom house in an old, crowded suburb just across the city's border. Fran has called a local tree surgeon, Sam Robustelli, to prune the oak tree in her yard. With a few expert passes of the chain saw, Sam cuts off the sick branches in order to save the healthy ones. When Fran gets out her checkbook, however, she's embarrassed: she doesn't have enough money to pay Sam, who makes thirty-five thousand a year.

How can a society decide what any given job is worth? Is a nurse more valuable to America than a tree surgeon? Does a secretary deserve to make as much money as a truck driver? Questions such as these mark the forefront of the debate on equal pay in the 1990's. Even among people devoted to correcting past employment discrimination, the answers are by no means obvious.

The key concept is that of equal pay for comparable worth. If two jobs have comparable worth, it means that they are equally valuable to society, even if the specific contents of the jobs are very different. For instance, if a teacher's job and an airline pilot's are equally valuable to society, they have comparable worth, and according to this theory they should be paid the same amount.

There's no problem in comparing worth when the two people involved are performing identical jobs. For instance, if a man and a woman graduate from the same police academy at the same time and both begin

as patrol officers in the same police department, it's obvious that they should receive the same salary. This has been national policy in the United States since the Equal Pay Act passed Congress in 1963.

However, what about the differences in pay between jobs in different fields? Advocates of the comparable worth theory claim that occupational fields such as nursing, teaching, and secretarial work have been historically undervalued. People entering these occupations have earned less money, on the average, than people entering business management or skilled, unionized blue-collar jobs. It's no coincidence that the lower-paid jobs are ones that have been predominantly filled by women. Women have been "crowded" into certain fields, and the pay rates in those fields reflect the discrimination against women in society as a whole.

Advocates of comparable worth have tried in recent years to establish new pay scales based on evaluations of jobs' value. Such job evaluations usually involve the measurement of four qualities: skill, responsibility, effort, and working conditions. The higher the levels of the first three factors, and the more dangerous the working conditions, the more pay deserved, under this theory.

Opponents of comparable worth efforts usually applaud the goal of equal pay, but point to dangers in the proposed remedy. For one thing, they say, there is simply no scientific way to compare the value of two different jobs. It is always a matter of personal judgment, and the question is, "Who is to judge?" Should the government step in? If so, a bureaucratic behemoth is likely to arise, and the results of its findings will always be, to a significant extent, arbitrary and controversial.

Opponents of comparable worth theory claim that the evaluation of jobs according to comparable worth will ironically set back the cause of higher pay for women. For example, if an evaluation decrees that secretaries deserve higher pay, business's likely response will be to hire fewer secretaries. They argue that the best way to close the gap between men's earnings and women's is to recruit more women for higher-paying, traditionally male-dominated jobs, rather than to revamp the pay scale. They also point out that if some men's wages are lowered after a job evaluation, it will harm their wives and children.

In sum, then, the issue of equalizing men's and women's earnings is more complicated than just paying both sexes the same for the same jobs. Our society faces the task of comparing different occupations—the apples and oranges of the labor force. Even if comparative values were agreed upon, the medicine might be more harmful than the ailment. Nevertheless, the fact that this is a difficult issue does not mean we can shirk it. One way or another, the gap between men's and women's earnings must be closed in future years, or painful societal conflicts will result.

Explores the subject by presenting differing viewpoints

Conclusion reinforces dominant impression: that society must find way to recognize comparable worth

WRITER TO WRITER

The greatness of a writer has nothing to do with subject matter itself, only with how much the subject matter touches the author.

Boris Pasternak, Russian poet and novelist

FOR YOUR
PORTFOLIO

1. Reflect on your writing. Take a few minutes to write a journal entry or an introductory note for your paper reflecting on your experience in writing this essay. In reflecting on that experience, you may want to consider the following questions.

- In what ways did your own understanding of your subject change as a result of your work on the essay? Do you now see your subject as even more complicated or as less complicated than you had thought?
- How adequately did you define your subject? What would it take to define it adequately? A book? A lifetime? Assuming that much more might have been written on your subject, how did you decide where to stop? What would you do next with your subject if you had more time and space and desire?

2. Apply your skills. To further explore the skills involved in explaining a concept, try one or more of the following.

- **Cross curricular** Choose a favorite subject at school. Make a list of complex ideas that are part of that subject. For example, if biology is your favorite subject, your list might include *pollination, adaptation,* and *photosynthesis*. Write a brief definition of each idea you list that might lead to a longer, more detailed explanation.
- **General** What do the concepts *social responsibility* and *community service* mean to you? Submit an essay on this subject to your local United Fund or volunteer organization for use in their fund-raising or recruitment campaigns.
- **Related assignments** Follow the suggestions on pages 132–142 to write a science report or do collaborative writing.

THE ULTIMATE MEDICINE

by Geoffrey Montgomery

A lively and creative scientific report can help readers who are not scientists become fascinated with complex subjects. As you write a scientific report, you must lure your readers into an unfamiliar world with your enthusiasm for and knowledge of your subject.

As you read this excerpt from an article on genetic surgery, notice how the writer uses a comparison to explain how genetic surgeons can revitalize ailing cells by using viruses.

The first time Richard Mulligan turned a virus into a truck, he swore softly in amazement. It was 1979, and Mulligan, then a 25-year-old graduate student at Stanford, had just performed an unprecedented feat of biological alchemy. Dressed in a modern-day mystic uniform of gloves, gown, boots, and mask, he had used the tools of recombinant DNA technology to splice a rabbit gene into a monkey virus.

Normally, viruses are vehicles for their own genes. In fact, they are little more than genetic material wrapped within a shell that allows the virus to travel from one cell to the next. They penetrate a cell, then commandeer the cell's genetic machinery into making thousands of virus copies. But with molecular sleight of hand, Mulligan had pulled out the genes that allow the virus to replicate and put in their place the genes for hemoglobin, the molecule in red blood cells—of both rabbits and people—that carries oxygen.

Mulligan hoped that the genetically modified virus upon entering a cell would no longer tell it to make more virus particles. It would just order hemoglobin proteins.

Mulligan assembled a fleet of his viral trucks, all with the rabbit hemoglobin gene in their cargo bay. Then he dumped a soupy solution of these viruses into a dish of cells cultured from a monkey's kidney. Kidney cells have no role in oxygen transport, and so they normally make no hemoglobin. But these kidney cells, after their invasion by Mulligan's viruses, underwent an astonishing transformation. Spurred on by the unloaded hemoglobin genes, the kidney cells began to churn out chains of hemoglobin molecules.

"It was incredible," says Mulligan. "The transferred hemoglobin gene caused the cells to make *tons* of hemoglobin protein."

With those clumps of protein, Mulligan had ushered in a revolutionary new vision of therapy for human genetic disease. His path-breaking gene-transfer experiment suggested that one could transform viruses, nature's genetic parasites, into molecular ambulances capable of shuttling beneficial genes into ailing cells. It was more than a major event in basic biological research. It signaled the dawn of a new era of medicine, in which physicians would be able to reach down into the molecular foundations of a disease and cure an ailment by correcting its cause.

Think AND Respond

To what does the writer compare a virus? What words does the writer use to develop this extended metaphor? Do you think the comparison makes the subject easier to understand? What scientific topic or new discovery would you like to explore? Could you use a comparison to explain your topic?

INVITATION TO Write

Geoffrey Montgomery's article shows how one writer used an extended comparison to explain the difficult concept of gene transfer. Select a scientific topic and present it in a clear and concise report.

Science reports often require the writer to present new concepts and ideas clearly to a general audience. Given the advances that occur daily in science and medicine, this skill has become increasingly important, not just to scientists but also to reporters who must cover these advances. Like writing a definition, writing about a scientific concept requires you to explore your topic from a number of different angles, using a variety of techniques. More important, however, thinking and writing about science will open your mind to a fascinating world that you might otherwise have overlooked and that will play an increasingly important role in determining the future of our planet and its people.

THINKING ABOUT A TOPIC

FOR HELP & PRACTICE

Writing Variables,
pp. 329–330

Figurative Language,
pp. 435–436

Presenting an Argument,
pp. 474–476

Using Source Material,
pp. 482–489

Finding the Best Source,
pp. 493–494

1. Select an intriguing idea. The best ideas for science reports stem from topics that fascinate you. Do not rule out a difficult subject if it interests you; as you write about it, you will come to understand it better. Think about intriguing concepts you've discovered in your science class—quarks or antimatter, for example. You might also find ideas by browsing through newspapers; science magazines such as *Discover, Scientific American,* or *Science News;* or the science columns of general news magazines such as *Time* and *Newsweek.* You might even form a small group with classmates or friends and brainstorm a list of unusual research projects.

2. Research your topic thoroughly. A recent edition of an encyclopedia may cover your topic. Depending on the topic, current books on the subject may also be available. However, since new developments in science occur so rapidly, the alphabetical subject headings in the *Readers' Guide to Periodical Literature* will probably be your best source of up-to-date information. Use at least three or four information sources for your report.

3. Envision your audience and your goal. Remember that your purpose is to explain your topic to an audience of your peers, not a group of scientists. As you take notes on your subject, your first goal is to understand the subject you are exploring yourself so that you can, in turn, explain it clearly to others.

Writing
— TIP —

You might find it easier to organize your notes if you write them on index cards. Use a separate card for each note.

DRAFTING YOUR REPORT

1. Set a purpose. Think about why you are fascinated with your topic. What aspect of your topic might your reader find most appealing? Write a controlling statement that sets a clear purpose for your report.

2. Evaluate your information. As you continue writing, keep your controlling purpose in mind so that you include only information that is relevant to your topic. Put yourself in the place of your reader. Are there any unfamiliar terms that need to be defined? Are there any gaps in logic or information in your report?

3. Look for ways to clarify or simplify your concept. Are there terms that should be defined in context? Can a difficult idea be paraphrased? Is there a comparison you could use, as Geoffrey Montgomery did, to make a difficult concept easier to understand?

4. Use a lively style. Avoid writing that is dry or highly technical. Instead, use lively descriptions, quotations, and appropriate comparisons to convey your enthusiasm for your subject. Notice how Geoffrey Montgomery uses an extended metaphor to describe the virus's vehicular function in transferring genes from one cell to another: "Mulligan assembled a *fleet* of his viral *trucks,* all with the rabbit hemoglobin in their *cargo bay.*" Later in the article, Montgomery continues the metaphor by referring to the viruses as "molecular *ambulances* capable of *shuttling* beneficial genes into ailing cells."

 Writer's Choice You can present your material objectively, or you can personalize it with a more informal tone. Which approach is more appropriate to your subject and purpose?

5. Consider a graphic aid. You might use a diagram, chart, or illustration. If you include a graphic aid from one of your sources in your report, you must credit the source. Another option is to design a graphic aid of your own.

6. Document your sources. Be sure that you give credit to your sources, whether you paraphrase, summarize, or use direct quotations. Use parenthetical documentation in the body of your report, and at the end provide complete publication information for each of your sources in a Works Cited list.

Writing
—TIP—

Most teachers accept MLA style for parenthetical documentation and Works Cited lists. See Workshop 9, pp. 284–290, for more information.

R EVIEWING YOUR WRITING

1. Ask a classmate to read your report. Did your report immediately engage your reader's interest? Ask your reader to state the controlling purpose of your report. Does your reader clearly understand the scientific concept you are presenting? If not, you may need to simplify your presentation of the material or provide additional information about your topic. Did your reader find your comparison helpful? Were your details vivid and precise?

2. Evaluate your style and tone. Have you presented your topic in an exciting new way? Is your writing dry or overly technical?

3. Proofread your writing. Review your work for any errors in grammar, usage, spelling, and punctuation, and make any necessary corrections. Then prepare a neat final copy of your report.

PUBLISHING AND PRESENTING

- **Make an encyclopedia.**   Along with your classmates, use your science reports to create a science and technology encyclopedia. Divide your encyclopedia into sections that reflect different scientific and technological disciplines: medicine, astronomy, computers, transportation, flight, botany, biology, and so on. Enhance the look of your encyclopedia by adding illustrations—photographs, drawings, photocopies—and other graphic aids, such as charts, graphs, timelines, and so on. Your completed encyclopedia would be a great resource for other students and an important addition to your science classroom or school library.

- **Write a news story.**   Imagine that the subject of your science report is a recent discovery, treatment, or advancement. Write a news story about it such as might appear in a major newspaper. Keep in mind that an effective news story tells *who, what, when, where,* and *why* about its subject. A news story also begins with an attention-getting "lead," the first few sentences that give the substance of the story.

Collaborative Writing

from

You Can't Take It with You

George S. Kaufman and Moss Hart

Do you like to work with others? Do you have friends with the skills to help you tackle a complex project? It sometimes makes sense to invite others to work with you collaboratively, in a partnership that can benefit you both and enrich your project.

Scientists often collaborate with one another. So do investigative reporters, songwriters, novelists, and playwrights. As you read the following scene, written collaboratively by George S. Kaufman and Moss Hart, think of ways they may have worked together to create and refine the dialogue.

Grandpa Well, what *I* feel is that Tony's too nice a boy to wake up twenty years from now with nothing in his life but stocks and bonds.

Kirby How's that?

Grandpa (*turning to Mr. Kirby*). Yes. Mixed up and unhappy, the way you are.

Kirby (*outraged*). I beg your pardon, Mr. Vanderhof, I am a very happy man.

Grandpa Are you?

Kirby Certainly I am.

Grandpa I don't think so. What do you think you get your indigestion from? Happiness? No, sir. You get it because most of your time is spent in doing things you don't want to do.

Kirby I don't do anything I don't want to do.

Grandpa Yes, you do. You said last night that at the end of a week in Wall Street you're pretty near crazy. Why do you keep on doing it?

Kirby Why do I keep on—why, that's my *business*. A man can't give up his business.

Grandpa Why not? You've got all the money you need. You can't take it with you.

Kirby That's a very easy thing to say, Mr. Vanderhof. But I have spent my entire life building up my business.

Grandpa And what's it got you? Same kind of mail every morning, same kind of deals, same kind of meetings, same dinners at night, same indigestion. Where does the fun come in? Don't you think there ought to be something

more, Mr. Kirby? You must have wanted more than that when you started out. We haven't got too much time, you know—any of us.

Kirby What do you expect me to do? Live the way *you* do? Do nothing?

Grandpa Well, I have a lot of fun. Time enough for everything—read, talk, visit the zoo now and then, practice my darts, even have time to notice when spring comes around. Don't see anybody I don't want to, don't have six hours of things I *have* to do every day before I get *one* hour to do what I like in—and I haven't taken bicarbonate of soda in thirty-five years. What's the matter with that?

Kirby The matter with that? But suppose we *all* did it? A fine world we'd have, everybody going to zoos. Don't be ridiculous, Mr. Vanderhof. Who would do the work?

Think AND Respond

Notice the differences in temperament and point of view between the two characters in this scene. What fairly apparent method of collaborative writing does this scene suggest? If you were to write a play with one or more partners, how would you split up the tasks? What tasks would you perform as a group?

INVITATION
—TO—
Write

This excerpt from a Kaufman and Hart play shows the variety and depth that can be achieved through collaborative writing. With one or more partners, plan and develop a piece of writing, such as a dramatic scene or an in-depth report.

Collaboration provides you with an opportunity to expand your potential by joining your skills with those of your collaborators. Just as sports teams can accomplish more when all the players work together, a collaborative writing team may attain a richness and scope in its writing that one writer alone could not achieve.

PLANNING A COLLABORATION

FOR HELP & PRACTICE

Planning/Organizing Strategies, pp. 348–357

Collaborative Planning, pp. 358–360

Peer Response, pp. 397–400

Presenting/ Publishing, pp. 412–413

1. Find a partner.   Look for someone who has similar interests or a similar goal to achieve. For example, if you want to write a screenplay, you might choose to collaborate with a classmate who has some acting experience. If you want to collaborate on a specific research project, ask your teacher to steer you to someone else who would benefit from working on such a report. Discuss your ideas with several potential partners until you find someone with whom you can work well.

Writer's Choice   You can work with a partner whose skills and interests parallel yours, or you can choose to work with someone whose abilities complement yours.

2. Explore your topic and goals.   Determine with your collaborator what your writing goals are. For a screenplay, for example, you might decide you want to compose a comedy that would satirize some aspect of life in the 1990's. Next, brainstorm your topic from every angle. Entertain all related ideas, no matter how odd or unusual. Even a single word or phrase can trigger an interesting association, and therefore a potential new direction.

3. Plan your collaboration. Think about how the individuals on your team can best work together. Will you discuss and shape ideas together verbally, then have one person draft and one or both revise? Or will you compose together, with one person acting as a scribe? In a creative piece such as a screenplay, you could role-play the characters with your collaborator, perhaps taping the exchanges for later analysis. You may want to consult the guidelines for Collaborative Planning on pages 358–360.

4. Assign different jobs. Assign a partner to each task. In a research project, for example, all collaborators can be entirely responsible for one part of the report, including all research, organization, and drafting; or you can allot one complete stage of the writing task to each member of the group. If you are composing a song collaboratively, one person could be responsible for the words, the other for the music. Another exciting method of assigning collaborative writing, usually used for fiction, involves writers taking turns writing various chapters. This approach allows each writer to experience the surprise and challenge of building on the other's unexpected plot twists.

COMPUTER
═**TIP**═

Input each person's contribution in the same file on your word processor. Experiment with different arrangements of material on screen.

DRAFTING YOUR MATERIAL

1. Organize the material. Gather together all your notes, research, or initial drafts and decide which material fulfills the group's purpose and goals. Then work together to discover an effective presentation. For a screenplay, you might discuss whether to experiment with flashbacks or to present events in chronological order.

2. Examine your options. Choose one person to read the prewriting aloud. Encourage others to elaborate on images and ideas. You might even create different versions of a segment or two and then discuss which version to use.

3. Draft your ideas. Write out a draft that incorporates everyone's comments. Use notations or symbols to mark the rough spots. Then read the draft aloud, discussing how to improve it.

Writing
TIP
As you read your writing aloud, have your collaborator mark the phrases or passages that sound awkward.

REVIEWING YOUR WRITING

1. Problem-solve. Read the completed draft aloud to make sure the pieces are now unified and the content or message is clear. Have you included all of the ideas or information each group member felt was important? Does the writing flow smoothly and logically? Look for problems in consistency. Do you need to create transitions between different segments? Work as a group to solve problems and answer questions.

2. Evaluate your work in relation to your goals. Review the group's stated goals and make revisions, if necessary, to meet those goals. If you have written a narrative or drama, stage readings or preliminary performances of your work.

PUBLISHING AND PRESENTING

- **Find a forum in which to present your collaborative work.** If it is a story or play, act it out. If it is a report, form a "panel of experts" and take turns speaking on the subject.
- **Create an anthology of collaborative works.** Illustrate, copy, and bind the anthologies.

Sentence
C O M P O S I N G

Varying Sentences

Various types of modifiers make up many of the sentence expanders used by professional writers to add detail and to create such effects as rhythm, suspense, and contrast. Notice the characteristics of each type of modifier below.

Adjectives and Adverbs

Adjectives and adverbs can be used singly or in combination.

Adverbs used singly	Quickly, frantically, he tried to slide back the hood with his left hand, but he had not the strength. **Roald Dahl, ''Beware of the Dog''**
Adverb and adjective in combination	The vast, arid plain, often deserted, today teemed with game of all sorts. **Isak Dinesen, *Shadows on the Grass***

Prepositional Phrases

Prepositions are words that show relationships (for example, *over, under,* and *around*). A prepositional phrase contains a preposition and related nouns and modifiers.

> On the table in the middle of the room lay the coffin.
> **Leo Tolstoy, *Childhood, Boyhood, Youth***

A. Combining and Imitating Sentences   Use the first sentence in each set as the foundation. Join the underlined part(s) of the next sentence(s) with the foundation in the position indicated in parentheses. Place s-v splits directly after the subject, and set them off with commas. Finally, write a sentence whose structure imitates that of the combined sentence.

1. Beth had resisted leaving for the day-care center. Beth was usually so pliable. (s-v split)   **Mary Higgins Clark, *A Cry in the Night***

2. A spring bubbled out of a rupture in the stone. The spring was high in the grey stone mountains. (opener) The spring was under a frowning peak. (opener)   **John Steinbeck, *The Pearl***

3. Dr. Killgruel was visited by Miss M. This happened on a summer day some months later. (opener)   **Joan Aiken, ''Follow My Fancy''**

4. He got up. He was vivid with excitement. (closer)
              F. Scott Fitzgerald, *The Great Gatsby*

Present Participial Phrases

Present participial phrases contain a present participle and related words.

Away she darted, <u>stretching close to the ground</u>.

Francis Parkman, *The Oregon Trail*

Past Participial Phrases

Past participial phrases contain a past participle and related words.

The all-powerful auto industry, <u>accustomed to telling the customer what sort of car he wanted</u>, was suddenly forced to *listen* for a change. **Jessica Mitford, *The American Way of Death***

B. Unscrambling and Imitating Sentences Unscramble the parts of each set to form a sentence whose structure matches the model. Then write a second sentence whose structure also imitates the model.

1. <u>Craning his head back</u>, he looked up along the wall.

Robb White, *Deathwatch*

   a. by the geraniums
   b. moving its body daintily
   c. the spider crawled down

2. Bigger laughed and approached the bed with the dangling rat, <u>swinging it to and fro like a pendulum, enjoying his sister's fear</u>.

Richard Wright, *Native Son*

   a. apologizing right and left like a penitent
   b. the salesperson returned and presented Winston with the refund
   c. soliciting his patronage

3. The room, <u>shadowed well with awnings</u>, was dark and cool.

F. Scott Fitzgerald, *The Great Gatsby*

   a. piled high with junk
   b. was forbidding but fascinating
   c. the attic

Appositive Phrases

An appositive is a noun or pronoun that identifies another noun or pronoun. Appositive phrases contain the appositive plus related modifiers.

The face of Liliana Methol, <u>the fifth woman in the plane</u>, was badly bruised and covered with blood. **Piers Paul Read, *Alive***

Absolute Phrases

An absolute is a sentence part, that, while related to the sentence as a whole, does not modify any specific word within the sentence.

> Then, very afraid, she shook her head warningly and touched a finger to her lips and shook her head again, <u>her eyes pleading with him</u>.
> **James Clavell, *Shogun***

C. Unscrambling and Imitating Sentences   Unscramble the parts of each set to form a sentence whose structure matches the model. Then write another sentence whose structure also matches that of the model.

1. Alice, <u>a cousin of Frederick's, a widow down on her luck</u>, came to Dorothy.
   Doris Lessing, *The Fifth Child*
   a. tried to get a weird haircut
   b. Dulcie
   c. a friend of mine, a person up on the latest styles

2. She returned to her bench, <u>her face showing all the unhappiness that had suddenly overtaken her</u>.
   Theodore Dreiser, *An American Tragedy*
   a. that had always characterized him
   b. Odysseus lunged for the Cyclops
   c. his response showing all the cunning

3. <u>The sharp edges gone</u>, he continued to work with the leaf, pulling off half-inch wide strips and laying them in a pile.
   Robb White, *Deathwatch*
   a. squirting streams of water and spraying the clowns in the ring
   b. the elephant started to prance around the ring
   c. its trunk raised

Application   From a recent piece of writing, choose six sentences to expand by adding adjectives and adverbs and the five kinds of phrases you have studied in this lesson. Use adjectives and adverbs and each kind of phrase at least once, and place them where they make the most sense in your sentences.

Grammar Refresher   For more on adjectives and adverbs, see Handbook 37; for more on prepositional phrases, see Handbook 33; for more on participial phrases, see Handbook 33; for more on appositives, see Handbook 33; for more on absolute phrases, see Handbook 33.

Sketchbook

As this movie poster from 1955 shows, the stereotype of lawless, uncontrollable teenagers is nothing new. In your view, how would a teenager be described?

Additional Sketches

What is the secret of your success?

Choose an issue or topic with which you are quite familiar and write as many questions as you can about it. When you find a question that seems impossible to answer, stop and explore it.

Informative Exposition: Analysis

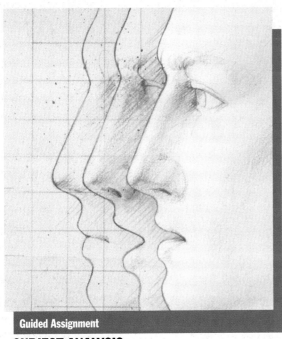

Guided Assignment
SUBJECT ANALYSIS

Related Assignment
GRAPHIC AID

Related Assignment
PROJECT EVALUATION

If you have ever met people who like to tinker with machines, you know they are constantly taking things apart—radios, computers, cars, and other devices—just to "see how they work." Indeed, taking a thing apart and examining the separate parts is a good way to understand or explain anything from an electronic gadget to a concept in philosophy. In thinking and writing, such a process is called analysis. In the next three assignments you will use analysis to explore a complex subject, to create a graphic representation of a subject, and to evaluate a project.

147

Subject Analysis

One way to understand a complex phenomenon is through analysis, the process of breaking down a subject into its constituent parts and studying how the parts fit together to make up the whole.

When writer Denise Grady's two-year-old son began to stutter, Grady decided to find out why, so she wrote a subject analysis about stuttering for a magazine. As you read this excerpt from the article, notice how Grady analyzes stuttering by identifying the various body parts involved and the many steps that lead to and comprise this complex behavior.

Nobody knows why people stutter. The disorder occurs in virtually every culture, and speech therapists estimate that it affects about one percent of the population around the world. The earliest explanations, dating from ancient Greece and persisting into the early 1800's, blamed the tongue: it was too weak, too wet, too dry, too hard, too cold, too large. By the early part of this

by Denise Grady

STUTT

century, the focus had shifted upward, and stuttering was seen first as a bad habit or the product of a neurosis, and later as the result of some unknown abnormality in the brain.

Today many speech researchers think that stuttering is both a physiological and a behavioral condition. The details may differ from one person to the next, but the basic scenario is that stuttering begins for an organic reason and persists, at least in part, because the anxiety generated by the stuttering then makes the stuttering worse, as do some of the habits that people fall into in their struggles to control their speech. Some experts believe that excessive concern with the mechanics of talking can throw the rhythm off, just as thinking too much about where to put your foot next can lead to a fall, and trying to perfect each sentence as you write it can lead to writer's block. Some researchers have even suggested that people become physically addicted to stuttering, perhaps to little jolts of adrenaline or other brain chemicals that may be released during stuttering.

In order to speak, one has to coordinate breathing, voice, and movements of the mouth, lips, and tongue. Almost a hundred muscles are involved, and all of them must receive nerve signals at certain instants to produce the right sequence of movements. Because the muscles are on both sides of the body, their movements must also be synchronized. The speech control center resides in the left half of the brain in most people; one popular theory suggests that in stutterers its control may be incomplete, and the right side may fire

ERING

out conflicting orders that throw the whole speech apparatus out of whack. The result may be a breakdown in timing—a failure of the mechanism that organizes the movements required for speech and that marks its rhythm. Some researchers say that mistiming may be a perpetual problem: stutterers may hear their own speech in a distorted way—with a delay, perhaps—that interferes with their ability to talk.

Male stutterers outnumber females by at least three to one, and the disorder often runs in families. It nearly always comes on during preschool years, when speech and language pass through their most intense phases of development. Many children, especially boys, have brief periods of stuttering or stumbling or fragmented speech. Most get over it. Why some never do remains a mystery. In one of his books, *The Nature of Stuttering*, Charles Van Riper describes a "monstrous collage of factors" of physiology, intelligence, personality, verbal skill, and environmental stress that may contribute to stuttering.

Think AND Respond

What steps lead to normal speech, according to Grady, and what steps lead to stuttering? What other aspects of the phenomenon does she consider? What evidence does she put forward to support her analysis? What subjects of personal interest to you could you explore in a subject analysis?

149

INVITATION
— TO —
Write

Denise Grady analyzed a subject that was important to her. Now it is your turn to choose a subject you consider important and analyze it by identifying and exploring its parts.

Even the most complicated subject is composed of simpler parts. Analysis can, therefore, be applied to almost any subject. A repair manual for an automobile shows thousands of parts and how they work together. A medical textbook may break a surgical procedure down to a series of steps. Each entry in an encyclopedia takes some whole subject and examines it part by part. A critic analyzes a play or movie to see how its various elements work—or fail to work—together. You, too, can take any topic and understand it better by writing a subject analysis, identifying the parts that comprise your subject and examining how they fit together.

PREWRITE AND EXPLORE

FOR HELP & PRACTICE

Gathering Information, p. 332

Limiting Your Topic, pp. 337–338

Analysis Frames, p. 343

1. Look for ideas.   You write best when you explore a subject that you care and know something about. Try one or more of the following exploratory activities to help you think of an interesting subject for analysis.

Exploratory Activities

- **Brainstorming**   With a group of classmates, brainstorm a list of noteworthy recent events in such fields as science, technology, politics, art, music, or international affairs. What topics for analysis do these events suggest?
- **Questioning**   Think of issues and topics that have raised questions in your mind recently, including ones mentioned at school, in conversation with friends, in your personal reading or research for school, or in the news. List your questions.

- **Interviewing** Talk to people with interesting occupations, hobbies, backgrounds, or fields of expertise. Listen for ideas you might like to write about.
- **Reading literature** Do you enjoy a particular type of literature—mysteries or science fiction, for example? How would you analyze the qualities of one genre of literature?

2. Choose a subject. Scan the ideas you have generated and choose a few that seem promising. Do a few minutes of freewriting to see where each one might lead. If you still can't choose a topic, look through your journal, review the writing you did for the Sketchbook on page 146, or check "Apply Your Skills" on page 161.

3. Explore your topic. Find out what you know and think about your subject by jotting down some notes about it. You might try "cubing" to discover new approaches to the subject. That is, picture your subject as a cube and let each of the six sides represent a different activity: *describe, compare, associate, analyze, apply,* and *argue for or against.*

One student, Zack, became fascinated with wolves after he observed them when he was on a wilderness trip. Here is how Zack cubed the subject of wolves. In this assignment you will follow Zack through the writing of his subject analysis of wolves.

**PROBLEM
SOLVING**

How can I discover the qualities or characteristics of my subject?

ONE STUDENT'S PROCESS

<u>Describe</u> A wolf against a full moon, howling. Large mammals with thick dense fur, skinny legs, powerful jaws. Lupine family.

<u>Compare</u> Wolves and people are alike: both are social. A wolf pack is like a large family and the whole pack raises the pups.

<u>Associate</u> When I think "wolf" I think of fierce animals. Also, of fairy tale wolves: the Big Bad Wolf in the "Three Little Pigs." Fables and sayings: the boy who cried wolf, a wolf in sheep's clothing.

<u>Analyze</u> Aspects of a wolf's life: hunting, mating, raising pups, traveling, communicating, dying.

<u>Apply</u> Wolves are an endangered species—what could I do to help preserve them? What can we learn from wolves?

<u>Argue for or against</u> I think wolves should be protected, not hunted. We should study the wolf for what it can teach us about the ways of the wilderness—and about ourselves.

4. Focus your exploration. Decide which aspect of your topic you want to focus on. After looking through his cubing notes, Zack decided he was most interested in the social life of wolves. He looked up wolves in an encyclopedia. Then he charted the main factors that make wolves social animals.

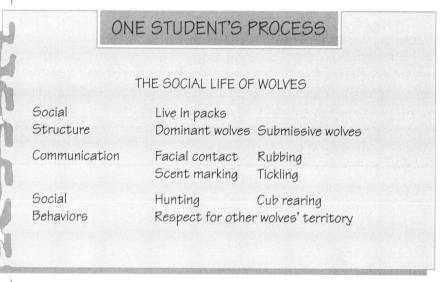

ONE STUDENT'S PROCESS

THE SOCIAL LIFE OF WOLVES

Social Structure	Live in packs Dominant wolves	Submissive wolves
Communication	Facial contact Scent marking	Rubbing Tickling
Social Behaviors	Hunting Respect for other wolves' territory	Cub rearing

As he created his chart, Zack realized that wolf communication lay at the heart of all the issues he wanted to raise in his analysis. He decided to focus specifically on this topic.

5. Break your subject into parts. To analyze, you must explore the subparts of your subject. These parts may be steps in a process, characteristics, stages, or any other logical division. Zack, for example, has already broken *communication* into four parts.

6. Frame your purpose and specific goals. Having brought your specific topic into focus, consider your purpose. Do you want to inform your readers? prove a point? rally support for some cause? Denise Grady wrote her analysis of stuttering to provide information—but she also wrote to gain a better understanding of a problem affecting a member of her family. What specific goals might you achieve by writing your subject analysis?

7. Gather information. Once you have a working purpose, you can gather information from interviews, books, magazines, reference works, videotapes, and other sources. Before you start, make a list of questions you have about your topic—questions you plan to answer in your analysis.

8. Write a thesis statement. First review the information you gathered and decide on the main idea you want to communicate. Then write one or two sentences that sum up this main idea. Keep in mind, however, that you may revise your thesis statement during the drafting and revising stages. Here is Zack's preliminary thesis statement for his essay on wolves.

ONE STUDENT'S PROCESS

Despite their reputation as vicious loners, wolves are social animals that communicate with each other in a variety of ways.

9. Think about your audience. Before you begin drafting your subject analysis, think about who will read your writing. Will your readers have any background in your subject? How much basic information will you need to provide? Which terms will you need to define? Also decide what level of language will be appropriate and what tone you should use.

DRAFT AND DISCOVER

1. Begin your draft. Look over your prewriting notes and then begin writing, keeping your overall purpose in mind. Try to get into the flow of your writing and set down everything you want to say. You will have time later to cut what you don't need, add what you forgot, and improve what you didn't express perfectly. Remember that drafting is an experimental stage. You may go back to the prewriting stage at any time to find more information, reorganize your approach, or redefine your purpose.

 Writer's Choice A compelling introduction is important, but it doesn't have to be written first. If you wish, write the introduction after you've written the rest of the draft. Then you'll know exactly what to say.

HANDBOOKS
FOR HELP & PRACTICE

**Introducing Nonfiction,
pp. 365–367**
**Elaborative Details,
pp. 376–378**
**Developing/
Presenting
Arguments,
pp. 474–477**

2. Organize your draft. The specific qualities of your subject will determine how you proceed, but subject analyses often follow this general form:

1. Provide a provocative introduction calculated to engage your readers' interest.
2. Identify the subject you intend to analyze, either in a single sentence or in a short paragraph.
3. Describe the parts that make up your subject.
4. Examine each part and its relationship to the others or to the subject as a whole.

3. Elaborate on ideas. Writing a subject analysis allows you to examine your subject from a variety of viewpoints, using a variety of strategies. The unique characteristics of your subject will determine which strategies you use, but you may need to use one or more of the following.

Strategies

- **Description** Elaborate on each subpart by examining its distinguishing characteristics in detail.
- **Comparison** Show how your subject or one of its parts resembles or differs from another relevant subject. Denise Grady, for example, compared the process of stuttering with that of normal speech.
- **Process analysis** If you are analyzing an event or procedure, discuss how each action or step follows from the preceding step and leads to the next one. Denise Grady used cause and effect to explain why some people stutter.
- **Definition** For some complex or technical subjects, an analysis may consist, at least to some degree, of clear, explicit definitions of key parts, characteristics, or terms.

 Writer's Choice Will charts, diagrams, or illustrations help clarify your analysis or make it more interesting? Include any graphic elements that may help you communicate with your readers.

When Zack wrote his subject analysis, he began by evoking the stereotype of wolves familiar to everyone. Then he used a variation of his thesis statement to introduce the analysis he hoped would change this stereotype. Here is the beginning of his unrevised draft.

PROBLEM
S O L V I N G

How can I explain the unique characteristics of my subject?

COMPUTER
TIP

If you are using a word processor to draft your analysis, triple-space and leave wide side margins. This will give you plenty of room to make changes and corrections after you have printed your draft.

When you think of wolves, you may think of the Big Bad Wolf who threatened the three little pigs in the fairy tale, or of the one who ate Little Red Riding Hood, or of the shepherd boy who cried "Wolf!" Or you might think of the lone wolf howling in the moonlight. All these images give a false picture. Wolves are not really vicious or mean animals at all, nor could you call them solitary hunters. In fact, wolves are very family- or pack-oriented and have a rich social life, which they maintain by communicating with each other in a variety of interesting ways. Some common wolf communication behaviors are facial contact, howling, and scent marking.

4. Take a break. Put your completed first draft away for a day or two to get some distance from it. Then read it over and see what you think of it. If possible, have a classmate read and respond to it as well. Here are some questions for you and your readers to keep in mind while evaluating your draft.

R E V I E W   Y O U R   W R I T I N G

Questions for Yourself

- Do I make my subject and purpose clear to the reader quickly?
- Have I covered all the points needed for a complete analysis of my subject? Should I leave out any of the information I have included?
- What could I add or change to make my analysis clearer? Do I need to explain any of the terms I have used? Would any graphic aids help the readers?
- Do I present the information in a logical order? Do the parts fit together smoothly?
- Have I achieved my purpose?

Questions for Your Peer Readers

- What did you learn about my subject? Did you find this information interesting?
- Are any parts of my essay unclear? Which parts? Do you understand all my terms or should I define any of them?
- Can you restate the main points of my analysis?
- Do you have any unanswered questions about my subject? What are they?

HANDBOOKS

FOR HELP & PRACTICE

Unity/Coherence, pp. 382–391

Improving Sentences, pp. 402–411

Varieties of Language, pp. 429–434

R E V I S E   Y O U R   W R I T I N G

1. Evaluate your responses. Think about your personal assessment of your draft and the responses you got from your peer readers. As you consider your draft, keep in mind that an effective subject analysis displays the characteristics listed on the following page.

Standards for Evaluation

An effective subject analysis . . .

- introduces the subject in an interesting and informative manner.
- identifies the individual parts that comprise the subject.
- uses appropriate strategies to examine and explain each part.
- presents information in a logical order.
- demonstrates an awareness of audience through the use of appropriate language and details.
- includes an effective and well-developed introduction, body, and conclusion.
- uses transitional words and phrases to illustrate the relationship among ideas, sentences, and paragraphs.

2. Problem-solve. Decide which responses you want to use and then rework your draft. Here are some of the changes Zack made as a result of the responses of one peer reader.

ONE STUDENT'S PROCESS

Howling is another way. You may thing that wolves
important *that wolves communicate*

howl because they are lonely. They usually howl for
,but in fact

social purposes. Barry Lopez says that wolves probably
, author of the book Of Wolves and Men,

don't howl during a chase, but often do howl after a

hunt "perhaps to celebrate a successful hunt (the

presence of food), their prowess, or the fact that they

are all together again, that no one has been injured".

Wolves howl most often during breeding and courtship

times, (in the winter), and more often in the evening or

early morning. *However, they don't howl at the moon, and they
don't howl any more often when there is a full moon.*

Seems a little choppy here.

Nice quote but who is Barry Lopez? Some authority?

I always heard that wolves howl at the moon. Is that true?

3. Proofread your work. Once you have finished revising your work, correct all errors in punctuation, grammar, and spelling. Make sure you have used appropriate punctuation marks to set off parenthetical definitions and other interrupting phrases. Then make a clean copy of your work that reflects all your changes.

LINKING
GRAMMAR AND WRITING
Punctuating Parenthetical Definitions

A parenthetical definition is a phrase that interrupts a sentence to explain or define something. You can set off a parenthetical definition with commas, parentheses, or dashes.

COMMAS: "Cartography, the science of map-making, developed slowly and painfully out of obscure origins."

Willis Lloyd

PARENTHESES: "Deer have a tremendous biotic potential (ability to reproduce and increase their population)."

Paul Winks

DASHES: "At the so-called House of the Tragic Poet, a mosaic shows a barking dog, with the inscription *cave canem*— 'Beware of the dog.'"

Robert Silverberg

See Grammar Handbook 39, pages 766–772, for more information on punctuating sentence interrupters.

PUBLISH AND PRESENT

HANDBOOKS
FOR HELP & PRACTICE

**Publishing,
p. 413**

- **Prepare a mini-encyclopedia.** Get together with a group of classmates and prepare a mini-encyclopedia in which each student's analysis comprises one entry.
- **Submit your work to your school or community newspaper.** If your paper doesn't usually print articles like the one you have written, suggest that the editors try a "Readers' Page" feature where work like yours could be published.
- **Present your paper to another class.** Try presenting an oral report based on your subject analysis to an appropriate class.

Wolf Communication—Part of Wolf Society

Zack N. Pauly

The Big Bad Wolf who threatened the three little pigs . . . the wolf who disguised himself as a grandmother and ate Little Red Riding Hood . . . the story of the little shepherd boy who cried "Wolf!" . . . a lone wolf howling in the moonlight—all these familiar images of the wolf have one thing in common: they give a false picture. Contrary to stereotypes born out of human fear, the wolf is not a cold-blooded killer of humans, nor is it a solitary hunter. In fact, wolves are very family- and pack-oriented and have a rich social life, which they maintain by communicating with each other in a variety of interesting ways. These wolf communication behaviors include facial contact, howling, and scent marking.

Facial contact behaviors, the most intimate type of wolf communication, closely resemble what humans do when they nuzzle their babies or hug and kiss one another as a greeting. Wolves use nose pushing, cheek rubbing, facial licking, and jaw wrestling to greet one another, to give a friendly welcome, or sometimes to show dominance. For example, jaw wrestling—a behavior in which two wolves mouth one another's jaws—can be a greeting or it can be a way of intimidating another, lower-ranking wolf. If one wolf puts its mouth over another's muzzle, it is giving a sign of friendship. But if the first wolf has its teeth bared, the greeting is not so friendly—it is the wolf's way of establishing itself

Introduces the subject in an interesting way

Establishes the purpose of the analysis

Identifies the parts of the subject

Examines each part separately in a logical order

Uses classification and cause and effect to examine this aspect of the subject fully

Subject Analysis **159**

Makes a smooth
transition to a second
aspect of the subject

Presents evidence to
support analysis

Completes analysis of
subject by examining
its third major part

Closes analysis with an
effective conclusion

as the more dominant, or more important, member of
the wolf pack.

Howling is another important way that wolves communicate. You may think that wolves howl because
they are lonely, but in fact they usually howl for social
purposes. Barry Lopez, author of the book *Of Wolves and
Men,* says that wolves probably don't howl during a chase,
but often do howl after a hunt, "perhaps to celebrate a successful hunt (the presence of food), their prowess, or the
fact that they are all together again, that no one has been
injured." Wolves howl often during breeding and courtship
times (in the winter), and more often in the evening or
early morning. However, contrary to popular belief, they
don't howl at the moon, and they don't howl any more often when there is a full moon.

Wolves also communicate by scent-marking. Wolves
leave scent marks to define their territory as if to erect
an invisible fence that only other wolves with their
keen sense of smell can detect. They mark their territory partly for the same reasons that we put our names
and initials on our books, mailboxes, sweaters, brace-
lets—to say, "This is mine." Scent marks help a wolf
to know if it is in its own territory. They may even
keep a pack together. How exactly do wolves leave scent
marks? They urinate, defecate, or scratch the ground
every few minutes as they are traveling. And wolves on
the move stop every few minutes to inspect scent
marks left by other wolves.

The more we learn about these and other forms of
wolf communication, the better we understand the complex social structure of wolf packs. Perhaps by gaining
insight into these magnificent animals—who form en-
during relationships, just as humans do—we can learn
more about ourselves and our place in the world of nature.

WRITER TO WRITER

There's something in life that's a curtain, and I keep trying to raise it.

Maxine Hong Kingston, novelist and memoirist

1. Reflect on your writing. Look back over your earliest writing on your topic and reflect on what you have learned in the course of completing your subject analysis. If you would like to pursue your topic further, how would you do it? Or are you now so tired of your topic that you hope never to think about it again? Finally, consider how satisfied you are with your paper and how you might be inclined to revise it further.

Use your reflections on the questions above to compose a brief introduction that tells something about what doing the paper has meant to you and where your interest might now take you.

2. Apply your skills. Try one or more of the following activities.

- **Cross curricular** Make a list of important words you've run across in your history studies, such as *crusade, Aztec, plague, Northwest Passage,* and *shogun.* Choose two and do some research about each. Jot down notes that would be helpful if you were writing a subject analysis of each word.
- **Literature** Look through magazines that publish nonfiction, such as *Discover, Smithsonian, Vanity Fair,* and *Travel & Leisure,* and find articles that contain subject analyses. Take notes about any words, passages, or techniques the writers used that you found particularly effective. Find examples of how the writers considered the background and needs of their audiences. For example, write down their techniques for defining unfamiliar words. Also highlight the thesis statement in each article if you can find one.
- **Related assignments** Follow the suggestions on pages 162–172 to develop a graphic aid or to write an evaluation of a school, community, or national project.

Graphic Aid

The United Nations System

Graphic aids, such as charts, tables, graphs, diagrams, or maps, can help explain a complex subject by breaking it down into parts and presenting the parts visually. You probably have come across many graphic aids in newspaper and magazine articles, textbooks, and library reference material. You also may have used, or even made, graphic aids in connection with school activities such as fund raising drives and sporting events.

As you examine this chart, notice how visual representations help explain the subject.

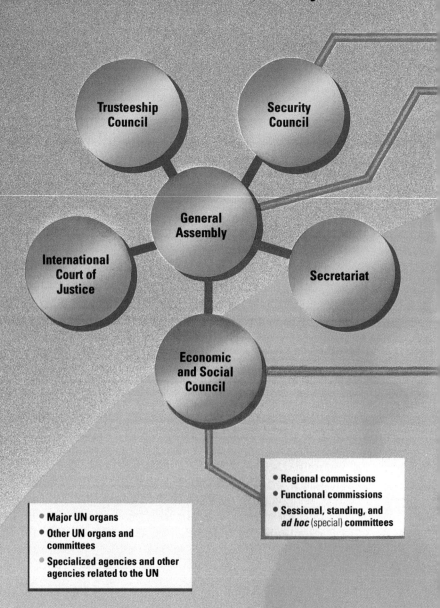

- Major UN organs
- Other UN organs and committees
- Specialized agencies and other agencies related to the UN

- Regional commissions
- Functional commissions
- Sessional, standing, and *ad hoc* (special) committees

- United Nations Disengagement Observer Force (UNDOF)
- United Nations Interim Force in Lebanon (UNIFIL)
- United Nations Truce Supervision Organization (UNTSO)
- United Nations Peacekeeping Force in Cyprus (UNFICYP)
- United Nations Military Observer Group in India and Pakistan (UNMOGIP)

- Military Staff Committee

- Main committees
- Standing and procedural committees
- Other subsidiary organs of the General Assembly

- United Nations Relief and Works Agency for Palestine Refugees in the Near East (UNRWA)

- International Atomic Energy Agency (IAEA)

- United Nations Conference on Trade and Development (UNCTAD)
- United Nations University (UNU)
- World Food Council (WFC)
- United Nations Environment Program (UNEP)
- United Nations Development Program (UNDP)
- United Nations Industrial Development Organization (UNIDO)
- United Nations Institute for Training and Research (UNITAR)
- International Research and Training Institute for the Advancement of Women (INSTRAW)
- UNICEF (United Nations Children's Fund)
- Office of the United Nations High Commissioner for Refugees (UNHCR)
- World Food Program (WFP)
- United Nations Fund for Population Activities (UNFPA)
- United Nations Center for Human Settlements (UNCHS), or Habitat

- World Intellectual Property Organization (WIPO)
- International Labor Organization (ILO)
- Food and Agriculture Organization of the United Nations (FAO)
- UNESCO (United Nations Educational, Scientific and Cultural Organization)
- World Health Organization (WHO)
- International Monetary Fund (IMF)
- International Development Association (IDA)
- World Bank
- International Finance Corporation (IFC)
- International Fund for Agricultural Development (IFAD)
- International Civil Aviation Organization (ICAO)
- Universal Postal Union (UPU)
- International Telecommunication Union (ITU)
- World Meteorological Organization (WMO)
- International Maritime Organization (IMO)

- General Agreement on Tariffs and Trade (GATT)*

*GATT has no formal relationship with the UN but cooperates with it and is considered part of the UN system.

Think and Respond

What can you learn about the United Nations by examining this diagram? What visual techniques did the writer use to present this information? Think of other ways you could visually present the information in the diagram.

INVITATION
=== TO ===
Write

The chart you have just examined presents the organizational structure of the United Nations. Now create a graphic aid that explains a complex subject by analyzing its parts.

Sometimes a subject analysis can best be presented through, or with the help of, a graphic aid. In the chart you have just examined, the writer analyzes the structure of a complex organization. As in any type of analysis, the writer breaks down the subject into parts, examines those parts, and shows how they fit together.

UNDERSTANDING GRAPHIC AIDS

FOR HELP & PRACTICE

Limiting Your Topic, pp. 337–338

Graphics for Exploring, pp. 339–342

Informal Sharing, p. 412

Reference Works, pp. 495–498

Many types of graphic aids can be used in a subject analysis. **Graphs** show relationships between groups, as well as development in time. **Tables** and **charts** are used to list and compare information. **Diagrams** show the parts or functions of the subject. **Maps** display geographical areas or distribution.

PLANNING YOUR GRAPHIC AID

1. Familiarize yourself with the variety of graphic aids. Look through books and magazines for examples of graphic aids that are used to help explain a complex subject. You may wish to get together with several classmates to share and discuss some of the more interesting examples you find.

2. Explore possible subjects for your graphic aid. Think about subjects in which a graphic aid might prove useful. Could a chart clarify a complex process in chemistry or biology class? Would a series of maps help explain territorial changes in a certain region of the world?

3. Gather information. Carefully research the subject you will be presenting. This may be done through library research, brainstorming sessions, and interviews; or through firsthand observation or experience.

4. Analyze the information. How can your subject be broken down for easier understanding? For example, in the UN chart, large groups are broken down into major UN organs, then further broken down into smaller UN commissions and committees, and finally into specialized agencies and other related bodies.

5. Choose the type of graphic aid to use. In doing so, consider which type is best suited to your subject and purpose. In general, charts and tables are most effective when you want to compare or list information. Diagrams are helpful when showing parts or functions of the subject. Maps are the best choice for displaying geographical information, while graphs can present quantitative relationships and development over time.

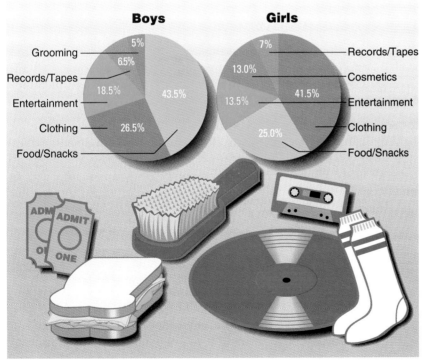

How Teens Spend Their Money

Boys

Grooming — 5%
6.5%
Records/Tapes —
18.5% 43.5%
Entertainment —
Clothing — 26.5%
Food/Snacks —

Girls

7% — Records/Tapes
13.0% — Cosmetics
13.5% 41.5% — Entertainment
25.0% — Clothing
— Food/Snacks

1. Organize your information.   Decide what information to include in your graphic aid and how best to present it. You may want to experiment with various organizational methods before settling on the best one to use in your subject analysis.

2. Draft your graphic aid.   Create the first draft of your graphic aid. As you draft, label your information where appropriate: in columns or rows for charts and tables, alongside graphs, and in keys or legends for diagrams and maps. Color-coding your graphic aid can also make interpretation easier for your readers. Give your graphic aid a title. The title should provide readers with a framework for interpreting the information.

Writer's Choice   Do you want to write a caption or other brief text to help explain or summarize the information in your graphic aid?

REVIEWING YOUR WRITING

1. Take another look at your graphic aid.   Ask yourself questions such as the following: Does my graphic aid clearly convey all the necessary information? Does it accomplish the goal I had in mind? Is it attractive and easy to read?

2. Share your graphic aid with several classmates.   To elicit helpful information from your classmates, ask them specific questions: Do you understand the information I am trying to communicate? Would a different organization make my graphic aid easier to understand? Would adding or eliminating color make the graphic aid clearer?

PUBLISHING AND PRESENTING

- **Copy your graphic aid onto a poster.**   Display the poster as you orally present your graphic aid to the class.
- **Submit your graphic aid to a newspaper.**   If your graphic aid deals with a subject of interest to the student body, submit it for publication in your school newspaper.

On the Lightside

SNIGLETS

Here are some humorous additions to your vocabulary study. "Sniglets" are words that don't appear in the dictionary, but should.

Accordionated (ah kor'de on ay tid) adj. Being able to drive and refold a road map at the same time.

Anaception (an a sep'shun) n. The body's ability to actually affect television reception by moving around the room.

B+ Stampede (bee' plus stam peed) n. The attempt by half the classroom to claim the paper with no name on it.

Bleemus (blee'mus) n. The disgusting film on the top of soups and cocoa that sit out for too long.

Brattled (brat'uld) adj. The unsettling feeling, at a stoplight, that the busload of kids that just pulled up beside you is making fun of you.

Burgacide (burg'uh side) n. When a hamburger can't take any more torture and hurls itself through the grill into the coals.

Cinemuck (si'ne muk) n. The combination of popcorn, soda, and melted chocolate which covers the floors of movie theaters.

Eurfirstics (yew fur'stiks) n. Two people waiting on the phone for the other to hang up first.

Flopcorn (flop'korn) n. The unpopped kernels at the bottom of the cooker.

Greedling (gree'dling) v. Pretending to read the inscription on the birthday card when you really just want to know how much the check is for.

Gription (grip'shun) n. The sound of sneakers squeaking against the floor during basketball games.

Hystioblogination (his' to o blahg in ay'shun) n. The act of trying to identify a gift by holding it to your ear and shaking it.

Multipochoholes (mul ti po'cho holz) n. Wounds left in test papers from overerasing.

Pigslice (pig'slys) n. The last unclaimed piece of pizza that everyone is secretly dying for.

Puntificate (puhn tih'fih kayt) v. To try to predict in what direction a football will bounce.

Sark (sark) n. The marks left on one's ankle after wearing tube socks all day.

Scribblics (skrih'bliks) n. Warm-up exercises designed to get the ink in a pen flowing.

Waftic (wahf'tik) adj. Describes any person in whose direction campfire or barbeque smoke always blows.

Rich Hall and Friends

Project Evaluation

Kids with Causes

Have you ever invested weeks or months of your free time working on a project that you cared deeply about? Were you filled with pride when the project came to a successful conclusion, or did you feel crushed when, despite all your best efforts, the project failed?

The evaluation of projects—judging their successes and failures, their strengths and weaknesses—can give you information that you can put to use in future projects. As you read this analysis of a project, note how the writer examines its successes and failures and how a failure led to a new achievement.

by Katrine Ames

For a growing number of teenagers, the sentiment "I'm OK, who cares about you?" no longer prevails. Though there are no firm numbers on teen activism, many teachers and counselors predict a comeback. Granted, it's not yet a tidal wave of altruism. But in groups or on their own, teenagers are running recycling programs and peer hot lines, staffing soup kitchens and recording senior citizens' oral histories. Peter Scales, deputy director of the Center for Early Adolescence at the University of North Carolina, says, "The desire is there. We just have to tap into it."...

This fish story is true. Six years ago the fledgling ecology club at Casa Grande High School in Petaluma, California, a middle-class city 35 miles north of San Francisco, began to clean up Adobe Creek. The trout stream, once a healthy home for steelhead, was polluted and neglected. After reeling in 10 tons of junk—car parts, sofas, a washing machine—the students learned a painful lesson. "We cleared the garbage to create the proper environment for fish to return," says vice president Brian Waits, 18. "What we didn't realize was that the community could put in litter as fast as we could clean it up."

With the help of teacher Tom Furrer, the students built a fish hatchery. Soon, they were fighting one another for the job of cleaning it out during their lunch hour; when the water got too hot, they raced to get ice. They released some 500 trout and catfish—fin-clipped so they could be recognized if they came back to spawn—into local waters.

Then, officials ruled that the hatchery did not meet earthquake standards and had to close down. Initially devastated, the club members soon resolved to build a better hatchery. It would release 20,000 steelhead and striped bass annually—and carried a $250,000 price tag. The students wrote a 186-page grant proposal and became articulate fund raisers. Donations flowed in (roughly $200,000 to date) and hatchery construction is now underway. "It will be our gift to the younger generation," says president Darcy Hamlow, 18. "Someday this stream will be full of life." This spring, a harbinger swam into view: a 29-inch steelhead, its clipped fins proof that it had been raised by the students.

Think AND Respond

What successes and failures does the writer of the project analysis describe? How would you evaluate a project you've worked on? Could you objectively examine the strengths and weaknesses of the project?

INVITATION
TO
Write

The excerpt from a news article evaluated an ambitious ecology project initiated by high-school students like yourself. Write an evaluation of a school, community, or national project, one that you can investigate either firsthand or through research.

In the working world, the project evaluation is a common type of written report. Businesses and other groups use it to determine the success of projects, programs, and procedures and to determine if any changes are necessary. This type of analysis has three main parts: (1) an explanation of the project; (2) an analysis and evaluation of its successes and/or failures; and (3) a summarizing conclusion or recommendation.

CHOOSING AND INVESTIGATING A PROJECT

FOR HELP & PRACTICE

Analysis Frames,
p. 343

Questioning,
pp. 376–377

Organizing
Your Work,
pp. 349–357

Introducing/
Concluding
Nonfiction,
pp. 365–371

Developing/
Presenting
Arguments,
pp. 474–476

1. Choose a project that interests you.   It might be a class or club project in which you are currently active or interested, or, like students at Casa Grande High, perhaps you'd like to organize an environmental clean-up. Does the Student Council sponsor a community-service program, or has a history class created a school museum? The program does not have to be local. For example, you might investigate a national program like Headstart.

2. Make a list of questions.   Think of what you want to know about the various aspects of the project or program. To explain the project, you need answers to certain basic questions. Who runs the project? What is the purpose of the project? How is it organized and operated?

3. Break down a complex project into its key parts or stages.   Some projects or programs have many aspects. If you were investigating a volunteer tutoring program, for example, you might want to examine such aspects as the selection of participants, the screening and training of volunteers, and the measurement of improvements made by participants.

4. Conduct your investigation. If you chose a project in your school or community, much of your investigation may consist of personal interviews and direct observations. If you chose a project outside your school or community, you will need to conduct library research.

5. Determine the criteria for evaluating the project. How will you judge whether a project, or an aspect of it, is successful? First, list any results or goals that the project, or one phase of it, was supposed to achieve. Then determine whether these goals were achieved. For some aspects, you may rely on the reports of those involved: find out what those people think of it and what benefits and drawbacks they see. In "Kids with Causes," the writer reported the setback to the project when the fish hatchery was closed because it did not meet earthquake standards. For other aspects, you might find useful statistics and other objective data: see if the data support people's opinions. Make your list of questions as specific and comprehensive as needed to achieve your goal, which is to explain clearly a particular project and analyze its successes and failures.

6. Organize your findings and draw some conclusions. Listen to your taped interviews and transcribe parts you can use. Read your notes and highlight the important parts. Draw conclusions and list the strengths and weaknesses of the project.

DRAFTING YOUR ANALYSIS

1. Write an introduction that provides a context. Let your readers know why the subject is important and why you are analyzing this project. Make your introduction interesting to capture your readers' attention. Notice how the writer of "Kids with Causes" both provided a context and captured your attention.

2. Organize the body of your analysis in a logical way. Begin by providing basic information about the project—what it is, why it was started, who runs it, and how it operates. Then proceed to describe the strengths and/or weaknesses of the project or each aspect of it. Include direct quotes and statistics or other data to support your evaluations.

3. End by drawing a conclusion or making a recommendation. The writer of "Kids with Causes" concluded by noting that the fin-clipped steelhead came back in the spring, a sign that the stream was clean enough to support life. Conclude your analysis by describing the overall success or failure of your project or by recommending improvements.

REVIEWING YOUR WRITING

1. Reread your draft with your goal in mind. Did you clearly explain the project and evaluate its strengths and weaknesses? Did you blend facts and human interest well?

2. Ask project participants to read your evaluation. Were any important events or details left out? Are the goals of the project explained clearly and completely? Are participants' roles and titles described accurately?

3. Check for accuracy. After making sure the content is on target, reread your analysis with an eye for improving the word choice and writing style. Proofread for correct spelling of project and participant names. Also check that direct and indirect quotations have been punctuated correctly.

PUBLISHING AND PRESENTING

- **Prepare a final copy of your evaluation.** Share your report with the members of the project. Encourage them to discuss their reactions with you.
- **Submit your evaluation.** Send it to the school or community newspaper for publication.
- **Prepare an oral report for your classmates.** Use visual aids such as charts, graphs, or diagrams if possible.
- **Prepare a videotape of your evaluation.** Include segments of interviews with project members and scenes of people participating in the project. Share the videotape with the project members and your classmates. Submit your videotape to a local television station as a feature about your community.
- **Save your project evaluation in your writing portfolio.** Compare it to other works you have written. How is your project evaluation different? How are you growing as a writer?

Sentence COMPOSING

Varying Sentence Openers

Experienced writers know that, by varying sentence openers, they can not only add detail but also build suspense and increase readers' interest. In the sentences below, notice the varying degrees of detail and suspense achieved with each type of opener.

Single Word	<u>Overhead</u>, the live oaks met, and it was as dark as a cave. **Eudora Welty, "A Worn Path"**
Prepositional Phrase	<u>To her astonishment</u>, she saw that the expression on his face was one of satisfaction. **Mary Lavin, "One Summer"**
Present Participial Phrase	<u>Changing into dry clothes from his cellophane pack</u>, Mr. Benjamin Driscoll lay down and went happily to sleep. **Ray Bradbury, *The Martian Chronicles***
Past Participial Phrase	<u>Amazed at the simplicity of it all</u>, I understood everything as never before. **Alphonse Daudet, "The Last Lesson"**
Absolute Phrase	<u>Pain shooting up my entire arm</u>, I lay panting on the edge of the pool and gingerly began to feel my wrist. **Theodore Taylor, *The Cay***

A. Imitating Sentences   Write a sentence to imitate the structure of each model. Openers are underlined.

1. <u>Stupidly</u>, Eugie gazed around the room to see if morning had come into it yet. **Gina Berriault, "The Stone Boy"**

2. <u>At the gate</u>, the servant opened the door a trifle and looked out at the waiting people. **John Steinbeck, *The Pearl***

3. <u>Weaving in and out among the rocks</u>, they carried bamboo baskets on erect heads, unmindful of the salt water leaking down on their half-dried hair. **Kim Yong Ik, "The Sea Girl"**

4. <u>Enchanted and enthralled</u>, I stopped her constantly for details. **Richard Wright, *Black Boy***

5. <u>His carpetbag in his hand</u>, he stood outside for a time in the barnyard. **Jessamyn West, "A Time for Learning"**

B. Unscrambling and Imitating Sentences Sometimes, as in the models below, professional writers use a combination of openers. Unscramble each set of parts to form a sentence whose structure matches that of the model. Then write a sentence of your own whose structure also imitates that of the model. Follow each opener with a comma. Openers are underlined.

Example   There, in the tin factory, in the first moment of the atomic age, a human being was crushed by books.   **John Hersey, *Hiroshima***
   a. the champions were defeated by Central High
   b. abruptly
   c. in the closing seconds of the fourth quarter
   d. on a freak play

Unscrambled   Abruptly, on a freak play, as time ran out in the fourth quarter, the champions were defeated by Central High.

Student Sentence   First, in the mortar, in the hooded work area of the chemistry lab, the dark chunks should be ground to powder.

1. Standing in the shadows, with the bright window behind him, he blazed with sunburned health.   **John Knowles, *A Separate Peace***
   a. with the difficult routine successfully behind her
   b. Monica finished with stunning grace
   c. tumbling across the gym floor

2. Pushing himself on up, pain throbbing into his legs, he looked around the outcrop.   **Robb White, *Deathwatch***
   a. Janet jackknifed from the high diving board
   b. her legs stretching to tautness
   c. arching her body way up

3. Oiled, with tube bones cut from bronze and sunk in gelatin, the robots lay.   **Ray Bradbury, *The Martian Chronicles***
   a. his car waited
   b. polished
   c. with its body double-coated in wax and gleaming in the sun

4. <u>In and out among the trees and bushes</u>, <u>across streams</u>, <u>over grassy places, now low to the ground</u>, <u>then just above my head</u>, the dodging butterfly led me far before I caught and held it with my hand.

Frank Lindermann, "Interview with a Crow Chief"

   a. now plummeting from a steep peak
   b. up and down along the tracks
   c. then climbing to a new precipice
   d. across bridges
   e. the roller coaster car sped us all around before the ride was done
   f. over the water

C. Expanding Sentences Write an opener or a combination of openers to begin each sentence below. Each of your openers should start with the words in parentheses and should make sense within the context of the sentence. After you finish, compare your sentences with the originals on page 322.

1. (Filled . . .), Vera took the letter. **Mary Lavin, "One Summer"**

2. (Sitting . . .), (gazing . . .), he spent a day in idleness.

   J. M. Coetzee, *Life & Times of Michael K*

3. Sometimes, (mounted . . .), (with . . .), Jody rode out beyond the room. **John Steinbeck, *The Red Pony***

4. (Although . . .), they always felt an anxiety in the house.

   D. H. Lawrence, "The Rocking-Horse Winner"

5. There, (between . . .), (against . . .), was a figure from a dream, a strange beast that was horned and drunken-legged, but like something he had never even imagined. **Doris Lessing, "A Sunrise on the Veld"**

6. (Trying . . .), (twirling . . .), (turning . . .), the officer, with his stalwart form and slight swagger, made a fine picture of a guardian of the peace. **O. Henry, "After Twenty Years"**

Application From a recent piece of writing, select three sentences at random. Write each sentence three times, adding a different opener each time. Vary the openers in content, length, and structure. Note how each adds detail and interest.

Grammar Refresher An opening phrase that does not refer clearly to the correct noun may create a dangling modifier. For information on avoiding dangling modifiers, see Handbook 33.

Sketchbook

What rules would you like to change? How would you change them, and why?

Additional Sketches

What was the best advice you ever received? What was the worst?

How would you improve your school or your community?

Informative Exposition: Synthesis

Related Assignment
REBUTTAL

Related Assignment
ORAL PRESENTATION

Guided Assignment
MAKING PROPOSALS

Have you ever thought of a plan for something and then tried to get others to go along with your plan? This is essentially what is involved in writing a proposal. Proposal writers identify a need and offer a specific plan to meet that need. Since a proposal is an offer to do something, the proposal writer's main goal is to convince an audience to accept the offer, that is, to adopt the proposal. As you complete your writing for this workshop, you will first learn how to make a written proposal. Then you will develop your skills in rebutting, or answering, the opinions or proposals of others and in presenting a proposal orally.

Guided
ASSIGNMENT

Making Proposals

Most proposals are written in response to an opportunity or need that the proposal writer becomes aware of. Many are written in response to a formal RFP, a Request for Proposals, that is announced by a private or public agency. RFP's are usually very specific about what kinds of proposals will be considered and the rules for submitting them. Notice the specifications outlined in the following RFP announcing the Clifton Awards.

THE CLIFTON AWARDS FOR
INNOVATIVE LEARNING PROGRAMS
REQUEST FOR PROPOSALS (RFP)

With the support of the Chester Clifton Memorial Fund, the Office of the Superintendent of Schools, in conjunction with the Tri-Cities Secondary Curriculum Council, invites proposals from individual students, groups of students, or combined student and teacher groups for innovative projects designed to supplement the learning opportunities available in Tri-Cities high schools. Projects selected as Clifton Award projects are eligible for funding of up to $1,200 to cover costs that may be necessary to initiate or sustain the innovative program for the academic year. Each proposal must be endorsed by the principal of the school where the project will be based.

Proposals selected for a Clifton Award must be directed toward improving learning opportunities for students, beyond those opportunities presently available in the curriculum. Funds may be used to cover such items as travel expenses, the purchase of books or supplies, the payment of lecture fees, or secretarial and clerical costs. Funds may not be used to provide salaries for faculty members or students.

Ordinarily, five to six proposals are funded each year, with funding ranging from $100–$1,200 for each project. The average award has been approximately $400. Projects requiring no funds are also eligible for awards. All recipients of awards will be honored at the annual Tri-Cities High School Honors Convocation.

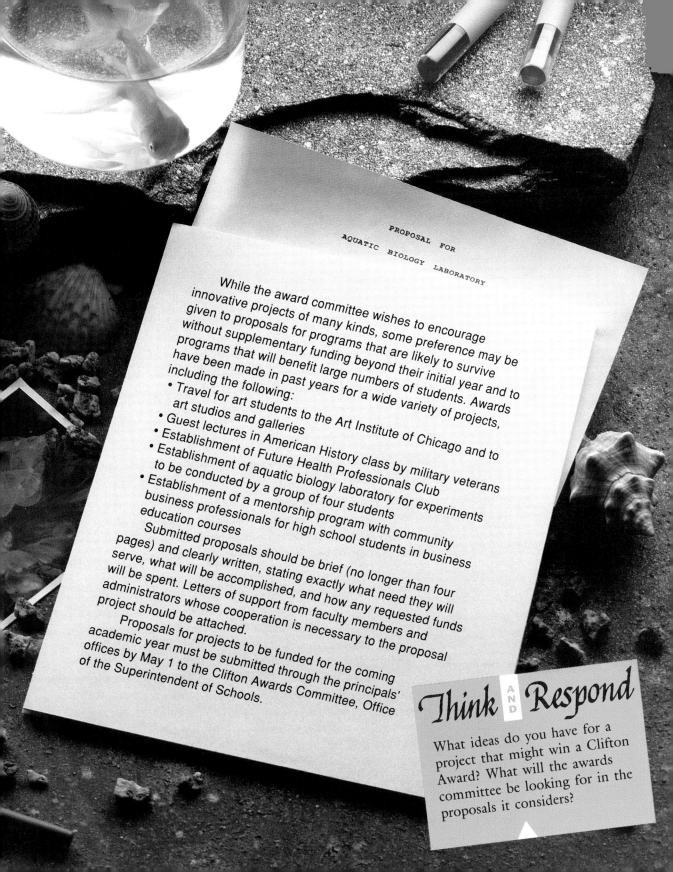

PROPOSAL FOR
AQUATIC BIOLOGY LABORATORY

While the award committee wishes to encourage innovative projects of many kinds, some preference may be given to proposals for programs that are likely to survive without supplementary funding beyond their initial year and to programs that will benefit large numbers of students. Awards have been made in past years for a wide variety of projects, including the following:

- Travel for art students to the Art Institute of Chicago and to art studios and galleries
- Guest lectures in American History class by military veterans
- Establishment of Future Health Professionals Club
- Establishment of aquatic biology laboratory for experiments to be conducted by a group of four students
- Establishment of a mentorship program with community business professionals for high school students in business education courses

Submitted proposals should be brief (no longer than four pages) and clearly written, stating exactly what need they will serve, what will be accomplished, and how any requested funds will be spent. Letters of support from faculty members and administrators whose cooperation is necessary to the proposal project should be attached.

Proposals for projects to be funded for the coming academic year must be submitted through the principals' offices by May 1 to the Clifton Awards Committee, Office of the Superintendent of Schools.

Think AND Respond

What ideas do you have for a project that might win a Clifton Award? What will the awards committee be looking for in the proposals it considers?

INVITATION
TO
Write

Think of an urgent problem or need in your school or community, and write a proposal for solving the problem or meeting the need. If you prefer, write a proposal for a project that meets the specifications for a Clifton Award.

The way a proposal is written is often important to its success. Your proposal may have to meet the following requirements. It must (1) define the problem or need you propose to address; (2) develop a clear plan of action for solving the problem or meeting the need; (3) meet the expectations and standards held by the readers who will evaluate your proposal and who will decide whether to grant or withhold their support.

PREWRITE AND EXPLORE

FOR HELP & PRACTICE

Writing Techniques, pp. 334–335
Interviewing, p.336
Collaborative Planning, pp. 358–360

1. Identify a problem or topic. A proposal must always answer an announced need or demonstrate that a need exists. Try one or more of the following activities to help you decide on the need or problem you would like to propose a solution for.

Exploratory Activities

- **Listing** Make a quick private list of problems, needs, or conditions that could use improvement in school or in your community. How might these problems be solved?
- **Researching and interviewing** Read recent issues of your school and community newspapers, looking for problems that need solutions. Then interview classmates, teachers, parents, and administrators. Ask them what they would like to see improved at school or in the community.
- **Sharing and collaborating** Share your more promising topics in a small group of writers and brainstorm ideas for solving those problems. Consider whether the solutions are realistic.

You should now have several possible ideas for a proposal. If you are still having difficulty finding a topic, look at the suggestions under "Apply Your Skills" on page 191. You might also consider the ideas you experimented with in the Sketchbook on page 176 or ideas you discover in your journal. List and evaluate all your ideas to see which ones you care about most, which ones seem most worthwhile for you to pursue, and which have the best chance of being adopted.

One student, Angela, listed and evaluated the following topics. In this workshop you will follow the development of her proposal.

PROBLEM
S O L V I N G

What should I look for in identifying a strong idea for a proposal?

ONE STUDENT'S PROCESS

Possible proposal ideas:

o Propose new sports team for girls so more girls can play team sports:
   I care about this topic. We don't get to travel or compete nearly as much as boys. Would like to make a league involving other schools. Too complicated for this assignment?

o Propose that Service Club hold a fund raising car wash in parking lot of downtown store, giving publicity to store. I really want to do this, but I could probably do it better by talking to them.

o Propose starting a health food snack bar in school to combat junk food addiction among students. This is a serious need and I really care about it. It could make money and be educational too. This is it!

2. Freewrite. Take ten minutes or so for some focused freewriting about your tentative proposal topic. Explain the problem, tell how you propose to solve it, and what sort of support you need.

3. Use collaborative planning. Working with a partner, share your freewriting and discuss your plans for a proposal. Pay special attention to the following areas.

- **Your audience** Who will be evaluating your proposal? What do they care about? What will it take to persuade them to give you what you are asking for?

- **The nature of the problem and its importance** How can you demonstrate its importance?
- **The details of your proposal** What, specifically, do you propose to do, and in what order?
- **The workability of your proposal** Will your proposal really work? How difficult will it be to put your plan into action? What are some arguments against it?
- **Your request** What are you asking for in order to implement your proposal, and how will you use what you are asking for? How will you spend any money that is given to you or use other resources (including time, materials, assistance) that you are requesting?
- **Research** What additional information might help you write a more effective proposal? Are there experts you ought to consult or books and articles you need to read? Could you conduct some research by doing your own observation, interviews, or surveys?

DRAFT AND DISCOVER

FOR HELP & PRACTICE

Facts and Statistics, p.379

Voice, pp. 418–422

Developing Arguments, pp. 474–476

Research Skills, pp. 479–490

Building Arguments, p. 504

1. Think about the parts of your proposal. Look over your freewriting and your notes from your collaborative planning session, and then begin a rough draft of your proposal. As you draft, you may want to look at the outline below, which presents a standard way of organizing a formal proposal.

> I. Preview summary of proposal (optional)
> II. Statement of need, supported by examples, testimony, and data, when appropriate
> III. Description of plan of action, detailing steps to be taken and describing benefits of the plan and how they will outweigh any disadvantages
> IV. Your request: exactly what you are asking for in money or other resources and how it will be used

 Writer's Choice If you are missing information (for example, statistics, costs, expert testimony), you might do more research now or go ahead with your rough draft, flagging places where you need to fill in blanks.

2. Employ effective writing strategies. You will probably want to use all or most of the following strategies at various points in writing your proposal.

Strategies

- **Summary** As a guide to readers, proposals often begin with a brief summary of what is being proposed.
- **Definition** Be sure to define any technical terms that your readers may not know.
- **Argumentation** A proposal makes two arguments: first, that a need exists and, second, that your plan can meet that need. To make your proposal persuasive, be sure to acknowledge any possible objections to it and refute those objections.
- **Quotation and documentation** An effective way to strengthen your argument is to present statistical data and expert testimony from books and articles or from your own original research through interviews and surveys.
- **Supplementary documentation** Proposal writers often attach to their proposals supplementary documents such as statistical charts, copies of published articles, letters of support, or résumés showing their qualifications and experience.

PROBLEM SOLVING

What strategies can I use to strengthen my proposal?

Angela wrote her rough draft quickly; she knew that she would be able to add additional material later. Here is the beginning of the first draft of her proposal.

ONE STUDENT'S PROCESS

SUMMARY. This is a proposal to establish a health food snack bar on campus to provide students with a healthy alternative to junk food snacks and, through better nutrition, to improve their ability to concentrate and learn.

NEED. In the three years I've been in Roosevelt High School, there is one complaint I've heard from everyone, students and teachers alike. There is no place at school where you can get healthy snacks. The cafeteria sells chips and sodas and candy, but very little fruit. Moreover, the cafeteria isn't open except at lunchtime.

3. Reread your draft and share it with others. After completing your rough draft, set it aside for a time. Then review it by yourself and share it with other readers. Ask yourself and your readers the following questions.

R E V I E W   Y O U R   W R I T I N G

Questions for Yourself
- Have I made a strong case that my proposal is a response to an important need? What further examples or data might help demonstrate the need?
- Am I clear about exactly what I propose to do, and am I sure that it can really be done?
- Have I noted possible objections or obstacles to implementing my proposed plan and answered them or shown how they can be overcome?
- Have I shown the advantages of my plan and how they outweigh the disadvantages?
- Have I made clear what I need to implement my proposal and what I'll do with the resources I get?
- Have I provided information about people who are ready to work with me once the proposal is approved?

Questions for Your Peer Readers
- Are you persuaded by the case I present that there is a real need for this proposal? Can you think of any other evidence I could use?
- Do you think my plan will work? What problems do you think might make it difficult to implement? Can you think of ways to improve the plan?
- Can you think of additional advantages and disadvantages of adopting my plan?
- Can you suggest anything else I might ask for to support my plan? Do you think I should ask for more or less money, more or fewer resources, more or less assistance?
- Can you think of influential people who might oppose my plan? Why would they oppose it?

1. Re-evaluate your proposal. Review your draft and reflect on your own response to it and on the responses of your readers. Decide how you want to revise your proposal. Before you begin rewriting, check the following list of features that reviewers usually look for in evaluating proposals.

Standards for Evaluation

An effective proposal . . .

- clearly defines a problem or describes a need, using such evidence as testimony, statistics, and examples.
- presents a clear plan for solving the problem or meeting the need, giving enough detail to demonstrate that the plan is workable.
- shows that the writer understands how to implement the plan and knows what expenditures it will entail.
- persuasively demonstrates how the advantages of the plan outweigh its disadvantages.
- addresses and respectfully refutes possible objections to the proposal.
- demonstrates a clear sense of the audience through the use of an appropriate tone and choice of details.
- makes clear how any requested funds will be spent and how other allocated resources will be used.

2. Problem-solve. Rework your draft to incorporate the changes you have decided to make.

HANDBOOKS

FOR HELP & PRACTICE

**Emphasis/
Tone/Mood,
pp. 423–428
Problem Solving,
pp. 472–473**

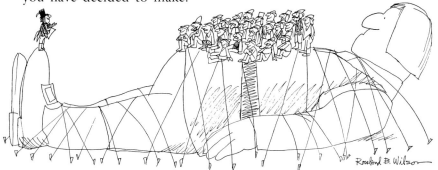

"First of all, let me congratulate everybody on the swell turnout and on the really bang-up job you all did on such short notice."

Drawing by Rowland B. Wilson; ©1964, The New Yorker Magazine, Inc.

Writer's Choice   Keep in mind that you do not have to incorporate all (or even any) of your readers' suggestions. Before making a change, consider whether it will improve your draft.

Notice how Angela improved two paragraphs of her draft by incorporating some changes suggested by one reader.

ONE STUDENT'S PROCESS

Health-conscious students and teachers have long
ʌEverybody has always complained about the absence
                    where students can   Mrs. DiLeo, who
of any place at school ʌto buy nutritious snacks. Health
chairs the Health and Physical Education Department, is convinced that "student
teachers say that students in our school would
concentration in most classes would improve and hyperactivity would diminish if kids
concentrate more better if they could buy such snacks
could eat healthy snacks in place of the sweets they now bring with them to school."
instead of the candy and chips they bring to school now.
                                        , she adds.Teenagers need
ʌForbidding snacks altogether is not the answer. ʌ
snacks during the day; they just need healthy snacks instead of junk food."
    Some administrators have argued that the cafeteria

is responsible for providing food for students and that it

can provide healthy snacks as well as lunches. But this
because the cafeteria is open only at lunch-time and is far removed from the
would not work, And even if the cafeteria did offer
classroom areas.
~~healthy snack, it would not affect students' snacking~~

~~habits much.~~

Maybe you should quote a health teacher to support your claim.

Why isn't forbidding snacks the answer?

You should tell why the cafeteria plan won't work.

3. Proofread your work.   After you have revised your proposal, read it again. Look for typographical errors and errors in spelling, punctuation, grammar, and usage. Minor blemishes can prejudice a reviewer against your proposal, especially if you are competing with other proposal writers for support.

Affect and *Effect*

Affect is a verb meaning "to influence." *Effect,* when used as a verb, means "to bring about or accomplish." When used as a noun, *effect* refers to the result of an action.

> Will eating junk food, snacks with little nutritional value, affect a person's mood? (verb)

> The school cafeteria, which is a well-managed facility, effected changes in the kinds of snacks being purchased. (verb)

> The changes will have a positive effect on student health. (noun)

Grammar
—TIP—

Set off nonessential appositives and clauses with commas.

ⓅUBLISH AND PRESENT

Here are some ways you might share your completed proposal.

- **Present your proposal orally.** Present your proposal to your class, to a school assembly, or to a community group that might be interested in the problem you are trying to solve. Afterward, lead a discussion of possible sources of support for the plan.
- **Submit your proposal to the school or community newspaper.** Choose the newspaper whose readers are concerned about the issue and who might have the power to help you implement the proposal.
- **Show your proposal to an expert on the problem.** That person might be able to suggest places where you can submit your proposal.
- **Send a copy to someone who might help implement it.** Prepare a list of individuals or agencies that might be in a position to support your proposal. Then send it to the most likely supporter first, reserving the others as back-ups to be used as necessary.
- **Save your work in your writing portfolio.**

HANDBOOKS

FOR HELP & PRACTICE

Publishing, p. 413

Food for Thought: A Proposal to Improve Nutrition and Student Learning

Angela Greentree

Summary

This proposal requests support for the establishment of a health food snack bar at Roosevelt High School to counteract the disabling effects of poor nutrition on student learning and, as a bonus, to contribute to student health education and business education.

Need

Clearly defines a problem, using expert testimony and statistics

According to Nathan Pritikin, a noted researcher on nutrition, junk food (soft drinks, candy, and so on) "gives you quick energy," but "it also gives you a quick letdown." Junk food snacks result after a short while in "lightheadedness, weakness, loss of concentration, and fatigue." Yet it is precisely such snacks that Roosevelt High students typically consume between classes. In a recent survey of students in three English classes (two at grade 11 and one at grade 12—meeting in the second, third, and sixth periods), it was found that almost half the students claimed to be hungry. Half said that they had snacked before class; and 85% of the snacks reported were high-sugar foods. For these students who want and need a snack during school hours, there is no real alternative to junk food.

Health-conscious students and teachers have long complained about the absence of any place at school where students can buy nutritious snacks. Mrs. DiLeo, who chairs the Health and Physical Education Department, is convinced that "student concentration in most classes would improve and hyperactivity would diminish if kids could eat healthy snacks in place of the sweets they now bring with them to school." Forbidding snacking altogether is not the answer, she adds.

"Teenagers need snacks during the day; they just need healthy snacks instead of junk food."

Some administrators have argued that the cafeteria is responsible for providing food for students and that it can provide healthy snacks as well as lunches. But this would not work because the cafeteria is open only at lunchtime and is far removed from the classroom areas. Moreover, even if the cafeteria should begin to stock healthy snacks, few students would purchase them. The fact is that most students have become accustomed to the quick rush of energy that sugar gives them and are unaware of the way sugar's quick energy is followed by the letdown that will deprive them of their energy and ability to concentrate. That is why my proposal, detailed below, includes an aggressive but entertaining campaign to educate students.

Proposed Solution

The solution is to provide a centrally located health food snack bar (an ideal location would be the main hallway near the auditorium, where most students pass between classes during an ordinary day) and to conduct a vigorous, schoolwide advertising campaign to change the snacking habits of students. Such a store would allow students and teachers to buy items such as fruit, bran muffins, health food snacks, fruit juices, and naturally sweetened sodas between classes throughout the day. The store would also serve three important educational purposes, described below.

First of all, students would manage the store themselves and thus get practical business experience of a kind not ordinarily available through regular business courses or through after-school jobs, where they are unlikely to be given management responsibilities. The store would require a staff for ordering, stocking, and selling snacks, and for record keeping, so a great many students could be involved in the project. Students could be restricted to working in the store only during periods when they would otherwise be in study hall or during free periods, so they would not miss any of

Addresses and respectfully refutes possible objections

Presents a clear plan for solving the problem, giving enough detail to show that the plan is workable

Persuasively demonstrates how the advantages of the plan outweigh its disadvantages

their regular academic classes. The store would also have academic supervision, because it would be operated under the general supervision of the Business Education Department, all of whose members have endorsed this proposal (see attached letters).

Another educational function of the snack bar would be to provide nutrition information for all students and staff at Roosevelt High. This would be accomplished through an advertising campaign conducted by the student managers, encouraging students to buy their snacks in the snack bar and to eat healthier foods in general. Mr. Gordon, in the English Department, has agreed to act as advisor to the snack bar on advertising strategies and Mrs. DiLeo will advise on the principles of nutrition (see attached letters).

The third educational function of the snack bar will be to improve learning in all classes at Roosevelt High by replacing junk food with healthy snacks in the diet of Roosevelt High students, thereby making those students better able to concentrate in class and more likely to learn whatever they are studying.

Support Requested

Implementing this proposal would entail relatively little expense on the part of the school administration. The establishment of a snack bar would cost approximately $600 for starting inventory, plus approximately $600 in lumber and supplies needed to build a structure that could be placed in the main hallway in front of the auditorium, where it would also be used for after-school events that are held in the auditorium. Mr. Kerwick, head of the Vocational Arts Department, has provided an estimate of construction costs and will guarantee that the snack bar can be built without any labor costs as a project of one or more shop classes (see attached memo). Once built and operating, the snack bar will be financially self-sufficient and should generate enough profit to repay construction and start-up costs and then provide additional income for other school activities.

Shows that the writer understands how to implement the plan

WRITER TO WRITER

Grant writing has to be persuasive. You must be able to market and sell your organization. The writing should be direct, compelling and concise.

Michael Chapman, former director of the American Indian Business Association, Chicago, Illinois

FOR YOUR
PORTFOLIO

1. Reflect on your writing. Review your prewriting materials and the various drafts you have written of your proposal. Reflect on how your proposal developed from your initial idea to a finished proposal. In what ways has your initial idea changed in this process? What were the influences that led to those changes? Summarize these reflections in a note that you attach to your proposal when you place it in your writing portfolio.

2. Apply your skills. Use the thinking and writing skills you have developed in writing your proposal to complete one or more of the following assignments.

- **Cross curricular** Identify a number of social problems that trouble or have troubled a society you are studying in history. Develop a proposal (with a clear sense of audience) that addresses one of the problems or needs of that society.
- **Literature** Consider the needs or problems of a character in a novel, play, or story you are studying. Try to describe the character's problem as if you were writing a "needs" section of a proposal. What proposal could you make to solve the character's problem? To what other character in the work would you address the proposal? Consider why proposals can't solve many important problems people have.
- **General** Use your proposal-writing experience to obtain funds or other support for a project that would be carried out by some group that you belong to.
- **Related assignments** Follow the suggestions on pages 194–202 to create a rebuttal and an oral presentation.

Seeing Blindness

Letter to the Editor of Harper's, *May 1989*

etters to the editor, editorials, and political debates are all examples of responses that argue with or try to refute a particular statement such as you might do in an argument with a friend. Such refutations are called *rebuttals*.

Joanne Lucas's letter to the editor of *Harper's* is a response to an article on temporary blindness that appeared in a previous issue of the magazine. As you read the letter, pay particular attention to how the writer responds to each of the points made by the author of the original article.

"Gone Blind," an essay by Otto Friedrich in the March issue, perpetuates some of the worst stereotypes and misconceptions about blindness. The journal that Friedrich kept during his four days of blindness, undergone for medical reasons, offers an interesting account of the sudden loss of vision. The anxieties that he experienced are shared by many newly blind persons, as well as their families and friends. But his assumptions about blindness are holdovers from the Dark Ages and should not remain unchallenged.

Friedrich's chronicle exemplifies what a sighted person *imagines* blindness to be. The blind do need help initially in gaining the training and tools that will allow them to participate fully in society and to hold jobs appropriate to their abilities. Such training is available. But blind persons wishing to work still face a high unemployment rate. This needless waste of human potential is, perhaps, largely due to ignorance and fear on the part of prospective employers. Friedrich's journal only reinforces such fears. For example, word processing equipment that uses synthetic speech technology can free a blind writer from dependency on—to use Friedrich's dismal phrase— "some suburban stenographer."

The assumption that a blind person cannot write well is ludicrous. Some of the best writers in the Western canon wrote in spite of blindness or severe vision impairment. Even if we are not sure that there was a Homer, we do know about Milton, Joyce, Borges, and Thurber, to mention a few. On what grounds does Friedrich base his conjecture that blind, he would be reduced to writing potboilers?

Friedrich even insinuates that thinking is impaired by loss of vision. Yet during his brief confinement, he gained new insights from the familiar material with which he passed the time.

Vision, in a poetic sense, is more than a matter of eyesight.

Joanne Lucas
Waldport, Ore.

Think AND Respond

The writer of this letter argued that Otto Friedrich's essay reinforced common stereotypes that portray blindness in a misleading way. Which of Otto Friedrich's observations about the blind did the writer attack in her rebuttal? Notice how Joanne Lucas went beyond merely refuting Friedrich's points to providing convincing examples for her own argument. Can you think of an article or position to which you would like to offer a similar rebuttal?

INVITATION
TO
Write

Joanne Lucas's letter refuted some common misconceptions about the blind that had appeared in a previous article in the magazine. Write your own rebuttal to an article, speech, proposal, or opinion that has provoked you.

Responding to ideas with which you disagree requires some of the same skills you use to present a proposal of your own ideas. To write a strong rebuttal, scrutinize your opponent's position and weigh the evidence he or she has used to build a case. Be sure to answer, or rebut, each argument with which you disagree with an example or counterargument that supports your own viewpoint.

PREPARING YOUR REBUTTAL

HANDBOOKS
FOR HELP & PRACTICE

Analysis Frames,
p. 343
Order of Importance,
pp. 353–354
Developing/Pre-
senting Arguments,
pp. 474–476
Rebuttals,
pp. 505–506

1. Find an issue that provokes you.   A news or magazine article, an editorial, or a television documentary can provide you with a one-sided argument that invites rebuttal. You could also write a rebuttal to a commonly held position or point of view with which you disagree. For example, you may want to attack common stereotypes about the disabled or about a racial or ethnic group.

2. Analyze the opinion you intend to rebut.   List all your opponent's arguments, whether you agree with them or not. Notice how Joanne Lucas commends Otto Friedrich's "interesting account of the sudden loss of vision." A rebuttal can gain credibility by conceding some advantages or good points to the opposing viewpoint.

3. Note the opposition's evidence.   Find the main weapons for your rebuttal in your opponent's ideas, in the evidence he or she uses to support them, or in your opponent's credentials to argue a particular viewpoint. For example, Joanne Lucas attacks Otto Friedrich's essay because Friedrich is a sighted person who can only imagine what it would be like to be permanently blind.

4. Collect supporting evidence and examples. Your purpose is to answer every point made by your opponent and to add any further information that will persuade your audience. Friedrich's assumption that he would be unable to write if blind, for example, is cleverly countered by Lucas's reference to several blind or visually impaired authors who are commonly regarded as geniuses.

DRAFTING YOUR REBUTTAL

1. Introduce your rebuttal with a strong statement of purpose. Look at Lucas's opening sentence. Although some of the first paragraph and much of the second concede that Friedrich makes some valuable points, you can tell exactly where Lucas's rebuttal is heading from the author's very first statement. Make sure your introduction states your viewpoint with equal power.

2. If possible, point out flaws in your opponent's arguments. Lucas says Friedrich's assumption that blindness leads to thinking impairment is belied by the very insights Friedrich reveals in his article. You may agree with some of your opponent's arguments but feel that they do not go far enough, or perhaps you'll argue that your opponent draws the wrong conclusion from the examples.

Writing
TIP

Ask for assistance from a member of your school's debate team. Debaters are trained to structure rebuttals that refute each argument of the opposing side.

3. Develop your points in order of ascending importance. Notice that Lucas first takes issue with Friedrich's assumption that blind people encounter insuperable technical obstacles to accomplishment. Then she attacks his more serious argument that sightlessness condemns a person to intellectual inferiority. Saving your strongest arguments for the end keeps your audience interested and helps you build to a more compelling conclusion.

4. Conclude with a forceful summary of your main points. Lucas's distinction between vision and eyesight in her last sentence drives home the observation that while blind people have lost the physical ability to see, they need not suffer a more fundamental lack of vision or insight.

◤R EVIEWING YOUR WRITING

1. Reread your rebuttal. List all the points you have included to argue your position. Have you answered every point made by your opponent? Can you think of any further examples that would strengthen your argument? Have you argued your points in ascending importance and ended with a strong conclusion?

2. Ask one or more classmates to read your rebuttal. Can your friend summarize your position in a one-sentence statement? Can he or she list all the points that prove your case? Are there any flaws in your ideas that your classmate can point out?

3. Rewrite your rebuttal. Proofread your draft for spelling, punctuation, and grammar. Incorporate your own and your friends' suggestions into a final draft that presents your rebuttal in the most compelling fashion.

◤P UBLISHING AND PRESENTING

- **Correspond with your opponent.** Send your rebuttal to the political figure, writer, or television commentator who presented the original viewpoint with which you disagreed. If you get a response, share it with your class.
- **Try to get your rebuttal into print.** Mail a copy of your rebuttal to your local or school newspaper.
- **Hold a debate.** If you are refuting a proposal made by one of your classmates, present your rebuttal as part of a structured debate.

On the Lightside

DENOTATIONS AND CONNOTATIONS

Many words have two kinds of meaning. The basic, direct meaning we call the *denotation*. The implied, suggestive meanings—*connotations*—are what give a word its individuality and color, its distinctive and unique personality.

Take the word *fist*. *Webster's Ninth New Collegiate Dictionary* defines *fist* as "the hand clenched with the fingers doubled into the palm and the thumbs doubled inward across the fingers." Okay, then, "The maiden held a white lily in her delicate fist" ought to be a perfectly effective sentence.

But it isn't; in fact, it's humorously incongruous. We smile at the clashing connotations of *maiden*, *white*, *lily* and *delicate* on the one hand, and *fist* on the other. The denotation of *fist* is correct, but its connotations make it a grotesque choice for a sentence about a maiden and a lily.

Giggle is defined in the dictionary as "to laugh with repeated short catches of the breath." But, because of its connotations, *giggled* is strikingly misplaced in a sentence like "The grizzled cowhand giggled at the tenderfoot's foolish suggestions."

Here are some entries from a magazine contest asking readers to create word-plays using connotation and denotation.

- I am traditional. You are old-fashioned. He is reactionary.
- I am beautiful. You have quite good features. She isn't bad-looking, if you like that type.
- I am righteously indignant. You are annoyed. He is making a fuss about nothing.

Try *your* hand at mixing the many hues of words. Create your own experiments in connotation and denotation by following these rules:

1. Each must proceed from *I* through *you* to *he* or *she*.
2. The basic denotation of the concept must be maintained. For example, "I am slender; you are skinny; he is a fat slob," would be unacceptable because the denotation changes.
3. In each grouping, the connotations must become increasingly mean as you move from first to second or third person.

The following examples were created by students.

- I have trouble keeping a tune. You can't sing. When he sings, all the female moose come running.
- I am good at procrastination. You are inactive. He is a lazy bum.
- I choose my friends with discrimination. You are standoffish. She is the snob of the century.

Richard Lederer

Oral Presentation

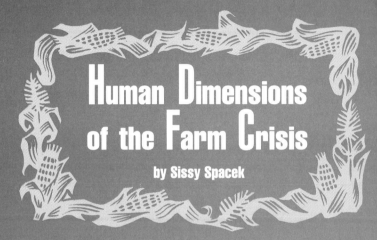

Human Dimensions of the Farm Crisis

by Sissy Spacek

Most people have the opportunity at some time in their lives to make a speech for the purpose of persuading others to change an opinion or take some action. Sissy Spacek had strong feelings about the farm crisis facing the country in the early 1980's, and she had a chance to share her concerns with a Congressional task force. As you read her speech, try to follow her main points. Why does she begin by talking about her family's long involvement in agriculture? What action does she want Congress to take?

The 1980's were difficult times for agriculture. Hundreds of thousands of farm families across the country faced bankruptcy and foreclosure because of falling farm prices. On May 6, 1985, actress Sissy Spacek appeared before a special House task force on agriculture to ask the federal government to help struggling farm families.

Mr. Chairman and Members of the Task Force, my personal connection to American agriculture goes beyond appearing in one of last year's "farm" movies. I am a product of rural America. I was born there. I grew up there. I was a 4-H'er.

My mother was a homemaker. My father served for 30 years as a county Agricultural Agent in Texas. My grandfather was a farmer and Deputy Agent of the Federal Farm Credit Administration under Franklin Roosevelt.

I am very proud that I come from a family that for generations has cared about American

farmers and American farmlands, and it is our conviction that the American family farmer is the most efficient, stable and productive of all of the world's farmers.

So I'm not here today to defend them on nostalgic grounds, but to support them as the best and wisest of farmers.

Right now the future of American agriculture looks pretty bleak. Young farmers can't afford to get started, and in an effort to make up losses, existing farmers plant every available scrap of ground, contributing to the worst soil erosion in history.

And corporate farms are learning the hard way what the family farmer has known for centuries: farming is no easy road to short-term profits.

I would be naive to assume that this is a simple problem with simple answers, but one thing I'm sure of: we can't turn our backs on these people who have fed us all so abundantly and cheaply throughout our history.

Our largest and most vital industry is disintegrating. It is not marginal producers, speculators or bad managers who are being squeezed out, but the solid core of our agriculture which is threatened.

And trouble on the farm spreads without regard for performance. As bankruptcies mount, land values fall—and since production loans are secured by land, without borrowing another dime, all farmers fall deeper into debt.

If we think this catastrophe affects only the farmers, we are dangerously naive.

The drugstore, the implement dealer, the grocery store and the bank in every agricultural community in this country is in trouble, and that trouble arrives in the cities when homeless farmers with their wives and children come to town to look for a job.

We have a responsibility to insure that our farmers make not only a fair living, but [can] afford to put back into the soil what they take out.

And the American public recognizes our responsibility in this crisis: According to recent *USA Today* and *New York Times* polls, more than 70 percent believe that the federal government has a clear obligation to save financially distressed farm families–families who are endangered by forces beyond their control, families who are the stewards of our homelands, this fertile American earth. . . .

A century ago, William Jennings Bryan said, "Burn down your cities and leave your farms, and cities will spring up again as if by magic, but destroy our farms and the grass will grow in the streets of every city in the country."

Thank you for this opportunity to appear before you today.

Think AND Respond

Do you find Sissy Spacek's appeal on behalf of American farmers persuasive? What are some of the arguments and techniques she uses to influence her audience to take action? What public issues do you have strong opinions about?

INVITATION
TO
Write

Sissy Spacek spoke out on an issue that was important to her. Think of some policy that you think needs changing—at school, in your local community, or for the entire nation. Write a speech in which you try to persuade others to join you in working for change.

Many efforts to persuade others are most effective when they are presented orally. A speaker has a more direct and immediate impact on an audience than a writer does, and can even change the delivery of the speech in response to the audience's reaction. Therefore, it is very important when preparing and delivering a speech to know your audience and to take advantage of your personal impact.

PLANNING AN ORAL PRESENTATION

HANDBOOKS

FOR HELP & PRACTICE

Organizing Your Work, pp. 349–357

Collaborative Planning, pp. 358–360

Introducing/ Concluding Nonfiction, pp. 365–371

Varieties of Language, pp. 429–433

Outline Form, pp. 826–827

1. Choose a topic about which you have strong feelings. Do you want to urge others to join you in changing a policy? Do you have a proposal for which you want support? Sissy Spacek, for example, knew that many farmers were facing a crisis in the early 1980's, and she believed that the federal government should help. Find an issue that really interests you. You might want to get together with a few classmates and examine the issues in your community—social, political, moral, or economic—which you would like to address.

2. Identify your audience. A speech is usually meant for a specific audience. For example, Sissy Spacek knew as she was planning her speech that she would be addressing a congressional committee. You may already have earmarked the group to whom you will be speaking. If not, now is the time to identify your listeners. Will they be young people or adults, or a mix of both? Choose your facts, tone, and approach with your intended audience in mind.

3. Discuss your plans with a friend.   Write the main idea you want to convey to your audience in a sentence or two. Then discuss with a friend some ways you might accomplish your goal. How can you get your audience's attention at the beginning of your speech? What key points should you cover? What tone, approach, and persuasive appeals would be most effective?

GETTING YOUR SPEECH ON PAPER

1. Make an outline.   Draw up an outline detailing what you want to say in the order you want to say it. Plan to cover only key points, since listeners may become confused by too long an introduction or too many arguments. If you find you are trying to cover too much, prune your outline.

2. Give some thought to the beginning of the speech.   Sissy Spacek started her speech by presenting her "credentials" to speak —her family roots in the rural community. She then used vivid description to re-create the farmer's plight. How can you capture your audience's attention?

3. Write your first draft.   Use your outline as a map or guide when you write your first draft. Be sure you include details and examples to support your arguments. Sissy Spacek, for example, showed that the economic trouble of some farmers led to bankruptcies and falling land values, which in turn affected other farmers and people in other occupations. As you write the first draft of your speech, try to build a case that clearly shows the importance of the issue you have chosen.

 Writer's Choice   After making their outline, some people like to dictate their speech directly into a tape recorder. Then they transcribe the speech from tape to paper. You may want to prepare your first draft in this manner.

4. Provide an effective conclusion.   In the last sentence or two of your speech, summarize your proposal, recap your main points, and request action. Spacek used a powerful quotation from William Jennings Bryan to accomplish these goals. In your conclusion, try not to trail off weakly, but end with a forceful restatement of your convictions on the issue.

Writing TIP

Speeches that attempt to persuade are most effective when they are short—three minutes is ideal. A typewritten speech of 1½ pages, double-spaced, is just about the right length for a three-minute speech.

5. Rehearse your presentation. After you finish your first draft, rehearse your speech. Stand up, face your imaginary audience, and deliver the speech orally. Practice varying your rate of delivery, volume, tone, pitch, and emphasis. Where can you pause for effect? Where could a soft or forceful tone help to communicate your meaning? Pay special attention to how you can deliver your opening remarks to capture the audience's attention and how you can deliver an effective conclusion that will move your listeners to agreement or action.

REVIEWING YOUR WRITING

1. Listen to your speech with a friend. Use a tape recorder to record your speech, and play it back with a friend. Is your message clear? Is it interesting? Can you think of ways to make it more persuasive?

2. Listen to the way the speech sounds. Remember that speaking is different from writing. Sissy Spacek used a conversational style for her speech, with many short sentences. She also made effective use of repetition. Could you improve your speech by using one of these techniques?

PUBLISHING AND PRESENTING

- **Participate in a round robin.** Schedule an informal round robin with other class members who are working on a speech. Take turns reading your speeches aloud. Discuss methods of making the speeches more effective.
- **Deliver your speech.** Recall the audience you had in mind when you first started to draft your speech. Make arrangements to deliver your speech to them.

Sentence

Varying S-V Splits

Effective writers often add details in the subject-verb split position to elaborate on the subject or provide a context for the action that follows.

In the sentences below, notice how the various kinds of s-v splits (underlined) prepare the reader for the main ideas of the sentences.

Appositive Phrase	The real estate agent, <u>an old man with a smiling hypocritical face</u>, soon joined them. **Willa Cather, ''The Sculptor's Funeral''**
Present Participial Phrase	August, <u>gasping for breath</u>, melted into September. **Robert Lipsyte, *The Contender***
Past Participial Phrase	The tent, <u>illumined by candle</u>, glowed warmly in the midst of the plain. **Jack London, *The Call of the Wild***
Absolute Phrase	An Arab on a motorcycle, <u>his long robes flying in the wind of his speed</u>, passed John at such a clip that the spirals of dust from his turnings on the winding road looked like little tornadoes. **Elizabeth Yates, ''Standing in Another's Shoes''**
Delayed Adjectives	The head of the filing department, <u>neat, quiet, attentive</u>, stood in front of the old man's desk. **James Thurber, ''The Catbird Seat''**

A. Sentence Combining In the first sentence in each set, locate the main subject and verb. Then place the underlined part of the second sentence directly after the subject of the first sentence. Enclose each s-v split in commas. The kind of phrase you will be inserting is identified in parentheses.

Example	When the light went out, the old man peeped into the little window. The old man was <u>trembling from agitation</u>. (present participial phrase)
Combined	When the light went out, the old man, trembling from agitation, peeped into the little window. **Anton Chekhov, ''The Bet''**

1. An open book lay beside it. The book was <u>something called *Totem and Taboo*</u>. (appositive phrase)   **Ralph Ellison, *Invisible Man***

2. Professor Kazan was first ashore. He <u>was wearing a spotlessly white tropical suit and a wide-brimmed hat</u>. (present participial phrase)
   Arthur C. Clarke, *Dolphin Island*

3. Daisy's face looked out at me with a bright ecstatic smile. Her face was <u>tipped sideways beneath a three-cornered lavender hat</u>. (past participial phrase)
   F. Scott Fitzgerald, *The Great Gatsby*

4. High in the air, a little figure stood staring out to sea. He had <u>his hands thrust in his short jacket pockets</u>. (absolute phrase)
   Katherine Mansfield, "The Voyage"

5. A man walked through the church-goers faced in the opposite direction. The man was <u>young and graceful and very much preoccupied</u>. (delayed adjectives)
   Esther Forbes, "Break-Neck Hill"

B. Sentence Expanding   For each sentence below, write some details that could be inserted in the s-v split position. Insert your addition at the (/) and enclose it in commas. Compare your sentences to the originals on page 323.

1. There had followed then a time of such happiness that Chips (/) hardly believed it could ever have happened before or since in the world.
   James Hilton, *Goodbye, Mr. Chips*

2. Old Mrs. Beal (/) was homeward bound from dinner with her daughter.
   Jessamyn West, "The Child's Day"

3. Across an immense ethereal gulf, intellects (/) regarded this earth with envious eyes and slowly drew their plans against us.
   H. Koch, "Invasion from Mars"

4. Mr. Cattanzara (/) lived on the next block after George's above a shoe repair shop.
   Bernard Malamud, "A Summer's Reading"

C. Unscrambling and Imitating Sentences   Unscramble each set of parts to form a sentence that matches the model. Then write a second sentence imitating the model. Enclose s-v splits in commas.

1. A wooded amphitheater, surrounded on three sides by precipitous cliffs of naked granite, sloped gently toward the crest of another precipice that overlooked the valley.   **Bret Harte, "The Outcasts of Poker Flat"**
   a. raced desperately toward cover in a cave that jutted out of the hillside
   b. the small cat
   c. terrified by a sudden streak of blinding lightning

2. He had already done it, and another face, grey, wet, and sour, was pushing into his, knocking him down and back as it scraped out under the plank. **Flannery O'Connor, "The River"**
   a. and the second horse
   b. as it tired out under the pressure
   c. Dandelion was clearly winning it
   d. out-classed, straining, and winded
   e. was slowing on the track, moving gradually behind and back

3. The class above, seniors, draft-bait, practically soldiers, rushed ahead of us toward the war. **John Knowles, *A Separate Peace***
   a. screamed above us at the band
   b. middle-schoolers, teeny-boppers, almost fanatics
   c. the row behind

4. At eleven o'clock, a man in a raincoat, dragging a lawnmower, tapped at my front door and said that Mr. Gatsby had sent him over to cut my grass. **F. Scott Fitzgerald, *The Great Gatsby***
   a. on the window seat
   b. a package in red ribbon
   c. and announced that Mike had sent a present to resolve their argument
   d. sat on a cushion
   e. gleaming in the sun

5. While we were waiting for coffee, the headwaiter, an ingratiating smile on his false face, came up to us bearing a large basket full of huge peaches. **Somerset Maugham, "The Luncheon"**
   a. the car
   b. as she was driving through Dallas
   c. emitting a dense cloud of black exhaust
   d. a suspicious rattle in its untrustworthy engine
   e. slowed to a crawl

Application Write a paragraph explaining how you cheer yourself up when your spirits get low. Into three of the sentences in your paragraph, insert s-v splits, varying the s-v splits in length and structure. Notice how efficiently these constructions can provide information essential to the main idea.

Grammar Refresher Expanders in the s-v split position may create confusion about subject-verb agreement. For a review of subject-verb agreement and intervening phrases, see Handbook 35.

Sketchbook

Can you see more than one side of issues? In an argument or debate, how do you decide who is right and who is wrong?

Additional Sketches

Resolved, that the United States should have a king. How would you debate this resolution?

Write a dialogue between yourself and a friend about some matter that perplexes both of you. Start your dialogue by describing what is bothering you. Then let your friend reply, and keep the dialogue going.

Persuasion

Guided Assignment
ARGUMENT ANALYSIS

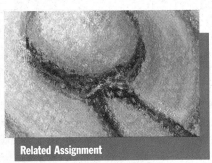

Related Assignment
ESTABLISHING CONFLICT

Related Assignment
DEBATE

Arguments can be used for many purposes. You are probably most familiar with persuasive arguments used to sway readers and argumentative arguments used to marshall evidence in support of one position. As long as you are intent on proving that your view is correct, however, you are not likely to come to see the point of view of the opposition—to look at your topic from an alternative perspective.

In the workshop that follows, you will learn to use arguments to look at a controversial issue from both sides with the intention of illuminating the issue, to develop a conflict between your own literary characters, and to engage in a debate.

207

Argument Analysis

from

Owl vs. Man

by Ted Gup

Examining arguments involves analyzing the two sides of a controversial issue, giving attention to all the available evidence that either side might use. In "Owl vs. Man," journalist Ted Gup presents both sides of a debate between conservationists and those who favor economic development of wilderness areas. As you read, consider whether the evidence seems to weigh more heavily on one side or another.

In Oregon's Umpqua National Forest, a lumberjack presses his snarling chain saw into the flesh of a Douglas fir that has held its place against wind and fire, rockslide and flood, for two hundred years. The white pulpy fiber scatters in a plume beside him, and in ninety seconds, four feet of searing steel have ripped through the thick bark, the thin film of living tissue and the growth rings spanning ages. With an excruciating groan, all 190 feet of trunk and green spire crash to earth. When the cloud of detritus and needles settles, the ancient forest of the Pacific Northwest has retreated one more step. Tree by tree, acre by acre, it falls, and with it vanishes the habitat of innumerable creatures. None among these

creatures is more vulnerable than the northern spotted owl, a bird so docile it will descend from the safety of its lofty bough to take a mouse from the hand of a man.

The futures of the owl and the ancient forest it inhabits have become entwined in a common struggle for survival. Man's appetite for timber threatens to consume much of the Pacific Northwest's remaining wilderness, an ecological frontier whose deep shadows and jagged profile are all that remain of the land as it was before the impact of man. But rescuing the owl and the timeless forest may mean barring the logging industry from many tracts of virgin timberland, and that would deliver a jarring economic blow to scores of timber-dependent communities across Washington, Oregon, and Northern California. For generations, lumberjacks and millworkers there have relied on the seemingly endless bounty of the woodlands to sustain them and a way of life that is as rich a part of the American landscape as the forest itself. For many, all that may be coming to an end. . . .

More than a contest for survival between a species and an industry, the owl battle is an epic confrontation between fundamentally different philosophies about the place of man in nature. At issue: Are the forces—and by extension, nature itself—there for man to use and exploit, or are they to be revered and preserved? How much wilderness does America need? How much human discomfort can be justified in the name of conservation? In the Pacific Northwest the nation's reinvigorated environmental movement is about to collide head on with economic reality. What happens here will shape the outcome of similar conflicts between ecological and economic concerns for years to come. It will also enhance or diminish U.S. credibility overseas, as America tries to influence other nations to husband their natural resources and protect their endangered species. From Brazil to Japan, the decision will be carefully observed. The stakes are that high.

Think AND Respond

What arguments does the writer present in favor of each side? Do you see any evidence that the author is partial toward one side over the other? Can you imagine a solution that would satisfy both sides? Does the piece suggest to you any other contemporary issues with two distinct and persuasive sides?

INVITATION TO Write

The excerpt you have just read presents both sides of a controversial environmental and economic issue. Write an essay in which you impartially examine both sides of some issue of interest to you.

When you examine arguments, your goal is to analyze both sides of a controversial issue. In some cases this examination will lead you to a proposal for a compromise solution—a solution that is satisfactory to both sides. In other cases you may be led to the conclusion that the arguments on one side are stronger than those on the other. It is your responsibility, however, to remain impartial in your analysis and refrain from drawing any conclusion until you have examined all of the evidence. Your assignment is not to choose a side or to solve a problem, but to illuminate an issue.

An argument analysis can be crucial to legislators who want to be sure that they understand an issue thoroughly before they pass legislation in a related area, to students or scholars who are more interested in understanding a controversial issue than in taking a side, and to judges who wish to make impartial rulings in cases with conflicting sides.

HANDBOOKS

FOR HELP & PRACTICE

Limiting Your Topic,
pp. 337–338

Collaborative Planning,
pp. 358–360

Reading Strategies,
p. 479

Using Source Materials,
pp. 482–489

Research Skills,
pp. 499–500

PREWRITE AND EXPLORE

1. Look for an issue. Try one or more of the following suggestions to explore ideas for your essay.

Exploratory Activities

- **Monitoring** As you listen to news broadcasts on television or radio, identify issues that intrigue you. Note these issues in your journal.
- **Inquiring** Ask teachers of other subjects to suggest issues that are appropriate for argumentative writing.

- **Brainstorming and listing** With a small group of classmates, brainstorm topics for argumentative writing in categories of your creation, such as current events, life at school, or teen concerns.
- **Scanning** The excerpt you read at the beginning of this workshop comes from an article that appeared in *Time* magazine. Scan copies of *Time, Newsweek,* and other newsmagazines for possible topics. Also check the letters to the editor printed in newspapers and magazines.
- **Reading literature** Make a list of issues in literature that have two sides. For example, is Stanley Kowalski, in Tennessee Williams's *A Streetcar Named Desire,* a hopeless, violent male chauvinist or just a man protecting his interests and those of his wife? Do some freewriting about the topics that interest you most.

2. Evaluate your topics. After you have come up with a variety of topics, you must decide which are suitable for an essay. Do some freewriting about the topics that interest you the most. Share your ideas with classmates. If you are not satisfied with your topics, check your journal for possibilities, consider the ideas you experimented with in the Sketchbook on page 206, or check the "Apply Your Skills" section on page 222. Also ask yourself questions about your topics such as the ones below.

PROBLEM SOLVING

How can I determine if my issue is appropriate for an argumentative essay?

Questions for Evaluating Topics

- Does the issue have two clear sides?
- Do both sides appear reasonable? Can I find strong arguments in support of both sides?
- Can I treat the issue impartially, or am I prejudiced toward one side?
- Do I find the issue interesting enough to spend time on it?

Jeremy thought of several possible topics for his argumentative essay and evaluated them as follows.

Possible Essay Topics	Comments
Should a national health insurance program covering all U.S. citizens be created?	Too complicated. Would require more research than I have time for.
Should there be a permanent site for the Olympic Games?	Possible but not exciting to me.
Should employers of workers who handle hazardous materials be required to provide protective clothing?	Too one-sided; no real controversy.
Should conservation or economic development be given a higher priority in our city?	Too general, and I'm prejudiced in favor of conservation. I'm really interested, though.

Jeremy found he was most interested in his last topic. He knew he had to narrow the focus and find a particular issue he could deal with impartially. He decided to write about a controversy in his city. This issue had two clear sides: one favored conservation and opposed construction of a new municipal airport on the proposed forested site, while the other supported the new airport.

3. Freewrite. Tentatively choose one topic and freewrite about it for ten minutes. Write what you know about the issue, the arguments advanced on both sides, and your questions about the issue.

4. Use collaborative planning. Share your freewriting with a partner. Discuss and take notes on what you must do to complete an effective argument analysis. Be sure to consider these questions:

- **About your topic** How can you find adequate information to present complete arguments on both sides? Do you need to make use of reading, interviews, observation, or your own experiences? Who are some experts you might consult?

Writing
TIP

It's a good idea to have two back-up topics in mind, in case your first, preferred topic turns out to be unsatisfactory for you.

- **About your purpose**   Aside from providing an impartial analysis of your issue, what do you hope to accomplish with your paper? Do you want to make up your own mind on a controversial topic or provide public officials with a clearer understanding of an important issue? Is it possible that an impartial airing of the issues could lead to a compromise or a solution that would satisfy all parties? How might your purposes influence how you proceed in conducting your analysis?
- **About your audience**   Who will read your analysis and what might your readers' purposes be? How familiar are your readers with the general topic? Should you avoid or use technical terms? Will you have to define some terms for your readers? How much background information will you need to provide? How biased are your readers likely to be and to which side and why? What can you do to help your readers give a fair hearing to both sides?

 Writer's Choice   Your planning efforts may have shown you unanticipated problems in pursuing your chosen topic. Do you now want to drop your initial choice of a topic and turn to one of your back-up choices?

5. Learn about your topic.   Use the library, newspapers, and magazines to read about your topic. Also talk to people who are experts. As part of his research on the airport controversy, Jeremy began by reading newspaper accounts of the controversy, along with editorials and letters to the editor in his local paper. When he thought he understood the major issues, he arranged to interview two of the people he had learned about from newspaper articles as leaders of the two opposing sides: the director of a local conservation group and the president of a regional business association.

6. Look for underlying assumptions.   See if you can classify the individual arguments advanced by both sides of your issue under the larger or deeper concerns that account for the arguments. Ted Gup, for example, in writing about the Oregon timberland controversy, found the roots of the controversy not in specific arguments about the fate of the northern spotted owl or the jobs of lumberjacks, but in "fundamentally different philosophies about the place of man in nature." Then he briefly explained the philosophies. What differences in values, philosophy, or outlook on life are at the root of the controversy you are analyzing? Will the differences allow for a meeting of the minds? Why can't a solution be worked out?

If you have access to a modem, you may be able to conduct some interviews by electronic mail.

How can I uncover the roots of the controversy?

FOR HELP & PRACTICE

**Comparison-
Contrast Order,
p. 352**

**Drafting Styles,
pp. 361–362**

**Developing/
Presenting
Arguments,
p. 474–476**

1. Begin your draft. The next step is to begin writing your first draft. You may use a variety of strategies to elaborate on your ideas, such as the ones below.

- **Narration** You can use this strategy to dramatize the controversy you are analyzing. In the opening paragraph of "Owl vs. Man," for example, the writer presents a dramatic account of a lumberjack cutting down a 200-year-old fir tree.
- **Explanation and definition** Much of an argument analysis entails explaining or defining the grounds for the argument. Even more important than the arguments on both sides is an explanation of why people are arguing in the first place. What values, or underlying assumptions, separate them?
- **Quotation and documentation** You will probably want to use quotations from spokespersons for the two sides of the controversy and to cite facts, statistics, and opinions from pamphlets, newspapers, or magazines.
- **Comparison and contrast** Your analysis is likely to consist largely of an examination of how the claims, goals, and assumptions of two disputing parties compare and contrast.

2. Introduce the issue. You might begin your essay with a narrative, a case history, or a scene. Another alternative is to give the historical background of the issue. Some writers begin by stating the issue in the form of a question.

3. Clearly state the two sides of the issue. Since the purpose of your essay is to examine both sides of an issue, it's important to give a clear statement of what the two sides are. Notice how Jeremy did this in the following sentence from his essay.

PROBLEM

S O L V I N G

**How can I best
present both
sides of my
issue?**

ONE STUDENT'S PROCESS

On one side of the issue are those who favor construction of the airport on the proposed site; on the other side are those who want to preserve Millers Woods in its natural state.

4. Present evidence to support both sides of the issue. As evidence, you can use facts, examples, expert opinions, statistics, or anecdotes. Try to present all important arguments on both sides of the issue. Remember that your goal is to accurately portray both sides, not to persuade your readers to support one or the other.

 Writer's Choice Which side of the issue do you want to present first? Often the side presented last assumes greater importance simply because it remains fresh in the reader's mind.

5. Organize your draft. After clearly stating both sides of the issue, in what order will you then present the evidence? As you compare and contrast the two sides, will you present all the evidence on one side of the issue, then all the evidence on the other side? Or is an item-by-item organization better?

6. Draw a conclusion. You may find that your examination of the two sides and your analysis of the underlying disagreements (or agreements) has led you to a conclusion. Your conclusion might be an opinion favoring one side over the other, a recommendation for a compromise solution, or a recognition that the underlying assumptions of the disputing parties make any resolution of their differences impossible. You might also conclude by summarizing the issues, leaving the issue of resolution to others.

In the following excerpt from the end of Jeremy's essay, he identified what he believed to be the underlying assumptions dividing the disputants in the airport controversy. Note that his analysis led him to take a surprising stand—surprising because it runs counter to the prejudice with which he began his study.

In a contest between the economic survival of people and that of a woodland preserve I see no alternative to standing up for people—which, unfortunately, means supporting airport construction at Millers Woods. Every effort to find a suitable alternative to building on the Millers Woods site has failed. We have a pressing need to reduce local unemployment and to promote economic growth—both of which the construction of an airport will achieve. At least for the short run, then, I feel we must act on behalf of the basic well-being of people over environmental preservation. In time we may be able to serve both interests without conflict.

Writing
—TIP—

In your first draft, concentrate on ideas. You will have time to clean up your writing in subsequent drafts.

7. Put your draft aside for a day or so. This allows you to put some distance between yourself and your writing. When you reread your draft, you will be able to evaluate it more objectively. Ask yourself and peer readers the following questions.

R E V I E W   Y O U R   W R I T I N G

Questions for Yourself

- Have I clearly stated the two sides of the issue?
- Have I presented the main supporting evidence for both sides? Have I treated both sides fairly?
- Have I identified and examined the underlying assumptions of the opposing parties?

Questions for Your Peer Readers

- Did my introduction make the controversy clear?
- What are the two sides of the issue? Did my writing give you a greater understanding of each side?
- Have I fairly presented the arguments on both sides of the issue? Does my analysis favor one side or the other?

REVISE YOUR WRITING

1. Evaluate your responses. Decide what changes you want to make. Keep in mind these qualities of good argumentative writing.

Standards for Evaluation

An effective argument analysis . . .

- clearly states the two sides of the issue.
- gives adequate background to understand the issue.
- impartially presents arguments on both sides of the issue.
- attempts to uncover basic underlying assumptions and values.
- concludes by summarizing the controversy or by stating the writer's conclusion about the issue.

2. Problem-solve. Now rework your draft, incorporating the changes you have decided to make.

Jeremy made the following changes to a paragraph from his draft.

FOR HELP & PRACTICE

**Unity/Coherence,
pp. 382–391**

**Peer Response,
pp. 397–400**

**Avoiding Wordiness,
pp. 406–408**

**Emphasis,
pp. 423–424**

**Sentence Variety,
pp. 439–444**

**Avoiding Logical
Fallacies,
pp. 477–478**

ONE STUDENT'S PROCESS

concerned citizens

Those who favor construction of the airport on the

our city's

proposed site point to the 20% rate of unemployment.

They note that construction of the airport would keep

biulding trades workers in our city busy for more than a

and   at least 200   e

year. The airport also would provide many permanant

new jobs for City residents. Either we build the airport or

According to   done by the Chamber of Commerce,

people will lose their jobs. A study showed that a new

airport would help make our city more attractive as a

tourist, and convention center. An increase in the tourist and
convention trade would bring more business to—and create more jobs in—local
hotels, restaurants, and retail stores.

Can you tell how
many new jobs would
be created?

Be more specific.
Who did the study?

Explain how our city
would benefit from
this.

Argument Analysis   **217**

3. Proofread your work. Make a clean copy of your essay. Then, read through it and correct errors in spelling, grammar, usage, and mechanics.

Writing
——**TIP**——

To check whether a word or phrase is redundant, cross it out and see if the sentence has exactly the same meaning without it.

LINKING
GRAMMAR **AND** WRITING
Avoiding Redundancy

Avoid using words and phrases that repeat the same idea as another word or phrase.

Original **People sit idly, doing nothing** and wondering if they ever will find work again.

Revised People sit idly, wondering if they will ever find work again.

PUBLISH AND PRESENT

FOR HELP & PRACTICE

Presenting Arguments, pp. 474–476

- **Conduct a panel discussion on the issue you have chosen.** Meet with classmates who are interested in that issue to plan your discussion. Present your paper orally as a starting point for the discussion.
- **Present your paper as a speech.** Contact an organization that is concerned with your chosen issue and propose that you speak at an upcoming event. Ask your librarian to help you locate appropriate organizations.
- **Send a copy of your argument analysis to representatives of the two sides of the issue you examined.** Ask them if they think you presented the issues fairly and how they feel about any compromise or solution your conclusion may propose.
- **Save your work in your writing portfolio.**

To Build Or Not to Build

Jeremy Yu

It's a beautiful spring morning at Millers Woods. The sun is shining brightly and birds are chirping. Some fifth-graders from a nearby elementary school are walking one of the nature trails with their teacher, identifying the various wild flowers they see and eagerly watching for any signs of animal life.

In the Chatham neighborhood on the other side of the city, the sun is shining but the mood is anything but cheerful. People sit idly on their front porches, wondering if they ever will find work again. Some have been unemployed for as long as two years, having lost their jobs in the first wave of layoffs at the auto plant. Others have been out of work since January, when the plant closed permanently.

A proposal to build a new municipal airport on the land that is now Millers Woods pits the interests of schoolchildren and unemployed workers—as well as other groups—against one another. On one side are those who favor construction of the airport on the proposed site; on the other side are those who want to preserve Millers Woods. Although numerous alternate sites for the airport have been proposed, none has been found to be suitable. Nor have proposals to expand the present airport turned out to be feasible.

Effective introduction—utilizes vivid description of site of the controversy

Introduces both sides of the issue—the need to preserve a wild area and the need to create jobs

Uses statistics to explain one argument

Those concerned citizens who favor construction of the airport on the proposed site point to our city's 20% rate of unemployment. They note that construction of the airport would keep building trades workers in our city busy for more than a year and would provide at least 200 permanent new jobs for city residents. According to a study done by the chamber of commerce, a new airport would help make our city more attractive as a tourist and convention center. An increase in the tourist and convention trade would bring more business to —and create more jobs in—local hotels, restaurants, and retail stores.

City residents who want to preserve Millers Woods emphasize its value as an educational and recreational resource. Each year, thousands of people visit the area to hike, picnic, and observe its abundant plant and animal life. If an airport is built on the site, the habitat of many animals native to our region will be destroyed.

Opponents of the airport also point out that the levels of noise and air pollution in our city will increase substantially if a new airport is built.

Underlying the debate are two different sets of priorities about what is important for our city. The question is whether aesthetic and environmental concerns take priority over the economic well-being of a large segment of our community, or vice versa. There is no doubt that if the airport is built, our city will lose a valuable educational and recreational resource and the habitat of many animals will be destroyed. In addition, we will have to deal with noise and air pollution. These are valid considerations and consequences to be avoided, even at great cost. But how do we weigh the seriousness of these consequences against the problem of chronic unemployment and underemployment for many of our city's residents? Their homes and lives are no less at risk than those of the woodland animals.

Explains underlying assumption

In a contest between the economic survival of people and that of a woodland preserve I see no alternative to standing up for people—which, unfortunately, means supporting airport construction at Millers Woods. Every effort to find a suitable alternative to building on the Millers Woods site has failed. We have a pressing need to reduce local unemployment and to promote economic growth—both of which the construction of an airport will achieve. At least for the short run, then, I feel we must act on behalf of the basic well-being of the people. In time we may be able to serve both interests without conflict.

Draws a conclusion from the analysis of the controversy

WRITER TO WRITER

If everybody is thinking alike then somebody isn't thinking.
General George S. Patton, U.S. Army, World War II

FOR YOUR PORTFOLIO ▶

1. Reflect on your writing.   Write a note about your experience in writing your essay and your present view of what you accomplished. Attach your note to your paper when you submit it or place it in your writing portfolio. Try to address some of these issues:

- To what extent did your analysis lead you to change your understanding of and opinion on the issue you were examining? What new insights did you gain and how?
- Do you think your analysis is really impartial or does it favor one side? Why is that the case?
- How adequately do you think you presented the two sides? Did the need to present both sides prevent you from doing a thorough job with either?
- What part of writing this essay was most difficult and why?

2. Apply your skills.   Draw upon the strategies you have used in your argument analysis to complete one or more of the following:

- **Social Studies/History**   Write an argument analysis of any controversial issue or public policy debate you have studied in history or social studies class. Look for underlying assumptions that account for the opposition between the two sides.
- **General**   Review the issues being debated in the letters to the editor in your local paper. Try to identify the assumptions underlying the arguments presented. What prospects for resolution or impasse are revealed to you through this analysis?
- **Literature**   Write a brief analysis of an argument or conflict at the center of a short story, play, or novel you are studying. This might be a conflict between characters, between a character and an external force, or within a character.
- **Related assignments**   Follow the suggestions on pages 224–232 in completing the related assignments in this workshop.

On the Lightside

DOUBLESPEAK

Please utilize a portable hand-held communications inscriber to input the digital readout that for each alphabetically identified episode will derive a positive informational response.

If you have not figured out that you're supposed to take a pencil and answer the following questions, you are already in danger of failing the doublespeak quiz. *Doublespeak* is a word for deceptive language and double talk. Also known as *gobbledygook* or *officialese*, it often conceals and obscures information rather than clarifying and communicating. See if you can match the governmental and institutional doublespeak below with plain English.

Unauthorized withdrawal

A. __ frame-supported tension structure
B. __ safety-related occurrence
C. __ experienced automobile
D. __ terminal episode
E. __ revenue enhancement
F. __ downsizing personnel
G. __ unauthorized withdrawal
H. __ wood interdental stimulator
I. __ philosophically disillusioned
J. __ social-expression products

1. toothpick
2. used car
3. accident
4. firing employees
5. greeting cards
6. death
7. scared
8. tent
9. bank robbery
10. taxes

Check the following answers to see if you are an incomplete success (a failure) at understanding doublespeak: A-8, B-3, C-2, D-6, E-10, F-4, G-9, H-1, I-7, J-5.

from The Garden-Party

by Katherine Mansfield

Conflict is a part of everday life. People argue among themselves; individuals struggle to make important personal decisions; political, social, and religious ideologies clash. However broad or narrow their scope, all conflicts represent a struggle between opposing sides—people, ideas, principles, beliefs, hopes, ideals.

Conflict is a driving force in literature, too. Study the following scene from Katherine Mansfield's short story "The Garden-Party." As you read, think about the nature of the conflict between Laura and Jose.

"There's been a horrible accident," said Cook. "A man killed."

"A man killed! Where? How? When?"

But Godber's man wasn't going to have his story snatched from under his very nose.

"Know those little cottages just below here, miss?" Know them? Of course, she knew them. "Well, there's a young chap living there, name of Scott, a carter. His horse shied at a traction-engine, corner of Hawke Street this morning, and he was thrown out on the back of his head. Killed."

"Dead!"

Laura stared at Godber's man.

"Dead when they picked him up," said Godber's man with relish. "They were taking the body home as I come up here." And he said to the cook, "He's left a wife and five little ones."

"Jose, come here." Laura caught hold of her sister's sleeve and dragged her through the kitchen to the other side of the green baize door. There she paused and leaned against it. "Jose!" she said, horrified, "however are we going to stop everything?"

"Stop everything, Laura!" cried Jose in astonishment. "What do you mean?"

"Stop the garden-party, of course." Why did Jose pretend?

But Jose was still more amazed. "Stop the garden-party? My dear Laura, don't be so absurd. Of course we can't do anything of the kind. Nobody expects us to. Don't be so extravagant."

"But we can't possibly have a garden-party with a man dead just outside the front gate. . . . And just think of what the band would sound like to that poor woman," said Laura.

"Oh, Laura!" Jose began to be seriously annoyed. "If you're going to stop a band playing every time someone has an accident, you'll lead a very strenuous life. I'm every bit as sorry about it as you. I feel just as sympathetic." Her eyes hardened. She looked at her sister just as she used to when they were little and fighting

together. "You won't bring a drunken workman back to life by being sentimental," she said softly.

"Drunk! Who said he was drunk?" Laura turned furiously on Jose. She said, just as they had used to say on those occasions, "I'm going straight up to tell mother."

"Do, dear," cooed Jose.

"Mother, can I come into your room?" Laura turned the big glass door-knob.

"Of course, child. Why, what's the matter? What's given you such a color?" And Mrs. Sheridan turned round from her dressing table. She was trying on a new hat.

"Mother, a man's been killed," began Laura.

"*Not* in the garden?" interrupted her mother.

"No, no!"

"Oh, what a fright you gave me!" Mrs. Sheridan sighed with relief, and took off the big hat and held it on her knees.

"But listen, mother," said Laura. Breathless, half-choking, she told the dreadful story. "Of course, we can't have our party, can we?" she pleaded. "The band and everybody arriving. They'd hear us, mother; they're nearly neighbors!"

Think AND Respond

Explain the argument between Jose and Laura and the specific reasons each uses to rationalize the position she has taken. How does Katherine Mansfield establish, or set up, this conflict? Can you recall any experiences in your life that were marked by clear conflict between opposing sides?

INVITATION
— TO —
Write

The excerpt from "The Garden-Party" establishes a conflict, in this case a disagreement between two characters. Write a fictional scene of your own that establishes a clear conflict between opposing sides.

A disagreement between fictional characters is usually based on opposing or at least strongly contrasting viewpoints. A realistic fictional disagreement must rise naturally out of the personalities and attitudes of the characters. Therefore, the arguments need not always be logical or reasonable. Instead, your characters may resort to fallacious reasoning and emotional appeals as real people do.

DEVELOPING A CONFLICT

HANDBOOKS

FOR HELP & PRACTICE

Analysis Frames, p. 343

Peer Response, pp. 397–400

Tone, pp. 424–425

Point of View, pp. 446–449

Developing/ Presenting Arguments, pp. 474–476

1. Choose an issue. Brainstorm a list of situations and personal experiences involving conflict between two sides. Include examples of both internal and external conflicts. You might list arguments you've had, difficult decisions you've made, or meetings where opposing ideas clashed. Select two or three conflicts and do some freewriting about each one. As you freewrite, notice which conflict stirs your creative energies the most. Try to state this conflict in a sentence or two, and use it as the basis of your writing.

2. Investigate both sides of your conflict. A diagram can help you to discover as much as possible about the conflict you have chosen. Start your diagram with two boxes, side by side. In each box, write one side of the conflict. Then draw additional boxes descending from the two main boxes. In each descending box, write an argument or reason to develop that side of the conflict.

3. Create a situation in which to present your conflict. How will you present the conflict you're developing? Katherine Mansfield's conflict came to life in a story about a garden party. You too might choose a fictional setting. Another option is to recreate the conflict situation from your life. If you choose the fictional approach, you must invent a setting, characters, and a plot. Be sure the characters representing each side of the conflict have contrasting personalities. Ask yourself, "What type of person would naturally take this position?" If you decide to write a nonfiction account, you still need a setting, characters, and a plot; these can be drawn from experience.

4. Consider an appropriate tone.   What tone will your story have? Will it be serious? comic? melancholy? angry? satiric? Choose a tone that reflects the way you feel about the conflict.

5. Reveal information subtly as you draft.   Provide necessary information about your characters gradually as they talk and react. Notice how in "The Garden-Party" Mansfield slowly reveals that Laura has a sister with whom she always disagrees, that an accident has occurred, and that a garden party is to take place. Also notice how the conflict is revealed entirely through dialogue. Introduce your own conflict and supporting arguments in a similar manner.

REVIEWING YOUR WRITING

1. Read your narrative to a friend.   Ask for help in evaluating it. Does the dialogue make the conflict clear? Does it sound natural? Have you given the characters personalities that fit their points of view? Have you provided enough information about the characters to make them seem real? Have you presented both sides?

2. Revise your draft.   Use your friend's comments and your own judgment to make your narrative clearer and more lifelike. When you've revised it, make a clean copy. Proofread for errors in grammar, usage, spelling, and mechanics.

PUBLISHING AND PRESENTING

- **Share your writing.**   In a small group compare your writing with others. Which papers showed the most effective use of dialogue? Which conflicts seemed most realistic?
- **Perform the scene.**   Stage a dramatic reading of your narrative, and record it on audiotape. Have the actors vary the pitch, tone, and volume of their voices to emphasize the drama of the conflict. Play your tapes as part of a class presentation.

Writing
TIP

Acting out the conflict with a partner can provide you with useful bits of dialogue.

Debate

In Bike-Happy Hollywood, Gary Busey's Crash Revs Up the Helmet Controversy Again

Jacob Young and Jack Kelley

"**I**t's a free country." This expression implies that, as a citizen, you're free to do whatever you want. Is this assumption true, or does government have the right to limit personal freedom in some circumstances?

This excerpt from a magazine article addresses these questions in the context of a dispute between motorcyclists and government leaders in California.

As you read the excerpt, think of the bikers and lawmakers as the two teams in debate about personal a freedom. Then decide which position you would argue in a debate.

Gary Busey couldn't wait to get rolling. The mechanics had finished installing a windscreen on his customized $15,000 [bike], and Busey wanted the big motorcycle right away. So even though Bartels' cycle showroom is closed on Sundays, salesman Gene Thomason opened the Culver City, California, shop to let Busey pick up his bike. The actor hit the starter, waved, then wheeled the custom-painted black-and-cream cycle into the traffic on Washington Boulevard.

As usual, Busey rode bareheaded. Hollywood's tough guys have had a long love affair with motorcycles, and the romance has recently heated up to the boiling point. . . . For many in the growing swaggering fraternity of bikers . . . helmets are for wimps. Barely 100 feet out of Bartels' door, Busey came face-to-face with the consequences of that macho style. As he tried to make a turn around a bus, his 625-pound [motorcycle] went into a skid. Instead of laying the bike down in the direction of the slide, as he should, "Gary high-sided," says Thomason. "The momentum threw him off. He landed on the curb on his back and his head hit."

Busey . . . was suddenly a statistic, one of an estimated 25,000 Californians to suffer serious injuries in biking accidents [that] year. Even as he struggled toward recovery, Busey also became the focus of a new battle over whether motorcyclists should have to wear helmets. . . . The day after Busey's accident, Assemblyman Richard Floyd angrily reintroduced his helmet bill. . . .

"Actors go out and buy these bikes because it's become a status symbol," says Marjoe Gortner, who owns four [motorcycles] and wears no helmet. "All this macho stuff comes into play. You feel invincible on a bike– you're Marlon Brando." . . . Salesman Thomason takes such play-riding philosophically. "We get a lot of celebrities," he shrugs. "They all ride; they all crash." And few wear headgear. . . .

Assemblyman Floyd doesn't care much for how bikers feel. By his estimate, the maimings and deaths from motorcycle accidents cost California $100 million each year, and helmets would cut both the carnage and the expense. The antihelmet forces argue that wearing headgear is a personal decision the government has no business legislating. They also claim that wearing a helmet cuts peripheral vision and muffles the senses, making accidents likelier. That may be so, but in a 1980 survey of Oklahoma crashes the fatality rate for riders who were not wearing helmets was almost six times that of those who were. . . .

Busey's manager and bike-riding partner, Herb Nanas, told a reporter that he believed "Gary would still take a position advocating freedom of choice" about helmets. In the end, however, Busey's injuries seemed a chilling price to pay just so he could feel the wind in his hair.

Think AND Respond

What is this particular controversy about? What position do the bikers take? How does the viewpoint of the lawmakers differ from that of the bikers? Which position comes closer to your own? In what other circumstances might government and citizens disagree about possible limits to personal freedom?

INVITATION TO Write

The article summarizes a dispute between California bikers and lawmakers about personal freedom. Write a four-minute constructive (opening) speech for the affirmative and negative teams in a debate about the right to freedom.

Like the essay you wrote for the Guided Assignment, the opening speeches in a debate present the pros and cons of a controversial issue. Arguments, even heated ones like the dispute between the bikers and the California lawmakers, do not have to be disagreeable confrontations. Even strong differences of opinion can usually be resolved through discussion, persuasion, and negotiation. The **debate** is a formal discussion in which rational arguments are put forth on both sides of an issue. In a debate, two opposing groups—the affirmative and the negative teams—express their reasons for supporting or not supporting a controversial proposal or proposition. The constructive (opening) speeches set forth the evidence and reasoning that support each team's case. Participating in a debate is a very effective way to develop your thinking skills because it requires you to look at the same issue from more than one angle.

FOR HELP & PRACTICE

Collaborative Planning, pp. 358–360

Unity/Coherence, pp. 382–391

Developing/ Presenting Arguments, pp. 474–476

Research Skills, pp. 479–489

Debating Techniques, pp. 501–506

RESEARCHING AND PLANNING YOUR SPEECHES

1. Write a proposition. Isolate the proposition, or controversial subject, the two teams will debate; for example:

> Resolved, that in certain circumstances government has the right to pass laws that limit personal freedom.

With some friends, brainstorm for subjects that have two clear sides about which people would disagree. The proposition you write should state only one main idea. Furthermore, the proposition should be worded precisely so that the debate does not become a quibble over semantics.

2. Assemble your evidence. First, list all the arguments that support the proposition. Next, list all the arguments against the proposition. From these, choose the strongest arguments to serve as the main points of each speech. Then consult books, magazines, newspapers, and other references for facts, statistics, reasons, quotations, and examples to develop each main point.

3. Determine appropriate content. The constructive speech of the affirmative team should show the need for change and the way to change. If the debate were on the issue discussed in the article, the arguments in favor of legislation requiring bikers to wear helmets would be presented. The constructive speech of the negative team should defend current conditions and show why proposed changes would be unwise. Evaluate the information you gathered earlier, and select the material that lends the strongest support to the position of each speech.

4. Outline each speech. Develop outlines you can use to guide you as you draft each speech. Each speech should have an introduction that captures the listeners' interest and states the proposition as clearly as possible. The body of each speech should present the main points in the order of increasing importance, with each main point followed by the supporting evidence you developed and selected in steps 2 and 3. Finally, each speech should have a strong, convincing conclusion that summarizes the main points and restates the speaker's position.

DRAFTING YOUR SPEECHES

1. Use persuasive devices cautiously. A constructive speech is a type of persuasive speech. Therefore, you can utilize elements and techniques of persuasion to make your points. As you draft, you may use either inductive or deductive reasoning, explaining your assumptions and their bases as you go along. You may also choose words whose connotations will influence listeners to accept your position. However, remember that the strength of an effective constructive speech rests on an appeal to the audience's reason, rather than on an overdependence on loaded language and emotional appeals.

2. Respond to arguments of the opposing side. In a debate, each team tries to anticipate and parry the arguments of the opposing team. In your constructive speeches, you should mention the main points that you expect the opposing side will make, and offer information or logic that counters or at least weakens those points.

3. Make your reasoning clear. Include transitional words, phrases, or clauses that show how sentences and ideas are related. This technique not only helps the listener to follow your reasoning, but also helps you to think clearly and avoid logical fallacies. When you revise, you can remove any of these "links" that seem unnecessary.

REVIEWING YOUR WRITING

1. Ask for reactions. Read your speeches to several students. Ask them to comment on the clarity and effectiveness of each speech. Do the main points and supporting facts, reasons, and examples persuade the listener to accept the position you are arguing? Is the listener influenced by the persuasive techniques you have used? Which arguments seem weak or unconvincing? How could the persuasive thrust of each speech be improved? Can your presentation itself be improved to stress important points?

2. Incorporate suggestions as you reread. Revise your speeches to include helpful suggestions made by peer readers and any new ideas that have occurred to you that will strengthen your arguments.

3. Rehearse your speeches aloud. Are there any series of words that are difficult to say aloud? Are there any sentences that are too long to be said in one breath? Make any changes that will make an oral presentation of the speeches smoother and easier.

PUBLISHING AND PRESENTING

- Present one of your speeches orally to your class.
- If you have strong convictions about one side of the issue of personal freedom, submit your speech in support of that view to the school or community newspaper.
- Prepare a class debate on the proposition. Form affirmative and negative teams. For each team, select the most persuasive constructive speech from all the speeches written for this assignment.

Writing
TIP

Tape the drafts of your speeches and time them. Remember that each speech should take only about four minutes to deliver.

Varying Sentence Closers

Effective writers use sentence closers to clarify or expand the information in a sentence and to add an interesting and unexpected rhythm.

Appositive Phrase   The room was empty, <u>a silent world of sinks, drainboards, and locked cupboards</u>.

Frank Bonham, *Chief*

Present Participial Phrase   He turned and ran, <u>dodging through the trees</u>.

Elliott Merrick, ''Without Words''

Past Participial Phrase   I seem forever condemned, <u>ringed by walls</u>.

Richard Wright, *Black Boy*

Absolute Phrase   The parrot was gone, <u>its cake a mess of crumbs and frosting on the ground</u>.

Shirley Jackson, ''Island''

Delayed Adjectives   Our father was younger than the landlord, <u>leaner, stronger, and bigger</u>.

James Baldwin,
Tell Me How Long the Train's Been Gone

A. Composing Sentences   Use a comma to join the underlined part of the second sentence to the end of the first sentence.

1. She lay and drowsed. She was <u>hoping in her sleep that the children would keep out and let her rest a minute</u>.

    Katherine Anne Porter, ''The Jilting of Granny Weatherall''

2. He had the appearance of a man who had done a great thing. It was <u>something greater than any ordinary man would do</u>.

    John Henrik Clarke, ''The Boy Who Painted Christ Black''

3. They were diggers in clay. They were <u>transformed by lantern light into a race of giants</u>.   **Edmund Ware, ''An Underground Episode''**

4. He trudged with his hands and tight fists in his pockets. He had <u>his head to the wind and the rain</u>.

    Walter Edmonds, ''Water Never Hurt a Man''

5. It was night now. It was <u>bright with moon fragment and stars and northern glow</u>.

    Paul Galico *The Snow Goose*

Sentence Composing   **233**

B. Unscrambling and Imitating Sentences Professional writers often use a series of phrases to create a long sentence closer. Unscramble each set of parts to form a sentence whose structure matches that of the model. Then write an imitation of the model. Punctuate your sentences as the models are punctuated.

1. My mother is waiting, and I nearly run into her, <u>choking with pounding, aching emotions, trembling with a dizzy swirl of ecstasy and fear.</u>
    Richard E. Kim, *Lost Names*
   a. falling with a desperate grab at the chair and table
   b. stumbling with a lurching, twisting movement
   c. the pup was sleeping, and Meg promptly tripped over it

2. She was now standing arms akimbo, <u>her shoulders drooping a little, her head cocked to one side, her glasses winking in the sunlight.</u>
    Harper Lee, *To Kill a Mockingbird*
   a. their boots knee-deep in the muck
   b. their shovels scooping the heavy mud into makeshift garbage pails
   c. they now worked with tools in hand
   d. their mops sopping up the water

3. You have to start by wanting to be a contender, <u>the man coming up, the man who knows there's a good chance he'll never get to the top, the man who's willing to sweat and bleed to get up as high as his legs and brains and his heart will take him.</u>   **Robert Lipsyte, *The Contender***
   a. a person who wants to persist and struggle to achieve as many dreams and goals and longings as this earth can provide
   b. a person fulfilling potential
   c. you have to begin by trying to be a self-confident individual
   d. a person who hopes that hard work and effort will eventually pay off

4. Katherine stood quietly at yet another window, this in the depot, and she saw in the distance the lantern mountains <u>glowing gold in all directions, catching the future sun.</u>
    Mark Helprin, "Katherine Comes to Yellow Sky"
   a. and it noticed across the field the large bull
   b. the calf waited listlessly for still more food
   c. chewing lazily on some grass
   d. this from its mother
   e. watching the others

5. There he stood, <u>tall, handsome, rubbing his hands that were red with cold</u>.　　　　**Virginia Woolf, "Lapin and Lapinova"**
   a. proud, confident
   b. up she strode
   c. accepting the plaque that was inscribed with her name

6. Her china blue eyes were bright as she watched the young couple go down the path, <u>he walking in an easy, confident fashion, with his wife on his arm</u>.　　　**D. H. Lawrence, "The Shadow in the Rose Garden"**
   a. Art singing in an off-key, cracked baritone
   b. the tall, dark trees seemed welcoming as we let the old trail lead us up the canyon
   c. without a care in the world

C. Sentence Expanding　Expand each sentence below by writing a closer that makes sense and joining it to the sentence with a comma. Write one each of the five types of closers you have been shown. Then compare your closers with the originals on page 323.

1. He grabbed the shield again.　　　　　　**Martin Raim, "The Cell"**

2. Towser roused himself under Fowler's desk and scratched another flea.
　　　　　　　　　　　　　　　　Clifford Simak, "Desertion"

3. Halfway there he heard the sound he dreaded.
　　　　　　　　　　　　　　　　John Steinbeck, *The Red Pony*

4. The other shoji slammed open, and unseen, Buntaro stamped away.
　　　　　　　　　　　　　　　　James Clavell, *Shogun*

5. In the fishpond, the hippo belched.
　　　　　　　　　　Leon Hugo, "My Father and the Hippopotamus"

Application　From a piece of recent writing, select three sentences. Write each sentence three times, adding a different closer each time. Vary the content, length, and structure of your closers. Note how each affects the rhythm and clarity of the sentences.

Grammar Refresher　A phrase added to the end of a sentence but not clearly modifying the intended noun can become a misplaced modifier. To learn to avoid misplacing modifiers, see Handbook 33.

Sketchbook

*T*he good critic is the one who tells of his mind's adventures among masterpieces.

Anatole France

*D*rooling, driveling, doleful, depressing, dropsical drips.

Sir Thomas Beecham

A true critic ought to dwell rather upon excellencies than imperfections, to discover the concealed beauties of a writer, and communicate to the world such things as are worth their observation.

Joseph Addison

*C*riticism is prejudice made plausible.

H. L. Mencken

What do you think a critic is? What do critics do? What *should* they do?

Additional Sketches

What books, films, or works of art have had a powerful impact on you? Why?

Would the story of your life be presented as a Broadway play, a major motion picture, a made-for-television movie, a situation comedy, or some other form of entertainment?

Writing About Literature

Guided Assignment
LITERARY ANALYSIS

Related Assignment
EXPLORING A PROVERB

Related Assignment
CRITICAL REVIEW

Whenever people have finished experiencing a particularly powerful or moving work of literature or art, they often wish to compare notes and responses. Through conversations, groups of readers and writers become a literary community—a community where individual perceptions about literary and artistic works are honored and common values are expressed. In the next assignment, your classroom will function as a literary community as you analyze a literary work. You will then apply these same skills examining the message in a proverb and evaluating a motion picture or television work.

Literary Analysis

FROM   A SUNRISE ON THE VELD

A literary analysis attempts to explain how a literary work communicates a particular set of meanings for a reader.

In the short story "A Sunrise on the Veld," Doris Lessing tells what happens early one morning when a fifteen-year-old sneaks away from his home in southern Africa to go hunting by himself on the nearby veld, or grassland. As you read this excerpt, write down phrases and sentences from the story that you find particularly significant, memorable, or striking in any way. Think about how these help you appreciate and find meaning in the story.

The first bird woke at his feet and at once a flock of them sprang into the air calling shrilly that day had come; and suddenly, behind him, the bush woke into song, and he could hear the guinea fowl calling far ahead of him. That meant they would now be sailing down from their trees into thick grass, and it was for them he had come: he was too late. But he did not mind. He forgot he had come to shoot. He set his legs wide, and he balanced from foot to foot, and swung his gun up and down in both hands horizontally, in a kind of improvised exercise, and let his head sink back till it was pillowed in his neck muscles, and watched how above him small rosy clouds floated in a lake of gold.

Suddenly it all rose in him: it was unbearable. He leaped up into the air, shouting and yelling wild, unrecognizable noises. Then he began to run, not carefully, as he had before, but madly, like a wild thing. He was clean crazy, yelling mad with the joy of living and a superfluity of youth. He rushed down the vlei under a tumult of crimson and gold, while all the birds of the world sang about him. He ran in great leaping strides, and shouted as he ran, feeling his body rise into the crisp rushing air and fall back surely on to sure feet; and thought briefly, not believing that such a thing could happen to him, that he could break his ankle any moment, in this thick tangled grass. He cleared bushes like a duiker, leaped over rocks; and finally came to a dead stop at a place where the ground fell abruptly

BY DORIS LESSING

away below him to the river. It had been a two-mile-long dash through waist-high growth, and he was breathing hoarsely and could no longer sing. But he poised on a rock and looked down at stretches of water that gleamed through stooping trees, and thought suddenly, I am fifteen! Fifteen! The words came new to him; so that he kept repeating them wonderingly, with swelling excitement; and he felt the years of his life with his hands, as if he were counting marbles, each one hard and separate and compact, each one a wonderful shining thing. That was what he was: fifteen years of this rich soil, and this slow-moving water, and air that smelled like a challenge whether it was warm and sultry at noon, or as brisk as cold water, like it was now.

There was nothing he couldn't do, nothing! A vision came to him, as he stood there, like when a child hears the word *eternity* and tries to understand it, and time takes possession of the mind. He felt his life ahead of him as a great and wonderful thing, something that was his; and he said aloud, with the blood rising to his head: all the great men of the world have been as I am now, and there is nothing I can't become, nothing I can't do; there is no country in the world I cannot make part of myself, if I choose. I contain the world. I can make of it what I want. If I choose, I can change everything that is going to happen: it depends on me, and what I decide now.

The urgency, and the truth and the courage of what his voice was saying exulted him so that he began to sing again, at the top of his voice, and the sound went echoing down the river gorge. He stopped for the echo, and sang again: stopped and shouted. That was what he was!—he sang, if he chose; and the world had to answer him.

And for minutes he stood there, shouting and singing and waiting for the lovely eddying sound of the echo; so that his own new strong thoughts came back and washed round his head, as if someone were answering him and encouraging him; till the gorge was full of soft voices clashing back and forth from rock to rock over the river. And then it seemed as if there was a new voice. He listened, puzzled, for it was not his own. Soon he was leaning forward, all his nerves alert, quite still: somewhere close to him there was a noise that was no joyful bird, nor tinkle of falling water, nor ponderous movement of cattle.

There it was again. In the deep morning hush that held his future and his past, was a sound of pain, and repeated over and over: it was a kind of shortened scream, as if someone, something, had no breath to scream. He came to himself, looked about him, and called for the dogs. They did not appear: they had gone off on their own business, and he was alone. Now he was clean sober, all the madness gone. His heart beating fast, because of that frightened screaming, he stepped carefully off the rock and went towards a belt of trees. He was moving cautiously, for not so

long ago he had seen a leopard in just this spot.

At the edge of the trees he stopped and peered, holding his gun ready; he advanced, looking steadily about him, his eyes narrowed. Then, all at once, in the middle of a step, he faltered, and his face was puzzled. He shook his head impatiently, as if he doubted his own sight.

There, between two trees, against a background of gaunt black rocks, was a figure from a dream, a strange beast that was horned and drunken-legged, but like something he had never even imagined. It seemed to be ragged. It looked like a small buck that had black rugged tufts of fur standing up irregularly all over it, with patches of raw flesh beneath . . . but the patches of rawness were disappearing under moving black and came again elsewhere; and all the time the creature screamed, in small gasping screams, and leaped drunkenly from side to side, as if it were blind.

Then the boy understood: it was a buck. He ran closer, and again stood still, stopped by a new fear. Around him the grass was whispering and alive. He looked wildly about, and then down. The ground was black with ants, great energetic ants that took no notice of him, but hurried and scurried towards the fighting shape, like glistening black water flowing through the grass.

And, as he drew in his breath and pity and terror seized him, the beast fell and the screaming stopped. Now he could hear nothing but one bird singing, and the sound of the rustling whispering ants.

He peered over at the writhing blackness that jerked convulsively with the jerking nerves. It grew quieter. There were small twitches from the mass that still looked vaguely like the shape of a small animal.

I t came to his mind that he should shoot it and end its pain; and he raised his gun. Then he lowered it again. The buck could no longer feel; its fighting was a mechanical protest of the nerves. But it was not that which made him put down his gun. It was a swelling feeling of rage and misery and protest that expressed itself in the thought; if I had not come it would have died like this: so why should I interfere? All over the bush things like this happen; they happen all the time; this is how life goes on, by living things dying in anguish. He gripped the gun between his knees and felt in his own limbs the myriad swarming of the twitching animal that could no longer feel, and set his teeth, and said over and over again under his breath: I can't stop it. I can't stop it. There is nothing I can do.

Think AND *Respond*

How does the boy change during this scene? What causes the change? In what ways does this boy remind you of yourself at age fifteen, or of fifteen-year-olds you have known?

INVITATION
—TO—
Write

Literary works like Lessing's draw a variety of responses and interpretations from readers. Guided by the activities in this assignment, analyze a literary work in order to explain the meaning the whole work or any of its elements has for you.

Most essays of literary analysis address two fundamental questions about a work of literature: "What does it mean?" and "How does it communicate its meaning?" Through reading, rereading, response, and analysis, you can arrive at your own interpretation of a literary work and account for the ways in which the work produces the meanings you find in it.

The skills of analysis and interpretation are applicable any time you wish to understand a work of literature, a written text of any kind, or any complex situation. For example, social scientists analyze and interpret human behavior, whereas marine biologists analyze and interpret the behavior of sea animals.

PREWRITE AND EXPLORE

1. Choose a literary work to explore. Think about works you are studying, writers and themes that interest you, or works that you have already read and found challenging or memorable. You might consider responding to "A Sunrise on the Veld," "The Handsomest Drowned Man in the World" by Gabriel Garcia Marquez, "Ode to My Socks" by Pablo Neruda, or "Miss Brill" by Katherine Mansfield.

2. Learn about the author. A reader's sense of the meaning of a text often depends upon knowing something about its author and the time when the text was written. Consult a reference work to see what you can find out about the author you choose.

HANDBOOKS

FOR HELP & PRACTICE

Reflecting/ Observing, pp. 331–332

Writing Techniques, pp. 334–335

Problem Solving, pp. 472–473

Outline Form, pp. 826–827

Readers of Lessing's story, for example, should know that from the time she was five years old until she was thirty, she lived on a farm in Rhodesia (Zimbabwe) in southern Africa. Her colonial experiences seem to have influenced her work, which characteristically reveals her concern with the experiences of exploited people.

3. Notice what you notice. The best readers understand that what they notice and wonder about as they read is important and therefore worth recording and reflecting on. You may already be keeping a reading log in which you record your questions, critical responses, and interpretations of the text you read. The following activities are other techniques you can use to focus your thinking on what you, as a reader, notice.

Exploratory Activities

- **Double-entry journal** Draw a line down the middle of a notebook page. On the left-hand side, write down short passages that strike you as you read. On the right-hand side, across from the passages, comment on what struck you.
- **Freewriting** Write a quick response to your first reading of the text, commenting on what you found interesting, puzzling, or memorable. Share your freewriting in a small group.

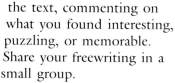

- **Text rendering** Work with others who have read the same text, and have each student read aloud interesting passages. If someone else chooses a passage you had picked, repeat it. A text can be heard best when it is read in different voices.

Jessica decided to write a literary analysis of "A Sunrise on the Veld." As she read the entire short story, she kept a double-entry journal. In this assignment you will follow Jessica's process in writing a literary analysis.

Writing TIP

When you freewrite, it is often helpful to limit yourself to writing for no more than ten minutes. If you try freewriting for longer periods of time, you may find yourself getting bogged down with decisions that you can make later.

Born Free, by Edwin Salomon (Publisher: Jacques Soussana Graphics, Jerusalem).

"All the great men of the world have been as I am now, and there is nothing I can't do; there is no country in the world I cannot make part of myself, if I choose. I contain the world. I can make of it what I want. If I choose, I can change everything that is going to happen: it depends on me, and what I decide now."

I guess this is just the way a young man might feel when he feels that his whole future is ahead of him and that he can conquer any obstacle. But something feels very immature about this. So he has to find out soon that he isn't in control of everything in his world. Why should he think he can make any country in the world a part of himself? What can he mean?

". . . and set his teeth, and said over and over again under his breath: I can't stop it. I can't stop it. There is nothing I can do."

Wow! Now I really see a theme clearly! What a contrast from the way the boy felt a minute before, when he thought he could control everything. I'm glad I wrote it down.

4. Examine the literary elements.   In addition to examining your reactions, think about how the writer manipulated literary elements to create a character, achieve a certain effect, make a point, or convey a theme. To focus your thinking, consider the following elements of a story.

- **Plot**   How predictable are the events in an unfolding story? Are there events that seem similar or contrasting? What is the central conflict? Are there events that don't relate to this conflict? Why not?
- **Characters**   What meanings are suggested by their names, their descriptions, their way of talking, or their actions? For example, do you think it is significant that the boy in Lessing's story has no name?

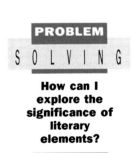

PROBLEM
S O L V I N G

How can I explore the significance of literary elements?

- **Setting**   Where and when does the story take place? What mood is created? How does the setting affect events? How are physical setting and psychological events related?
- **Point of view**   From whose point of view is the story told? Why might the author have made that choice? How much does the narrator know? Is the narrator reliable? Notice that Lessing used an omniscient third-person narrator—one who sees, hears, and knows everything.
- **Language and imagery**   What words, phrases, images, or figures of speech seem to be repeated? Do any objects or events seem to have symbolic value? For example, could Lessing's story be symbolic of the political situation that exists in southern Africa?
- **Theme and ideology**   Does the story address any universal problem or experience, or does it teach a lesson? Are there other stories it reminds you of? Does it reflect any particular set of religious or political beliefs?

5. Reread and reflect.   As you reread, notice how much more you are able to observe. In a five-minute freewrite, focus on how your understanding of the text changed on subsequent readings. Also record what remains unclear to you.

6. Develop an interpretation.   To focus your thinking on an interpretation, try one or more of the following activities.

- **Retelling**   Working with a partner, retell the story. Vary the story to fit your own style of retelling. After you have retold the story and have heard your partner's retelling, discuss how similar or different your two stories are from each other and from the original. Discuss how these differences may reflect or lead to different views of the meaning of the story.
- **Problem solving**   Select a passage that you don't fully understand. In a focused freewriting, explain what you don't understand about it and what you do know about other parts of the text that surround the problem section. Share your writing with a small group who have read the same text.
- **A striking sentence**   Select from the text a sentence or a short passage that strikes you or that seems to be very important. Use it as a starting point for a focused freewriting on why it stands out and how it influences your interpretation of the text.

Jessica used freewriting to focus her emerging interpretation.

I want to write about two closely related passages, and what strikes me about them is the way they almost repeat each other yet say opposite things. The passages are the one that says "there is nothing I can't become, nothing I can't do" and then the passage that echoes it, saying "I can't stop it. There is nothing I can do." These passages contain the whole idea behind the story. That is, the story is about a boy's experience of his adolescent fantasy of omnipotence and his recognition of his fantasy as a fantasy. So it's sort of about disillusionment. Yet it's not clear if the boy is actually disillusioned.

What else do I want to say? I don't think girls have such fantasies of power and control. So perhaps the story is trying to show the foolishness of male fantasies. I mean I think that Lessing is trying to mock male fantasies at the same time that she appreciates the boy who has the experience of growing up slightly. So it's not a put-down of males either, but a showing of their limitations. And maybe of some strength? I want to think more about this. Does the boy's having no name suggest that he could be any boy or all boys at a certain age?

7. Test a tentative interpretation. The value of your interpretation within a community of readers will depend on how much your interpretation can help others see the same text more clearly. This does not mean that your readers must agree with your interpretation, but that they must be able to see how you arrived at it—what evidence from the text will support the interpretation that you advance. To test your interpretive argument and the evidence available, try the following.

- **Nutshelling** Put your tentative interpretation in writing in a nutshell of two or three sentences.
- **Believing and doubting** Share your interpretation with a partner. Provide each other with reasons to support and reasons to doubt each other's interpretation. Consider how you might want to revise or clarify your interpretation.

COMPUTER TIP

Enter into your computer file your nutshell interpretation and all the supporting and contradictory information. Later you can organize the evidence for use in your essay.

Literary Analysis   **245**

- **Brainstorming for evidence**   Using a cluster or a list, write down all the evidence in support of your interpretation. When you think of evidence that would be inconsistent with your interpretation, write it down too.
- **Evaluating the evidence**   Review the evidence supporting and contradicting your interpretation. Try to figure out how you can use the contradictory information to revise or clarify your interpretation.

8. Plan your essay.   As you think about ways to organize and present your essay, you may want to use one or both of the following strategies.

Strategies

- **Collaborative planning**   Get together with a partner and dis- cuss your plans for drafting your essay. Make sure you discuss the main point you want to make in your essay; the evidence in support of your point; the contradictory evidence and how to deal with it; and your plan for organizing your information and structuring your essay.
- **Outlining**   Use an outline form or a tree diagram to organize your material into main points and subordinate points.

DRAFT AND DISCOVER

1. Begin drafting.   Your writing plan or outline can help you organize your thoughts, but keep yourself open to new ideas and interpretations that occur to you as you draft. Writers often find their best ideas or even change their minds about what they are going to say while they are in the middle of writing.

 Writer's Choice   To start your draft, you might begin with a thesis statement, with a piece of freewriting you have already completed, or with a brief summary of the story.

2. Organize your draft.   As you write your essay, keep in mind the following points for making your analysis effective.

- In the introduction to your literary analysis, identify the title and author of the work you are analyzing, and briefly state your main point.

- Provide enough of a summary of the work so that your essay will be clear to readers unfamiliar with the work. Avoid giving a detailed plot summary.
- Show your reader how you get from the words in the literary text to your interpretation. Use quotations from the text to show that your claims are valid, but don't count on quotations alone. Explain how the quotations support the claims you make about the text.
- Don't misrepresent your understanding of a literary work for the sake of a convenient interpretation. Sometimes a work of literature will reflect two opposing value systems or suggest two contradictory views of human nature. Let your interpretation reflect such complexities; discuss and analyze the conflicting ideas you find.
- Don't avoid evidence that may seem to contradict your interpretation. Tell how you account for such evidence, or acknowledge the plausibility of an alternative interpretation. If you can dispute the evidence, do so.

Notice that Jessica began her draft with an opening paragraph that gave the title and author of the literary work and also stated her main point.

Sunset over Lake Kou, Burkina Faso, West Africa

ONE STUDENT'S PROCESS

Doris Lessing's short story "A Sunrise on the Veld" is an initiation story about one dramatic moment during one morning in the life of a fifteen-year-old boy—a moment that forces the boy to begin the process of maturing into an adult. Although the story focuses on one person, the events in the boy's life represent experiences that are universal. During a moment of joy and confidence, the boy suddenly encounters pain and death, and he begins to change and mature. This experience is like the experiences that all persons must have in order to move into adulthood.

3. Reread and reflect. When you review your essay, ask yourself the following questions. Have your peer readers respond also.

Questions for Yourself

- Does my essay say what I want it to say?
- Is the writing unified, or did I change my mind or wander as I wrote?
- Have I provided evidence from the text—including quotations—to support my interpretation?
- Have I acknowledged the possibility that the story can be interpreted in another way and explained why I have interpreted it my way?

Questions for Your Peer Readers

- Do I give enough of a summary of the story so you can follow it? Do I tell you more than you need to know?
- What is the main idea of my interpretation?
- Summarize the evidence I present for my interpretation.
- What confirming or contradicting evidence to my interpretation did I leave out?
- Are you persuaded that my interpretation is the most plausible one? Why or why not?
- What questions remain for you about my paper?

R EVISE   YOUR   WRITING

HANDBOOKS

FOR HELP & PRACTICE

Unity/Coherence, pp. 382–391

Peer Response, pp. 397–400

Using Source Materials, pp. 482–489

1. Evaluate your responses. Be sure to treat the responses of your readers as information about their reading of your draft and not as the last word on what you need to do. Trust yourself as a reader too. As you decide what to do, keep in mind these guidelines, which are often used to evaluate literary analyses.

Standards for Evaluation

An effective literary analysis . . .

- identifies clearly the title and author of the literary text.
- presents an interpretation of a literary text that clarifies the meaning of the text or reveals how the text operates.

- provides textual evidence for the interpretation it advances and shows how the evidence supports the interpretation.
- takes into account any plausible alternative interpretations and any contradictory evidence.

2. Problem-solve. Taking into account your review of your paper and the responses of your readers, revise your paper. Jessica responded to suggestions from her peer readers this way.

ONE STUDENT'S PROCESS

Two particular passages in the story echo one another

ironically to reveal the theme of the story and the

—unnamed because he could be any boy—

content of the lesson that the unnamed boy has to learn.

Here is the first of these passages, reflects the boy's sense of his

own power and approaching manhood:

"There was nothing he couldn't do, nothing! . . . He felt

his life ahead of him as a great and wonderful thing,

; and he said aloud, with the blood rising to his head: all the great men of the world

have been as I am now, and there is nothing I can't become, nothing I can't do;

something that was his . . . If I choose, I can change

everything that is going to happen: it depends on me,

and what I decide now"

Almost immediately after uttering these words to

himself, he is drawn by a scream of pain to a nearby

being devoured alive by a thick swarm of black ants.

wooded area where he discovers a young buck. Moved by

pity for the helpless buck, he considers shooting it to end

its misery, but decides not to. Recognizing that he is

merely witnessing a natural event, one that perhaps he

no right to interfere with.

Is it significant that he is unnamed?

Nice choice of quotations. Could you include more to clarify the boy's feelings?

Shouldn't you tell why the buck is screaming?

Good that you've shown the conflict he's beginning to feel.

3. Proofread your work. Reread your revised draft aloud at least twice, listening for places where your reading stumbles. Your ear can help you hear where your essay may need additional editing. Then correct any mechanical errors that you see.

LINKING

GRAMMAR **AND** WRITING

Long Quotations

In a literary analysis, long quotations—usually those of four lines or more—should be set off from the text. Double-space the quotation, indent from the left, do not use quotation marks, and place the page reference in parentheses after the final period.

> The urgency, and the truth and the courage of what his voice was saying exulted him so that he began to sing again, at the top of his voice, and the sound went echoing down the river gorge. (159)

See Grammar Handbook 41, pages 807–815 for additional help with quotations.

P UBLISH AND PRESENT

- **Collect essays on a particular author in a single volume.** Place it in the school or classroom library as a reference work for other interested students.
- **Exchange essays.** If students in another class have read and written about the same literary works, trade literary analyses and see how the interpretations of their community of writers differs from yours.
- **Read your essay aloud.** The best audience would be composed of people who have read your chosen literary work.
- **Participate in a read-around.** Meet with other writers who have written about the same text. Pass the papers around in a circle until everyone has had a chance to read one another's paper. Use the papers as the basis for a round-table discussion of the literary text.
- **Save your literary analysis in your writing portfolio.**

The Dawning of Awareness

Jessica Schaeffer

Doris Lessing's short story "A Sunrise on the Veld" is an initiation story about one dramatic moment during one morning in the life of a fifteen-year-old boy—a moment that forces the boy to begin the process of maturing into an adult. Although the story focuses on one person, the events in the boy's life represent experiences that are universal. During a moment of joy and confidence, the boy suddenly encounters pain and death, and he begins to change and mature. This experience is like the experiences that all persons must have in order to move into adulthood. In addition, the story may have even a larger message since the boy is from a white family in southern Africa. Perhaps his story might be representative of the white males who govern southern Africa.

On the morning portrayed in the story, the boy comes across a young buck with a broken leg that is being eaten alive by ants. The boy is shocked and sickened by the sight of the suffering animal and is forced to recognize how little control he has over the world and its tragic and cruel forces.

Two particular passages in the story echo one another ironically to reveal the theme of the story and the content of the lesson that the unnamed boy—unnamed because he could be any boy—has to learn. The first of these passages reflects the boy's sense of his own power and approaching manhood.

> There was nothing he couldn't do, nothing! . . . He felt his life ahead of him as a great and wonderful thing, something that was his; and he said aloud, with the blood rising to his head: all the great men of the world have been as I am now, and there is nothing I can't become, nothing I can't do; . . . If I choose, I can change everything that is going to happen: it depends on me, and what I decide now. (25)

Mentions title, author, and theme immediately

Presents larger theme—the boy represents an exploitive government

Provides short summary of important plot event

Includes interpretation of subsequent quotation

Cites quotation that supports interpretation

Gives descriptive
details of pivotal event
in plot

Almost immediately after uttering these words to himself, he is drawn by a scream of pain to a nearby wooded area where he discovers a young buck being devoured alive by a thick swarm of black ants. Moved by pity for the helpless buck, he considers shooting it to end its misery, but decides not to, recognizing that he is merely witnessing a natural event, one that perhaps he has no right to interfere with.

Supports interpretation
of boy's growing
awareness with
quotation

> . . . if I had not come it would have died like this: so why should I interfere? All over the bush things like this happen; they happen all the time; . . . He gripped the gun between his knees and felt in his own limbs the myriad swarming that the twitching animal could no longer feel, and set his teeth, and said over and over again under his breath: I can't stop it. I can't stop it. There is nothing I can do. (26)

Relates two passages
and draws conclusions

The last line of the passage above is an ironic echo of the boy's reflection a few moments earlier that "there is . . . nothing I can't do." Moving from his adolescent fantasy of power to recognition of helplessness represents the beginning of his progression into manhood. Until that moment, Lessing seems to be saying, the boy's development was in the direction of a false sense of unlimited control and power.

Summarizes evidence
that was given above

Uses author's
background to
substantiate
interpretation

Given the southern African setting of the story and Lessing's position as an opponent of all forms of exploitation, it is almost impossible not to read the story as a political parable. Perhaps Lessing sees the adolescent, white, southern African boy as a representative of the society into which he was born—a society dominated by a distinctly male sense of power and control. The boy's identification with "all the great men of the world" links him with an even larger tradition of the male ambition for control over other humans and nature.

Provides symbolic
interpretation

Concludes by tying the
ideas in the essay
together

Whether we read this story as an account of one boy's experience or of a country's experience, the character's recognition that he is not omnipotent indicates that the possibility for growth and change always exists in life.

WRITER TO WRITER

Criticism, analysis, reflection is a natural response to the existence in the world of works of art. . . . Without it, works of art would appear in a vacuum, as if they had no relation to the minds experiencing them. It would be a dismal, unthinkable world with these shooting stars arousing no comment, leaving no trace.

Elizabeth Hardwick, novelist

Elizabeth Hardwick, American novelist

1. Reflect on your writing. As an introduction to your essay, write a note to your reader telling the story of the writing of your essay. Tell about which activities helped you most in developing your interpretation, whose responses or ideas may have influenced you, and how your essay developed through the stages of the writing process. Now that you have read other literary analyses, tell what changes you would make to yours. Attach your note to your essay when you submit it to your teacher.

2. Apply your skills. Use your skills to do an interpretive analysis of one of the following:

- **General** Write an essay that analyzes and interprets the social significance of the seating pattern of students in the school cafeteria.
- **Cross-curricular** Write an essay that analyzes and interprets an eyewitness account of a historical event, such as the shots fired on Lexington Green, or a historical document, such as the Gettysburg Address.
- **Literature** Write an essay that analyzes and interprets a poem such as "The Tyger" by William Blake or "Hope" by Emily Brontë. Remember that interpreting symbols is often an important part of any analysis of a poem.
- **Related assignments** Using the suggestions on pages 256–264, write an analysis of a proverb or a review of a movie or television show.

FOR YOUR
PORTFOLIO

Exploring a Proverb

"**A**ctions speak louder than words." "The early bird catches the worm." You have probably heard proverbs like these all your life. Such sayings seem to express undeniable truths about the way people act or feel. However, you may well wonder if these age-old sayings are still true. Do actions still speak louder than words? Does the early bird catch the worm every time?

The excerpt you are about to read questions the truth of a different proverb, "Spare the rod and spoil the child." As you read, notice the evidence the author uses to make his main point.

"You Know What They Say..."

by Alfie Kohn, *Psychology Today*

"Spare the rod and spoil the child." Few proverbs have been so thoroughly disproved—or have caused so much harm—as this one. Nearly 40 years of research have shown conclusively that the "rod" produces children who are more aggressive than their peers. "Physical punishment teaches that the way to solve problems is to beat up others," says Leonard Eron, a research psychologist at the University of Illinois at Chicago. He and others explain that having children focus on what they did wrong and why it was wrong encourages them to internalize control of their own actions. But physical punishment, while suppressing misbehavior in the short run, ultimately promotes nothing more than a determination to avoid getting caught.

In 1960 Eron and his colleagues studied 870 8-year-olds in rural New York and found a clear-cut relationship between the severity of the physical punishment they received—ranging from none at all to slaps and spankings—and how aggressive other children judged them to be. Twenty-two years later, the researchers tracked down some of these same people and found that the aggressive kids were now aggressive adults. And those adults now had aggressive children of their own.

Think AND Respond

Alfie Kohn's argument against the proverb includes a quote from an authority and research results from several studies. What is the most convincing part of Kohn's argument? Can you think of other proverbs that may benefit from a similar reinterpretation or reappraisal?

INVITATION TO Write

The excerpt you just read claims that the proverb "Spare the rod and spoil the child" has been thoroughly discredited by research. Analyzing a proverb of your own choice, present a persuasive argument that it, too, should be reinterpreted.

For generations, truths about human nature have been handed down in the form of proverbs. Human nature hasn't changed so much over the years, and many of the old sayings still ring true. However, our familiarity with these proverbs sometimes prevents us from taking a critical look at how traditional sayings apply to current situations. The skills of critical review and analysis can help you discover how much truth a particular proverb still contains.

HANDBOOKS

FOR HELP & PRACTICE

Sharing Techniques, pp. 335–336

Introducing Nonfiction, pp. 365–368

Peer Response, pp. 397–401

Problem Solving, pp. 472–474

Developing/ Presenting Arguments, pp. 474–477

EXPLORING A PROVERB

1. Brainstorm a list of proverbs. With a group of friends, or perhaps with your family, try to recall as many old sayings as possible. Here are a few examples: "Make hay while the sun shines." "You can't teach an old dog new tricks." "Look before you leap." A class brainstorming session will produce many proverbs, perhaps including parallel examples from different cultures. For example, a Nigerian proverb, "Seeing is better than hearing," echoes the Chinese saying "A picture is worth a thousand words." A Japanese equivalent of "Spare the rod" is "To pamper children is to desert them." Libraries also have books of proverbs.

2. Choose a proverb. It doesn't matter whether you agree or disagree with the proverb you select. You are looking for a saying that will benefit from analysis and interpretation.

Writer's Choice Could you analyze a proverb by comparing it to another similar proverb or to a contrasting version?

3. Freewrite about the meaning of your proverb. Without imposing any order on your thoughts, begin to write about what the proverb seems to mean and your own reaction to it. Tell whether you agree with it. To what situations does the proverb refer? Is it always true? How might the words of the proverb be interpreted in a different way?

4. Determine your approach to the analysis. Your purpose is to persuade your reader that your proverb is not true, is still true, or is true but needs to be reinterpreted. Select the approach that you can support most effectively. You might choose to rely on research, as did the author of the excerpt, or you could argue from personal experience, telling a story to make your major point. Reading may provide you with more examples to support your argument. Consider taking an informal poll to determine if people agree or disagree with your proverb, and then use the results of your poll to bolster your conclusion.

WRITING YOUR ANALYSIS

1. Introduce your proverb in a way that suggests your approach. Depending on the approach you select, you could begin by stating your proverb as a question: "Is beauty really only skin deep?" Similarly, you can grab your readers' attention with a negative statement about a proverb with which you disagree: "Misery does not love company." If you are going to tell a story, you might choose a narrative hook such as, "Last summer I learned to my chagrin that honesty is not always the best policy."

2. Examine the commonly accepted meaning of your proverb. Even if you choose to disagree with your proverb, you should still explain what it means and explore why people have believed it for so long.

3. Analyze whether the accepted meaning still holds true. Present your research or your story, making clear how these examples support your main point.

4. Conclude your analysis. Summarize the arguments you have already presented or bring your story to its natural conclusion. Adding just one more example, as the author does in the excerpt, can leave your reader with something new to think about that cements the argument.

1. Read your analysis.   Have you anticipated and addressed all the possible criticisms of your approach? Do your examples or story support your conclusion? Have you omitted any possible examples that would strengthen your case?

2. Ask a classmate to read your paper.   Have you accomplished your purpose, persuading your reader that your argument is sound? Can your friend think of additional examples that would help to prove your point, or arguments against it that you hadn't thought of? Solicit ideas about how to make your introduction or conclusion more arresting to readers.

3. Read your paper to an older person.   You may learn something about why your proverb seemed to be true in an earlier time.

4. Proofread and rewrite your analysis.   Check your paper for grammar, spelling, and punctuation. If you have told a story, make sure that you have been consistent in your use of tenses.

P UBLISHING AND PRESENTING

- **Create a booklet.**   Compile your classmates' analyses along with your own into a booklet entitled "A New Look at Some Old Proverbs."
- **Enter your analysis in a nonfiction writing contest.**
- **Hold a debate.**   If two students have written contradictory analyses, have them present their arguments in the form of a debate.

On the Lightside

WHERE THERE'S A WILL

It is high time people realize the impact William Shakespeare had on the English language. *The long and the short of it* is that our everyday speech is filled with words and phrases that have been taken from his plays and poems. Anyone who underestimates his contribution is *living in a fool's paradise.*

Over the centuries Shakespeare's expressions—such as the ones in italics above—have become some of the most familiar in the English language. Some have been overused to the point that they are now clichés. A British journalist, Bernard Levin, once showed how much Shakepeare contributed to common speech by stringing together sixty of his phrases in one giant sentence. It reads, in part:

If you cannot understand my argument, and declare "It's Greek to me," you are quoting Shakespeare; . . . if you have *played fast and loose*, if you have been *tongue-tied*, *a tower of strength*, *hood-winked* or *in a pickle*, . . . why, *be that as it may*, *the more fool you*, for it is *a foregone conclusion* that you are *(as good luck would have it)* quoting Shakespeare; . . . even if you *bid me good riddance* and *send me packing*, if you wish I was *dead as a doornail*, if you think I am *an eyesore*, *a laughingstock*, *the devil incarnate*, . . . then—*by Jove! O Lord! Tut, tut! for goodness' sake! what the dickens! but me no buts*—it is all one to me, for you are quoting Shakespeare.

The genius of Shakespeare lives on, not only in his great plays and sonnets, but also in our common, everyday speech.

Critical Review

Rep Puts Play to Music and Throws It Into TEXAS

By Chris Sanders

Although you may not view yourselves as such, you and your friends often play the role of critical reviewers. You discuss movies, television shows, books, plays, and other forms of entertainment and art, and you make judgments about what you like and what you dislike.

The following critical review of a play performed by the Repertory Theatre of St. Louis was written by a college student. As you read the review, notice how the writer evaluates different elements of the play.

LESLIE COBER

A Shakespearean musical? Set in Texas circa 1870? With a live country and western band on stage?! When I first heard that the Rep was adapting one of Shakespeare's lesser known comedies into a musical, I was admittedly apprehensive. But, as this job requires, I put my preconceptions behind me and began my research.

The Merry Wives of Windsor, Texas, the Shakespearean comedy John L. Haber adapted for the Rep, has a curious history. A well-known theatrical legend explains that the play was commissioned by a royal mandate. To allegedly satisfy Queen Elizabeth's desire to see a play about Falstaff in love, Shakespeare wrote *The Merry Wives of Windsor* within a fortnight.

First performed in 1597, the play was a tremendous success and continued to be a popular favorite until the early 19th century when it fell into disfavor. It has since been considered critically as an aberration, too banal or trite to be taken seriously: Shakespearean fluff, if you will.

Which brings us to Mr. Haber's adaptation, although perhaps "adaptation" is too mild a word to describe the incredible transformation the play underwent. Although he borrows Shakespeare's plot, the characters and some of the dialogue, this stuff is more like *Bonanza* than Shakespeare, albeit a very amusing *Bonanza.*

Director Edward Stern has taken the otherwise weak script firmly in hand and created a comic world where barbecues, stampedes and a live band are just part of the fun. . . .Sight gags abound, and simply hearing the characters drawling Shakespeare's lines is good for an occasional guffaw.

The Rep has assembled a strong cast for the production. . . . Although country music is not one of my favorite musical spheres, I must confess that the sounds of the Red Clay Ramblers kept the action flowing briskly throughout and was quite infectious. The Ramblers. . . provide us with two, count 'em *two* hoedowns, as well as a hilarious second act curtain-opener entitled "The Moo Song." The musical highlight of the evening, however, was the performance by John Foley, who played (believe it or not) the yodelling cowboy. One of his two numbers, "Count On My Love," a ballad sung with Deborah Jean Culpin, was truly beautiful.

The set, designed by Kevin Rupnik, worked well on the Rep's thrust stage and created a Texan atmosphere through the use of an impressive array of eclectic southern curios. Candice Donnelly's costumes were similarly impressive, as was Peter Sargent's lighting design, which gave us neon beer signs and a lariat made of Christmas lights.

So if you're looking for an evening of fine Shakespeare, don't go see the Rep's season opener. But if you are looking for some light entertainment and musical fun, and a rib or two at the Bard, you just might enjoy *The Merry Wives of Windsor, Texas.*

Think AND Respond

What strengths and flaws in *The Merry Wives of Windsor, Texas* does the writer point out? What is the writer's overall conclusion about the play? Have you seen any plays or films recently about which you would like to comment?

INVITATION
═ TO ═
Write

Chris Sanders's critical review analyzes the strengths and shortcomings of a performance of *The Merry Wives of Windsor, Texas.* Write a critical review of your own, evaluating a play, movie, painting, or another work of art.

Like an analysis of any literary work, a critical review has three main parts: a description of the subject, an in-depth evaluation of the subject's various elements, and a conclusion about its overall value. The purpose of a critical review is to offer readers a useful analysis of the subject and to suggest whether seeing it, reading it, or listening to it is worth their time. That's why critical reviews most often appear in newspapers and magazines. Some critics also offer their views on radio and television programs, and others have had their work collected in books.

CHOOSING AND ANALYZING A SUBJECT

1. Choose a subject that engages you personally. Your subject might be a movie or a television show you enjoyed—or one that you disliked. You might also choose to review a live performance, such as a play, a rock concert, an opera, or a dance recital. Perhaps there is a painting, drawing, photograph, sculpture, or other work of art you have seen and admired. Do you have a favorite tape or CD?

Begin your search for a topic by brainstorming a list of specific subjects you might review. Discuss your list with friends, and write down any additional suggestions they may have. After reviewing your list, choose the subject that interests you the most, the one you feel most compelled to write about.

FOR HELP & PRACTICE

Analysis Frames,
p. 343
Introducing/
Concluding
Nonfiction,
pp. 365–371
Elaborative Details,
pp. 376–381
Unity/Coherence,
pp. 382–391
Developing/
Presenting
Arguments,
pp. 474–477

2. Identify key elements of your subject.
Theme is an element that is common to all forms of art. Beyond theme, however, each form of art has its own inherent characteristics. For plays, these elements include plot, dialogue, acting, staging, sets, lighting, and costumes. When evaluating paintings, you might look at color, technique, and composition. A review of a song or album would consider such elements as melody, rhythm, and lyrics. Think about your subject, and make a list of the key elements that relate to that specific art form.

3. Analyze each element of your subject. Examine each element on your list, and jot down some notes about how your subject expressed that element. You don't necessarily need to evaluate every element of a subject. You might instead choose to focus on just a few elements. Look for strengths or weaknesses in each area you want to evaluate. You might do this in chart form to use later as a guide to writing. Don't worry about searching for a "right" response. Critical reviews are largely a matter of opinion. Your review should give your honest, personal reactions.

D RAFTING YOUR REVIEW

1. Write an introduction. In the introduction, identify the subject, set the tone, and express your general opinion. Notice how the reviewer of *The Merry Wives of Windsor, Texas* identifies the subject and sets a lighthearted tone in the first two paragraphs. He also lets the audience know that he was "admittedly apprehensive." The tone of your review—whether it's objective, sarcastic, laudatory, humorous, or negative—will be shaped by your opinion of the subject.

2. Organize the body of your review logically. Let your subject guide the organization of your review. For a play or movie, you might first describe the plot and then discuss the merits and flaws of the script, acting, and staging. For a painting, you might describe the work as a whole first, and then evaluate color, technique, and composition in turn. Remember to support your opinions with specific details or examples.

3. Be specific. In your descriptions and evaluations, avoid the use of vague adjectives, such as *great, good,* and *poor*. Instead, make your descriptions and evaluations meaningful by carefully choosing your words. Notice Chris Sanders's use of such descriptive words as *inventive, briskly, infectious, hilarious,* and *eclectic.*

4. Sum up your general impression. Reread the concluding paragraph of Chris Sanders's review, and note how he sums up his overall view of the play. Write a concluding paragraph to your review that reinforces the opinions you've expressed.

REVIEWING YOUR WRITING

Writing
—TIP—

As you write a critical review of a performance, replay scenes in your mind. Keep asking yourself, "What *exactly* is it I liked or disliked? What *exactly* made me feel the way I did?"

1. Check your draft for specific, detailed evaluations. Did you clearly state your opinion of each element of your subject, using specific, expressive vocabulary? Did you support your evaluations with details and examples?

2. Be sure the tone of your review is consistent. Have you maintained the tone you intended throughout your review? If not, you may want to rewrite some sentences or change some vocabulary so that your tone remains consistent.

3. Make sure your criteria are clear. Have you clearly indicated the standards by which you are judging your subject? Can your readers understand the reasons for your reactions? If not, you may want to add further explanations to some parts of your review.

4. Prepare a final copy. After revising your review, prepare a final copy incorporating all of your changes. Proofread your final copy for errors in grammar, usage, spelling, and mechanics.

PUBLISHING AND PRESENTING

- **Collect all the reviews in a class binder.** Organize the binder by subject, so that classmates can read one another's reviews.
- **Submit your critical review to the school or community newspaper.**
- **Stage a Critic's Circle.** On many radio and TV shows, critics review and rate current movies. Form teams to stage similar presentations of your class's reviews.

Sentence

Combining Sentence Variations

Often, professional writers mix sentence expanders (openers, s-v splits, closers) within one sentence. Contrast the two versions of each sentence below. Notice not only the increased information and vividness, but also the changes in rhythm.

MODELS

1. The two girls sank into the kitchen chairs.
2. Then Sylvia makes her perilous way down again.
3. Mr. Aaa heard the voices outside in the stone cause-way.

Original Sentences

1. With opener and closer: <u>Laughing</u>, the two girls sank into the kitchen chairs, <u>their feet sprawled out in front of them</u>.   **Mary Lavin, ''One Summer''**
2. With s-v split and closer: Then Sylvia, <u>well satisfied,</u> makes her perilous way down again, <u>not daring to look far below the branch she stands on, ready to cry sometimes because her fingers ache and her lamed feet slip</u>.   **Sarah Orne Jewett, ''A White Heron''**
3. With opener and s-v split: <u>Half an hour later</u>, Mr. Aaa, <u>seated in his library sipping a bit of electric fire from a metal cup</u>, heard the voices outside in the stone causeway.   **Ray Bradbury, *The Martian Chronicles***

A. Unscrambling and Imitating Sentences Unscramble each set of parts to form a sentence whose structure matches that of the model. Follow the punctuation in the model. Then write a second imitation of the model. Openers, s-v splits, and closers are underlined in the models.

1. Two boys, <u>in gym clothes and boxing shoes</u>, were balancing themselves on their shoulders, <u>kicking their legs up in the air</u>.
          Robert Lipsyte, *The Contender*
   a. slowing their speed slightly at the sharp bend
   b. several stock cars
   c. with garish paint and donut tires
   d. were hurling themselves against the third turn

2. Poppa, <u>a good quiet man</u>, spent the last hours before our parting <u>moving aimlessly around the yard, keeping to himself and avoiding me</u>.

Gordon Parks, ''My Mother's Dream for Me''

a. lying peacefully in the old cradle
b. the only Bronte boy
c. gurgling in contentment and being admired
d. Branwell
e. spent the first weeks of his life

3. <u>For a day and a night</u>, the great flakes drove down upon us, <u>swirling and swooping in the wind, blotting out the summit, the shoulder, everything beyond the tiny, white-walled radius of our tent</u>.

James Ramsey Ullman, *Top Man*

a. stirring and moving the air
b. the ancient ceiling fan spun above the tourists
c. the papers within the charming little room of the quaint hotel
d. with a whir and a rattle
e. ruffling the curtains, the bedclothes

4. <u>And so, lost and wandering on the sea</u>, <u>with topsails and spritsails torn</u>, the rotten hulk drifted, rather than sailed, <u>into the harbor of Berehaven on Bantry Bay on June 11th, 1593</u>.

Bruce Chatwin, *In Patagonia*

a. on Monday morning
b. with branches and trunk pummelled
c. the plum tree drooped, rather than stood
d. and so, bent and broken by the wind
e. in the garden outside his window

B. Combining Sentences   Use the first sentence in each set as a foundation. Insert the underlined parts of the following sentences into the foundation. Each combined sentence should contain expanders in two of the three positions, opener, s-v split, and closer. Compare your sentences with the originals on page 323.

1. I show the pass to a young Japanese private. I show it to him <u>at the gate</u>. The private is <u>the sentry</u>.   **Richard E. Kim, *Lost Names***

2. Janet stood there as if painted. She was <u>pausing half-way down to say something to someone above</u>. She seemed <u>distinct and unreal</u>.

Elizabeth Bowen, ''Foothold''

3. He went about with a sort of stealth. He was <u>absorbed, taking no heed of other people</u>. He was <u>seeking inwardly for luck</u>.
D. H. Lawrence, "The Rocking-Horse Winner"

4. He slipped from the wooden ledge and fell onto his back on the windowsill. He slipped <u>after perhaps a seventh attempt</u>. He fell <u>fluttering his wings</u>. **Virginia Woolf, "The Death of the Moth"**

C. Unscrambling Sentences Unscramble the parts in each set to form a sentence that makes sense. Each sentence should contain expanders in two of the three different positions, opener, s-v split, and closer.

1 a. she covered the tear
  b. her shoulders bunching to hide her face
  c. with a quick, guilty hand **Zenna Henderson, "The Believing Child"**

2 a. braced for a new concussion
  b. brought him leaping out of bed
  c. pouring in on Father Kleinsorge's half sleep
  d. the sudden flood of light **John Hersey, Hiroshima**

3 a. she got up in an apologetic sort of way and moved toward the better protected rear of the car
  b. feeling the empty seats as she went in a palpable search for hot pipes
  c. at last, her teeth chattering **Henry Sydnor Harrison, "Miss Hinch"**

4 a. looked neat and snug
  b. in the frosty December dusk
  c. with pale blue smoke rising from the chimneys and doorways glowing amber from the fires inside
  d. their cabins **Harper Lee, To Kill a Mockingbird**

Application From a piece of your recent writing, select six sentences at random. To each sentence, add expanders in two of the three different positions, opener, s-v split, and closer. Vary the content, length, and structure of your expanders. Notice the increased vividness and detail and the variations in rhythm that the various combinations of expanders bring to your writing.

Grammar Refresher For more on absolute phrases, see Handbook 33, page 599. For more on present and past participial phrases, see Handbook 33, page 598. For more on appositive phrases, see Handbook 33, page 593.

Sketchbook

What purpose did the builders of Stonehenge have in mind? Why did the Anasazi abandon their cliff dwellings? Who built the Great Zimbabwe structures?

The past is filled with mysteries. Which ones would you like to explore?

Additional Sketches

What is your area of expertise?
How do you find things out?

Reports

Guided Assignment

A scientist peering through a telescope and comparing mathematical formulas makes a fascinating discovery about matter at the edge of the universe. A medical researcher studying data from dozens of experiments unlocks the mystery of a deadly disease. A scholar poring through ancient manuscripts compiles a startling picture of a lost civilization. All these people are conducting research to answer particular questions. Research can also give you access to the information discovered by humankind through the ages. In this workshop you will apply your research skills to write a research report and to learn about careers you might enter in the years to come.

Research, or the systematic gathering of information from a variety of sources, can take us deep into new worlds of the future, present, and past.

Novelist John Steinbeck's childhood fascination with the legends of King Arthur led him to research the literature of medieval England, and this research led him eventually to write a new translation of Sir Thomas Malory's classic *Morte d'Arthur.* As you read this introduction to Steinbeck's translation, think about the impact Malory's work had on him and how he acted on his fascination.

FROM

Introduction to Medieval Literature

by John Steinbeck

ome people there are who, being grown, forget the horrible task of learning to read. . . . I remember that words—written or printed—were devils, and books, because they gave me pain, were my enemies.

Some literature was in the air around me. The Bible I absorbed through my skin. My uncles exuded Shakespeare, and *Pilgrim's Progress* was mixed with my mother's milk. But these things came into my ears. They were sounds, rhythms, figures. Books were printed demons—the tongs and thumbscrews of outrageous persecution. And then, one day, my aunt gave me a book and fatuously ignored my resentment. I stared at the black print with hatred, and then, gradually, the pages opened and let me in. The magic happened. The Bible and Shakespeare and *Pilgrim's Progress* belonged to everyone. But this was mine—it was a cut version of the Caxton *Morte d'Arthur* of Thomas Malory. . . .

Later, because the spell persisted, I went to the sources—to the *Black Book of Caermarthen*, to "The Mabinogion and Other Welsh Tales" from the *Red Book of Hergist*, to *De Excidio Britanniae* by Gildas, to *Giraldus Cambrensis Historia Britonum*, and to many of the "Frensshe" books Malory speaks of. And with the sources, I read the scholarly diggings and scrabblings —Chambers, Sommer, Gollancz, Saintsbury—but I always came back to Malory, or perhaps I should say to Caxton's Malory, since that was the only Malory there was until a little over thirty years ago, when it was announced that an unknown Malory manuscript had been discovered in the Fellows Library of Winchester College. The discovery excited me but, being no scholar but only an enthusiast, I had neither the opportunity nor the qualification to inspect the find until in 1947 Eugène Vinaver, Professor of French Language and Literature at the University of Manchester, edited his great three-volume edition of the works of Sir Thomas Malory, for Oxford University, taken from the Winchester manuscript. . . .

For a long time I have wanted to bring to present-day usage the stories of King Arthur and the Knights of the Round Table. . . . I wanted to set them down in plain present-day speech for my own young sons, and for other sons not so young—to set the stories down in meaning as they were written, leaving out nothing and adding nothing—perhaps to compete with the moving pictures, the comic-strip travesties which are the only available source for those children and others of today who are impatient with the difficulties of Malory's spelling and use of archaic words. If I can do this and keep the wonder and the magic, I shall be pleased and gratified. In no sense do I wish to rewrite Malory, or reduce him, or change him, or soften or sentimentalize him. I believe the stories are great enough to survive my tampering, which at best will make the history available to more readers, and at worst can't hurt Malory very much.

INVITATION TO Write

You have read how John Steinbeck acted on his interest in the King Arthur legends. Now research and write a paper that examines in depth a subject that interests you. Use the suggestions in this workshop as guidelines.

A good research paper poses a question or problem and takes the reader on a purposeful quest for the answer. In writing such a paper you have to exercise your own thinking and judgment to locate relevant information and to mold and shape it into an interesting, readable form. The skills you acquire in this workshop will enable you to write papers on many academic topics. You also can apply these research skills in many situations outside of school, from deciding which brand of a particular product to buy, to investigating which college to attend or what career to pursue.

PREWRITE AND EXPLORE

HANDBOOKS

FOR HELP & PRACTICE

Writing Variables,
pp. 329–330

Tree Diagrams,
pp. 339–340

Limiting Your Topic,
pp. 337–338

1. Look for ideas.   As Steinbeck's experience shows, personal interest can be your best guide in choosing a topic to research. Sometimes, however, a teacher may assign a general subject for your research paper. In either case, the following suggestions may help you explore ideas for your paper.

Exploratory Activities

- **Skimming your journal**   If you are free to write about any subject you choose, read some of the entries in your journal, looking for broad areas that interest you. List these areas and then freewrite to find possible topics within them.
- **Brainstorming**   Get together with several classmates and brainstorm ideas for your research paper assignment. Don't reject any of the ideas that come up or stop the discussion; just keep trying to generate more.

- **Freewriting** Start writing about your assigned subject or a broad area of interest, and see where the words take you. Don't worry about logical progression: your purpose is simply to explore ideas. Decide beforehand how many minutes you will write and don't stop or look back until the time is up. Then review your writing to see if you generated any new research topics.
- **Tree diagraming** Write down your assigned subject or a broad area of interest. Then write down any related ideas that come to mind as branches of that subject, and keep branching out as long as ideas keep coming to you. One of these idea branches may be refined into a specific writing topic for a research paper.
- **Reading literature** What authors or literary works inspire you? Are you drawn to such writers as George Orwell, Nadine Gordimer, or Doris Lessing, or to the subjects they write about? How might research help you explore any of these subjects further?

2. Share ideas. After generating a list of topics, get together with a group of classmates to share and discuss ideas. Notice how your classmates react to your topics and see if the ones they suggest give you any fresh ideas.

3. Choose a topic. If you're not satisfied with the topics you came up with on your own or in discussion with your peers, look back at the ideas you generated for the Sketchbook on page 268 or check the "Apply Your Skills" section on page 300 for other options. Then review your possibilities and choose a topic that you want to learn more about and that you think will hold your interest over time.

4. Narrow your topic. Once you've identified a subject to research and write about, check to see if the subject is too broad to cover in the research report you plan to write. Doing some preliminary reading in reference works—such as encyclopedias and specialized dictionaries—and scanning the tables of contents and the indexes of books about your topic may help you see how your topic can be divided into smaller parts. One of those parts may be just the right size for a report. Be careful, however, that your topic isn't so narrow that you won't be able to find enough sources of information on it. You may continue to refine and limit your topic as you conduct your research.

PROBLEM
S O L V I N G

How can I decide if my topic is suitable for a research paper?

Students in Michele Lin's English class were assigned to write research reports examining the influence of history on literature. In this workshop you will follow Michele's progress as she selected, researched, and wrote about her topic. Here is some freewriting she did to help her select and narrow her topic.

Richard Harris as King Arthur, Vanessa Redgrave as Guinevere, and Franco Nero as Sir Lancelot in the film *Camelot*.

ONE STUDENT'S PROCESS

It would be fun to do research about the legend of King Arthur and his knights of the Round Table. Steinbeck's right—the stories about Arthur are really interesting. I never read Thomas Malory's book—but I read A Connecticut Yankee in King Arthur's Court last summer. Also saw the movie Camelot. Maybe I could write about all the different versions of King Arthur throughout history—I could summarize and compare them. No, sounds too broad and like a lot of reading. And not like a topic I could research in outside sources. It's funny—what I know about the times in which Arthur supposedly lived (6th century) is from contemporary fiction. I wonder what really was happening in that period of history though. Maybe I could read about the history and analyze what parts of the different legends are really true and what parts are purely fiction.

5. Find a goal. Ask yourself what you want to accomplish by researching and writing about your topic. Do you want simply to learn more about your subject and satisfy your own curiosity, as Michele did? Do you want to prove a point, settle an argument, or elicit a strong response from your audience? In "Introduction to Medieval Literature," for example, John Steinbeck says that his goal was to rewrite the legends he loved in "plain present-day speech" so that the stories would be more accessible to today's readers. Your personal goals can help keep you focused as you research and write your paper. Keep in mind, however, that your goals may change during the writing process.

6. Identify your purpose. Your purpose can serve as a compass, guiding you through your research and giving you direction as you write. It may also give you an interesting angle on or approach to your topic. The following chart lists several possible purposes and examples of paper topics.

Purpose of Paper	Example of Topic
To inform	King Arthur: the many versions of an English legend
To examine cause and effect	The influence of Arthurian legend on culture—art, music, theater, literature
To compare and contrast	King Arthur and Robin Hood
To analyze	Fact and fiction in different Arthurian legends

7. Write a statement of controlling purpose. A statement of controlling purpose tells what your paper will be about. The statement helps guide the beginning stages of your research, and it gives you a standard by which you can judge the relevance of the information you gather.

The statement of controlling purpose you write now should be flexible. As you alter or refine your topic during the research stage, you must also update your controlling-purpose statement. Later, when you've completed your research and are getting ready to organize your information into an outline for your paper, you will revise this statement into a thesis statement. Here is the statement of controlling purpose Michele wrote to guide her work:

> I will analyze the legends of King Arthur and determine which aspects are historically accurate and which are fictional.

RESEARCH YOUR TOPIC

1. Prepare to do research. Before you can begin to write your paper, you will need to research your topic thoroughly. As with any search, you have a better chance of success if you know what you're looking for. Before you go to the library, therefore, consider making a list of the questions you will try to answer through your research. Michele made the list of questions shown on the following page before she began researching her topic. Note that all of her questions relate in some way to her controlling purpose.

FOR HELP & PRACTICE

**Research Skills,
pp. 479–489**

**Library, Reference
Works, and Other
Sources,
pp. 491–500**

**Outline Form,
pp. 826–827**

- What are the earliest known versions of the Arthur legend?
- How did the story change over the course of time?
- What was happening in British history at the time that Arthur supposedly lived?
- Was there really a King Arthur and if so, what is known about him?
- What parts of the story of King Arthur belong to legend rather than to history?

2. Begin your research. Doing research involves finding facts and ideas in a variety of reliable sources. Begin your library research by consulting one or more good encyclopedias and other reference works that contain entries on your subject. Also ask your librarian for any specialized reference books geared to your topic. Consulting such works will give you an overview of your topic and may suggest directions for further research and study. Next, check the *Readers' Guide to Periodical Literature* for a list of articles on your subject. Your library's card or computer catalog will provide you with titles and call numbers of books you'll want to examine.

3. Explore different types of sources. Depending on your field of study, you may wish to examine both primary and secondary sources. **Primary sources** provide direct or firsthand reports about events. Diaries, letters, journals, and original documents—such as the Constitution and the Emancipation Proclamation—all qualify as primary sources. **Secondary sources** provide indirect or second-hand information, including analyses of primary sources. Most books, newspaper and magazine accounts, encyclopedia articles, and research studies—such as your paper—are examples of secondary sources. Secondary sources are more plentiful and, in some cases, easier to obtain than primary sources.

You can also gather information on your topic through interviews, television and radio programs, recordings, and graphic aids. The Internet offers a vast array of secondary sources and also provides easy access to on-line versions of many primary sources such as historical documents.

Research
—TIP—
Many writers, particularly historians, include excerpts from primary sources in their works to support their conclusions.

4. Evaluate your sources. The guidelines below can help you determine whether the sources you find on your topic contain useful and accurate information.

Evaluating Source Materials

- **Is the author an unbiased authority?** Someone who has written several books or articles on your subject and whose name is included in various bibliographies may be considered an authority. However, try to determine to what extent an author's point of view is influenced by his or her politics, gender, or ethnic background. You'll want to be sure to read a variety of viewpoints, especially if your topic is a controversial one.

- **Is the source up-to-date?** Depending on your subject, a source's publication date may make a difference in the quality and timeliness of its data. Using recently published books and articles is particularly important in fields that are constantly changing, such as computers, science, and medicine. Most likely, a source published in 1975 will not be as relevant or accurate as one published last year.

- **Where was the article published?** If an article's title sounds promising, consider the kind of publication it appears in. In general, popular-interest magazines and tabloid newspapers are not suitable sources for a report.

- **For what audience is the source intended?** You may find books or articles that have been written about your topic for young readers. Because these often present information in an oversimplified form, they are not suitable sources for research reports. Sources of a highly complex, technical nature may also be inappropriate for your purposes.

---

5. Keep digging for more information. Don't be satisfied with the material you find in two or three good sources. There may be gems of information lying just beneath the surface of your data, and it will take some investigation on your part to unearth them. If the books and articles you've consulted contain bibliographies of resources the authors used in conducting their own research, check to see if any of those sources pertain to your report topic. Also try searching the library's card or computer catalog again, using different key words to describe your topic.

TECHNOLOGY TIP

Pages 854–857 of the Access Guide explain how to make the most of electronic resources, such as on-line information services, that your library may provide.

6. Make source cards. For each source you find, record complete publication information on a three-by-five-inch index card. You will need this information when you give credit to the source of an idea in the body of your paper and when you create a list of works cited. The guidelines below tell you what information you should record for three common types of sources.

Guidelines for Source Cards

- **Books** Write the author or editor's complete name, the title, the name and location of the publisher, and the copyright date.
- **Magazines and Newspapers** Write the author's complete name, the article's title, the name and date of the magazine or newspaper, and the page number(s) of the article.
- **Encyclopedias** Write the author's complete name (if given), the entry title, and the name and copyright date of the encyclopedia.

It's also a good idea to include on each source card a library call number and a note about where you found the source, in case you ever need to find the source again. It's even more important, however, to number your sources in the upper right-hand corner of the cards for easy reference during note taking. When you use sources that you will need to credit, note their source-card numbers on your note cards instead of rewriting the title and author each time. Three of Michele's source cards are shown on the next page.

Research
TIP

Basic Forms for Works Cited Entries, on pages 288–290, can help you see what information you should include on source cards for a wider variety of source types.

A Modern English version of Sir Thomas Malory's *Le Morte Darthur*

Source Card for Book

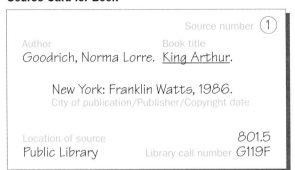

Source number ①

Author   Book title
Goodrich, Norma Lorre. <u>King Arthur</u>.

   New York: Franklin Watts, 1986.
City of publication/Publisher/Copyright date

Location of source   801.5
Public Library   Library call number G119F

Source Card for Magazine or Newspaper Article

②

Article title
Williams, Mary. "King Arthur in History

Name and date of publication
and Legend." <u>Folklore</u> Summer 1962:

73–88. Page numbers(s)

Public Library

Source Card for Encyclopedia Entry

③

Entry title   Encyclopedia title
"Arthurian Legend." <u>Encyclopaedia</u>

   <u>Britannica: Micropaedia</u>. 1993 ed.
Copyright date

School Library

7. Read your sources and take notes. Keep your topic, controlling purpose, and research questions in mind as you review your sources and look for useful information. Use the following techniques to take notes when you find material that suits your purpose.

- **Paraphrase** Restate the material in your own words. A paraphrase is approximately the same length as the original. Use this method when your notes need to be especially detailed.
- **Summary** Record the main idea of a passage in your own words. A summary is about one-third the length of the original. Use this method when you want to remember a general idea.
- **Quotation** Copy from the original text word for word, including all punctuation. Use quotation marks to signal the beginning and the end of the quotation. Use this method when the original text is particularly well said and you think the author's exact words would enhance a point you'll make in your report.

Drafting your report will be easier if your notes are accurate and complete. See Handbook 24, pages 482–489, for more information about writing quotations, paraphrases, and summaries and about using them effectively in your writing.

To take notes efficiently, look through the table of contents and the index of each book, or the headings and subheadings of each encyclopedia or magazine article. Closely read and take notes on only the parts that pertain to your limited topic.

The following guidelines can help you take notes efficiently.

Guidelines for Note Taking

- Use a separate four-by-six-inch index card for each piece of information, idea, or quotation. At the top of each card, write a brief heading that indicates the note's main idea. Later, you can group your cards according to their main ideas and arrange them into a logical order to guide your draft.

- In the upper right-hand corner of each note card, record the number of the source card for the source of information.

- Indicate whether what you have written is a paraphrase, a summary, a quotation, or an idea of your own. This will help you to remember whether the idea needs to be credited to a source if you use the note in your draft.

- Record the number of the page on which you found the material in your source. This information is essential for giving proper credit to the source in your report; you'll also need the page number if you want to go back to the source to verify a fact or a quotation or to gather more information.

- As you take notes, keep your controlling purpose and research questions in mind, so that you record only relevant information. However, you should also keep an open mind as you learn about your topic; you may wish to revise your controlling purpose, add questions to your list, and use new material you find.

Here are two note cards Michele wrote as she read one of her sources.

Source number

Similarities Among Legends   Main idea

For hundreds of years, many different legends about King Arthur have been written and told throughout England, Wales, and Scotland. Most of these legends agree that Arthur will return to save his people one day. 11–12 Page number(s)

(Summary) Type of note

Suit of Italian armor made of steel, leather, and velvet, about 1490

Geoffrey of Monmouth's Version

Three books of Geoffrey of Monmouth's twelve-book <u>History of the Kings of Britain</u> tell the story of Arthur, who appears to be Geoffrey's favorite king. "Here, for the first time in a written work, Arthur appears as the great romantic hero of Celtic tradition, with a splendid court [and] a magical sword." 17
(Paraphrase and quotation)

8. Write a thesis statement.   Now that you have researched your topic, you should have a more precise idea of what you want to accomplish in your writing. Recast your statement of controlling purpose as a thesis statement that expresses the main idea you will develop in your report. Since a thesis statement is most often a part of the introduction, it may indicate the organizational pattern you will follow. Your thesis statement should also reflect your perspective and tone.

Remember Michele's controlling purpose:

> I will analyze the legends of King Arthur and determine which aspects are historically accurate and which are fictional.

After conducting in-depth research on her topic, she discovered that this was not so easy to do, since for centuries historians have recorded different versions of what actually happened. Michele's first thesis statement reflected this fact:

> Although historians don't agree on the specifics, throughout the centuries they have agreed that the legend of King Arthur contains elements of both fantasy and reality.

Still, this thesis statement didn't make it clear what Michele's own point of view was or what she hoped to accomplish in her paper. She revised it again for her final draft:

> In order to determine what is real and what is fiction in the legend of King Arthur, it is necessary to examine the legend's many forms against the backdrop of what is now known about early British history.

Writing
━TIP━

The thesis statement tells the main idea of a piece of writing in the same way that a topic sentence tells the main idea of a paragraph. See pages 365 and 382 for more information on thesis statements and topic sentences.

Research Report   **281**

Young Arthur
successfully pulls
the sword from the
anvil and becomes
king of England.

9. Organize your material. Even though you may later decide to rearrange your main points, it's a good idea to create an organizational plan, or outline, before you begin to write. An outline for your paper is like a road map: your thesis provides a point of departure, and your conclusion is your destination. Each subheading for the body of your paper names a point of interest along the way. Your outline can help keep you from wandering off the road and straying in different directions as you draft.

Begin organizing your information by grouping your note cards according to their main ideas. Then arrange your groups in a logical order—one in which there is a coherent flow from each main idea to the next. You may find it useful to sketch out your ideas graphically (in a cluster map, a time line, or a tree diagram, for example) before drafting an outline. Guidelines for standard outline form and models of sentence and topic outlines can be found in the Appendix, pages 826–827.

Here is the beginning of Michele's topic outline. Notice that she used chronological order for historical information.

ONE STUDENT'S PROCESS

King Arthur: The Myth and the Monarchy
Introduction—the place of a legendary king in British history
   I. The legend of King Arthur
      A. Early versions of the story
         1. Written by Geoffrey of Monmouth (1135)
         2. Written by Wace of Jersey (1155)
         3. Written by Chrétien de Troyes (1175)
      B. Later version (1485) by Malory—the tale as we know it
   II. King Arthur's real place in history
      A. Mentions of Arthur in 6th–9th century chronicles
      B. Arthur in broader context of British history

Writer's Choice Chronological order often works for historical information or for steps in a process. Order of importance, order of impression, and comparison and contrast are other organizational patterns you can use.

1. Begin writing. At this stage just try to get your ideas down on paper, using your outline as a guide. Depending on how detailed your outline is, you'll want to write one or more paragraphs for each topic and subtopic. As you write, remember that even though you are drafting a formal research report, you don't want your language to be so formal that it sounds stilted and pretentious. Just be yourself and use a natural, comfortable writing voice.

2. Look for more information if necessary. You may find as you draft that you don't have enough information on a topic in your outline; your note cards simply don't tell the whole story. At this point you may wish to stop drafting and return to your sources for more information. You may even need to go back to the library to conduct further research. If you'd rather keep writing, just go on to another section of your outline and do additional research when you're ready.

3. Support your analysis. Remember that your goal is not simply to restate the information you find in a number of reliable sources. It is to synthesize that information, make inferences, analyze and interpret evidence, and reach a reasonable conclusion. Therefore, use the facts, statistics, examples, and other evidence you've gathered and recorded on note cards to support your own original ideas. Direct quotations—as well as paraphrases and summaries—may be used to help support your points.

4. Avoid plagiarism. The only material in your report that you do not need to credit, or document, is information that is considered common knowledge and your own interpretations and ideas. You therefore need to credit the sources of all direct quotations, paraphrases, and summaries you use in your writing. If you neglect to do so, you will be committing **plagiarism,** the dishonest—and unlawful—presentation of someone else's words or ideas as your own. You can credit your sources by means of footnotes, endnotes, or parenthetical documentation. Check with your teacher to see which method you should use.

HANDBOOKS

FOR HELP & PRACTICE

Organizing Your Work,
pp. 349–357
Elaborative Details,
pp. 376–378
Problem Solving,
pp. 472–474
Using Source Materials in Writing,
pp. 482–489

In medieval art, King Arthur was often identified by three crowns.

5. Document your sources. Parenthetical documentation is the most common way of crediting sources in the body of a paper. In this method of documentation, a detailed list of sources—including publication information—appears at the end of the report, and parenthetical notes in the text provide readers with specific details about where you found your material.

Therefore, provide a reference to a source and page number(s) in parentheses following each quotation, paraphrase, or summary you use. Follow these guidelines for parenthetical documentation; you can consult the final draft of Michele's report, pages 292–299, for examples.

A detail of a fifteenth-century woodcut depicts King Arthur and his knights gathered at the Round Table.

Guidelines for Parenthetical Documentation

- **Work by one author** Put the author's last name and the page reference in parentheses: (Jones 58–59). If you mention the author's name in the sentence, put only the page reference in parentheses: (58–59).

- **Work by more than one author** Put the authors' last names and the page reference in parentheses: (Smith and Klein 87). If a source has more than three authors, give the first author's last name followed by et al. and the page reference: (Norbert et al. 23).

- **Work with no author given** Give the title (or a shortened version of it) and the page reference: ("Sir Lancelot" 398).

- **One of two or more works by the same author** Give the author's last name, the title or a shortened version, and the page reference: (Laver, Holy Grail 398).

- **Two or more works cited at the same place** Use a semicolon to separate the entries: (O'Shea 132; Musick 95).

6. Take a break. Set your completed draft aside for a while to gain some perspective on it. Then read it again and share it with a classmate. The questions on the next page can help you and your peer readers review your draft.

Questions for Yourself

- Have I written a clear thesis statement? Have I developed and supported it in the body of my report?

- Have I provided enough elaboration of each main point in my outline? Where do I need to add more information?

- Have I included material that does not relate to my overall purpose? What information should be deleted?

- Have I presented my information in a logical order? How can I organize my material more effectively?

- Have I used too many direct quotations? Would paraphrasing any of them increase the readability of my report?

- Are my facts and quotations accurate? Have I correctly documented my sources?

- Have I achieved my overall purpose and personal goals for the report? What changes might I make to help me attain these goals?

- If this research report is a response to an assignment, have I met the requirements of the assignment?

Questions for Your Peer Readers

- What did you like most about my paper?

- Is the main idea of my paper clear? Tell me its subject and purpose in your own words.

- Which parts, if any, seem confusing or out of place?

- What do you need more information about? What parts can I leave out?

- Did the introduction capture your interest? Did the conclusion satisfy you, or did it leave you hanging?

HANDBOOKS
FOR HELP & PRACTICE

Concluding Nonfiction, pp. 368–371
Unity/Coherence, pp. 382–391
Revising Effectively, pp. 392–396
Peer Response, pp. 397–401

R E V I S E   Y O U R   W R I T I N G

1. Evaluate your responses. Think about your own reactions to your draft and about the responses you got from your readers. What changes will you make? As you consider this question, keep in mind that a good research report has certain characteristics.

Standards for Evaluation

An effective research report . . .

- begins with an interesting introduction that includes a thesis statement identifying the subject and the writer's approach to it.
- uses evidence and details from a variety of sources in the body of the paper to develop and support the thesis.
- correctly credits the sources of all direct quotations and paraphrases and summaries of other people's ideas.
- includes a Works Cited list with complete publication information for all the sources credited in the report.
- follows a logical pattern of organization and includes appropriate transitions so that ideas flow smoothly.
- ends with an effective, satisfying conclusion.

2. Problem-solve.   Rework your draft, taking both your own and your readers' responses into account. Here are the changes Michele made in part of her first draft on the basis of those responses.

ONE STUDENT'S PROCESS

I didn't know much about it before now.

¶ This story is familiar to most readers.
~~Everyone knows this familiar story.~~ It is part of what

most famous   in the Western world
may be the ~~greatest~~ legend ~~ever told~~—the tale of

Britain's King, Arthur. The story has all the elements

What are the elements of a classic legend?

a kind and noble king, magic spells, knights in armor, and a misty other world.
of a classic legend; But although some legends are

pure
fantasy, others including this one have a basis in fact.

s
What part of the King Arthur legend are true? Al-

~~though they don't agree on the specifics, historians~~

I'm not sure what your thesis is.

haven't always told the same story. In order to
throughout the centuries ~~agree that the legend of King~~

determine what is real and what is fiction in the legend of King Arthur, it is
~~Arthur has elements of both fantasy and reality.~~

necessary to examine the legend's many forms against the backdrop of
what is now known about early British history.

286   Workshop 9

3. Prepare your list of works cited. At the end of your research report, you must list the sources you actually used in writing the paper. Gather the cards for all the sources you have used and prepare your final list of works cited in accordance with the following guidelines.

Guidelines for a List of Works Cited

- Center the heading *Works Cited* and double-space between the heading and the first entry. Double-space each entry, and double-space between the entries.

- Begin the first line of each entry at the left margin; indent all subsequent lines five spaces.

- Arrange all entries alphabetically by the last name of the author or editor. If no name is given, alphabetize the entry according to the first word in its title. If the first word is *A, An,* or *The,* alphabetize according to the second word of the title.

- Alphabetize two or more sources by the same author by the first words in their titles. Give the author's name in the first entry only; after that, replace the author's name with three hyphens followed by a period (---.).

- Punctuate your entries correctly; use the examples on the following three pages for punctuation guidelines.

- If you wish, you may break your list of works cited into sections for the different types of sources you used. Centered subheadings for the sections might be *Books, Articles,* and *Other Sources;* alphabetize each section separately.

Written materials are not the only sources of information. These medieval paintings show some 14th-century amusements.

These guidelines are general rules for the Works Cited section of your paper. The following basic forms of entries will help you use correct punctuation and list sources with different elements.

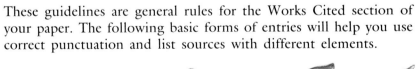

Basic Forms for Works Cited Entries

Whole Books

A. One author

Wilson, Anne. <u>The Magical Quest: The Use of Magic in Arthurian Romance</u>. Manchester: Manchester UP, 1988.

UP is an abbreviation of "University Press."

B. Two authors

Gilbert, Sandra M., and Susan Gubar. <u>The Madwoman in the Attic: The Woman Writer and the Nineteenth Century Literary Imagination</u>. New Haven: Yale UP, 1979.

C. Three authors

Heppelwhite, Charles W., Jeannette M. Meyerhoff, and Gerhardt B. Kassenbaum. <u>The Effects of High Technology on Smokestack America</u>. Litchfield: Litchfield, 1988.

D. Four or more authors

Gatto, Joseph, et al. <u>Exploring Visual Design</u>. 2nd ed. Worcester: Davis, 1987.

Et al. is an abbreviation of a Latin phrase meaning "and others." You can use *et al.* instead of listing all authors.

E. No author given

<u>Literary Market Place: The Directory of American Book Publishing</u>. 1990 ed. New York: Bowker, 1990.

F. An editor, but no single author

Saddlemyer, Ann, ed. <u>Letters to Molly: John Millington Synge to Maire O'Neill</u>. Cambridge: Harvard UP, 1984.

This form may be used when you have cited several works from a collection. Instead of writing separate entries for each work, you may write one entry for the entire work, listing the editor or editors first.

G. Two or three editors

Chipps, Genie, and Bill Henderson, eds. <u>Love Stories for the Time Being</u>. Wainscott: Pushcart, 1987.

Parts Within Books

Page numbers of selections follow publication dates in entries for parts within books and for articles and reviews in magazines, newspapers, and journals.

H. A poem, short story, essay, or chapter in a collection of works by one author

Angelou, Maya. "Remembering." Poems. New York: Bantam, 1986. 11.

I. A poem, short story, essay, or chapter in a collection of works by several authors

Welty, Eudora. "The Corner Store." Prose Models. Ed. Gerald Levin. San Diego: Harcourt, 1984. 20–22.

J. A novel or play in a collection of novels or plays published under one cover

Serling, Rod. Requiem for a Heavyweight. Twelve American Plays. Ed. Richard Corbin and Miriam Balf. New York: Scribner's, 1973. 299–327.

Steinbeck, John. Cannery Row. The Short Novels of John Steinbeck. New York: Viking, 1963. 355–649.

Magazines, Newspapers, Journals, Encyclopedias, and Reviews

K. An article in a quarterly or monthly magazine

Batten, Mary. "Life Spans." Science Digest Feb. 1984: 46–51.

L. An article in a weekly magazine

Powell, Bill. "Coping with the Markets." Newsweek 27 Apr. 1987: 54.

M. A magazine article with no author given

"How the New Tax Law Affects America." Nation's Accountants 24 Sept. 1986: 66–69.

N. An article in a daily newspaper

Faust, Joan Lee. "Tulips: A History of Success." New York Times 12 Sept. 1990, B18.

If no author is given, begin with the title.

O. An editorial in a newspaper

> "Is America Set for the Hypermarket?" Editorial. <u>Chicago Tribune</u> 4 Jan. 1988, sec. 1: 10.

If no author is given, begin with the title.

P. An article in a journal

> Aumiller, Emily P. "<u>Lord of the Flies</u> as a Musical." <u>English Journal</u> 71.8 (1982): 32.

The volume number, the number of the issue, the date, and the page reference follow the title of the journal.

Q. An encyclopedia article

> Faulk, Odie B. "Western Frontier Life." <u>The World Book Encyclopedia</u>. 1993 ed.

If the article is unsigned, begin the entry with the title.

R. An unsigned, untitled review

> Rev. of <u>Harry and Son</u>. <u>American Film</u> Mar. 1984: 78.

S. A signed, titled review

> Ludlow, Arthur. "Glass Houses." Rev. of <u>Rolling Breaks and Other Movie Business</u>, by Aljean Harmetz. <u>Movies</u> Aug. 1983: 76.

Other Sources

T. A personal interview

> Farquharson, Reginald W. Personal interview. 26 May 1988.

U. Information in private files

> Students of Paul D. Schriener. "Of Our Lives: A History of the 1960's and 1970's." Department of Social Studies, Munster High School, 1981.

V. An article in an on-line database

> Lankard, Bettina A. "Career Development in Generation X." <u>ERIC Clearinghouse on Adult, Career, and Vocational Education</u> (1995). Online. Internet. 3 Dec. 1996.

For the information to include in entries for other electronic sources, see page 857 of the Access Guide.

4. Proofread your work. Carefully reread your final draft and correct any errors you might have made in grammar, spelling, and mechanics. Double-check the accuracy of your quotations by proofreading them against your note cards or the original sources. Then make a clean final copy of your report, following these Modern Language Association guidelines for manuscript preparation.

MLA Manuscript Guidelines

- **Typing or printing** Type your final draft on a typewriter, or if you are using a word processor, print out a letter-quality copy. Do not justify the lines. If you have to write your final copy by hand, use dark blue or black ink and make sure your handwriting is neat and legible. Use only one side of the paper.

- **Paper** Use $8\frac{1}{2}$-by-11-inch, white, nonerasable paper.

- **Margins** Except for page numbers, leave one-inch margins on all sides of the paper. Indent the first line of each paragraph five spaces from the left margin. Indent set-off quotations (those of more than four lines) ten spaces from the left margin. Do not indent long quotations from the right.

- **Spacing** The entire paper—including the heading and title on the first page, the body of the paper, quotations, and the Works Cited list—should be double-spaced.

- **Heading and title** One inch from the top of the first page and flush with the left margin, type your name, your teacher's name, the course name, and the date on separate lines. Below this heading, center the title on the page. Do not underline the title, put it in quotation marks, or use all capital letters.

- **Page numbers** Number all pages consecutively in the upper right-hand corner, one-half inch from the top. You may type your last name before the page number to identify your work in case a page is misplaced.

5. Present your paper, then save it in your portfolio. The members of one or more of your classes may be interested in the topic of your paper. Consider using illustrations, graphs, models, or music to add interest to your oral presentation. Alternatively, you could turn your report into an electronic multimedia presentation. For help, see pages 861–863 of the Access Guide.

Michele Lin

Mrs. DeVry

English IV

12 May 1994

King Arthur: The Myth and the Monarchy

Catches the reader's attention with an engaging introduction in the form of an exciting narrative

King Arthur gazed across the battlefield. A hundred thousand knights, allies and enemies alike, lay dead. The king looked about and saw his enemy, Mordred, leaning on his sword. "Traitor!" cried the king as he ran and plunged a spear into Mordred's belly. But with his dying breath, Mordred swung his sword in a mighty arc. The blade cut through the king's helmet and sank into his skull. The king and Mordred fell.

"My time passes fast," said the wounded king to Sir Bedivere, his only surviving knight. "Take my good sword, Excalibur, and go with it to yonder water's side and throw it into the water." Sir Bedivere did so, and as the sword flew, a mysterious hand reached up from the deep, caught it by the handle, waved it three times in farewell, and disappeared.

Documents the source of the story

Then Bedivere set Arthur on a barge at the water's edge. "I must go into the vale of Avalon to heal me of my grievous wound," said the king as he sailed off into the mist. Never again was he seen (Hibbert 54–56).

This story is familiar to most readers. It is part of what may be the most famous legend in the Western world—the tale of Britain's King Arthur. The story has all the elements of a classic legend: a kind and noble king, magic spells, knights in armor, and a misty other world. Although some legends are pure fantasy, others, including this one, have a basis in fact. What parts of the King Arthur legend are true? Historians throughout the centuries haven't always told the same story. In order to determine what is real and what is fiction in the legend of King Arthur, it is necessary to examine the legend's many forms against the backdrop of what is now known about early British history.

States the central problem of the paper in a thesis statement and establishes the writer's approach

For more than a thousand years, people have been telling stories about the deeds of King Arthur and his knights. During the 700's, and even earlier, storytellers spread tales of the king's adventures across England, Scotland, Wales, Ireland, France, and the rest of Europe (Hibbert 11; Morris 117, 119). The tale differs from region to region. For example, in Cornwall, the legend goes that the land swarmed with giants until Arthur vanquished them. In Northumberland, Arthur, his queen, and his dogs are said to be asleep beneath a castle. All the legends agree on one point, however—that one day Arthur will return to save his people (Hibbert 11–12).

Presents a historical analysis, using chronological order

The tale of Arthur, "the once and future king," probably gained its greatest popularity during the twelfth century. In 1135 Geoffrey of Monmouth completed his twelve-book History of the Kings of Britain, devoting three entire books to King Arthur (Hibbert 17). Scholars agree that Geoffrey's work is a masterpiece, yet few people think that the work recounts true history. Most of his tales come from ancient stories and legends or from Geoffrey's own rich imagination. Geoffrey's purpose, many insist, was not to present historical fact but to create a national hero (Hibbert 19–21;

Williams 77, 88; Ashe 4, 25; Morris 118).

Geoffrey's tales inspired other writers (Ashe 9, 12). In 1155 Wace of Jersey wrote a long poem in French that included an account of Arthur's reign, adding information about the Round Table where Arthur's chivalrous knights met (Hibbert 21; Williams 77–78). Twenty years later, the French poet Chrétien de Troyes created another version of the tale. Set in a mystical land, the story included new characters, such as Sir Lancelot, and introduced into Arthurian legend the search for the Holy Grail, the cup used by Jesus at the Last Supper (Hibbert 21; Ashe 169; "Arthurian Legend" 603).

Over the next two hundred years, the legend spread across Europe and even Asia. New writers added stories of lost loves, noble searches, chivalrous knights, and valiant battles (Hibbert 26; Morris 118).

Finally, England's Sir Thomas Malory wove together many Arthurian tales, legends, and poems. Malory's work, published in 1485 as Le Morte Darthur (The Death of Arthur), became the classic English version of the legend, basically the tale as it is known today (Hibbert 33–34; "Arthurian Legend" 604).

In Malory's version Uther Pendragon, king of England, falls in love with the beautiful Igrayne, the wife of a mighty duke. Merlin, the king's wizard, helps Uther win Igrayne's love. In return, however, Merlin demands that the king give him the son who will be born to them. The wizard sends the son, Arthur, to live with a knight named Sir Ector (Hibbert 34–36).

Years later, according to Malory, King Uther dies

Uses concrete details and examples to develop the writer's analysis

Gives credit to several sources that agree on this point

Includes summaries of information in the writer's own words

with no known heir. Merlin advises England's leaders to wait for a sign, a miracle that will show them who should be the next king. Suddenly, a rock appears with a sword plunged into an anvil that is mounted on it. Around the sword is written, "Whoso pulleth out this sword . . . is rightwise king. . . ." Powerful knights cannot loosen the sword, yet Arthur, a young squire, easily pulls the sword from the anvil. "We will have Arthur for our king," the crowd cheers (Hibbert 36–37).

Uses an exact quotation to establish authenticity and flavor

In this way, says Malory, Arthur becomes king of England and goes on to fight evil barons, kill a thirty-foot giant, and defeat the legions of Rome. At the height of Arthur's power, the land's bravest, most honest knights join Arthur at his court, Camelot, and become part of what is known as the Round Table. The story turns tragic, however, when Arthur's queen, Guinevere, and his friend, the noble and courageous Sir Lancelot, fall in love. Arthur ultimately loses his wife, his best friend, and the knights of the Round Table who leave Camelot to search for the Holy Grail. As for Arthur, he disappears, sailing toward Avalon and suffering from a deadly wound (Hibbert 38–53).

Are these legends just myths created and embellished by storytellers and poets, or is there some truth in this tale of a powerful, noble king? Historical records are scanty, but they do provide a rough picture of a real, historical King Arthur.

Returns to the central problem

In 548, the British monk-historian Gildas wrote a work referring to a major victory over the Germanic Saxons at Mount Badon about fifty years earlier. He talks about a great leader in the battle but never mentions Arthur by name. A later biography of Gildas suggests that Arthur had killed the monk's brother in battle. For that reason, Gildas most likely hated Arthur and refused to include his name in the account of the Mount Badon victory (Hibbert 91, 93; Williams 74, 80–81).

Later historians do mention Arthur by name. In the early ninth century, the Welsh monk Nennius briefly refers to Arthur as a military commander in twelve sixth-century battles against Saxon invaders, including Mount Badon (Williams 74–75). A tenth-century chronicle, The Annals of Wales, also describes King Arthur's victory at Mount Badon and his last battle against Mordred's forces ("Arthur" 602).

Presents background information important to the central problem

To be understood, however, these clues of Arthur's existence and accomplishments must be seen against the background of British history of the fourth through sixth centuries. At the beginning of the fourth century, Britain was the western boundary of the great Roman Empire. By the late fourth century, though, that empire had begun to crumble, with barbarian tribes pressing against its borders. By the fifth century, the Romans could no longer defend their entire empire, so they gave up control over Britain (Hibbert 59; Ashe 28).

Moves coherently through a chronological sequence of key ideas

The British were not happy about their new-found freedom, however. Over the years they had become civilized and peaceful and were unable to protect their lands without help from the mighty Roman troops (Hibbert 60; Ashe 27). Yet British lands were in danger. Saxons threatened the island from lands across the

North Sea. These rugged, bearded warriors, with their short swords, iron spears, and axes, may have looked like monstrous giants to the peaceable British (Hibbert 61). The British faced other barbarian enemies too— fierce Picts from Scotland and Scotti from Ireland (Hibbert 60; Ashe 28–29).

The British searched for powerful rulers to lead them against the invaders. The first of these warrior-kings was Vortigern, who already controlled parts of Britain (Hibbert 70). Vortigern made a serious mistake, however. He allowed a band of Saxons to settle in Britain in return for their help in fighting the Picts. The plan went well at first, but the Saxons brought more and more of their warriors to Britain. These began to attack their neighbors, and the country was in a state of continual warfare (Hibbert 70–71; Ashe 38–41).

Then, around 460, a new British ruler, Ambrosius, arose. Ambrosius halted the advance of the Saxons, but when his rule ended sometime between 470 and 480, the Saxons could no longer be stopped (Morris 108). They renewed their invasion of Britain, extending their settlements as warriors won new lands (Ashe 57–58). Only a powerful new ruler could save Britain from the devastation of the Saxon advance.

Uses transitions to link paragraphs

The reign of Arthur began at this time, and records suggest that British forces began gaining ground on the Saxons. Mounted British troops defeated Saxon foot soldiers in a series of battles. After a final victory at Mount Badon, sometime between 500 and 516, the Saxon threat was temporarily halted (Morris 110–114);

Ties the background information to the central problem

Arthur had ended Britain's crisis.

Even Gildas, who did not mention Arthur by name, described the years of Arthur's reign as a time of good government and stable rule, years of "truth and justice" (Morris 117). These years were the basis of tales of a "golden age" that lasted until Arthur's death at Camlann (Morris 117, 123, 132, 140).

Can this historical background help reveal a picture of the true Arthur? He surely was not the king in shining armor and crown of Malory's story. The real Arthur probably wore the leather tunic and simple iron headpiece of a fifth-century warrior. For weapons, he would have carried a heavy iron sword and a wooden spear with an iron point. His home was most likely not a grand castle but a squat stone fortress, and his companions, rather than the courteous knights of the Round Table, were probably rugged cavalrymen like Arthur himself (Hibbert 129; Ashe 14; Goodrich 9).

Still, the historical picture of Arthur does show that there is truth in the legend. Arthur, it seems, truly did rescue his land from devastation and extend the boundaries of the British domain. He did rule as the powerful but honorable leader of a just government. Most likely, jealous lords like Mordred finally did succeed in killing Arthur and ending his "golden age."

They would never kill the people's memory of King Arthur, however. "The future needed a legend, not a history" (Morris 87, 119). It was the story of Arthur that provided the legend, one of a good and noble ruler and the everlasting "gleam of a golden age" (Morris 87).

Brings together different strands of information to draw a new conclusion about the topic

Steers the reader toward closure

Brings the paper to a satisfying conclusion by summing up the implications of the writer's research

Works Cited

"Arthur." <u>Encyclopaedia Britannica: Micropaedia.</u>
1993 ed.

"Arthurian Legend." <u>Encyclopaedia Britannica:
Micropaedia.</u> 1993 ed.

Ashe, Geoffrey. <u>The Discovery of King Arthur.</u> Garden
City: Doubleday, 1985.

Goodrich, Norma Lorre. <u>King Arthur.</u> New York:
Franklin Watts, 1986.

Hibbert, Christopher. <u>The Search for King Arthur.</u> New
York: American Heritage, 1969.

Morris, John. <u>The Age of Arthur.</u> New York: Scribner's,
1973.

Williams, Mary. "King Arthur in History and Legend."
<u>Folklore</u> Summer 1962: 73–88.

LEARNING FROM YOUR WRITING PROCESS

FOR YOUR
PORTFOLIO

1. Reflect on your writing. Think about the process you used in writing your research paper. Read the questions below to see what thoughts they stimulate. Note your answers and insights in your writing log or in an afterword that you can attach to your paper and keep in your portfolio.

- What did you learn about gathering information during the process of writing your research paper? What other applications could you find for this skill?
- How did your view of your topic change as you researched and wrote your paper? What caused your view to change?
- Are there aspects of your subject that you would like to research further?
- What did you learn about yourself from researching and writing this paper?

2. Apply your skills. Try one or more of the following activities.

- **Cross curricular** Choose any current event or circumstance that raises questions in your mind—such as a dispute between two countries, a government policy, or the rising cost of music concerts. Gather enough information to arrive at an opinion about the issue and then defend your position in a debate or discussion.
- **Literature** Think of a nonfiction book you have read that you found interesting. Do some research to see if you can independently confirm the position or point of view presented by the author of that book.
- **Related assignments** Follow the suggestions on pages 301–302 to write a plan for a career search.

Career Search

You can apply the skills you have acquired in completing this Guided Assignment to many other types of research tasks, both inside and outside of school. For example, at this time you may be getting ready to make a career choice. Before making a decision about which career to pursue, it's a good idea to do some research on the career or careers that interest you. Many of the research techniques you used in this workshop can be applied to doing research on a variety of professions that interest you. Suggestions for using these techniques appear below.

1. Examine your goals. Begin your career search by taking a good look at yourself. How important do you think a satisfying career will be to your future happiness? What are you looking for in a job or career? Where do you want this career to take you? Write in your journal about your personal goals and what types of careers you might pursue to fulfill them.

2. Examine your skills. What do you do well? What do you enjoy doing most? Make a list of your skills, and then think about which skills you'd like to use on the job. For what jobs and careers are your skills most suited?

3. Choose careers to explore. Use your goals and skills to identify careers you would like to know more about. Then choose one or more and begin your search.

4. List career search questions. Think about what you want to find out about your chosen field and make a list of questions such as the following:

- What responsibilities does a professional in this field have?
- What level of education or training is required?
- Where must people live to pursue this career?
- What is the starting salary? What is the earning potential of this career?
- What is the employment outlook for this career?
- What are the opportunities for advancement and growth in this career?
- Is there an opportunity for travel on the job?
- How satisfied are people currently working in the field?
- What political issues or economic trends are challenging people in the profession?

HANDBOOKS

FOR HELP & PRACTICE

Interviewing,
p. 336
Sources,
pp. 482–489
Evaluating Sources,
pp. 493–494
Evaluating Your
Career Options,
pp. 507–509

5. Begin searching.   As with researching a school report, you will probably want to consult a variety of sources. Your school counseling office can direct you to many sources. Here are some additional suggestions:

- **Library sources**   Consult your librarian to find out what employment reference works your library has, such as career encyclopedias and the *Occupational Outlook Handbook*. Libraries often carry professional and trade journals and magazines as well. These are helpful for finding out the latest issues, concerns, and trends in a given field.
- **Professional, trade, and union associations**   Associations often produce brochures and other materials about vocational career opportunities.
- **Interviews**   Talk to people in the career you are exploring. If you know people who do this type of work, ask them about it. If not, contact a company directly. The personnel director can give you information over the phone or make an appointment with you for an informational interview.

6. Record your findings.   Since the information you gather is for your own use, you may not choose to make a formal presentation of your findings. However, you will probably find it helpful to write about your experiences in your journal as a way of reviewing and evaluating what you have learned. This process can help you decide whether to pursue a particular career or whether to search for alternatives. You also might consider writing up your findings as a report for the school guidance office that could be useful to other students researching careers.

Sentence

Reviewing Sentence Composing Skills

In the preceding sentence composing exercises, you have studied how professional writers use openers, s-v splits, and closers singly and in combination to increase the information in their writing, to provide variety, and to create the rhythms of their style. In this lesson, you will review and practice the skills you have learned. You will also apply those skills to a piece of your own writing.

REVIEWING VARIETY IN SENTENCE OPENERS

Skill 1: Single Words as Sentence Openers (pages 173–175)

Sighing, he sat down and put on the other shoe.
Elizabeth Bowen, "Foothold"

Skill 2: Phrases as Sentence Openers (pages 173–175)

Prepositional Phrase To her astonishment, she saw that the expression on his face was one of satisfaction.
Mary Lavin, "One Summer"

Present Participial Phrase Changing into dry clothes from his cellophane pack, Mr. Benjamin Driscoll lay down and went happily to sleep.
Ray Bradbury, *The Martian Chronicles*

Past Participial Phrase Amazed at the simplicity of it all, I understood everything as never before.
Alphonse Daudet, "The Last Lesson"

Absolute Phrase Pain shooting up my entire arm, I lay panting on the edge of the pool and gingerly began to feel my wrist. **Theodore Taylor, *The Cay***

REVIEWING VARIETY IN S-V SPLITS

Skill 3: Phrases as S-V Splits (pages 203–205)

Appositive Phrase The real estate agent, an old man with a smiling, hypocritical face, soon joined them.
Willa Cather, "The Sculptor's Funeral"

Present Participial Phrase August, gasping for breath, melted into September. **Robert Lipsyte, *The Contender***

Past Participial Phrase	The tent, <u>illumined by candle</u>, glowed warmly in the midst of the plain. **Jack London, *The Call of the Wild***
Absolute Phrase	An Arab on a motorcycle, <u>his long robes flying in the wind of his speed</u>, passed John at such a clip that the spirals of dust from his turnings on the winding road looked like little tornadoes. **Elizabeth Yates, "Standing in Another's Shoes"**
Delayed Adjectives	The head of the filing department, <u>neat, quiet, attentive</u>, stood in front of the old man's desk. **James Thurber, "The Catbird Seat"**

REVIEWING VARIETY IN SENTENCE CLOSERS

Skill 4: Phrases as Sentence Closers (pages 233–235)

Appositive Phrase	The room was empty, <u>a silent world of sinks, drainboards, and locked cupboards.</u> **Frank Bonham, *Chief***
Present Participial Phrase	He turned and ran, <u>dodging through the trees.</u> **Elliott Merrick, "Without Words"**
Past Participial Phrase	I seem forever condemned, <u>ringed by walls.</u> **Richard Wright, *Black Boy***
Absolute Phrase	The parrot was gone, <u>its cake a mess of crumbs and frosting on the ground.</u> **Shirley Jackson, "Island"**
Delayed Adjectives	Our father was younger than the landlord, <u>leaner, stronger, and bigger.</u> **James Baldwin, *Tell Me How Long the Train's Been Gone***

304 Sentence Composing

23. My brother's voice, <u>sounding very suspicious</u>, spoke from within.

24. In it was a little boy in short trousers, <u>his thin legs bent under one another</u>, <u>his eyebrows cocked up rather snobbishly</u>, and <u>his twisted hand held tightly to keep it still</u>.

25. <u>Writing them down on paper with my left foot to look at them in sort of wonder</u>, I played with words like a child fascinated with a new toy.

B. Identifying Sentence Composing Skills For each sentence in Exercise A, identify the sentence composing skills the underlined parts illustrate. Some sentences illustrate more than one of the four skills.

Application Like Christy Brown, you can play with words. Without using models or writing imitations, write four sentences, each illustrating a different sentence composing skill. You may write four unrelated sentences, or you may include your sentences within a longer piece of writing.

Application The sentences below are from *Grendel,* a modern retelling of the Beowulf epic from the monster's point of view, by John Gardner. They give portions of the sequence of events when the monster Grendel raids the hall of the king. Imitate each sentence. Then choose one of your imitations and use it as the first sentence in a paragraph. Your paragraph should explain the sequence of events in an activity you have performed often, perhaps doing a household chore, practicing one technique in a sport, or going from your house to a friend's house. Use varying openers, s-v splits, and closers as you write your paragraph.

1. Behind my back, at the world's end, my pale slightly glowing fat mother sleeps on, old, sick at heart, in our dingy underground room.

2. Eleven years now and going on twelve I have come up to this clean-mown central hill, dark shadow out of the woods below, and have knocked politely on the high oak door, bursting its hinges and sending the shock of my greeting inward like a cold blast out of a cave.

3. The old Shaper, a man I cannot help but admire, goes out the back window with his harp at a single bound, though blind as a bat.

Sketchbook

Since the sixteenth century, the picaresque novel has been a popular literary form. This type of novel recounts the zany adventures of a sharp-witted rogue, or *picaro,* who often unwittingly gets into trouble. Create a picaresque hero of your own. Relate one episode from your hero's story.

Additional Sketches

Newspaper columnists often give personal accounts of or opinions about current events. Find a short, objective newspaper article about an event or incident of interest to you. Write a personal, subjective account of the event or give your opinion of the event described.

Think of a celebration that you have either participated in or seen covered in newspapers, magazines, or on television, such as a Fourth of July picnic or a Chinese New Year parade. Write a description of the celebration.

Writing for Assessment

Guided Assignment

RESPONDING TO READINGS

By now, you have quite a bit of experience using your writing skills to answer test questions. Sometimes, however, you need to call on more than your writing skills; you must use your reading comprehension skills as well. In this workshop you will study ways you can develop your ability to interpret written selections and then write effective essays about them.

Reading, as well as writing, is an essential skill for test taking. In many instances, you must apply your skills at comprehending texts before you can use your writing skills to convey the meaning you have discovered.

The two reading selections on these pages deal with the idea of "home." John Gardner describes the medieval English home, and Witold Rybczynski examines the modern home. As you read each selection, think about the similarities and differences in what each writer describes.

From

THE LIFE *and* TIMES *of* CHAUCER

by John Gardner

A modern visitor might be distressed, too, by the living arrangements: no glass windows except in the houses of the rich—places like John Chaucer's house on Thames Street and, better yet, John of Gaunt's palace on the Savoy, where the glass was stained. At night all light that might have labored in through the coarse glass windows, or the parchment windows or nothing-covered windows in poorer houses, was tightly sealed out by wooden shutters. (It made, of course, for a coziness we miss.) There were no chairs, only benches or cushioned trunks for a lady or a gouty old gentleman to sit on; at mealtimes the servants brought out trestles and table boards. There was no privacy, even in a vintner's big house. Whereas the poor lived in only one room, or at most two, in company with their chickens, pigs, geese, cats, and mice, a vintner's house might have numerous rooms, but none to be alone in. A house like Chaucer's father's would be a large building with a high stone wall and gardens around it, perhaps a few fruit trees, a house with a steeply pitched tile roof and

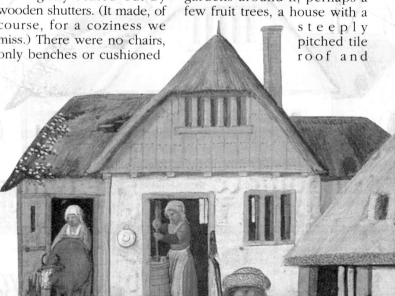

leaded-glass bay windows projecting from the second and third floors. There were various outbuildings, including a pigpen (the livestock of the citizenry was a persistent problem for town magistrates, who repeatedly issued ordinances forbidding the inhabitants to let their horses, swine, and geese run loose in the streets); and inside the house lay a labyrinth of corridors and chambers, dark arches, stairs. There would be a garret, or coalhouse, set over the great gate opening onto Thames Street and extending over whatever humble tenantries were built into the wall; there would be a "pastry house" or bakehouse, connected with the kitchen, which stood next to the central hall; a vaulted cellar and a larder house, with a buttery above, and above that a chamber, all connected by stairs; beyond the hall, the great parlor, with small chambers around it, a chapel, perhaps a privy; and there would probably be, else-where, a cloth house with closets, a bolting house, third floor garrets, and various chambers for storage, laundry, and so forth. A rich splay of rooms; but the rooms—queerly small, from a modern point of view—were for working in, never for getting away by oneself. For living there was only the great parlor and the hall, which doubled as a dining room. In the bedrooms the inhabitants slept several to a bed, usually naked, though sometimes in heavy, long nightgowns and nightcaps. (Nightgowns and nightcaps are frequently mentioned in medieval wills.) Though today we might object to sleeping several in a bed, no objection seems to have crossed medieval minds; even the gentlemen-servants to the king slept two to a bed, as Edward's Ordinances show. It may be, however, that we pay dear for our privacy. The loneliness, ennui, and alienation now so common seem to have been rare diseases in the late Middle Ages. 🐚

In 1977, on the other hand, when *Better Homes and Gardens* magazine surveyed its readers, only 15 percent preferred furniture in the "latest modern style." What the majority wanted, and continue to want, was old-fashioned—not necessarily old—furniture and traditional decor.... If department stores or home-decorating magazines are any indication, most people's first choice would be to live in rooms that resemble, as much as their budgets permit, those of their grandparents.

No one finds this peculiar. But, as Adolf Loos pointed out, such nostalgia is absent from other aspects of our everyday lives. We do not pine for period cuisine. Our concern for health and nutrition has altered the way that we eat, as well as what we eat; our admiration for the slim physique would be puzzling to the corpulent nineteenth century. We have changed our way of speaking, our manners, and our public and private behavior. We do not feel the need to revive the practice of leaving visiting cards, for example, or of indulging in extended, chaperoned courtship. A return to eighteenth-century decorum would ill suit our informal way of life. Unless we are collectors, we do not drive antique cars. We want automobiles that are less expensive to operate, safer, and more comfortable, but we do not imagine that these improvements can be achieved by resurrecting car models from previous periods. We would feel as odd in a Model T as we would in plus fours or a hooped skirt, yet although we would not think of dressing in period clothes, we find nothing strange in dressing our homes in period decor. . .

Nostalgia for the past is often a sign of dissatisfaction with the present. I have called the modern interior "a rupture in the evolution of domestic comfort." It represents an attempt not so much to introduce a new style—that is the least of it—as to change social habits, and even to alter the underlying cultural meaning of domestic comfort. Its denial of bourgeois traditions has caused it to question, and reject, not only luxury but also. . . intimacy. Its emphasis on space has caused it to ignore privacy just as its interest in industrial-looking materials and objects has led it away from domesticity. Austerity, both visual and tactile, has replaced delight. What started as an endeavor to rationalize and simplify has become a wrong-headed crusade; not, as is often claimed, a response to a changing world, but an attempt to change the way we live. It is a rupture not because it does away with period styles, not because it eliminates ornament, and not because it stresses technology, but because it attacks the very idea of comfort itself. That is why people look to the past. Their

nostalgia is not the result of an interest in archaeology, like some Victorian revivals, not a sympathy for some particular period, like Jeffersonian classicism. Nor is it a rejection of technology. People appreciate the benefits of central heating and electric lighting, but the rooms of a Colonial country home or of a Georgian mansion—which had neither—continue to attract them, for they provide a measure of something that is absent from the modern interior. People turn to the past because they are looking for something that they do not find in the present—comfort and well-being.

Think AND Respond

What themes do the selections explore? What similar ideas do Gardner and Rybczynski present? How do the selections differ? What qualities do you think are important about the concept of "home"?

A number of essay tests that are administered by classroom teachers, school districts, state agencies, colleges, and national testing organizations require you to demonstrate your ability to understand and interpret difficult reading passages at the same time that you show yourself proficient in English composition. Rather than measuring what facts you have learned and retained, such tests reveal whether you can analyze, interpret, or evaluate material. Although traditional study techniques may not be helpful, you can take several steps that will help you present your thoughts clearly within a limited time period.

This workshop will provide you with guidance and practical strategies you can use to perform effectively on tests that require you to read one or more passages and to write an essay dealing in specific ways with those passages.

PREWRITE

1. Read the question. Before you turn to the reading selection, read the question or "prompt" that will direct your writing. The prompt will give you guidance about what to look for as you read the passage.

2. Read the passage carefully. A deliberate reading is a good investment of your time. Make sure you understand the passage as you read. Don't hesitate to go back over complicated sentences or paragraphs, and don't feel discouraged by the difficulties the passage may pose for you—it was probably selected to provide a challenge. The test of a good reader is in his or her willingness to accept that challenge and to keep trying.

HANDBOOKS
FOR HELP & PRACTICE

Writing Prompts,
pp. 327–330
Graphics for
Organizing,
pp. 343–347
Reading Strategies,
p. 479
Testing,
pp. 521–532

Responding to
Readings

3. Annotate the text. As you read, mark up the text—unless you are directed not to—and make notes to help you keep track of the ideas in it. Keep these guidelines in mind.

- Look for the thesis or main idea and underline it or draw a box around it to help you refer to it later.
- Underline or put check marks next to key points and important details.
- Write your comments and questions in the margins.
- Use notes or arrows to show connections or similarities between ideas or important distinctions.
- Write brief definitions of unfamiliar terms that you figure out from context.

4. Re-read the passage. Unless it is a very long passage or a very short test, you will probably have time to re-read the reading selection. You may be surprised about how many details and important ideas slipped your attention on your first reading. Don't be surprised if your re-reading changes your mind about what the passage means.

5. Re-read the question or prompt. One key to answering essay questions is to understand what you are expected to do. Look for the words in the prompt that give you directions: *compare and contrast, define, explain, analyze, discuss.* The following lists include most of the tasks you are likely to be asked to perform in an essay test and what such tasks may entail. Note that most of the suggestions listed are really strategies for writing.

Strategies

Descriptive Tasks

If you are asked to *describe, show,* or *tell about* your subject, follow these guidelines.

- Identify the major characteristics of your subject.
- Gather details from the reading to describe your subject.
- Use a logical method of presenting your description (such as top to bottom, left to right, near to far, or most important to least important).

Explanatory and Analytic Tasks

If you are asked to *explain, analyze, interpret, examine,* or *discuss* a text or subject, use one of these methods.

- Break your subject down into its component parts or its main and subordinate ideas and then examine these parts to determine how each works or to determine the meaning of the whole.
- Analyze your subject in terms of causes and effects, problem and solution, advantages and disadvantages, or pros and cons.
- Show how the evidence presented in the text supports or fails to support the main idea or how it is sometimes contradictory.
- Explain how some parts of the passage are difficult to understand or unclear to you.

PROBLEM SOLVING

Which strategies should I use to respond to the prompt?

Defining, Classifying, and Evaluating Tasks

If you are asked to *define,* to *compare and contrast,* to *classify,* or to *evaluate* a text or subjects, use one of these approaches.

- Define a subject by describing its features and showing what distinguishes it from similar subjects.
- Classify a subject by placing it in a larger class along with other members of that class and describing the key features that unify them.
- Evaluate a topic by comparing it against a standard or set of criteria for judging.
- Compare and contrast subjects, that is, discuss their similarities and differences either feature by feature or by describing all the features of one and then of the other.

Argumentative Tasks

If you are asked to *argue for a point of view, persuade* somebody, *agree or disagree, take a side,* or *give your opinion* on a controversial question, use one of these methods.

- State your position and then give clear and logical reasons to support your position.
- Acknowledge opposing arguments and deal with them.
- Acknowledge complexity and ambiguity—that neither position may be entirely right or the issues not clear.
- Show the strengths and weaknesses of both sides and refuse to take a side, if you think neither is more correct.

Reflective Tasks

If you are asked to *reflect on, respond to, comment on, give your opinion on* or *discuss* a subject, you might use any of the following approaches.

- Elaborate on your own point of view on your subject.
- Talk about how your view of the subject changed from your first reading to the second.
- Discuss other texts that illuminate or might be illuminated by your text.
- Discuss how the text influenced your thinking, surprised you, made you angry, or moved you in some other way.
- Agree or disagree with the position taken in the text and give your reasons.

6. Plan your response. Some students find it helpful to jot down words and phrases without worrying about logical order. Then they organize their notes by numbering them. Others like to take notes in a modified outline form. Reread the selection as necessary to increase your understanding and gather pertinent details.

Whatever organizational method you use, keep the time factor in mind. Pacing is very important. Plan out how much time you can devote to each part of your outline or each point you will cover. In this way, you will not be left with a great deal to say and no time to respond.

To respond to the prompt on page 312, Paula first identified her basic writing decisions. Then, because she was asked to compare and contrast, she made notes by listing information in two columns and in order of their importance.

Gardner
describes medieval house—not
comfortable in modern sense—
purpose not to provide a place
of comfort but to provide rooms
for working—point is that homes
did not foster privacy but
community and warmth

Rybczynski
writes about the modern
home and how we furnish
our homes in ways that
evoke the past

DRAFT AND DISCOVER

1. Develop a thesis statement. A thesis statement contains your main idea and shows that you understand the question. It keeps you on track as you write. Paula wrote this thesis statement.

> Both Gardner and Rybczynski agree that although home life in the past was not physically comfortable or convenient, it provided a sense of well-being and intimacy that, according to Rybczynski, we try to recreate in our homes today.

2. Organize your draft. Compose your answer in three parts: an introduction, a body, and a conclusion. The introduction includes your thesis statement and briefly previews points you will cover. The body supports each point with specific details, appropriate facts, and opinions from the selection. Use transition words to connect ideas smoothly. You may end in one of these ways:

- referring to your thesis statement (in different words);
- summarizing your points;
- drawing a conclusion about the importance of your points; or
- making a recommendation or stating your opinion.

3. Write to your audience. Remember that one goal of assessment is to determine how effectively you can communicate in standard formal English. Therefore, you should use a friendly straightforward style. Avoid trying to impress your readers with unnaturally inflated diction. The use of slang or trite expressions is also inappropriate.

HANDBOOKS
FOR HELP & PRACTICE

**Thesis Statements,
p. 349
Elaborative Details,
pp. 376–378
Unity/Coherence,
pp. 382–391**

4. Reread your draft. Once you complete your draft, take time to look it over. Ask yourself the following questions.

R E V I E W   Y O U R   W R I T I N G

- Does my response directly address the reading selections?
- Have I included specific evidence from the selections?
- Is my response in an appropriate form?
- Is my response organized effectively?

R EVISE YOUR WRITING

FOR HELP & PRACTICE

Introductions/ Conclusions, pp. 365–375

Revising Effectively, pp. 392–396

Improving Sentences, pp. 402–411

Varieties of Language, pp. 429–433

Avoiding Logical Fallacies, pp. 477–478

1. Compare your work against criteria for evaluation. Because you are writing specifically for evaluation, keep in mind the qualities most evaluators will be looking for.

Standards for Evaluation

An effective essay on a reading selection . . .

- demonstrates an understanding of the reading selection or selections at more than a superficial level.
- fulfills the task assignment specified in the prompt.
- is organized around a clear, single, central idea or thesis or main idea.
- is expressed clearly, using precise language and a style that is neither overly casual nor pretentiously academic.
- demonstrates a willingness to think seriously and honestly about a subject rather than to sacrifice intellectual honesty to presumptions about what readers want to hear.
- shows a willingness to learn from a writing assignment, even if it entails acknowledging changes in thinking in the middle of an essay.

2. Evaluate your response. You won't have much time to change your essay, but you should take time to reread the question and be sure you understood and responded to the key words. Also review your prewriting notes to make sure you included everything you planned to. You can neatly strike out passages or insert additional words or lines with a carat. As a last step, go back and correct any spelling and punctuation errors. Paula's final essay follows.

ONE STUDENT'S PROCESS

NAME <u>Paula Guajardo</u>   GRADE   <u>12</u>

In these passages, both John Gardner and Witold Rybczynski write about the idea of home. Gardner describes how people lived in the late Middle Ages, and Rybczynski writes about contemporary homes. They agree that, although home life in the past was not physically comfortable or convenient, it provided a sense of well-being and intimacy that, according to Rybczynski, we are trying to recreate in our homes today.

Gardner depicts the medieval house as dark and small and sometimes airless—but cozy. The rooms were small and tacked on to one another haphazardly; and there were, in the houses of the rich, numerous rooms to provide space for work and storage but not for providing individuals with privacy. There were no designated areas for public and for private space. Gardner suggests, though, that the lack of privacy and enforced community were not necessarily bad. He notes that people in the Middle Ages seemed not to have suffered from the boredom and loneliness so common in modern American life.

Rybczynski agrees with Gardner that contemporary Americans are seeking peace at home. He says that is why we look to the past when we furnish our homes— to recreate the sense of well-being and satisfaction missing from modern home life with its clinical-looking stark colors and sharp interiors. We don't want to give up electricity and central air, he argues, but we are trying to create more liveable environments.

These ideas appeal to me because I am most comfortable when I have the happy clutter of my things about me and when people I care about are near. I see the desire to create intimacy more and more—in the dentist's waiting room that looks like a den and in classrooms that feel warm and cozy. Although no one would want the total lack of privacy characteristic of Medieval home life, it is psychologically important for humans to feel comfortable and connected to others at home— and both Gardner and Rybczynski seem to agree.

Explores similarities and differences between two essays

Uses specific detail from the selection

Identifies point of agreement between the two selections

Interior of a Kitchen, Beuckelaer, The Louvre, Paris

Responding to Readings

The more you practice responding to written prompts the more comfortable you will feel. Try these topics for practice.

Topic 1

This passage from Willa Cather's *A Lost Lady* introduces the character Ivy Peters. Describe the kind of person Ivy seems to be and explain how the passage achieves this impression. Finally, predict what kind of activity Ivy will involve himself in.

> George and Niel hated to look at Ivy,—and yet his face had a kind of fascination for them. It was red, and the flesh looked hard, as if it were swollen from bee-stings, or from an encounter with poison ivy. This nickname, however, was given him because it was well known that he had "made away" with several other dogs before he had poisoned the judge's friendly water spaniel. The boys said he took a dislike to a dog and couldn't rest until he made an end of him. Ivy's red skin was flecked with tiny freckles, like rust spots, and in each of his hard cheeks there was a curly indentation, like a knot in a tree-bole,—two permanent dimples which did anything but soften his countenance. His eyes were very small, and an absence of eyelashes gave his pupils the fixed, unblinking hardness of a snake's or a lizard's. His hands had the same swollen look as his face, and were deeply creased across the back and knuckles, as if the skin were stretched too tight. He was an ugly fellow, Ivy Peters, and he liked being ugly.

Topic 2

Edward Abbey writes about his home state of Arizona in the following passage. Analyze Abbey's attitude toward his home state and explain how the style and tone of the passage function in expressing that attitude.

> But Arizona is something different. Or was. There is nothing in Arizona that much resembles Europe or the East except the slums along the railroad tracks in Flagstaff. Arizona has some pretty mountains too, like Colorado, but mostly and essentially, Arizona is desert country. High desert in the north, low desert in the south, ninety percent of my state is an appalling burnt-out wasteland, a hideous Sahara with a few oases, a grim bleak harsh overheated sun-blasted . . . inferno. Arizona is the

native haunt of the scorpion, the solpugid, the sidewinder, the tarantula, the vampire bat, the conenose kissing bug, the vinegarroon, the centipede, and three species of poisonous lizard: namely, the Gila monster, the land speculator, and the real estate broker. Arizona is where the Apaches live, who used to suspend their prisoners head-down above a slow fire . . . . Arizona is where the vultures swarm like flies about the starving cattle on the cow-burnt range. In Arizona the dust storms carry lung fungus . . . . Arizona is the land-fraud capital of the world. Keep a firm grip on your shirt. Because of the parched air and the hard water, Arizonans come down with more kidney stones per pelvis than any place outside of Chad and southern Libya. In Arizona the trees have thorns and the bushes spines and the swimming pools are infested with loan sharks, automobile dealers and Mafiosi. The water table is falling and during a heavy wind you can see sand dunes form on Central Avenue in Phoenix. We have the most gorgeous sunsets in the Western World—when the copper smelters are shut down. I am describing the place I love. Arizona is my natural native home. Nobody in his right mind would want to live here.

Sentence

Author's Expansions
Adding Phrases and Clauses, Exercise C, page 111

1. Wanting to whistle, to do something to bring noise and movement into the house, she turned and opened the door on her right and stepped into the dim crowded parlor.

2. Professor Kazin, wearing a spotlessly white tropical suit and a wide-brimmed hat, was the first ashore.

3. He moved restlessly, looking round as though expecting to see someone sneaking up on him.

4. He had become part of the group of young unemployed, who hung about on pavements, sat around in cafés, sometimes did odd jobs, went to the cinema, rushed about on motorbikes or in borrowed cars.

Varying Sentence Openers, Exercise C, page 175

1. Filled with joy, Vera took the letter.

2. Sitting in the mouth of his cave, gazing up at the farther peaks on which there were still patches of snow, he spent a day in idleness.

3. Sometimes, mounted on an old saddle, with shrill cries of encouragement, Jody rode out beyond the room.

4. Although they lived in style, they always felt an anxiety in the house.

5. There, between two trees, against a background of gaunt black rocks, was a figure from a dream, a strange beast that was horned and drunken-legged, but like something he had never even imagined.

6. Trying the doors as he went, twirling his club with many intricate and artful movements, turning now and then to cast his watchful eye down the pacific thoroughfare, the officer, with his stalwart form and slight swagger, made a fine picture of a guardian of the peace.

Varying S-V Splits, Exercise B, page 204

1. There had followed a time of such happiness that Chips, remembering it long afterward, hardly believed it could ever have happened before or since in the world.

2. Old Mrs. Beal, her Sunday black billowing in the wind, was homeward bound from dinner with her daughter.

3. Across an immense ethereal gulf, intellects vast, cool, and unsympathetic, regarded this earth with envious eyes and slowly drew their plans against us.

4. Mr. Cattanzara, a stocky, bald-headed man who worked in a change booth on an IRT station, lived on the next block after George's, above a shoe repair shop.

Varying Sentence Closers, Exercise C, page 235

1. He grabbed the shield again, twisting it as he pulled.

2. Towser roused himself under Fowler's desk and scratched another flea, his leg thumping hard against the floor.

3. Halfway there he heard the sound he dreaded, the hollow, rasping cough of a horse.

4. The other shoji slammed open, and unseen, Buntaro stamped away, followed by the guard.

5. In the fishpond the hippo belched, not softly.

Combining Sentence Variations, Exercise B, pages 266–267

1. At the gate, I show the pass to a young Japanese private, the sentry.

2. Janet, pausing half-way down to say something to someone above, stood there as if painted, distinct and unreal.

3. Absorbed, taking no heed of other people, he went about with a sort of stealth, seeking inwardly for luck.

4. After perhaps a seventh attempt he slipped from the wooden ledge and fell, fluttering his wings, onto his back on the windowsill.

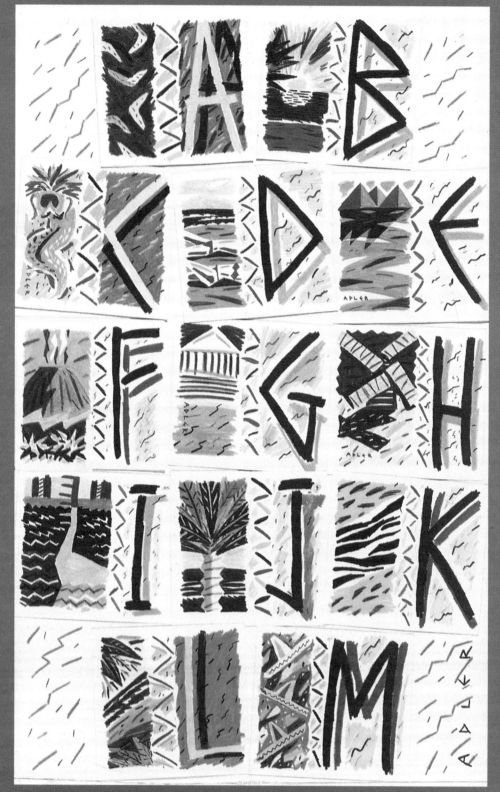

Travel Alphabet, Alan Nils Adler, 1983

Writing Handbook

Sketchbook

One evening I was walking along a path, the city was on one side and the fjord below. I felt tired and ill. I stopped and looked out over the fjord—the sun was setting, and the clouds turning blood-red. I sensed a scream passing through nature; it seemed to me that I heard the scream. I painted this picture, painted the clouds as actual blood. The colour shrieked.

Edvard Munch
DIARY

The Scream, by Edvard Munch, 1893

For Norwegian artist Edvard Munch, the surrounding landscape and his own state of mind combined to produce a powerful emotional response—so powerful that he "sensed a scream passing through nature." Have you ever experienced anything like that? Have you ever felt like the figure in the painting? What emotions does this painting stir in you?

Additional Sketches

Think of a color. Then think of a memory you associate with that color.

The humorist Roy Blount once wrote a song entitled, "I'm just a Bug on the Windshield of Life." What are you?

Writing Prompts and Writing Decisions

Before beginning a writing project, you probably will find it helpful to analyze the activity as a whole and the individual parameters you will have to consider. Questions such as the following may help you focus your thinking.

- What is my purpose in writing this piece? Who will read it?
- What do I already know about the topic, and what do I need to research?

WRITING PROMPTS

There are three major categories of writing: self-prompted, prompted by others, and done for assessment. Self-prompted writing is personal writing done to fulfill your own purposes or for your own pleasure. Writing prompted by others includes class assignments, reports, and memos. Writing done for assessment purposes includes college entrance examinations and job applications.

Self-Prompted Writing Some writing that you do for yourself is utilitarian, or practical, such as filling out forms and writing letters of complaint. Other self-prompted writing you will do simply because you enjoy it. This type of writing includes poems, journal entries, and personal letters.

The variables of practical self-prompted writing are largely predetermined. If you write a letter requesting information about summer-school programs at a local college, for example, your topic, form, purpose, audience, and tone are already established. In doing creative self-prompted writing, on the other hand, you have complete freedom to determine all of the variables of your work.

WRITER TO WRITER

Each time I write, no matter what the form or subject, it is an expression of me.

Brandy Barton, student
Cedar Rapids, Iowa

Writing Prompts and
Writing Decisions   **327**

Writing for Others In school, you often write in response to prompts supplied by your teachers. Some of the writing you do

after you graduate will also be prompted by others. Some jobs, including newspaper reporting and writing advertising copy, require people to write all the time. Even nonwriting jobs involve writing: for example, scientists write proposals, lab reports, and articles for journals; accountants and salespeople write business letters and reports.

Writing for Assessment A unique kind of writing prompted by others is writing done for assessment purposes. This kind of writing occurs throughout your academic life—on essay tests, college entrance examinations, and entrance exams for many training programs. Often, job applicants also must submit letters explaining their qualifications for employment. Many jobs require people to pass written examinations for promotions to higher positions. The following guidelines should help you respond to a writing prompt on a test or application.

Guidelines: Writing for Assessment

1. Read the question over until you understand all of its parts. Look for key words, such as *explain, describe, analyze,* and *classify* that give specific directions.

2. Briefly consider your topic, purpose, form, and audience.

3. Make some notes or an informal outline on a piece of scrap paper or in your head.

4. Develop a thesis statement that sets a goal for your writing, and state it at the beginning of the piece.

5. Make a list of the main points that you will present to support the thesis statement.

6. As you write, use transitions to connect your ideas.

7. End with a strong conclusion.

8. If you have time, reread and revise your work.

WRITING VARIABLES

Analyzing a writing prompt by breaking it down into its parts, or variables, enables you to make decisions about each variable separately, and then to examine the relationships of all the variables to one another. Some of the key writing variables are listed in the following chart.

Writing Variable	Definition	Examples
Topic	what you write about	*perestroika*, recycling
Form	the shape of the piece of writing	research paper, radio script, memo, blank verse
Purpose	overall goal to be accomplished by the piece of writing	to explain, to entertain, to persuade, to teach, to figure something out
Personal Goals	specific goal(s) that you want the writing to accomplish	to work out a problem, to create a particular mood, to impress your boss
Audience	the people for whom you are writing	your co-workers, yourself, your classmates, your friends and neighbors
Voice	your tone and personal writing style	objective or subjective, formal or informal, serious or mocking, disapproving or supportive

Although writing involves making decisions about these variables, there are no strict rules about when in the writing process you should consider them. In fact, some decisions may not be made until you are well into the drafting process. However, when you examine a writing prompt, identify which variables have already been specified and which you can select.

Sometimes a predetermined writing variable can make the task of writing seem impossible. For example, what can you do if you must write about a topic that doesn't interest you or for an audience that intimidates you?

Try not to let your writing process be undermined by a topic that bores you. Instead, look for an aspect of the topic that has some interest for you and start writing about that aspect. Getting involved in part of an assigned topic may help you find a personal approach to the topic as a whole.

"Fellow octopi, or octopuses...octopi?...Dang, it's hard to start a speech with this crowd."

If you must write for a difficult audience, before you write ask yourself, "What is hard for me about this audience?" Many people find it easier to write for classmates or for a teacher they know than for strangers. You might try writing a draft for your favorite audience first, and then revise it for the audience you find difficult.

Remember that your most important audience is *yourself*. It is often helpful to write early drafts just for *yourself*—so you can feel safe to experiment with new techniques. Then you can revise these drafts to suit the needs of other audiences.

Practice Your Skills

For each of the following writing prompts, decide which writing variables are given and which still need to be determined. Then provide the missing writing variables for each prompt, including reasons for your choices. If any of the variables is problematic for you, indicate how you would deal with the problem.

- Your history teacher asks you to write about the civil rights movement.
- Your boss tells you to write a memo briefing other employees on changes in the sick-day policy.
- You decide to write a personal letter.

Generating Ideas for Writing

Have you ever wondered where the really successful writing ideas come from—the ones behind popular books, movies, and television programs? There's really nothing mysterious about the process of coming up with writing ideas. You can generate compelling ideas for your own writing by learning a few simple techniques for stimulating creative thinking.

REFLECTING AND OBSERVING

Two basic approaches to idea generation are (1) recalling and reflecting and (2) observing and responding. The first is directed inward; the second, outward.

Recalling and Reflecting

If you sit quietly and let your mind drift back into the past, you can often **recall** vividly the sights, sounds, smells, tastes, and feelings of a previous event in your life. If you start to **reflect** about the significance of the event, relating your recollection to your present-day experience and observations, you will often experience the surprise of discovery and find the germ of a writing idea starting to take shape in your mind.

To illustrate, suppose you begin by thinking about a camping trip you once took in the mountains. Soon you might start asking yourself what made the trip so memorable. After reflection, you might decide that camping always brings out the best in people. Now you have the glimmer of a writing idea. Perhaps you could write a play in which two enemies find themselves in a situation where they must camp in the woods together.

WRITER TO WRITER

For me the initial delight is in the surprise of remembering something I didn't know I knew. . . . There is a glad recognition of the long lost, and the rest follows. Step by step the wonder of unexpected surprise keeps growing.

Robert Frost, writer and poet

Observing and Responding

When you **observe** and **respond,** you see beyond the surface of things. You might look at a friend as she talks and hear her words but not recognize what she is thinking. If you are a sensitive observer, however, you will watch her eyes, listen to the tone of her voice, and draw inferences about what she is feeling. Such active, responsive observation can lead you to new insights and provide you with new ideas for writing.

Suppose that you are at an aquarium and you notice a child watching a brightly colored fish swim in and out of the tentacles of an anemone. Observing this child might lead you to think about how people often lose their sense of wonder as they grow up. Later, in a quiet moment of contemplation, you might decide to write a poem on that subject.

GATHERING INFORMATION

You can learn to supplement your own reflections and observations with those of other people. Several techniques can help you tap this information as a new source of writing ideas.

Gleaning

When you **glean,** you gather bits and pieces of information from conversations, newspapers, television programs, and other sources you encounter. You can glean at any time and in any place. All you need to do is collect interesting details, looking for a "writable" idea. You then examine all its different facets and ramifications.

Browsing

Casually leafing through books and magazines, called **browsing,** often helps you find new ideas for writing. You can browse through subject area sections of bookstores, libraries, or even computer information services.

Clip Files

If you come across an article that you want to keep for future reference, you might clip it out and file it, or else photocopy it. It's a good idea to record the name, date, and page number on the clip so that you can document quotations you may later use.

ELABORATING ON YOUR OBSERVATIONS

There are many techniques for "mining" your observations and reflections for ideas, including thinking techniques, writing techniques, sharing techniques, and others. At first you may choose to respond simply by thinking. Later, you may want to write your ideas down, share them, or interpret them with graphics, questioning, and research.

Thinking Techniques

The most immediate way you can expand upon what you've observed or recalled is through creative thinking processes such as imaging, conducting a knowledge inventory, and using trigger words and pictures.

Imaging Much of what you've experienced is stored in your brain as mental images. You can respond to what you've observed, recalled, or reflected on by using a technique called **imaging.** When you image, you recall ideas and memories by clearing your mind of distractions and concentrating only on the sensory qualities of your remembered subject—its look, sound, feel, taste, and smell. List all the details you can envision.

Knowledge Inventory A **knowledge inventory** helps you discover what you already know about a subject, which will often be much more than you are aware of knowing. You complete a knowledge inventory by jotting down, in list form, every fact you can think of regarding a subject. Then you can list questions you still have about the subject.

Trigger Words and Pictures **Trigger words** are words that stimulate your idea-generation process. Finding trigger words can be as simple as flipping through a dictionary or browsing through a magazine. To use a trigger word, start by thinking about its traditional meaning. Then free-associate or cluster to discover alternate meanings, metaphorical relationships, or other less ordinary meanings. Here are some examples of trigger words.

blackout	treasure	detention	masquerade
cult	crisis	graduation	solstice
xenophobia	fantasy	hoax	avalanche
ingenuity	accomplice	opportunity	waterhole

Just as words can trigger your imagination, so can visual images in the world around you or in fine art or photographs. Look at a picture and ask yourself questions such as the following: How could I describe what I see in this picture? How does this picture make me feel? What might have occurred just prior to the scene shown? Could the people in this picture make good characters in a story?

Breeze at Work, Sandy Skoglund, 1987

Writing Techniques

Once you've discovered ideas through reflecting and responding to your observations, you can use the following prewriting techniques to build on those ideas: using a journal, freewriting, looping, listing, and internal dialogue.

Journals A **journal** is your creation, your own place to record your thoughts. It can also become one of the most powerful writing tools you will ever use. As your entries accumulate, your journal becomes a sourcebook for your writing ideas, a place to collect memorable passages from other people's writing, and a laboratory for trying out ideas and writing styles.

Freewriting and Looping **Freewriting** is the written equivalent of letting your mind wander. Without paying attention to grammar, mechanics, or logic, you write continuously for a given amount of time. Freewriting helps you find new approaches to a topic. **Looping** takes freewriting a step farther. After you freewrite, you examine what you wrote to find your best idea. This idea then becomes a new subject for a second loop of freewriting. Repeat the loop at least once. By the end of your third or fourth loop, you should be able to identify and narrow your writing topic.

Listing Making a **list** can help you organize ideas, examine them, and identify areas where you need to do further research. Listing parts of a whole or steps in a process will help you determine order and relationships as well as provide you with an outline for your writing. By annotating the list with questions, you can often discover other possible ideas for writing.

Internal Dialogue Here are three different ways to use **internal dialogue** to generate writing ideas.

1. Interview yourself thoroughly about a topic. Write down your questions and answers.
2. Hold a dialogue between two parts of yourself—between your mind and your emotions, your studious self and your playful self, your angry self and your loving self.
3. Take on the roles of two characters, or of a character and some idea or object, to debate an issue.

Regardless of whether or not the conversation makes sense, it will still help you generate ideas and see ideas and issues from different perspectives.

Sharing Techniques

Other people can often provide valuable perspectives on your ideas. Some effective sharing techniques that you can use to generate useful ideas include brainstorming, interviewing, discussion, and idea exchanges.

Brainstorming Free generation of ideas in a group setting, or **brainstorming,** can be an exciting way to expand on your observations. When you brainstorm, you and others simply come up with as many ideas as you can without stopping to critique or examine them. A brainstorming session should have the atmosphere of a free-for-all, and no idea should be discarded.

Interviewing   One of the most useful ways to explore a topic is **interviewing.** Simply find someone who knows a great deal about your topic, and talk to him or her about it. The interview can be informal, or it can involve elaborate planning, with questions written out beforehand and a formal appointment for a question-and-answer session.

Discussion   A **discussion,** of course, is simply the act of getting together with others to talk about a topic. Perhaps you will have a discussion leader, who helps the group define key terms, keeps order during the conversation, and summarizes the main points.

Idea Exchange   You may wish to organize a group of friends or classmates into a writing group that meets frequently and exchanges ideas. You might also set up a file of writing ideas to which everyone contributes and from which everyone can draw. Such a file is called an **idea exchange.**

Practice Your Skills

Follow the directions given below. After completing each activity, record your writing ideas in your journal or write them on a page to be saved in your writing portfolio. You can refer to your collection of writing ideas later when you need a subject about which to write.

1. Think about a special place you have visited. Make a chart listing your memories of the place. What sights, sounds, smells, and feelings do you associate with the place?
2. Browse through an encyclopedia or dictionary and choose some physical object that interests you. Conduct a knowledge inventory to investigate what you already know about the object. Then come up with at least three different writing ideas—one for a factual piece, one for a persuasive piece, and one for a literary work such as a poem or short story.
3. Choose an important decision or crisis currently facing politicians in your city or state, or in the country as a whole. Write a dialogue in which two characters take opposing viewpoints on your subject. Based on your dialogue, jot down three or four ideas for pieces that you might write.
4. Imagine that you are going to write an article for your school newspaper on an aspect of the arts in your school—dance, art, film, or music. Interview a teacher or student involved in the art program you have chosen to investigate. Use the results of the interview to write down several ideas for your article.

Focusing Ideas

Once you have generated some writing ideas and have reflected, observed, and expanded on your observations, you can begin to focus on a topic suitable for your writing activity.

LIMITING YOUR TOPIC

Is it better to write about African music or about the group Ladysmith Black Mambazo? The answer depends on what kind of writing you want to do.

Determining Factors

The principal factors that determine how you should limit a topic are your purpose, intended audience, and length and format requirements.

Purpose If your purpose is to provide a general survey of a topic, you can choose a fairly broad topic. Usually, however, you will want to include as much detailed information as possible, so you will need to narrow your topic.

Audience If your audience is well informed about your subject, you can either present your topic in broad terms or focus on very specialized information. If your audience is unfamiliar with your subject, you will need to focus on a narrow aspect of the topic, providing a great deal of detailed information.

Length and Format Requirements When you are writing in response to a classroom or publication prompt, you must consider length and format requirements. Usually you will want to limit your topic so that you can elaborate it fully in the available space.

Techniques for Limiting a Topic

Several techniques that you can use to explore and elaborate on a topic can also help you focus your topic. These techniques include brainstorming, questioning, browsing in books and magazines, and using graphic devices.

Brainstorming Enlist the help of other writers in a brainstorming session. Present your general topic to your group and see what specific aspects of the topic occur to them.

Questioning Asking questions about a general topic can help you generate a list of more focused topics related to it. For example, you might ask yourself the following questions.

- What issue or aspect of this topic matters most to me?
- What is at stake for me or my audience with regard to this topic?
- What is the most interesting aspect of this topic?

Other types of questions that can help you focus a topic—action questions, category questions, and creative questions and Aristotelian invention—are discussed in "Using Questioning Techniques," pages 376–378.

Browsing and Research Sometimes, just leafing through books, magazines, or reference works can give you ideas for a focused topic. If you are writing a factual piece, make a list of questions for research. As you use reference works to find answers, you may discover an aspect of your topic that you want to pursue further.

Graphic Devices Charting, clustering, and mapping are a few of the graphic devices that might help you to narrow a topic. For more specific information on using graphic devices like these, see Writing Handbook 4, pages 339–347.

W R I T E R   T O   W R I T E R

As soon as I pick a topic, I write that topic in the center of my paper and make a cluster map.

Ryan Fiel, student
San Marcos, California

Practice Your Skills

Match each broad topic from the list on the left with a writing format from the list on the right. Then, limit each broad topic by questioning, brainstorming, or using a graphic device.

Broad Topics	**Writing Formats**
Careers	six-page short story
The Future	fifteen-page story
Community Problems	three-minute speech
Other Cultures	ten-minute oral report

Applying Graphic Devices

A **graphic device** is a visual representation of things, ideas, and the relationships among them. Writers often use graphic devices throughout the writing process to limit or focus topics, to gather or generate ideas, and to organize their material.

Each graphic you'll learn about can function in more than one way and at different stages of your writing process. The usefulness of all types of graphic devices is limited only by your imagination.

GRAPHICS FOR EXPLORING IDEAS AND FOCUSING TOPICS

Some graphic devices are useful for exploring ideas—for developing writing topics, gathering general information and specific details, and limiting and focusing topics. These graphics include cluster maps, tree diagrams, observation charts, pro-and-con charts, and evaluation matrices.

Cluster Maps and Tree Diagrams Graphic devices that help you explore ideas related to a general topic or central idea include **cluster maps** and **tree diagrams** (or spider maps). Graphics like these can help you both broaden the range of your thinking and limit the focus of your ideas. In a cluster map, the central idea is broken down into subordinate or related ideas connected to it with lines.

Cluster Map

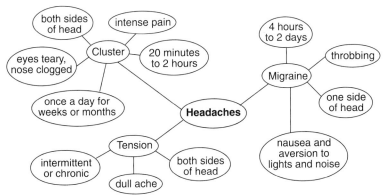

Applying Graphic
Devices   **339**

A tree diagram differs from a cluster map in certain respects, but it functions in the same way. The main idea is at the bottom or top, and the related ideas "branch out" from there.

Tree Diagram

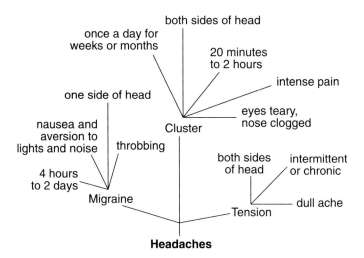

Pro-and-Con Charts   You can explore and compare the positive and negative aspects of an idea or course of action by making a **pro-and-con chart.** This type of chart can help you explore two sides of an issue. If you were preparing for a debate on the subject of nuclear energy, for example, you could list arguments in a chart as shown below.

Pro-and-Con Chart **Nuclear Energy**	
Pros	**Cons**
Decreases dependence on foreign oil.	Produces hazardous wastes that cannot be disposed of safely.
Does not create adverse greenhouse effects like the burning of fossil fuels.	Creates potential for a major accident (as at Chernobyl).
Can be abundantly produced.	Is associated with leaks of radiation into environment.

Observation Charts If you plan to write about a place or situation, you can make an **observation chart** to record information gathered through the five senses. The following chart was created by a student who was planning to write about her scuba-diving experience.

Observation Chart	
Diving on a Coral Reef	
Sight	Underwater things appear closer and larger; as you descend, lose colors: first the reds, then the yellows, finally, the blues
	Elkhorn, staghorn, and other corals; enormous multicolored sponges; starfish; urchins; angelfish; burrfish; porcupine fish; puffers; giant flounder; trumpetfish; moray eels; bull shark, lemon shark, tiger shark
Touch	Weightlessness in water, like an astronaut (hydronaut?); tightness of dive mask; caution not to touch anything under water because of damage that can be done to the marine life
Taste	Taste of salt water; bitter rubber of mouthpiece
Hearing	Sound amplified under water; faraway boat sounds as if it is about to run over you; wonderful quiet of the deeper water—no conversation, no cars, no telephones, no loud radios—just a meditative calmness and the sound of your own breathing through the regulator
Smell	Smell of salt sea air; diving equipment (rubber and silicone); fish

Evaluation Matrices An **evaluation matrix** is used for making evaluations, or judgments. Begin by listing the parts of the subject or idea that you want to evaluate. Then list criteria by which each part should be judged. Finally, make judgments based on each of your criteria. Suppose, for example, that you want to write a review of a short story you've read. You might make an evaluation matrix like the one shown on the next page.

Evaluation Matrix
Short Story by Classmate

Narrative Element	Criteria	Evaluation
Character	1. Dialogue is natural, distinct.	1. Yes, especially dialect of main character.
	2. Characters have distinct personalities, histories, values, and motivations.	2. Antagonist is a bit weak.
	3. Interactions are interesting.	3. Yes!
Setting	1. Time and place are clear.	1. & 2. Could make setting clearer with fewer and more precise details.
	2. Details are included that create the texture, the feel, of the setting.	
	3. The setting evokes a mood.	3. Yes—of hilarity.
Plot	1. A conflict is introduced and resolved.	1. Yes.
	2. Twists in the plot are surprising.	2. The resolution is particularly surprising—well done.
Theme	1. The message of the story is significant and original, not a cliché.	1. Yes—humorously depicts human nature.
	2. Theme grows out of the events in the story.	2. Yes—characters' interactions make it clear.

GRAPHICS FOR ORGANIZING IDEAS

Graphic devices are useful for organizing ideas and information during the writing process. Graphics that are particularly useful for organizing ideas include analysis frames, category charts, compare-and-contrast charts and Venn diagrams, flowcharts, inductive reasoning frames, plot diagrams, and time lines. Organizing your information in one of these graphics may help you get ready to write. You may, however, prefer to organize your ideas visually in the middle of the drafting process or when you're ready to make revisions.

Analysis Frames   You can use an **analysis frame** to break down a subject into its component parts. To construct an analysis frame, write the subject at the top of the chart. Then list its parts as column headings, and describe each part in the appropriate column.

If you were writing a report on different ways the media handle a major news item, you might first break the subject into its parts as in the following analysis frame to ensure your full coverage of the topic.

Analysis Frame
National Media

Print	Broadcast	Narrowcast
newspapers magazines	television networks radio, AM and FM	cable television pay television computer networks

Category Charts   You can use a **category chart** to classify things or ideas according to their qualities, characteristics, or membership in a group. Note how the following chart categorizes some of the most popular television shows of the 1970's.

Category Chart Hit Prime-Time Television Programs in the 1970's		
Serial Comedy	**Serial Drama**	**Variety Shows**

All in the Family
The Brady Bunch
Sanford and Son
Happy Days
The Odd Couple
Laverne and Shirley
	The Waltons
	Family
	Little House on
	  the Prairie
	Kojak
	Mission Impossible
	Marcus Welby, M.D.
		Sonny and Cher
		The Carol
		  Burnett Show
		Hee Haw
		Donny and Marie
		Captain and
		  Tenille

Comparison-and-Contrast Charts and Venn Diagrams   To organize ideas by their similarities and differences, use either a **comparison-and-contrast chart** or a **Venn diagram.** Like the cluster map and tree diagram, these two graphics have different structures but function in the same way. Note how similarities and differences between the novel and the epic poem are organized in the following graphics.

Comparison-and-Contrast Chart Epic Poem Versus Novel	
Similarities	1. Narrative 2. Relatively long 3. Subplots 4. Room for character development
Differences	1. Novel originally and most often deals with realistic material; epic usually fantasy. 2. Divine forces often intervene in epics; gods usually don't play a role in novel. 3. Epic usually told in poetry; novel in prose.

Venn Diagram

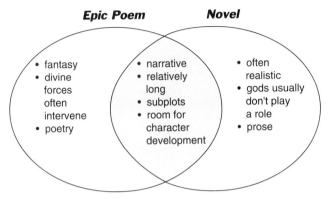

Epic Poem   **Novel**

- fantasy
- divine forces often intervene
- poetry

- narrative
- relatively long
- subplots
- room for character development

- often realistic
- gods usually don't play a role
- prose

Flowcharts   You can use a **flowchart** to help you organize the stages in a process or the steps necessary to complete an activity. In flowcharts used by professionals such as businesspeople and computer scientists, an oval usually stands for start or stop, a diamond for a question or point of decision, and a rectangle for an action. Use these symbols or any other shapes you like. In a flowchart like the one shown below, the stages or steps are listed in order and are connected by arrows that show direction of movement.

Flowchart
Portion of Videogame: Finding the Safe in Lord Grimley's Castle

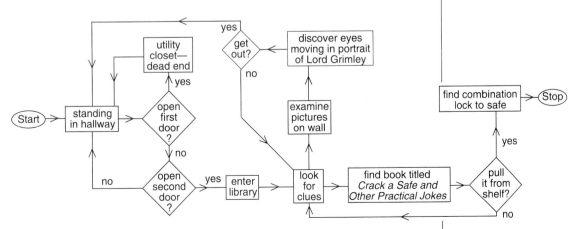

Applying Graphic Devices

Plot Diagrams If you were writing a short story or a play, you might make a **plot diagram** showing all the major events in your plot. A plot diagram can help keep you on track during the drafting process.

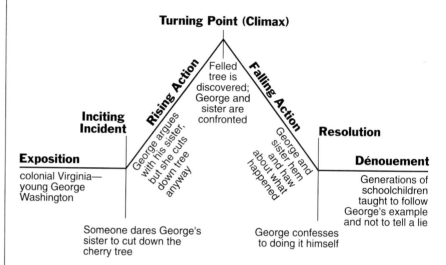

Plot Diagram:
Story Idea—History as It Might Have Happened

Turning Point (Climax)

Rising Action — Falling Action

Felled tree is discovered; George and sister are confronted

Inciting Incident

Exposition
colonial Virginia— young George Washington

George argues with his sister, but she cuts down tree anyway

George and sister tell him about what happened

Resolution

Dénouement
Generations of schoolchildren taught to follow George's example and not to tell a lie

Someone dares George's sister to cut down the cherry tree

George confesses to doing it himself

Time Lines Although a time line doesn't show story development in the same way a plot diagram does, this graphic can help you keep track of the order of major developments or discoveries. Whether you are writing a mystery or an essay on the history of comic strips, a **time line** can help you organize information in chronological order.

Time Line
Development of the Comic Strip in the United States

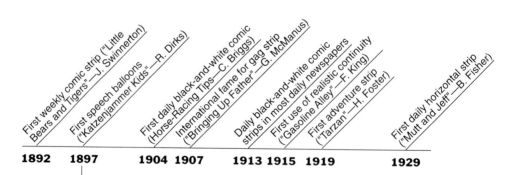

First weekly comic strip ("Little Bears and Tigers"—J. Swinnerton)

First speech balloons ("Katzenjammer Kids"—R. Dirks)

First daily black-and-white comic ("Horse-Racing Tips"—C. Briggs)

International fame for gag strip ("Bringing Up Father"—G. McManus)

Daily black-and-white comic strips in most daily newspapers

First use of realistic continuity ("Gasoline Alley"—F. King)

First adventure strip ("Tarzan"—H. Foster)

First daily horizontal strip ("Mutt and Jeff"—B. Fisher)

1892   1897   1904 1907   1913 1915 1919   1929

Inductive-Reasoning Frames   You can use an **inductive-reasoning frame** to list separate facts or examples that support a general conclusion, or induction. To make an inductive-reasoning frame, list the specific facts and draw an arrow to the conclusion based on these facts. Do not make overgeneralizations in your conclusions.

Inductive-Reasoning Frame
Writers' Early Work

Fact 1: *A Portrait of the Artist as a Young Man,* James Joyce's first novel, is, in part, an autobiographical work in which the protagonist comes of age and asserts his identity as an artist.

Fact 2: Ernest Hemingway's first major work, *In Our Time,* is a collection of stories revolving around Nick Adams, a character whose experiences roughly parallel those of young Hemingway.

Fact 3: F. Scott Fitzgerald's first novel, *This Side of Paradise,* deals with a young Princeton man like himself.

▼

Conclusion: Novelists sometimes begin their careers by writing about what they know best—themselves.

Practice Your Skills

A. Make an observation chart that could be used to plan a piece of writing about one of the following topics.

- auditioning for the school play
- gridlock on the city streets

B. Make a pro-and-con chart for one of the following topics.

- campaigning for political candidates
- making long-range career plans

C. In small groups, discuss which type of graphic device would be most helpful for planning an essay on each of the following topics.

- a description of a vista seen from a helicopter
- ways of dealing with poverty in the U.S.
- the history of papermaking
- an analysis of recent Supreme Court decisions on an issue
- a comparison of network newscasts

Planning and Organizing Strategies

A novelist may begin writing with only a sketchy idea of the plot, characters, and setting of a story. A news reporter may make a list of questions and interview several people before writing an article. A student may make a detailed outline and do extensive research before beginning a report. Different writing activities—and different writers—require different types of planning. Knowing the various strategies that writers often use can help you choose an approach that is right for you and your writing situation.

PLANNING YOUR WORK

It usually is helpful to plan your writing carefully before drafting if you are constrained by predetermined requirements. For example, if you are writing an essay for a history class, the material you use and its organization may be determined by the topic you have been asked to cover. You might therefore decide to outline your topic and gather information to support each point in the outline before you begin writing. However, if you are writing an original story, play, or poem, you may want to begin drafting immediately and see where your ideas take you.

The amount of initial planning that you do also depends on your personal style. Some people feel more secure when they have a careful plan to follow. Others prefer the challenge of working out their structure as they go along. Use the method that works for you and for the particular activity you are working on.

WRITER TO WRITER

My first draft is generally a jumble of all my ideas on a given subject. In my next draft, I choose those ideas that are most important and pertinent to each other. From there on, it is simply a matter of refining the paper.

Adam Shoughnessy, student
Watertown, Massachusetts

Whether you organize your ideas before you draft, as you draft, or as you revise, you will at some point want to order the presentation of your material. Writing that is well organized has unity and coherence—each idea is relevant and leads logically and smoothly into the next. See "Unity and Coherence," pages 382–391, for more information.

There are many different ways to organize your writing. Generally, your material itself will suggest the most effective method. As you write, ask yourself how your ideas are related to one another. Try not to force them into a preconceived organizational mold. The form of organization that is closest to the natural relationships among your ideas will probably also be the most natural, and the most effective, way to organize your writing.

Some common ways to organize paragraphs—as well as longer pieces of writing—include main idea and supporting details; chronological, spatial, and comparison-and-contrast orders; organization by classification and division or by degree; and cause-and-effect, dialectic, and inductive and deductive organizations.

Main Idea and Supporting Details

In most pieces of expository writing, you can organize your material by first stating a main idea and then supporting it with details, such as examples or reasons. In a single paragraph, your main idea may be stated in a topic sentence. In longer pieces of writing, your main idea may be expressed in a one-or-two-sentence thesis statement in your introduction. The paragraph below begins with a topic sentence stating the main idea; the sentences that follow provide supporting details.

▼

> Friendship appears to be a unique form of human bonding. Unlike marriage or the ties that bind parents and children, it is not defined or regulated by law. Unlike other social roles that we are expected to play—as citizens, employees, members of professional societies and other organizations—it has its own subjective rationale, which is to enhance feelings of warmth, trust, love, and affection between two people.
> **Mary Brown Parlee and the Editors of *Psychology Today***

PROFESSIONAL
M O D E L

Chronological Order

Many types of writing that present a series of events—short stories, biographies, and historical accounts, for example—are most effectively presented using chronological order. Notice how the following paragraph from a science fiction story uses chronological order to dramatize the hardship of the characters' journey:

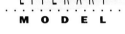
> The summer was waning when Shann took his two sons and went ahead to explore the way. For three days they climbed, and for three nights slept as best they could on freezing rocks, and on the fourth morning there was nothing ahead but a gentle rise to a cairn of gray stones built by other travelers, centuries ago.
>
> **Arthur C. Clarke, "History Lesson"**

Writers sometimes follow chronological order strictly, starting with the first event. Variations on this order are possible, however. In the **flashback,** a writer interrupts the forward movement in time to relate an event that occurred in the past. In **foreshadowing,** a writer hints about something that may happen in the future. Foreshadowing can help build suspense or arouse curiosity.

Spatial Order

Physical descriptions of persons and places are most naturally organized by spatial order. When describing a medieval cathedral, for example, you might describe it first as seen from a distance and then up closer; you might describe it from the top down; or you might describe it from the inside out. Notice how the following description uses both top-down and bottom-up spatial order.

> The sky too has its changes, but they are less marked than those of the vegetation and the river. Clouds map it up at times, but it is normally a dome of blending tints, and the main tint blue. By day the blue will pale down into white where it touches the white of the land, after sunset it has a new circumference—orange, melting upwards into tenderest purple.
>
> **E. M. Forster, *A Passage to India***

Writing
TIP

If you choose to use flashback or foreshadowing, be sure that you give your reader clear signals that you have temporarily suspended the normal chronological presentation of events.

Zoom in and zoom out are two camera techniques that also can be particularly effective in writing an introduction or conclusion. If you are using a zoom-in organization, you begin by describing a panoramic view. Then you describe the same scene as you move closer, focusing on progressively finer and finer details. You end with a close-up description of one aspect of the scene. In the following excerpt, the author uses the zoom-in technique to describe the main character's home.

Mia Farrow and Robert Redford starred in the 1972 film, *The Great Gatsby.*

The lawn started at the beach and ran towards the front door for a quarter of a mile, jumping over sundials and brick walks and burning gardens—finally when it reached the house drifting up the side in bright vines as though from the momentum of its run. The front was broken by a line of French windows, glowing now with reflected gold and wide open to the warm windy afternoon, and Tom Buchanan in riding clothes was standing with his legs apart on the front porch.

F. Scott Fitzgerald, *The Great Gatsby*

Another variation of spatial order is **order of impression.** In this type of organization, the writer begins with the image that creates the most powerful impact and then describes the peripheral or less compelling images. For example, if you were describing a crying child, you might describe his face first, then his drooping shoulders and clenched hands.

Comparison-and-Contrast Order

In expository and persuasive writing, you will often want to discuss the similarities and differences between two or more persons or things. You can do this by using comparison-and-contrast order, organizing your information in any of three ways: by subject, by similarities and differences, or by features.

1. When organizing your material by **subject,** you discuss one subject completely and then the other.

2. When organizing your material by **similarities and differences,** you discuss the similarities between the two subjects first and then describe all their differences (or vice versa).

3. When organizing your material by **features,** you compare and contrast the two subjects with respect to each characteristic.

Here is a review that compares and contrasts two television programs by feature.

> NBC's "Cosby Show" and Fox's "In Living Color" are very different half-hour comedy shows controlled primarily by black performers. Bill Cosby's humor tends to be warm and gently didactic: eat your veggies; stay in school. Keenen Ivory Wayans's approach is hip-hop brash and iconoclastic; neither whites nor blacks are exempt. But both shows share a distinctively black sensibility. . . .
>
> **John J. O'Connor, The New York Times**

Organization by Classification and Division

If you are writing about a number of related subjects, you can classify the subjects into groups according to criteria such as related characteristics or membership in a specific class. The following excerpt from *Moby Dick* uses classification to describe porpoises.

DUODECIMOES—These include the smaller whales. I. The Huzza Porpoise. II. The Algerine Porpoise. III. The Mealy-mouthed Porpoise.

To those who have not chanced specially to study the subject, it may possibly seem strange that fishes not commonly exceeding four or five feet should be marshalled among WHALES—a word, which, in the popular sense, always conveys an idea of hugeness. But the creatures set down above as Duodecimoes are infallibly whales, by the terms of my definition of what a whale is—i.e. a spouting fish, with a horizontal tail.

Herman Melville, *Moby Dick*

Organization by Degree

When you are describing a number of persons or things that share a particular characteristic, you might organize your material by degree—either from more to less of the characteristic or from less to more. For example, you might describe a variety of jobs by the amount of creativity required to do each one. You might describe a group of actors according to their ability to play a wide variety of roles. Notice how the following excerpt from *Sports Illustrated* is organized by degree.

Wayne Gretsky of the Los Angeles Kings will make $3 million this season, counting deferred payments. Mario Lemieux of the Pittsburgh Penguins will earn $2.3 million. But these two players are in a separate universe—nobody fills seats the way they do. The next-highest-paid player last season in straight salary—bonuses, deferred payments and perks promised by handshakes not included—was the Edmonton Oilers' Mark Messier, the league MVP, who made $832,000.

Jay Greenberg, *Sports Illustrated*

Variations on the organization-by-degree format include **organization by order of importance** and **organization by familiarity.** For example, a report on types of seashells could be organized by familiarity—from most familiar to less well known.

The inverted pyramid is a special type of organization by order of importance. Newspaper articles are often organized this way so readers can get information quickly. The "lead" typically answers six questions about the event being described: *who, what, where, when, why,* and *how.* In subsequent paragraphs the writer presents background details in the order of their importance. In a newspaper article, paragraphs are often no more than three sentences long. Here is a graphic representation of the inverted pyramid.

Inverted Pyramid Organization

Who, What, Where, When, Why, How
Most important detail
Next most important detail
Next most important detail
Least important detail

Notice how this organization is used effectively in the following paragraphs from a classic news report.

PROFESSIONAL
. . . .
M O D E L

HOUSTON, July 20—Man stepped out onto the moon tonight for the first time in his two-million-year history.

"That's one small step for a man," declared pioneer astronaut Neil Armstrong at 10:56 P.M. EDT, "one giant leap for mankind."

Just after that historic moment in man's quest for his origins, Armstrong walked on the dead satellite and found the surface very powdery, littered with fine grains of black dust.

A few minutes later, Edwin (Buzz) Aldrin joined Armstrong on the lunar surface and in less than an hour they put on a show that will long be remembered by the worldwide television audience.

Thomas O'Toole, *Washington Post*

The first paragraph of this story explains **who** the event is about (man), **what** happened (he set foot on the moon), **where** it took place (the surface of the moon), and **when** it occurred (July 20). The subsequent paragraphs provide additional details about **why** and **how** this historic event took place.

Cause-and-Effect Order

Events—personal, historical, political, or scientific—often form causal chains. For example, the discovery of atomic structure led eventually to the development of the hydrogen bomb. The novelist Jack London used this type of organization to describe the causes and effects of a famine on a northern tribe.

▼

In the summer the salmon run had failed, and the tribe looked forward to the winter and the coming of the caribou. Then the winter came, but with it there were no caribou. Never had the like been known, not even in the lives of the old men. But the caribou did not come, and it was the seventh year, and the rabbits had not replenished, and the dogs were naught but bundles of bone. And through the long darkness the children wailed and died, and the women, and the old men; and not one in ten of the tribe lived to meet the sun when it came back in the spring.

Jack London, "The Law of Life"

LITERARY
M O D E L

The failure of the salmon run and the disappearance of the caribou are causes; the effects include intense suffering and the death of ninety percent of the population.

Cause-and-effect writing is often organized into one of the following patterns.

Cause-to-Effect Pattern

Cause

Effect   Effect   Effect

(1)   (2)   (3)

Effect-to-Cause Pattern

Effect

Cause   Cause   Cause

(1)   (2)   (3)

In the **cause-to-effect pattern,** you state the cause or causes first and then proceed to describe the effect or effects. In the **effect-to-cause pattern,** you begin with an effect and gradually reveal its cause or causes.

Dialectic Organization

In **dialectic organization,** you present one position (the thesis), then its opposite (the antithesis), and finally describe a compromise position between the two (the synthesis). The Greek philosopher Aristotle proposed this method of seeking the "Golden Mean," or middle ground, as the basis of all ethics. In writing, this organization is particularly useful in persuasion or argumentation. Dialectics are often used for working out solutions to dilemmas or other difficult problems.

You might, for example, use dialectic organization in a report on a dispute between renters and landlords in your community. You might first present the renters' position—that they want to establish a renters' rights commission to protest landlords' raising rents, demanding too much rent in advance, and refusing to return security deposits. Then you would discuss the property owners' stance—that the renters' allegations are untrue and that a commission would make it more difficult for owners to pay their taxes and make a profit. Finally, you could present a compromise solution— establishment of a renters' commission composed of both renters and landlords so that the rights of both groups could be protected.

Inductive and Deductive Organization

Inductive and deductive organization are two other means of presenting an argument. **Inductive arguments** begin by presenting specific facts or examples and end with a general conclusion based on the facts and examples. **Deductive arguments** begin with a general statement and then present facts and examples that support the generalization. An example of deductive argumentation follows.

▼

[A] host of studies have found many children with low social competence are at risk for adverse effects [on their academic performance]. One of the most striking findings was a study of 200 kindergarteners reported in the August issue of *Child Development* by Gary Ladd at the University of Illinois.

Those kindergarteners who were socially rejected in October, Dr. Ladd found, did only half as well as other children on tests of academic readiness when tested the following May. At the start of the year both groups were at the same level.

Daniel Goleman, *The New York Times*

Practice Your Skills

A. Tell what method of organization you might use for each of the following pieces of writing and why you would choose it.

1. A humorous play about an ordinary high school student who is mistaken for a famous rock-and-roll star.

2. An essay that presents the reasons why, in your opinion, all beachfront property should (or should not) be government owned.

3. A newspaper story about an automobile accident caused by a flock of Canada geese strolling across a freeway.

4. A review of events that brought about the Solidarity-led revolution in Poland.

5. An essay that argues that the nation swings between periods of conservatism and periods of liberalism.

6. A description of Loch Ness in Scotland.

B. Read two articles from contemporary magazines that are appropriate for a general audience. Think about the method of organization used in each article. Bring the articles to class and, in small groups, discuss the methods used by the writers of the articles to organize their material.

Collaborative Planning

Whether you make a formal plan for your writing before you begin, or plan as you work, you often complete this aspect of your writing process alone. However, if you choose to plan before you begin, you may prefer to engage in a process called **collaborative planning.** This process involves sharing or "talking out" your writing plan with someone else. Explaining your plan aloud allows you to see your writing from a larger perspective and gives you the opportunity to test ideas before you put them in writing.

USING THE PLANNER'S BLACKBOARD

Every writing situation demands a different kind of plan. Nevertheless, all good writing plans address these elements: topic, purpose, audience, form, and the connections among them.

One useful way to consider the relationships among these writing variables is by using a graphic representation called a **planner's blackboard.**

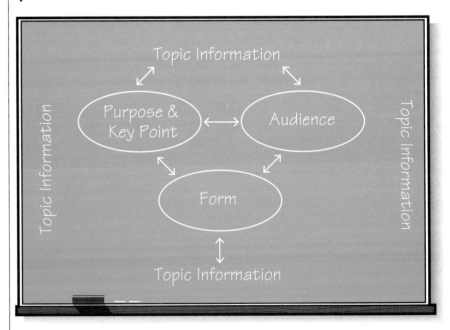

As a writer, you can use the planner's blackboard to remind you to consider all the components of planning as you explain and develop your writing plan. Information about your topic serves as the background of your plan, and as you assess the purpose, audience, and form of your writing, you consider how each decision you make affects the other variables. In doing so, you work forward and backward as the arrows in the diagram indicate to elaborate your writing plan.

Once you understand how the writing variables work together, you'll be able to make decisions that result in an effective piece of writing. You will become a more flexible and confident writer by using the planner's blackboard alone and in collaboration with others.

ENLISTING SUPPORT
FOR YOUR WRITING PLAN

A collaborator, or partner, can help you create and formalize your writing plan by giving you encouragement, objectivity, and a fresh perspective. He or she can read your plan and then ask probing questions or make suggestions to improve it. You can also identify the plan's weak points by reading it aloud to your collaborating partner.

Your collaborator may also notice that you have forgotten a certain writing consideration—such as the characteristics of your audience, for example. He or she may then offer suggestions for resolving that specific problem, suggesting, for example, that you establish a checkpoint in your planning process for evaluating the needs of your readers.

Your Role as a Writer The most important thing to remember in the collaborative planning process is that you, the writer, are in charge. Your collaborator can help you by facilitating your efforts to develop your writing plan. Your role is to present your plan clearly and to listen carefully to your collaborator's responses and questions about your plan. However, you evaluate all responses and decide if and how you will change your plan.

The planner's blackboard can be very useful to you in presenting your plan to your partner. It will give you a framework for explaining your ideas about your writing and clarifying the relationships among your topic, form, audience, and purpose.

COMPUTER
TIP

If you have a computer with a graphics program, you can save the planner's blackboard on your computer and use it whenever collaborative planning seems most appropriate.

Collaborative
Planning

Your Role as a Supporter Supporters are neither teachers nor critics. A supporter neither tells you how to write nor criticizes your work; rather, he or she helps and supports your effort to develop and elaborate your writing plan. As a supporter, you can also help the writer by using the following guidelines.

Guidelines for Providing Collaborative Support

- Listen carefully to what the writer has to say. Afterward, try to summarize the writer's plan in a few words. For example, you might say, "What I hear you saying is that _____. Is that what you mean?"

- Ask the planner to elaborate. "You just said _____. Tell me more about what you mean or why you said that."

- Ask about key parts of the blackboard planner that the writer has not explained fully. "If your purpose is _____, what form will you use? Is it the best choice? What are your specific personal goals?"

- Ask the writer to consider how different parts of his or her writing plan are connected, especially if you detect weak links or potential problems. For example, you might ask, "If your key point here is _____, how do you think your readers will respond?" You might also encourage the writer to think about each of the writing variables individually in relation to his or her writing purpose, considering whether each best serves that purpose. Mention any problems you notice, and offer suggestions if the writer asks for your advice.

Practice Your Skills

Imagine that you are going to collaborate with a writer who has made the following initial statement about her writing: "I think I want to write about the process new immigrants to this country must go through in becoming citizens in order to explain the complexities of this privilege we take for granted."

Write out a list of questions or responses that will help the writer pinpoint missing variables, inconsistencies, or potential problems in her plan. To assess this plan objectively, prepare a planner's blackboard based on her statement.

Drafting to Discover Meaning

Drafting is the process of making meaning with your writing. Therefore, when you draft, concentrate on what you have to say, not on how you are saying it. Don't worry about matters such as spelling or mechanics, and don't think that you have to have everything worked out beforehand. In fact, you may have only a vague idea of what you want to say as you begin.

Perplexity, not certainty, is the ideal state in which to start writing. As you draft, explore your confusion. Raise questions and see where they lead. Don't be afraid to experiment. Concentrate on getting your thoughts down on paper. You will have the chance to bring your writing into sharper focus later, when you start to revise.

WRITER TO WRITER

When you write, you lay out a line of words. The line of words is a miner's pick, a woodcarver's gouge, a surgeon's probe. You wield it, and it digs a path you follow. Soon you find yourself deep in new territory. Is it a dead end, or have you located the real subject? You will know tomorrow, or this time next year.

Annie Dillard, *The Writing Life*

Although drafting is important, that doesn't mean that when you're writing a critical or informative piece you don't have to plan beforehand. However, with any type of writing, you need to leave yourself open to new ideas that emerge.

DRAFTING STYLES

Certain general patterns—drafting, getting feedback from others, rereading, rewriting—are all part of the writing process. However, writers and writing styles differ widely. Some writers begin by writing freely; others make plans and follow them carefully. Still others combine planning and experimentation.

Adventuresome Drafting When you aren't sure what you want to say or how to organize your information, you may choose simply to set your thoughts freely down on paper. Don't worry about form, style, audience, or purpose at this point. Just concentrate on getting all of your ideas out. Writing of this kind, done without much planning, is called **adventuresome drafting.** One expert on composition calls it *raw writing*. Raw writing is worth doing in the early stages of your work because it frees you from the constraints of form and lets you concentrate on finding meaning.

Raw writing often produces fresher, more evocative language than does careful writing. Give yourself the freedom to use some of this livelier writing in your final product. Consider, for example, the informal tone that this student retained in the final draft of these paragraphs.

▼

My mother was a writer? The thought made me laugh when I first considered it, but as I sat at the kitchen table with her that Sunday evening . . . listening to her talk, that silly thought I had quickly diminished.

I have to admit now that I wasn't very excited about doing the interview, just because I didn't think that my mother would have anything interesting to say about writing. Wrong again. My mother's always been one who loves to talk, so it turned out that I'd ask a simple question, and she'd go on supplying me with such a long, elaborate answer that I couldn't keep up with her!

Careful Drafting The direct opposite of adventuresome drafting is **careful drafting.** When writing a careful draft, you work slowly, getting each paragraph the way you like it before moving on to the next one.

As you might expect, careful drafting requires extensive planning. You must decide beforehand what you are going to say and how you are going to say it. For example, you might prepare a formal outline and an elaborate set of notes before you start to write. Some writers always prepare a set of 3″ × 5″ note cards that they can arrange and rearrange as they work out an organization.

Intermediate Drafting If you are like most writers, you often have a rough idea of what you are going to say before you start a piece of writing. In that case, you will probably be most comfortable with a drafting process that lies somewhere between adventuresome and careful.

Bridge-building is an excellent way of writing an intermediate draft, because it allows you to organize your ideas as you write. You start by identifying the key ideas, sections, or events that you want to include in your writing. Then you begin writing your draft. As you work, ask yourself questions like these: How can I get from point A to point B? What details do I need to include to make the connections among my ideas clear? Martha Grimes, the well-known mystery writer, uses the bridge-building technique. She jots down notes about characters, plot, and setting over the course of several months, traveling to various places in England to get ideas. Then she goes back home and weaves her notes together into an intricately plotted, evocatively written novel.

Drafting is a process of constant self-discovery. When you begin, you can never be quite sure what your finished piece of writing will look like. Because they often make surprising discoveries about themselves and their topics, many writers say that drafting is the most enjoyable part of writing. Once you learn to draft without inhibition and restraint, you will experience the true joy of writing.

DRAFTING AND REVISION

Overlapping Processes   Rarely do writers wait until they have completed a draft before they begin to revise. Some revise and shape their writing as they draft, blending the two processes into one. Others draft a few paragraphs, revise, and then go on to draft some more. Still others wait until they have a complete draft before doing any revisions. Draft and revise in the manner that works best for you.

Knowing When to Stop   Strange as it might seem, knowing when to stop is an important part of the drafting process. Typically, you will revise your draft several times, do more research, and perhaps rethink your entire topic before you decide it's time to stop. Ultimately you will stop drafting and begin to fine-tune your piece.

It is a good idea to take a break between drafts; when you return to your writing, you will be able to evaluate it with a fresh eye. When you have worked on a piece for some time and cannot look at it objectively anymore, a peer reader can provide you with new perspectives on your writing. For more help on working with peers during the writing process, see "Peer Review and Response," pages 397–401.

Drafting When You Can't Revise   You probably will not have time to revise your draft when you are writing an answer to an essay question during an examination. The best strategy for answering essay questions on tests is to spend a few minutes drawing up a quick but explicit writing plan.

Begin by jotting down the main ideas that you want to cover in a brief, informal outline. This will help guide your writing and remind you to include all the important points in your answer. If you cannot write a brief outline or list, make one up in your head.

Begin by restating the question as a topic sentence or thesis. Then, use a simple method of organization, such as chronological order, order of importance, or the inverted pyramid form. Use transitions that indicate the form of organization you are using, such as *first . . . second* and *least important . . . more important.* Readers of essay exams are impressed by good organization.

Practice Your Skills

A. Meet with a group of three or four students to discuss the following questions.

1. What drafting technique did each person in your group use on his or her last piece of writing? What drafting technique does each writer generally prefer? Why?
2. Have you ever switched from one topic to another in the middle of the drafting process? Discuss how and why this happened.

B. Choose one of the following writing prompts and draft a response to it. Then, in a small group, share your writing with other students. Discuss any difficulties that you had during the drafting process. Solicit suggestions for alternative ways you might have proceeded.

1. Briefly discuss three people whom you admire, and explain what personal and professional qualities or attributes make these people worthy of respect.
2. Imagine you were Secretary of Education of the United States and write a short speech discussing the two issues you would make priorities and why.
3. Think of a part-time, after-school job for which you would like to apply. Write a short letter of application discussing your qualifications.
4. Write a critique of a book you have recently read and enjoyed or a popular song that you like. Include specific reasons why you think others might enjoy it too.

Writing Introductions and Conclusions

You probably feel that it's important for you to make a good first impression when you meet someone new. You also want to leave a positive final impression. Introductions and conclusions are also important in your writing, because they are the first and last impressions you make on your readers.

INTRODUCING NONFICTION

In the next few pages, you'll review a number of different strategies for writing effective introductions to nonfiction—introductions that will capture your readers' attention and entice them to keep reading.

Begin with a Thesis Statement An introduction to a piece of nonfiction—an explanation, persuasive essay, literary analysis, essay for assessment, or report, for example—often includes a **thesis statement,** one or two sentences that clearly state the main idea of the writing that follows. A thesis statement may be woven into both the beginning and the ending of a piece of writing.

An effective thesis statement does more than tell what the paper is about, however. A thesis statement may convey the writer's point of view or perspective on his or her topic, and it may signal the paper's overall organization. Here are three thesis statements: one for a persuasive essay, one for a literary analysis, and one for an explanation.

- The government should ban pesticides that preliminary scientific investigations have linked to cancer in humans. The possibility of saving lives by banning these chemicals outweighs the risks of waiting until the evidence against them is conclusive.
- In Arthur Miller's *Death of a Salesman,* Willy Loman is a tragic hero who fails to live up to other people's expectations of him.
- In the United States, the majority of people over the age of sixty-five are women, and they face special problems in the areas of health care, housing, and social security simply because of their gender.

You may or may not wish to include a thesis statement in the introduction—the first paragraph or two—of every piece of nonfiction you write. However, all your introductions should capture your readers' attention and interest them in reading more. Study the following techniques for creating engaging introductions.

Relate an Anecdote   Beginning with a brief anecdote, or story, can hook readers and help you make a point in a dramatic way. The following anecdote is an effective beginning to an essay on people's confusion about enormous numbers.

> The renowned cosmogonist Professor Bignumska, lecturing on the future of the universe, had just stated that in about a billion years, according to her calculations, the earth would fall into the sun in a fiery death. In the back of the auditorium a tremulous voice piped up: "Excuse me, Professor, but h-h-how long did you say it would be?" Professor Bignumska calmly replied, "About a billion years." A sigh of relief was heard. "Whew! For a minute there, I thought you'd said a *million* years."   **Douglas R. Hofstadter, "On Number Numbness"**

Make a Surprising Statement   Opening with a startling, unusual, or interesting fact or opinion is particularly effective for explanations; it can work in some descriptions too, as this introduction to a personality profile shows.

> Govan Brown has been driving a city bus in Manhattan for just over 20 years, putting in nearly enough miles—220,000 —to reach the moon. No wonder he's retiring.
> **Douglas Martin, *The New York Times***

Address Readers Directly   Speaking directly to your readers in your introduction establishes a friendly, informal tone and involves readers in your topic right away.

> If you like to search the stores for bargains, you'll probably find exactly what you're looking for—in catalogs.   ***USA Today***

Present a Description   A description of your subject—a person or a place, for example—can set a mood. This description evokes the lush atmosphere of the Virgin Islands.

> They look like a tropical paradise is supposed to look: the steep, green hills of sun-drenched islands rising out of a clear blue sea. Tucked into the nooks and crannies of the irregular coastline of these islands are small secluded white-sand beaches washed by a warm crystal-clear sea. An almost constant breeze wafts in from the ocean, rustling the palms and cooling the beach.   **Scott Frier, "Island in the Sun"**

Begin with a Quotation   You can use a quotation in your introduction, as the writer of the model below does to open his article about acupuncture. Quotations from experts can add credibility to your writing.

> "People think of energy as something we get out of the Middle East, or out of the wall plug," says acupuncturist Charles Lo, M.D. "But everything living has energy—what the Chinese call *qi* [pronounced *chee*]."   **Bryan Miller, *The Reader***

Pose a Question   A question draws readers into your writing; even if they know the answer, they'll want to continue reading to see what you have to say. Notice how this student writer combines introduction techniques by both asking questions and addressing her readers directly.

> Have you ever heard of a dandy brush? How about a hoof pick? Or a sweat scraper? Confused? If you were a horse lover, you wouldn't be. In fact, you would use these words every day, because these words name some vital pieces of equipment needed to keep a horse clean and safe.

Draw an Analogy   Try making a dramatic point by comparing your subject to something else. The following introduction to an essay about water pollution compares rivers to veins.

Introductions and
Conclusions   **367**

> Rivers are the veins of the earth. Like blood vessels carrying oxygen to a body's vital organs, rivers transport precious life-giving water across the landscape to the edges of the globe. Poison the bloodstream and the body will die. Pollute the rivers and Mother Earth will perish and die too.

CONCLUDING NONFICTION

After reading a conclusion, the reader should have a sense of closure and resolution. A conclusion that gives a reader this kind of satisfaction usually has the following characteristics.

- It follows logically from what has been presented or covered in the text.
- It does not introduce new, unrelated material.
- It makes a lasting impression by leaving the reader with something to think about.

There are, of course, many ways of meeting these criteria. The following are some effective ways to write a conclusion.

Restate Your Thesis   One way to conclude a piece of writing is by restating your thesis, or main idea, in different words. In the essay "Pines Above the Snow," the main idea is that pines, and woodlands in general, are of great spiritual and emotional value to human beings. Here is the essay's conclusion.

> It is in midwinter that I sometimes glean from my pines something more important than woodlot politics, and the news of the wind and weather. This is especially likely to happen on some gloomy evening when the snow has buried all irrelevant detail, and the hush of elemental sadness lies heavy upon every living thing. Nevertheless, my pines, each with his burden of snow, are standing ramrod-straight, rank upon rank, and in the dusk beyond I sense the presence of hundreds more. At such times I feel a curious transfusion of courage.
>
> **Aldo Leopold, "Pines Above the Snow"**

Summarize the Ideas of Your Body Paragraphs   When you present a series of ideas in a piece of writing, your reader may find it useful to read a summary of these ideas in the conclusion. You might begin the conclusion by summarizing the ideas of the body paragraphs and then end it by summarizing, in a single sentence, the main point, or thesis, of the entire piece.

> As we have seen, coral reefs take thousands and thousands of years to build. However, they can be destroyed within a matter of years, days, or even minutes by pollutants, by untrained divers, by anchors, and by ships going aground. Given these perils and the extraordinary fragility of the coral environment, it is vital that protected marine parks be established to preserve the living coral reef.

Generalize About the Information You Have Given   At times you may wish to end by drawing a general conclusion from the specific information that you have presented. In the following example, Bill Lovin reaches a general conclusion about a moving experience and about the photographer's need to make visual records.

> I overcame the romanticism of the moment enough to hold my camera out as far as I could and let the film roll, filming Jovita [his dive buddy] and the manta's point of view. I almost wish I hadn't.
>
> In 25 years of diving with whales, dolphins, sharks, to name but a few, I had never felt such a kinship with any of the ocean's creatures. The whole experience lasted for 280 feet of film, 7 minutes and 42 seconds. It might seem absurd for an underwater photographer to suggest leaving the camera at home in order to feel the experience and not be compelled to record it. You do not need a camera at Cocos Island to remember it forever.   **Bill Lovin, "Impressions of Cocos"**

Make a Prediction   Readers are interested in matters that are going to affect them and are therefore moved by conclusions that predict the future. The conclusion on the following page was written for a photographic essay on endangered species. In it the author makes a thought-provoking prediction.

PROFESSIONAL
M O D E L

▼

> Perhaps these images can play a small part in helping us find our way home out of that long exile from nature. But until we become much more skilled at listening to the voices of nature in and around us, all animals—including the one we call human—are in jeopardy. The unspeakable tragedy is that our learning process will be too slow to prevent some of the extraordinary animals on these pages from being among the last survivors of their species.
>
> **James Balog, "A Personal Vision of Vanishing Wildlife"**

Issue a Call for Action Writers of persuasive pieces often use their conclusions to ask readers to take action. Coretta Scott King, for example, urges people to support a full-employment statute.

PROFESSIONAL
M O D E L

▼

> For myself, if the alternative to full employment is simply to wait, to tolerate in silence the shattered dreams of jobless youth and the broken hearts of laid-off men, then my choice is clear.
>
> America's jobless cannot "wait," not only because waiting is no solution and not only because waiting has social consequences that are frightening to contemplate, but because to do nothing when we have the capacity to act is morally and socially wrong. **Coretta Scott King, "Why We Still Can't Wait"**

Ask a Question Just as beginning a piece of writing with a question can engage readers' attention, concluding with a question can make your readers think about the issues you have raised.

PROFESSIONAL
M O D E L

▼

> The only question left to be settled now is: Are women persons? And I hardly believe any of our opponents will have the hardihood to say they are not. Being persons, then, women are citizens; and no State has a right to make any law, or to enforce any old law, that shall abridge their privileges or immunities. Hence, every discrimination against women in the constitutions and laws of the several states is today null and void. **Susan B. Anthony, "A Woman's Right to Suffrage"**

End with a Quotation As in an introduction, a quotation is a good way of focusing readers' thinking. To conclude an essay about accepting losses in sports, Charles Kuralt uses an apt quotation.

> Winning isn't the only thing, Coach Lombardi. Defeat is not like death, Coach Allen. I noticed the daffodils came up in my garden the morning after the Marquette game, even though North Carolina lost. Life goes on, even for us losers. I have a new maxim for the dressing room walls: Berton Brayley's sportsman's prayer, which says, "If I should lose, let me stand by the side of the road and cheer as the winners go by."
>
> **Charles Kuralt, *Dateline America***

INTRODUCING AND CONCLUDING NARRATIVES

The introduction of a narrative should draw readers into the story; the conclusion of a narrative should leave readers with something to think about.

Introducing a Narrative

Most narratives follow this advice: "Begin at the beginning . . . and go on till you come to the end: then stop." However, some stories start in the middle of the action, or *in medias res*.

> Basil Duke Lee shut the front door behind him and turned on the dining-room light. His mother's voice drifted sleepily downstairs:
> "Basil, is that you?"
> "No, mother, it's a burglar."
>
> **F. Scott Fitzgerald, "The Captured Shadow"**

Other types of introductions provide readers with information that will help them to understand and enjoy the story. This information will often establish an important story element or theme. The following are some ways to introduce a narrative.

Set the Scene   Writers often choose to begin a piece of writing by setting the scene for their readers. Consider the following introductory paragraph from the Middle English romance *Sir Gawain and the Green Knight*.

> Winter lay upon the land. Cold held forest and field in its grim clutch, and in the night sky the stars glittered like gems. The wolf slid from shadow to shadow, stalking hapless prey, falling upon the unwary with death in his fangs. Deep in caverns the great trolls and other monsters mumbled in uneasy sleep, seeking warmth. Over the moor and fen the mists rose and fell, and strange sounds troubled the chill silence.
>
> **Y. R. Ponsor, translator, *Sir Gawain and the Green Knight***

Describe the Main Character   Many narratives begin with a revealing description of the main character. Remember that a character can be described by a narrator, by another character, or by his or her own words. Charles Dickens's characterizations are considered to be among the most vivid and well drawn in all of literature. The following characterization is the first paragraph of "The Madman's Manuscript," a chapter from Dickens's novel *The Pickwick Papers*. Notice how the reader learns about the character from his speech patterns, his exclamations, and the frightening thought processes they reveal.

> Yes!—a madman's! How that word would have struck to my heart many years ago! How it would have roused the terror that used to come upon me sometimes, sending the blood hissing and tingling through my veins, till the cold dew of fear stood in large drops upon my skin, and my knees knocked together with fright! I like it now though. It's a fine name. Show me the monarch whose angry frown was ever feared like the glare of a madman's grip. Ho! ho! It's a grand thing to be mad! to be peeped at like a wild lion through the iron bars— to gnash one's teeth and howl through the long still night, to the merry ring of a heavy chain—and to roll and twine among the straw, transported with such brave music. Hurrah for the madhouse! Oh, it's a rare place!
>
> **Charles Dickens, "A Madman's Manuscript"**

Introduce the Central Conflict Most stories are based on the working out of a conflict, and a narrative may begin by introducing this conflict. The following newspaper article begins by establishing the alignment of countries in a potential confrontation.

▼

PROFESSIONAL
M O D E L

WASHINGTON, Aug 3—Powerful Iraqi forces wheeled into position for a possible attack on Saudi Arabia today, while the United States and its allies continued to search, so far without discernible success, for a way to force Iraq to pull back from its rapid conquest of Kuwait on Thursday.

R. W. Apple, Jr., "U.S. Weighs Action"

Present a Major Symbol Sometimes an image that appears in the introduction of a story will later be developed into a major symbol. For example, in the course of William Saroyan's story "Gaston," the peaches come to symbolize the liveliness and compassion that a girl discovers in her father and for a time also experiences within herself. In the introductory paragraph, the writer both presents the symbol and gives a description of the main characters, the narrator and her father.

▼

LITERARY
M O D E L

They were to eat peaches, as planned, after her nap, and now she sat across from the man who would have been a total stranger except that he was in fact her father. They had been together again (although she couldn't quite remember when they had been together before) for almost a hundred years now, or was it only since day before yesterday? Anyhow, they were together again, and he was kind of funny. First, he had the biggest mustache she had ever seen on anybody, although to her it was not a mustache at all; it was a lot of red and brown hair under his nose and around the ends of his mouth. Second, he wore a blue-and-white striped jersey instead of a shirt and tie, and no coat. His arms were covered with the same hair, only it was a little lighter and thinner. He wore blue slacks, but no shoes and socks. He was barefoot, and so was she, of course.   **William Saroyan, "Gaston"**

Introductions and
Conclusions   **373**

Concluding a Narrative

Did you ever find that you were enjoying reading a story, only to be sadly disappointed by the ending? Just as there are many ways to begin a story, there are many ways to end one. Consider the following methods to conclude a narrative.

Present the Last Event Often a story simply ends with the last event. The interpretation of the event is left to the reader's imagination. One famous American novel, for example, ends with the event that comes immediately after the death of the narrator's beloved.

> But after I had got them [the doctors and nurses] out and shut the door and turned off the light it wasn't any good. It was like saying good-by to a statue. After a while I went out and left the hospital and walked back to the hotel in the rain.
>
> Ernest Hemingway, *A Farewell to Arms*

End with a Climactic Event The climax is the point in a story where the conflict reaches its greatest tension. De Maupassant's "The Necklace" ends with a stunning revelation.

> "You mean to say you bought a diamond necklace to replace mine?"
>
> "Yes. You never noticed then? They were quite alike."
>
> And she smiled with proud and simple joy. Mme. Forestier, quite overcome, clasped her by the hands. "Oh, my poor Mathilde. But mine was only paste. Why, at most it was worth only five hundred francs!" **Guy de Maupassant, "The Necklace"**

Resolve the Conflict Many stories show the resolution of the central conflict in the conclusion. Often, the resolution follows the climactic event. In the conclusion to his short story "The Long Winter," writer Walter Havighurst resolves a conflict between his two main characters, a rancher and his son. In the story, the rancher has been estranged from his son, whom he has blamed for his wife's death. At the end of the story, the rancher has saved his son's life, and the rift between the man and boy has begun to close.

> "Summer is getting here at last," the rancher said. "It's late season. We had a long winter, but it's over now." He turned in the saddle. "You're not saying much, Danny. What's on your mind?"
>
> The boy smiled. "Oatmeal and corn bread," he said, "bacon and pancakes. I'm starved."
>
> **Walter Havighurst, "The Long Winter"**

Practice Your Skills

A. Two of the three sample thesis statements below need to be revised. Rewrite them so that each clearly states a main idea or focus for a piece of nonfiction and reveals a plan of organization or a point of view. Then write introductory paragraphs or conclusions for all three topics, using the techniques described in this handbook. If you wish, include the thesis statement in your introduction or rephrase it in your conclusion.

1. Scientific studies have shown that birds possess intelligence comparable to that of human beings. Like people, birds make and use tools, communicate with one another and with other species, plan, play, love, and grieve.

2. You won't become a victim of a street crime if you take certain precautions.

3. Mandatory participation in the after-school sports program would help students learn the connection between physical fitness and good health. Improving the nutritional value of school lunches would also help students feel better.

B. Read the following scenario for a piece of fiction or use your imagination to create a scenario of your own. In your journal, freewrite about the different ways you might begin or end the story, using the strategies described in this handbook. Then share your ideas with your classmates in a group discussion.

- *Setting:*   a small town in your state, present day
- *Characters:*   four restless high school seniors eagerly awaiting graduation
- *Conflict:*   a weekend camping trip that turns tragic when one student slips and hits his head, falling into a coma

COMPUTER
═TIP═

As you revise, remember to print a hard copy of your story every so often, or else save your drafts on disks. That way you won't lose material if you change your text and then decide to go back to your original version.

Introductions and
Conclusions   **375**

Techniques for Elaboration and Development

Elaboration is the process of developing a writing idea by generating specific supporting details. Elaboration can take place at any point during the writing process.

FINDING DETAILS FOR ELABORATION

To find details to elaborate your writing, you can use any of the information-gathering techniques in Writing Handbook 2, pages 331–336, or the graphic devices described in Writing Handbook 4, pages 339–347. Questioning is another useful technique.

Using Questioning Techniques

Questioning is a particularly useful method for determining the types of details that will help you elaborate your topic. The following list suggests types of questions you might consider.

Action Questions These questions, which begin with the words *who, what, where, when, why,* or *how,* are particularly useful in generating detailed descriptions of events or actions. Examples of these questions are listed below.

- What is happening? What has happened? What will happen?
- Who is, was, or will be responsible? Who else is involved?
- Where does, did, or will it happen?
- Why did, does, or will it happen?
- How did, does, or will it happen?

Category Questions You can use category questions, such as those listed below, to explore and analyze various aspects of a topic.

- **Definition**
  How does the dictionary define my subject? How would I define it?
  To what group does it belong?
  What are some specific examples of it?
  What are its parts? How might they be divided?

- **Comparison**
  What is my subject similar to? In what ways?
  What is it different from? In what ways?
  What is it worse than? In what ways?
- **Cause and Effect**
  What causes my subject?
  What effects does it have?
  What is its purpose?
- **Conditions and Events**
  Is this subject possible? Why or why not?
  Is it practical? Why or why not?
  Has it happened before? When? How? To whom?
- **Documentation**
  What facts or statistics do I know about my subject?
  What have I seen, heard, or read about it?
  What saying, proverb, song, or poem do I know about it?
  How could I find out more about it?

Creative Questions These can help you shift your perspective and stretch your imagination by considering fanciful approaches to your subject.

- What if I combined two objects that are normally separate?
- What if I used something in a new or unusual way?
- What if something had never happened?
- What if someone had never existed?
- What if I changed the material, shape, color, or location?
- What if I put unlikely or opposing ideas together?
- What if people changed their roles or actions?

Aristotelian Invention Questions based on techniques developed by the Greek philosopher Aristotle can also help stimulate creative thinking about your subject. Some of the most useful techniques are listed below and on the following page.

- Compare and contrast your subject with other things.
- Think of synonyms for your subject and of the differing implications, or connotations, of these synonyms.
- Consider your subject over time.
- Relate the subject to yourself.
- Define your subject; think of the different meanings of words used to name your subject.
- Think of the parts of your subject.
- Look for examples and see if you can generalize from them.
- Look for causes, effects, pros, and cons.

- Look for analogies and draw conclusions based on them.
- Contrast the actual or current state of your subject with its possible future state.
- Consider common opinions concerning your subject, and determine whether these opinions are factually based.

Finding Answers to Your Questions

You can find the answers to your questions in several ways, including holding a dialogue, conducting an interview, and checking reference works such as encyclopedias, almanacs, dictionaries, and collections of short biographies.

Holding a Dialogue   You can use internal dialogue in several ways to develop writing ideas. Holding a dialogue allows you to consider more than one side of an issue. Here are some ways to use dialogue to generate ideas.

- Interview yourself about the subject. Write down both your questions and answers.
- Hold a dialogue between two parts of yourself, such as your confident side and your insecure side, or your brave self and your frightened self. Use your contradictory feelings to explore different sides of an issue or idea.
- Take on the roles of two characters, or one character and an inanimate object or abstract idea.

Conducting an Interview   You can gather up-to-date information on a topic by interviewing. Quoting experts or experienced persons can add interest and authenticity to your writing. You should prepare for an interview by doing research beforehand and compiling a list of questions to ask your expert. This will allow you to focus on the information you need when you are conducting the interview.

Using Library Resources   Checking reference works can help you answer questions you might have about a topic. Don't allow the number and size of reference works to daunt you. Take the following steps to save time and energy when trying to locate information.

- Begin by **skimming.** Move your eyes quickly over the page to find out if the information you need is there.
- **Scan** promising material, again moving your eyes quickly until you locate the information you want.
- Do **in-depth reading** of the relevant information.

Writing
TIP

Use phone directories or local government listings to find experts in the topic you are researching.

The types of details that you need to elaborate a piece of writing depend on your purpose, audience, and form.

Facts and Statistics A **fact** is a statement that can be verified, and **statistics** are simply facts expressed as numbers.

> According to the *1990 Universal Almanac,* edited by John W. Wright, there are currently 1.5 million Native Americans and 64,000 Native Alaskans (Eskimos and Aleuts) living in the United States. This represents a significant increase since the 1960 census, when only 524,000 Native Americans and 42,500 Native Alaskans were counted.

W R I T E R   T O   W R I T E R

Include many specific details and examples so that the reader knows exactly what you are saying and can visualize the images you describe.

Jason Moneymaker, student
DeSoto, Texas

Sensory Details Details that appeal to the senses are particularly helpful in enlivening descriptions. Notice how they are used below.

> The village matchmaker came to my family when I was just two years old. No, nobody told me this, I remember it all. It was summertime, very hot and dusty outside, and I could hear cicadas crying in the yard. We were under some trees in our orchard. The servants and my brothers were picking pears high above me. And I was sitting in my mother's hot sticky arms. I was waving my hand this way and that, because in front of me floated a small bird with horns and colorful paper-thin wings. And then the paper bird flew away and in front of me were two ladies. I remember them because one lady made watery "shrrhh, shrrhh" sounds. When I was older, I came to recognize this as a Peking accent, which sounds quite strong to Taiyuan people's ears. **Amy Tan, *The Joy Luck Club***

LITERARY
M O D E L

Incidents An incident—an interesting or significant event—can illustrate a persuasive argument very well.

PROFESSIONAL
M O D E L

> Average United States consumers continue to face what appears to me to be more direct and blatant overcharges in phone rates. . . . A recent attempt to place a call on a pay phone from Lower Manhattan directly across the Hudson River to Jersey City—a distance of perhaps one mile—brought a request to deposit $1.90 for one minute. The charge seemed ludicrous, given that I could have physically delivered my message by train for $1. **Mark Solof, *The New York Times***

Specific Examples Examples are often effective in building a convincing thesis, as in the following paragraph.

PROFESSIONAL
M O D E L

> That's the individual she is: neither Kennedy nor Onassis nor even her own glamorous public image, but a woman who remains serious, hardworking, sensitive, funny, and even slightly outrageous. (In conversation, she's the sort of person to whom you find yourself saying things you had previously only thought, indiscreet things that her own gentle rebelliousness encourages you to say.)
> **Gloria Steinem, *Outrageous Acts and Everyday Rebellions***

Quotations A pertinent quotation can breathe life into nonfiction.

The time-honored methods of teaching home economics are changing in high schools across the country. As family structures and eating habits change from the two-parent, mother-at-home, meat-and-potatoes form on which the original curriculum was based, home ec classes move with the times. "Two out of three meals are eaten away from home; everybody works," points out Jewell Deene Ellis, director of Home Economics Education for the Kentucky Department of Education.

Opinions Many different kinds of opinions—including judgments and proposals—can be used for elaboration.

There is no reason that a country with one of the highest standards of living in the world, the United States, should be nineteenth in its infant mortality rate. Clearly, this problem should be a top priority among human-service professionals and legislators. We need better prenatal care, better education for young mothers, and more financial support for indigent mothers and their children.

Visual Aids   Charts, graphs, maps, and tables can sometimes illustrate a complicated point more effectively than words. For example, the following table might help you discuss the comparative amounts spent on defense by various NATO countries.

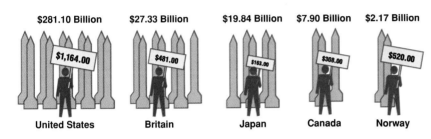

$281.10 Billion	$27.33 Billion	$19.84 Billion	$7.90 Billion	$2.17 Billion
$1,164.00	$481.00	$163.00	$308.00	$520.00
United States	Britain	Japan	Canada	Norway

Practice Your Skills

A. Consider each of the following main ideas, and choose the three you can elaborate into a paragraph most effectively. Follow the suggestions for elaboration in parentheses.

1. Some of the most important work is that for which people usually do not get paid. (Elaborate with examples.)

2. The developing countries of the world suffer under a great burden of debt. (Consult some almanacs to find statistics.)

3. The opening of the film _____ established a mood of _____. (Fill in the blanks. Use sensory details to re-create the event.)

4. Few things in life are irrevocable. However . . .(Elaborate with an incident from your life.)

B. Read the following statistics. Then use them to create a pie chart, a bar chart, or a table. Write a brief report in which you draw a conclusion from the statistics. Use the graphic aid in your report.

Region	Population
Asia	3,031 million
Africa	615 million
North America	413 million
South America	282 million

COMPUTER
TIP

If you have a computer graphics program, you can use it to develop visual aids.

Mastering Unity and Coherence

What makes one piece of writing seem solid and well crafted and another seem patched together and makeshift? The answer is unity and coherence. Writing has **unity** when all the sentences and paragraphs work together toward the same goal and are directly related to the main idea. Writing has **coherence** when all the sentences and paragraphs are clearly and logically linked together.

TECHNIQUES FOR ACHIEVING UNITY

Writing has unity when all the sentences support and develop one stated or implied main idea. Unity is important both in individual paragraphs and in longer pieces of writing.

Unity Within Paragraphs

The following writing techniques will help you create unified paragraphs.

Write a Topic Sentence State the main idea of a paragraph in a clear, concise topic sentence, and support that idea in all the other sentences. A topic sentence may be effective at the beginning of a paragraph, but it may also appear later in the paragraph or at the end to summarize or reinforce the main idea. In this paragraph from Theodore Barber's *The Human Nature of Birds*, the topic sentence appears at the beginning.

> Birds, like humans, can play and have fun. Their play varies from simple enjoyable activities to complex organized games. Many kinds of birds have been reliably observed to play with sticks, leaves, feathers, pinecones, and many other objects; to repeatedly drop a small object in midair and catch it before it hits the ground; to ride down a rapid tidal current or to slide down a snowbank feet first, walk back up, and ride or slide down again apparently for the sheer joy of it.

Relate All Sentences to an Implied Main Idea Write a paragraph that does not have a formal topic sentence, but make sure that all the sentences support one implied idea. In the following paragraph from Diane Ackerman's *A Natural History of the Senses*, the sentences support the idea that pain is subjective.

In the sand-swept sprawl of the panoramic film *Lawrence of Arabia* a scene of quintessential machismo stands out: T. E. Lawrence holding his hand over a candle flame until the flesh starts to sizzle. When his companion tries the same thing, he recoils in pain, crying "Doesn't that hurt you?" as he nurses his burned hand. "Yes," Lawrence replies coolly. "Then what is the trick?" the companion asks. "The trick," Lawrence answers, "is not to mind."

Delete Unrelated Ideas During revision, delete any sentences that clearly don't contribute to the main idea of a paragraph.

Consider what animals people find attractive, and you'll see an interesting pattern emerge. People generally love to look at the young of any species—kittens, puppies, chicks, and so on. ~~Young animals grow up quickly, though, and mature animals don't capture our imaginations in quite the same way.~~ People also love adult animals that have childlike features, such as big-eyed, small-nosed pandas and koalas. We are drawn to the young—and the young-looking—in other species, which remind us of our own babies.

Create Two Paragraphs from One A paragraph lacks unity if it contains more than one main idea. During revision, analyze each paragraph to make sure it is built around a single idea. Create new paragraphs wherever necessary.

Rosa climbed the stairs to her ballet class reluctantly that day. She knew that she would hear disappointing news: Inéz, not she, was going to dance the part of Giselle. I'll never get a break, she thought to herself. It's almost enough to make me hate her. ¶Meanwhile, Inéz had started to board the Fifth Avenue bus when a man in a business suit, obviously in a hurry, pushed by her, knocking her back onto the sidewalk. Inéz's left leg twisted in one direction, her foot in the other. Her leg would be in a cast for six weeks.

Unity in Description

A good description creates a unified impression. Consider the following paragraph from a story about a poor woman whose husband and children are dying of starvation. On the way to a temple, where there is supposed to be food, the woman's husband falls, obviously near death. Notice how all the details in this passage work together to create a unified impression of the mental anguish the woman is suffering.

> What do I remember? Every word, every detail. I remember walking along the wet deserted street by the wall of the temple; I remember looking up for the flare that had ever burnt on the top of the temple, and it was quenched; and the black demons of fear came shrieking at my ear and would not be silenced, for all that I repeated like a madwoman, "Fire cannot burn in water." I saw the faces of men who were not there and of children from whom the life had been filched, and yet it was black night, blacker than black since the stars were hidden.
>
> **Kamala Markandaya, *Nectar in a Sieve***

TECHNIQUES FOR ACHIEVING COHERENCE

A piece of writing is coherent when the ideas flow smoothly from one to the next, with no gaps in logical organization. The reader should be able to follow the ideas and readily understand the connections between them. Like unity, coherence is important both within single paragraphs and in longer writing as a whole.

WRITER TO WRITER

Logical consequences are the scarecrows of fools and the beacons of wise men.

Thomas Henry Huxley, British biologist

Coherence Within Paragraphs

A paragraph is coherent when each of its sentences logically flows to the next. Three major techniques help achieve coherence.

- Present your ideas in a logical order.
- Use pronouns, synonyms, and repeated words to show that ideas previously mentioned are connected.
- Use transitional devices to show the relationships among ideas.

Word Chains One way to create coherence in a piece of writing is by repeating key words from sentence to sentence or by referring to a previously stated idea in different words. As you read the following passage, notice how the repetition of the word *crab* creates a chain within the first paragraph and also between the first paragraph and the second.

L I T E R A R Y
· · · · · · · · · · · · · · ·
M O D E L

> I was not too fond of **crab,** ever since I saw my birthday **crab** boiled alive, but I knew I could not refuse. That's the way Chinese mothers show they love their children, not through hugs and kisses but with stern offerings of steamed dumplings, duck's gizzards, and **crab.**
>
> I thought I was doing the right thing, taking the **crab** with the missing leg. But my mother cried, "No! No! Big one, you eat it. I cannot finish." **Amy Tan, *The Joy Luck Club***

Another way to structure a word chain is by using synonyms, near synonyms, or pronouns instead of a key word. This technique creates coherence and adds interest and variety to your writing. Notice how the last two paragraphs of the passage that follows are linked by repetition of the word *dress,* by use of the near synonyms *red taffeta* and *green velvet,* and by use of the pronoun *it* in place of *red taffeta.*

Grammar
—**TIP**—

Be sure your reader can tell which nouns are referred to by the pronouns you choose.

> "He's a nice young man, a scholar, from college. You'll like him."
>
> "I won't." Naomi glared. "You're wearing my favorite **dress** for him."
>
> **The red taffeta. It** was the only nice **dress** Ruthie had, although she had put a dollar down on a **green velvet** now in layaway. **Marge Piercy, *Gone to Soldiers***

L I T E R A R Y
· · · · · · · · · · · · · · ·
M O D E L

Transitional Devices Another way to achieve coherence in your writing is to use words and phrases that indicate specific relationships and provide necessary links between ideas. Such words and phrases are called **transitional devices.** They can be used to achieve coherence both within a paragraph and between paragraphs in a longer piece of writing.

Occasionally, two ideas are so obviously connected that no transitional device is needed. In the following example, no transition is necessary because the reader can infer the connection between the bad weather described in the first sentence and the postponement of the trip reported in the second.

> The surf was pounding and there was a storm brewing. We decided to postpone our snorkeling trip.

More often, however, you need to add a specific word or phrase to show how two ideas are connected. In the next example, the word *nevertheless* signals the contrast between the idea in the first sentence and the idea in the second.

> Many people suffer from phobias—such as fear of heights, dogs, or driving—that make their lives very difficult. **Nevertheless,** through therapy, a person suffering from a phobia can gradually learn to deal with the object of his or her fear.

A transition can, of course, connect two paragraphs as well as two sentences. In the next passage, the transition *for example* shows how the second paragraph is connected to the first—it gives an example of the idea the first paragraph expresses.

PROFESSIONAL
· · · · · · · · · · · · · ·
M O D E L

> Persi Diaconis and Frederick Mosteller of Harvard have spent ten years collecting thousands of stories of coincidences. They have concluded that nearly all the coincidences were statistically likely events.
>
> **For example,** a few years ago a New Jersey woman won her state lottery twice within four months. This was widely reported as a one in 17 trillion long shot. But the odds were actually closer to one in 30. Why? One in 17 trillion is the odds that a given person who buys a single ticket for each of two lotteries will win both times. But the odds that *somebody,* out of all the millions who buy lottery tickets in the United States, will win twice in her lifetime are better than one in 30.
>
> *The New York Times*

Some of the most common transitions are those that show relationships of time or sequence. Other transitions show more abstract relationships, such as cause and effect, similarity, degree, or contrast. The following chart lists some of the most useful transitional devices.

Transitional Devices

	Words or Phrases	Example
Time or Sequence	before, during, after, earlier, then, later, soon, first, next, finally, once, eventually, in time	My legs felt heavier and heavier as the marathon continued. **Finally,** I saw the finish line.
Logical Relationships	since, therefore, as a result, because, inevitably, besides, consequently	Construction of the new reactor began that summer. **Inevitably,** public reaction was mixed.
Similarity	as, like, and, again, too, also, likewise, equally, similarly, another, moreover, in addition	The candidate's campaign workers were quite effective in delineating the issues. **Equally** important were their efforts to get the voters to vote.
Degree	better, best, more, most, worse, worst, less, least, greater, greatest	The story I wrote won a prize! **Even better,** it was published!
Contrast	but, yet, not, still, nevertheless, however, in contrast, otherwise, although, on the other hand, nonetheless	Smith's book treats its subject lightheartedly. **In contrast,** Vonnegut's novel treats the same topic with dark humor.

In addition to showing relationships, transitions can signal that an example is about to be given, that the material following the transition is being emphasized, that additional information follows, or that explanation or clarification is being offered to the reader.

Transitions That Introduce Examples

as	for example	for instance
like	such as	to illustrate
that is	namely	in particular

Transitions That Signal Emphasis

indeed	in fact	in other words

Transitions That Signal More Information

in addition	besides	furthermore
moreover	also	as well

Transitions That Signal Explanation

for example	that is	in other words

UNITY AND COHERENCE
IN LONGER WRITING

The same techniques you use to achieve unity and coherence within single paragraphs are useful for creating unity and coherence in longer pieces of writing such as essays and reports. In longer pieces, not only should each sentence build on the topic of its paragraph but each paragraph should also clearly contribute to the main idea of the composition. In addition, each paragraph should develop logically from the one that precedes it.

As you consider the following passage, notice how the sentences within each paragraph and the paragraphs themselves contribute to the writer's thesis. In addition, observe the various techniques the writer uses to create coherence in the piece.

According to a recent survey conducted by the Center for the Study of Public Information, a full 60 percent of American voters get all their information about political issues from nightly television programs. A democracy that gets most of its news from such shows is a democracy in great jeopardy, for half-hour news programs provide the public with the illusion of information, not the substance. This insubstantiality is the result not of a conspiracy to misinform or underinform; it is an inherent shortcoming of television as an information medium, at least as it is currently organized.

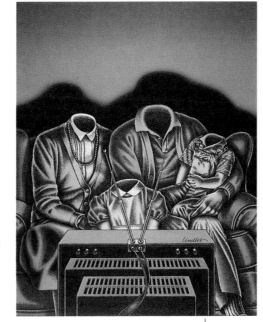

The importance of solid information to a democracy did not escape Thomas Jefferson, who felt most strongly that a democracy could survive only when the public was well informed. In his view, an informed public would have the ability to evaluate political issues and make political decisions on the basis of reason, not as a result of preconceptions or whims. He feared a public that received false or inadequate information; people would be unable to make intelligent decisions. Jefferson could not have foreseen television, but he clearly anticipated its impact.

To achieve coherence, the writer makes particularly effective use of repeated words such as *democracy,* of synonyms such as *not the substance* and *insubstantiality,* and of pronouns. The transition between paragraphs is provided by the phrase *the illusion of information,* the subject of the first paragraph, and the contrasting phrase, *the importance of solid information,* that begins the second.

Practice Your Skills

A. Revise the following paragraphs for unity and coherence. Delete unrelated ideas, reorganize the paragraphs, and add transitions so that the relationships among the ideas are clear.

1. Adopting a child from another country usually involves several steps. You travel to the country, go through the legal adoption procedure there, and then bring the child back to the United States. Once back in the United States, you go through additional legal procedures so that the adoption can be finalized under U.S. law. The first thing that happens, though, is that you contact an agency that deals with international adoptions, and this agency does a home study report on your family. After the home study is done, you have to get together many, many documents, including health certificates, birth certificates, marriage certificates, letters of recommendation, police checks, immigration and naturalization papers, and many others besides. These documents have to be notarized, certified, and sent to the country before you can travel there to adopt the child. To call this a complicated procedure is an extreme understatement. Marrying someone from another country is quite easy.

2. There are many, many approaches to painting a landscape in oils. You paint any large, background areas such as mountains, bodies of water, the ground, or the sky. You then add on smaller, middle-ground features such as grasses, trees, and clouds. Turner was a master at painting clouds. So was Winslow Homer. You add finishing details like branches, birds, fence posts, ice caps, ripples on the water, highlights, and shadows. Basically, you work from back to front. Begin with a really careful sketch. (If your sketch is good, it's hard to spoil it with paint.) Assemble your materials—oil paints, a palette, paint thinner, turpentine, brushes, a palette knife, cloths, canvas, an easel, and charcoal. Do your background sketch in charcoal. This is the approach that I usually take. Sketch right on the canvas. Your paint will cover up the sketch.

Breezing Up,
Winslow Homer

3. Until recently, the main source of information in the United States was the newspaper. By its very nature as a print medium, the newspaper can be read at the reader's own pace. Many people have even taken speed-reading courses to help them read faster. The newspaper provides long and careful analyses of issues and events. Recent polls show a sharp decline in readership. Some people read only the cartoons or the sports section. The in-depth analyses newspapers provide require higher levels of literacy and longer attention spans. Each year, more Americans get most of their information from television. Television is an inadequate medium for communicating information in depth. Because television is a visual medium, relying on stories that can be filmed, it cannot probe the subtlety of the issues that confront the citizens of a complex world. Television news programs must take periodic commercial breaks and the brief stories can never provide the depth that is possible in newspapers. The visual image encourages a focus on personalities rather than issues, a preoccupation that is demonstrated by the newscasters themselves, since they make tremendous amounts of money.

B. Read the following pairs of sentences. The first sentence of each pair comes at the end of one paragraph and the second comes at the start of the next. Identify the type of transitional device that links each pair.

1. [This system of streets] persisted in the Roman [town], the medieval eastern German towns, and the [towns] of southern France, in certain European cities of the seventeenth and eighteenth centuries, and, of course, in the modern cities of North America.
     Even more important than those practical criteria for the design of cities were the habits that governed the lives of their inhabitants.   **René Dubos**

2. The nights are always cold on Thorn. There's no fog there up on the mountainside, but the wind always blows.
     But Thorn was behind me now.   **Ursula Le Guin**

3. If you just press ENTER instead of keying in numbers for the day, month, and year, the robot will interpret this as an instruction to perform the requested tasks at the same time every day.
     After you enter the time, [it] will ask you to confirm that you entered the date and time correctly, and will then say, "Next."
                                                                                   Mike Higgins

Revising Effectively

WRITER TO WRITER

I do a lot of revising. Certain chapters six or seven times. Occasionally you can hit it right the first time. More often, you don't.

John Dos Passos, novelist

Revision is an integral part of the writing process entailing three different types of changes: rethinking content, reworking structure, and refining mechanics, or proofreading. You don't have to wait until you have completed a draft to begin revision, and you can often do more than one type of revision at a time.

REVISING FOR CONTENT

Rethinking content is the most important part of the revision process. You must make sure that your work has a clear focus, that the ideas are developed fully, and that all material included is relevant to your thesis. Consider the following issues as you revise.

Checklist for Rethinking Content

- **Is my thesis clear? Does my writing have a central focus?** Check that you have expressed your main idea clearly and that you have provided all the information your readers need.

- **Have I incorporated adequate detail?** See where you can insert a telling detail, a revealing statistic, or a vivid example.

- **Have I eliminated material that is unnecessary, irrelevant, or confusing?** Check your writing for unity, making sure that all the ideas and supporting details advance your thesis.

As you read the following first draft of an editorial for a high school newspaper, think of ways the content could be made stronger.

Three cheers for the Durfee Ecology Club! A few months ago some students at Durfee Community High decided that they wanted to improve their environment. They organized the Durfee Ecology Club, and one of their first projects was an extremely successful Clean-Up-Durfee Day on March 13. Last year fourteen trash containers were placed throughout the school. This constituted a major effort to keep Durfee clean; but how did all that litter get in the halls in the first place? And on the grounds. The answer is obvious, of coarse. Students put it there—careless, inconsiderate, thoughtless students. A lot of students prefer littering the school with trash and didn't make much use of the containers.

The student body should feel honored to have such civic-minded students in their school.

In rereading his draft, the writer realized that it lacked specific details about the number of students involved in the cleanup campaign and the number of trash bags they filled. He also decided to elaborate on the results of the campaign and to add a concluding paragraph urging students to make an ongoing commitment to the ecology effort.

REVISING FOR STRUCTURE

In addition to considering the content of your writing, you must examine its organization and sentence structure. The following questions will help you focus your structural review.

In considering the structure of his editorial, the writer realized that the last six sentences of the first paragraph were out of place, and he moved them to a more logical position. He also created paragraphs, added transitional words to clarify relationships, and reworded several sentences to eliminate unnecessary repetition.

REVISING FOR MECHANICS

When you proofread, or refine the mechanics of your writing, you look for and correct errors in grammar, usage, and mechanics. The following questions can help you identify these errors.

As the writer proofread his editorial, he indicated all content, structural, and mechanical alterations using the following standard editorial symbols.

Writing
TIP

As you proofread, have a dictionary, thesaurus, and style book available for easy reference.

Three cheers for the Durfee Ecology Club! A few months ago
some ∧*twenty-six* students at Durfee Community High decided that they

wanted to improve their environment. They organized the Durfee

Ecology Club, and one of their first projects was an extremely

successful Clean-Up-Durfee Day on March 13. ∧Last year fourteen
¶ This was not the first clean-up effort at Durfee, however.

trash containers were placed throughout the school. This constitut-

ed a major effort to keep Durfee clean, but how did all that litter get

in the halls in the first place? And on the grounds. The answer is

obviously, of coarse. Students put it there—careless, inconsiderate,

thoughtless students. ∧*Apparently* A lot of students prefer littering the school

with trash and didn't make much use of the containers. *to using*

The student body should feel honored to have such civic-

minded students in their school.

∧ *¶ It is time that all Durfee students take a look at their environment. The Ecology Club challenged students to participate in a clean-up day. Now I am challenging them to eliminate the need for clean-up days.*

Practice Your Skills

Revise the following expository piece, making content, structural, and mechanical changes as necessary.

Inertia is the tendensy of a physical body to stay in motion or at rest until it is acted upon on by an outside force. I have always been fascinated by that old parlor trick. You know, the one where someone snatches a tablecloth from a dining room table. That will work in principle, but in practice, you would find that friction between the dinnerware and the tablecloth creates enough force to overcome the effects of inertia. It starts everything moving right off the table.

Last night I tried a little experiment. It demonstrates the effects of inertia just as dramaticly but with far less mess! I followed these steps: I put a cup of water on the table, two inches from the edge. I centered a cake pan on the cup. I set a box in the middle of the cake pan. I balanced a hard-boiled egg on top. I positioned a broom in front of the setup and pinned it to the floor with my foot. Of course, I had to gather all the material first: a cup, a broom, an 8-inch cake pan, and a small, empty box with a slick surface. And don't forget the hard-boiled egg.

Once everything was ready, I pulled back the broom handle and aimed for the center of the cake pan. Then I let fly. Thwack! Clatter! The cake pan flew across the table. It crashed to the floor. Where was the egg? Sitting in the water. Because of inertia, the egg did not fly off the table, it just dropped into the cup.

I had to try the experiment several times before I could make it work. The trick is to hit the cake pan in the middle. Squarely. Some people like to use a raw egg. It makes the experiment more dramatic. My advice is don't.

Peer Review and Response

Although you are ultimately responsible for your own writing, you will find that a peer reader can be a valuable asset, serving as a sounding board when you want to try out ideas and providing feedback when you get stuck and need help in getting back on track.

WORKING WITH A PEER READER

Both you and your peer reader will find the relationship profitable, but you have to be clear about the ground rules at the outset. You want your reader to act as an audience, not as an editor. You want to know what he or she thinks about your writing, but it is up to you to decide what changes to make—or even whether to make changes at all. You may not agree with what your reader says. In that case, you may decide to keep your writing as it is.

It is not always easy to establish a satisfactory working relationship with a peer reader. Communication is crucial. You have to be specific in telling your reader just what kind of feedback you need. Here are a few suggestions for working with a peer reader that others have found effective.

Using a Peer Reader as a Sounding Board   Ask your peer reader to listen as you read your piece aloud. You can tell a great deal about your writing by sharing it this way. When someone is listening to you, you are more aware of what you're saying. Using your reader as a sounding board is especially useful in the early stages of the writing process, when you have just started to explore a topic and are not yet ready for criticism. Similarly, you may not want your reader to offer criticism after you finish a piece of writing. You will certainly hope that your reader likes the finished product, but you may be more interested in just having your work heard.

Focusing on the Positive   At times, you may become discouraged about a piece of writing. That's when you can go to your peer reader for some positive feedback, saying, "I need help. I want you to point to specific things in the piece that work especially well for you or that stick in your mind."

You may even be able to read between the lines of your reader's positive response to learn what doesn't work. For example, if you've written a story and your reader has not commented on one important character, you may wonder if that character is as effectively portrayed as he or she might be.

Clarifying Your Purpose   You can ask your peer reader to help you with your writing purpose by asking questions like this: "Can you help me see what my words actually accomplish?" One benefit of this is that you might find out whether you are saying what you think you're saying. Another is that you might come up with new ideas about your purpose that will take you in interesting directions.

Honing Your Ideas   You may want to ask your peer reader to ignore your language and focus only on your ideas. Phrase your questions something like this: "Talk to me about *what* I've said, not about *how* I've said it. What are your ideas on this topic? Where do you agree or disagree with me? What do you want to hear more about?" These questions will probably elicit some of your most valuable peer responses. They may help you establish your audience and purpose more clearly as well as find out whether your current ideas work.

Analyzing Specific Features   At some point, you may want to ask your peer reader for help in a specific area, such as word choice, organization, sentence structure, or mechanics. For example, you might ask for help on something concrete like transitions, saying: "Would you check this piece to see if you can find ways I can connect my ideas more closely?" Or you might ask for help on something more general like organization, saying: "What do you think about my organization? Is it easy to follow? Does it make sense?"

Here are other types of questions you could direct to your peer reader.

1. Listen as I read this speech aloud. Have I included enough examples to support my main point? Does the speech sound convincing?

2. Will you read this editorial I wrote for the school newspaper? Does it help you see my position, or at least make you question your own?

3. Will you check the paragraphing in this report? I tried to begin a new paragraph each time I began a new idea, but I am not sure of myself.

4. I really feel nervous about writing this letter of application. I want to appear calm and confident. Will you read the letter for me and tell me how I come across?

Writing
—**TIP**—

Listen carefully as your peer reader offers constructive criticism. Later, when you are alone and have time to think, you can sort out which ideas you think are really helpful.

Eliciting Spontaneous Feedback   Give your peer reader your piece of writing, saying: "Let me stop you a few times as you read so you can tell me what's going on in your mind—moment to moment." This type of response is trustworthy because it gives you your reader's immediate, unmodified reactions. Your reader might respond this way, for example: "Well, I was a little confused in the first paragraph because you quoted someone I've never heard of. Just now, though, I was really getting interested in this idea about America's changing demographics."

Here are some specific issues to consider when asking for spontaneous feedback from your reader.

1. You need to know your reader fairly well and trust him or her before you ask for this kind of honesty. The reader may feel something negative at the moment when you ask for a comment. He or she may say, "I'm really annoyed about this disorganized paragraph because it's interrupting my train of thought." Be sure you are prepared for the possibility of a negative response.

2. Your reader may say something too general, such as, "I pretty much like it." Try to find out exactly what caused this response. For example, ask, "What do you like in the sentence you just finished reading?"

3. Your reader may not want to be interrupted while reading. One alternative is for you to read your piece aloud, stopping once in a while to ask, "What are you thinking or feeling now?" Another option is to ask your reader to read silently, stopping to comment after each paragraph or page. A third option is to ask the reader to jot down brief responses as you read your piece aloud or to take marginal notes as he or she reads silently. You can then ask the reader to share those comments with you.

MAKING THE MOST OF PEER RESPONSE

You may get many varied or even contradictory responses to your writing. Not only do different readers respond differently to one piece of writing, but the same reader may respond differently to the same piece at different times. When you get multiple responses, the best strategy is to wait until you've heard all the responses. Take them all in, ponder them, and then make up your own mind.

Again, you're in control of your own writing. Don't feel that you have to argue with your peer reader or defend your own choices. Eventually, you will probably become relatively comfortable with peer response and find it an essential component of your writing process.

WRITER TO WRITER

The writer should receive another writer's opinion before trashing questionable ideas.

Kathleen O'Brill, student
Northfield, Illinois

ACTING AS A PEER READER

Try to take your responsibilities seriously when you act as a peer reader. Remember that the person whose writing you read today may be the one who reads yours tomorrow. Be constructive, and try to frame your criticisms diplomatically. For example, instead of saying, "Your grammar is abominable," say, "You might want to check the usage in this sentence. I don't think the subject agrees with the verb."

When you act as a peer reader, think of the type of feedback you find most helpful in your own writing, and respond accordingly. Here are some specifics.

- **Acting as a sounding board** Listen when your writer feels the need to read his or her piece aloud. Don't interrupt, and don't volunteer comments unless the writer asks for them.

- **Focusing on the positive** Whenever possible, comment on some aspect of the writing that you think is particularly effective. Volunteer suggestions for improving the piece only when asked.
- **Analyzing specific features** Follow the writer's lead in deciding what specific feature to focus upon. If the writer asks you to read the dialogue in a short story to see if it sounds natural, do it. If the writer just asks for help in punctuating the dialogue, however, don't offer unsolicited advice about whether or not it sounds realistic.

Practice Your Skills

In a small group, practice responding to the following rough draft in each of the six ways described in this lesson. Afterward, revise the piece of writing based on the group's comments.

Have you ever been to a stand-up comedy show in which the comic was not at all funny? You squirm in your chair and look the other way, trying to pretend that you don't notice anything wrong. Though you're thoroughly embarrassed, you know that the comic would like to be in another galaxy right now.

I believe that comedians, though they can make the audience believe they are artless and flaky, are actually the hardest-working, most courageous, and most talented of all performers. They have to be willing to do lots of stuff other performers don't have to worry about. Like actors on pretaped soaps.

Like Rodney Dangerfield, comedians rarely get any respect. But put yourself in their shoes. I wouldn't try to do it. No way.

The Far Side Cartoons by Gary Larson are reprinted by permission of Chronicle Features, San Francisco, CA.

"Larry? Betty? . . . Stand up, will ya? . . . These are some friends of mine, folks, who flew all the way in from the dump."

Improving Your Sentences

Some carpenters work on large, rough structures such as frames for houses. Other carpenters do more delicate work such as building cabinets, stairways, and wood moldings. Drafting is like rough carpentry. It's all about putting up the rough overall structure. After drafting you start to do the delicate work—the fine-tuning that will make your writing exceptional. One important part of this fine-tuning is the process of revising individual sentences.

CORRECTING EMPTY SENTENCES

To create effective sentences, you need to revise sentences that are grammatically correct, yet lack substance. Empty sentences often contain the following problems.

Circular Reasoning This problem occurs when the second part of a sentence merely restates what was said in the first part. Circular reasoning cheats the reader, who is led to expect details and reasons that are never supplied.

Circular	The increase of traffic problems in major urban areas results from having too much traffic congestion on the roads in the city.
Analysis	The writer promises to tell why traffic problems have increased, but then says in effect that there are traffic problems because there are traffic problems.
Revised	Traffic problems in major urban areas have increased because the number of vehicles on most roads and highways now dramatically exceeds the volume that city planners had anticipated.

Unsupported Opinions Sentences that contain opinions without reasons, facts, or examples force the reader to guess at the writer's full meaning. Such sentences need further development.

Unsupported	Automobile insurance rates are unfair.
Analysis	No reasons or facts are supplied to support the claim.
Revised	Automobile insurance rates are unfair because they discriminate against male drivers under the age of twenty-five.

Statement of the Obvious Some statements are so obvious that they do not need to be made. Everyone knows, for example, that Shakespeare was an important writer or that mountain climbing is difficult and dangerous. Your writing will be more effective if you learn to weed out the obvious.

Obvious   Dickens was a popular writer.

Revised   Dickens's popularity was due to his wide range of memorable characters and his intricate and suspenseful plots.

Practice Your Skills

Rewrite the following sentences to correct problems of circular reasoning, unsupported opinions, or statement of the obvious.

1. Leonardo da Vinci, a demanding perfectionist, never finished many of his artistic projects because he found it difficult to complete a work of art.
2. School sports can be dangerous.
3. Martin Luther King, Jr., received a doctorate in systematic theology from Boston University in 1955, the same year that people began to call him "Doctor."
4. The extremes in contemporary fashion are interesting.
5. Since its founding, the United States has always been a nation of immigrants.
6. Ambition can be potentially harmful.
7. Some critics argue that the poetry of Edgar Allan Poe sounds better when translated into French because the poems achieve a more musical quality in French.
8. Cross-country skiing, a popular recreational sport in many countries, is enjoyed during the winter.
9. Abraham Lincoln was a remarkable President.
10. *Mrs. Dalloway* was the most challenging novel I have ever encountered, owing to its complexity.

REDUCING OVERLOADED SENTENCES

For the same reason that a machine should have no unnecessary parts, a sentence should have no unnecessary words. Lively writing is concise. For example, consider the following statement written by Barley T. Campbell.

Distance lends enchantment to the view.

Now read the same idea expressed in another sentence.

> Sometimes you have to step back from a scene in order to really see it, because if you are too close you may not appreciate it as fully as possible.

In the first sentence, the writer focused precisely on his idea. The second sentence, with five times the number of words, is **overloaded.**

Overloaded sentences may contain unrelated details, too many ideas or details, or unclear relationships among ideas.

Unrelated Details   Unrelated details interrupt the main ideas and distract the reader.

Overloaded   The poet Carl Sandburg, who once lived in Kansas, was the author of a biography of Abraham Lincoln.

Revised   The poet Carl Sandburg wrote a biography of Abraham Lincoln.

Too Many Ideas   Putting too many ideas or details in a sentence can make you forget what you started to write and will confuse the reader. When you find overloaded sentences in your writing, you will need to eliminate some details or put them in a new sentence.

Overloaded   Everyone should learn a second language because this knowledge will expand his or her cultural horizons, while it may lead to practical career benefits as well, considering our need for businesspeople who are fluent in more than one language.

Revised   Everyone should learn a second language to expand his or her cultural horizons. Bilingual ability may also have practical benefits, since many businesses need bilingual employees.

Stringy Sentences   Some sentences become overloaded when the writer strings a series of ideas together with *and's*. In the resulting run-on sentence, no single idea stands out, and the reader will find it difficult to understand how the ideas are related. When revising, you can correct a stringy sentence in two ways:

1. Choose conjunctions that will show a more precise relationship between your ideas. A subordinating conjunction such as *because, in order that, although,* or *whenever* is more specific than *and.* For more information, see Grammar Handbook 31, pages 562–564.

Writing
— TIP —

You may find it helpful to list all the ideas in a sentence you suspect of being wordy. Then you can decide which ideas belong in the sentence and which should be deleted or put in another sentence.

2. Divide the sentence into two or more statements.

Stringy   There is a water shortage in many parts of the country, *and* this shortage is causing concern, *and* the U.S. Department of the Interior is trying to find economical methods of changing sea water to fresh water.

Revised   The water shortage in many parts of the country is causing concern; *consequently,* the U.S. Department of the Interior is trying to find economical methods of changing sea water to fresh water.

Stringy   Scientists today are working in an invisible world, *and* they are dealing with atoms, ions, electrons, and quarks, *and* no one has ever seen these things, *and* some of them may not even exist in the usual sense of the word.

Revised   Scientists today are working in an invisible world of atoms, ions, electrons, and quarks. No one has ever seen these things; *indeed,* some of them may not even exist in the usual sense of the word.

Practice Your Skills

Rewrite the following overloaded sentences by choosing more precise conjunctions, eliminating details, or creating new sentences.

1. She had just been promoted to book critic for our newspaper, and she decided to write her own novel and quit her job, and we were in a quandary about who could be hired to replace her.
2. Building a tunnel beneath the English Channel is a sensible idea though a difficult engineering feat, and also expensive, because the tunnel will ease travel between England and the Continent.
3. Scientists dreamed long ago of transmitting power through the air without the use of wires, and they experimented for many years, developing their ideas, and at last they seem to be near the realization of their dream.
4. San Francisco, the famed "City by the Bay," with its breathtaking hills, scenic waterfronts, and pastel-colored houses that excite the senses, not to mention the russet-hued majesty of the Golden Gate Bridge, is one of America's most enchanting cities.
5. We usually finish our chores on Saturday, which is the last day of the week, and buy groceries for the next week.
6. Art lovers enjoy Florence, Italy, which my aunt Florence says she was named after, because of the city's great art treasures.
7. Our first day of traveling brought us to the outskirts of Houston, and just as we were about to stop for the night, the car stalled, and we later learned that it would need extensive repairs.

8. Ryan, who won the soccer award last year after recuperating from an extended illness early in the season, went skiing in the Colorado Rockies with his friends.
9. The emergency crew was able to tow away the truck that had burned, since the tires had not been damaged, though no one who saw it thought the truck could be repaired, despite the owner's hopes to the contrary, which probably reflected an understandable lack of perspective.
10. Ben Jonson wrote one of his most famous poems to commemorate the death of his seven-year-old son, who died after he became a victim of the plague in 1603, and this loss was deeply mourned by the father, who considered his son his "best piece of poetry."

AVOIDING WORDINESS

A sentence containing unnecessary words is usually hard to read because the extra words obscure the meaning. Consider the following sentence.

> The world is full of both advantages and disadvantages, and for every advantage that we enjoy we have to compensate for it by accepting some disadvantage at the same time.

Now read a sentence by Ralph Waldo Emerson in which the same idea is expressed more concisely.

> Every advantage has its tax.

You can correct wordiness in your writing in two ways: by eliminating repetition and by reducing sentences.

Redundancy   One kind of wordiness results from needless repetition. Correct redundancies by deleting words, using pronouns, or rewriting.

Wordy   We thought we had provided an adequate supply of food with enough for everyone to eat.

Revised   We thought we had provided an adequate supply of food.

Wordy   I have chosen a topic that is a frequent topic of debate. My topic is the exploitation of our natural resources.

Revised   I have chosen a topic that is frequently debated today— the exploitation of our natural resources.

Wordiness can result from using several words instead of one.

Wordy *At the present time* she thinks that she will be able to join us, but since her schedule may change, she cannot be certain until *a later point in time.*

Revised Now she thinks that she will be able to join us, but since her schedule may change, she can't be certain yet.

Sentence Reduction Sometimes you need to reduce a sentence to avoid wordiness. At other times you may want to reduce one for stylistic reasons. You can often convert wordy sentences into shorter ones in one of three ways:

1. Change a clause to a phrase.
2. Change a clause to an appositive.
3. Change a phrase to a single modifier.

Clause *When pajamas were brought from India to England,* they caused a tremendous sensation.

Phrase *Bringing pajamas from India to England* caused a tremendous sensation.

Clause My cousin Leslie likes to hear me tell "The Three Bears," *which is a favorite story of many children.*

Appositive My cousin Leslie likes to hear me tell "The Three Bears," *a favorite story of many children.*

Phrase One of the *players on the team that represents Detroit* was hurt badly.

Modifier One of the *Detroit players* was hurt badly.

If the clauses of a compound sentence have the same subject, you can reduce the sentence by changing it to a simple sentence with a compound predicate. If, on the other hand, the clauses of a compound sentence have the same verb, you can reduce the sentence by using a compound subject.

Compound Sentence The quarterback's feeble pass floated lazily, and it was easily intercepted.

Simple Sentence The quarterback's feeble pass floated lazily and was easily intercepted.

Compound Sentence All the cups of the new china set shattered upon falling, and the saucers shattered too.

Simple Sentence All the cups and saucers of the new china set shattered upon falling.

Practice Your Skills

A. Rewrite the following sentences, eliminating wordiness.

1. The activity of weather forecasting is not new, for humans have been trying or attempting to predict the weather correctly with accuracy for many years.
2. Three hundred years ago, people believed that with confidence that they would be able to predict changes in patterns of weather.
3. In 1593 the thermometer had been invented, and less than a hundred years later a simple barometer was invented in 1643.
4. With these two instruments, which measured temperature and which measured air pressure, humans were able to tell how cold the air was and how heavy the air was that they were measuring.
5. In the year 1686, the Englishman Edmund Halley, who was an English astronomer, made the first weather map in existence.
6. Weather maps of the early 1800's showed weather systems, and those maps showed and indicated that the weather systems moved with the prevailing winds.
7. At that time scientists could predict the approach of storms, but scientists could not warn people about the approaching storms.
8. Because there was no radio or television available or possible at that time, reports of weather observations were then sent by mail through the postal system.
9. Unfortunately, the storms often arrived, as luck would have it, before the mail had a chance to arrive.
10. Now, we have better and more accurate methods of forecasting weather, and we have better methods of relaying our weather forecast information.

B. Rewrite the following paragraph. Avoid wordiness by eliminating redundancies and reducing overloaded sentences.

On May 25, 1981, Dan Goodwin dressed in a Spiderman suit, which he wore as a costume, and set off to climb Sears Tower in Chicago, the city which is on Lake Michigan, and which is also the tallest of the world's tall buildings, or skyscrapers. Dan used a homemade claw and cups that had a suction capacity to climb the 110-story building, and officials were not amused, and Dan's stunt or process of climbing violated city laws which prohibited trespassing. As Goodwin was climbing the skyscraper, people who were permanent employees of the fire department were lowered from the top of the building in an attempt to stop him, but he evaded them successfully, and when Dan Goodwin finally reached the top of the Sears Tower, he was arrested and taken into police custody.

PREVENTING AWKWARD BEGINNINGS

Just as first impressions are difficult to alter, it is hard to regain the attention of a reader who has been bored by a weak beginning.

WRITER TO WRITER

Fiction writing is very seldom a matter of saying things; it is a matter of showing things.

Flannery O'Connor, short story writer and novelist

A less skillful writer than Flannery O'Connor might have begun the sentence above with *It is a commonly recognized fact that* or *In my opinion.* Avoid beginning sentences with phrases that unnecessarily delay expressing the main ideas. The most common of such phrases are *the fact that, due to the fact that, what I believe is, in my opinion,* and *the reason is.* Also be careful of overusing phrases such as *there are* and *here is,* which are often unnecessary.

Study these solutions to the problem of awkward beginnings.

Awkward	There are many useful experiments being conducted at the University of Michigan.
Revised	Many useful experiments are being conducted at the University of Michigan.
Awkward	Due to the fact that Joan's injury is serious, she was unable to compete in the race.
Revised	Because Joan's injury was serious, she was unable to compete in the race.
Revised	Joan's injury was serious, so she was unable to compete in the race.

Practice Your Skills

Rewrite the following sentences to avoid awkward beginnings.

1. What a waterfall is, is a sudden and steep descent of a stream or river from one level to another.
2. The reason that a waterfall exists is because the soft rock of the stream bottom has worn away, and the water plunges over the ledge of hard rock that remains.

3. What a small volume of falling water is called is a cascade, while a large volume of falling water is called a cataract.
4. There is Niagara Falls, one of the most spectacular cataracts in the world, but this is due to the volume of water and not the depth of the drop.
5. In my opinion, Niagara's fame can be partially attributed to the daredevils who have attempted death-defying stunts there.
6. The fact of the matter is that there are at least twelve cataracts in North America that are higher than Niagara Falls.
7. What I want to point out is that the drop of Ribbon Falls in Yosemite, California, is almost twice as steep as that of Niagara.
8. In point of fact, there are six waterfalls in Yosemite alone that are higher than Niagara Falls.
9. Then, too, it should also be recognized that there are at least fourteen other cataracts in the world higher than Niagara Falls.
10. You can believe it when I tell you that Angel Falls in Venezuela has a total drop of 3,212 feet, while Tugela Falls in South Africa has a total drop of 2,014 feet.

LINKING SENTENCE PARTS

Anyone reading your writing has certain expectations because of the way you have constructed your sentences. If your sentence parts are not linked correctly, your sentences will be awkward or difficult to understand.

Parallel Sentence Parts   Parts of a sentence that have parallel meanings should be parallel in structure. When *and* is used to join sentence parts of equal value, such as noun and noun, verb and verb, or phrase and phrase, the constructions are said to be **parallel.** One error in parallel structure occurs when *and* is used to join unequal constructions.

Not Parallel   I like *football, soccer,* and *playing softball.* (two nouns and a gerund)

Parallel   I like *football, soccer,* and *softball.* (three nouns)

A particular type of faulty parallelism occurs with *which* and *who. And* should never appear before these words unless *which* or *who* appears earlier in the sentence.

Incorrect   Shanghai, China, one of the world's largest cities, *and which* has a densely populated city center has a high standard of living by Chinese standards.

Correct	Shanghai, China, *which* is one of the world's largest cities, *and which* has a densely populated city center, has a high standard of living by Chinese standards.

Related Sentence Parts Certain sentence parts derive much of their meaning from their relation to each other: subject and verb, verb and complement, the parts of a verb phrase. When these related sentence parts are separated by intervening words, the resulting sentence is confusing. Keep closely related sentence parts together.

Confusing	The Seminoles *were,* after several fierce wars with the U.S. Army, *defeated* and *moved* to reservations. (parts of verb phrase separated)
Revised	After several fierce wars with the U.S. Army, the Seminoles *were defeated* and *were moved to* reservations.
Confusing	In 1970, the U.S. government *awarded* to the Seminoles, as partial compensation for lands taken from their ancestors 150 years earlier, *twelve million dollars.* (verb and direct object separated)
Revised	In 1970, the U.S. government *awarded twelve million dollars* to the Seminoles as partial compensation for lands taken from their ancestors 150 years earlier.

Practice Your Skills

Rewrite the following sentences to make sentence parts parallel or to connect related sentence parts.

1. I sat and watched and was hoping she would not drop the baton.
2. The kneeling chair has an unconventional design and which is quite comfortable was developed in Scandinavia.
3. After we arrived, we took a cab to the train station, had lunch, and were looking at the train schedule.
4. As in a Chagall painting, people had the ability to fly and floating in space.
5. On the trip to Belize, the students were able to try scuba diving and to snorkel.
6. The dog trainer was able, after several classes on heeling and staying, to help Geoffrey control the spaniel.
7. In Rome we bought, as a present for Julia's birthday, a purse.
8. Liane practiced long-distance running, swimming, and the bicycle for the triathlon.
9. New arrivals to San Juan crowd its streets and who search for jobs often live in substandard housing.
10. We were, as the sun set slowly, completely satisfied just to watch.

Presenting and Publishing Your Writing

Through writing, you can teach people, persuade them, make them laugh, or move them to tears. You already know how rewarding it can be to have people read and respond favorably to your work. Until now, though, you may have limited your writing audience to your teachers and closest family and friends. There are many ways, however, for you to expand your audience.

WRITER TO WRITER

What I love about writing is the finished product.

Victoria Reilly, student
Bethpage, New York

IDEAS FOR INFORMALLY SHARING YOUR WRITING

You can share your writing at any point during the writing process. Here are some ways to share your writing with others.

Sharing Your Writing in Process

- Have someone sit at your word-processing terminal, reading and responding to what you have written.

- Have someone read your manuscript and comment on it in the margins, and then return it to you.

- Meet with your teacher to discuss a particular piece of writing or your writing portfolio as a whole.

- Form a writing exchange group with friends or classmates. Meet regularly to read and comment on one another's work.

- Keep a portfolio of your writing. When you want to share your work, find there the pieces that you want others to read.

If you feel ready to share your writing with an audience, take steps to get your work published. Here are some options you might consider for self-publication and for formal publication.

Self-Publishing Options

- Make copies of your work to distribute to friends, relatives, classmates, and teachers.
- Present your work orally at speech tournaments or in similar situations.
- Save your work on a computer diskette and give the diskette to others who have access to a computer.
- Write pieces for production or interpretation by a drama club or other fine-arts groups.
- Make a home video or cassette recording of your work.
- Through collaboration with others, create a class anthology, magazine, or newspaper, and distribute it.

Formal Publishing Options: Publishing at Your School

- Submit writing to your school newspaper. Some school papers publish short stories, essays, and poems as well as news stories and features.
- Yearbook editors sometimes need short pieces to accompany photographs of various school activities.
- Your school may publish a literary magazine that contains poems, essays, and short stories by student writers. If not, consider starting one yourself, with a faculty sponsor and a staff of fellow students.
- Give a multi-media presentation of your work at a school assembly or special-interest club meeting.

COMPUTER TIP

If you have access to the necessary software, try experimenting with the layout of your writing. See how various designs can affect the dramatic impact or reading of your work.

Formal Publishing Options: Publishing in the Larger Writing Community

- Write and send a letter or even a long commentary for publication on the editorial page of a local newspaper. Your community paper may also print news stories or feature articles by nonstaff writers.

- Submit your work to a local or national writing contest. Some communities have contests sponsored by newspapers, arts organizations, historical societies, or public-service groups. These are often announced through the local newspaper. In addition, *Atlantic Monthly, English Journal,* National Federation of Press Women, National Council of Teachers of English, the Poetry Society of America, *Redbook,* and Scholastic Magazines, Inc., all sponsor writing contests. *Writer's Digest* and *The Writer* magazines are also good sources for information on writing contests.

- Send your work to trade magazines that publish work by young adults. Publications such as *Market Guide for Young Writers* and *Writer's Market* list these magazines as well as other publishing opportunities.

MANUSCRIPT PREPARATION

For formal publication, you will need to prepare your writing in standard manuscript format. Here are some basic guidelines.

- Type or word-process your piece double-spaced.
- Place your name and the page number in the upper right-hand corner of each page.
- Leave ¾-inch margins all around the page.
- If you have a title for your piece, center it on the top line.
- Keep your pages together with a staple or paper clip at the upper left-hand corner.

There are some variations in manuscript preparation guidelines, so check to find out what your prospective publisher prefers. It is important to follow these guidelines meticulously. Doing so will increase the chances of your manuscript being given adequate consideration and even being accepted for publication.

Beyond manuscript preparation, you may be interested in designing your own work, that is, doing your own layout and graphic design. **Layout** is the process of preparing a printed page in which you divide the page into carefully measured columns and indicate space for pictures and art. **Graphic design** is the art of designing a printed page. A graphic designer makes decisions about layouts, typefaces, borders, art, photographs, and graphic elements such as symbols and bars. Some computer programs make it possible for writers to experiment with various graphic elements and influence the way their work will look on the page. Consult your local computer dealer or the manuals for the software programs to which you have access for further information about how you can design and style the look of your writing.

Practice Your Skills

A. Think of an idea for a short story or a nonfiction article. Choose a local newspaper or a magazine to which you'd like to submit the piece and find out what specific guidelines the publisher requires writers to follow. Write your piece, prepare a final copy following the guidelines, and mail it to the appropriate office.

B. Working with your classmates, publish a newsletter of students' stories, essays, poems, and dramatic sketches. First, develop a design for your newsletter; decide on its overall size, the size of its margins, the number and width of the columns, whether it will have photos or illustrations and other graphic features. Collect writing from classmates typed to fit your column sizes, and then cut and paste the writing onto pieces of paper. Also paste up artwork to accompany the writing. Finally, make copies of your finished newsletter and distribute them.

Sketchbook

"I judge a man by the shoes he wears, Jerry."

What is your personal style?

Additional Sketches

Can you remember a time when something you said was completely misunderstood? Tell about the experience.

Think of a person whose style you admire. You could select a writer, actor, musician, artist, or someone from any walk of life. Why does this person's style appeal to you?

Understanding Voice and Style

No two people use language in exactly the same way. A given writer or speaker's particular way of using language is known as his or her **style.** Writers often find that the more they write, the stronger and more distinctive their writing style becomes. Most professional writers have developed styles that are as distinct and recognizable as their signatures.

W R I T E R   T O   W R I T E R

Interest and style vary between people, just as much as people themselves vary.

Alison Elgin, student
Seattle, Washington

YOUR UNIQUE STYLE

The following elements work together to create a writing style. To develop a style that is distinctly your own, you need to make choices about how you want these elements to work in your writing. Of course, you may make different choices with each piece of writing, depending on your audience and purpose. However, your individual writing style will be the basis of every set of decisions.

Sentence Structure   Certain aspects of sentence structure help define the style of each piece of your writing. Will you write short, simple sentences or long ones with several phrases and clauses? Will the verb always follow the subject or will you vary the sentence structure?

Diction   Your diction, or word choice, greatly affects your writing style. In some circumstances—and for some audiences—common, general words like *brave* or *dog* are most appropriate. In other situations, precise words like *intrepid* or *terrier* are best. If your diction is good, you'll consistently choose strong nouns and verbs rather than modifiers, and you'll avoid redundancy, jargon, and clichés.

Imagery   The way you use images or descriptive pictures affects the style of your writing. Will you describe things in a direct, literal way? Or will you draw on figures of speech to color your descriptions?

COMPUTER
TIP

If your word-processing program has a thesaurus, it will help you choose the best word by offering you a list of synonyms. Choose the synonym that is most appropriate for your context and the voice you have chosen.

Voice and Style   **417**

Mechanics Will you use exclamation points often in your composition? Are you fond of the dash? The way you use punctuation is also part of your writing style.

Tone What is your attitude toward the subject you are writing about? Sympathetic? Curious? Lighthearted? Ironic? Outraged? The way you feel about your subject influences the language you use and sets the tone of your writing.

Voice Voice is the individual "sound" of your writing, closely interwoven with all the previously mentioned elements of style. Note how the author's voice comes through even in the following paragraph about iguanas.

> They stare at the surf, beneath which their pastures of algae are now buried by the risen tide. They shift their positions as the sun shifts, as their bodies warm, and seldom otherwise move. I want to see them swim. But they don't oblige. Occasionally the big male bobs his head, a quick series of three or four jerky nods that seem to say: *Believe it, Jack, I'm the baddest dude on this piece of beach.*
>
> **David Quammen, *The Flight of the Iguana***

Together, Quammen's varied sentence structure, precise language, evocative imagery, humorous slang, and lighthearted tone contribute to the voice of the paragraph.

Y OUR UNIQUE VOICE

Writing is like having your own private canyon in New Mexico where you can go to be alone with your thoughts, to shout your ideas and feelings without inhibition, and then to listen to their echoes. Writing allows you to hear yourself clearly and to recognize your own uniqueness. Discover your true voice in your writing and see what makes it different from anyone else's. The following guidelines will help you assert your individual voice in your writing.

Write for yourself. When you write without thinking about an audience, you are not tempted to change your voice to impress other people. The voice that emerges is your own. Write often just for yourself. Journal writing is an excellent vehicle for this.

Write about things you care about. If you feel passionately about your subject, your caring will be evident in your voice. Even when your choice of writing topics is limited, you can usually find some part of the topic that you care about.

Use everyday language. Don't upgrade your vocabulary to impress your audience. Avoid the fifty-cent word when a nickel word will convey your meaning just as well. Try to capture the flavor of your own conversational tone.

Delete superfluous words. Many deadwood expressions and wordy phrases can be whittled down for more effective writing. For example, you can change phrases such as the following to make your prose clear and precise.

make an attempt to	>	*try*
in a hasty manner	>	*hastily*
owing to the fact that	>	*because*
gain an understanding of	>	*understand*

Read your work aloud. The best way to hear how your writing voice sounds is to read your words aloud. Revise passages that sound silly, wooden, or phony. Also replace words or phrases that are difficult to pronounce aloud with language that can be spoken smoothly.

Use other writers' voices. You can actually develop your own style of writing by imitating other writers' voices. Try imitating writers whose styles you admire. You'll soon be integrating the elements you feel most comfortable with into your own work.

CHOOSING DIFFERENT VOICES

Inevitably, your style will change to suit the purpose of each piece of writing you do. You must find the most appropriate stylistic options in every writing circumstance. In some writing situations, for example, you may need to choose a voice other than your own or to use a voice that exaggerates some of the characteristics of your own voice. If you were writing a poem about a young child, you might choose to speak in the child's voice, using short sentences and simple vocabulary. You might also use nonstandard speech to present your child speaker realistically. On the other hand, if you were writing a scientific report, you might decide to use careful, precise language and an objective tone to reflect the seriousness and reliability of your content.

Writing TIP

Tape-record your ideas before writing to help you retain some of the natural elements of your spoken language.

Voice and Style **419**

As you read the following two passages by E.B. White, listen to the two different voices of the writer. Both passages are descriptions of summer, but one comes from a book White wrote for children, and the other comes from an essay he wrote for adults.

LITERARY
M O D E L

> The early summer days on a farm are the happiest, fairest days of the year. Lilacs bloom and make the air sweet, and then fade. Apple blossoms come with lilacs, and the bees visit around among the apple trees. The days grow warm and soft. School ends, and children have time to play and to fish for trouts in the brook. Avery often brought a trout home in his pocket, warm and stiff and ready to be fried for supper. . . .
>
> In early summer there are plenty of things for a child to eat and drink and suck and chew. Dandelion stems are full of milk, clover heads are loaded with nectar, the Frigidaire is full of ice-cold drinks. Everywhere you look is life; even the little ball of spit on the weed stalk, if you poke it apart, has a green worm inside it. And on the underside of the leaf of the potato vine are the bright orange eggs of the potato bug.
>
> **E.B. White, *Charlotte's Web***

LITERARY
M O D E L

> Summertime, oh, summertime, pattern of life indelible, the pasture with the sweet fern and the juniper forever and ever, summer without end; this was the background and the life along the shore was the design, the cottages with their innocent and tranquil design, their tiny docks with the flagpole and the American flag floating against the white clouds in the blue sky, the little paths over the roots of the trees leading from camp to camp and the paths leading back to the outhouses and the can of lime for sprinkling, and at the souvenir counters at the store the miniature birch-bark canoes and the postcards that showed things looking a little better than they looked.
>
> **E.B. White, "Once More to the Lake"**

In *Charlotte's Web,* White uses short, simple sentences; monosyllabic, familiar words; and concrete images. In "Once More to the Lake," he uses a very long, complex sentence; less common words; and poetic images. By modifying various stylistic elements in each passage, White adapts his voice to his audience.

Practice Your Skills

A. Read each of the following passages. Consider the sentence structure, diction, imagery, mechanics, and tone of each. Write a paragraph comparing and contrasting the two writers' styles.

1. To an anomalous species of terror I found him a bounden slave. "I shall perish," said he, "I must perish in this deplorable folly. Thus, thus, and not otherwise, shall I be lost. I dread the events of the future, not in themselves, but in their results. I shudder at the thought of any, even the most trivial, incident, which may operate upon this intolerable agitation of the soul. I have, indeed, no abhorrence of danger, except in its absolute effect—in terror. In this unnerved—in this pitiable condition—I feel that the period will sooner or later arrive when I must abandon life and reason together, in some struggle with the grim phantasm, FEAR."
    Edgar Allan Poe, *The Fall of the House of Usher*

2. The woman of Pablo could feel her rage changing to sorrow and to a feeling of the thwarting of all hope and promise. She knew this feeling from when she was a girl and she knew the things that caused it all through her life. It came now suddenly and she put it away from her and would not let it touch her, neither her nor the Republic, and she said, "Now we will eat. Serve the bowls from the pot, Maria."   **Ernest Hemingway, *For Whom the Bell Tolls***

Voice and Style   **421**

B. Read each of the following passages. In a small-group discussion, compare and contrast the three writers' voices. Explain what you like most about each writer's voice.

1.   My life changed completely when I was twelve, the summer the heavy rains came. The Fen River which ran through the middle of my family's land flooded the plains. It destroyed all the wheat my family had planted that year and made the land useless for years to come. Even our house on top of the little hill became unlivable. When we came down from the second story, we saw the floors and furniture were covered with sticky mud. The courtyards were littered with uprooted trees, broken bits of walls, and dead chickens. We were so poor in all this mess.

Amy Tan, *The Joy Luck Club*

2.   Nobody in this family lies in the sun. You work in the sun, you lie in the shade. We don't have air-conditioning, of course. "If you'd work up a little sweat out there, the shade ought to feel good enough for you" is Dad's thinking. Air-conditioning is for the weak and indolent. This isn't the Ritz, you know. Be thankful for a little breeze.

Garrison Keillor, *Lake Wobegon Days*

3.   Elizabeth, however, had never been blind to the impropriety of her father's behaviour as a husband. She had always seen it with pain; but respecting his abilities, and grateful for his affectionate treatment of herself, she endeavoured to forget what she could not overlook, and to banish from her thoughts that continual breach of conjugal obligation and decorum which, in exposing his wife to the contempt of her own children, was so highly reprehensible. But she had never felt so strongly as now, the disadvantages which must attend the children of so unsuitable a marriage, nor ever been so fully aware of the evils arising from so ill-judged a direction of talents; talents which rightly used, might at least have preserved the respectability of his daughters, even if incapable of enlarging the mind of his wife.

Jane Austen, *Pride and Prejudice*

4.   Polly sat for a little time on the side of the bed, crying. Then she dried her eyes and went over to the looking glass. She dipped the end of the towel in the water jug and refreshed her eyes with the cool water. . . . Then she went back to the bed again and sat at the foot. . . . She rested the nape of her neck against the cool iron bedrail and fell into a reverie. There was no longer any perturbation visible on her face.

James Joyce, ''The Boarding House''

Creating Emphasis, Tone, and Mood

The process of writing is more than just an intellectual activity. It is an emotional one as well—both for you as a writer and for your audience who shares your artistry. Emphasis, tone, and mood work together to create the emotional impact of all writing.

WRITER TO WRITER

Write your heart out.

Bernard Malamud, fiction writer

EMPHASIS

Good writers have an appreciation for sentence rhythm and an ability to create varied and interesting effects in their writing. **Emphasis** is the special stress given to words and phrases to make them stand out and have an impact on the reader. Good writers avoid relying on exclamation points, underlinings, and words like *very, really,* and *quite* to achieve emphasis.

By changing your syntax, or word order, you can make a whole paragraph or certain parts of it emphatic. You can, for example, repeat important words and phrases or use parallel or varied sentence structure.

Repetition　Repeating words and phrases can create emphasis within a sentence or paragraph. To be effective, repetition must not simply be a lack of variety. Use repetition only when the repeated word underscores an idea you want to emphasize. Notice how the repetition of the word *hunger* serves to unify the following passage. The reader can actually feel the narrator's urgency.

> Hunger stole upon me so slowly that at first I was not aware of what hunger really meant. Hunger had always been more or less at my elbow when I played, but now I began to wake up at night to find hunger standing at my bedside, staring at me gauntly.
> **Richard Wright, *Black Boy***

Parallelism   By expressing related concepts in similar structural and grammatical forms, parallelism achieves emphasis. Note how Gwendolyn Brooks uses parallelism and the repetition of phrases to emphasize the importance of ritual at Christmastime.

> The world of Christmas was firm. Certain things were done. Certain things were not done.
>
> **Gwendolyn Brooks, *Report from Part One***

Position   One of the simplest ways to achieve emphasis and make your writing more interesting is to change the position of words or phrases. When a modifier is moved to the front of the sentence as shown below, it immediately gains importance.

> Instinctively, I pulled my quilt over my face to stifle a cry of terror.   **Nien Cheng, *Life and Death in Shanghai***

A second possibility is to invert a sentence's customary word order; a subject can follow a verb, or a verb can follow an adverb.

> In the high heavens rode a veiled moon, magnified by the mist of an early spring day.   **Colette**

Notice how Katherine Mansfield uses this technique successfully in the passage on page 427 of this handbook.

passage on page 427 of this handbook.

Writing
━TIP━

Remember that your tone must remain consistent throughout a piece of writing. During revision, check to be sure that your attitude —or that of your narrator—has not changed.

T O N E

Tone is the expression of the attitude you have toward the subject of your writing. You communicate tone through your choice and placement of words and the complexity of your sentence structure. The tone of a piece of writing is conveyed through the voice of the narrator, the speaker, or the actual writer.

A list of various tones you can communicate through your writing would be virtually endless. The following box, however, includes a few of the more common ones.

Types of Tone in Writing

formal	amused	admiring	humorous
informal	condescending	bitter	sympathetic
romantic	optimistic	ironic	serious
satirical	critical	pessimistic	cynical

Your audience and writing purpose should help you determine your tone. For research reports, you will want to adopt a fairly objective or scientific tone that focuses attention on the content of your writing and allows the reader to make his or her own judgments. For essays and for fiction writing, you can use a more informal, subjective tone.

The following passage from an encyclopedia illustrates the use of objective tone.

> The Indian Meteorological Department recognizes four seasons. . . . In effect, however, there are only three noticeable seasons—the cold season, from about November to the end of February; the hot season (when it can be intensely warm, particularly in central and northern India), from about March to June; and the rainy season, from about June to October, by which time the southwest monsoon expends itself.
>
> **Encyclopaedia Britannica**

In contrast, a writer crafting an essay on the same general subject may adopt a highly subjective tone.

> I cannot describe the *oppression* of such afternoons. It is a physical oppression—heat pressing down on me and pressing in the walls and the ceiling and congealing together with time which has stood still and will never move again. And it is not only those two—heat and time—that are laying their weight on me but behind them, or held within them, there is something more which I can only describe as the whole of India.
>
> **Ruth Prawer Jhabvala, *An Experience of India***

In this highly personal account, Ruth Jhabvala expresses a pessimistic attitude toward her adopted land. Her choice of words like *oppression, pressing, congealing, weight,* and phrases like *time which has stood still and will never move again,* leaves no mistake that on afternoons like these, the writer feels oppressed by India— its summers, its past, its present.

Fiction, editorials, magazine articles, biographies, and autobiographies are usually written with an identifiable tone that can range from sarcastic and critical to admiring and even lighthearted. The author's diction provides the most important clue to tone.

For example, if you describe the chemistry laboratory of your school as "bursting with creative energy," you are conveying a positive, enthusiastic tone. On the other hand, if you describe that same classroom as "disorganized and chaotic," your tone becomes critical and disapproving.

Emphasis, Tone, and Mood

MOOD

While tone is the deliberate stance the writer takes toward the subject of his or her writing, mood is the overall climate of feeling or emotional setting a writer creates as a backdrop for the action.

Mary Shelley creates a powerful mood in the following excerpt from her novel *Frankenstein*. Read the passage slowly, and consider how it makes you feel.

> It was on a dreary night of November that I beheld the accomplishment of my toils. With an anxiety that almost amounted to agony, I collected the instruments of life around me, that I might infuse a spark of being into the lifeless thing that lay at my feet. It was already one in the morning; the rain pattered dismally against the panes, and my candle was nearly burnt out, when, by the glimmer of the half-extinguished light, I saw the dull yellow eye of the creature open; it breathed hard, and a convulsive motion agitated its limbs.

Mary Shelley, *Frankenstein*

Shelley creates a mood of gloom, horror, and suspense with words and phrases such as *dreary night, lifeless thing, pattered dismally, dull yellow eye,* and *convulsive motion.* She chooses words whose connotations will evoke these feelings in her audience.

A writer's diction affects both tone and mood. Word choice, details, images, figurative language, and repetition all contribute to the mood of a piece of writing; these elements invite the reader to participate in the moment, to become part of a scene, and to feel the same feelings. Notice how strong adjectives determine the melancholy mood of the following paragraph.

There was a cold bitter taste in the air, and the new-lighted lamps looked sad. Sad were the lights in the houses opposite. Dimly they burned as if regretting something. And people hurried by, hidden by their hateful umbrellas.

Katherine Mansfield, "A Cup of Tea"

Practice Your Skills

A. Identify the tone and mood and any devices used for emphasis in the following passages. How effective is the use of each device?

1.   It was a beautiful college. The vines and the roads gracefully winding, lined with hedges and wild roses that dazzled the eyes in the summer sun. Honeysuckle and purple wisteria hung heavy from the trees. . . . I've recalled it often . . . How the grass turned green in the springtime and how the mocking birds . . . sang, how the moon shone down on the buildings, how the bell in the chapel tower rang out the precious, short-lived hours; how the girls in bright summer dresses promenaded the grassy lawn.

Ralph Ellison

2.   Some experts believe that teen-agers' nuclear fears are greater today than at any time since the first atom bombs were dropped on Japan in 1945. One reason is pretty obvious, says Tony Wagner, executive director for Educators for Social Responsibility: Nuclear weapons are more powerful and more numerous than they have ever been before.

Sara E. Lewis

3.   Oh, yes, . . . I know what they all say about our "youthful exuberance"—our music, our clothes, our freedom and energy and go-power. And it's true that, physically, we're strong and energetic, and that we dance and surf and ride around on motorbikes and stay up all night while the parents shake their heads and say "Oh, to be young again. . . ." What sticks in my head, though, is another image. I hear low, barely audible speech, words, breathed out as if by some supreme and nearly superhuman effort, I see limp gestures and sedentary figures. Kids sitting listening to music, sitting rapping, just sitting. Or sleeping—that, most of all. Staying up late, but sleeping in later. We're tired, often more from boredom than exertion, old without being wise, worldly not from seeing the world but from watching it on television.

Joyce Maynard

4.   Suddenly it all rose in him; it was unbearable. He leaped up into the air, shouting and yelling wild, unrecognizable noises. Then he began to run, not carefully, as he had before, but madly, like a wild thing. He was clean crazy, yelling mad with the joy of living and a superfluity of youth.

Doris Lessing

5.   Then he rose, lightly, and, as always now when he left me, stooped to kiss me. Usually he made stay there by the fire, while he went out into the night, but this time I got up and followed him to the cave entrance, and waited there to watch him go. The light was behind me and my shadow stretched, thin and long. . . . It was almost night, but over beyond Maridunum in the west, a lingering bar of light hinted at the dying sun. It threw a glint on the river skirting the palace wall where I was born, and touched a jewel spark on the distant sea. Near at hand the trees were bare with winter, and the ground crisp with the first frost. Arthur trod away from me across the grass, leaving ghostprints in the frost. He reached the place where the track led down to the grove, and half turned. I saw him raise a hand.

Mary Stewart

B. Choose one of the passages from exercise A and rewrite it, using a different tone or mood from the original. For example, if the original paragraph has a serious tone, rewrite it with a humorous or ironic one. If the mood is quiet and reminiscent, make it sad or melancholy.

C. Choose a special place in nature or a favorite city street corner. Observe the place carefully at different times of day—in the morning and again at sunset, for example. Write a description contrasting the place at those two times, choosing evocative images and details to establish two different moods.

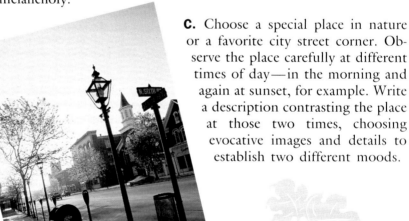

Varieties of Language

Because communication involves both *what* we say and *how* we say it, good writers understand and draw on all the varieties of English, using them to communicate effectively with different audiences for different purposes. For example, in factual writing such as for reports, you generally would use straightforward, formal language to present ideas clearly to your reader. In narrative writing, on the other hand, you might use different levels of language such as slang and dialect to create vivid and believable characters.

Standard English is language that is acceptable in any writing or speaking situation. It falls into two categories—formal and informal. **Nonstandard English** is language that does not conform to the conventional rules of grammar, usage, and mechanics, and is generally not used in writing.

FORMAL AND INFORMAL ENGLISH

Formal English This level of language is suitable for serious lectures and speeches, scholarly journals, business reports, legal documents, and textbooks. It has a serious tone and is devoid of contractions and slang. Notice how the use of formal English conveys the serious tone and purpose of the following passage.

> The language we use about war is inappropriate, and its inappropriateness is designed to conceal a reality so odious that we do not wish to know it. The language we use about politics is also inappropriate; but here our mistake has a different purpose.   **Aldous Huxley, *The Language of War***

**LITERARY
M O D E L**

Informal English This is the language that is used in casual, everyday circumstances. Also known as **colloquial English,** it is the language of conversation and informal writing and is characterized by a relaxed tone; generally nontechnical, simple words; and use of contractions and sentence fragments. Newspaper and magazine journalists often use informal language, as you can see in the example on the next page.

> It wasn't an ideal way to study nature. Last month Alvaro Garza, Jr., decided to take a close look at a dead squirrel on a frozen river near his Minnesota home, fell through the ice, and spent 45 minutes submerged. At the time of his rescue he was considered clinically dead, yet within days he was acting like an ordinary kid.　**Newsweek**

Sᴘᴇᴄɪᴀʟ ʟᴀɴɢᴜᴀɢᴇ

A writer or speaker can also use special varieties of language such as idioms, slang, euphemisms, clichés, jargon, and gobbledygook to create specific effects. Because these varieties of language can be confusing or inappropriate, they should be used with caution.

Idioms An idiom is a group of words whose intended meaning differs from the literal meanings of the individual words. For instance, in the sentence "After a heated discussion, we voted to *turn down* the proposal," the words *turn down* are an idiom meaning "to veto or decline." Some common idioms are listed below. Avoid using idioms in formal writing or when they may cause confusion, such as when speaking with people from another country.

bottle up [one's] feelings	*in the same boat*
called on the carpet	*lock, stock, and barrel*
good ear	*sitting pretty*

Slang This informal, vivid language is created by a particular group within a culture, becomes popular within that group, and then either passes out of use or becomes part of the standard vocabulary. Expressions such as *groovy, dig* (as in "Can you dig it?"), and *cool cat* were popular in the middle part of this century but have mostly fallen out of use. However, although the word *rap* (meaning "talk"), for example, is of the same vintage as the words *groovy* and *dig,* it has been accepted into general use.

Because of the specialized nature of slang, it is best to consider your audience and your intention before using it. Slang is inappropriate in formal writing, but it is often used in informal conversation and in the dialogue of fiction and drama.

Euphemisms   Euphemisms are expressions that sound less offensive than the words they replace. For example, *sanitation engineer* is a euphemism for *garbage collector*. You may decide to use a euphemism out of courtesy, but avoid using euphemisms to hide the truth.

Clichés   Expressions that have lost their descriptive power through overuse are called **clichés.** Phrases such as *sad but true, pretty as a picture, cold as ice, clear as a bell,* and *chip off the old block* detract from good writing. Replace clichés with fresh, precise words.

W   R   I   T   E   R   T   O   W   R   I   T   E   R

The difference between the right word and the wrong word
is the difference between lightning and a lightning bug.
Mark Twain, American novelist and humorist

Jargon   The specialized, technical vocabularies of particular professions or activities are called **jargon.** For example, medical professionals use words such as *infarction, peritonitis,* and *toxin.* Computer operators use words like *mainframe, access, printout, hardware,* and *software.* Such words provide a shortcut to meaning for those within the profession but may confuse others. Unless you define your terms, do not use specialized vocabulary if your audience will not understand it. Study the following example.

Jargon	The plaintiff's legal representative was shocked to learn that her client had brought suit against the company prior to the present litigation.
Standard English	The man's lawyer was shocked to learn that her client had sued the company before.

Gobbledygook   Language that is inflated, pretentious, and often intentionally confusing is called **gobbledygook**. It is often found in legal, technical, and business writing and is characterized by overloaded sentences and vague, abstract, uncommon, or technical words.

> In view of the previous and projected voluntary personnel reductioning, we anticipate no unilaterally enforced retirement except under the most compelling circumstances unforeseen at this point in time.

Avoid gobbledygook by using direct and understandable language such as the following.

> Because enough people have resigned, we will not have to lay off anyone.

Dialects A **dialect** is a version of a language that is spoken by people of a particular region or social group. Everyone speaks a particular dialect, and although dialects can differ in vocabulary, pronunciation, and even grammar and punctuation, each is entirely adequate and "correct." Examples of dialects include the Hispanic dialect of English spoken in American cities such as Miami, the dialect spoken by educated people from Great Britain, and the Midland dialect spoken in the American Midwest.

In recent years, widespread education and national media have tended to reduce the differences between regional dialects in the United States. However, differences in regional dialect still remain. In major urban areas distinct English dialects are used by people of different economic, racial, and ethnic backgrounds.

Not only the pronunciations of words, but the words themselves, may vary from dialect to dialect. The lowly earthworm is a good example. In various parts of the United States it is called *angle dog, angleworm, bait worm, dew worm, fish bait, fishing worm, fish worm, mud worm, rain worm*, or *red worm*.

Writers such as William Faulkner used dialect very effectively to evoke the setting of a story and to create vivid, memorable characters. Here is a passage from one of his novels set in the rural South of the 1920's.

"Is you all seen anything of a quarter down here," Luster said.

"What quarter."

"The one I had here this morning," Luster said. "I lost it somewhere. It fell through this here hole in my pocket. If I dont find it I cant go to the show tonight."

"Where'd you get a quarter . . ."

"Got it at the getting place," Luster said. "Plenty more where that one come from. Only I got to find that one. Is you all found it yet."

"I aint studying no quarter. I got my own business to tend to."
William Faulkner, *The Sound and the Fury*

Practice Your Skills

A. Below is the first draft of a factual paragraph written in informal English. Identify examples of clichés, slang, idioms, and dialect. Then rewrite the paragraph in formal English.

> There's like about 800 ponies living free, all by themselves, on this fab island called Assateague, somewheres off the coast of Maryland. I'm not putting you on. Every year, the Chincoteague Volunteer Fire Department like herds the ponies across the water to another island, it's called Chincoteague. This way, some of the foals can be sold as pets and the rest of the herd can be checked for illness or injury. And that keeps the population stable so the ponies have enough vittles and water on their island, Assateague. Really it's the Chincoteague Volunteer Fire Department that owns the ponies, like officially. But the ponies be free as the wind on their own island all through the year, except for roundup week at the end of July. After the July roundup, the firemen swim the ponies back to their island for another year of sitting pretty in freedom and protection.

B. Below is a brief glossary of jargon used in the world of the theater. Choose another discipline, such as medicine, law, psychology, or sports, and create a similar glossary of specialized vocabulary used in that field. Then write a paragraph using terms from your list or the list below.

stage left	the actor's left as he or she faces the audience
block	to plan the movement and placement of the actors
mug	overact, especially with facial expressions
cross upstage	to move away from the audience

C. Find some technical or government pamphlets or official regulations in your local library. Among these publications, you should be able to find examples of gobbledygook. Copy them, and then rewrite them in simple, straightforward English.

Varieties of Language

Using Poetic Language

I think that to transfuse emotion—not to transmit thought but to set up in the reader's sense a vibration corresponding to what was felt by the writer—is the peculiar function of poetry.

A. E. Housman, poet

Poetry is the oldest form of literature. Long before people learned how to communicate through written symbols, they shared information by chanting it in rhythmic patterns that could be easily remembered. Because of this long tradition, it is not surprising that poets have developed many effective techniques for using language to communicate moods and emotions. You can use these techniques, or **poetic devices,** to enrich your own writing of both poetry and prose.

IMAGERY

As a writer you should attempt to show your readers what you mean rather than just tell them. In other words, your writing is most effective when it vividly creates a concrete experience or picture in your readers' minds. One way you can give your readers this concrete experience is by using images.

An **image** is a representation in words of a sensory experience—a sight, sound, touch, taste, or smell. Collectively, the images used by a writer are called **imagery.** As the poet Archibald MacLeish eloquently exemplified in his poem "Ars Poetica," the way to enable readers to feel an emotion—in this case, grief—is to present them with images that evoke that feeling.

> For all the history of grief an empty doorway and a leaf.
> **Archibald MacLeish, "Ars Poetica"**

Now suppose you read the following sentence in an essay about the Okefenokee Swamp.

> I assumed that hiking across the swamp would be difficult.

This statement doesn't give readers enough sensory information to engage their imaginations and enable them to re-create the difficult experience. Compare the following passage.

> I had imagined that five days of slogging across the Okefenokee Swamp would offer such heights of discomfort and travail that the experience would be exhilarating for its pure intensity. Tangled vegetation, oppressive heat, no solid ground for miles, fetid water, biting insects, ten thousand alligators, and the continent's foremost selection of poisonous snakes— that sort of thing. I had to put it to Red like one of those old recruiting ads for the Peace Corps: "Bad pay and long hours, but at least you'll be hungry and in danger."
>
> **David Quammen, "Swamp Odyssey"**

The second passage provides many sensory details and images that allow the reader to form a lively picture of the swamp—insects, poisonous snakes, and all.

FIGURATIVE LANGUAGE

As you have seen, one way to create a powerful experience for a reader is to use sensory language, or imagery. Another way is to use **figurative language,** language that evokes associations that go beyond the literal meaning of the words. Some specific types of figurative language are **simile, metaphor, personification, symbolism, hyperbole, understatement,** and **synesthesia.**

Simile A simile is a comparison using words such as **like** or **as** that enriches the reader's understanding. Consider the following line by the novelist Joseph Conrad.

> The mysterious East faced me, perfumed like a flower, silent like death, dark like a grave. **Joseph Conrad, "Youth"**

Notice how, by using three similes, Conrad provides a concrete sensory experience of the East in a single sentence.

Metaphor Like a simile, a metaphor also compares something with something else that is concrete and familiar. However, it merely implies the comparison, rather than stating it explicitly through the use of the words *like* and *as.* In the following passage, the main character in a play describes the play and its setting to the audience before the action begins, using two metaphors.

If everything goes well for me tonight, this should be a waltz, one-two-three, one-two-three; a no-holds-barred romantic story, and since I'm not a romantic type, I'm going to need the whole valentine here to help me: the woods, the willows, the vines, the moonlight, the band.

Lanford Wilson, *Talley's Folly*

By comparing the story to a waltz and the sets to a valentine, the character helps to create a romantic mood for the action that will follow in the play.

Personification Writers often provide an additional dimension to their readers' experience by using **personification,** the attribution of human qualities to animals or inanimate objects. Notice how the poet Shelley uses personification to convey the desolate sound of the wind.

Rough wind, that moanest loud
Grief too sad for song   **Percy Bysshe Shelley, "A Dirge"**

Symbolism A word functions as a **symbol** when it is used to indicate not only its usual referent, but also something quite different. Some symbols have traditional associations. For example, the word *flag* refers not only to a cloth banner, but it also symbolizes the country that flies it. Other conventional symbols include a circle—perfection; the sun—power or reason; greenery—youth; winter—old age; and a road—the path of life. For example, when Walt Whitman used the symbol of the "ship of state" in his poem "O Captain! My Captain!" readers knew that the poem was actually referring to the ship of the United States and its lost captain, Abraham Lincoln.

Writers can also create their own associations between unlike things, establishing **personal symbols.** For example, notice in the following lines how the poet Dylan Thomas uses opposing symbols —both conventional and personal—to express a basic paradox of human experience.

Time held me green and dying
Though I sang in my chains like the sea.

Dylan Thomas, "Fern Hill"

The conventional symbol for youth and life—greenery—is combined with its opposite—death, and the personal symbol—the sea—both sings freely and is chained. These powerful symbols convey Thomas's deep understanding of the mingled joy and despair of life.

Writing
TIP

You can use symbols as the framework of an entire work, as Herman Melville did in *Moby-Dick,* or as a way of supporting a single point in your writing.

Hyperbole The word *hyperbole* is derived from the Greek word meaning "excess." It denotes the use of exaggeration to say something in a highly dramatic way that captures the reader's attention. For example, the writer Constance Urdang uses hyperbole in the lines "Papa's got a job in a miracle factory . . . in an old building taller than God." Notice that the hyperbole establishes a dramatic contrast between an ordinary, man-made object, a building, and the boundlessness and otherness of God.

Understatement Writers often use understatement, the opposite of hyperbole, for comic effect. For example, in James Goldman's play *The Lion in Winter,* King Henry II of England is threatening to disown his sons, who are conspiring for the throne, and to have his wife put to death. In a masterful example of understatement, Queen Eleanor sums up the situation: "Well, what family doesn't have its ups and downs?"

Synesthesia In using this type of figurative language, writers describe a sensory experience as if it were perceived through another sense. For example, people often describe a painter's colors—a visual experience—in auditory terms—as clashing or loud. The following lines from William Blake's poem, "London," use synesthesia to describe an auditory phenomenon—a soldier's sigh—in visual terms: "And the hapless soldier's sigh/Runs in blood down palace walls."

Sound Devices

In addition to imagery and figurative language, you can use the sounds of words to make your writing lyrical and to reinforce an idea, create a mood, or express a theme. These sound devices include **rhyme, onomatopoeia, alliteration, assonance,** and **consonance.** Since these poetic devices are used mainly to create special effects, use them judiciously in your prose writing.

Rhyme This common sound device involves the repetition of syllables with the same consonant and vowel sounds. Writers usually use this repetition at the end of a line of poetry for maximum effect. Notice how rhyme enhances these lines in the modern English rendering of Chaucer's *The Canterbury Tales:* "When in April the sweet showers fall/And pierce the drought of March to the root, and all/The veins are bathed in liquor of such power/As brings about the engendering of the flower. . . ."

Onomatopoeia When writers use a word with a sound that suggests its meaning, they are using **onomatopoeia.** For example, in the sentence "The telephone wires *whined* a reply," the word *whined* suggests the actual sound of a whine. Other onomatopoeic words include *crack, hiss, rumble,* and *pop.*

Alliteration Repetition of the initial sounds in words, **alliteration,** lends a musicality and depth to writing. The repeated *s* and *h* sounds create rhythm and lilt in this line: "The **s**ecret **s**ide of the **h**unted **h**eart."

Assonance Repetition of a vowel sound usually preceded and followed by unlike consonant sounds is called **assonance.** The poet Richard Wilbur used assonance to enrich the reader's experience in the following line: "F**oa**m was in upr**oa**r where he dr**o**ve bel**ow**."

Consonance This sound device involves the repetition of a consonant sound internally in words, as in this line by the poet John Keats: "Much ha**v**e I tra**v**e**l**ed in the rea**l**ms of go**l**d."

Practice Your Skills

A. Identify the poetic device used in each example—simile, metaphor, personification, symbolism, hyperbole, understatement, or synesthesia.

1. Because I could not stop for Death—
   He kindly stopped for me— **Emily Dickinson**
2. Your absence has gone through me
   Like thread through a needle **W. S. Merwin**
3. A work in progress . . . is a lion you cage in your study.
   Annie Dillard

B. Identify the use of rhyme, onomatopoeia, alliteration, assonance, or consonance in the following examples.

1. Give me the splendid silent sun with all his beams
       full dazzling. **Walt Whitman**
2. Many times man lives and dies
   Between his two eternities. **William Butler Yeats**
3. My husband and child smiling out of the family photo;
   Their smiles catch onto my skin, little smiling hooks. **Sylvia Plath**

C. Write two paragraphs describing a scene at a carnival. In the first paragraph, create a mood of festivity and frivolity. In the second, create a mood of suspense and horror. Use imagery, figurative language, and sound devices that contribute to each mood.

Establishing Sentence Variety

Read the following paragraph, and notice your response to it.

> The community has been divided by politicians' tactics. The campaign has been extremely negative. The commercials have concentrated on name-calling and mudslinging. The climate has been aggressive, and the voters have been the victims. The election has represented a triumph of sensationalism and publicity antics over well-reasoned debate and decision.

The paragraph sounds choppy because the sentences all have the same structure—subject followed by verb. They all begin with *the*. The sentences are correct, but they give the passage no life. The following suggestions will help you avoid this problem.

VARIETY IN SENTENCE OPENERS

When every sentence begins the same way, a paragraph is dull. Avoid beginning too many sentences with a subject followed by a verb. This most common sentence structure is often overused.

Varying Sentence Openers

- **Begin with a subject and verb.**
  Alicia worked conscientiously at the job until evening.
- **Begin with a single-word modifier.**
  Conscientiously, Alicia worked at the job until evening.
- **Begin with one or more prepositional phrases.**
  Until evening, Alicia worked conscientiously at the job.
- **Begin with a participial phrase.**
  Working conscientiously, Alicia stayed at the job.
- **Begin with an appositive.**
  A model employee, Alicia worked at the job until evening.
- **Begin with an infinitive phrase.**
  To finish the job, Alicia worked at it until evening.
- **Begin with a subordinate clause.**
  Since Alicia was determined to finish, she worked conscientiously at the job until evening.

COMPUTER TIP

When using a word processor for revisions, try underlining, boldfacing, or otherwise highlighting any sentence you plan to adjust to create more variety.

Practice Your Skills

A. Rewrite the following sentences, beginning each with the form suggested in parentheses.

1. Wanda walked over to the bank in the morning to cash the check. (prepositional phrase)
2. Someone evidently notified the Coast Guard that our boat had not returned. (adverb)
3. The value of gold usually increases when the value of the U.S. dollar decreases. (subordinate clause)
4. Virginia Woolf used the stream-of-consciousness technique to reveal a character's thoughts. (infinitive phrase)
5. John Maynard Keynes was an English economist, and he profoundly influenced economic policy in the United States during the Roosevelt administration. (appositive)

B. Identify the italicized structure as Prepositional Phrase, Participial Phrase, Appositive, Infinitive Phrase, or Subordinate Clause.

1. *Although they lived in style,* they felt always an anxiety in the house. **D. H. Lawrence**
2. *To judge by the goat and sheep pens,* this was the den of a giant, and this was no mild vegetable-eater. **Iain Finlayson**
3. *Breathing slowly,* Peter Lake stared at the ceiling. **Mark Helprin**
4. *One of eleven brothers and sisters,* Harriet was a moody, willful child. **Langston Hughes**
5. *At daybreak on the next morning* all hands were roused out to weigh anchor. **W. H. G. Kingston**

VARIETY IN
SENTENCE STRUCTURE

Writing is repetitious if too many sentences have the same structure. Basically, there are four different kinds of sentences.

- A **simple sentence** has one independent clause.
- A **compound sentence** has two or more independent clauses.
- A **complex sentence** has one independent clause and one or more subordinate clauses.
- A **compound-complex sentence** has two or more independent clauses and one or more subordinate clauses.

Notice how the overuse of compound sentences in this passage produces a monotonous, singsong rhythm.

> The storm arose without warning, and waves started to bounce our boat around. Herb pulled in the anchor, and I reeled in the lines. It was impossible to get back to the dock, so Herb steered for the point. The wind was behind us, or we never would have made it. We sailed into the beach, and then we jumped into the water and pulled the boat ashore.

You can achieve more variety in sentence structure by applying strategies such as the following.

Varying Sentence Structure

- **Create a simple sentence with a compound predicate.**
  We were delayed by a flat tire and missed the first inning.
- **Create a simple sentence with a participial phrase.**
  Delayed by a flat tire, we missed the first inning.
- **Create a complex sentence with a subordinate clause.**
  Because we were delayed by a flat tire, we missed the first inning.
- **Create a compound-complex sentence with two independent clauses and one or more subordinate clauses.**
  We were delayed because we had a flat tire, and we missed the first inning.

Notice how applying these strategies improves the sample paragraph.

> The storm arose without warning. As waves started to bounce our boat around, Herb pulled in the anchor and I reeled in the lines. It was impossible to get back to the dock, so Herb steered for the point. With the wind behind us, we sailed into the beach, jumped into the water, and pulled the boat ashore.

Practice Your Skills

A. Revise the following compound sentences by following the directions in parentheses.

1. Jon shot the puck into the goal, and he raised his arms in joy. (Create a simple sentence with a compound predicate.)

2. The lecturer spoke about cancer, and she said that this illness could turn out to be several diseases. (Create a simple sentence with a participial phrase.)
3. I know the radius; I can compute the diameter. (Create a complex sentence with one subordinate clause.)
4. Spices such as pepper enhance taste, but they can be hard to digest if used too generously. (Create a complex sentence with two subordinate clauses.)
5. Influenza vaccine is available to everyone, but some people do not bother to get a shot, and epidemics still occur. (Create a compound-complex sentence with two independent clauses and one subordinate clause.)

B. Revise the following paragraph. Vary the sentence structure to include at least one simple sentence and one complex sentence.

> We reached Trinidad, Colorado, in the evening, and in the morning we headed south through Raton Pass. We ate lunch at Eagle's Nest, New Mexico, and then we took a roundabout route through the mountains. The gravel road was better than we expected, and the mountains were strikingly beautiful.

VARIETY IN
SENTENCE LENGTH

Using variety in sentence length can create powerful writing. Notice how Ernest Hemingway varied the length of his sentences in the following paragraph. Notice how the mix of long and short sentences mimics the rhythm of the hiker's physical activity.

LITERARY
MODEL

> He walked along the road feeling the ache from the pull of the heavy pack. The road climbed steadily. It was hard work walking uphill. His muscles ached and the day was hot, but Nick felt happy. He felt he had left everything behind, the need for thinking, the need to write, other needs.
>
> **Ernest Hemingway, "Big Two-Hearted River"**

Sometimes writers deliberately use a series of short sentences, a device that can be especially effective in building suspense or emphasizing action. However, the unintentional use of short sentences often produces the opposite effect—dullness. When you detect this problem, you can easily combine some of the short sentences in a passage by using the strategies suggested in the following chart.

Varying Sentence Lengths

- **Use a single-word modifier.**

Weak	Quietly we walked into the hall. It was dark.
Revised	Quietly we walked into the dark hall.

- **Use a prepositional phrase.**

Weak	The concert will be held at The Civic Forum. The date is May 7.
Revised	The concert will be held at The Civic Forum on May 7.

- **Use a participial phrase.**

Weak	The Van Allen belts are two fields of charged particles. They extend 600 miles to 15,500 miles above the earth.
Revised	The Van Allen belts are two fields of charged particles extending 600 miles to 15,500 miles above the earth.

- **Use an appositive.**

Weak	Susan Stein won first prize in the state competition. She is a violin soloist in our orchestra.
Revised	Susan Stein, a violin soloist in our orchestra, won first prize in the state competition.

- **Use a simple sentence with a compound predicate.**

Weak	I stained the cabinet. Then I coated it with shellac.
Revised	I stained the cabinet and coated it with shellac.

- **Use a compound sentence.**

Weak	The plane stopped in Okinawa for repairs. We landed in Tokyo three hours late.
Revised	The plane stopped in Okinawa for repairs, so we landed in Tokyo three hours late.

- **Use a subordinate clause.**

Weak	Yuki sprained her right ankle. She was practicing fencing.
Revised	Yuki sprained her right ankle while she was practicing fencing.

A writer may err by making his sentences too compact and periodic. An occasional loose sentence prevents the style from becoming too formal and gives the reader a certain re-lief. Consequently, loose sentences are common in easy, un-studied writing. The danger is that there may be too many of them.

William Strunk, Jr., and E. B. White, *The Elements of Style*

Practice Your Skills

A. Combine each set of short sentences by using the form suggested in parentheses.

1. Ellen paged carefully through the book. It was old. (single-word modifier)
2. The judge came in. The spectators stood up. (subordinate clause beginning with *when*)
3. You can reach the planet Jupiter in about thirty minutes. You must travel at the speed of light. (participial phrase beginning with *traveling*)
4. Grover Cleveland was elected to a second term. The country was on the verge of financial panic. (subordinate clause beginning with *when*)
5. The engineers landed their helicopters on Ellesmere Island. It was the dead of winter. (prepositional phrase beginning with *in*)

B. Revise the following paragraph to create more variety in sentence structures and lengths.

A chinook is a dry wind that blows down from the Rocky Mountains in winter and early spring. It is an unseasonably warm wind. The wind's temperature increases as the chinook moves down the slopes. The temperature increases about 1 degree for every 180-foot drop. A chinook helps grazing cattle. It melts snow in the lowlands and exposes grass. Chinooks can cause snow to melt very rapidly. Lowland areas are often flooded.

C. Revise the paragraph about an election on page 439. Create a natural rhythm by varying the sentences. Use the guidelines suggested in this handbook to help you make appropriate revisions.

On the Lightside

THE DING-DONG THEORY

Listen to the sound of *bash, clash, crash, lash, mash, slash,* and *thrash.* The short *a* sound and the hiss of the *-sh* give them all the sound of violence.

Sense the rapid movement the *fl* sound gives to *flicker, flutter, flurry, fly,* and *fling.*

Notice how your nose wrinkles from the *sn* in *snort, sneer, sniff, snarl,* and *snout.*

Hear the metallic resonance of *bong, gong, ring, clang,* and *ding-dong.*

All these words seem to echo their meanings. Such **echoic** words have fascinated people throughout history. The eighteenth-century British poet Alexander Pope marveled at them, writing that "the sound must seem an echo to the sense."

The ancient Greek philosophers Pythagorus, Heraclitus, and Plato went even further. They subscribed to the theory that the universe is like a great bell, and every object in it has a special ring. Speaking a word is like ringing a bell—the word's own special sound rings out. The theory has been called the "ding-dong" theory of language origin. The name may sound like a nursery school concept, but for many words, it has the ring of truth.

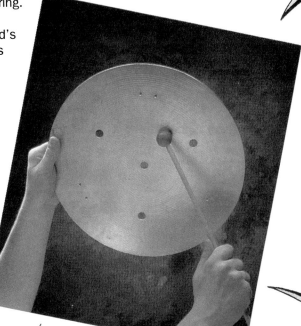

Examining Point of View

The **point of view** in a piece of writing is the perspective from which a story or a nonfiction account is told. You may write from the first-person, second-person, or third-person point of view. Read each example below. How do you react to each point of view?

First-Person Point of View

The bases are loaded. If I strike out, we'll lose the game. I feel paralyzed.	*Narrator participates in the action and uses the pronoun* I *to refer to himself or herself.*

Second-Person Point of View

When you're up to bat, you've got to forget the crowd. Just concentrate on the ball.	*Narrator uses the imperative mood and the pronoun* you *to refer to the reader. The narrator does not refer to himself or herself.*

Third-Person Point of View

It's the bottom of the ninth inning. The Sox are winning 3–2, but the Jets have the bases loaded. Smith is coming up to bat.	*Narrator does not participate in the action. Instead, the action is described "at a distance," as happening to some* he, she, *or* it.

IDENTIFYING POINT OF VIEW IN NONFICTION

First-Person Point of View   A writer will choose to write in the first person when he or she wants to let readers know that the personal experiences or ideas expressed are his or her own. Typically, writers make this choice when writing personal essays, letters, and autobiographies or memoirs. The following letter is an example of nonfiction writing from the first-person point of view. Samuel Johnson writes in a wry tone to an earl who claimed to be his benefactor.

Second-Person Point of View   The second-person point of view is often used in nonfiction, especially in speeches, essays, and educational materials. In speeches and essays, the writer often tries to elicit a personal response or action from individuals in the audience. Many writers find the second-person point of view very effective in these cases. Technical writing, such as a computer- or bicycle-repair manual, also commonly uses the second-person perspective. Below is an example of second-person nonfiction taken from a travel guide.

> *Pack light*. Lay out everything you think you'll need, pack only half of it, and take more money. Remember that you can buy almost anything you'll need in Europe, and that the more luggage you carry, the more you'll look and feel like a tourist.
>
> ***Let's Go: The Budget Guide to France***

Third-Person Point of View   Writers of nonfiction use the third-person point of view when the emphasis is on the message rather than on the message-giver. Most general nonfiction is written from this point of view. The following passage is an example.

> Several years ago, *Time* photographer Steve Northup, who had covered Vietnam and Watergate, took a group of students around Cambridge shooting pictures. He quietly insisted that they ask every [subject] for permission. His attitude toward private citizens was one of careful respect for the power of "exposure."   **Ellen Goodman, *Close to Home***

First-Person Point of View   In fiction, the first-person point of view can be very powerful. The speaker is not the writer, but rather a character created by the writer's imagination. In first-person fiction, everything is seen from the perspective of that character, who is also the narrator. In the following passage, the narrator is Lemuel Gulliver, a ship's surgeon who describes his adventures in an imaginary land.

> The Queen, giving great allowance for my defectiveness in speaking, was however surprised at so much wit and good sense in so diminutive an animal. She took me in her own hand, and carried me to the King, who was then retired to his cabinet.
> **Jonathan Swift, *Gulliver's Travels***

You might compare first-person fiction to acting. The writer takes on the role, or persona, of someone else and expresses that person's thoughts, emotions, and reactions. The writer is limited to expressing only what that character can see, hear, or experience. By inhabiting the world of one character fully, a writer can use first-person narration to create intimate and moving portrayals of individuals and their stories.

Third-Person Point of View   When writing fiction from a third-person perspective, a writer must decide whether to use a limited or omniscient point of view. In writing from the **third-person limited point of view,** the narrator speaks from the perspective of one character. For example, the point of view in the following passage is limited to the perspective of Louise Mallard as she anticipates the news that her husband has been killed in a train accident.

> There was something coming to her and she was waiting for it, fearfully. What was it? She did not know; it was too subtle and elusive to name. But she felt it, creeping out of the sky, reaching toward her through the sounds, the scents, the color that filled the air.   **Kate Chopin, "The Story of an Hour"**

In writing from the **third-person omniscient point of view,** the narrator is able to reveal the unspoken thoughts of all the characters. The word *omniscient* simply means "all-knowing." In the following passage, three brothers and their sister discuss their plans for the future. An omniscient narrator records the scene.

> But the consultation amounted to nothing. There was a strange air of ineffectuality about the three men, as they sprawled at table, smoking and reflecting vaguely on their own condition. The girl was alone, a rather short, sullen-looking young woman of twenty-seven. She did not share the same life as her brothers. She would have been good-looking save for the impressive fixity of her face, "bulldog," as her brothers called it.   **D. H. Lawrence, "The Horse-Dealer's Daughter"**

EXPERIMENTING WITH POINT OF VIEW

Point of view is one of the writer's most powerful tools. Investigating different points of view can help you write imaginatively and effectively.

Write in the third person about yourself. Attribute your own experiences to a character with a name other than your own. Many fiction writers have done this. For example, in *A Portrait of the Artist as a Young Man,* James Joyce writes about his own boyhood in Ireland, giving himself the name Stephen Dedalus.

Use an omniscient first-person narrator. Write a story told by someone who knows everything that goes on in the other characters' minds. This is only possible, of course, in fiction about really exceptional characters—as in a science fiction story about a person with telepathic powers.

Use the first person to explore a nonhuman narrator. You might choose an animal, a mountain, a river, even a cockroach, as in Don Marquis's *archy and mehitabel.* This is often done in poetry.

Write from a point of view unlike your own. This experiment can help you to grow both as a writer and as a citizen. It can broaden your awareness and understanding of others.

Tell a story from several different points of view. You can investigate different perspectives by shifting point of view within a story. In her novel *Gone to Soldiers,* Marge Piercy tells different parts of her story from different characters' points of view.

Use the second person in fiction. The second-person point of view is seldom used in fiction, though some authors such as Italo Calvino and Jay McInerny have used it effectively.

Use an unreliable narrator. Edgar Allan Poe, for example, often wrote from the point of view of narrators who were portrayed as insane. A villain like the narrator of Ring Lardner's story "Haircut" is another kind of unreliable narrator.

Use the first person to tell someone else's story. Ghostwriting is a common example of this. Autobiographies are not always written by the people they're about. Some celebrities ask professional ghostwriters to tell their stories for them.

Writing
—**TIP**—

Try writing different drafts of a work from different points of view. When you revise for your final draft, choose the point of view that works best.

ANALYZING VANTAGE POINT

The physical location from which a writer views a subject is called the **vantage point.** In the essay "Shooting an Elephant," George Orwell recalls when he was called upon to deal with a rampaging elephant. By the time he arrived, the elephant was grazing placidly. Orwell uses the vantage point of a narrator surrounded by two thousand hostile villagers.

L I T E R A R Y
M O D E L

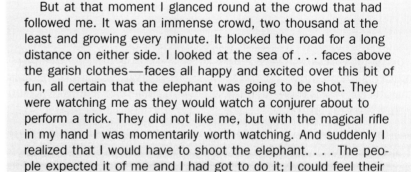

But at that moment I glanced round at the crowd that had followed me. It was an immense crowd, two thousand at the least and growing every minute. It blocked the road for a long distance on either side. I looked at the sea of . . . faces above the garish clothes—faces all happy and excited over this bit of fun, all certain that the elephant was going to be shot. They were watching me as they would watch a conjurer about to perform a trick. They did not like me, but with the magical rifle in my hand I was momentarily worth watching. And suddenly I realized that I would have to shoot the elephant. . . . The people expected it of me and I had got to do it; I could feel their two-thousand wills pressing me forward, irresistibly.

George Orwell, "Shooting an Elephant"

Telling the story from this vantage point helps the reader gain a greater appreciation of the pressures and circumstances that led Orwell to shoot the elephant. How would the emotional impact of the passage differ if Orwell had made the decision from the safety of the police station?

Vantage point can also refer to a distancing in time. For example, George Orwell wrote "Shooting an Elephant" long after the incident took place. Looking back at the event from the vantage point of time contributes to the ironic tone and sense of shame that permeate the essay.

Practice Your Skills

A. Read the following passages by Annie Dillard and Stephen Crane. Identify the point of view used in each excerpt. Then discuss why you think it might have been chosen and what impact it makes on the reader.

1.   I do not so much write a book as sit up with it, as with a dying friend. During visiting hours, I enter its room with dread and sympathy for its many disorders. I hold its hand and hope it will get better.   **Annie Dillard, _The Writing Life_**

2.   The oiler, steering with one of the two oars in the boat, sometimes raised himself suddenly to keep clear of water that swirled in over the stern. It was a thin little oar, and it seemed often ready to snap.

      The correspondent, pulling at the other oar, watched the waves and wondered why he was there.

      The injured captain, lying in the bow, was at this time buried in that profound dejection and indifference which comes, temporarily at least, to even the bravest and most enduring when, willy-nilly, the firm fails, the army loses, the ship goes down.   **Stephen Crane, "The Open Boat"**

B. Write a poem or short story using one of the unusual points of view discussed in "Experimenting with Point of View" on pages 449–450.

C. Describe a tornado from two different vantage points. First describe it from the vantage point of a weather forecaster tracking it on radar. Then describe the same tornado from the vantage point of someone caught in its path. Remember to determine the response you want to elicit in your readers and choose an appropriate point of view for describing the tornado.

Mastering Dialogue

When you skim a page of a novel or magazine article, **dialogue** is one element in the writing that draws you in. Dialogue adds life to all kinds of writing. In fiction, dialogue reveals subtleties of character, moves the action, and provides information. In poetry, conversation adds variety. In nonfiction, quotations give articles authenticity as well as a human dimension.

W R I T E R   T O   W R I T E R

For me as an author, cultivating an astute ear for dialogue is a lifelong process.

Anne Chamberlain, fiction writer

U SING DIALOGUE IN FICTION

Any kind of imaginary prose narrative—a play, short story, legend, myth, or novel—is **fiction.** In any given piece of fiction, three modes of writing are woven together: **narration,** which presents events; **description,** which presents details of setting and character; and **dialogue,** which presents characters' words. Through dialogue the characters reveal themselves directly.

The passage below is from a short story by Katherine Mansfield. Notice how the dialogue reveals the insensitivity of the two young people to the older woman.

LITERARY
M O D E L

> Just at that moment a boy and a girl came and sat down where the old couple had been. They were beautifully dressed; they were in love. The hero and heroine, of course, just arrived from his father's yacht. And still soundlessly singing, still with that trembling smile, Miss Brill prepared to listen.
> "No, not now," said the girl. "Not here, I can't."
> "But why? Because of that old stupid thing at the end there?" asked the boy. "Why does she come here at all— who wants her? Why doesn't she keep her silly old mug at home?"
> **Katherine Mansfield, "Miss Brill"**

For information about punctuating dialogue, see Grammar Handbook 41, "Apostrophes and Quotation Marks," on pages 808–810.

Writing
—TIP—

To write realistic dialogue, have your characters speak in relatively short exchanges, not in long sentences or paragraphs.

USING DIALOGUE IN DRAMA

Dialogue is the main component of drama. Therefore it must provide information about the setting and plot, as well as the characters. Notice how George Bernard Shaw uses dialogue in the following passage to reveal character, provide background information, and move the story line forward. We learn that the note taker is self-confident, even smug, and that he makes his living by teaching millionaires how to speak proper English. We also get a hint of the conflict to come when the note taker boasts that he could transform the way the flower girl speaks in just three months.

LITERARY
M O D E L

THE FLOWER GIRL *(quite overwhelmed, looking up at him in mingled wonder and deprecation without daring to raise her head).* Ah-ah-ah-ow-ow-ow-oo!

THE NOTE TAKER *(whipping out his book).* Heavens! what a sound! *(He writes; then holds out the book and reads, reproducing her vowels exactly.)* Ah-ah-ah-ow-ow-ow-oo!

THE FLOWER GIRL *(tickled by the performance, and laughing in spite of herself).* Garn!

THE NOTE TAKER. You see this creature with her kerbstone English: the English that will keep her in the gutter to the end of her days. Well, sir, in three months I could pass that girl off as a duchess at an ambassador's garden party. I could even get her a place as lady's maid or shop assistant, which requires better English. That's the sort of thing I do for commercial millionaires. And on the profits of it I do genuine scientific work in phonetics, and a little as a poet on Miltonic lines.

George Bernard Shaw, *Pygmalion*

In the script of a play, each new passage of dialogue is signaled by the speaker's tag. Stage directions in parentheses convey information about gestures and tone of voice, and they provide suggestions for staging, music, and sound effects.

Poets often use dialogue in narrative poetry to give their readers a sense of immediacy and involvement. In his poem "Channel Firing," Thomas Hardy describes the terrible disruption of warships firing their guns through the voices of the dead, whom it has awakened. Notice in the concluding lines of the poem shown below how the dead speak not only for themselves, but for the living as well.

LITERARY
M O D E L

> So down we lay again. "I wonder,
> Will the world ever saner be,"
> Said one, "than when He sent us under
> In our indifferent century!"
>
> And many a skeleton shook his head.
> "Instead of preaching forty year,"
> My neighbour Parson Thirdly said,
> "I wish I had stuck to pipes and beer."
>
> Again the arms disturbed the hour,
> Roaring their readiness to avenge,
> As far inland as Stourton Tower,
> And Camelot, and starlit Stonehenge.
>
> **Thomas Hardy, "Channel Firing"**

GUIDELINES FOR WRITING DIALOGUE IN FICTION

- Use words and expressions that reveal your characters' backgrounds, ages, personalities, and feelings. When appropriate, use special language like dialect, jargon, or slang.
- Make your characters sound natural. People often use sentence fragments, idioms, and contractions when speaking.
- In your speaker tags, use verbs that describe emotions. If a speaker is annoyed, it is more revealing to write "Nelson snapped" than "Nelson said."
- In a play, you can use stage directions to describe a character's voice, facial expression, body language, and actions.
- Test your dialogue by reading it aloud. If it sounds unnatural when you say it, then it needs to be revised.

USING DIALOGUE
IN NONFICTION

News stories, histories, biographies, and most essay writing—all forms of **nonfiction**—often contain dialogue. Dialogue in nonfiction is a transcription of the actual words of actual people and must, therefore, accurately reflect what was said.

Journalists add human interest to news stories by using dialogue. The following excerpt from a newspaper article describes a battle of wills between New Jersey's Governor Florio and the chairman of Hartford Insurance Company, who threatened to refuse car insurance to New Jersey drivers.

> What the state did was tell ITT Hartford, one of the biggest insurers in the nation, that if it wanted to pull out of the auto insurance business in New Jersey, it would have to give up lucrative business in lines like health and homeowner's policies as well. "If they won't play by the rules," an angry Mr. Florio said, "we won't let them sell anything."
>
> **Wayne King, "Going Toe-to-Toe Over Car Insurance Bills"**

PROFESSIONAL
M O D E L

Practice Your Skills

Complete one of the following activities. Work alone or with a partner, as your teacher directs.

1. Write a short story. Create a strong beginning, and give your characters dialogue that reveals their personalities.

2. Write a one-act play. Create stage directions and dialogue that will convey the setting and mood and carry the plot forward.

3. Write a newspaper article about an event or issue of local interest. Interview participants, witnesses, and people affected by the event or issue, and include quotes from them.

Sketchbook

What is success?
Is it doing your own thing
or to join the rest?
Or should you truly believe
and keep trying over and over again
living in hopes
that some day you'll be in with the winners?

Allen Toussaint
"WHAT IS SUCCESS"

What is success?

Additional Sketches
What will you be doing ten years from today?
Write a letter of complaint about something that has been bothering you.

Developing Your Vocabulary

A calligrapher dips into his pot of ink and his handwriting flows elegantly from the brush. That fluidity, however, was developed only after much practice with the tools of his trade. In the same way, by immersing yourself in words, you can develop the fluidity that will enable you to express your thoughts clearly and elegantly.

You can begin by applying the following techniques for analyzing words from their component parts and their context. Then, just practice, practice, practice.

MAKING A PERSONAL PLAN

You have two distinct vocabularies. Your **passive vocabulary** contains words that you understand when you hear or read them. Your **active vocabulary** contains words that you comprehend well enough to use yourself.

Both of your vocabularies grow over time. A word enters your passive vocabulary when you first encounter it in the speech or writing of others. You recognize and understand the word in context but do not yet use it yourself. By applying certain strategies you can integrate the word into your active vocabulary and begin to use it in your speech.

By following a personal plan for vocabulary improvement, you will gain precision in expressing yourself. Your higher degree of sophistication in the use of language will benefit you in job and college interviews. By using the techniques discussed below, you can also improve your performance on the standardized tests that are part of the college and job application process.

Develop Curiosity Instead of passing over an unfamiliar word in your reading, or ignoring a new word you hear on the evening news, jot it in a special section in your journal. The list that you collect becomes the basis for your personal program of vocabulary improvement. Also take the opportunity to explore new words while using a thesaurus.

Learn the Definitions Familiarity with a word begins with understanding its meaning. Look up unfamiliar words in a dictionary. In addition to discovering the definition, research the background of a new word. A colorful **etymology,** or word history, may help you remember the definition.

Writing
—TIP—

If a somewhat unfamiliar word pops into your head while you are writing, use it and keep going. When you have finished writing, you may go back and look up the word in the dictionary.

Put New Words to Use Once you have discovered a new word and researched its meaning, try to work the word into your speech and writing as soon as possible. It's been said that if you use a word twice, it is yours.

Set Goals The list of new words you gather in your journal is only the beginning for your vocabulary-improvement plan. In addition, set a goal of learning a specific number of words in a particular time period. Remember to set reasonable goals—perhaps two new words a day—to ensure that you continue your plan.

Make a Plan Establish a personalized method for acquiring and practicing new words. You might begin with the following list of sixty-nine words for vocabulary study. Apply your personal program for vocabulary development to make these words a part of your passive and active vocabularies.

Words for Vocabulary Study

abstruse	exigency	onerous
acquisitive	fatuous	overt
aesthetic	frenetic	paucity
anachronism	germane	pedantry
banal	histrionic	penchant
cacophonous	ignominy	propitious
chronic	impecunious	quintessence
coalition	importune	raze
collusion	incumbent	rebuff
congeal	inexorable	rectitude
conjecture	laconic	recumbent
credence	manifest	sequester
decimate	mélange	somnambulist
demur	mesmerize	taciturn
deprecate	misanthrope	tirade
derogatory	monotheism	unequivocal
disarray	mutable	unremitting
dissident	myopic	utopian
ebullient	nadir	vacillate
eclectic	neologism	verbiage
efficacy	non sequitur	viscous
errant	nuance	visionary
ethereal	obtuse	zealot

In addition, start browsing through books on vocabulary available in the library and in bookstores. Pay attention to books specifically designed to help you with the vocabulary portions of the college entrance examinations.

Build a strategy for practice into your vocabulary-improvement plan. You may wish to write new words on index cards so that you can review them at free moments, or you might record new words on tape to listen to and review.

Extend Your Plan   Integrate your pursuit of new words into as many of your activities as possible. For example, word games and crossword puzzles are enjoyable activities to help build and review vocabulary.

Practice Your Skills

A. For the next five days, work on your own personal vocabulary-development program. Follow the steps in this list.

1. Each day record two unfamiliar words in your journal.
2. Use a dictionary to find the meaning of each word and learn its definition.
3. Use index cards or a tape recorder to drill each word; then introduce it into your speaking and writing.
4. Every week write a sentence for each of your new words.

B. Read this passage, then follow the directions on the next page.

> The side of the ship made an *opaque* belt of shadow on the shimmer of the sea. But I saw at once something elongated and pale floating very close to the ladder. Before I could form a guess a faint flash of *phosphorescent* light, which seemed to issue suddenly from the naked body of a man, flickered in the sleeping water with the *elusive,* silent play of summer lightning in a night sky. With a gasp I saw revealed to my stare a pair of feet, the long legs, a broad *livid* back *immersed* right up to the neck in a green *cadaverous* glow. One hand, *awash,* clutched the bottom rung of the ladder.

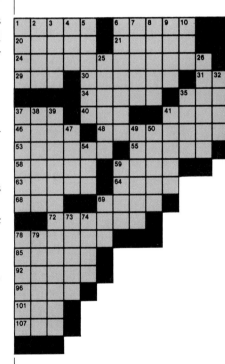

Developing Your
Vocabulary   **459**

He was complete but for the head. A headless corpse! The cigar dropped out of my *gaping* mouth with a tiny plip and a short hiss quite *audible* in the stillness. . . . The moment of *vain* exclamations was past. . . . I only . . . leaned over the rail as far as I could, to bring my eyes near to the mystery floating alongside.   **Joseph Conrad, *The Secret Sharer***

1. Make five columns on your paper and label them *Word, Definition, Unknown, Passive Vocabulary, Active Vocabulary.*
2. Enter each italicized word from the passage in the column marked *Word.* Check the appropriate place in the last three columns to indicate whether the word is unknown, in your passive vocabulary, or currently in your active vocabulary.
3. Under *Definition* write a complete meaning for each word. If a word is unknown to you, use a dictionary.
4. Reread the passage noting any words that were unknown.
5. Write a sentence using each of the italicized words.

EXTRACTING MEANING FROM CONTEXT

You can use a dictionary to find the meanings of unknown words. However, you can also get a clue to the meanings of an unfamiliar word from its **context,** the sentence or the group of sentences in which the word appears. Using context clues is a simple but powerful method for increasing your passive vocabulary. Six common types of context clues are definition, restatement, example, comparison, contrast, and cause and effect.

Definition and Restatement   The most obvious type of context clue is direct **definition.** Clues of this type are usually signaled by a form of the verb *to be* (*am, is, are, was, were*).

> A *sycophant* **is** someone who tries to win favor by using flattery.

Sometimes a writer will explain a term by restating it in other words. Be alert for such words or phrases as *in other words, that is, to put it another way, or,* and *this means,* which may often signal **restatements.** The demonstrative pronouns *this, that, these,* and *those* may also indicate restatements. Finally, a restatement may be signaled by the use of commas, parentheses, or dashes. Such restatements are called *appositives.*

Jane Eyre was *ambivalent* about Mr. Rochester; **that is,** her feelings about him were contradictory.

Irv is studying *topology*. **This** branch of mathematics deals with those properties of geometric figures that do not change even when the figure is distorted.

The symbols etched on the magnificent sword were *runes,* characters from an early German alphabet.

Example Sometimes a writer will give examples that reveal the meaning of a word. Words that signal examples include *such as, like, especially, particularly, for example,* and *for instance.*

All *arachnids*—scorpions and ticks, **for example**—have four pairs of legs.

When the example word itself is unfamiliar, you must examine the words that precede the example, and even the whole sentence, for context clues.

Nicole's poise, particularly her *composure* when speaking to an audience, made her an ideal student leader.

Comparison Occasionally a writer will make a comparison that enables you to grasp the meaning of an unfamiliar word. Words often used to indicate comparisons include *similar, like,* and *as.*

He approached his work *meticulously,* **like** a landscape painter who must render every leaf in precise detail.

Contrast Sometimes a writer will supply a contrast, allowing you to determine a word's meaning. Contrasts may be signaled by words such as *but, although, unlike,* and *on the contrary.*

Although she strode confidently up to the horse and grasped the bridle, Ann was a complete *novice* at horseback riding.

Cause and Effect When a writer sets up a cause-and-effect relationship between the ideas in a sentence, you often can deduce the meaning of one word from its effect on another. Cause-and-effect relationships are signaled by the words *because, since, when, consequently, therefore,* and *as a result.*

Because the candidate had lied so often in the past, the public suspected that he was *mendacious.*

When the chemist noted that the acid had not damaged the metal, he concluded that the metal was *impervious* to acid.

The six types of context clues that you have just studied provide direct information concerning the meanings of words. Sometimes, however, context clues are more subtle. Often, you must study an entire paragraph to **infer** the meaning of a word; that is, you must draw a conclusion from specific facts.

When you encounter an unfamiliar word, search the context to see what information is provided. Then try to determine the connection between those facts and the unknown word.

Supporting Details   Notice how details in the following passage lead you to a definition of the italicized word.

> He always kept the *talisman* in his pocket. Once he'd gone skiing without it and had broken his arm. It didn't pay to take chances.

The context tells you that the object called a *talisman* can be kept in a pocket and that the owner once thought going out without it brought bad luck. Therefore, you can infer from the details that a talisman must be something like a good luck charm.

Context Clues   Inferences can also be drawn from any of the context clues discussed earlier. The following passage develops a series of contrasts that help you to infer the meaning of *scrupulous*.

> She was such a *scrupulous* housekeeper that her neighbors were suspicious when her windows remained open during a rainstorm. Their concern grew when the newspapers began to pile up at her door. Finally, someone called the police.

You note the contrast that is developed between a scrupulous housekeeper and one who would allow windows to remain open in the rain or newspapers to accumulate. Therefore, you can infer that *scrupulous* means "careful and exacting."

Structure Clues   Occasionally the structure of the writing offers clues to word meaning. An intentionally repeated sentence pattern, such as the one in the example below, may suggest an association between familiar and unfamiliar words.

> The speech *slandered* the senatorial candidate. Suggestions of dishonesty *defamed* his character.

The parallel placement of *slandered* and *defamed* as verbs suggests that *slander* means "to speak ill of."

Practice Your Skills

A. Define the italicized words by using context clues. Identify the method by which the clue reveals the meaning.

1. Since his last case of severe indigestion, Pat has *eschewed* his own cooking.
2. Charlene did not resist the suggestion. On the contrary, her *acquiescence* was immediate and enthusiastic.
3. Louis Pasteur investigated *rabies,* the disease that makes dogs, bats, and other animals go mad.
4. Our unusual neighbor, Mr. Robson, is generally known for his *eccentricity.* Thus we were not surprised to learn that he has over seventy-five pet cats and dogs.
5. The points at which bones make contact or unite with one another are called *articulations.*
6. This *burgeoning* community is quickly depleting its water supply. Its growing population must look to a new source.
7. The fact that lower vertebrates do not depend very much on the *cerebrum* can be demonstrated by removing that part of the brain and observing the general behavior of the animal.
8. Their drafting technician requested the *calipers,* several protractors, and a ruler.
9. Like a child who is reluctant to go to bed, Elizabeth *dawdled* all the way up the stairs.
10. Many *Porifera,* including the elephant-ear sponge, are used commercially for cleaning and cosmetic purposes.

B. Infer the meaning and write your own definition for each italicized word in the following sentences. Check your definition in a dictionary.

1. Eleanor, who has always suffered from *acrophobia,* could not be induced to go to the top of the Washington Monument when her class toured the capital.
2. In my hometown there is a law against smoking in public, but the law has fallen into *desuetude.* Until recently, people have not felt it was their concern whether another person was smoking or not, and the law has not been used in forty years.
3. Since the days of President Johnson's War on Poverty in the United States, many Americans have improved their standard of living: yet it is still possible to find people living in *destitution* in our wonderful land of plenty.
4. An *indefatigable* worker, Thomas Edison spent days and nights on his experiments, not even taking time to eat and sleep.

5. After trying countless fad diets without success, Mom found that the most *efficacious* way to lose weight was to take smaller portions and to avoid snacking between meals.

6. Lawrence's *effrontery* at the Christmas party surprised everyone. He asked my grandfather's guests personal questions, though he had scarcely made their acquaintance.

7. Frustrated and jealous because he believed himself less talented than the younger composer, Antonio Salieri belittled Mozart at every opportunity. He *disparaged* both Mozart's talent and his personal habits.

8. Each of the pianists is an erstwhile *prodigy*. Gould is supposed to have been able to read notes before he could read the printed word. He started playing the piano at the age of three and gave his first recital at fourteen.

9. Jogging lost some of its popularity as people realized that it was not without risk. Many former joggers have taken up race walking instead, an activity that does not *jeopardize* the knees and joints.

10. The first national parks were established because people feared that commercial development of all lands would leave nothing in the *public domain* and would eventually destroy the magnificent scenic wealth of the continent.

11. Coach Hernandez *extolled* the benefits of aerobic exercise as a way to maintain fitness. As a way to achieve flexibility and suppleness, he praised yoga.

12. Suddenly the brake lights of the car in front flashed. Seeing this, Sam prepared to *decelerate*.

C. Examine the following passages, and write your own definitions for each italicized word. Check your definitions in a dictionary.

1. One of the great *visionaries* of the architectural world is Paolo Soleri, who came to the United States from Italy thirty-one years ago. Soleri's fame does not rest on the structures he has actually built, for these are few in number: a striking glass-domed house, a ceramics factory on the Amalfi coast, and the so-called earth colony where he and his followers lived in Arizona. His impact on the world of design has been made almost entirely through his *intricate,* detailed drawings for the city of the future—in which he fully intends to live. These drawings have astonished and *mesmerized* visitors to museum shows around the country.

Joseph J. Thorndike, Jr.

2. Mr. Bingley had soon made himself acquainted with all the principal people in the room; he was lively and *unreserved,* danced every dance, was angry that the ball closed so early, and talked of giving

one himself at Netherfield. Such *amiable* qualities must speak for themselves. What a contrast between him and his friend! Mr. Darcy danced only once with Mrs. Hurst and once with Miss Bingley, *declined* being introduced to any other lady, and spent the rest of the evening in walking about the room, speaking occasionally to one of his own party. His *character* was decided. He was the proudest, most disagreeable man in the world, and everybody hoped that he would never come there again. **Jane Austen**

3. Although it is difficult to generalize, too many of our universities have become huge circuses in which the sideshows overshadow the main attraction. "When a university president makes a speech calling for intellectual leadership," writes Dr. Hutchins, "he cannot be heard over the din his publicity man is making about the newest campus queen." Our colleagues have involved themselves in activities that have only the most *tenuous relation* to the *academic function*. **Martin B. Margolies**

4. Jade was the link in China between earth and heaven, the bridge from life to immortality. A Chinese gentleman paced his life by altering his *gait* to make jades dangling from his belt tinkle to a measured beat. Confucius compared the *virtues* of such a gentleman with the virtues of jade, applying such traits as intelligence, loyalty, justice, humanity, truth, and more. Just as we use the word gold to *embellish* a phrase, the Chinese *incorporate* jade into thousands of expressions: "Jade person" is a beautiful woman; "fragrant jade" is a woman's skin; "jade shattered" is a beauty's death. **Fred Ward**

ANALYZING WORD PARTS

You have already learned how to use context clues to determine the meanings of unfamiliar words. Another technique that you can use for the purpose of unlocking word meaning is the analysis of **prefixes, suffixes, base words,** and **roots.** These are the **word parts** from which words are made.

- **Prefix**   a word part added to the beginning of another word or word part
- **Suffix**   a word part added to the end of another word or word part
- **Base Word**   a complete word to which a prefix and/or suffix can be added
- **Root**   a word part that can never stand alone but to which a prefix and/or a suffix is added

Prefixes

A careful reader or listener can apply several strategies, such as analyzing prefixes to unlock the meanings of unfamiliar words. When using this technique, remember that many prefixes have more than one meaning. If you encounter an unfamiliar word with such a prefix, decide which of the meanings fits the context or consult a dictionary. The following is a list of common prefixes in English.

Common English Prefixes

Prefix	Meaning	Example
bene-	good	benefit
circum-	around	circumscribe
com-, con-	with	compassion
		consequence
dia-	through, across	dialogue
dis-	the opposite of	disapprove
epi-	upon	epidermis
equi-	equal, even	equidistant
eu-	good	eulogy
hyper-	excessive	hypercritical
hypo-	under	hypodermic
il-, im-, in-, ir-	not, in	illogical, impossible, input, irregular
inner-, intra-	within	innermost, intramural
intro-	into	introspection
macro-	large, long	macrocosm
mal-	bad	malnutrition
mis-	wrong	mismatched
non-	not	nonflammable
omni-	all	omnivorous
pan-	all	panorama
para-	beside	parallel
poly-	many	polysyllabic
re-	again	recover
sub-	under, less than	substandard
super-	above, beyond	supersonic
sym-	together	sympathy
trans-	across	transoceanic

Suffixes

Suffixes affect the function as well as the meaning of a word. **Noun suffixes,** for example, are used to create nouns from other parts of speech. **Adjective suffixes** can be used to create adjectives.

You can increase your vocabulary considerably by analyzing suffixes you encounter on unfamiliar words and by adding suffixes to familiar words. If you have any doubts, consult a dictionary to assure yourself that the suffix you are using fits the context and the meaning you wish to convey.

Noun Suffixes

Suffix	Meaning	Example
-ade	act, condition	blockade
-age	act, condition, collection, home	marriage, parsonage
-an	belonging to, born in	American
-archy	form of government	monarchy
-ary	member, doer	missionary
-cide	killer, killing	insecticide
-dom	state, condition	freedom
-ectomy	surgical removal	tonsillectomy
-ee	recipient	appointee
-eer, -er	doer, maker	puppeteer, winner
-hood	condition	priesthood
-ician	doer	diagnostician
-ics	science, skill	mathematics
-ism	ideology	Romanticism
-ist	doer, maker	violinist
-itis	inflammation	tonsillitis
-ization	state, quality	colonization
-ment	result, agency, state, condition	government, internment
-mony	result, condition	testimony
-ness	quality	happiness
-or	doer	director
-ster	doer, member	youngster
-ion, -sion, -tion	state, condition	inflation
-tude	state, quality	quietude
-ure	act, result	censure

Adjective Suffixes

Suffix	Meaning	Example
-able	able, capable	washable
-al	like, suited to	musical
-ar	of, pertaining to	solar
-en	made of	wooden
-esque	relating to	statuesque
-fic	causing	honorific
-ful	having qualities of	wonderful
-ic	pertaining to	volcanic
-ish	like, similar to	impish
-ive	tending to or toward	instructive
-less	without	penniless
-like	similar to	lifelike
-oid	relating to	humanoid
-ose	full of, having	verbose
-ous	full of, having	nervous
-some	like, showing	worrisome
-ward	in the direction of	homeward

Base Words

Words that can stand by themselves or be used with suffixes and/or prefixes are called **base words.** When a prefix or suffix is added to a base word, the meaning of the base word will alter slightly. Notice how the meaning of the base word *provision* changes when different suffixes are added to it:

provision   provisional   provisioner

Once you fully comprehend the meanings of prefixes and suffixes, you will be able to discern the complete definitions of words comprised of a base word and word parts.

Word Roots

Sometimes, when a prefix or suffix is removed from a word, the part remaining will not stand by itself. Such a word part is a **root.** A root has a specific meaning that can help you determine the meaning of the entire word. Many English words are derived from Greek and Latin roots. The following two charts list some of these common roots.

Writing
TIP

When using a thesaurus, notice the different word roots within the selection. Knowing the definitions of the roots will enable you to select the perfect word to express your thoughts.

Roots Derived from Greek

Root	Meaning	Example
aesthet, esth	perception	aesthetic
anthrop	human	anthropology
arche, archae	ancient	archaeology
bibl	book	Bible
bio	life	biography
cryptos	secret, hidden	cryptic
dogma	opinion	dogmatism
dynamo	power	dynamo
ge, geo	earth	geology
gnos	know	diagnostic
graphein, gram	writing, write	graphic
homo	same	homogeneous
kine, cine	movement	cinema
log	word, thought	dialogue
mania	madness	maniac
paleo	old	paleolithic
patho	suffering	sympathy
phil	love	philharmonic
phobe	fear	phobia
pneum	air, breath	pneumonia
scope	seeing, look at	oscilloscope
sophos	wise, wisdom	sophisticated
therme	heat	thermometer

Roots Derived from Latin

Root	Meaning	Example
alius	other	alien
amo, ami	love	amity
animus	mind, life	animate
cogn	know	recognize
corpus, corporis	body	corporeal
credere, creditus	believe	creed
dicere, dictus	say, tell	dictate
gratia, gratus	kindness, favor	gratitude
grex, gregis	flock	segregate
init	beginning	initiate
just, juris	law, right	injury
lumen, luminis	light	illuminate
mandare	command	reprimand
manus	hand	manipulate
mon	advise, warn	premonition
mut	change	mutate
rid	laugh	ridicule
rumpere, ruptus	break	rupture
sequor, secutus	follow	sequence
tact, tang	touch	tangible
unus	one	universe
ver	truth	veracity
videre, visus	see	visit
void	empty	devoid

Word Families

The same root may serve as the source for a large number of related words. A group of words with a common root is called a **word family.** For example, the word *logic* belongs to a word family that includes *logistics, monologue, dialogue, logo,* and *logarithm.* This family contains the Greek root *log* and each word has a meaning that includes the ideas "word" or "thought." By combining this knowledge with the fact that the suffix -*ic* means "science or skill," you arrive at "the science or skill of thought" as a definition for *logic.* This approximates the formal meaning of *logic,* which is "the science of correct reasoning." By adding word families to your personal vocabulary plan, your word power will grow rapidly.

Practice Your Skills

A. Each of the words given below contains two or more of the following word parts: a prefix, a base word, a suffix, or a root. First, write the word and then identify these word parts. Write a definition for each whole word based on the meanings of its parts. Check the meaning of each word in a dictionary and alter your definition if necessary. Finally, use each word in a sentence.

1. benefactor	11. euphonious	21. tenacious
2. ingratitude	12. pathology	22. cryptography
3. injurious	13. malefactor	23. inconsequential
4. confluence	14. demographic	24. symmetrical
5. geothermal	15. technician	25. paraprofessional
6. inalienable	16. geopolitical	26. contender
7. paleontology	17. nonconformist	27. psychopath
8. superfluous	18. germicide	28. pneumatic
9. archaic	19. bibliographer	29. incognito
10. philanthropist	20. kinetic	30. gregarious

B. Read the following passage, list the italicized words, and identify prefixes, roots, and suffixes. Use your knowledge of word parts, context clues, and inference to write a definition of each word. Examine the etymological portion of a dictionary entry for assistance with word parts. Check your definitions in a dictionary.

Up in her bedroom window Sally Carrol Happer rested her nineteen-year-old chin on a fifty-two-year-old sill and watched Clark Darrow's ancient Ford turn the corner. The car was hot—being partly *metallic* it *retained* all the heat it *absorbed* or *evolved*—and Clark Darrow bolt upright at the wheel wore a pained, strained expression as though he considered himself a spare part, and rather likely to break. He *laboriously* crossed two dust ruts, the wheels squeaking *indignantly* at the *encounter,* and then with a terrifying expression he gave the steering gear a final wrench and deposited self and car approximately in front of the Happer steps. There was a *plaintive* heaving sound, a death-rattle, followed by a short silence; and then the air was rent by a startling whistle.

Sally Carrol . . . continued to silently regard the car, whose owner sat brilliantly if *perfunctorily* at attention as he waited for an answer to his signal. . . . Sally Carrol sighed *voluminously* and raised herself with *profound inertia* from the floor. . . .

F. Scott Fitzgerald

Refining Critical Thinking and Writing Skills

You can't write without thinking; therefore, whenever you are writing, you are also developing your thinking skills—particularly the skills of hypothesis testing and problem solving.

W R I T E R   T O   W R I T E R

How do I know what I think until I see what I say?

E. M. Forster, British novelist

WRITING AS HYPOTHESIS TESTING

Writing is a process that enables you to explore what you know and to try new ideas. Every writing idea is an untested **hypothesis** or assumption, an experiment that may or may not work.

As you draft, you test ideas, developing them to see where they lead. If they take you somewhere you don't want to go or if they don't lead anywhere, you can revise your draft or begin again.

Not every writing idea leads to a successful piece of writing. However, every time you experiment with an idea, you can learn something valuable.

WRITING AS PROBLEM SOLVING

When reality is different from your expectations, a problem exists. For example, you have a problem if you can't find the car keys where you thought you left them and you need to drive to the airport. You also have a problem if you must write a paper for your social studies class and you have no idea where to begin. Any writing activity can be viewed as a problem to be solved.

You can apply the following strategies to any kind of problem, but consider, specifically, applying them to writing problems.

Strategies for Understanding and Solving Problems

Understanding Problems

1. **State the problem.** Putting the problem into simple, clear language is an important step toward solving it.

2. **Explore the problem.** Describe the problem in detail. Analyze it, freewrite about it, and ask questions about it. Make a sketch, diagram, chart, or map to explore the problem graphically.

3. **Define the problem.** Use the goal-oriented method to zero in on components of the problem. Ask yourself, "What is the situation like now?" Then, ask yourself, "What will the situation be like when the problem is solved?"

Solving Problems

1. **The trial-and-error method.** Think of all the possible solutions that you can and list them. Then look at each solution and imagine its consequences. Beginning with the most promising solution, try each one successively until the problem is solved.

2. **The divide-and-conquer method.** Divide the problem into parts and solve each part, one at a time.

3. **The past-experience method.** Think of similar problems that you have solved before. Evaluate your past solutions to see if any can be applied to the new problem.

4. **The simplification method.** Determine the core of the problem and solve it first; then work on the details.

5. **The "what-if" method.** Ask "what-if" questions to stimulate your imagination. This process may lead you to a creative solution you would not have seen otherwise.

6. **The "two-heads-are-better-than-one" method.** Include friends, relatives, and teachers in your problem-solving process.

7. **The pros-and-cons method.** Make a pro-and-con chart listing possible solutions. You may want to assign a number value to each pro and con so that you can evaluate the relative "weight" of each and not just the number of items in your chart.

Suppose Jill is writing a letter to her congressional representative to voice her concerns about impending restrictions in government guidelines for granting student loans. After reading over the first draft of her letter, Jill identifies a serious problem: her main point—that students from middle-income families may no longer be eligible for education loans—has gotten lost among several other ideas, including that there is no community college in her area.

Jill can use various problem-solving strategies in the process of revision. For example, she might first state the problem in writing, using simple, clear language. "I have lost the focus of my letter." Once she defines the problem clearly for herself, she might use the simplification method, stating her main point and then listing and prioritizing other ideas that support and clarify that point. If she still feels unsure of the clarity of her argument, she might use the "two-heads-are-better-than-one" method, asking friends or relatives how she could make her letter more focused and convincing.

Practice Your Skills

In a small group discuss each of the following writing problems and their possible solutions.

1. You have three ideas for the conclusion of a human-interest story that you are writing for your school paper. How might you use the trial-and-error method to decide which to use?
2. For a comparative government class, you must write a paper on similarities and differences between the Soviet Union and the United States. Use the divide-and-conquer method to help you come up with a narrower topic.
3. You are trying to come up with an idea for a science-fiction story. Use the "what-if" method to come up with some ideas that might work for your story.
4. You are preparing a persuasive speech about requiring companies to offer day care to employees with children. Use the pros-and-cons method to gather information.

DEVELOPING AND PRESENTING AN ARGUMENT

Critical thinking skills play a major role in persuasive writing, or argumentation. Many situations, in and out of school, call for the ability to argue persuasively in writing. For example, a student may write a paper for science class, arguing that the songs of whales are a form of communication but do not meet certain criteria necessary to be classified as a true language; or a film critic may review a new movie, arguing that it is trite and predictable. Each piece of writing must clearly convey the writer's point of view.

Types of Arguments

Drawing conclusions from available information—and finding the appropriate structure for it—is a key to producing effective argumentative writing. Deduction and induction are two logical processes of argumentation with opposite structures.

Deductive Arguments   A **deductive argument** begins with a general statement of fact. Following that generalization is a specific conclusion that can be deduced, or derived, from it, as in the example below.

Generalization	A winning team is one that wins more games than it loses.
Specific fact	Our softball team has a 9–8 record.
Specific conclusion	Our softball team should be recognized as a winning team.

Inductive Arguments   An **inductive argument,** on the other hand, begins with specific observations that lead to a general conclusion, as in the following example.

Specific fact	In every softball game we've won this year, the pitcher rested three days between games.
Specific fact	In every softball game we've lost this year, the pitcher rested only two days between games.
General conclusion	Pitchers need at least three days rest between games for them to be most effective and to win games for the team.

Notice, however, that this general conclusion is not necessarily true. It doesn't take into account other factors that contribute to winning and losing games, such as the quality of the team's offense. The conclusion needs to be qualified: *Some* pitchers need at least three days rest between games for them to be most effective. Be sure to use qualifiers such as *some, few, often, many,* or *most* to limit the scope of the generalizations you derive in an inductive argument.

Writing
——TIP——
Test the clarity and completeness of your argument by reading it aloud to a reliable listener who is unfamiliar with your topic. Then ask the person to restate your main point.

Application of Induction and Deduction to Writing You can use both inductive and deductive thinking processes as you write argumentative essays. You can use induction when you begin to gather material for your writing, since you don't always know what hypothesis you will prove or what conclusion you will draw before you begin your research. If you wanted to write about the efficacy of job-internship programs, you might begin by gathering facts.

Specific fact	Of the students who go to work, 80 percent are rehired by the companies they interned for while still in high school.
Specific fact	Nineteen percent of those who go to work are hired by companies that receive written recommendations from intern employers.

What generalizations can you draw from your list of facts? You might come up with the following.

General conclusion	Participating in a job-internship program helps students to succeed after graduation.

You can use the deductive process as you write your draft. Begin with your general conclusion, which becomes the thesis of your paper, then provide your audience with enough information and specific details to prove your point. You can expand the range of the specific facts and details you initially have gathered by adding information about students who do not participate in the program, or by adding case histories and interviews with graduates. When you write, each specific fact should be fleshed out with details in full paragraphs. Your conclusion—a restatement of your original premise—is inevitable if you've provided convincing evidence.

Practice Your Skills

A. Tell whether each of the following arguments is inductive or deductive. Change the conclusions if necessary to make them true.

1. Environmentalists want to preserve the natural environment.
   Development damages the natural environment.
   Environmentalists want to restrict development in order to preserve the natural environment.

2. Any level of dioxin is unsafe.
   Wood preservatives with penta (pentachlorophenol) contain dioxin.
   Wood preservatives with penta are unsafe.

B. Choose a controversial issue that interests you as a topic for an argumentative essay. Explore the issue using inductive reasoning, gathering facts and information that will support your point of view. Then, using deduction, write an outline for your essay.

AVOIDING LOGICAL FALLACIES

Mistakes in reasoning are **logical fallacies.** Because persuasive writing must be logical, you need to evaluate your logic to avoid the following types of fallacious arguments.

Circular Reasoning Supporting a statement by repeating it in different terms is **circular reasoning,** as in the following example: "Experts prefer Gothic architecture to modern architecture because people who know about architecture believe Gothic architecture is superior." The second part of this sentence rephrases but does not support the first part.

Evasion of Issues Supporting an opinion with arguments that do not address its central point is **evading the issue.** For example, substantial evidence indicates that exhaled smoke—or secondary smoke—may be harmful to nonsmokers. Imagine a smoker opposing a ban against smoking in enclosed public areas, saying, "Smokers have rights, too. Why should a smoker put out a cigarette just to make a short pass through a lobby? Nonsmokers can stay out of lobbies if they are offended." The smoker's argument evades the central issue: secondary smoke may be harmful to nonsmokers.

False Analogy A **false analogy** assumes that two things share a similarity that they do not actually share, as in this example: "People in cities are like rats crowded in cages. When subjected to high levels of stress, they instinctively attack one another." The analogy is not totally false, because—like rats—people do respond to a stressful environment. However, reason, as well as instinct, guides human behavior. The analogy between rats and humans is false because it implies that human behavior is guided only by instinct.

Overgeneralization A generalization that is too broad is an **overgeneralization.** A visitor to the United States who observes overflowing garbage cans on the streets of five large cities may conclude: "All large cities in the United States have inadequate garbage collection." However, this conclusion would be an overgeneralization because it is based on a limited sample.

THE FAR SIDE By GARY LARSON

© Chronicle Features, 1983

"Wait a minute! Isn't anyone here a real sheep?"

The Far Side Cartoons by Gary Larson are reprinted by permission of Chronicle Features, San Francisco, CA.

Stereotyping The most dangerous type of overgeneralization is the **stereotype.** Stereotypes are broad generalizations made about people on the basis of their gender; ethnicity; race; or political, social, professional, or religious group. Stereotyping not only prevents people from responding authentically to each other as individuals, but it also can provide justification for repressive social and political policies.

Oversimplification Explaining a complex situation by omitting relevant information is **oversimplification.** For example, saying that heart disease is strictly inherited overlooks other factors that may influence susceptibility, such as diet, smoking, and exercise.

Either/Or Fallacy Advocating a polarized position, leaving no room for alternatives, is the **either/or fallacy.** For example, believing that a decision must be based on either reason or emotion—not on a combination—is fallacious.

False Cause Attributing a specific response to the wrong stimulus is citing a **false cause.** The statement "The pilot landed his plane in the cornfield because the straight rows provided him with a visual runway," contains a false cause. He landed in the cornfield because he didn't have enough fuel to get to the airport.

Only Reason Attributing an event with more than one cause to a single reason is an instance of **only reason.** Note the following example, "Professional football team owners say they want the instant-replay rule abolished because it takes away a referee's authority." The argument is fallacious if the owners also have unstated reasons for wanting to abolish the rule.

Practice Your Skills

A. Identify the error in logic in each of these statements, and revise each statement to correct the error.

1. The country must increase taxes or cut services.
2. Everyone enjoys a good comedy.
3. Dietary fat is harmful.
4. Europeans love soccer because that's the sport they enjoy in every European country.
5. Violence in society is the result of excessive violence on TV.

B. Write a paragraph based on a logical fallacy. Exchange paragraphs with a classmate, identify the fallacy, and rewrite your classmate's paragraph so that it makes sense.

Research Skills

As you face exams, research projects, and preparing for college or a career, the work may often seem overwhelming. However, even if you have a stack of textbooks to review or a dozen library books to consult, you can manage the reading and the documentation of source materials in an efficient and straightforward way. The following guidelines for reading rapidly, studying effectively, and using source materials in your writing should help.

APPLYING READING STRATEGIES

You have different purposes in reading—whether in school, at work, or at home—and it is important that you match your reading method to your material and purpose. The three primary methods of reading are *skimming, scanning,* and *slow, careful reading.*

Skimming   This type of rapid reading involves moving your eyes quickly over a text, glancing at headings, topic sentences, highlighted phrases, and graphic aids. Skimming is useful when you want to get a general idea of what the material is about and whether it will be useful to you. For example, you might want to skim a newspaper to see if you can find information about a particular current event. You can also skim possible source materials for a research paper.

Scanning   You scan materials to find a specific fact or piece of information, such as a percentage or a definition. Scanning is particularly useful when you review for a test or when you are trying to find a specific item of information to use in a paper.

To scan, place a card over the first line of a page and then move the card down the page quickly, taking in whole lines or groups of lines at a time. You will notice key words and phrases that indicate that you are close to the information you need. Then you can slow down and read carefully.

Slow and Careful Reading   When you must thoroughly understand material in depth, you will want to read slowly and carefully. This process involves taking notes, asking questions, identifying main ideas, finding relationships between ideas, and drawing inferences, or conclusions, about what you read.

Study skills will be important to you all your life, in school and at work. Now, more than ever, professionals need to study manuals, reports, memoranda, specifications, and other written materials to do their jobs well.

The most effective way to study an assignment is to divide it into manageable sections and approach it systematically using the study and research techniques described on this and the following page.

Preview the Assignment   When you preview an assignment, you prepare to learn by getting a general idea of what the material is about and establishing a context for what you will learn by recalling what you already know. In previewing written material, take the following steps.

1. Read the first two paragraphs of the assignment.

2. Read the first sentence of each paragraph that follows.

3. Read the last two paragraphs.

4. Read any information presented in special type—such as captions, headings, and boldfaced words—or in graphics, such as photos, graphs, diagrams, and charts.

Take Notes as You Read   Even if you don't refer to the notes after you take them, the note-taking itself will help fix what you read in your mind. Translating what you read into your own words and then writing them down involves more of your brain than just reading does. Consequently, taking notes increases the likelihood that you will remember what you are studying.

Predict   As you read, try to guess what will happen next. When you're studying literature, you may find predicting especially useful and enjoyable. Ask yourself questions like these: "What will this character do next? How will these characters get along? What will happen to this character as a result of his or her personality and actions? What will result from this event? How will this conflict be resolved?" By making predictions, you will become more involved in your reading and improve your retention of what you read.

Question   Before reading, make a list of questions that you hope to answer. Write down the answers as you find them. As you read, add questions as they occur to you. Questions that remain unanswered after you've finished reading can be raised in a class discussion or in a conference with your teacher.

Identify Main Ideas Don't get sidetracked by details as you read: it's important to recognize the main ideas in the material. Topic sentences of paragraphs, particularly in introductory or concluding paragraphs, often state main ideas. Because main ideas are sometimes implied rather than directly stated, however, be particularly attentive to the total context of a passage.

Identify Relationships As you read, look for passages that either imply or specifically state relationships between things or ideas. Common types of relationships include sequence, cause and effect, part to whole, spatial order, order of importance, order of value, comparison and contrast, and negation.

Make Inferences You make inferences when you draw conclusions based on what you know or observe. For example, if you read in a newspaper that unemployment and prices are rising while wages and sales are falling, you can infer that the economy is heading toward a recession. Write down any inferences you draw from the material you read.

Respond with Your Own Ideas and Opinions As you read, you may want to write comments to yourself about the material you're reading. For example, if you disagree with an author, make a note of the reason for your disagreement. Remember, you don't have to accept everything that you read as fact. Use your own experience, knowledge, and opinion to challenge the author.

Review What You Have Read Review your notes and skim over the material again to get an overview of it after you have familiarized yourself with the details. You may decide to organize your notes into questions and answers, main ideas and key terms, and ideas or opinions that you plan to follow up on later.

Practice Your Skills

At the top of the following page is a passage from a book called *The Minutemen and Their World*.

1. Skim the passage. Does the passage contain any information about the American Revolution?
2. Scan the passage. What powers did the colonial town have?
3. Now read the passage carefully. How was the town run? How much power did it have? How does it compare with towns today?

When the eighteenth-century Yankee reflected on government, he thought first of his town. Through town meetings, he elected his officials, voted his taxes, and provided for the well-ordering of his community affairs. The main business of the town concerned roads and bridges, schools, and the poor. . . . But the colonial New England town claimed authority over anything that happened within its borders. It hired a minister . . . and compelled attendance at his sermons. It controlled public uses of private property. . . . And it gave equal care to the moral conduct of its inhabitants.

USING SOURCE MATERIALS IN WRITING

In addition to culling information from books, you must be able to incorporate material written by others into your own writing. You can do this three ways: by quoting directly, by paraphrasing, or by summarizing. The method you choose depends on the nature of the material and how you are using it.

Direct Quotation

Citing a writer's words exactly can be very effective if they are particularly important or well stated. Notice how Pearl Bailey's own words make a point forcefully and succinctly.

As Pearl Bailey said, "There's a period of our lives when we swallow a knowledge of ourselves and it becomes either good or sour inside." In other words, at some point we come to terms with ourselves; we either make peace with who we are, or we struggle against our nature.

If a direct quotation is longer than four lines, set it off from the text by beginning the quote on a new line and indenting it ten spaces from the left margin. Because the quote is already differentiated from the text, you do not need to add quotation marks.

Grammar
—TIP—
Use single quotes to indicate quotations within quotations.

WRITER TO WRITER

By necessity, by proclivity, and by delight, we all quote.
Ralph Waldo Emerson, American essayist and poet

482 Writing Handbook

Paraphrase

Sometimes you will want to **paraphrase,** or rewrite a passage from someone else's work in your own words, instead of quoting it directly. You might want to paraphrase material rather than quote it directly in order to simplify the material or to maintain a consistent style in your writing. You can use paraphrasing to incorporate material into your writing or to review material that you have read. For example, compare the following passage from *The Flamingo's Smile* by Stephen Jay Gould with a paraphrase of the material done by a student.

Original Passage

> In most birds (and mammals, including us), the upper jaw fuses to the skull; chewing, biting, and shouting move the mobile lower jaw against this stable brace. If reversed feeding has converted the flamingo's upper jaw into a working lower jaw in size and shape, then we must predict that, contrary to all anatomical custom, this upper beak moves up and down against a rigid lower jaw. The flamingo, in short, should feed by raising and lowering its upper jaw.
>
> **Stephen Jay Gould, *The Flamingo's Smile***

Paraphrase

> For the most part, birds and mammals have rigid, immobile upper jaws and loose, mobile lower jaws. This is the situation with humans, for example. However, the flamingo is a special case. It typically feeds with its head upside down, and its upper jaw looks like a lower jaw in both size and shape. Therefore, it would be reasonable to expect the flamingo's upper jaw, since it acts like other animals' lower jaws, to move like other animals' lower jaws (Gould 85).

Notice that the paraphrase in the example above is approximately the same length as the original passage and that the source is cited in parentheses. Consider the paraphrasing guidelines in the box at the top of the following page when you are writing a paraphrase.

Guidelines for Paraphrasing

1. **Locate the main idea.** Find the stated or implied main idea and write it down in your own words.

2. **List supporting details.** Jot down the details that support the main idea.

3. **Determine the tone.** Convey the same attitude that the author of the original does.

4. **Refine the vocabulary.** Simplify the wording of the original. One way to do this is to replace difficult words in the original selection with more familiar synonyms.

5. **Revise the paraphrase.** Reread the paraphrase to be sure that it expresses the meaning and tone of the original.

Summary

Like a paraphrase, a summary, or précis, presents the basic meaning of a piece in your own words. Whereas a paraphrase is about the same length as the original, a summary condenses a passage to about one-third of its original length without sacrificing its basic meaning.

You read and listen to summaries daily. The lead paragraph of a news article that appears in a newspaper or magazine is a summary.

Radio and television broadcasts present the important events of the day in brief, summarized form. Summaries also often serve as the conclusions of compositions, reports, and research papers.

In addition to summarizing source materials in your writing, you can write summaries as you are reading to help you understand complex material.

Read the following passage by Jacques Costeau and compare it with the summary on the following page.

Original Passage

About a hundred years ago, Thomas Henry Huxley, the English biologist, could say with confidence: "I believe that probably all the great sea fisheries are inexhaustible; that is to say that nothing we do seriously affects the number of fish." Huxley, of course, did not foresee the technological advances that would be made and applied within a century to fishing, as well as to every other aspect of man's activities. Sadly, Huxley's prediction has proved wrong. Today's fishing fleets consist of entire flotillas equipped with electronic devices and include floating ships that process the catch at sea. Planes are often used as spotters to locate schools of fish. Radio telephones direct boats to the fish. Radar and echo sounders find schools that cannot be seen from the air or on the water's surface. Moreover, oceanic sciences have determined the conditions of salinity and temperatures required for various species to thrive. Today, thermometers and salinometers are used by fishing fleets. These ultramodern fishing fleets can stay in the open water almost indefinitely, sweeping the sea of much of its life. The herring population in the Atlantic, the most heavily fished area of the world, is decreasing. Haddock may have been wiped out. Similarly, modern whaling methods have all but eliminated several types of whales from the face of the earth. Helicopters and swift, engine-driven catcher boats with sounding equipment spot the whales. Explosive harpoons fired from guns mounted on the catchers find their marks. Humans have become by far the greatest predators of all time. **Jacques Cousteau**

S T U D E N T
M O D E L

Summary

▼

A hundred years ago, the English biologist Thomas Henry Huxley predicted that despite anything we might do, our supply of fish would remain inexhaustible. Technological and scientific advances have proved him wrong. Today's year-round fleets are aided by electronic detectors, radio telephones, radar, echo sounders, and spotter planes. Advances in oceanic sciences have further improved their efficiency. As a result, the herring population has been seriously decreased; haddock and several kinds of whales have been almost wiped out. Humans are the greatest destroyers of all time (Cousteau 131).

Follow these steps when writing a summary.

Guidelines for Summarizing

1. **Locate the important points.** Identify the core of the writer's argument.
2. **Reduce the information.** Look for ways to reduce or eliminate unnecessary details, examples, anecdotes, and repetition. Also shorten long phrases and combine sentences.
3. **Revise the summary.** Check to make sure that all essential ideas in the original are contained in the summary.

Documentation of Sources

Whenever you use material from another writer, whether you are quoting directly, paraphrasing, or summarizing, you must document your source.

Using Parenthetical Documentation In using **parenthetical documentation,** you list the author's last name and the page number from the source in parentheses after the paraphrased, summarized, or quoted material. Notice, for example, the following documentation from a research paper about baseball.

Baseball was played in a form called rounders in England in the early eighteenth century, and until 1845 was popular in various forms in America (Voigt 11).

If you are using two or more works by the same author, the parenthetical reference should include the author's last name, the source's title or a shortened version of it, and the page number—for example, (Voigt, Baseball 64).

If you use an author's name in the sentence introducing the quotation, paraphrase, or summary, you need to supply only the page number in parentheses.

> David Voigt says that baseball's "Golden Age" was in the
> 1880's (25).

If you're using more than one work by the author named in the sentence, your parenthetical reference should include the title or a shortened version of it, as well as the page number.

When citing the source of a brief quotation that ends a sentence, place the reference between the closing quotation mark and the period. For a set-off quotation, place the reference after the quotation's final punctuation.

> The popularity of the sport had ramifications in other
> aspects of life: "baseball sold newspapers" (Voigt 61).

To cite two or more works in one reference, separate the citations with a semicolon—for example, (Voigt 25–27; Mackie 6).

If the source of your information has a corporate author, such as the Environmental Protection Agency or the State Department, be sure to say so in your parenthetical reference (State Department 15), or mention the corporate author in the text.

If your source contains a quotation from another source that you want to use, you may begin your parenthetical reference with the abbreviation *qtd. in,* for "quoted in."

When you use in-text parenthetical documentation, be sure to provide complete publication information for each source in a Works Cited list. See "Research Report," pages 287–290, for detailed information on preparing this list.

Using Other Methods of Documentation Instead of parenthetical references, you may document your sources in **footnotes** or **endnotes.** For both methods, you number consecutively all paraphrases, summaries, and direct quotations from the beginning to the end of your paper, using a superscript Arabic numeral (set slightly above the line) following each passage's final punctuation. Documentation notes should then appear at the bottom of relevant pages (footnotes) or in a list beginning on a separate page at the end of the paper (endnotes).

Writing
—TIP—

The publication information you provide in a footnote or an endnote is essentially the same as the information you include in a Works Cited entry. However, the format —the spacing and the punctuation— is different. Ask your teacher for format guidelines if you are instructed to use footnotes or endnotes.

Avoiding Plagiarism Presenting someone else's words or ideas as your own is **plagiarism;** it is a serious offense, and it can carry severe penalties. These guidelines may help you avoid plagiarism:

- Write complete bibliographic information on a 3″ × 5″ index card for each source you are likely to use. Give each card a source number.
- Write material from your sources on note cards. If you copy material from a source word for word, be sure to put quotation marks around it. Write the relevant source number on each note card so that you can document your information.
- If you write a summary or a paraphrase on a note card, label the card accordingly.

When writing your paper, follow these guidelines:

- **Document all direct quotations.** Make sure that you have copied down each quotation word for word and that the punctuation is the same as in the original.
- **Document information you glean from your sources.** This includes ideas and expressions that you didn't think of yourself but that you copied, paraphrased, or summarized from your sources.
- **Do not document common knowledge.** Information is considered common knowledge if it can be found in several different sources or if it is knowledge that many people have.

For more information on writing complete and accurate source cards and note cards, see "Research Report," pages 278–281.

Practice Your Skills

A. Write a paraphrase of the following passage. Try to retain all the basic ideas of the original, but make sure you use your own words.

Americans seem to live and breathe and function by paradox; but in nothing are we so paradoxical as in our passionate belief in our own myths. We truly believe ourselves to be natural-born mechanics and do-it-yourself-ers. We spend our lives in motor cars, yet most of us—a great many of us at least—do not know enough about a car to look in the gas tank when the motor fails. Our lives as we live them would not function without electricity, but it is a rare man or woman who, when the power goes off, knows how to look for a burned-out fuse and replace it. We believe implicitly that we are the heirs of the pioneers; that we have inherited self-sufficiency and the ability to take care of ourselves. . . . There isn't a man among us in ten thousand who knows how to butcher a cow or a pig and cut it up for eating, let alone a wild animal. . . . Americans treasure the knowledge that they live close to nature, but fewer and fewer farmers feed more and more people; and as soon as we can afford to we eat out of cans, buy frozen TV dinners, and haunt the delicatessens.   **John Steinbeck, *America and Americans***

B. Write a summary of this passage. Condense it to one-third its original length without sacrificing its essential meaning.

[Dinosaurs] were unintelligent machines; their actions were automatic, and lacking in the flexibility needed to cope with unfamiliar situations. Flexibility means intelligence, and the dinosaurs had little. Their small brains held a limited repertoire of behavior, with no room for varied response. The brain of the dinosaur was devoted mainly to the control of his huge bulk; it served simply as a telephone switching center, receiving signals from his body and sending out messages to move his head and limbs in unthinking reaction. If the eye of Tyrannosaurus registered a moving object, he pursued it; but his hunt lacked cunning. If the eye of Brontosaurus registered movement, he fled; but his flight was mechanical and mindless. And some other dinosaurs were still less intelligent; Stegosaurus, a ten-ton vegetarian, had a brain the size of a walnut. Dinosaurs were stupid animals; incapable of thought, moving slowly and ponderously, they waded through life as walking robots. . . . There was no need for greater intelligence in their lives, and therefore it never evolved.   **Robert Jastrow, *Until the Sun Dies***

CLAW YOUR WAY TO THE TOP

Humorist Dave Barry's educational plan for a successful future

ELEMENTARY SCHOOL

This is where you should learn to add, subtract, multiply, and divide, which are skills that are essential for filling out expense reports; you should also develop lifelong chumships with anybody whose name ends in "II," or, even better, "III." You might also consider learning to read. This is not really necessary, of course, inasmuch as you will have a secretary for this purpose, but some businesspersons like to occasionally do it themselves for amusement on long airplane trips.

HIGH SCHOOL

The point of high school is to get into a good college. The way you do this is by being well rounded, which is measured by how many organizations you belong to. Many college admissions officers select students by actually slapping a ruler down on the list of accomplishments underneath each applicant's high school yearbook picture. So you should join every one of the ludicrous high school organizations available to you, such as the Future Appliance Owners Club and the National Honor Society. If they won't let you into the National Honor Society, have your parents file a lawsuit alleging discrimination on the basis of intelligence.

Another thing you need to do in high school is to get good SAT scores, which are these two numbers you receive in the mail from the Educational Testing Service in Princeton, New Jersey. They have a whole warehouse filled with numbers up there. To get yours, you have to send some money off by mail to Princeton, then you have to go sit in a room full of other students with number-two pencils and answer questions like "BRAZIL is to COMPENSATE as LUST is to . . ." Then you have to figure out what kind of mood the folks up at the Educational Testing Service were in on the day they made up that particular question.

Nobody has the vaguest idea anymore how this elaborate ritual got started, what it has to do with anything in the real world, or how the Educational Testing Service decides what numbers to send you. My personal theory is that it has to do with how much money you send them in the mail. I think the amounts they tell you to send are actually just Suggested Minimum Donations, if you get my drift.

Dave Barry

Library, Reference Works, and Other Sources

REVIEWING CLASSIFICATION SYSTEMS

Most of the important human accomplishments have come about because someone asked a question and got an answer. In fact, this simple process is the basis for all research. Libraries hold the answers to so many important questions that they need their own unique organizational system.

Card and Computer Catalogs

Any search for materials in the library should start with the catalog listings. The card catalog allows you to locate a listing for a book by **title,** by **author,** and, for nonfiction books, by **subject.** Next to every listing in a card catalog, you will find an identification number, the **call number,** which will help you locate the book. Some libraries have recently supplemented or replaced the card catalog with a computer catalog. For more about computer catalogs, see page 854 of the Access Guide.

The Classification of Books

All libraries organize books similarly. The most elementary categorization of books in libraries is as fiction or nonfiction.

Fiction   In most libraries, novels are arranged alphabetically by the author's last name. Books by the same author are shelved alphabetically by title. Short-story anthologies may be shelved with novels by the author's last name, placed in a separate section at the end of fiction, or classified as literature in the nonfiction section.

Nonfiction   Factual material, or nonfiction, is organized in one of two ways. Many libraries use the Dewey Decimal System to classify their nonfiction. Major disciplines—technology, for example—are further divided into subcategories, such as 608 for inventions and patents. The Dewey Decimal numbers form the call number that is displayed on the book spine to help you locate the book on the library shelves.

COMPUTER TIP

When using a computer catalog, print out the sources you find listed. This saves time, ensures accuracy, and eliminates having to come back to find more sources.

Dewey Decimal Classifications

000–099	General Works (encyclopedias, bibliographies)
100–199	Philosophy (conduct, psychology)
200–299	Religion (the Bible, mythology, theology)
300–399	Social Science (law, education, economics)
400–499	Language (grammars, dictionaries, foreign languages)
500–599	Science (mathematics, biology, chemistry)
600–699	Technology (medicine, inventions, cooking)
700–799	The Arts (painting, music, theater, sports)
800–899	Literature (poetry, plays, essays—but not novels)
900–999	History (biography, geography, travel)

Melvil Dewey, American librarian, 1851-1931

Some libraries use the Library of Congress, or LC, system. This system has twenty-one broad categories, designated by letters of the alphabet. Subcategories are identified with a second letter. Fiction is shelved in the P section in the LC system.

P1880
G672.1
A701.3
P934.41
Q434.0
T114.91

Library of Congress Classification

A	General Works	M	Music
B	Philosophy, Psychology, Religion	N	Fine Arts
		P	Language and Literature
C-F	History	Q	Science
G	Geography, Anthropology, Recreation	R	Medicine
		S	Agriculture
		T	Technology
H	Social Science	U	Military Science
J	Political Science	V	Naval Science
K	Law	Z	Bibliography and Library Science
L	Education		

LOCATING MATERIALS

Your research will be more efficient if you learn about the special sections or rooms that libraries have.

Sections of the Library

Stacks   The stacks, or shelves, in a library may be open or closed. Although only library personnel can use **closed stacks,** you can browse freely in open stacks to locate resources.

Periodicals   Current magazines and newspapers are often displayed on open racks in a separate section or room. Back issues of periodicals may be bound and shelved in the periodical room.

Nonprint   Microfilm and microfiche, photographic reductions of printed material, are often housed in a separate room, along with machines for reading them. Filmstrips, films, cassettes, records, compact discs, art prints, and framed photographs also may be found there.

Reference, Biography, and Vertical File   These areas are discussed later in this handbook.

FINDING THE BEST SOURCE

Although browsing in the stacks can help you find sources of information, following some proven research methods will save you effort and produce more reliable results.

Indexes

Indexes are sources that lead to other sources. Indexes list names, places, topics, people, titles, and first lines of works alphabetically, and they supply the titles of specific reference books that contain information on the listing.

Readers' Guide to Periodical Literature   Suppose that you are writing a publicity article for the school paper on an upcoming sixties dance and you need some background on the twist. Skimming subject entries in the bound volumes of the *Readers' Guide* for the sixties would provide you with a list of magazine articles on the twist.

TECHNOLOGY
—— TIP ——

There are also several computerized and on-line indexes you can use. For more about electronic reference sources, see pages 854–856 of the Access Guide.

The excerpt from the *Readers' Guide* below shows typical listings.

Martinez, Ricardo, and others — Author entry
    Neuronal pp60 contains a six-amino acid
    insertion relative to its non-neuronal
    counterpart. bibl f il *Science* 237:411-15 Jl
Marvin, Lee, 1924–1987 — Subject entry
          about
    Obituary
    People Wkly il por 28:42   S 14 '87. B.
    Darrach
Marx, Groucho, 1891–1977
    Anecdotes, facetiae, satire, etc.
    A Harvard prof tells runners: on your Marx;
    get set; Groucho! [T. McMahon says
    jogging like Groucho is better for the
    body] il *People Wkly* 28:85 S 21 '87
Marx, Julius H. *See* Marx, Groucho, — "See" cross-reference
    1891–1977
Marx, Richard
          about
    Richard Marx's commercial background.
    S. Hochman. il por *Roll Stone* p20–1
    S 24 '87
Marx Brothers
         see also — "See also" cross-reference
    Marx, Groucho, 1891–1977

Labels: Name of magazine; Volume number, page number; Illustrated article; Author of article; Author entry; Subject entry; Date of magazine.

The New York Times Index   If you are researching an incident or an issue that made the national news, *The New York Times Index* will have abstracts of articles about your topic. This index lists articles by subject in chronological order for each year.

Biography and Genealogy Master Index   There are over 350 commonly used biographical dictionaries. The *Biography and Genealogy Master Index* tells you which biographical sources contain information on the person you are researching. The index lists pseudonyms as well as real names.

Granger's Index to Poetry   Suppose your literature text does not include Shelley's poem "Ozymandias," but you need a copy of the poem by tomorrow. *Granger's Index to Poetry* lists this poem by author, title, and first line and identifies books containing it.

Other Indexes   Similar to *Granger's,* the *Short Story Index* and the *Play Index* help you locate books that contain a certain literary work. The *National Geographic Magazine Cumulative Index* can help you locate articles in *National Geographic* magazine published from 1899 to 1976. The *American Heritage Cumulative Index* is useful for research of American history.

Parts of a Book

An examination of the parts of a book will help you decide if the book is going to be useful to you.

Title Page   The title page lists the full title, author or editor, and publisher. Publication by a special-interest group may affect the credibility of the material.

Copyright Page   The publication date will help you determine if the information in the book is current enough for your purpose.

Foreword, Preface, Introduction   Skim this preliminary material to learn how the author approached the subject.

Contents   This chapter outline of the book's contents will indicate coverage of your topic.

Index   This detailed alphabetical list of subjects, found in the back of the book, directs you to the page(s) you need.

Text   Sample the text itself. A useful source will treat the subject thoroughly in language that you can understand.

End Matter   You may find that one source is superior to others because it includes maps and charts in an **appendix** or because it contains a **glossary** of special terms. **Notes** and **bibliographies** list the author's sources. If one source is mentioned repeatedly in the bibliographies that you check, this source may be an especially reliable one for you to consult.

R E F E R E N C E   W O R K S

Dictionaries, encyclopedias, yearbooks, atlases, and almanacs are usually cataloged as reference works. Such sources are often located in a separate room or section of the library and are marked with an *R* or *Ref* above the call number.

Dictionaries

Abridged dictionaries, sometimes called college or desk dictionaries, are useful for discovering the meanings of unfamiliar words. **Unabridged dictionaries,** like the *Oxford English Dictionary* and *Webster's Third New International Dictionary,* contain longer, more detailed entries than those in abridged dictionaries.

Specialized Dictionaries

You might consult one of the many specialized dictionaries available if you are researching a topic that requires specialized or technical knowledge.

Dictionaries About Language   You can trace the origin of a word in either an abridged or an unabridged dictionary, but if you try to learn the etymology of a phrase such as "heavens to Betsy," you may need one of several dictionaries that treat specific aspects of language. These aspects include phrases, idioms, slang, jargon, rhyme, etymologies, and elements of usage.

Thesaurus   The word *thesaurus* comes from a Greek word meaning "treasure." This dictionary of synonyms and antonyms is indeed a treasure to a writer who is looking for a word with just the right shade of meaning.

Special-Purpose Dictionaries   Special-purpose dictionaries are available for many subjects, such as music, law, and medicine. If you wanted to explain the distinction between watercolor, gouache, and casein paints, for example, you probably would find a dictionary of art terms to be most helpful.

Encyclopedias

Encyclopedias, like dictionaries, can provide either general or specialized information.

General Encyclopedias   The word *encyclopedia* comes from a Greek word meaning "general education." Thus, the alphabetically arranged collection of articles on nearly every subject that makes up the volumes of an encyclopedia provides a quick reference on a subject. Yearbooks provide updated supplementary information.

The respected *Encyclopaedia Britannica* is composed of three parts: the *Propaedia,* or Outline of Knowledge and Guide to the *Britannica;* the *Micropaedia,* an index and short-entry encyclopedia; and the *Macropaedia,* which contains knowledge in detail.

Specialized Encyclopedias   Just as you may need to consult a specialized dictionary for technical vocabulary, you may need to consult a specialized encyclopedia on a specific subject for more exact, more detailed information than a general source offers. For example, a discussion in your economics class centers around monopolies and how they differ from cartels. Your assignment is to

TECHNOLOGY
— TIP —

Consider checking an on-line encyclopedia for the most up-to-date statistics and facts about a subject. Remember that not all encyclopedias you find on a computer are actually on-line. For more information, see page 855 of the Access Guide.

write a comparison-contrast paper. You might supplement what you learn from a general encyclopedia with material from a specialized work such as Donald Greenwald's *Encyclopedia of Economics*.

Almanacs, Yearbooks, and Atlases

Because almanacs and yearbooks are published annually, they provide an excellent source for current facts and statistics. They also cover matters of historical record in government, economics, sports, and other fields. Examples include the *Statistical Abstract of the United States* and the *World Almanac and Book of Facts*.

Atlases, such as the *National Geographic Atlas of the World,* are books of maps that also contain information about weather, global statistics, and geography.

Biographical References

In some libraries, biographies are part of the 900 Dewey Decimal classification and are marked with a number that begins with 92. Other libraries create a separate biography section and mark each book with a *B* and the first letter of the last name of the person the book is about.

If you want only to learn or confirm simple facts, such as someone's birth date or career history, a special dictionary such as *Webster's Biographical Dictionary* would be a good choice. If you require more information but do not need a full-length biography, consult sources such as the following for information on your subject: *Who's Who, Who's Who in America, Current Biography,* and *Dictionary of American Biography*.

Literary Reference Works

Literary research may involve a variety of tasks. You may need to learn about writers and their works or investigate some aspect of literary history. Occasionally, you might need to identify a quotation or locate a poem or short story. Literary reference works meet these needs.

Books About Authors   Sources such as *Twentieth Century Authors* and *Contemporary Authors* provide biographical information about authors. More extensive entries in *American Writers: A Collection of Literary Biographies and Writers at Work* also identify the connections between the authors' own experiences and those of their fictional characters.

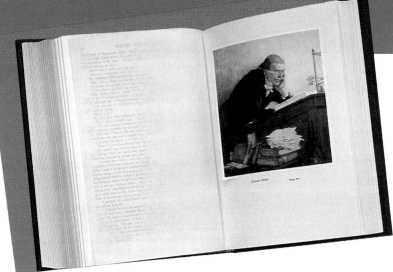

Book Review Digest   Suppose that you are responsible for writing the book reviews in your school newspaper. By consulting articles in the *Book Review Digest,* arranged alphabetically by author, you can compare your reviews with those of professional reviewers.

Cyclopedia of Literary Characters   The *Cyclopedia of Literary Characters* identifies the main characters in 1,300 novels, dramas, and epics from world literature. For example, a glance at the listing "Uriah Heep" in the character index leads you to a listing for Charles Dickens's *David Copperfield* and tells you that Heep was a hypocritical embezzler.

Books of Quotations   *Bartlett's Familiar Quotations* is a popular source for identifying quotations and well-known sayings. You may search for a quotation by author, subject, or first line. *Bartlett's* also contains a short section with often-quoted passages from religious works, such as the Bible, the Koran, and the Book of Common Prayer.

Bergen Evans's *Dictionary of Quotations* is another useful source. It extends beyond *Bartlett's* to include the comments of contemporary literary, political, and scientific figures.

Other Literary Sources   Your library offers many reference works on the history of literature. Among them you will find the Oxford Companion Series. Suppose you know that the character John Falstaff appears in a number of Shakespearean plays. How can you quickly learn which ones? You will find this kind of information in *The Oxford Companion to English Literature.* You will also find short biographies of authors, discussions of literary movements, awards and lists of winners, and explanations of literary allusions. Other books in the Oxford series focus specifically on American literature, classical literature, and the theater.

The process of research, like a road map, suggests a network of possible directions for you to follow. At times, you may decide to alter your techniques or explore sources beyond the library.

Altering Your Techniques

If you seem to have reached a dead end in your research, try some of the following strategies.

1. Examine how your topic fits a category. Suppose you fail to find a listing in the card catalog for the topic *chaos theory*. Chaos theory is a subcategory of the cosmos. You may be able to find information about chaos theory listed under the entry for *cosmos*.

2. Expand your search words. Consult a specialized dictionary or a thesaurus for additional terms related to your topic. For example, if you are investigating genetically transmitted diseases, you could start by looking for source material about genetics. Then you could look for information listed under the related headings *heredity* and *inherited traits*.

3. Follow up cross-references. Catalog listings and encyclopedia articles often include related subject headings called **cross-references.** DNA and Mendel's law, for example, might be cross-reference leads for the genetic disease topic.

4. Be alert to possible sources in bibliography lists. Skim the bibliographies found at the end of encyclopedia and journal articles and in the backs of nonfiction books.

5. Remember: the librarian is a valuable resource. Your library is staffed with knowledgeable people who are anxious to help you with your research.

WRITER TO WRITER

The single most important thing to remember when using the library is this: *if you have a question, ask someone.* A reference librarian can help you match your needs to the sources of information available in the library.

Milton H. Crouch, librarian

Exploring Sources Beyond the Library

The U.S. government and special-interest groups may be able to provide information not available elsewhere.

U.S. Government as a Source The Government Printing Office and many government agencies publish material on a multitude of subjects. Consult the *United States Government Organizational Manual,* which gives the purpose of each government agency and indicates the agencies to consult for special information. Also examine the *Selected List of United States Publications* to obtain the titles of possible useful publications.

Information Networks Special-interest groups or organizations often distribute excellent pamphlets. These are sometimes housed in a set of library file cabinets called the **vertical file.** Names and addresses of special-interest organizations may be found in the *Encyclopedia of Associations.*

TECHNOLOGY
—— TIP ——

Many government agencies and institutions, along with private associations, now have sites on the Internet. For more about accessing these sites, see pages 855–856 of the Access Guide.

Practice Your Skills

A. Choose a suitable topic for a research paper. Use the card catalog or computer catalog in your library to compile a working bibliography for the topic. List at least three books.

B. Continue researching the topic you chose for Exercise A by finding two related listings in the *Readers' Guide* and one listing in another index mentioned in this handbook. Copy the entry information for each listing.

C. Use reference works to complete the following items.

1. List the almanac, yearbook, or atlas that supplies the following statistics: (a) last year's PGA winner; (b) average rainfall in Buenos Aires, Argentina; (c) primary export of the United States.
2. What does a computer user mean by saying that a program needs "handshaking"?
3. How favorable were the reviews of John Steinbeck's *The Grapes of Wrath* when it was first published?
4. What is the plot of Frank Norris's novel *The Pit?*
5. Complete this quotation, and identify the speaker: "Let us never negotiate out of fear . . ."

D. List three sources found in the card or computer catalog that provide information on the French Revolution. You may need to search alternative headings and cross-references.

Debating Techniques

A **debate** consists of two opposing teams arguing a controversial subject called the question, or **proposition.** In a formal debate, the proposition is stated as a **resolution.** That is, it begins with the words, "Resolved, that. . ." and then makes a positive statement that advances an opinion, a solution, or an action. A typical proposition might be: "Resolved, that Puerto Rico should become the fifty-first state."

The speakers in a debate are divided into two teams. The **affirmative team** argues that the resolution should be upheld and accepted. The **negative team** argues that the resolution should be rejected. Each team tries to collect enough reasons and evidence to convince an audience that its stand is the correct one.

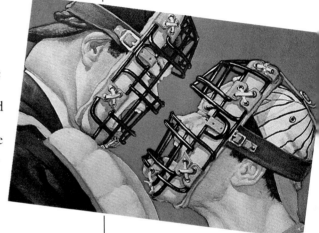

Debating helps sharpen your ability to analyze facts, evaluate evidence, and see logical connections. It also teaches you how to support your own views and to listen critically to the ideas of others. The following guidelines and techniques will enable you to argue your position on any subject effectively according to the rules of formal debate.

THE DEBATE PROPOSITION

All debates concern one of three types of propositions.

- **Propositions of fact** make a claim that a particular state of affairs can be proved to exist.

  Resolved, that acid rain is destroying forests.

- **Propositions of value** state that something is good or ethical.

  Resolved, that reporters are justified in maintaining the confidentiality of their sources.

- **Propositions of policy** recommend particular actions. Almost every topic for high-school debate is a proposition of policy.

  Resolved, that grades in elective classes should be abolished.

Every debate proposition must have the following characteristics.

1. The proposition must be stated in the affirmative. For example, a proposition might state that "Warren High School should abolish its dress code," but would never state that "Warren High School should not have a dress code."

2. The proposition should state only one main idea.

3. The proposition should be arguable. Neither side should be obviously right or wrong.

4. The proposition should be expressed in precise language so that the debate does not become a quibble over words.

THE DEBATE FORMAT

Following is a traditional debate format.

1. The affirmative and negative teams have the same number of debaters and the same amount of time to speak.

2. Members of the two sides alternate speaking. The affirmative team opens and closes the debate.

3. Each of the team's speakers gives an opening speech called the **constructive speech** and a closing speech called the **rebuttal.** The constructive speech contains the evidence and reasoning that support the speaker's case. The rebuttal contains a defense of each team's arguments and an attack on the opposition's.

Constructive Speeches (8 minutes each)

First Affirmative	First Negative
(Speaker 1)	(Speaker 2)
Second Affirmative	Second Negative
(Speaker 3)	(Speaker 4)

Rebuttals (4 minutes each)

First Negative	First Affirmative
(Speaker 1)	(Speaker 2)
Second Negative	Second Affirmative
(Speaker 3)	(Speaker 4)

A chairperson presides and maintains order during the debate. A speaker may appeal to the chairperson if he or she feels that the opposing team has violated legitimate procedures. Either a panel of judges or the audience votes to decide which team wins.

PREPARING FOR DEBATE

The debate itself may take only an hour or so, but many hours of studying, planning, and practicing must come first. The box below describes these steps as they relate to debate preparation.

Steps in Preparing for Debate

1. Research the proposition
2. Plan your case.
3. Write a constructive speech.
4. Practice your constructive speech.
5. Prepare for rebuttal.

Researching the Proposition

The first step in preparing for debate is to learn as much as possible about the subject. The more you know, the better you can argue either side of the proposition. To ensure systematic and thorough research, use the following guidelines.

Researching the Proposition

1. Do preliminary reading to gain background information on the proposition. Consult books, encyclopedias, atlases, magazines, newspapers, and other reference works.
2. Prepare a bibliography. Since most debate topics are current issues, current sources of information are most important. Consult such indexes as the *Readers' Guide to Periodical Literature,* the vertical file index, and the *Monthly Catalog of U.S. Government Publications.*
3. Collect as much material on your topic as you can find in the resources available to you.
4. Study the material you have collected. Record any facts, examples, or reasons that support your arguments. Be sure to gather a variety of materials.
5. Organize your notes by topic for easy access.

Building an Argument

Once you have researched and studied your subject, you are ready to plan your case and build an argument.

1. Analyze the proposition. Go over every important word of the proposition to make sure you know what you are to prove or disprove.

2. Determine the issues. The issues are the main differences between the affirmative and the negative positions. To determine the issues, list all the reasons you have for supporting your side of the proposition. Then list what your opponents' contrasting reasons might be. Devise a list of questions to help determine the issues.

Affirmative	*Negative*
a. Why does the current state of affairs need changing?	a. Why is there no need to change?
b. Why will the proposed change improve conditions?	b. Why will the proposal not improve conditions?
c. What other advantages will the change bring?	c. What bad effects would the change bring?
d. Why is it wrong to attack this proposition?	d. What more desirable idea could be suggested?

Writing
—**TIP**—

In selecting evidence, be sure that your facts are correct and that they support your arguments. Avoid evidence that can be reinterpreted to bolster contentions of the opposing side.

3. Choose your contentions, or main points. From the reasons you have for supporting your position, choose the ones you will use to build your case.

4. Select your evidence. Go over the notes from your reading to select items of evidence that support each of your points. Record each item of evidence and its source on a separate note card. Your case will appear stronger if you use various types of evidence, including statistics, examples from past experience, quotations from recognized authorities, and analogies to similar situations.

5. Prepare an outline. Separate your note cards according to topic. Your main points should become the main topics of your outline and the pieces of evidence the subtopics. Arrange the arguments in your outline in an order you think would have the greatest impact.

PREPARING CONSTRUCTIVE SPEECHES AND REBUTTALS

Once you have an outline, you can prepare your constructive speech and take notes to help in your rebuttal.

Constructive Speeches

The constructive speech should include an introduction, a body, and a conclusion. Avoid long, convoluted sentences that are difficult for the judges to follow. Use transitions between points to keep your speech flowing smoothly.

Introduction   The introduction should arouse interest by presenting questions, facts, illustrations, or anecdotes. It should also state the debate proposition as clearly and precisely as possible.

Body   The body of an affirmative or negative speech states the main points of the argument and presents evidence to support each point. However, affirmative and negative speeches differ in the following two ways.

1. The constructive speeches of an affirmative team show the need for change, the way to change, and the advantages of change.

2. The constructive speeches of a negative team defend the current conditions, show how proposed changes will be harmful, and suggest possible counterplans.

Conclusion   The conclusion of a constructive speech should simply summarize the main points listed in the body. Conclusions should never introduce new material, and they should not repeat the evidence used to support the main points. A clear restatement of the main position should end the constructive speech.

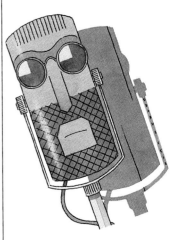

Rebuttal

The rebuttal affords debaters a final opportunity to attack their opponents' arguments and defend their own. Rebuttals do not include new issues, although they may introduce new evidence. Unlike constructive speeches, which are completely written ahead of time, rebuttals must be prepared while the debate is in progress.

Methods of Rebuttal   Each debater listens carefully to the opponents' constructive speeches, takes notes, organizes the material in his or her head, and prepares an extemporaneous rebuttal. This can be done in the following ways.

1. Prove that the opponents' evidence is not sufficient.

2. Prove that the evidence is inaccurate.

3. Prove that the evidence is from an unreliable source.

4. Prove that the evidence could lead to a different conclusion.

Rehearsing and Presenting the Debate

You and your partner should rehearse your constructive speeches many times. Presenting your speeches to parents or friends and asking them to list arguments against your position helps you find gaps in your thinking. For more help in evaluating arguments, see "Developing and Presenting an Argument," pages 474–476.

During the debate, stand so that you can see your audience. Vary the speed, pitch, and volume of your voice, and speak clearly and confidently. Avoid sarcasm and arrogance.

Practice Your Skills

A. Decide whether each of the following statements is a valid, well-worded proposition. If not, explain why and revise it.

1. Resolved, that public employees do not have the right to strike.
2. Resolved, that women have made sufficient gains in the work world in the last few years.
3. Resolved, that TV debates between political candidates do not change voters' opinions.

B. Choose one of the following propositions. Prepare to debate this proposition, taking either the affirmative or the negative side. Research the proposition, prepare a bibliography, gather evidence, and prepare an outline for your constructive speech and for a hypothetical rebuttal.

1. Resolved, that states should eliminate parole for prisoners who commit violent crimes.
2. Resolved, that medical and scientific experimentation with animals should be outlawed.

C. Write a constructive speech based on one of the propositions from Exercise B, or on another proposition of your own choice. Make sure that your introduction states the proposition and arouses a significant amount of interest among your listeners.

Occupational Interests and Career Choices

About this time, people may start asking you, "What are you going to do after graduation?" This may seem like a simple enough question, but when you give it some thought you just might find the entire issue a bit overwhelming. After all, you're being asked to map out your future, to make decisions that will affect the course of your life.

Here is some help. The following techniques for self-evaluation, preparing résumés and letters of application, and choosing a college or career will help you to plan the next few years of your life carefully and intelligently.

EVALUATING YOUR OPTIONS

You may have already identified an occupational interest or a definite career choice. Perhaps, however, your future goals are more general: to become independent, to provide for yourself or for a family, to find a challenging job, to work in an area of service to others. To clarify your goals, you will find it worthwhile to sit down and evaluate your options for the future.

Analyzing Your Interests, Abilities, and Needs

Your research and critical thinking skills are as valuable in finding answers to what to do with your life as they are in solving problems in school, at work, and with friends. Carefully consider the questions below. Discuss your answers to the questions with your guidance counselor, your parents, and anyone else whose opinion you value.

Identifying and Evaluating Your Interests   The following questions may help you to identify and evaluate your interests.

- What school subjects do I enjoy most and least? why?
- Which hobby, extracurricular activity, or volunteer work gives me the greatest satisfaction?
- What types of leisure reading do I choose?
- What have I enjoyed most and least about a job I've had?
- Do any of my interests relate to a possible career?

Identifying Your Strengths and Preferences   The following questions will aid you in identifying your strengths and weaknesses, your special skills and personal preferences.

- How do I view myself as a student? Have I been an underachiever or an overachiever? What is my grade-point average and class rank?
- What are my strongest and weakest school subjects?
- How well have I done on college entrance tests (SAT, ACT)?
- Do I enjoy working with ideas, numbers, people, machines, tools, plants, or animals?
- Do I enjoy working independently or with others?
- Do I prefer variety or routine? indoor or outdoor work? sedentary work or physical activity and/or travel?

Exploring Your Options   The following questions will aid you in exploring your options after high school.

- Shall I take a year off to work or travel after graduation?
- Shall I join the armed forces as a career or as a way to obtain training?
- Shall I attend college full time? Should I attend a community college and live at home to save money?
- Would a trade or technical school give me the training I need?
- Does a specialized school—in the arts, design, mechanical arts, or computers—match my interests and goals?

Considering Your Financial Options   The following questions will be helpful as you consider your financial options.

- After graduation, how much of my living expenses must I provide?
- How much financial help will or can my parents provide? What savings or other financial resources do I have?
- Will I need additional help in financing my education?
- Can I qualify for any scholarship money?
- Am I willing to apply for and repay loans?
- Can I work part-time or apply for work-study programs?
- Can I finance my education through the armed forces?–

   After you have answered the preceding questions, examine your answers with care. Then begin to narrow your choices about possible careers and fields of study. Base your choices on a realistic look at your options, your interests, and your abilities.

Researching Your Prospects

The following are some valuable sources of information about occupations and schools. Most of the books listed are available in either counseling offices or libraries.

1. *Dictionary of Occupational Titles* and *Occupational Outlook Handbook*
2. Career-planning manuals, such as *What Color Is Your Parachute?*
3. Parents, guardians, and friends who have attended college and pursued various careers
4. College catalogs or school bulletins
5. *Comparative Guide to American Colleges*
6. Peterson's Guides, including *After Scholarships, What?* and *Creative Ways to Lower Your College Costs and the Colleges That Offer Them*

INVESTIGATING JOB OPPORTUNITIES

You may decide that you want to get a job immediately after graduation. Looking for a job can be a stressful experience, but you'll probably find that thinking about it is worse than doing it. The best way to combat your anxiety is to plunge into job-search activities with as much enthusiasm as possible.

Ways to Find Jobs   Once you know what sort of job you want to pursue, there are a number of ways you can learn what jobs are available.

- Check the classified ads in a local newspaper.
- Contact local employment agencies.
- Network with people whom you know.
- Write letters to possible employers.
- Arrange to talk with potential employers informally, without requesting a job, to gather information.

When you are seeking information about a particular job, it's sometimes better to find out the name and title of the person who is responsible for the department in which you want to work rather than talking to someone in the human resources or personnel department. By contacting the department directly, you'll be speaking to people with whom you might be working. It's important to find out what those people are like.

You might be surprised to find how willing people are to talk with you about what they do. Most managers welcome an opportunity to discuss how they became interested in their professions and what they like and dislike about their jobs.

Writing Résumés and Letters of Application   In preparing your résumé or letter of application, be sure you conform to one of the commonly accepted formats. Once you've done that, you can infuse your letter or résumé with your own individuality. For additional information about writing résumés and letters of application, see "Applying for a Job" on pages 516–518.

Job Application Forms   If an employer asks you to come to his or her place of business for a job interview or to complete a job application, ask whether any tests will be a part of the application process.

When you visit the potential employer, you will want to bring with you all the information necessary to complete an application. Have on hand, for example, the names, titles, addresses, and telephone numbers of people who will give you personal and professional references. You will want to read the entire application form before filling in the blanks. In fact, it's a good idea to write your answers on a sheet of scrap paper first before completing the form.

Interviewing   The following guidelines will help you in an interview.

1. Prepare yourself beforehand. Employers will probably ask you about the information in your résumé. They may also ask you questions that will reveal your interpersonal skills and your plans for the future.

2. Dress appropriately for the interview.

3. Arrive at the interview on time. Make sure you have good directions.

4. Come prepared. Bring with you any information that you might need, including extra copies of your résumé.

5. Be courteous and enthusiastic during the interview. Greet the interviewer with a friendly handshake. During the interview, maintain eye contact and good posture. Think about what you are going to say before you say it. At the end of your interview, thank the interviewer for his or her time.

6. Write a follow-up letter. Thank the interviewer for considering you for the position. Follow proper business letter form.

You may decide that you want to go to college before settling on a career. To learn more about a particular college, send a letter or a postcard to its admissions office, requesting a catalog and an application for the academic year in which you plan to attend.

Handling a College Interview and a Visit to the Campus Some colleges and universities recommend an interview as part of the formal application process. Use the interview to help you decide whether to apply to that particular college.

If you schedule an interview, be sure to allow enough time to tour the campus. Most colleges offer scheduled campus tours for prospective students and their parents. Try to allow some extra time for exploring the campus on your own so that you can begin to get a "feel" for the place and some idea about whether you would be comfortable there.

Evaluating College Information After you have gathered information on various schools that interest you and perhaps visited a few of them, it's time to narrow the field and select a handful of colleges or universities to which you will apply.

The following lists of questions should help you narrow down your choice of schools.

Choosing a School: Questions to Ask Yourself

Academics

- What is the academic reputation of the school?
- Does my record make this a realistic prospect?
- Does the school offer quality programs in my fields of interest?

Costs

- What is the cost of tuition, fees, and housing?
- Does the school offer scholarships, loans, work-study programs, or other financial opportunities?

Size

- Are students given individual attention, or is the freshman year a "sink-or-swim" experience?
- How large are the lecture courses? If a class is too large for a student to get to know a professor, are teaching assistants easily accessible?

Facilities

- Are the dormitory and dining facilities adequate?
- Does the school have a good library?
- Do the departments in my areas of interest have any special facilities?
- Does the school have adequate recreational and sports facilities? Are these facilities open to all students?

In addition to the preceding questions, keep your personal needs and preferences in mind. Ask yourself whether you want—or need—to attend a school close to home. If you are considering a college located far from home, remember to include travel costs for at least two or three trips home as part of your annual expenses. Would you prefer a school located in a big city, or is a quiet college town more appealing? If you have your heart set on a particular college, is your goal realistic?

One effective way to compare colleges is to construct a chart that contrasts their important features. Across the top of a sheet of paper, list the names of the schools. In a left-hand column, write the headings *Academics, Costs, Size,* and *Facilities.* Then fill in the spaces under each school's name.

From the information on your chart, make a list of the schools that best fit your needs. Many guidance counselors suggest that this list number no more than six to eight. Include both the school you would most like to attend and a "safety" school that you would be satisfied to attend—one to which you feel certain of gaining admission.

Completing a College Application   After narrowing your prospects to no more than six schools, the next step is to complete your admissions applications. Since your college application is your formal presentation to the admissions committee, you will want to make sure it represents you well.

Preview the entire application before you even pick up a pen. An overview will give you the chance to plan what you want to emphasize about yourself and your accomplishments.

Many schools require written recommendations from teachers and/or school counselors. Select your references carefully. Choose people who know you well and who will write positively and informatively about you.

As you fill out your application, keep these points in mind.

1. Read and follow all the application's instructions carefully. A completely accurate application tells the reader that you are a candidate for whom detail is important.

2. If possible, photocopy the application before you fill it out. Use this copy as a draft and then copy the information onto the actual form. Carefully type or print your final form.

3. Note all application deadlines on a calendar, or list deadlines on a flowchart. Allow plenty of time for the school to receive transcripts, test scores, and recommendations.

4. Emphasize your key interests and those activities to which you devote the most time and energy. Highlight areas in which you excel and activities or attributes that make you unique.

Writing an Essay   Your application may require an entrance essay. A well-written one can help tip the balance toward admission in cases where the decision could go either way. Other than a personal interview, the entrance essay is the only place in the application procedure where you can convey a real sense of your personality, values, and style.

Writing TIP

Make photocopies of everything you submit to the admissions office in case your application is lost in the mail.

Practice Your Skills

A. Answer the questions on pages 507–508 under the heading "Analyzing Your Interests, Abilities, and Needs." Then analyze your answers and write a short paragraph that summarizes what you find out about yourself.

B. Write down three careers in which you are interested. Research each one by consulting sources such as those listed on page 509. Then answer the following questions.

1. What specific academic skills and personality traits are required for the job?
2. What special training or education must a person receive before entering this career?
3. What is the typical work environment for someone in this job? Are there any health restrictions?
4. What financial return can someone working in this job expect to receive, both immediately and over the long run? What types of benefits are offered?
5. Is there a demand for new workers in this field? Will that demand remain steady?

C. The following chart is taken from the Common Application, an admissions form currently used by more than 100 private colleges. Complete this section as if you were applying for college admission. Write your answers on a separate sheet of paper.

EXTRACURRICULAR AND PERSONAL ACTIVITIES

Please list your principal extracurricular, community, and family activities and hobbies in the order of their interest to you. Include specific events and/or major accomplishments such as musical instruments played, varsity letters earned, awards from clubs or organizations, etc.

Activity	Grade levels	Hours per week	Weeks per year	Positions held, Honors won

D. On a separate sheet of paper, complete the following part of an application for admission to a fictitious school. Save the information you provided on the form to use as a guide when completing your real applications.

Application for Admission to General University

Please return to Office of Admissions, General University, College Junction, Idaho 83539, with an application fee of $30.

1. _____
   Last name (type or print)   First (legal)   Middle

2. _____
   Permanent address   City   State   Zip

3. _____
   Social Security number   Telephone (area code)

4. Place and date of birth _____

5. Name of parent or guardian _____

6. Permanent address of parent or guardian _____

7. Father's occupation _____ Employer _____

   Mother's occupation _____ Employer _____

8. What college did your father attend? _____

   Your mother? _____

9. Name of any relative who is now attending or has attended General University _____

10. Name of high school _____

11. City and state of high school _____

12. Date of graduation _____

13. Have you taken the ACT? _____ When? _____

    SAT? _____ When? _____

14. What semester do you wish to enter?

    Fall _____ Winter _____

15. Division and major _____

16. On a separate sheet of paper, write an essay that gives us a personal statement about yourself. Choose one of the topics below.

    a. Explain and discuss the significance of a personal experience or achievement that has special meaning for you.

    b. Identify and describe a person who has had a significant influence on you and explain that influence.

E. Answer this Common Application essay question: "Briefly discuss which of these activities (extracurricular and personal activities or work experience) has had the most meaning for you, and why." Limit your answer to no more than one typed page.

Business Writing

The writing you do in school prepares you for the kind of writing you'll need to do after you graduate—in the job application process, in your work, and in conducting your day-to-day affairs. One of the most common types of business writing is the letter, which incorporates many of the elements of persuasive writing. Whether you are writing to request information, order or return products, state your opinions, complain, or say thank you, business letters attempt to get the reader to agree with you and comply with your requests.

To ensure that your letter has the desired effect on your reader, you must first realize that every business letter sends a double message: the factual information conveyed in the letter and the impression it makes about you, the writer. You can control the impact of your letter's content by using proper grammatical form, present tense, and accurate, clearly-stated facts. You can control the reader's impression of you by always using a businesslike tone—straightforward and polite, but not overly formal and stodgy. These simple, yet crucial, guidelines should be followed in all types of business writing, including job applications or cover letters, follow-up letters, and the writing you do on the job.

APPLYING FOR A JOB

Your first contact with a prospective employer usually will be a cover letter, accompanied by a résumé. Prepare these documents with care and make sure they are error-free.

Cover letters   When writing a **cover letter** or letter of application, follow proper business letter format (see the Appendix, pages 828–829.) Address your letter to a specific person, such as a personnel director, and make certain that the person's title and the spelling of his or her name are correct. State the purpose of your letter in your first sentence. Briefly explain why you want the job and outline your special qualities or qualifications that make you the perfect candidate.

Type your letter single-spaced—double-spaced between paragraphs—on 8 1/2 × 11-inch paper. If your letter is very brief, double space the entire letter to improve its appearance. A sample letter of application is shown on the next page.

1402 Welles Avenue
Grover's Mill, New Jersey 04562
January 28, 19—

Ms. Marion Robinson
Director of Human Services
<u>Grover's Mill Telegraph</u>
566 Main Street
Grover's Mill, New Jersey 04562

Dear Ms. Robinson:

I would like to apply for an internship as a copy editor
for the <u>Grover's Mill Telegraph</u>. I hope to work for your
paper this summer before entering the Indiana University
School of Journalism in the fall.

As you will see from the enclosed résumé, I have
considerable experience as a writer and copy editor on the
staff of the Grover's Mill High School newspaper, the
<u>Clarion</u>. I have written news stories on school and
community events and features on bicycle racing, toxins in
the home, and Outward Bound programs for high-school
students. I have enclosed clippings of my writing from the
school paper for your review.

In addition to my experience on the school paper, I have
many other skills that qualify me for this job. I am
familiar with several word processing programs and my
communication skills are superb. I can provide excellent
recommendations from teachers, previous employers, and
co-workers who will attest to my industriousness and
dependability.

Thank you for considering my application. Please write
or call to let me know when I can come in for an
interview. My telephone number is (201) 555-1616. I look
forward to hearing from you soon.

Sincerely,

Philip Yani

Enc: Résumé; clippings

Résumé A résumé is a list of information about you that would be of interest to potential employers. It should be a self-advertisement, highlighting your experience and qualifications in the best possible way.

A clear, easy-to-read résumé is divided into separate sections, each with its own heading. If you know exactly what kind of job you are looking for, you can say so under the job objective heading which always falls at the beginning of a résumé as shown in the sample below. If you are applying for a variety of jobs, you can write a general résumé without an objective. Both forms are accepted in the business world.

Organize your résumé to emphasize your strong points. For example, if you have held several important jobs, list your work history in reverse chronological order immediately after your job objective. If you have little work experience, emphasize your education, including any awards or specialized training you may have received, and your skills, such as leadership, business or teaching.

A résumé should be written in phrases or clauses, not in complete sentences. Use positive, active verbs to describe your work and achievements. Do not include references to your gender, weight, height, age, race, or religion, since they are legally irrelevant to your job qualifications. Including wage or salary expectations on a résumé is also considered inappropriate. Type your résumé on good-quality 8 1/2 × 11-inch stationery, preferably white, off-white, or buff, or have it professionally typeset. Proofread the final copy carefully. To make the best impression, your résumé must be clear, concise, and completely error-free.

Philip Yani
1402 Welles Avenue
Grover's Mill, New Jersey 04562
(201) 555-1616

OBJECTIVE	Summer intern at a local newspaper
QUALIFICATIONS	• Three years' experience as writer and copy editor, Grover's Mill High School Clarion • Knowledge of Associated Press Stylebook • Thorough understanding of newspaper production process
WORK EXPERIENCE	September 1990–Present Part-time cashier/stockboy, Best Food Market August 1988–Present Writer and copy editor for Grover's Mill High School Clarion. Researched, wrote, and edited a variety of news, features, and sports stories. Wrote headlines, assisted in layouts, trained new staff members.
EDUCATION	Grover's Mill High School, Grover's Mill, New Jersey, 1988–1992; B+ average.
AWARDS	Winner of Tri-State "Young Authors" Composition Contest, 1990.
INTERESTS	Journalism, modern American literature, history, tennis
REFERENCES	Available on request.

The writing you do to apply for a job gives employers an idea of the skills you will bring to writing activities required on the job. Of all the different types of writing you are likely to do in the business world, memoranda and technical writing are two of the most common.

Memoranda   Written communications to convey information and make announcements to company employees are called **memoranda,** or **memos.** When writing a memo, include the mandatory header information as shown in the example below. Although the tone of a memo may be more informal than a business letter, the message should still be brief, clear, and concise.

                            Memo
TO: Newspaper staff
FROM: Mary Rutkowski, Production Dept.
SUBJECT: Deadlines for special "Graduation Day"
            issue
DATE: April 23, 1992

All copy for the special "Graduation Day" issue is to be submitted on or before April 30th. Please let me know if you anticipate any problems in meeting this deadline. We expect this to be our finest "Graduation Day" issue ever.

WRITER TO WRITER

The greatest thing a human soul ever does in this world is to see something and tell what it saw in a plain way.
Galileo, Italian astronomer and physicist

Technical Writing   Technical writing is a broad term used to cover various types of writing done in science, industry, and other specialized fields. Assembly instructions, on-line documentation, and manuals are all forms of technical writing. Use the following guidelines when doing technical writing.

Technical Writing Guidelines

1. When possible, use the second-person imperative. For example, write "Tighten the bolt," not "The bolt should be tightened."

2. Break a process down into separate steps, and include in your writing every step that the reader must take to complete it. Assume that the reader will do nothing unless specifically told to do it.

3. Present the steps in chronological order. Use transitions such as *first, second, third,* and *finally.*

4. Use simple sentences and familiar vocabulary. Make sure that everyone who reads your directions can follow them.

5. Use visual aids such as diagrams and flowcharts. Good technical writing uses all means available to make complex information clear and understandable. A picture sometimes says a thousand words.

6. Try your directions as part of the revision process. This will test whether or not your directions are clear, logical, and complete.

Practice Your Skills

A. Write a business letter of complaint (about damaged merchandise, late delivery, or a cockroach in a plate of spaghetti served at a restaurant, for example); a letter of apology (for a missed appointment or a late report, for example); or a letter of request (for college brochures, time extension, or information for a research report).

B. Find a job in the "Help Wanted" ads that might be appropriate for a high-school student. Then prepare a job application letter and a résumé that you might use if you were applying for this job.

C. Imagine that you are the director of a student production of *South Pacific.* Write a memo to the cast members announcing a change of opening night from May 4th to May 9th.

D. Choose an activity that you are good at but not everyone can do, such as videotaping a scene, changing a tire, or preparing a meal. Write directions for completing that activity.

Testing for College Admission

College-bound students usually take one or more college entrance exams. Two widely used tests are the Scholastic Aptitude Test (SAT) and the test of the American College Testing Program (ACT). You already may have taken one of these tests. However, you should be aware that you can retake either one in the fall of your senior year and still receive your scores in time to meet college admission and scholarship deadlines.

TYPES OF TESTS

The Scholastic Aptitude Test and the ACT Assessment are the two most common entrance tests taken by college applicants. Many students, however, will also take achievement tests and advanced-placement tests during high school, and most colleges and universities give placement tests to incoming freshmen.

The Scholastic Aptitude Test   The SAT is a multiple-choice test. Its format is being revised during the early 1990's, but it currently contains two verbal and two math sections.

The ACT Assessment   The ACT has multiple-choice questions measuring skills in English, mathematics, social studies, and natural sciences, and requires some knowledge of American history, chemistry, and biology. The ACT is divided into four sections: English usage, mathematics usage, social studies reading, and natural sciences reading.

Achievement Tests   The College Entrance Examination Board offers one-hour achievement tests in such subjects as English, foreign languages, history and social studies, mathematics, and sciences.

Advanced-Placement Tests   Some students are able to pursue the equivalent of college-level studies while they are still in high school. Advanced-placement tests measure students' understanding and in some cases award them college credit and appropriate placement at participating colleges. These examinations are offered each May. The tests contain an essay or a problem-solving section and a multiple-choice section on a wide range of subjects.

Last-minute cramming does not help you on aptitude tests such as the ACT and the SAT. The best scores are achieved through regular reading, writing, and studying in the courses that are part of your high-school curriculum. However, practicing with commercially prepared manuals or with sample tests from the testing organization will familiarize you with the test content and formats, and will help you develop strategies for answering the questions. On the day of the test, follow these guidelines.

1. Bring to the test center all required materials named in the booklet you receive with your registration form. Typically, you need several sharpened number-two pencils, an admission ticket, a form of personal identification, and a watch (to help you budget your time).

2. Plan to arrive at the test center thirty minutes before the test is scheduled to begin.

3. Listen carefully to all instructions given by the test supervisor. Begin as soon as the command to begin is given.

4. Completely darken each appropriate space on the answer sheet. Thoroughly erase any stray marks or changed answers. Check your answer sheet periodically to make sure that the numbers on the spaces you are marking coincide with the numbers of the questions you are answering in the booklet.

5. Approach each test section with a comprehensive strategy. Note the number of questions and the time available. Answer all the easy questions on a quick first read-through. Then go back for the more difficult questions, keeping an eye on your time.

QUESTIONS AND STRATEGIES

Standardized tests typically contain questions of the following types: antonyms, analogies, sentence completion, reading comprehension, usage, sentence correction, and construction-shift. In order to be well prepared for taking standardized tests, you should learn specific strategies for answering questions of each kind.

Antonyms Antonym questions provide a single word and ask you to choose from five words the one most nearly opposite in meaning.

> FERMENTING: (A) improvising (B) stagnating (C) wavering (D) plunging (E) dissolving

You will find the following strategies helpful for answering antonym questions.

1. Try to determine the meaning of the given word before you look at the answer choices. Note any prefixes, suffixes, base words, or roots. Think of a synonym (a word that has most nearly the same meaning) for the given word, or create a sentence that uses this word.

2. Once you have determined the meaning of the given word, look carefully at the answer choices. Remember to look only for words with *opposite* meanings. Do not be thrown off by synonyms. In some test items, synonyms are deliberately included, and they can fool students who automatically choose the first related word they find.

3. If you cannot readily identify the correct answer, try to eliminate any obviously incorrect answers. Also, since most words have multiple meanings, try looking for antonyms of the word's other meanings.

4. Remember that few words are exact opposites; find the word most nearly opposite in meaning. In the example, both *dissolving* and *stagnating* can be related to *fermenting,* which signifies a kind of chemical breakdown or turbulence and unrest. However, *dissolving* implies a melting or disintegration into a liquid, not the molecular simplification of fermentation. *Stagnating,* meaning "becoming sluggish or inactive," is a much clearer opposite. The correct answer is *B.*

Practice Your Skills

Each of the following antonym examples consists of a word in capital letters, followed by five lettered words or phrases. Choose the word or phrase most nearly opposite in meaning to the word in capital letters.

1. VERSATILE: (A) unadaptable (B) mediocre (C) impatient (D) egocentric (E) vicious
2. FRAUDULENT: (A) rather pleasing (B) extremely beneficial (C) courteous (D) authentic (E) simplified

3. BOLT: (A) cleanse (B) slide (C) look upon
   (D) move sluggishly (E) exhibit proudly
4. IMPUGN: (A) speak well of (B) describe in detail
   (C) forget to complete (D) dissociate (E) stimulate
5. EPHEMERAL: (A) lasting (B) inhumane (C) contemporary
   (D) destructive (E) appropriate

Analogies Analogy questions ask you to note the relationship in a pair of words, to understand the basis of the relationship, and to recognize a parallel relationship in another word pair.

> TERRESTRIAL : LUNG :: (A) marsupial : pouch (B) floral : root
> (C) perennial : seed (D) aquatic : gill
> (E) canine : mouth

The following strategies will help you to complete analogies.

1. Determine the relationship between the first two words, and state the relationship in a sentence: *Terrestrial* creatures breathe by means of their *lungs*.

2. Decide which of the choices expresses a similar relationship: *Aquatic* creatures breathe by means of their *gills*.

The correct answer is *D*.

Types of Relationships in Analogy Questions	
Type of Analogy	**Example**
object to its function	BRUSH : PAINTING :: scissors : cutting
object to its material	STREET : ASPHALT :: memorial : granite
cause to effect	ICE : COOLING :: acid : etching
action to object	HURL : DISCUS :: fire : cannon
part to whole	THREAD : FABRIC :: brick : wall
item to category	*MACBETH* : DRAMA :: *Lord Jim* : novel
item to characteristic	MERCURY : LIQUID :: diamond : hard
worker and tool	ARTIST : BRUSH :: dentist : drill
worker and creation	SCULPTOR : STATUE :: composer : sonata
worker and workplace	CHEMIST : LABORATORY :: actor : theater
word to antonym	GLORIOUS : INFAMOUS :: haughty : meek
word to synonym	OMINOUS : SINISTER :: succinct : concise
time sequence	PREMATURE : TIMELY :: punctual : late

Practice Your Skills

Each of the following analogy items begins with a related pair of words. Select the lettered pair whose relationship most closely resembles that of the original pair.

1. VOLUME : SPHERE :: (A) altitude : triangle
   (B) diagonal : square (C) area : circle
   (D) angle : rectangle (E) length : cube
2. RAMSHACKLE : COLLAPSE :: (A) intact : explode
   (B) threadbare : hem (C) waterlogged : sink
   (D) dilapidated : repair (E) flammable : quench
3. TRICK : ROGUE :: (A) stratagem : friend
   (B) sentence : criminal (C) accident : witness
   (D) conspiracy : traitor (E) novel : reader
4. CALIPERS : MEASURING :: (A) nails : hammering
   (B) crops : harvesting (C) glasses : polishing
   (D) decisions : weighing (E) scissors : cutting
5. WHEEDLE : FLATTERY :: (A) inspire : creations
   (B) accuse : denials (C) scrutinize : clues
   (D) intimidate : threats (E) appreciate : offers

Sentence Completion To answer sentence-completion questions successfully, you must recognize relationships among parts of a sentence, and you must recognize and know the meanings of key words. A sentence-completion question consists of a sentence from which one or two words have been removed. You must choose the lettered word or set of words that completes the meaning of the sentence most logically. Study the following example.

> Although Spalding _____ the importance of the physical necessities of life, her most successful endeavor was the _____ of the condition of the impoverished.
> (A) deprecated . . . alleviation
> (B) emphasized . . . investigation
> (C) accentuated . . . amelioration
> (D) epitomized . . . delineation
> (E) disregarded . . . desecration

Use these strategies to answer sentence-completion questions.

1. Read the incomplete sentence carefully, noting any key words that show the following relationships: contrast (*but, although, however*); similarity (*another, the same as, and*); cause and effect (*therefore, as a result, consequently, because*). In the example, *although* suggests a contrasting relationship.

2. Try each choice in the sentence, eliminating those that are nonsensical or grammatically incorrect.

3. Make sure that *both* words fit the sentence logically. In the example on the preceding page, the second word in answer *C* makes sense, but the first word does not.

4. Make sure that *both* words are the correct part of speech and form.

The answer to the sample question is *A*.

Practice Your Skills

The blanks in these sentences indicate an omission. Following each are five lettered words or sets of words. Choose the answer that best fits the meaning of the sentence.

1. In the North Pacific, the number of whales has been so drastically reduced that the sighting of even one is _____ event.
   (A) a newsworthy   (B) a treacherous   (C) an everyday
   (D) an elaborate   (E) an expected

2. Musicians' salaries have risen so much faster than concert admission prices and donations that some famous _____ are threatened with _____.
   (A) composers . . . silence   (B) orchestras . . . bankruptcy
   (C) works . . . oblivion   (D) conductors . . . strikes
   (E) soloists . . . taxation

3. In view of the _____ value of the new treatment for this complicated case, _____ with another physician is advisable.
   (A) questionable . . . a consultation
   (B) necessary . . . an interlude
   (C) accepted . . . an exploration
   (D) impossible . . . a confrontation
   (E) presumed . . . an argument

4. Parental devotion, especially if too solicitous, has its _____, one of which is _____ a child's progress toward maturity.
   (A) delusions . . . envisioning (B) excesses . . . abetting
   (C) targets . . . ensuring   (D) rewards . . . ameliorating
   (E) pitfalls . . . protracting

5. The validity of her experimental findings was so _____ that even the most _____ investigators could not refrain from extolling her scientific genius.
   (A) enigmatic . . . officious   (B) fallacious . . . credulous
   (C) unassailable . . . disputatious   (D) inevitable . . . convivial
   (E) dubious . . . skeptical

Reading Comprehension Reading-comprehension questions test your ability to read and understand passages of various kinds. Typically, a reading passage is followed by five questions, which may ask the student to (1) identify a central idea, a specific detail, or a specific technique used by the author; (2) interpret meanings of words; (3) see relationships between ideas in the passage; (4) draw a conclusion based on information in the passage; or (5) apply information given in the passage.

Study the following reading-comprehension passage.

> However one chooses to define weather and climate, there is a simple, practical distinction between them: weather is a matter of everyday experience, whereas climate is a statistical generalization of that experience. Weather is what usually interests us, but to interpret it correctly we must first determine what the underlying climate is in general; otherwise, we have no yardstick for comparison. In a sense, climate is like the carrier wave in radio broadcasting on which the irregular signals of programming—weather—are superimposed. We have to study the "normal" distribution of the meteorological elements before we can begin to understand the "variability around the norm" that constitutes weather.

Which of the following comparisons most closely parallels the relationship between weather and climate in this paragraph?

(A) A particular game to a team's season record
(B) A heat-seeking missile to a fighter plane
(C) A bacterium to its colony
(D) An element to a compound
(E) A waterfall to a lake

To answer reading-comprehension questions, use the following strategies.

1. Identify the main idea as you read. Pay attention to transitions and words that show relationships.

2. Read all the choices before you select an answer.

3. Do not choose an answer just because it's a true statement; make sure it answers the question being asked.

4. Base your answer on the information in the passage, not on your knowledge or opinion.

The answer to the sample question is *A*.

Practice Your Skills

Read the following passage. Then answer the reading-comprehension questions on the next page.

My grandmother's notorious pugnacity did not confine itself to the exercise of authority over the neighborhood. There was also the defense of her house and her furniture against the imagined encroachments of visitors. With my grandmother, this was not the gentle and tremulous protectiveness of certain frail people who infer the fragility of all things from the brittleness of their own bones and hear the crash of mortality in the perilous tinkling of a teacup. No, my grandmother's sentiment was more autocratic: she hated having her chairs sat in or her lawns stepped on or the water turned on in her sinks; for no reason but pure administrative efficiency, she even grudged the mailman his daily promenade up her sidewalk. Her home was a center of power, and she would not allow it to be insulted by easy or democratic usage. Under her jealous eye, its social properties had withered, and it functioned in the family structure simply as a political headquarters. Family conferences were held there, consultations with the doctor and the clergy; unruly grandchildren were there for a lecture or an interval of thought-taking; wills were read and loans negotiated. The family had no friends, and entertaining was held to be a foolish and unnecessary courtesy required only by the bonds of a blood relationship. Holiday dinners fell, as a duty, on the lesser members of the organization; sons and daughters and cousins respectfully offered up baked Alaska on a platter, while my grandparents sat enthroned at the table, and only their digestive processes acknowledged the festal nature of the day.

1. The author's main purpose in this passage is to
   (A) review childhood impressions and fears
   (B) mourn the vanishing unity of the nuclear family
   (C) create a vivid portrait of a strong personality
   (D) revive the memory of a dimly recalled ancestor
   (E) commend some of a grandmother's firmly held principles

2. It can be inferred from the passage that all of the following are characteristic of the author's grandmother EXCEPT
   (A) desire for order   (B) pride in authority
   (C) disdain for sentiment   (D) reluctance to compromise
   (E) jealousy of youth

3. The tone of the passage is best described as
   (A) sympathetic and sentimental   (B) restrained and cautious
   (C) apathetic and aloof   (D) satirical and candid
   (E) bitter and loathing

English Usage   English-usage questions test your ability to recognize errors in word choice, punctuation, capitalization, grammar, and usage. Study the following example.

> An idealist is not always $\underline{as}$ $\underline{ignorant}$ of realities as $\underline{their}$ critics
> $\quad\quad\quad\quad\quad\quad\quad\quad\quad\quad$ **A** $\quad$ **B** $\quad\quad\quad\quad\quad\quad\quad\quad$ **C**
> would $\underline{like\ to}$ believe. No $\underline{error}$
> $\quad\quad$ **D** $\quad\quad\quad\quad\quad\quad$ **E**

To answer English-usage questions, keep these points in mind.

1. Read the entire sentence slowly and carefully, not just the underlined parts.

2. Look for errors in word choice, punctuation, capitalization, grammar, and usage.

In the example, since the possessive pronoun *their* does not agree with its antecedent, *idealist,* the correct answer is *C.*

Practice Your Skills

In each sentence, four words or phrases are underlined. Choose the underlined word or phrase that contains an error in usage. If the sentence is correct, choose *E, No error.*

1. It is $\underline{rumored\ that}$ the names $\underline{of\ them}$ $\underline{to\ be\ promoted}$ will be
   $\quad\quad\quad$ **A** $\quad\quad\quad\quad\quad\quad\quad\quad$ **B** $\quad\quad$ **C**
   announced today, but the choices $\underline{have\ not\ been\ made}$ yet. $\underline{No\ error}$
   $\quad\quad\quad\quad\quad\quad\quad\quad\quad\quad\quad\quad$ **D** $\quad\quad\quad\quad\quad\quad$ **E**

2. For <u>many people</u>, hang gliding, an <u>increasingly</u> popular sport, seems
A   B
<u>satisfying</u> the urge <u>to fly</u>. <u>No error</u>
    C   D   E

3. Late in the war, the Germans, <u>retreating</u> <u>in haste</u>, <u>left many</u> of <u>their</u>
                               A   B   C   D
prisoners go free. <u>No error</u>
              E

4. <u>Throughout</u> the Middle Ages, women <u>work</u> <u>beside</u> men, knowing
    A   B   C
that the efforts of men and women alike were <u>essential</u> to survival.
                                         D
<u>No error</u>
E

5. <u>Because of</u> extreme weather conditions, starvation <u>exists</u> in some
   A   B
countries where <u>they</u> must struggle every day <u>to stay alive</u>. <u>No error</u>
            C   D   E

Sentence Correction   Sentence-correction questions test your ability to identify errors in different parts of a sentence. All or part of a sentence is underlined. Following the sentence are five ways of changing the underlined part. Select the answer that produces the most effective, grammatically correct sentence. The first choice always repeats the underlined words. The correct answer will be the one that best expresses the meaning of the sentence. A typical sentence-correction question follows.

> <u>Because she was a woman was why Sharon Frontiero, a lieutenant in the United States Air Force, felt that she was being treated unfairly.</u>
>
> (A) Because she was a woman was why Sharon Frontiero, a lieutenant in the United States Air Force, felt that she was being treated unfairly.
> (B) Sharon Frontiero, a lieutenant in the United States Air Force, felt that she was being treated unfairly because she was a woman.
> (C) Because she was a woman, Sharon Frontiero felt that this was why she was being treated unfairly as a lieutenant in the United States Air Force.
> (D) Sharon Frontiero, a lieutenant in the United States Air Force, feeling that was being treated unfairly because she was a woman.
> (E) A woman, Sharon Frontiero, felt that because she was a lieutenant in the United States Air Force, that she was being treated unfairly.

Even if you believe that the sentence is correct as written, read all of the suggested answers. In this case, the original sentence is awkwardly stated, so answer *A* is incorrect. Answer *C* is wrong because it begins with a misplaced adverb clause. Answer *D* is incorrect because it is a sentence fragment. Answer *E* is incorrect because it changes the meaning of the sentence.

The correct answer is *B*.

When answering a sentence-correction question, try to decide which version sounds best. Avoid wordy versions, unnecessary shifts of verb tense, run-on sentences, and expressions that are not considered acceptable in standard written English.

Practice Your Skills

Each of the following sentences contains an underlined portion. Following each sentence are five ways of rephrasing the underlined part. Select the answer that produces the most effective and grammatically correct sentence. Answer *A* always repeats the original sentence.

1. In the nineteenth century, trains were more than <u>machines they were</u> expressions of the greatness of the United States.
   (A) machines they were
   (B) machines and were
   (C) machines; they were
   (D) machines; although they were
   (E) machines, but were

2. The widespread slaughter of buffalo for their skins profoundly <u>shocked and angered Native Americans</u>.
   (A) shocked and angered Native Americans
   (B) shocked Native Americans, angering them
   (C) shocked Native Americans, and they were also angry
   (D) was a shock and caused anger among Native Americans
   (E) was shocking to Native Americans, making them angry

3. <u>Many memos were issued by the director of the agency that</u> had an insulting tone, according to the staff members.
   (A) Many memos were issued by the director of the agency that
   (B) Many memos were issued by the director of the agency who
   (C) The issuance of many memos by the director of the agency which
   (D) The director of the agency issued many memos that
   (E) The director of the agency, who issued many memos that

4. Joseph Conrad was born and educated in Poland and he wrote all of his novels in English.
   (A) Joseph Conrad was born and educated in Poland and he
   (B) Joseph Conrad, being born and educated in Poland,
   (C) Although being born and educated in Poland, Joseph Conrad
   (D) Although Joseph Conrad was born and educated in Poland, he
   (E) Being from Poland, where he was born and educated, Joseph Conrad

Construction-Shift Sentences Construction-shift sentences, found in the English Composition Test given by the College Board, ask you to rephrase sentences according to specific directions without changing the meaning of the original.

> Although the composer Ethel Smyth was famous in England in the early years of this century for her operas and symphonies, she is almost unknown in this country.
> Begin with <u>Almost unknown</u>.

   (A) country, despite being famous for
   (B) country, the composer
   (C) country, the English
   (D) country, although she was famous
   (E) country and famous

The rephrased example sentence would read as follows: Almost unknown in this country, the composer Ethel Smyth was famous in England in the early years of this century for her operas and symphonies. Thus the correct answer is *B*.

Practice Your Skills

Rephrase each of the following construction-shift sentences according to the directions that follow it. Make only those changes that the directions require. Keep the meaning of the revised sentence as close as possible to the meaning of the original sentence.

1. The appreciation of painting, as well as of other forms of art, demands the interplay of judgment and imagination.
   Begin with <u>The interplay</u>.

   (A) demands
   (B) is demanded by
   (C) is essential to
   (D) are essential to
   (E) demand

2. Gandhi started out with the normal ambitions of a young Indian student and adopted his nationalist opinions only by degrees as he grew older.
Begin with <u>Starting</u>.

(A) he only adopted
(B) Gandhi adopted
(C) only adopting
(D) Gandhi had only adopted
(E) and only adopted

3. The supervisor was able, or so he thought, to make the decision himself.
Change <u>able</u> to <u>capable</u>.

(A) to be making
(B) of having made
(C) of making
(D) to have made
(E) to make

4. The computer's most profound impact arises less because of its usefulness as a calculating machine than because of its potential for communication.
Eliminate both occurrences of <u>because</u>.

(A) not only is it useful
(B) and it has the potential
(C) as well as its potential
(D) more from being useful
(E) more from its potential

Content-Specific Questions Content-specific questions, found in the College Board achievement tests, measure your knowledge of facts and concepts in subjects such as English, history, mathematics, science, and foreign language. The following is an example of a content-specific question.

The Marshall Plan can best be described as an attempt to achieve

(A) military goals through political means.
(B) political goals through economic means.
(C) economic goals through military means.
(D) political goals through military means.
(E) economic goals through political means.

The correct answer is *B*.

Understanding and Evaluating the Media

Information about the world—in the form of radio and television news reports and written stories in newspapers and news magazines—is available twenty-four hours a day, seven days a week. Keeping abreast of current events, as well as ongoing social, political, and economic trends, can seem like an impossible chore. However, once you learn to think critically about the sources of news stories, you may find that understanding the news is not only possible, but is essential to being an informed citizen.

UNDERSTANDING BROADCAST MEDIA

Broadcast media include radio and television programs. Broadcast news reports can be short and succinct, providing only headlines and brief details, or long and analytic, providing in-depth discussion and varying points of view.

Radio News

Nearly all radio stations report the news at different times during the day. News broadcasts range in length from roughly five minutes every hour during morning and afternoon rush hours to around-the-clock news broadcasting.

News Briefs Brief, five-minute reports include abbreviated local and international news stories—complete with short quotes taken from interviews with eyewitnesses and experts—as well as sports, weather, and traffic information.

Advantage
- News briefs give you basic, essential information you can investigate more fully through other broadcast or print media.

Disadvantages
- Radio news only informs through one of the senses; it provides no visual images or photographs to enhance the text of the stories.

- Short news stories do not provide any in-depth coverage.

News Analysis Public radio and all-news stations provide news analysis, often conducting lengthy interviews with experts and providing a forum for discussion and debate.

Advantage

- Analytical reports provide more perspectives than you can usually find in another single source of news.

Disadvantage

- Although they provide depth of coverage on selected issues, news analysis programs do not present a broad overview of important issues of the day.

Television News

Like all television programming, newscasts compete for your viewership. Newscasts hold viewers' interest with captivating video pictures, eyewitness interviews, and warm, congenial newscasters. However, news stories often are selected for their potential to increase the ratings of the network, and may be sensationalized accordingly. Television news coverage, therefore, can provide a distorted impression of what is really important.

Several kinds of news programs—each with unique advantages and disadvantages—can be seen throughout the day.

Local Newscasts The coverage provided by half-hour news programs focuses primarily on local, city, or statewide news, providing only a few world headlines.

Advantages

- Powerful visual information supports and extends the text of the reporters' stories.

- Live and on-tape reports include brief interviews with news-makers, experts, and eye-witnesses to bolster interest and provide comprehensive analysis of events.

Disadvantage

- Newscasts are limited to short reports on selected local stories.

National Newscasts Broadcast nightly from such cities as Washington, D.C., and New York, these newscasts focus on national and international events, sometimes providing several sides to a single story.

Advantage

- On-the-scene reporters stationed all over the country and around the world provide viewers with international perspectives on the news.

Disadvantage

• Network newscasts sometimes fail to supply adequate background information.

News Analysis Programs Public television stations—as well as some networks—air news analysis shows which provide a forum for in-depth discussion and debate on topical events.

Advantages

• News analysis shows provide a comprehensive analysis of selected issues from a variety of perspectives.

• Viewers can gather information from primary sources and make judgments for themselves.

Disadvantage

• News analysis programs do not provide a broad sense of daily local, national, or international news.

U N D E R S T A N D I N G   P R I N T   M E D I A

Print media include news transmitted to an audience in writing. The primary sources are newspapers and news magazines.

W R I T E R   T O   W R I T E R

He had been kicked in the head by a mule when young, and believed everything he read in the Sunday papers.

George Ade, humorist

Newspapers

Major daily newspapers report not only local and world news, but most also offer editorials and cover sports, business, employment opportunities, cultural events, and human interest stories.

Advantage

• Newspapers can be scanned quickly for an overview of news issues; headlines flag articles of particular interest.

Disadvantage

• Some papers are perceived to be liberal or conservative; the editorial philosophy of the paper can affect the way news events are explained and which events are included.

News Magazines

News magazines are published weekly or monthly, rather than daily, like newspapers. They contain objective news reporting, in-depth analyses of major issues, and subjective reviews and editorials. They also include articles on topics of general interest, such as art, music, dance, medicine, science, economics, and politics.

Advantages

- News magazines provide colorful visual and graphic information to supplement each story.

- News magazines often include well-rounded stories that explain the broad personal and social effects of news events.

- You can browse through a news magazine at your leisure, reading the stories that are of particular interest while ignoring the rest.

Disadvantage

- Like newspapers, some magazines are perceived to be liberal or conservative; the editorial philosophy can affect the way news events are explained and which events are included in the coverage.

EVALUATING THE MEDIA

Since there are so many different kinds of news stories, written from a range of perspectives, you need to evaluate news sources in your pursuit of the truth.

Understanding Angles

No single news story could begin to capture all aspects of an issue—nor should it try. Just as you often begin with a broad, general idea and then narrow your focus to a manageable size in your own writing, journalists narrow their focus for stories by choosing an angle, or perspective, for each report. If you piece together reports on an event from a number of different news sources, you will get a more complete picture than if you examine only one. The following guidelines can help you analyze the news you see and hear.

Consider Timing   Journalists often want to be the first to report on a breaking news event. Initial reports of events—ranging from local warehouse fires, to outbreaks of disease, to federal budgets—often include only rough outlines of the news with few, sketchy details. Sometimes initial reports turn out to be highly inaccurate. When you hear news reports, ask the following questions.

- When did the event happen?
- How soon after the event are the media revealing it to the public?
- How many and what kinds of details does the story include?
- What information seems to be missing from the initial reports? What do I still want to know?

It is very important that you follow the developments of news stories over time. If you first read a story in a newspaper, watch for related stories in the same paper through the following weeks. See what initial information turned out to be true, and what information was revised.

Consider Content   When you read or listen to a news story, think carefully about the facts and details presented. You may find a story to be deficient because a journalist has not fully investigated his or her story; or an insignificant story may be blown out of proportion for its entertainment or shock value. Ask these questions as you consider the content of news stories.

- What information does each news story include? What information does it exclude? What can I infer by reading between the lines?
- Did the writer interview representatives from more than one side of a controversial issue? Does the story seem balanced? If not, is it an editorial representing the views of a particular columnist?

Consider Style   The language a journalist uses to report the news is critical to your understanding events as they truly happen. It's one thing for language that reflects value judgments to be used on the editorial page, but quite another for it to be used on the front page. Know what you're reading, and ask questions like these as you evaluate news styles.

- Who is the intended audience for the story?
- Does the writer use value-laden language, or is the writing style objective and matter-of-fact?

Writing
—TIP—

Any editorial you write will be more convincing if you understand perspectives other than your own before you begin. Conduct interviews with several people so that you understand the range of thinking about your topic.

To most effectively interpret and evaluate the media, you must combine what you already know with what you learn from the news. Decide what to accept, what to reject, and what to find out more about. Remember, too, that no two news sources are alike, since the news is investigated, written, and reported by different people who bring their own perspectives to each story and who write from different angles on the same topic. Gather your news, then, from a variety of sources to get the most complete story possible.

Practice Your Skills

A. Over the course of a week, take in as much broadcast news as you can. Try to listen to an analytical news program on the radio in the morning or pay special attention to the headlines presented on shorter radio newscasts. Watch television news in the late afternoon, and listen to another radio news program in the early evening, perhaps on a public broadcasting station. Compare the pros and cons of these media and write about your preferences in your journal. Answer these questions.

- How does the presence or absence of pictures influence the way you understand news reports?
- How are your emotions affected by radio and TV news?
- Did you respond differently to the same news story presented on radio and television?
- What information does your imagination supply when you listen to radio news?

B. Choose a local, national, or international story that interests you and follow it in print for a week. Read as much as you can about the issue in your city's daily newspaper, in national newspapers, and in news magazines. Check to see if that story is also covered in broadcast news and compare the information you get from different sources.

C. Some analysts say that the news media serve three vital functions with regard to the government.

- gatekeeper—deciding which stories get attention
- watchdog—reporting waste, mismanagement, criminal activity
- scorekeeper—making judgments about politicians, policies, bills, and the like.

For one week, study various kinds of news coverage on the air and in print. Find two examples of each of these functions.

Drought, Kenneth Noland, 1962

Grammar and Usage Handbook

Directions   One or more of the underlined sections in the following sentences may contain errors of grammar, usage, punctuation, spelling, or capitalization. Write the letters of each incorrect section. Then rewrite the item correctly. If there is no error in an item, write E.

Example   Renoir, the <u>artist,</u> told his son, <u>whom</u> later became a
                         A   **B**
<u>filmmaker,</u> that to know people one <u>need</u> to study their hands
   C   **D**
and faces. <u>No error</u>
              E

Answer   B—who; D—needs

---

1. "<u>Don't no one</u> know <u>who</u> invented the <u>wheel?</u>" the student <u>asked,</u> incredulously.
       A   **B**   **C**   **D**
   <u>No error</u>
   E

2. <u>Jacques Cousteau</u> is a great innovator; <u>him</u> and Emil Gagnan <u>invented</u> the aqua-
       A   **B**   **C**
   lung <u>used in scuba diving.</u> <u>No error</u>
           D   **E**

3. Whether <u>a real, verifiable</u> <u>King Arthur</u> ever lived <u>is</u> a subject of <u>considerable</u> debate
               A   **B**   **C**   **D**
   among historians. <u>No error</u>
                        E

4. The <u>Encyclopedia</u> article describes estivation <u>as similar</u> to hibernation, but
          A   **B**
   <u>they don't</u> say <u>what the difference is.</u> <u>No error</u>
       C   **D**   **E**

5. The first <u>Arabian horses</u> were brought to the <u>West</u> in the early <u>Twentieth Century</u>
                 A   **B**   **C**
   by two English <u>aristocrats, today,</u> the descendants of those Arabians are being bred
                       D
   and raised on a horse farm in Arizona. <u>No error</u>
                                             E

6. <u>Gilbert's and Sullivan's</u> operetta *<u>The Pirates of Penzance</u>* became widely popular
       A   **B**
   again because of a <u>Broadway</u> production starring Kevin Kline and the
                          C
   <u>pop singer Linda Ronstadt.</u> <u>No error</u>
       D   **E**

7. Executing fantastic pirouettes, loops, and tumbles in the clear skies of Washington,
   <u>A</u>
   the audience watched the stunt pilot, David Rahm, perform. No error
   B   C   D   E

8. Long ago, well before the invention of the Printing Press, poets often sung their
   A   B   C   D
   poetry to small, interested audiences. No error
   E

9. Sanskrit, the ancient language of India, is a distant relative of english,
   A   B
   which is evident when two common words such as "brother" and "phrater" are
   C   D
   compared. No error
   E

10. One wonders whether the artist who sculpted Mount Rushmore might have began
    A   B   C
    to have second thoughts when he realized that the work was going to take him an
    D
    entire lifetime. No error
    E

11. Belize's many atractions include the following tropical jungles, Mayan ruins, and
    A   B   C
    magnificent coral reefs. No error
    D   E

12. Colors that are opposite one another on a color wheel—red and green, for
    A   B   C
    example—are known as complimentary colors. No error
    C   D   E

13. Most of the desserts of the world lie in two bands, north and south of the tropics.
    A   B   C   D
    No error
    E

14. Many studies have tried to determine whether seeing violence on television makes
    A   B   C
    children behave more violent. No error
    D   E

15. Archbishop Desmond Tutu recieved the Nobel Peace Prize for his efforts to end
    A   B   C
    the system of apartheid in South Africa. No error
    D   E

16. Marion <u>didn't</u> feel too <u>good</u> after her <u>accident, but</u> she <u>choose</u> to keep an optimis-
    A   B   C   D
    tic attitude. <u>No error</u>
                    E

17. The <u>Museum of Man</u> in Paris <u>is</u> a major source of <u>scientific</u> information about
          A   B   C
    <u>human anatomy.</u> <u>No error</u>
          D   E

18. <u>Researchers</u> concluded that chimpanzees like Nim Chimpsky <u>doesn't</u> really <u>have</u> the
    A   B   C
    ability <u>to learn language.</u> <u>No error</u>
              D   E

19. A crowd <u>gathered,</u> hoping <u>to see</u> the huge rocket ship <u>raising from</u> <u>its</u> launch pad.
              A   B   C   D
    <u>No error</u>
      E

20. Thomas <u>Hardy's</u> novel <u>was called</u> *Far from the Madding Crowd,* <u>not</u> *Far from the*
              A   B   C   D
    Maddening Crowd. <u>No error</u>
                        E

21. <u>Them</u> place names throughout California <u>such as Los Angeles and San Luis Obispo</u>
    A   B
    <u>reflect</u> the <u>Spanish</u> heritage of the state. <u>No error</u>
    C   D   E

22. Roman Gabriel, <u>who</u> played football for <u>Los Angeles and Philadelphia,</u> <u>holds</u> the
                    A   B   C
    <u>record. For the greatest number of fumbles in a career.</u> <u>No error</u>
                    D   E

23. In <u>500 B.C.</u> Iran <u>was called</u> Persia and <u>was</u> the <u>nucleus</u> of a vast empire. <u>No error</u>
          A   B   C   D   E

24. Archimedes, <u>the Greek mathematician,</u> invented a giant <u>magnifiing</u> glass that was
                    A   B
    used to set fire to enemy <u>ships;</u> according to ancient historians, this ship burner
                                C
    worked <u>beautiful.</u> <u>No error</u>
              D   E

25. The adobe bricks were <u>sat</u> in the sun to <u>dry,</u> and then, after a few days, the bricks
                            A   B
    were <u>lain</u> to make the foundation and walls. <u>No error</u>
    C   D   E

Sketchbook

Tomorrow, and tomorrow, and tomorrow
Creeps in this petty pace from day to day
To the last syllable of recorded time

William Shakespeare
MACBETH, act 5, sc. 5, lines 21–23

Think of something that you would love to do but have always postponed. Devise a plan to do it. To express a sense of urgency, use only simple sentences.

Additional Sketches

When was the last time you watched clouds roll by, enjoying the parade of weightless and ever-changing forms, perhaps imagining that they were something else? Look up in the sky and write down what you see, using expressive adjectives and verbs.

Create a detailed sketch of a character for a story. Make notes describing his or her appearance and personality. Include in your sketch things your character might say or do.

Review of Parts of Speech

PARTS OF SPEECH

This handbook reviews the eight parts of speech. The first section contains a test that will enable you to check your knowledge of these basic elements of the English language. Each of the following sections reviews one of the parts of speech: **nouns, pronouns, verbs, adjectives, adverbs, prepositions, conjunctions,** and **interjections.**

First, do the following diagnostic exercise and compare your answers with the answer key at the bottom of page 567. If you find that you need review on any part of speech, study the appropriate section in this handbook. Then, use the Application and Review on pages 566 and 567 to recheck your skills.

As you complete the exercises in this handbook, keep the following rule in mind:

The part of speech of any particular word is determined by the function of the word in the sentence.

For example, the word *photograph* can function as a number of different parts of speech. Its use in context determines its part of speech.

> Jo took a *photograph* of the food-laden picnic table. (Noun)
>
> Many parents *photograph* their babies often. (Verb)
>
> The *photograph* album belongs to my family. (Adjective)

Diagnostic Exercise   Write the italicized words from the following literary excerpt. After each word, write its part of speech as it is used in the context of the story.

When you have completed the exercise, check your answers with the key on page 567.

> (1) "*Oh,* this heat!" said Mrs. Baumgartner, *and fanned herself gracefully* with her straw hat.
> (2) *Something* had alarmed the children on the beach *below, and* Mrs. Otis, turning to look at them again, saw them abruptly immobilized; then, as *silently* and as swiftly as sharks, they led the horse away and disappeared *into* the *pine* grove, leaving *no traces* of themselves behind. (3) *Until* she saw them go, she had not been *aware* that the skies *were darkening,* and she wondered how long ago the transforma-

tion *had begun.* (4) Now, *from* miles away, there rolled up a *thunderclap, and,* as always in the tropics, the rain came *abruptly,* battling the trees and lashing the vines, beheading the flowers, crashing onto the *tin* roofs, and belaboring the jalousies of Captain Sundstrom's pretty house. (5) *Blue* blossoms *showered* the head *of* Pan. (6) Wrapping the field glasses in *her* sash to protect *them* from the rain, *Mrs. Otis* returned *to* the gallery.

(7) "See?" said Captain Sundstrom to his guests, *with* a *gesture toward* the storm. (8) "We told *you this* heat *was* only an interlude." **Jean Stafford, *A Modest Proposal***

Nouns

A noun is the name of a person, place, thing, quality, or action.

Nouns can be classified in several ways. Notice that all nouns can be placed in at least two classifications, and some nouns can be placed in more than two.

All nouns are either *common* or *proper.* A **common noun** is the general name for a person, place, thing, or idea. It is common to an entire group: *comedian, city, organization, religion.* A **proper noun** names a specific person, place, thing, or idea. It always begins with a capital letter and may consist of more than one word: *Charlie Chaplin, Rome, League of Women Voters, Mormonism.*

All nouns are either *concrete* or *abstract.* A **concrete noun** names something that can be perceived by the senses—sights, sounds, odors, tastes, and textures: *mountain, pizza, jeans, sand, waves, lizard.* An **abstract noun** names something that cannot be observed by the senses, such as ideas and beliefs: *intelligence, loneliness, theory.*

A **collective noun** is a singular noun that names a group of people or things: *audience, clan, jury, crew, herd, class.*

A **compound noun** is a noun formed from two or more words that express a single idea. Compound nouns can be written as one word, as separate words, or with hyphens: *backpack, night owl, Fifth Avenue, sister-in-law.* A dictionary gives the correct form for compound nouns.

Grammar Note Gerunds are verbals ending in *-ing* that function as nouns:

Laura did the *organizing* of the library books; we all helped with the *shelving.*

Writing TIP

Precise, accurate word choice contributes to strong writing. Use specific rather than general nouns— *terrier* for *dog,* or *canoe* for *boat.*

Practice Your Skills

A. CONCEPT CHECK

Nouns List the nouns in this literary excerpt. Identify the *Collective, Abstract,* and *Proper* nouns.

(1) "Uranium," said the captain. (2) "Uranium 235." (3) The words glittered on his tongue like sparks from a gold-stopped tooth.

(4) There was no crew. (5) The only answer came from the wind, which sang in the rigging of his crazy old ship like the music of Orpheus. . . . (6) The decks were clear. (7) The sails were stowed, since there would be no need for them. (8) Insofar as was possible, old *Argo* was trim and ready for the voyage.

Joan Aiken, "Follow My Fancy"

B. DRAFTING SKILL

Precise Word Choice A writer's choice of specific words contributes to effective writing. Replace the vague italicized nouns in the passage below with more exact nouns. You may wish to experiment with the effect achieved by more than one set of answers.

(1) The *person* huddled over the table in the almost deserted *room*. (2) *Items* scattered about gave testimony to the morning's *activity*. (3) Outside the *weather* continued, giving no signal of *change*. (4) In the distance were *sounds* of *things*. (5) Unmistakable was the *feeling* that lay over the entire scene. (6) A *smell* permeated the air of the *place*. (7) Suddenly a loud *noise* was heard outside. (8) The *person* at the table walked to the door and peered out at the *surroundings*.

PRONOUNS

A pronoun is a word used in place of a noun or another pronoun.

The noun to which a pronoun refers is called its **antecedent**.

> Kim said that *she* would win a bowling trophy. (*Kim* is the antecedent of the pronoun *she*.)

> The horses rushed past the farmer and kept on running until *they* reached the meadow. (*Horses* is the antecedent of the pronoun *they*.)

There are seven main categories of pronouns.

Personal Pronouns

Personal pronouns are pronouns that change their form to express person, number, gender, and case. All these pronouns are listed in the box below.

	Nominative	Objective	Possessive
Singular			
First Person	I	me	my, mine
Second Person	you	you	your, yours
Third Person	he, she, it	him, her, it	his, her, hers, its
Plural			
First Person	we	us	our, ours
Second Person	you	you	your, yours
Third Person	they	them	their, theirs

Person   When a personal pronoun refers to the person speaking, it is a **first-person** pronoun. If a pronoun refers to the person being spoken to, it is a **second-person** pronoun. A pronoun that refers to a person or thing spoken about is a **third-person** pronoun.

Number   Pronouns that refer to one person, place, thing, or idea are **singular** in number. Pronouns that refer to more than one are **plural.**

Gender   Pronouns that refer to males are in the **masculine** gender. Pronouns that refer to females are in the **feminine** gender. Pronouns that refer to things are in the **neuter** gender.

Writing
TIP

Avoid ambiguity in your writing by checking for clear antecedents of pronouns.

Case   Personal pronouns change form to show how they function in a sentence. This change in form is called **case.** The three cases are nominative, objective, and possessive. Nominative pronouns are used as subjects or as predicate pronouns. Objective pronouns can be used as objects of verbs and objects of prepositions.

Possessive pronouns show ownership. The forms *mine, yours, hers, its, ours,* and *theirs* can be used in place of nouns: The bright blue umbrella is *mine.* The forms *my, your, her, his, its, our,* and *their* are used to modify nouns: *Their* umbrella is striped.

For more information on pronoun case, see Grammar Handbook 36, pages 693–694.

Reflexive and Intensive Pronouns

Intensive and reflexive pronouns are formed by adding *-self* or *-selves* to certain personal pronouns.

Reflexive and Intensive Pronoun Forms

First Person	myself, ourselves
Second Person	yourself, yourselves
Third Person	himself, herself, itself, themselves

Although reflexive and intensive pronouns look alike, each is used in a different way; neither can be used without an antecedent.

A **reflexive pronoun** is a pronoun used as the object of a verb or preposition.

> During the Boston Tea Party, the colonists disguised *themselves* for protection. (The reflexive pronoun *themselves* is the object of the verb *disguised.*)

An **intensive pronoun** is used in apposition to a noun or pronoun to add emphasis.

> Theseus *himself* found the way out of the maze.

Demonstrative Pronouns

The **demonstrative pronouns** are *this, that, these,* and *those.* They are used to point out or identify specific people or things.

> *That* is the path to the lake.
> Are *these* the horseshoes that you were looking for?

Interrogative Pronouns

The **interrogative pronouns,** which are used to ask questions, are *who, whom, whose, which,* and *what.*

> *What* are the ingredients in shish kebab?
> *Who* painted that picture of knights in armor?

Indefinite Pronouns

Pronouns that do not refer to a specific person or thing are called **indefinite pronouns.** Indefinite pronouns usually have no antecedent.

> *Everyone* was on the edge of his or her seat at the movie's end.

> *All* of Alfred Hitchcock's films have conclusions that are full of suspense.

Commonly Used Indefinite Pronouns

Singular			Plural	Singular or Plural	
another	everybody	no one	both	all	most
anybody	everyone	nothing	few	any	none
anyone	everything	one	many	more	some
anything	much	somebody	several		
each	neither	someone			
either	nobody	something			

Grammar Note Demonstrative, interrogative, and some indefinite pronouns can also function as adjectives: *These* jumping beans are lively.

Relative Pronouns

The relative pronouns *who, whose, whom, which,* and *that* introduce a subordinate clause and relate it to a word in the sentence.

> Jane Goodall is the naturalist *who* studied the behavior of chimpanzees. (The antecedent of the relative pronoun *who* is the noun *naturalist.*)

> The statesman *whom* everyone admires is the nominee. (The antecedent of the relative pronoun *whom* is *statesman.*)

Practice Your Skills

CONCEPT CHECK

Pronouns   Write the pronouns in the following sentences. Identify each pronoun according to kind: *Personal, Reflexive, Intensive, Demonstrative, Interrogative, Indefinite,* or *Relative.*

1. What is the state of "robotics," or robot technology, today?
2. Already many of the more technologically innovative companies are using "service" robots for cleaning offices and guarding buildings.
3. One of these uses the "Hansel and Gretel principle" to sweep a floor.
4. The robot first circles a room, using sonar to place itself correctly.
5. Then it goes around the room again, leaving a trail of fluorescent paper, which the robot itself follows and sweeps up, along with dirt and dust, on its next circuit.
6. If robotics researchers are successful, robots themselves will be able to "see" and "sense" where they are.
7. Robots such as these would be capable of humanlike movements, and each would be able to adjust itself to an environment.
8. Eventually a service robot will deliver meals in hospitals; it will "memorize" and negotiate hospital corridors on its regular rounds.
9. There may also be house robots that serve us breakfast and do chores.
10. Who wouldn't like a robot like that?

V ERBS

A verb is a word or group of words that expresses an action, a condition, or a state of being.

The verb is the key part of every sentence. There are two main categories of verbs: action verbs and linking verbs.

Action Verbs

An **action verb** tells what the subject does. The action may be physical or mental.

Physical Action	The albatross *landed* awkwardly on the beach.
	We *flung* ourselves into the icy stream.
Mental Action	Most people *dream* every night.
	Amanda *considered* her father's promise again.

Linking Verbs

A **linking verb** does not express action. Instead, it links the subject of a sentence to its complements. A complement may be one of the following: a predicate noun, a predicate pronoun, or a predicate adjective.

> The Everglades *are* swamplands in Florida. (The verb *are* links the subject *Everglades* with the predicate noun *swamplands.*)

> The audience walking out of the theater *seemed* pleased with the performance. (The verb *seemed* links the subject *audience* with the predicate adjective *pleased.*)

The most common linking verb is *be* in its various forms. Many linking verbs relate to the senses: *sound, taste, appear, feel, look, smell.* Others express the condition or placement of the subject: *become, remain, seem, stay, grow.*

Although some linking verbs such as *be* and *seem* are never action verbs, others can function as either linking or action verbs depending on how they are used.

Linking Verb	Action Verb
The avocado *tasted* bland.	We *tasted* the guacamole dip.
Ed *felt* tired today.	Lee *felt* the wind on her face.
The casserole *smelled* spicy.	George *smelled* the pine trees.

Auxiliary Verbs

In many sentences the verbs—whether action or linking—consist of more than one word. They are a combination of a **main verb** and one or more **auxiliary verbs.** A main verb with its auxiliaries is called a **verb phrase.** The main verb is always the last word in the phrase.

Auxiliary	+	Main Verb	=	Verb Phrase
was		driving		was driving
should have		remembered		should have remembered
will have been		doing		will have been doing
can		embroider		can embroider

The most frequently used auxiliaries are the forms of *be, have,* and *do.* These are other common auxiliaries:

must	may	shall	could	would
might	can	will	should	

The verbs in a verb phrase are often separated by one or more words that are not part of the verb phrase.

The hinges *haven't been oiled* in years.

The orchids *could* probably *benefit* from more frequent spraying.

Did you *participate* in the school talent show?

Should they *have been waiting* in the rain?

Transitive and Intransitive Verbs

Action verbs may be transitive or intransitive. A **transitive verb** is a verb that has a direct object. The verb carries the action from the subject to the object. An **intransitive verb** has no object.

Transitive	Intransitive
Polo players *hit* a wooden ball.	The players *ride* expertly.
Elena *bought* an oboe.	Elena *practiced* in the garage.
You *forgot* your ticket.	Ian *arrived* today.

A few verbs in English are only transitive; a few others are only intransitive. Most verbs, however, can be either.

Transitive	Intransitive
Sudi *moved* the furniture.	Sudi *moved* to Phoenix.
I *packed* my suitcase.	I *packed* for the trip hastily.
We *ran* a fast race.	We *ran* down the block.

Grammar Note Linking verbs do not have objects and so may be considered intransitive. When passive voice verbs are changed to their active form, they are always transitive.

For more information on verbs, see Grammar Handbook 34, "Verb Usage," pages 631–667.

Practice Your Skills

CONCEPT CHECK

Verbs and Verb Phrases Write all of the verbs or verb phrases in the following sentences. Then label each verb either *Action* or *Linking*. Identify each action verb as *Transitive* or *Intransitive*. Most sentences will have more than one verb.

1. The Chinese were probably the first users of fireworks since they had already invented the gunpowder necessary for pyrotechnics.
2. Between the sixteenth and eighteenth centuries in Europe, fireworks became the toys of kings, who often used them in court celebrations.

3. Court fireworks masters would construct elaborate decorated "machines," stage settings that served as background for the fireworks explosions and added to the excitement.

4. King Louis XIV of France was a lover of fireworks, and once he ordered a show that continued for five days.

5. Handel wrote his famous "Fireworks" music for a display in England; its fireworks machine was 410 feet long and 114 feet high and included eleven thousand fireworks.

6. Before the 1830's, fireworks must have seemed dull because their colors included only amber and greenish blue; since then, however, the use of new chemicals has produced many other vibrant colors.

7. Today, Fourth of July celebrations all over the United States sparkle and reverberate with the sights and sounds of sophisticated pyrotechnic displays.

8. Americans specialize in "multi-shell fireworks" that explode in one cluster of light after another as the shells fall.

9. We also like "willow" fireworks, which emit long, thin tendrils of light that bloom in the sky with just the smallest puff, while the Chinese prefer round fireworks that produce a quick burst of stars like a spread of chrysanthemums.

10. Fireworks specialists are always seeking even more extraordinary effects so that they can further amaze and thrill us spectators.

ADJECTIVES

An adjective is a word that modifies a noun or a pronoun.

Adjectives change or limit the meaning of nouns or pronouns by answering one of the following questions:

Which One?	*this* keyboard, *that* suggestion, *those* test tubes
What Kind?	*thick* sandwich, *hasty* decision, *portable* computer
How Many?	*twelve* eggs, *many* floats, *few* comedians
How Much?	*little* experience, *enough* money, *abundant* rainfall

Position of Adjectives An adjective generally precedes the word it modifies. Sometimes, for variety, a writer will place adjectives after the words they modify.

> The house, *isolated* and *eerie,* resembled a set for a horror movie.

> Last week's weather, *hot* and *humid,* forced us to stay indoors.

Writing
TIP

Keep your writing lively by using fresh, imaginative adjectives and avoiding trite expressions.

Predicate Adjectives   A **predicate** adjective is an adjective that follows a linking verb and modifies the subject.

> The bench was *wet* from the rain. (The predicate adjective *wet* modifies the subject *bench*.)

> The acoustics in the auditorium seemed *excellent*. (The predicate adjective *excellent* modifies the subject *acoustics*.)

Proper Adjectives   Proper adjectives are formed from proper nouns and are always capitalized.

> *Hawaiian* pineapples   *Chaucerian* age
> *Atlantic* coast   *French cooking*

Articles   The most common adjectives are the articles *a, an,* and *the.* Articles modify the nouns they precede.

The word *the* is called the **definite article** because it usually refers to a specific person, place, or thing.

The words *a* and *an* are the **indefinite articles.** They indicate that a noun is not unique but is one of many of its kind. Use *a* before a word beginning with a consonant sound: *a* diary, *a* union. Use *an* before a word beginning with a vowel sound: *an* apricot, *an* understanding. Remember, it is the sound and not the spelling that determines the correct choice.

Other Words Used as Adjectives   Many words that are generally thought of as other parts of speech can also function as adjectives. These include nouns and certain classes of pronouns including possessive, demonstrative, interrogative, relative, and indefinite pronouns. Certain verbals ending in *-ed* and *-ing* may also function as adjectives. The following list shows some examples.

Nouns	*cattle* drive, *tennis* racket, *traffic* jam, *wall* phone, *desk* pad, *graduation* cap
Pronouns	*her* chopsticks, *this* parabola, *which* idea, *some* artifacts, *all* legends
Verbals	*sparkling* icicles, *wilting* flowers, *congested* streets, *fast-paced* comedy, *often-visited* spot

Practice Your Skills

A. CONCEPT CHECK

Adjectives Find at least twenty-five adjectives in the following passage from a novel by Mark Twain. Do not include articles.

Writing Theme
Mark Twain

(1) Now when I had mastered the language of this water and had come to know every trifling feature that bordered the great river as familiarly as I knew the letters of the alphabet, I had made a valuable acquisition. (2) But I had lost something, too. . . .

(3) All the grace, the beauty, the poetry had gone out of the majestic river! (4) I still keep in mind a certain wonderful sunset which I witnessed when steamboating was new to me. (5) A broad expanse of the river was turned to blood; in the middle distance the red hue brightened into gold, through which a solitary log came floating, black and conspicuous; in one place . . . the surface was broken by boiling, tumbling rings, that were as many-tinted as an opal; . . . the shore on our left was densely wooded, and the sombre shadow that fell from this forest was broken in one place by a long, ruffled trail that shone like silver; and high above the forest wall a clean-stemmed dead tree waved a single leafy bough that glowed like a flame in the unobstructed splendor that was flowing from the sun. **Mark Twain, *Life on the Mississippi***

B. DRAFTING SKILL

Using Adjectives Rewrite the following paragraph, inserting adjectives for the blanks. Insert proper adjectives as indicated.

(1) Samuel Clemens grew up in the _____ Midwestern town of Hannibal, Missouri, on the Mississippi River. (2) Clemens was fascinated by the _____ life that the river offered. (3) _____ towns such as St. Louis and New Orleans with their (Proper) names seemed _____ to him. (4) The _____ chance he got, Clemens left home to become a cub pilot on a steamboat. (5) Although he was _____ as a pilot, he eventually grew restless. (6) He spent three years as a pilot, and then the _____ year he went west to _____ frontier country. (7) In Nevada, Clemens began to write _____ short stories, which were so amusing they earned him a job on a (Proper) newspaper; these stories, which he signed "Josh," were the beginning of a _____ career. (8) Later, he took the pen name of Mark Twain from the _____ term for "two fathoms."

Parts of Speech   **557**

C. APPLICATION IN WRITING

Describing a Scene In the passage at the top of page 557, Mark Twain shows himself to be a skillful painter with words. Write a paragraph in which you describe a scene that you have experienced. It could be a path in a forest, a view from a mountaintop, or even the view from your window.

The Champions of the Mississippi, Currier and Ives print, 1866

ADVERBS

An adverb modifies a verb, an adjective, or another adverb.

Adverbs tell *where, when, how,* or *to what extent* about the words they modify. Note that nouns can sometimes function as adverbs.

Where?	floated *away,* went *home* (noun), sauntered *forward*
When?	worked *late,* heard *before,* left *already*
How?	fell *noisily,* wrote *legibly,* cooks *well*
To What Extent?	*very* rare, *rather* hot, *hardly* begun

Many adverbs are formed by adding *-ly* to an adjective: *foolish*—adjective, *foolishly*—adverb.

Intensifiers   Adverbs that modify, and add emphasis to, adjectives and other adverbs are called **intensifiers.** Some common intensifiers are *too, very, quite, rather, really, fully, barely, completely, scarcely,* and *little.*

Directive Adverts   Adverbs that tell *where* (place or direction) about the verb are **directive adverbs.** Many directive adverbs combine with verbs to make idioms: *put through, break off, check in.* An idiom's meaning cannot be understood from the meanings of its separate words.

   For more information about adverbs, see Grammar Handbook 37, "Adjective and Adverb Usage."

Practice Your Skills

CONCEPT CHECK

Adverbs   Write the adverbs in the following sentences and tell which word or words each modifies. Then find and label the idioms in the sentences.

Writing Theme
Deception

1. Arthur Ferguson, of Scotland, was a phenomenally successful salesman; he was also extraordinarily dishonest.
2. In the 1920's Ferguson quite deviously pulled off a series of cons that made him one of history's most notorious flim-flam artists.
3. One day in the early 1920's, Ferguson saw a tourist gazing admiringly at Nelson's column, a monument in Trafalgar Square, in London.
4. Ferguson immediately approached the tourist and explained very sadly that England was going to have to sell the monument in order to pay its debts.
5. Then Ferguson formally introduced himself as a government broker officially commissioned to carry out the sale of the monument.
6. The apparently wealthy tourist, excited at the news, rather foolishly gave Ferguson a $30,000 check for the valuable monument.
7. The tourist gradually realized that he had been completely duped. Ferguson had already cashed the check at the nearest bank.
8. For several years Ferguson ran a quite steady business selling monuments to tourists.
9. Ferguson sold, among other monuments and national treasures, Big Ben, Buckingham Palace, and even the White House in the United States, but he was eventually caught and imprisoned.
10. Ferguson's schemes broke down when he tried, totally unsuccessfully, to sell the Statue of Liberty to a man who wisely reported Ferguson to the New York police.

PREPOSITIONS

A preposition is a word used to show the relationship between a noun or a pronoun and another word in a sentence.

Men of fashion commonly wore three-cornered hats during the 1700's. (The preposition *of* relates the noun *fashion* to the noun *men;* the preposition *during* relates the verb *wore* to the noun *1700's.*)

The relationships most often expressed by prepositions are location (*by, near*), direction (*up, off*), and association (*of, with*). Some prepositions are **compound,** formed by combining two or more words. Study these lists carefully.

Commonly Used Prepositions

about	before	down	of	throughout
above	behind	during	off	to
across	below	except	on	toward
after	beneath	for	onto	under
against	beside	from	out	underneath
along	between	in	outside	until
among	beyond	inside	over	up
around	but	into	past	upon
as	by	like	since	with
at	despite	near	through	without

Commonly Used Compound Prepositions

according to	in place of
as well as	in relation to
because of	in response to
by means of	in spite of
by way of	inside of
except for	instead of
in accordance with	on account of
in addition to	

"Wait a minute! ... McCallister, you fool! *This* isn't what I said to bring!"

Objects of Prepositions

A preposition is always followed by a word or a group of words called the **object of the preposition.** The preposition, its object, and any modifiers of the object form a **prepositional phrase.**

> Black peppercorns are the dried berries *of a woody climbing vine.* (*Of* is a preposition; *vine* is its object; *woody* and *climbing* modify *vine.*)

The object of a preposition may be a noun, a pronoun, or a clause.

> The first diesel engine was invented by *Rudolf Diesel.* (Noun)
> A thick fog swirled around *me.* (Pronoun)
> Extra test tubes are here for *whoever needs them.* (Clause)

For more information on prepositional phrases, see Grammar Handbook 33, pages 591–592.

Practice Your Skills

CONCEPT CHECK

Prepositions   Write the prepositions from each of the following sentences. For each preposition, write its object.

1. Places on earth are often named after famous people or by geographic features, but how are places in space named?
2. In the past, each observatory chose its own names for planetary features and then battled for its choices with other observatories.
3. Because of these arguments, in 1919 it was decided that the naming would be done by a union of astronomers.
4. After years of haggling, the union has developed rules for naming.
5. The features on Venus, itself named for the Roman goddess of love, are named for women from myths and literature in accordance with the decision.
6. The names of many of Saturn's features are based upon characters from the King Arthur legend.
7. Many places on Mars are named after science-fiction writers like Edgar Rice Burroughs and H. G. Wells.
8. The name of Ray Bradbury, author of *The Martian Chronicles,* will probably also appear on Mars.
9. According to the established rules, if satellites discover any new moons orbiting Neptune, these will be named after sea spirits from cultures throughout the world.
10. The decision seems to be an appropriate one since Neptune, a Roman diety, ruled the world beneath the sea.

Writing
——TIP——

For clarity, always place a preposi- tional phrase close to the word it modifies.

◀ **Writing Theme**
Planetary Names

A conjunction is a word that connects words, phrases, or clauses.

The three kinds of conjunctions are coordinating, correlative, and subordinating conjunctions. In addition, conjunctive adverbs function as conjunctions.

Coordinating Conjunctions

A **coordinating conjunction** is used to connect words or groups of words that have the same function in a sentence. The following are coordinating conjunctions:

and	but	or	for	so	yet	nor

Coordinating conjunctions can join various parts of speech or sentence parts: nouns, pronouns, verbs, adjectives, adverbs, prepositions, phrases, or clauses.

> The attic was dark, airless, *and* dusty. (Adjectives)
> The play's plot was old, *but* the dialogue was witty. (Clauses)

Correlative Conjunctions

Correlative conjunctions function like coordinating conjunctions, but they are always used in pairs. These are correlative conjunctions:

both . . . and	neither . . . nor	whether . . . or
either . . . or	not only . . . but (also)	

> *Both* Monet *and* Renoir were impressionist painters.

Subordinating Conjunctions

Subordinating conjunctions introduce subordinate clauses. They connect clauses that are not complete sentences to clauses that are. A subordinating conjunction expresses relationships of time, manner, cause or reason, comparison, condition, or purpose.

> ┌── **independent clause** ──┐ ┌── **subordinate clause** ──┐
> Many students take chemistry, although it is not required.
> (The subordinating conjunction *although* connects the subordinate clause to the independent clause and shows their opposition.)

Subordinating Conjunctions

Time	after, as, as long as, as soon as, before, since, until, when, whenever, while
Manner	as, as if
Place	where, wherever
Cause or Reason	because, since
Comparison	as, as much as, than, whereas
Condition	although, as long as, even if, even though, if, provided that, though, unless, while
Purpose	in order that, so that, that

For more information about clauses, see Grammar Handbook 33, "Phrases and Clauses," pages 605–615.

Conjunctive Adverbs

Conjunctive Adverbs are used to connect clauses that can stand by themselves as sentences.

> The number of apples to pick seemed endless; *nevertheless,* we continued at the task steadily.

> Under Kublai Khan, China extended its empire from the Pacific Ocean into Poland; *furthermore,* China flourished culturally at that time.

> Rita spent long hours in the chemistry laboratory at the university; *consequently,* she was far better prepared for the exam than her classmates.

Conjunctive Adverbs

accordingly	finally	indeed	still
also	furthermore	moreover	then
besides	hence	nevertheless	therefore
consequently	however	otherwise	thus

Punctuation Note A conjunctive adverb is usually preceded by a semicolon and followed by a comma.

Practice Your Skills

CONCEPT CHECK

Conjunctions Write each conjunction and identify it as *Coordinating, Correlative,* or *Subordinating,* or as a *Conjunctive Adverb.*

1. Dragons appear in the Old English epic *Beowulf* and in many other medieval English tales.
2. These stories were probably brought to England when the Danes invaded, during the years following A.D. 750.
3. In Old English, the word *wyrm* "worm" referred to any creeping, crawling thing; accordingly, the word was used to refer to dragons.
4. In *Beowulf* neither warriors nor the monster Grendel can match the strength and cunning of the hero; however, in the end a fire-breathing "wyrm" overcomes the hero.
5. The dragons in *Beowulf* are well known, but even more famous is the dragon who fought with England's patron saint, St. George.
6. According to legend, St. George saved his own life and that of a princess by killing a dragon during a crusade.
7. During the Middle Ages, St. George became a favorite of the crusaders because they believed he could protect them in battle.
8. The episode of St. George and the dragon came to be celebrated not only in English literature, but also in painting, sculpture, and architecture.
9. Dragons appeared in medieval literature and art so often because they represented the evils fought by humans in every land.
10. In European stories, dragons are ferocious beasts, whereas in Asian legends the animals are considered friendly—an interesting contrast in cultures.

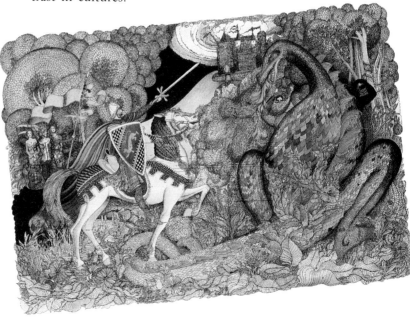

INTERJECTIONS

An interjection is a word or word group used to express surprise or other emotions. It has no grammatical relationship to the other words in a sentence.

Some common interjections are *oh, o, great, hello,* and *ouch.* An interjection may be followed by an exclamation point, or it may be included in a sentence but set off by commas.

Great! I bowled two strikes.
You heard me. *Never!*

Well, what's wrong now?
Hurrah! We won.

Writing
—**TIP**—

Overuse of interjections results in loss of impact.

Practice Your Skills

A. DRAFTING SKILL

Using Interjections Fill in the blanks in the following passages with appropriate interjections.

"_____" Michiko said, stopping her friend. "Want to hear something weird?"

"Sure," Carmen responded. "What's up?"

"_____, in science class we were talking about meteorites. It seems that in 1902, in a rural part of the Soviet Union, a crash occurred that leveled the trees in a fifty-mile-diameter circle."

"_____! Can a meteor do that?"

"_____, that's what's really strange. There wasn't an impact crater. In fact, all the trees at the center of the circle were still standing."

"_____! So it wasn't a meteor."

"No one knows. It's one of the great unexplained mysteries of science."

"_____! The idea gives me goose bumps!"

B. APPLICATION IN WRITING

Creating a Dramatic Scene Try your hand at mystery writing. Imagine that you have been hired to create a drama for television. First, think of a general plot line and characters. Then focus on a scene showing a moment of tension and excitement, such as the discovery of the crime or the unmasking of the criminal. After briefly describing your characters and setting, write a dialogue for this emotional scene using at least four interjections. Make sure the interjections are appropriate and natural for your characters.

Writing Theme
Mysteries

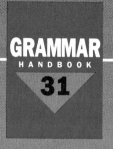

GRAMMAR
HANDBOOK
31

Writing Theme
Native American Culture

A. Recognizing the Parts of Speech Identify the part of speech of each italicized word as it is used in the following literary excerpt. Then write *Noun, Pronoun, Verb, Adjective, Adverb, Article, Preposition,* or *Conjunction.*

(1) *I* have heard talk and talk, but nothing is done. (2) Good words do not last *long* unless they amount to something. (3) Words do not pay for my *dead* people. (4) They do not pay for my country, now overrun *by* white men. (5) They do not protect my father's *grave.* (6) They *do* not *pay* for all my horses and cattle. (7) Good words will not give me *back* my children. (8) Good words will not make good *the* promise of your War Chief General Miles. (9) Good words will not give my people good health and *stop* them from dying. (10) Good words will not get my people a home *where* they can live in peace and take care of themselves. (11) I am tired of talk *that* comes to nothing. (12) It makes my heart sick *when* I remember all the good words and all the broken promises. (13) There has been *too* much talking by men who had no right to talk. (14) Too *many* misrepresentations have been made. (15) Too many misunderstandings have come up *between* the white men about the Indians. (16) If the white man wants to live in *peace* with the Indian he can live in peace. (17) There will be *no* trouble. (18) Treat all men *alike.* (19) Give them the *same* law. Give them all an even chance to live and grow. (20) All men were made by the *Great Spirit Chief.* They are all brothers.

**Chief Joseph of the Nez Percé,
"Nez Percé Surrender and Outcome"**

B. Using Parts of Speech Identify the part of speech of each italicized word. Then write a new sentence using the word as a different part of speech. Indicate which part of speech you have used.

1. Early inhabitants of the Americas valued *sports* activities.
2. Even though there were *many* different Native American societies, almost all played games.
3. Some would *train* warriors to win honor by requiring them to engage in competitive games.
4. *One* of the most popular sports was the footrace.
5. *In* the southwestern United States some footraces were thirty miles long.
6. Native Americans also played many different kinds of *ball* games.
7. In these games, the players did not *touch* the ball with their hands.

8. The game of lacrosse developed from one of *these* games.
9. In another game the players rolled a hoop *along* the ground and threw spears or sticks at it.
10. Of course, shooting arrows at a target was very popular and was also *good* for training hunters and warriors.

C. Understanding Parts of Speech Read the poem and locate within it the items listed below. Write the word or words for each item.

1. compound noun
2. verbal as an adjective
3. possessive pronoun as an adjective
4. adverb
5. subordinating conjunction

6. interjection
7. abstract noun
8. verb phrase
9. three pronouns
10. three prepositions

> O our Mother the Earth, O our Father the Sky,
> Your children are we, and with tired backs
> We bring you the gifts you love.
> Then weave for us a garment of brightness;
> May the warp be the white light of morning,
> May the weft be the red light of evening,
> May the fringes be the falling rain,
> May the border be the standing rainbow.
> Thus weave for us a garment of brightness,
> That we may walk fittingly where birds sing,
> That we may walk fittingly where grass is green,
> O our Mother the Earth, O our Father the Sky.
>
> **A Tewa Indian ballad, ''Song of the Sky Loom''**

Answer Key for Diagnostic Exercise, Pages 546–547

1. Oh—interjection; and—Conjunction; fanned—Verb; herself—Pronoun; gracefully—Adverb
2. Something—Pronoun; below—Adverb; and—Conjunction; silently—Adverb; into—Preposition; pine—Adjective; no—Adjective; traces—Noun
3. Until—Conjunction; aware—Adjective; were darkening—Verb; had begun—Verb
4. from—Preposition; thunderclap—Noun; and—Conjunction; abruptly—Adverb; tin—Adjective
5. Blue—Adjective; showered—Verb; of—Preposition
6. her—Adjective or Pronoun; them—Pronoun; Mrs. Otis—Noun; to—Preposition
7. with—Preposition; gesture—Noun; toward—Preposition
8. you—Pronoun; this—Adjective; was—Verb

On the Lightside

WHEN NOUNS GO BAD

Let's face it: . . . If language wore clothing, nouns would be the nonstarters in horn-rimmed glasses and cardigan sweaters who loiter on the threshold of ambition, discussing abstracts, and whether their modifiers have dangled lately. In the versatile English language, however, nothing is impossible, and nouns have been known to yearn for a walk on the wild side. But when they aspire to linguistic licentiousness, nouns don't just swap their specs and sweaters for sunglasses and leather jackets. No, when nouns go bad, they go where the action is: They become verbs.

Take, for example, the opening of this essay: *Let's face it.* The principal verb there is *face*—a verb because it conveys an action. *Face* began in English as a noun signifying that area at the front of your head viewed in the mirror every morning. . . .

Actually, no law—save for that of good taste—prevents nouns from opting for life in the fast lane. In fact, the fast lane is congested with the malodorous traffic of the exotic models that whiz by. People are *ambulanced* to the hospital, where physicians *office, source* their medical libraries, and *chair* committees and *debut* expensive operations. Once there, patients are *impacted* by treatments, *gifted* by visitors, maybe even *flowered* by relatives. . . . Then it's back to the fast lane to *motor* the patients home, where cars are *garaged,* and their human cargo once again *hosts, parties, romances,* [and] *parents.* . . .

Of the nominal or nounal verbs (or maybe just *nerbs,* a suitably nerdy word) in the above paragraph, the *American Heritage Dictionary* gives whole-hearted recognition only to *chair, motor, garage, and parent.* . . . What does all this expert opinion mean? Not much.

The English language is one of the purest forms of active democracy. . . . In other words, if a sufficient bloc of delegates in the electoral college of language . . . nerbs the noun *contact*—as in "I'll contact you tomorrow"—then let the experts rail and wail for all they're worth. *Contact* becomes a working nerb in the marketplace of the language, where only the fit survive.

Charles Marsh

The Parts of a Sentence

GRAMMAR
H A N D B O O K
32

SUBJECTS AND PREDICATES IN SENTENCES

A sentence is a group of words that expresses a complete thought. Every complete sentence has two parts: the subject and the predicate.

The subject of the sentence is the person, place, thing, or idea about which something is said.

The predicate tells what the subject did or what happened to the subject.

Subject	Predicate
Lava	flows.
The lava from a live volcano	flows hot and smooth.

The **complete subject** includes all the words that name the person, place, thing, or idea the sentence is about. The **complete predicate** includes all the words that tell what the subject did or what happened to the subject.

Each complete subject contains a **simple subject** that names exactly whom or what the sentence is about, and each complete predicate contains a **simple predicate,** hereafter referred to as the **verb.** The simple subject and the verb are the key words that express the core idea of each part of the sentence.

The simple subject (most often called the **subject**) tells whom or what the sentence is about. The subject may be a single word or a group of words, but it does not include modifiers.

The verb tells what the subject does or is. It may be one word or a verb phrase. The verb phrase may be interrupted by modifiers, but the modifiers are not part of the verb.

In each of the following sentences, a vertical line separates the complete subject and complete predicate. The simple subjects and the verbs are in bold type.

The **flowers** in Ms. Rivera's garden | **perished** in the frost.

This broken **camera** | **will** not **take** any pictures.

Which **bus** | **can take** me to the stadium?

Sentence Diagraming   For information on diagraming the subjects and verbs of sentences, see page 834.

The Parts of a
Sentence   **569**

Writing
TIP

Avoid repetition. Combine ideas from two sentences into one by using compound sentence parts.

Compound Sentence Parts

The subject, the verb, or both can be compound. A compound subject consists of two or more subjects that share the same verb. The subjects are joined by a conjunction.

Firefighters and *paramedics* worked to free the victim.

A **compound verb** has two or more verbs that share the same subject and are joined by a conjunction.

The contractor *erected* the walls and *installed* insulation.

Sentence Diagraming For information on diagraming sentences with compound subjects and verbs, see page 836.

Practice Your Skills

CONCEPT CHECK

Subjects and Predicates Rewrite the following sentences. Label the complete subject and complete predicate. Then underline the simple subject and the verb. Watch for compounds. Notice that some sentences contain verbals (see pages 594–601 for explanation); do not confuse these with verbs.

1. L. T. Felty is the official Chili Adviser to the governor of Texas.
2. Felty also acts as vice-president of Waxahachie Bank and Trust Company.
3. This remarkable man discovered and pursued an unusual way to improve the ailing economy of his town.
4. He helps movie producers find sets and extras in the area.
5. One downtown building can be converted overnight into a jailhouse, a barbershop, or a haberdashery.
6. Three Academy Award-winning movies were shot there in just four years.
7. Horton Foote won an Academy Award for best screenplay for *Tender Mercies.*
8. He returned to Waxahachie to produce three more films.
9. More than twenty movies and hundreds of TV shows have been filmed in Waxahachie in the past twenty years.
10. Waxahachie today calls itself "the Hollywood of Texas."

Robert Duvall starred in the 1982 film, *Tender Mercies.*

SUBJECTS IN DIFFERENT TYPES OF SENTENCES

In English sentences, the subject generally precedes the verb. In some types of sentences, however, this order is reversed. This part of the handbook presents different kinds of sentences and points out unusual subject-verb patterns. Sentences can be classified into four types according to the purpose of the speaker or writer.

Declarative Sentences

A **declarative sentence** states a fact, wish, intent, or feeling and ends with a period. Most declarative sentences are in subject-verb order. However, the sentence order may be inverted to signal special emphasis or effect.

Normal Order   One extra second was added to 1987 to adjust for the slowing rotation of the earth.

Inverted Order   Just one mile from the cottage was a sandy beach with a lifeguard on duty.

In sentences beginning with *here* or *there,* the subject-verb order is often inverted, with the verb before the subject. *Here* and *there* are adverbs. *There* can also be an **expletive,** a word that helps to get the sentence started but has no other grammatical function in the sentence.

Here is the street I live on. (*Here* is an adverb.)

There are the books you ordered. (*There* is an adverb.)

There was no gas in the car. (*There* is an expletive.)

Interrogative Sentences

An **interrogative** sentence asks a question and ends with a question mark. The subject of an interrogative sentence may appear before the verb, after the verb, or between parts of a verb phrase.

Which pianist will perform at the White House?

Why is the economic forecast so uncertain?

Will postage rates go up again this month?

Sentence Diagraming For information on diagraming interrogative sentences, see page 834.

Imperative Sentences

An **imperative sentence** gives a command, request, or direction. It usually ends with a period, but if the command is strong, the sentence may end with an exclamation point. The subject of an imperative sentence is usually not expressed, but it is understood to be the pronoun *you*.

(You) <u>Leave</u> a deposit for the videotape rental.

(You) <u>Be</u> home by eleven!

Don't (<u>you</u>) play in the park.

Sentence Diagraming For information on diagraming imperative sentences, see page 834.

Exclamatory Sentences

An **exclamatory sentence** expresses strong feeling or excitement. It ends with an exclamation point unless it begins with an interjection such as *oh* or *hey,* in which case it can end with either an exclamation point or a period.

Hey! This <u>boat</u> <u>is leaking</u>!

Oh no! I can't find my keys.

Any declarative, interrogative, or imperative sentence can be considered exclamatory when it expresses strong feeling. Even if it is interrogative, it will end with an exclamation point.

<u>Will</u> <u>you</u> <u>stop</u> making that noise!

Practice Your Skills

A. CONCEPT CHECK

Types of Sentences Identify each sentence in the following selection as *Declarative, Interrogative, Imperative,* or *Exclamatory,* and name the end punctuation it needs.

(1) Have you ever watched a flying squirrel fly (2) What a wonderful sight it is (3) The little animal doesn't really fly, of course, but it executes amazing glides (4) How can it glide 20, 60, or even 150 feet (5) A fold of loose skin, called a patagium, connects the wrist of each foreleg to the ankle of each hind leg (6) The squirrel glides by extending its legs, using the patagium as an airfoil

Writing
——**TIP**——

In most writing, use exclamatory sentences sparingly. Overuse dilutes the impact.

Writing Theme
Unusual Creatures

(7) Do you think that, as you get to know this delightful animal, you might want to adopt a flying squirrel as your pet (8) Don't do it (9) Though flying squirrels are often interesting and amusing, they can also be messy, and they sometimes bite (10) Enjoy them in their natural habitat

B. PROOFREADING SKILL

Sentences and End Punctuation Rewrite the following passage, correcting any errors that you find. Be sure to pay particular attention to end marks.

In 1825, on the island of St. Vincent in the caribbean, someone discovered what seemed to be a snail. Without a shell. Picture a creature with too antennae like those of a snail, thirty pairs of legs and a length of about three inches After carefull study, scientists decided it wasn't related to the snail but they couldn't determine what it was related too The mystery remained unsolved for eighty-six years.

What finally produced the answer A fossil found in canada in 1911 provided the key A comparison of the fossil with the snail-like creature proved both to be members of a group of prehistoric sea creatures called peripati that are neither arthropods nor true worms, but organisms that have their own seperate branch on the evolutionary tree. Others of this family can be found in tropical regions today think of it These creatures have remained in existance, relatively unchanged, for 450 million years

COMPLEMENTS

Some sentences use just a subject and a verb to express a complete thought. Other sentences require another word or group of words to complete their meaning. These words are called complements.

A complement is one or more words used to complete the meaning of the verb in a sentence.

Since it completes the meaning of the verb, the complement is considered part of the predicate.

In this part of the handbook, you will study the four kinds of complements: direct objects, indirect objects, objective complements, and subject complements.

Direct Objects

A **direct object** is a word or group of words that receives the action of an action verb in a sentence. The direct object answers the question *whom?* or *what?*

> Tanya debated *Juan* on American foreign policy. (debated *whom?*)
>
> In 1990 the Germans reunited their *country*. (reunited *what?*)

The direct object may be just one word, as in the sentences above. It may also be a phrase or a clause, as shown below.

> Each day, Kim practices *swimming a mile* for next month's triathlon. (phrase)
>
> Rosa knows *how the word-processor operates*. (clause)

Sentence Diagraming   For information on diagraming direct objects, see page 835.

Direct Object or Adverb?   Do not mistake an adverb after an action verb for a direct object. Adverbs serve a different function in the sentence. A direct object following an action verbs tells *whom* or *what*. An adverb tells *where, when, how,* or *to what extent.*

> The salesperson called *customers* all day. (direct object—called *whom?*)
>
> The salesperson called *patiently* all day. (adverb—called *how?*)

Indirect Objects

An **indirect object** is a word or group of words that tells *to whom, to what, for whom,* or *for what* the action of the verb is performed. A verb can have an indirect object only if it also has a direct object. The indirect object comes before the direct object.

> The proctor gave each *student* two sharpened *pencils*. (*Student,* the indirect object, answers the question *to whom? Pencils* is the direct object.)
>
> José built his *beagle* a new *dog house*. (*Beagle,* the indirect object, answers the question *for what? Dog house* is the direct object.)
>
> The tour guide told *us* wonderful *stories*. (*Us,* the indirect object, answers the question *to whom? Stories* is the direct object.)

Do not mistake a noun or pronoun preceded by *to* or *for* for an indirect object. Such a noun or pronoun is the object in a prepositional phrase. The word *to* or *for* does not appear before a noun or pronoun used as an indirect object.

> The subway conductor gave the *visitors* directions. (*Visitors* is an indirect object.)

> The subway conductor gave directions to the *visitors*. (*Visitors* is the object of the preposition *to*.)

Sentence Diagraming For information on diagraming indirect objects, see page 835.

Practice Your Skills

A. CONCEPT CHECK

Direct and Indirect Objects Make three columns on your paper. Label them *Verb, Indirect Object,* and *Direct Object*. For each sentence, write the verb and any objects in the appropriate columns. Watch for compound objects.

1. A *pascal* measures the pressure or force of an area.
2. A religious philosopher as well as a scientist, Blaise Pascal gave the scientific world this term and many other important contributions.
3. Pascal's father controlled what the boy learned.
4. The elder Pascal taught his son only certain subjects.
5. Curiously, his father would not teach Pascal mathematics or science.
6. However, Pascal gave his father quite a surprise.
7. At age twelve he taught himself nearly all the principles of Euclid's geometry.
8. At age sixteen he wrote *The Geometry of Conics*.
9. Some years later he developed the theory of probability and also a calculating machine.
10. With this calculating machine, Pascal may have provided future generations the prototype of the modern computer.

B. APPLICATION IN WRITING

Explaining a Process Blaise Pascal was known for his ability to explain complex concepts very clearly and simply. Choose a process you understand well. Write a short explanation of the process that a young child could understand. Use a variety of precise direct and indirect objects to help make your explanation clear.

Writing Theme
Blaise Pascal

The Parts of a Sentence

Objective Complements

Another type of complement that can occur in a sentence with a direct object is the **objective complement.** An objective complement is always a noun or an adjective; it follows the direct object and identifies or describes it. Any of these verbs (or synonyms for any of them) may take an objective complement: *appoint, call, choose, consider, elect, find, make, keep, name, think.*

> This extreme cold makes some **people** *fearful.* (The objective complement, *fearful,* describes the direct object, *people.*)

> Ruth considers the **Alvin Ailey Dance Company** *a unique troupe.* (The objective complement, *a unique troupe,* describes the direct object, *Company.*)

Subject Complements

A **subject complement** comes after a linking verb and identifies or describes the subject. (For information on *be* and other linking verbs, see page 553.) The subject complement can be a *predicate nominative* or a *predicate adjective.*

Predicate Nominatives A **predicate nominative** is a word or group of words that comes after a linking verb and renames or identifies the subject of a sentence. Predicate nominatives are either *predicate nouns* or *predicate pronouns.*

> The lead guitarist is also the group's *singer.* (predicate noun)

> The newest member of the team is *she.* (predicate pronoun)

Predicate Adjectives A **predicate adjective** is an adjective that follows a linking verb and modifies the subject of a sentence.

> Darlene seems *happy* with her new after-school job.

Sentence Diagraming For information on diagraming subject complements, see page 836.

Usage Note Gerunds sometimes act as predicate nominatives, and participles sometimes act as predicate adjectives. Do not confuse such gerunds and participles with progressive (*-ing*) verb forms.

> The most exciting part of our vacation last summer was *rafting through the Grand Canyon.* (gerund phrase as predicate nominative)

> The senator's speech was hardly *inspiring.* (participle as predicate adjective)

Writing
TIP

Hold your readers' attention by varying sentence types, subject placement, and types of complements.

Practice Your Skills

A. CONCEPT CHECK

Object and Subject Complements Identify each italicized word as *Direct Object, Objective Complement, Predicate Nominative,* or *Predicate Adjective.*

1. The horse is *unique* in its connection to the history of the Americas.
2. First appearing in North America about 55 million years ago, the earliest ancestor of the modern horse stood only about fifteen inches high, and it had *toes,* not hooves.
3. Scientists have labeled this earliest horse *Eohippus.*
4. The descendants of Eohippus grew *larger* and crossed into Asia and the Middle East.
5. Meanwhile, horses became *extinct* in the Americas.
6. No one knows who first made horses *beasts* of burden.
7. However, by early historic times, the horse had become an important *element* in warfare in the Middle East and throughout Asia.
8. When the Greeks first saw warriors from the east on horseback, they called these people *centaurs,* thinking that they were half-human and half-horse.
9. To Arabs and Spaniards of the Middle Ages and Renaissance, the horse was especially *important.*
10. The Arabs and the Spaniards were outstanding *riders* who displayed remarkable horsemanship.
11. During their exploration of North America, the Spaniards brought *horses* back to the continent of their origin.
12. Horses that were lost or released in New Spain, as the area of Spanish exploration was called, eventually became *wild.*
13. Today we call the descendants of these wild horses *mustangs.*
14. For the settlers of the American West, the horse was both a draft animal and an indispensable *means* of transportation.
15. Historians agree that the horse played a central *role* in Native American culture.

B. DRAFTING SKILL

Sentence Imitation Identify each italicized word or phrase as *Direct Object, Objective Complement, Predicate Adjective,* or *Predicate Nominative.* Then write a sentence of your own that has the same structure as the one containing the italicized word(s).

Among those competent to judge, Don Vito Cantú was the best (1) *horseman* ever seen in New Spain. . . .

They christened (2) *him* (3) *Evaristo Rodrigo Cantú,* but they called (4) *him* (5) *Vito.* He rode (6) *horses* from the time his infant hands could hold reins. Destiny made (7) *him* a (8) *man* of consequence to savage spaces of a new world across an Ocean Sea: in the year 1552 he brought from Spain to the City of Mexico two Barbary (9) *stallions* and five (10) *mares* of exceptional worth. . . . I remember (11) *how he rode,* like a god of horsemanship. I remember (12) *how he looked when he dismounted.* . . . His hair was (13) *gray* and so were his spiked mustachios. His face bore (14) *marks* of hard years and hard weathers. . . . His quilted buff-leather doublet, his leathern and baize trunk hose, his tall jackboots were (15) *those* of a soldier familiar with rough employment and open sky.

Tom Lea, *The Hands of Cantú*

Little Blue Horse, A Children's Picture, 1912, Franz Marc

CHECKPOINT
PAGES 569–578

Make two columns on your paper. For each sentence write the complete subject in one column and the complete predicate in the other. Underline each complement and identify it by writing *Direct Object (D.O.)*, *Indirect Object (I.O.)*, *Objective Complement (O.C.)*, or *Subject Complement (S.C.)*.

1. The waters off the coast of New England are cold and murky year-round.
2. Divers find this area attractive because of its marine life.
3. Cape Ann is a favorite diving spot in New England.
4. Two outstanding dive spots—Folly's Cove and Back Bay—give Cape Ann a solid reputation among divers.
5. One denizen of these waters is especially popular with divers.
6. Scientists call this creature *Homarus americanus*.
7. Divers simply call it tasty.
8. This creature is the famous East Coast lobster.
9. The succulent flesh of the lobster's tail and claws makes it a prized catch.
10. The laws of the New England states regulate lobstering by divers.
11. Limits on lobstering give the lobsters a chance to maintain their populations.
12. Many divers allow themselves lobster-watching holidays in the waters off Cape Ann.
13. Viewing underwater life affords them great pleasure.
14. Divers today are more ecology-minded than in the past.
15. Many consider the lobster a great but endangered resource.

AVOIDING SENTENCE FRAGMENTS

By definition, there are two requirements for a sentence: it must express a complete thought and have both a subject and a verb. A sentence fragment fails to satisfy one or both requirements.

A sentence fragment is only part of a sentence.

In some fragments, either the subject or the verb is missing.

Fragment   Seems difficult to complete. (What seems difficult? The subject is missing.)

Sentence   This new tax *form* seems difficult to complete.

Fragment	In the *Arabian Nights,* the queen Scheherezade. (What did the queen do? The verb is missing.)
Sentence	In the *Arabian Nights,* the queen Scheherezade *saved* her life with 1,001 suspenseful tales.

In other fragments, both subject and verb are missing.

Fragment	Popular among bikers and joggers.
Sentence	Tiny tape *players* with earphones *are* popular among bikers and joggers.

Sentence fragments result from incomplete thoughts or incorrect punctuation.

Fragments Resulting from Incomplete Thoughts

When you think faster than you can put your thoughts on paper, you may end up writing fragments and confusing your readers. For example, you may intend to express these complete thoughts:

> Calligraphy, the art of beautiful handwriting, began in China more than two thousand years ago. Today, many Americans study calligraphy and use it to make personalized invitations and greeting cards.

As your thoughts move quickly and your hand struggles to keep up, however, you may write something like the following:

> Calligraphy, the art of beautiful handwriting, began in China more than two thousand years ago, using calligraphy to make personalized invitations and greeting cards.

Writing
—TIP—
Writers of advertisements often deliberately use fragments for effect.

Emperor Ming-Huang's Journey to Shu, later copy of an 8th-century original

The example passage on the previous page contains a confusing fragment. Readers may think you meant that the main use of calligraphy in China is for invitations and greeting cards—which was not your meaning at all.

Practice Your Skills

DRAFTING SKILL

Correcting Sentence Fragments Combine each incomplete thought in Column A with an incomplete thought in Column B to make a complete sentence.

Writing Theme
Mysteries of Peru

Column A

1. The Nazca people of ancient Peru
2. Little is known
3. However, they left an astonishing memorial of their existence
4. The giant plateau in an extremely dry area of southern Peru
5. One of the most impressive of these designs shows a spider,
6. The shapes of giant lizards, cats, birds,
7. Perplexed by these ancient markings,
8. Only from a point in the air high above the earth
9. Since the Nazca left no written explanations of their design,
10. Perhaps sometime during the twenty-first century

Column B

a. scientists are investigating how they might have been carved by a primitive people who had no way of viewing the designs they were making.
b. it is highly likely that these astonishing designs will remain shrouded in mystery for a long time.
c. inhabited the Nazca desert more than a thousand years ago.
d. the mystery may eventually be solved.
e. on a high, forty-mile-long plateau.
f. and other creatures can also be found on the high Nazca Plateau.
g. about these mysterious people.
h. can these designs be seen clearly!
i. contains enormous designs the Nazca or some other ancient people carved into the surface of the earth.
j. its eight legs stretching along the plateau for an extraordinary 150 feet.

Fragments Resulting from Incorrect Punctuation

A complete sentence begins with a capital letter and ends with a period, a question mark, or an exclamation point. Many sentence fragments are caused by the period fault, which occurs when a writer inserts an end punctuation mark before he or she finishes writing a complete thought.

Fragment	*On this notebook-size computer.* Jan does all her accounting
Sentence	On this notebook-size computer, Jan does all her accounting.

Practice Your Skills

A. CONCEPT CHECK

Eliminating Sentence Fragments   Write *Sentences* after the number of each item that contains only complete sentences. Rewrite the other items, eliminating the fragment(s) by adding necessary words or correcting a period fault.

1. The largest mountain range in the world is the Andes. North to south along the entire western edge of the continent of South America.
2. This astonishing mountain range is being raised by the collision of geological plates. Along the western coasts of the South and North American continents.
3. Inhabiting the Andes are three relatives of the camel. That are especially adapted to living at high elevations.
4. These interesting creatures are the guanaco, the alpaca, and the llama. Two of these animals have proved most useful to Andean peoples.
5. The guanaco is a wild beast, but the alpaca and the llama, which may be descendents of the guanaco, have long been domesticated. By the inhabitants of the Andes.
6. A llama is four feet tall at the shoulders. It resembles a large, long-necked sheep.
7. Some say a llama looks like a small camel. Unlike a camel, however, no humps.
8. Serves as a beast of burden. Carrying great loads to enormous heights.
9. Also prized for its meat and milk. Which are consumed mainly by local peoples.
10. In addition, the people harvest the llama's fine wool. Which is dried, spun, and woven into wonderful designs for hats, scarves, and sweaters.

Writing Theme
Llamas

B. PROOFREADING SKILL

Sentence Fragments   Rewrite the following passage, correcting all errors. Correct all sentence fragments, adding words and changing punctuation as necessary.

Helen Bodington operates an unusual school in San Francisco. An obedience school for llamas. She started her business nearly fourty years ago by training dogs. She taught her first llama to carry backpacks on hiking trips. And to jump into the bed of her pickup truck. Some other things she teaches llamas are how to pull a cart, jump, walk with their owners. And respond to simple commands.

For five thousand years the Incas bred llamas as beasts of burden. Llamas are work animals. Not really suitable as pets. Ms. Bodington says her own llama is a dignified companion, a "nice person." Llama ownership is an expensive proposition. With llamas selling for $1,000 to $7,000 depending on there gender and age. A person needs at least an acre of land to give a llama proper excercise. According to Ms. Bodington, llamas can live for twenty-five years. On one bale of hay a Month.

AVOIDING RUN-ON SENTENCES

Sometimes a writer fails to use an end mark to signal the end of a sentence. The result is a run-on sentence.

A run-on sentence is made up of two or more sentences written as though they were one sentence.

Run-on   Cross-country skiing is more than just an invigorating winter activity it provides excellent conditioning for all major muscles.

Correct   Cross-country skiing is more than just an invigorating winter activity. It provides excellent conditioning for all major muscles.

The Comma Fault or Comma Splice

A writer sometimes mistakenly separates two sentences with a comma instead of a correct end mark. This error is called a **comma fault** or **comma splice.** It results in the most common type of run-on sentence.

Comma Fault	Why is the main street in town blocked off today, is there going to be a parade?
Correct	Why is the main street in town blocked off today? Is there going to be a parade?
Comma Fault	Homeless people must find shelter in public buildings on nights like this one, no one should be exposed to this bitter cold.
Correct	Homeless people must find shelter in public buildings on nights like this one. No one should be exposed to this bitter cold.

Correcting Run-on Sentences The run-on sentences above were correctly rewritten as two separate sentences. In other cases, it is more appropriate to create one compound sentence. Several ways to correct run-on sentences by creating compounds are explained below. Notice that each correct example is a compound sentence with two independent clauses.

1. You can combine related ideas in one sentence by using a comma and a coordinating conjunction.

Run-on	Snowshoes seemed awkward at first, we grew used to them.
Correct	Snowshoes seemed awkward at first, but we grew used to them.

2. You can combine related ideas in one sentence by using just a semicolon.

Run-on	During the late 1800's, huge herds of cattle grazed on the open range they were tended and guarded by hired cowhands.
Correct	During the late 1800's, huge herds of cattle grazed on the open range; they were tended and guarded by hired cowhands.

3. You can combine related ideas by using a semicolon, a conjunctive adverb, and a comma.

Run-on	Long exposure to below-zero temperatures often makes car batteries go dead, my car started in this morning's record cold without any problem.
Correct	Long exposure to below-zero temperatures often makes car batteries go dead; nevertheless, my car started in this morning's record cold without any problem.

Writing
―TIP―

Vary the ways you join clauses. Too many *and*s sound childish; too many semicolons seem stiffly formal.

Practice Your Skills

A. CONCEPT CHECK

Run-on Sentences   Correct each run-on sentence below, using one of the following methods: (1) a capital letter and a period, (2) a semicolon alone, (3) a comma and a conjunction, or (4) a semicolon and one of these conjunctive adverbs followed by a comma: *however, nevertheless,* or *moreover.*

Writing Theme
William Faulkner

1. William Faulkner was born in Mississippi in 1897, that state was destined to be his home for most of his life.
2. He lived in the town of Oxford, Mississippi, where his house still stands, every year it is visited by crowds of tourists.
3. Some consider Faulkner the greatest novelist that America has produced he is one of the few Americans to win the Nobel Prize in literature.
4. Faulkner never finished college, as a young man he worked odd jobs and trained as a military pilot.
5. While working as a journalist in New Orleans, Faulkner met Sherwood Anderson the older novelist encouraged the young Faulkner to write novels.
6. In 1926 Faulkner wrote his first novel, *Soldier's Pay,* he followed this with a second novel, *Sartoris.*

7. *Sartoris* began a series of novels, all of them dealt with Faulkner's major theme— the decline of the Old South.
8. One fascinating aspect of Faulkner's novels is that he made up his own mythical Mississippi city, Jefferson, he created a mythical county, Yoknapatawpha.
9. Each novel is complete in itself, readers enjoy the fact that the same people, families, and places turn up in novel after novel.
10. Some readers find Faulkner's prose occasionally difficult to follow they invariably discover that his work is richly rewarding.

The Parts of a
Sentence   **585**

B. APPLICATION IN LITERATURE

Run-on Sentences   Sometimes a writer will break the customary rules of usage to create particular effects. Read the following passage from one of William Faulkner's great novels. Notice that Faulkner wrote the passage as one long run-on sentence, omitting all punctuation, even apostrophes. Rewrite the passage, adding or deleting words and inserting punctuation and capitalization as necessary to make complete sentences. Compare your version with the original. Discuss with your classmates why Faulkner might have written the passage as he did. What effect is created by his use of the run-on?

> I didnt look back the tree frogs didnt pay me any mind the grey light like moss in the trees drizzling but still it wouldnt rain after a while I turned went back to the edge of the woods as soon as I got there I began to smell honeysuckle again I could see the lights on the courthouse clock and the glare of town the square on the sky and the dark willows along the branch and the light in mothers windows the light still on in Benjys room and I stooped through the fence and went across the pasture running.

William Faulkner, *The Sound and the Fury*

CHECK POINT
PAGES 579–586

Correct the following fragments and run-on sentences, adding, changing, or dropping words, punctuation, and capital letters wherever necessary.

1. On the plain of Judea, near the Dead Sea, there is a huge, mesalike rock. Known as Masada.
2. There, about 160 B.C., a Jewish leader built a fort, this was later expanded into a great citadel.
3. In A.D. 66 the people of Judea rose against the Romans. Who were ruling their land.
4. At the time of the revolt, Masada was occupied by a garrison of Roman soldiers, however, Jewish patriots drove this first group of soldiers out.
5. The Romans crushed the rebellion elsewhere in Judea, to their great dismay, though, Masada held out against them.
6. In A.D. 72, therefore, an entire Roman legion marched against Masada. Included three to six thousand experienced soldiers.

7. Massed against a small force of Jewish men, women, and children. Fewer than a thousand in all.

8. Despite their meager numbers, the people of Masada held out against the Romans, their strong beliefs and leadership sustained them.

9. Unable to take the citadel by sheer force of numbers, the Romans devised a plan they decided to build a ramp and to erect on it a stone siege tower, catapults, and a battering ram.

10. One can only imagine the feelings of the defenders of Masada. As they watched this fateful construction progressing.

11. Eventually it became clear that the Romans would succeed in their efforts, the people of Masada chose to take their own lives rather than be captured and killed by their enemies.

12. Of the original 967 Masadans, only seven survived. Two women and five children.

13. When they finally breached the walls of Masada in A.D. 73. The Romans were amazed at what they found, they marveled at the courage of their slain enemies.

14. Gazing upon their bodies, the Romans could only "wonder at their immovable contempt of death." As a contemporary Jewish historian put it.

15. Over the centuries some people claimed that the story of Masada was simply a legend. Only one contemporary written account of it.

16. However, in 1838 an American expert identified an enormous rock near the Dead Sea. As the legendary Masada.

17. Then, between 1963 and 1965, the area was excavated by a team led by an Israeli archaeologist. Modern techniques used in the task.

18. These modern excavations proved the Jewish historian correct the siege of Masada had actually taken place.

19. Many important finds have been made at Masada, these include ancient scrolls and fragments of scrolls.

20. However, the most important find was the place itself. A site that has become symbolic of human determination in the face of overwhelming odds.

The Parts of a
Sentence

Writing Theme
Whales and Whaling

APPLICATION AND REVIEW

A. Sentence Types Identify each sentence as *Declarative, Interrogative, Imperative,* or *Exclamatory.* Then name the appropriate end punctuation for each sentence.

1. Who has not heard of the great white whale, Moby Dick
2. Go to Nantucket, the island off Massachusetts
3. There, it's not hard to imagine the whaler *Pequod* and her crew preparing to set sail
4. In his epic novel *Moby Dick,* author Herman Melville captures the spirit of the whalers
5. How many a whaler has, like Melville's young seaman Ishmael, felt a "damp, drizzly November" in the soul
6. However, the novice Ishmael was certainly in for a few surprises as he set out to sea
7. Think about waking up to find that your roommate is a tattooed Polynesian prince named Queequeg
8. There is the matter of what Queequeg carries in his sack
9. How Ishmael's eyes bulge when Queequeg pulls out a shrunken head
10. How would you like to find that your captain is ready to risk the whole crew to satisfy his own obsession

B. Identifying Complements Identify each italicized complement as *Direct Object, Indirect Object, Objective Complement, Predicate Nominative,* or *Predicate Adjective.*

1. The blue whale is the largest *animal* that has ever lived.
2. To many people, such size is *intimidating.*
3. Adventure tales, such as the story of Moby Dick, have made whales *villains* in the eyes of many.
4. For example, because of its name, most people mistakenly consider the killer whale *ferocious;* the killer whale is, in fact, a large dolphin.
5. Actually whales, and even killer whales, are quite *harmless* to humans.
6. Moreover, whales of all kinds exhibit rather sophisticated social *behavior.*
7. Consider that humpback whales occasionally give *each other* affectionate hugs.
8. Although whales generally travel in herds, their basic social unit is the *family.*
9. Whales, like other mammals, bear their young live and feed *them* milk.
10. Furthermore, as you might expect, a mother whale is highly *protective* of her young.

C. Sentence Fragments and Run-ons Rewrite any fragments and run-ons to make complete sentences. Write *Sentence* for any numbered item that is correct.

1. Because many of the larger whales face extinction.
2. Since the 1970's the United States, Canada, and some European countries. Have protested the continuation of whaling.
3. In the past few years, only a few countries have continued widespread whaling operations, one of the most active of these is the Soviet Union.
4. The Soviets have maintained a large whaling fleet. Since the end of World War II.
5. Therefore, it came as a surprise a few years ago. When the Soviets rescued some beluga whales in the frigid Bering Sea, off Alaska.
6. The weather had grown sharply colder, the belugas had become trapped in an ever-shrinking area of open water in the middle of an ice field. While they were feeding on a school of fish.
7. The whales thrashed about in the water, unable to escape, they faced inevitable doom as the ice closed in.
8. News media publicized the giant creatures' plight around the world; people from many nations expressed concern and sympathy for the imperiled whales.
9. For days the situation made the headlines, it concerned environmentalists and casual observers alike.
10. Fortunately for the whales, the Soviets sent an icebreaker to the area. To clear a channel to open water.
11. The Soviet ship broke through the ice and then, to the sound of classical music from its loudspeakers, led the whales to freedom in the open sea.
12. Proved to be a very difficult and expensive undertaking.
13. Altogether, the Soviets spent well over $80,000 to free the belugas. A fact that surprised many observers since the Soviets have been among the world's leading killers of whales.
14. Praise came from around the world, this was for the captain and crew of the Soviet icebreaker.
15. This was one whaling adventure with a happy ending.

On the Lightside

HEADLINE BLOOPERS

New Vaccine May Contain Rabies
Daily Press (Newport News, Va.) 5/1/78

Complaints about NBA referees growing ugly
Chicago Sun-Times 5/23/79

Squad helps dog bite victim
Grant County (Wisc.)
Herald Independent 4/29/76

Dr. Tacket Gives Talk On Moon
Indiana Evening Gazette 3/13/76

Bill Would Permit Ads on Eyeglasses
Tulsa World 11/30/76

Shouting Match Ends Teacher's Hearing
Newsday 7/13/77

Child teaching expert to speak
Birmingham Post-Herald
3/28/77

Farmer Bill Dies In House
The Atlanta Constitution 4/13/78

Jumping bean prices affect poor
Eugene (Ore.)
Register-Guardian
2/27/74

Bond issue is readied for city incinerator
The Berkshire Eagle (Pittsfield, Mass.) 10/21/78

27 dental hygiene students to receive caps at MCC
Woodbridge (N.J.) News Tribune 2/5/74

Solar system expected to be back in operation
Libertyville (Ill.) Herald 3/15/78

PLO invited to raid debates
Dallas Morning News 12/5/77

Branch Avenue Bridge To Be Fixed Before Fall
Providence Evening Bulletin 8/8/74

Air head fired
Chicago Sun Times 9/18/90

Phrases and Clauses

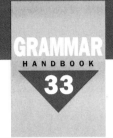

PREPOSITIONAL PHRASES

A phrase is a group of related words that does not have a subject and predicate. It functions in a sentence as a single part of speech. A **prepositional phrase** is one of several kinds of phrases.

A prepositional phrase consists of a preposition, its object, and any modifiers of the object in the phrase.

> Charlie Chaplin has long been a favorite *of filmgoers.*

The object of a preposition may be a noun, a pronoun, or a word or group of words used as a noun.

> Margaret Mitchell's masterpiece is about the American Civil War *era.* (The noun *era* is the object of *about.*)

A preposition may take a compound object. A conjunction joins the parts of the compound object.

> Aside from her famous *novel* and a *collection* of her letters, Mitchell published nothing else.

In some sentences, a prepositional phrase modifies the object in a phrase that precedes it.

> Concerned citizens are protesting the excess *of violence in some TV programs.*

Prepositional phrases can function as adjectives or adverbs.

Adjective Phrases

An **adjective phrase** is a prepositional phrase that functions as an adjective, modifying a noun or a pronoun. Usually an adjective phrase immediately follows the noun or pronoun it modifies.

Modifying a Noun	Details *about Shakespeare's private life* are obscure. (Which details?)
Modifying a Pronoun	Few *of his works* shed much light on the author. (Few what?)

Adverb Phrases

An **adverb phrase** tells *where, when, how, why,* or *to what extent.* Like an adverb, it can modify a verb, an adjective, or another adverb. Study the following examples.

Charlie Chaplin in the silent film, *The Kid,* 1921

Modifying a Verb	The incriminating letter was found *inside a book.* (Found where?)
Modifying an Adjective	The *Apollo* moon flights were successful *beyond anyone's dreams.* (Successful to what extent?)
Modifying an Adverb	The smoke alarm sounded late *in the morning.* (Late when?)

Sentence Diagraming For information on diagraming prepositional phrases, see page 837.

Sentence Diagraming For information on diagraming prepositional phrases, see page 837.

Writing Theme
The American South

Practice Your Skills

CONCEPT CHECK

Adjective and Adverb Phrases Write each prepositional phrase in the numbered sentences in the following literary excerpt. Then write the word *Adjective* or *Adverb* to identify how the phrase functions. Notice how the use of phrases adds detail to the passage.

(1) When Katie went back to Fayetteville at the end of the year Amanda was lonely for her. Within a month she had gotten in the habit of going up there to visit.

The first time she drove to Arkansas she left before dawn, planning on making the long drive in one day. (2) She crossed the Mississippi River at Greenville so close to home she could smell it, then drove on up through the Arkansas delta . . . .

(3) In Little Rock she stopped at a Waffle House for an omelet, pouring maple syrup all over the eggs like a bad child, eating the last bites with her fingers, full of some outlandish feeling of freedom. (4) She licked the syrup from her fingers and began the last leg of her journey.

(5) At Alma the real hills began, the Boston Mountains, the oldest mountains in the United States. (6) As Amanda drove up into the mountains they reached out to her and took her heart away . . . . (7) Something about the lay of the land seemed exactly right to her . . . .

Ellen Gilchrist, *The Annunciation*

Leonardo da Vinci's *Angel of the Annunciation* (detail) appears on the front cover of the novel *The Annunciation* by Ellen Gilchrist.

An **appositive** is a noun or pronoun that usually comes directly after another word in a sentence to identify or provide further information about that word.

> The English poet *Elizabeth Barrett* secretly married Robert Browning. Her father, *a tyrant,* was very angry and vigorously opposed the marriage.

An **appositive phrase** is made up of an appositive and all of its modifiers. The modifiers may be single words, phrases, or clauses.

> The California Institute of Technology, *a famous university that is located in Pasadena,* attracts students from all over the world. (The adjective *famous* and the clause *that is located in Pasadena* are both modifiers of the appositive *university.*)

Appositives occasionally precede the noun or the pronoun to which they refer.

> *A strong skier,* Meera won a medal in the slalom.

An appositive or appositive phrase may be either essential or nonessential. An **essential appositive** must be included in a sentence to make the meaning clear.

> The singer *Bruce Springsteen* was born in New Jersey and continued to live there as an adult. (The appositive is necessary to identify the singer.)

A **nonessential appositive** is one that is not needed to make the meaning of a sentence clear. In the following example, the italicized appositive is nonessential. If it were omitted, the basic meaning of the sentence would be the same.

> January, *the coldest month in many northern regions,* is named for the Roman god Janus.

Punctuation Note Use one or two commas to set off a nonessential appositive from the rest of the sentence. Do not use commas with an essential appositive.

Sentence Diagraming For information on diagraming appositives and appositive phrases, see page 839.

Writing
TIP

Appositives provide a means of achieving emphasis and streamlining your writing.

Practice Your Skills

CONCEPT CHECK

Appositives and Appositive Phrases   Rewrite each of the following sentences that contains an appositive or appositive phrase. Underline the appositive construction, inserting *commas* where needed. If a sentence has no appositive, write *None*.

1. Benjamin Banneker an inventor, surveyor, mathematician, and astronomer was a prominent person in early U.S. history.
2. His grandmother an Englishwoman and a former indentured servant taught him to read and write.
3. In 1753, with only two models an old pocket watch and a picture of a clock he constructed a clock that kept perfect time for more than fifty years.
4. An amateur astronomer Banneker accurately predicted a solar eclipse on April 14, 1789.
5. In 1791, he assisted Major A. Elliott the surveyor appointed by George Washington to design the city of Washington, D.C.
6. Later, he made all the astronomical calculations and weather predictions for an almanac he published.
7. Other material antislavery essays and medical advice was also included.
8. Other people often prominent Americans contributed articles for Banneker's publication.
9. The almanac evidence of the accomplishments of African Americans was especially important in an age of discrimination.
10. A supporter of the rights of African Americans Banneker also advocated free public education and elimination of the death penalty.

VERBALS AND VERBAL PHRASES

A **verbal** is a verb form that is used as a noun, an adjective, or an adverb. A group of words made up of a verbal, its modifiers, and its complements is called a **verbal phrase.**

In this section, you will review the three kinds of verbals and verbal phrases: **infinitive, participle,** and **gerund.**

Infinitives and Infinitive Phrases

An **infinitive** is a verbal that is made up of *to* (called the sign of the infinitive) and the base form of a verb. An infinitive may be used as a noun, an adjective, or an adverb.

Noun	*To write* demands discipline, time, and great effort. (subject)
	The only ambition Lian has in life is *to write*. (predicate nominative)
Adjective	I don't understand Alan's obsession *to succeed*. (modifies the noun *obsession*)
Adverb	The basketball team was playing *to win*. (modifies the verb *was playing*)

Auxiliary verbs are added to the present infinitive to form three other kinds of infinitives.

> We are expecting *to be invited*. (passive present)

> *To have invited* them was a mistake. (active perfect)

> Frank was surprised *to have been invited*. (passive perfect)

Sometimes an infinitive is used without the word *to*.

> Sylvia did not dare question the judge's statement. (Sylvia did not dare *to* question. . . .)

An infinitive phrase is a group of words made up of an infinitive, its modifiers, and its complements.

Subject of an Infinitive	The committee wanted Rosita to run for office. (*Rosita* is the subject of *to run*.)
Object of an Infinitive	A delegation went to greet the senator at the airport. (*Senator* is the object of *to greet*.)
Complement of an Infinitive	No one expected the winner to be Robert. (*Robert* is the predicate nominative identifying *winner*.)

Because it is a verb form, the infinitive in an infinitive phrase may take one or more complements.

> I will try *to save her a seat near the stage*. (*Her* is the indirect object of *to save*, and *seat* is the direct object.)

Usage Note The objective form of the pronoun is used as *the subject, the object,* or *the predicate pronoun* of an infinitive.

> The coach signaled *us* to play. (*Us* is the subject of the infinitive *to play*.)
> We wanted to beat *them*. (*Them* is the object of the infinitive *to beat*.)

As a verb form, the infinitive in an infinitive phrase can have adverbs and adverb phrases as modifiers.

> *To walk briskly* is one of the best forms of exercise. (The adverb *briskly* modifies the infinitive *to walk.*)

> Flight 309 to Paris will be ready *to board in approximately fifteen minutes.* (The adverb phrase *in approximately fifteen minutes* modifies the infinitive *to board.*)

An infinitive phrase can function as a noun, an adjective, or an adverb.

Noun	On Inauguration Day, the President swears *to execute the laws of the United States faithfully.* (object)
Adjective	An optometrist or an ophthalmologist is the specialist *to see about eye problems.*
Adverb	The students hurried *to board the bus.*

In most cases, a skilled writer avoids placing words between *to* and the verb form in an infinitive. Such placement creates a **split infinitive,** a form that is usually awkward.

Awkward	Good comedians get their audience *to frequently laugh.*
Better	Good comedians get their audience *to laugh frequently.*

Usage Note Experts disagree about split infinitives. Some say a split infinitive is always incorrect. Others feel that a split infinitive sounds better, as in "The corporation expects *to very nearly double* its earnings." Discuss these opinions with your teacher.

Sentence Diagraming For information on diagraming infinitives and infinitive phrases, see page 839.

Practice Your Skills

A. CONCEPT CHECK

Infinitive Phrases   Write the infinitives or infinitive phrases in the quotations below and identify the functions of each as *Adjective, Adverb,* or *Noun.* Label the use of each noun infinitive as *Subject, Object,* or *Predicate Nominative.*

1. There is a great difference between an eager man who wants to read a book and a tired man who wants a book to read.
   G. K. Chesterton
2. Almost anyone can be an author; the business is to collect money and fame from this state of being.   **A. A. Milne**
3. Writers, if they are worthy of that jealous designation, do not write for other writers. They write to give reality to an experience.
   Archibald MacLeish
4. You must not suppose, because I am a man of letters, that I never tried to earn an honest living.   **George Bernard Shaw**
5. To write books is difficult. To read books is more difficult still, because of the tendency to go to sleep.
   Felix Dahn, paraphrased by Sir Stanley Unwin
6. The greatest part of a writer's time is spent in reading, in order to write. A man will turn over half a library to make one book.
   Samuel Johnson
7. Nothing you write, if you hope to be any good, will ever come out as you first hoped.   **Lillian Hellman**
8. Biography is to give man some kind of shape after his death.
   Virginia Woolf
9. What I like . . . is to treat words as a craftsman does his wood or stone or what-have-you.   **Dylan Thomas**
10. When anyone sits down to write, he should imagine a crowd of readers looking over his shoulder.   **Robert Graves**

B. REVISION SKILL

Sentence Combining   Combine each of the following sentences by adding to one sentence an infinitive phrase taken from the other sentence. Eliminate unnecessary words. Some rewording of the base sentences may be needed.

1. William Faulkner traveled to Sweden in 1949. He went to accept the Nobel Prize for literature.
2. In his acceptance speech, Faulkner spoke about the duty of a writer. According to Faulkner, this duty is to celebrate the nobility of the human spirit.

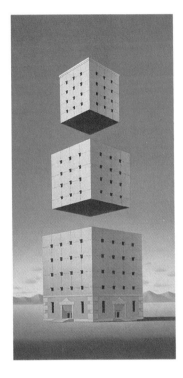

3. Faulkner said that writers serve an important purpose. He said this purpose is to remind other people of "the courage and honor and hope and pride and compassion and pity and sacrifice" of which people are capable.
4. He said that "the poet's voice" can help mankind. It can help mankind "to endure and prevail."
5. By reminding people of qualities like courage, honor, and pride, writers give their fellow human beings strength. This strength is needed to overcome the fears and anxieties of modern life.

C. APPLICATION IN WRITING

A Maxim   Maxims are wise sayings that express truths that most people believe, for example: There is a time *to speak* and a time *to keep silence*; *To err* is human, *to forgive* divine. Like many others, these maxims include infinitives. Write five maxims, each with an infinitive phrase. As your teacher directs, combine your ideas with those of other students to create a class booklet entitled *Maxims for Moderns*.

Participles and Participial Phrases

A participle used as an adjective is another type of verbal.

A participle has various forms: *encouraging* (present), *encouraged* (past), *having encouraged* (perfect), and *having been encouraged* (passive perfect).

Since participles act as adjectives, they can modify either nouns or pronouns.

Modifying a Noun   The magazine editor sent an *encouraging* letter to the young writer.
Encouraged, the writer continued writing short stories.

Modifying a Pronoun   *Having been encouraged,* she developed more confidence in her ability to write.

Do not confuse a participle with the verb of a sentence. A present participle or a past participle can be used with an auxiliary verb to form a verb phrase. (See pages 552–554.) The participle in a verb phrase acts as a verb. A participle used as a verbal acts as an adjective. Study the following examples.

Verb   The young writer *had completed* another story before receiving the editor's letter.

Verbal   She submitted the *completed* short story to the magazine for publication.

A participle with its modifiers and complements is called a participial phrase. A participial phrase acts as an adjective.

> *Waiting anxiously for the editor's reaction,* the writer tried to begin another story.

Participles are verb forms and may be modified by both adverbs and adverb phrases. In the example sentence above, the adverb *anxiously* and the adverb phrase *for the editor's reaction* modify the participle *waiting.*

Like verbs, participles may have complements.

> The editor, *having received the writer's manuscript,* read it immediately. (In the participial phrase, *manuscript* is the direct object of the participle *having received.*)

Absolute Phrases An **absolute phrase** is made up of a participle and the noun or pronoun it modifies. Although an absolute phrase has no direct grammatical connection with a particular word in the rest of the sentence, it does modify the independent clause by indicating time, reason, or circumstance.

Time	*Our discussion finished,* we all shook hands.
Reason	*Her wallet having been stolen,* Nadine could not pay the dinner check.
Circumstance	The child dutifully answered the questions, *his eyes filling with tears.*

Sentence Diagraming For information on diagraming participles and participial phrases, see page 838.

Practice Your Skills

A. CONCEPT CHECK

Participles, Participial Phrases, and Absolute Phrases Write the participles and participial phrases in the following sentences. If the participle or participial phrase modifies a particular word, write the word that it modifies. If the participial phrase is an absolute phrase, write *Absolute.*

1. Hanged as a spy, Nathan Hale was nonetheless a famous patriot.
2. Hale was a member of a small, respected group of patriots known to history as the Rangers.
3. Their fighting skills and daring exploits were legendary.
4. The captain of the Rangers, having asked for a volunteer, chose Hale to spy on the British.

Writing
═TIP═
Participial phrases may be essential or nonessential. Set off nonessential phrases with commas.

Writing Theme
Espionage

5. Hale being untrained, the espionage attempt was sure to fail.
6. Pretending to be a Dutch schoolmaster, he crossed British lines.
7. A cousin dedicated to the British cause may have betrayed him.
8. Stopped by a British officer, Hale did not know what to do.
9. The arresting officer questioned him.
10. Hale answered the questions, his face betraying his fear.
11. Hale, condemned to hang, was refused a trial.
12. Facing death bravely, Hale reportedly said, "I only regret that I have but one life to lose for my country."
13. His body, dangling from a rope, served as a grim message to other patriots.
14. Several monuments honor Hale as one of America's most revered heroes.
15. A boulder in Halesite, New York, marks the place believed to be the site of his capture.

B. DRAFTING SKILL

Sentence Combining Rewrite the following paragraph, adding information or combining sentences according to the directions given in parentheses.

(1) Elizabeth Van Lew lived in Richmond, Virginia, during the Civil War. She is known to history as a spy for the Union forces. (Combine the sentences using a participial phrase.) (2) She helped runaway slaves and Northern prisoners who escaped. (Use *escaped* as a participial modifier.) (3) She sent letters to Washington. The letters told officials in Washington what was happening in Richmond. (Combine the sentences using a participial phrase.) While her neighbors knitted for the men in gray, Van Lew sent intelligence reports to help the men in blue. (4) Van Lew tended prisoners at Libby Prison in Richmond. She gathered information all the while. (Combine the sentences using a participial phrase.) (5) She sent messages to General Grant. The messages were coded. (Use *coded* as a participle.)

Runaway slaves, such as those helped by Elizabeth Van Lew, went north to join one of the 166 black Union regiments.

Gerunds and Gerund Phrases

A gerund is the *-ing* form of a verb used as a noun.

Gerunds can perform many of the functions of nouns.

Subject	Fast *driving* is dangerous on any road.
Direct Object	Most people really enjoy *sailing*.
Object of a Preposition	Before *leaving,* the senator called her office.
Predicate Nominative	Ted's most irksome habit is *interrupting*.
Appositive	A fairly new hobby, *spelunking,* is increasing in popularity.

A gerund, its modifiers, and its complements make up a gerund phrase.

Since the gerund in a gerund phrase is a verb form, it is often modified by an adverb or an adverb phrase.

> *Eating sensibly in the morning* is a wise practice. (The gerund *eating* is modified by the adverb *sensibly* and the adverb phrase *in the morning.*)

Practice Your Skills

CONCEPT CHECK

Gerunds and Gerund Phrases   Write the gerunds and gerund phrases in the following sentences. Tell whether each is a *Subject, Direct Object, Predicate Nominative, Object of a Preposition,* or *Appositive.* If there is no gerund or gerund phrase, write *None.*

Writing Theme
Eclipses

1. In ancient China, watching the heavens was the responsibility of court astrologers.
2. Another responsibility of court astrologers was informing the Emperor, in advance, about exceptional heavenly events.
3. One day, legend has it, a dragon began eating the sun.
4. The people drove the dragon away by beating drums and gongs.
5. The people's actions, making noise and frightening the dragon, saved the sun from certain destruction.
6. However, the Emperor was not at all pleased.
7. He had his two astrologers, Hsi and Ho, beheaded for failing to warn him about the sun-eating dragon.
8. At that time, foretelling any future event was based on magic.
9. Today predicting an eclipse is not difficult at all.
10. Astronomers wait for the periodic alignment of the earth, the sun, and the moon.

It is usually best to place every modifier as close as possible to the word it modifies. Also, it should be obvious which word in a sentence is being modified.

Misplaced Modifiers

A **misplaced modifier** is one that is placed so far away from the word it modifies that the intended meaning of the sentence is unclear and perhaps even humorous. The examples below show how misplaced modifiers can distort the meaning of a sentence.

Misplaced	The helpful librarian pointed out the book to the boy *on the shelf.* (The prepositional phrase *on the shelf* seems to modify *boy.*)
Clearer	The helpful librarian pointed out the book *on the shelf* to the boy.
Misplaced	Tourists see many historic sites *walking the Freedom Trail in Boston.* (The participial phrase *walking the Freedom Trail in Boston* seems to modify *sites.*)
Clearer	Tourists *walking the Freedom Trail in Boston* see many historic sites.

Dangling Modifiers

Like misplaced modifiers, dangling modifiers can distort meaning or cause unintended humor. A **dangling modifier** does not clearly modify any noun or pronoun in a sentence. Dangling modifiers often appear at the beginnings of sentences. To correct a dangling modifier, make sure the sentence names the thing modified.

Dangling	To receive the free booklet, a stamped, self-addressed envelope must be enclosed. (Who or what will receive the booklet?)
Clearer	To receive the free booklet, you must include a stamped, self-addressed envelope.
Dangling	*Studying the American Revolution,* Paul Revere was captured before he could complete his historic ride. (Who was studying the American Revolution?)
Clearer	*Studying the American Revolution,* the *students* learned that Paul Revere was captured before he could complete his historic ride.

Writing
―TIP―

Dangling phrases occur most often when the verb is in the passive voice. Using the active voice may make dangling modifiers less likely.

Practice Your Skills

A. CONCEPT CHECK

Misplaced and Dangling Modifiers Rewrite each sentence that contains a misplaced or dangling modifier, correcting the error. If a sentence has no error, write *Correct*.

1. Known for ruthless efficiency, spy novels about the Cold War often feature the KGB.
2. The KGB was created in 1954 in the Soviet Union, which stands for "Committee for State Security."
3. Acting as the Communist Party's watchdog the KGB's responsibilities include both domestic and international security.
4. In fact, composed of seventeen directorates, the KGB is the largest secret police and intelligence organization in the world.
5. Discredited for its part in a political purge, the KGB undertook a campaign in the eyes of Soviet citizens to revamp its image.
6. Acclaimed as heroes of Soviet espionage, the Soviet government in the 1950's proudly admitted to using spies.
7. In fact, some agents were secretly sent to the United States to gain information from the Soviet Union.
8. Using the alias of Emil Goldfus, in 1957 the United States captured and convicted a KGB agent.
9. To transmit military secrets, shortwave radio equipment had been installed in his Brooklyn apartment.
10. The spy, whose real name was Rudolf Abel, had worked in New York City for nine years as an artist and a photographer.

B. PROOFREADING SKILL

Using Phrases Correctly Rewrite the following sentences, eliminating misplaced and dangling participles and correcting errors in capitalization, punctuation, and spelling.

The Central Intelligence Agency (CIA) an organization that was founded in 1947 does intelligence work for the United States. Wishing to learn the secrets of freinds as well as enemies, more than a million agents are employed worldwide. To carry out its secret missions, many electronic devices are used. For example, tiny microphones called *bugs* are planted by agents in walls and telephones. CIA Agents obtain useful intelligence from overheard conversations listening on receivers located far away from the bugs. Among other devices used by agents are hidden cameras, secret codes, and disguises. The life of a CIA agent is fasinating but the possibility of discovery or even death is always present.

A. Tell whether the italicized phrase in each of the following sentences is an *Appositive Phrase,* an *Infinitive Phrase,* a *Participial Phrase,* or a *Gerund Phrase.* Also list any prepositional phrases used as modifiers in the italicized phrases.

1. *Pushing Native Americans from their lands* was a dark aspect of westward expansion.
2. Red Cloud, *war chief, medicine man, and popular leader of the Oglala Sioux,* believed that his land should not be taken from him.
3. His land had become a highway for homesteaders *traveling along the Oregon Trail.*
4. The Oregon Trail and the nearby Bozeman Trail, *both parts of the Powder River Indian country,* were located in the territory of the mighty Sioux.
5. *Protecting these sacred lands and hunting grounds* became the consuming purpose of the Sioux.
6. These hunting grounds, *given to Red Cloud by the Great Spirit,* were crucial to the Sioux culture.
7. *Swarming down from the nearby hills,* Red Cloud and the Sioux fiercely defended their land.
8. After many years of fighting, Red Cloud signed a treaty *to make the Powder River country Sioux land forever.*
9. He was the first—and only—Native American *to win a war with the United States.*
10. In 1980, the Supreme Court ordered the federal government *to pay the Sioux 122.5 million dollars as restitution for the illegal seizure of Sioux land in 1877.*

Caroline Kills in Water (below), resident at the Sioux Indian Reservation, Rosebud, South Dakota (right)

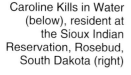

B. Write each verbal phrase in the following sentences and label it *Infinitive Phrase, Participial Phrase,* or *Gerund Phrase.* Identify its function by writing *Noun* or *Modifier.*

1. Not all Native Americans believed in resisting with violence.
2. The Navajos, for example, chose not to fight the American settlers.
3. Peacefully raising sheep in the American Southwest, the Navajos did not believe in war.
4. When American soldiers rounded up the Navajo people, most of their leaders did not seriously consider fighting the troops.
5. Destroying crops and canyon homes, however, the soldiers terrorized the Navajos.
6. The soldiers thus made it impossible for the Navajos to return to their homes.
7. A tragic chapter in history continued when the Navajos, forced by the soldiers, endured a 300-mile march to Fort Sumner.
8. Exhausted from the long journey and uprooted from their homeland, many Navajos did not survive.
9. To make the Long Walk required more strength than some of the young and old people had.
10. Others found adjusting to new lands and a new culture impossible.

C. Rewrite each sentence to eliminate the misplaced or dangling modifier.

1. Rushing westward in the mid-1800's, Indian lands were crossed on the route to California.
2. To seek instant fortune, many hardships were endured and untold dangers were faced.
3. Eastern farmers joined the thousands of "forty-niners" seeking gold along the Oregon Trail.
4. In wagons called "prairie schooners," historians estimate that more than 80,000 people headed west to California.
5. Squalid living conditions and lawlessness prevailed as fortunes in gold were mined in the hastily built towns.

CLAUSES

A clause is a group of words that contains a subject and a verb.

A clause always has a subject and a verb; a phrase never does. Remembering this will help you differentiate between phrases and clauses.

In this section, you will study and use two kinds of clauses: **independent clauses** and **subordinate clauses**.

Independent Clauses

An independent clause can stand alone as a sentence.

There are two independent clauses in the following sentence. The subject of each clause is underlined once; the verb is underlined twice.

> A young West German <u>pilot</u> <u>landed</u> his plane in Moscow's Red Square, and the <u>police</u> <u>arrested</u> him immediately.

Each clause in the sentence above can stand alone as a sentence because each clause has a subject and a predicate and expresses a complete thought. The conjunction *and* is used to join the two clauses. Notice that independent clauses can be written as sentences.

> A young West German <u>pilot</u> <u>landed</u> his plane in Moscow's Red Square.
> The <u>police</u> <u>arrested</u> him immediately.

Subordinate Clauses

A subordinate clause cannot stand alone as a sentence.

The following subordinate clause has a subject and a verb. However, since it does not express a complete thought, it cannot stand alone as a sentence.

> After Nansen and his partner had survived the Arctic winter in a hand-built stone hut . . . (What happened then?)

To use the subordinate clause in a sentence, add an independent clause to complete the thought.

> After Nansen and his partner had survived the Arctic winter in a hand-built stone hut, *they were rescued by a party of British explorers.*

Practice Your Skills

CONCEPT CHECK

Types of Clauses Identify each italicized word group in the following sentences. Write *P* for each phrase, *I* for each independent clause, and *S* for each subordinate clause.

1. Many writers of great literature have had *to overcome physical or psychological adversity.*
2. The poet John Keats wrote some of his best-known works while suffering from tuberculosis, *a common disease of his era.*

Writing
─TIP─

To avoid faulty subordination, place important ideas in independent clauses and lesser ideas in subordinate clauses.

Writing Theme
Overcoming Adversity

3. The epileptic seizures of the Russian novelist Feodor Dostoevski were so severe that it took him days to recover; for much of his career *he was also overwhelmed with debts.*

4. *At various stages in her career,* Virginia Woolf experienced bouts of mental illness that prevented her from writing.

5. *John Milton wrote his most famous poem* after he had completely lost his sight.

6. The novelist Richard Wright overcame a childhood of hunger and prejudice, *and he became a powerful writer.*

7. Flannery O'Connor continued *writing short stories,* though she had an incurable disease which eventually took her life.

8. O. Henry, *who became a master of the short story,* continued his writing career while in prison.

9. While *working as a hotel busboy,* Langston Hughes showed Vachel Lindsay his poems; soon a book of Hughes's poems was published.

10. The power *of Elie Wiesel's novels* can be traced to his childhood experience in concentration camps.

11. *After his father was imprisoned for debt,* the twelve-year-old Charles Dickens went to work in a factory.

12. *As a child Alice Walker was blinded in one eye;* writing fiction helped her escape from the taunts of her classmates.

13. *How the young orphan Jerzy Kosinski survived in war-torn Europe* be-came the subject for his highly praised novel.

14. *Katherine Mansfield spent her last years as an invalid,* yet during that time she wrote some of her best stories.

15. The Argentine writer Jorge Luis Borges wrote many of his finest short stories *after he became totally blind.*

The three kinds of subordinate clauses are **adjective clauses, adverb clauses,** and **noun clauses.**

Adjective Clauses

A subordinate clause that is used to modify a noun or a pronoun is called an **adjective clause.**

Like an adjective, an adjective clause answers the questions *Which one?* or *What kind?* Usually the adjective clause follows the noun or pronoun it modifies.

> The man *who examined the mummy* was Myron Marx, a hospital radiologist. (Which man?)
>
> Marx X-rayed the mummy of Ta-bes, a woman *who lived in Egypt 3,000 years ago.* (What kind of woman?)

Words That Introduce Adjective Clauses Many adjective clauses begin with **relative pronouns** such as *who, whom, whose, that,* and *which.* The relative pronoun relates the adjective clause to the noun or pronoun it modifies. The modified noun or pronoun is the antecedent of the relative pronoun. An adjective clause that begins with a relative pronoun is sometimes referred to as a **relative clause.**

In an adjective clause, the relative pronoun may function as the subject, the direct object, the object of a preposition, or a modifier.

Subject	Rosa Bonheur was the French artist *who created those wonderful paintings of horses.* (*Artist* is the antecedent of *who. Who* is the subject of the verb *created.*)
Direct Object	Her father, *whom she greatly respected,* taught her the basics of painting. (*Father* is the antecedent of *whom. Whom* is the direct object of the verb *respected.*)
Object of a Preposition	The painting *for which Rosa Bonheur is most admired* is called *The Horse Fair.* (Painting is the antecedent of *which. Which* is the object of the preposition *for.*)
Modifier	She also painted a portrait of Buffalo Bill, *whose Wild West Circus toured Europe in the 1800's.* (*Whose* modifies the noun *Wild West Circus.*)

Some adjective clauses begin with relative adverbs such as *after, before, since, when, where,* and *why.* Like a relative pronoun, a **relative adverb** relates the adjective clause to the word it modifies. The relative adverb also modifies the verb in the clause.

> The house *where President John F. Kennedy was born* is in Brookline, Massachusetts. (*Where* relates the clause to the noun *house* and modifies the verb *was born.*)

In some cases, the relative pronoun or adverb can be omitted from the sentence.

> Paris is a city *I want to see someday.* (*That* has been omitted from the clause.)

Essential and Nonessential Clauses An adjective clause can be essential or nonessential. An **essential adjective clause** must be included to make the intended meaning of a sentence complete. Do not set off essential clauses with commas.

> Fish *that swim in the waters of totally dark caves* have no eyes. (Without the clause, the intended meaning would be incomplete.)

A **nonessential adjective clause** is one that adds additional information to a sentence whose basic meaning is already complete. One or two commas are needed to set off nonessential clauses from the rest of the sentence.

> The tour guide on the African camera safari spoke Swahili, *which we do not understand.*

Sentence Diagraming For information on diagraming adjective clauses, see page 840.

Practice Your Skills

A. CONCEPT CHECK

Adjective Clauses Write each adjective clause and identify the introductory word as a *Relative Pronoun* or a *Relative Adverb*. If the introductory word is omitted, write *Omitted.* Last, write the word in the independent clause that is modified by the adjective clause.

1. Belladonna, which is also known as "poison cherry" and "deadly nightshade," is a poisonous herb.
2. According to Greek myth, it was Hecate who first cultivated deadly nightshade.

Writing
TIP

In formal speech and writing, use *that* to introduce essential adjective clauses and *which* to introduce nonessential clauses. (The antecedent of *which* can never be a person.)

Writing Theme
Exotic Plants

3. Hecate, who was a goddess, kept the plant in a garden.
4. The garden where the plant grew was guarded by demons and could not be entered by mortals.
5. *Belladonna,* which is a compound of two Italian words meaning "beautiful woman," is the plant's scientific name.
6. At one time, having large eyes was a popular "look" Italian women tried to achieve.
7. Women treated their eyes with belladonna drops, which caused the pupils to dilate.
8. Eyes into which the drops were placed appeared larger and therefore more beautiful.
9. However, this was an age before the dangers of belladonna were widely recognized.
10. Now belladonna is recognized as a plant that can bring on madness or even death.

B. REVISION SKILL

Sentence Combining   Combine each of the following sentence pairs into one sentence that contains an adjective clause. When using relative pronouns, remember to use *that* for essential clauses and *which* for nonessential clauses. Punctuate all clauses correctly.

Example   There are some very unusual plants. These plants are meat-eaters.

There are some very unusual plants that are meat-eaters.

1. Sundews, bladderworts, and Venus' flytraps are meat-eaters. They trap insects.
2. A sundew has many little hairs on its leaves. The hairs are sweet and sticky.
3. Any insect will get stuck. The insect stands on the sticky leaf.
4. Another meat-eater, the bladderwort, fascinates botanists. These botanists study its little hollow holes, or bladders.
5. Each bladder has a kind of trap door. This trap door is surrounded by tiny hairs.
6. The trap door opens and the bladder sucks in the prey. The door is very sensitive to the touch of passing insects or fish.
7. A third carnivorous plant is the Venus' flytrap. The Venus' flytrap is familiar to most people.
8. The flytrap's leaves encircle the prey. The leaves lock together.
9. The insect is then trapped in a place within the plant. In that place it is slowly digested.
10. Stories have been told about people being eaten by huge meat-eating plants. These stories have no basis in fact.

Adverb Clauses

An adverb clause is a subordinate clause that is used as an adverb to modify a verb, an adjective, or an adverb.

Verb	Kareem carries his calculator *wherever he goes.*
Adjective	Marian's cold got worse *after she walked in the rain.*
Adverb	Can any animal run faster *than a gazelle can?*

An adverb clause can also modify a verbal.

Infinitive	The team members vowed *to practice* harder *as soon as exams were over.*
Participle	*Proud* of herself *after she won,* Janet smiled.
Gerund	*Arguing* with Peter *because he refused to work* accomplished nothing.

Words That Introduce Adverb Clauses Most adverb clauses begin with a **subordinating conjunction** that relates the clause to the word it modifies and establishes a specific relationship between them.

Time	as, as soon as, after, before, since, until, when, whenever, while
Cause	because, since
Comparison	as, as much as, than
Condition	if, although, as long as, though, unless, provided that
Purpose	so that, in order that
Manner	as, as if, as though
Place	where, wherever

Adverb clauses answer these questions: *Where? When? How? Why? To what extent?* and *Under what circumstances?*

Follow your dreams *wherever they take you.* (Follow *where?*)

When you visit Tokyo, shop along the Ginza. (Shop *when?*)

Since she has a bad cold, the mayor postponed her meeting. (Postponed *why?*)

The agitated lion acted *as if it might attack.* (Acted *how?*)

Myra plays the guitar much better *than most professionals do.* (Better *to what extent?*)

If the snow continues, all flights will be canceled. (Will be canceled *under what circumstances?*)

Writing
—TIP—
Use a comma after an adverb clause that begins a sentence.

Elliptical Clauses When there is no possibility that readers and listeners will misunderstand the meaning, one or more words may be left out of an adverb clause. A clause from which a word or words have been omitted is called an **elliptical clause.**

> When competing in a chess tournament, the champion was totally absorbed. (The words *she was* have been dropped: When *she was* competing in a chess tournament. . . .)

> She usually wins because she can concentrate on the game far more intently than her opponents. (The word *can* has been omitted: . . . than her opponents *can.*)

Sentence Diagraming For information on diagraming adverb clauses, see page 840.

Practice Your Skills

A. CONCEPT CHECK

Adverb Clauses Write the adverb clause in each sentence, and underline the subordinating conjunction. Then write the word, or words, modified by the clause. If the clause is elliptical, write *E*.

1. When Pearl Buck's novel *The Good Earth* was published in 1931, no one suspected that it would gain worldwide popularity.
2. If Buck had not grown up in China, she might not have written so movingly about the poor Chinese peasant named Wang.
3. Because Buck's parents were Presbyterian missionaries, the family lived in a Chinese community.
4. Though Buck was an American, Chinese was the first language she learned.
5. She returned to the United States to attend college when she was seventeen years old.
6. After she had graduated from college, she went back to China to teach.
7. While she lived in a small village with her missionary husband, she formed the ideas and impressions she would later use in *The Good Earth*.
8. *The Good Earth* has been translated into more than fifty languages so that people the world over can enjoy the story of Wang and his life.
9. None of Pearl Buck's later works became as popular as *The Good Earth*.
10. Before she died, Buck earned the distinction of being the first American woman to win the Nobel Prize for literature.

B. DRAFTING SKILL

Sentence Expansion   Expand each sentence by adding an adverb clause. Begin each clause with a subordinating conjunction that expresses the relationship indicated in parentheses. Do not always place the adverb clause at the beginning of the sentence.

1. Remember that good books can vicariously transport you. (place)
2. Try a good mystery or adventure novel. (condition)
3. Don't sneak a look at the ending. (time)
4. Some readers enjoy competing with a fictional detective to solve a crime. (cause)
5. Perhaps science fiction suits your tastes better. (cause)

Noun Clauses

A noun clause is a subordinate clause that is used as a noun in a sentence.

A noun clause can perform all the functions of a noun: subject, direct or indirect object, predicate nominative, object of a preposition.

Subject	*What the committee suggested* was an outdoor beautification project.
Direct Object	Scientists may have determined *where Noah's Ark landed.*
Indirect Object	The teacher gave *whoever had been absent from class* a review of the lesson.
Predicate Nominative	An unsolved mystery is *where Atlantis was located.*
Object of a Preposition	The reporter offered scanty proof for *what he claimed in his article.*

Phrases and Clauses   **613**

Noun clauses also function as direct objects of verbals.

> Spanish explorers of the Americas tried unsuccessfully to discover *where the fabled El Dorado was.* (The noun clause is the direct object of the infinitive *to discover.*)

> Hearing *what the second baseman called him,* the umpire threw the player out of the game. (The noun clause is the direct object of the participle *hearing.*)

Words That Introduce Noun Clauses   A pronoun or a subordinating conjunction can introduce a noun clause.

Pronouns	who, whom, whose, which, that, whoever, whomever, what, whatever
Subordinating Conjunctions	how, that, when, where, whether, why (More subordinating conjunctions are on pages 562–564.)

Some words that introduce noun clauses may also introduce adjective and adverb clauses. To avoid confusing one type of clause with another, consider the context and determine how the clause functions within the sentence.

> April 4, 1968, was *when Martin Luther King, Jr., was assassinated.* (functions as a noun—a predicate nominative.)

> It is the anniversary of the day *when Martin Luther King, Jr., was assassinated.* (functions as an adjective modifying *day*)

> The whole nation grieved *when Martin Luther King, Jr., was assassinated.* (functions as an adverb modifying *grieved*)

The introductory pronoun in a noun clause can act as a subject or an object within the clause.

> *What is needed in the world* is a little more love and laughter. (*What* is the subject of the verb *is needed* in the clause.)

> *What the world needs* is a little more love and laughter. (*What* is the direct object of the verb *needs* in the clause.)

Usage Note   At times, the introductory word *that* may be omitted from a noun clause.

> Did you know *the numeral representing a trillion has twelve zeros?* (*That* has been omitted at the beginning of the clause.)

Sentence Diagraming   For information on diagraming noun clauses, see page 840.

Writing
—TIP—

When a noun clause follows verbs such as *see, feel, think,* and *say,* it is often necessary to retain the word *that* for clarity.

Practice Your Skills

A. CONCEPT CHECK

Noun Clauses Write whether each italicized noun clause is used as a *Subject, Indirect Object, Direct Object, Object of a Preposition,* or *Predicate Nominative.*

Writing Theme
Stories of Love
and Grief

1. The Taj Mahal is *what many people describe as the most beautiful tomb in the world.*
2. The Indian ruler Shah Jahan knew *that he wanted a spectacular monument to his favorite wife and constant companion.*
3. *That Mumtaz Mahal (Chosen One of the Palace) had died in childbirth* brought great sorrow to the Shah.
4. Agra, in northern India, is *where the Taj Mahal is located.*
5. The Taj Mahal affords *whoever sees it* great pleasure and delight.
6. Part of *what makes this great tomb so astoundingly beautiful* is the intricate carving and inlaid precious stones.
7. It is staggering to think of *how many workers were needed to complete the building.*
8. *That the whole complex of buildings took twenty-two years to complete and cost 40 million rupees* is well known.
9. Visitors can see *that the tomb is built of pure white marble.*
10. To preserve this impressive complex, Indian authorities spend *whatever it takes to keep the Taj Mahal in perfect condition.*

B. DRAFTING SKILL

Sentence Combining Combine each of the following sentence sets. Form one sentence with a noun clause that has the introductory word and function indicated in parentheses.

Example Love, murder, or deception are story elements. These can make a story intriguing. (*what,* subject)
What can make a story intriguing is love, murder, or deception.

1. Something fooled Sampson. It was Delilah's deceptive charm. (*what,* subject)
2. Everybody knows about Romeo and Juliet. They were caught in a web of tragic misunderstanding. (*that,* direct object)
3. Cleopatra brought about the downfall of Mark Antony. Several ancient Roman authors tell this story. (*how,* direct object)
4. An event caused the ruin of Eleanor of Aquitaine. It was the betrayal of her husband, King Henry II. (*what,* predicate nominative)
5. Lady Macbeth became a victim. She became a victim of the things guilt can do. (*what,* object of a preposition)

You already know that sentences are classified according to purpose and may be declarative, interrogative, imperative, or exclamatory. In this part of the chapter, you will learn that sentences are also classified according to structure, that is, by the number and kinds of clauses they have. There are four kinds of sentences included in this classification: **simple, compound, complex,** and **compound-complex.**

Simple Sentences

A simple sentence has one independent clause but no subordinate clauses.

The trains made ninety-seven stops.

A simple sentence contains no subordinate clauses, but it may contain a number of phrases.

Carrying passengers and freight, *the trains* of the Trans-Siberian Railway *made ninety-seven stops* at large and small stations on their trips across the vast expanses of Asian Russia.

Some simple sentences have compound parts.

Turkey and pumpkin pie may not have been part of the original Thanksgiving feast. (compound subject)

Compound Sentences

A compound sentence has two or more independent clauses that are joined together.

The independent clauses in a compound sentence may be connected (1) by a comma and a coordinating conjunction such as *and, but, or, nor, for, so,* or *yet;* (2) by a semicolon; or (3) by a semicolon and a conjunctive adverb followed by a comma.

The people of ancient times built the Seven Wonders of the World, *but* only the Great Pyramid of Khufu still stands.

Sonja Henie won three Olympic figure-skating championships; this led to her being given starring roles in Hollywood films.

Mary Martin played Nellie Forbush in the Broadway version of *South Pacific; however,* she did not play this role in the film version.

Sentence Diagraming For information on diagraming simple and compound sentences, see pages 834 and 841.

Practice Your Skills

A. CONCEPT CHECK

Sentences Write *Simple* or *Compound* to describe each sentence. Also tell if a sentence has a *Compound Subject, Compound Predicate, Compound Direct Object,* or *Compound Predicate Nominative.*

Writing Theme
Mexico

1. Both the original Indian culture of the Aztecs and the Spanish culture from Europe influenced the Mexico of today.
2. In fact, the past seems to be present everywhere in Mexico, and the present seems to be deeply rooted in the past.
3. In Mexico today, the three main groups of people are those with Spanish ancestry, those with Indian ancestry, and those with mixed Spanish and Indian ancestry.
4. The majority of Mexicans are mestizos (of mixed ancestry), but some follow an Indian way of life and are considered Indians.
5. Most Indians live in isolated groups in remote areas; therefore, their traditional ways of life define them.
6. For example, many Indians wear traditional clothing, follow the customs of their ancestors, and worship ancient gods.
7. The people of Spanish descent are the smallest and wealthiest group; the mestizos comprise the middle class.
8. Skilled workers, government workers, and businesspeople make up the middle class.
9. Mexico is a large country and a rapidly growing one, and it benefits from its basically homogeneous population.
10. Most Mexicans share their common Indian-Spanish heritage, their religious beliefs, and their language.

Sentence Combining   Compound sentences and sentence parts can be used to express ideas efficiently. Rewrite each of the following sentence sets, combining each set to form a compound sentence or a sentence with compound parts.

1. Mexico is a modern, industrialized nation. It is also an ancient land.
2. Mexico City is the capital of Mexico. It is one of the largest urban centers in the world.
3. For years this city was the world's largest. Now Tokyo holds that position.
4. All the glories of modern Mexico can be seen in Mexico City. A great deal of rich local color can be seen in Mexico City.
5. You can also see all the overwhelming problems of rapid population growth. All the problems of poverty are also evident.
6. Mexican citizens have been drawn to the city in increasing numbers for years. Now the city has become the industrial center of the nation.
7. More than 50 percent of Mexico's industry is located in Mexico City. Almost all of Mexico's leading banks and businesses are located there.
8. Some people live in great comfort. Others have inadequate housing, housing without plumbing, or no housing at all.
9. Wealthy neighborhoods can be found in Mexico City. Slums can also be found in this city of fourteen million people.
10. For the tourist, Mexico City offers picturesque plazas. It also offers open market places. The extraordinary cultural attractions make it a magnet for tourism.

Complex Sentences

A complex sentence has one independent clause and one or more subordinate clauses.

> The passengers grumbled *when the airline announced the third postponement of their flight.*

In a complex sentence, a subordinate clause functions as a *noun* or a *modifier*. As a modifier, it modifies a word in the independent clause.

> W. C. Fields was the film comedian *who wore a tall top hat and had a large red nose.* (The clause modifies the noun *comedian*.)

When Whoopi Goldberg participated in the television program "Comic Relief", she donated her talents to raise funds for the homeless. (The clause modifies the verb *donated.*)

If the subordinate clause functions as a noun in a complex sentence, it can be the subject, object, or complement in the independent clause.

Subject	*What we saw on our whirlwind vacation* is just a blur in my memory.
Direct Object	We photographed *whatever looked important or interesting.*
Predicate Nominative	Scuba diving was *what we wanted to try first.*
Object of a Preposition	I will tell you about *where we were* if I can remember.

In each of the preceding examples, the subordinate clause is a part of the independent clause; the two cannot be separated. Each sentence has one independent clause and at least one subordinate clause. Therefore, all the sentences are complex.

Sentence Diagraming For information on diagraming complex sentences, see page 841.

Complex yet simple, the humor of W. C. Fields and Whoopi Goldberg delights movie audiences.

Writing Theme
Life in the
Middle Ages

Practice Your Skills

CONCEPT CHECK

Types of Sentences   Identify each sentence as *Simple, Compound,* or *Complex.* If it is complex, write the subordinate clause or clauses.

1. In the great hall of a French castle, servants light torches signaling that the evening meal is about to begin.
2. A long board has been laid on a series of trestles and covered with cloths.
3. On one side, the cloth goes all the way to the floor so that the dogs can't crawl under the table in search of scraps.
4. The year is 1200, and neither permanent tables nor individual chairs are common yet.
5. On a side table sits a bronze container called an *aquamanile,* which means it is used for washing hands.
6. Hands are publicly washed so that everyone knows fingers are clean when they are dipped into serving bowls.
7. There are no utensils, bowls, or napkins to greet diners.
8. Instead of plates, diners are handed trenchers, thick slices of bread.

9. The guests help themselves with bare hands to the many platters, and they put the food on their trenchers.
10. An occasional carved or cast spoon may be used for serving, but the fork isn't yet known in Western Europe.

Compound-Complex Sentences

A compound-complex sentence has two or more independent clauses and one or more subordinate clauses.

Independent clauses are joined (1) by a coordinating conjunction preceded by a comma, (2) by a conjunctive adverb preceded by a semicolon and followed by a comma, or (3) by a semicolon alone.

Subordinate clauses either modify a word in one of the independent clauses or act as a noun in one of the independent clauses.

Each of the following compound-complex sentences has two independent clauses. The second independent clause in each sentence has one subordinate clause, which is italicized.

> The crew from the United States entered the sailing race off the coast of Perth, Australia, and they won the cup *that the Australian crew coveted so much.*
>
> Perth is normally a quiet place; however, it became a beehive of frenzied activity *while the America's Cup race was in progress.*

The following compound-complex sentence has two independent clauses, each of which contains a subordinate clause.

> Holmes asked Watson what clues suggested a solution to the mystery, but he smiled condescendingly when his doctor companion nervously hazarded a guess.

Independent Clause 1	Holmes asked Watson what clues suggested a solution to the mystery
Independent Clause 2	he smiled condescendingly when his doctor companion nervously hazarded a guess
Subordinate Clause 1	what clues suggested a solution to the mystery (a noun clause that functions as the direct object of independent clause 1)
Subordinate Clause 2	when his doctor companion nervously hazarded a guess (an adverb clause that modifies the verb *smiled* in independent clause 2)

Sentence Diagraming For information on the diagraming of compound-complex sentences, see page 841.

Practice Your Skills

CONCEPT CHECK

Kinds of Sentences Identify each of the following sentences as *Simple, Compound, Complex,* or *Compound-Complex.* Write each subordinate clause and indicate its function as *Noun* or *Modifier.*

(1) No one could remember when the tribe had begun its long journey. (2) The land of great rolling plains that had been its first home was now no more than a half-forgotten dream. (3) For many years, Shann and his people had been fleeing through a country of low hills and sparkling lakes, and now the mountains lay ahead. (4) This summer they must cross them to the southern lands. (5) There was little time to lose. (6) The white terror that had come down from the Poles, grinding continents to dust and freezing the very air before it, was less than a day's march behind. (7) Shann wondered if the glaciers could climb the mountains ahead, and within his heart he dared to kindle a little flame of hope. (8) This might prove a barrier . . . which even the remorseless ice would batter in vain. (9) In the southern lands of which the legends spoke, his people might find refuge at last.

Arthur C. Clarke, "History Lesson"

AVOIDING PHRASE AND CLAUSE FRAGMENTS

A **sentence** is a group of words that contains a subject and a predicate and that expresses a complete thought. Keep this definition in mind to avoid mistaking fragments for complete sentences.

Phrases as Fragments

Prepositional phrases, appositive phrases, and verbal phrases are sometimes used incorrectly as sentences; however, they are fragments because they have no subjects or verbs.

Fragment *After their appearance on the Ed Sullivan Show in the United States* (a series of prepositional phrases)

Sentence *The Beatles became world-famous* after their appearance on the *Ed Sullivan Show* in the United States. (An independent clause has been added.)

Fragment	*Madame Tussaud's, a wax museum located in London* (appositive phrase)
Sentence	Madame Tussaud's, a wax museum located in London, *features a Chamber of Horrors.*
Fragment	*Still standing on the north bank of the Thames River* (participial phrase)
Sentences	*The Tower of London,* still standing on the north bank of the Thames River, *is a reminder of England's past.* (The phrase is used as a modifier in a sentence.)
	The Tower of London is still standing on the north bank of the Thames River. (The participle in the phrase is used as part of the main verb in a verb phrase.)

Practice Your Skills

A. CONCEPT CHECK

Types of Fragments   Each example below contains a sentence and a fragment. Write a new sentence, joining the two parts. Then tell what kind of phrase the fragment has become in the new sentence: *Prepositional, Participial, Gerund,* or *Infinitive.*

1. Armadillos are small burrowing animals. With armored coats of overlapping plates and scales.
2. *Armadillo* is a word in the Spanish language. Meaning "little armored one."
3. Having a strong suit of armor. The armor protects the armadillo from its enemies.
4. Unlike the protective shell of the turtle. The armadillo's "armor" is flexible and moves with its body.
5. Armadillos also have powerful claws. To dig their way into their burrows.
6. When an armadillo senses danger, it will dig quickly. Into the ground and out of sight.
7. Rolling itself up into a ball. This is another technique necessary for protection.
8. Hoping its armor alone will protect it. An armadillo might simply crouch on the ground.
9. It takes an animal with extremely strong teeth or claws. To penetrate the tough scales and plates of an armadillo's hide.
10. To fight off an attacker. An armadillo will also use its claws as a last resort.

B. DRAFTING SKILL

Correcting Fragments Expand each fragment by adding details to make a complete sentence. Add any needed punctuation.

1. A defense mechanism called "protective coloration"
2. To hide from predators by blending with the surroundings
3. On land and in the water all over the world
4. For example, the chameleon's ability to change color
5. The walking stick, an insect resembling a twig
6. Spotted like the bottom of a stream bed
7. With the coloration of coral reefs
8. Changing from brown fur to white fur in winter
9. Unnoticed against the white of the Arctic winter
10. To blend with the tall grasses of the African plain

Subordinate Clauses as Fragments

A subordinate clause can be mistaken for a sentence because the clause has a subject and a verb. The introductory word in a subordinate clause, however, makes the clause a fragment.

Sentence	The Star of Africa and Cullinan II are diamonds of enormous value.
Subordinate Clause	Because the Star of Africa and Cullinan II are diamonds of enormous value.

A capitalized word at the beginning of a subordinate clause and an end mark after it do not make the clause a sentence. The clause is always a fragment until it is combined with an independent clause.

Fragment	Before the diamond cutter began to divide the huge stone. She examined it from various angles.
Sentence	Before the diamond cutter began to divide the huge stone, she examined it from various angles.

The fragment above was combined with a related independent clause in order to make it a sentence. A subordinate-clause fragment can also be corrected by rewriting the clause as a sentence.

The diamond cutter divided the large stone into six pieces. All of which would be polished and set in a new tiara for the princess.

The diamond cutter divided the large stone into six pieces. All of them would be polished and set in a new tiara for the princess.

Practice Your Skills

CONCEPT CHECK

Correcting Clause Fragments Rewrite the fragments in the paragraph below as complete sentences. In some cases the fragment may be combined with the word group that precedes it. If a sentence is correct, write *Correct*.

(1) Orienteering is a sport. (2) That the entire family can enjoy. (3) Although it resembles cross-country running. (4) Orienteering involves finding one's way through an unknown area to a pre-selected place by using a map and a compass. (5) Long before the contestants gather their equipment. (6) The course planner has marked control points along the route. (7) Teams and individual competitors must proceed along the course to these marked points. (8) Where they have a score card punched. (9) A winner's prize is awarded. (10) To whoever has the fastest time. (11) Because participants will be navigating around obstacles. (12) They must plan a strategy. (13) One big help is the topographical map. (14) Which shows the lay of the land, including features such as stone walls, buildings, and streams. (15) The contestant must get oriented to the landmarks and find a path. (16) It should be the fastest route to the next control point. (17) Because courses vary in difficulty. (18) An event may last from one to three hours. (19) Although most participants proceed on foot. (20) Some adventurers orienteer on skis, in canoes, in wheelchairs, and even on horseback.

C H E C K P O I N T
PAGES 605–623

A. Write each subordinate clause in the following sentences. Tell whether the clause functions as a *Noun,* an *Adjective,* or an *Adverb.*

1. In the United States, cars are necessary for people who need to get around.
2. However, bicycles are the main transportation in Beijing, which has a population of over five and a half million.
3. Wherever they need to go, the Chinese rely on their bicycles.
4. What is hard to obtain is a bicycle coupon.
5. One factory worker complained that three years passed before she could get her bicycle coupon.
6. Whoever does not want to be fined must obtain a license as well as a license plate.

7. Accidents happen frequently, although police officers and volunteer traffic wardens are everywhere.
8. Whenever riders do not obey the regulations, the police are required to issue fines.
9. Giving someone a ride and not obeying the lights are what police officers watch for.
10. Also, bicycle owners must have government-specified equipment, which includes a bell, brakes, and a lock.

B. Write *Simple, Compound, Complex,* or *Compound-Complex* to identify each of the following sentences. Then label each italicized group of words as an *Adjective Clause, Adverb Clause, Noun Clause,* or *Phrase.*

1. The first emperor *of China* was an extraordinary man.
2. He is credited with many great reforms *that changed his empire.*
3. *That he unified the system of writing* is in itself an enormous accomplishment.
4. *To foster better communication and trade,* he also standardized the currency system and the system of weights and measures.
5. *In an age of travel by wagon,* his legislation of a uniform length for wheel axles advanced transportation.
6. *Obsessed with immortality,* he drank potions *to prolong his life,* and he had an enormous mausoleum built for himself.
7. The potions, *which contained mercury,* are probably *what killed him.*
8. Excavation *of his tomb* has been ongoing *in China for years.*
9. An entire army of six-foot-tall terracotta figures and three-foot-tall bronze figures has been found *surrounding the perimeter of the burial area.*
10. Each of these figures was meticulously cast, carefully painted, and equipped with weapons *to protect the entombed emperor in the afterlife.*
11. The wooden weapons have crumbled, but styles of clothing and hairdos are details *that have endured over the centuries.*
12. *What this tomb will yet reveal about life in early China* cannot be guessed.
13. *After a farmer found a terracotta figure on his land,* the site was established, and archaeological research began.
14. The site is so large *that it is housed in an airplane hangar,* and only a small part has been excavated so far.
15. *Since the excavation began,* thousands of tourists have visited the site *where the buried emperor rests amid the glories of his empire.*

Writing Theme
Money

A. Identifying Phrases Write *Prepositional, Participial, Gerund,* or *Infinitive* to identify each italicized phrase in the following sentences. Identify the function as *Noun, Adjective,* or *Adverb.*

1. *Counterfeiting money* is not a new practice.
2. Since about the fourth century B.C., counterfeiters have worked hard *to distribute fake money.*
3. *To demonstrate the seriousness of the crime,* the Chinese cut off the hands of counterfeiters.
4. The Romans took a different approach by *offering handsome rewards* to reporters of the crime.
5. If a Roman reported a counterfeiter, his taxes were waived for life *as a reward.*
6. A slave was rewarded *with freedom* for such a report.
7. On the other hand, the jailer paid with his own life if a counterfeiter was allowed *to escape.*
8. In England during the early 1800's, counterfeiters *hanging from the gallows* were a common sight.
9. The English felt that this was the most certain way *to send a message* about the seriousness of the crime.
10. In contrast, *abolishing the death penalty for counterfeiting* became a focus of crusaders who didn't view it as harshly.

B. Placing Modifiers Correctly Identify each modifier error as *Misplaced* or *Dangling.* Then rewrite the sentence, correcting the error.

1. To prohibit the printing of paper money in the American colonies, strict regulations were imposed on the colonists.
2. Defying the British, the money was still printed even though it was not backed by gold or securities.
3. In 1787 the United States minted the first coin that bore the country's name, the Fugio cent.
4. Having engraved the coin with the motto "Mind Your Business," a clear message of independence was sent.
5. Now engraved with the motto "In God We Trust," the U.S. Treasury mints all paper money and coins.

C. Recognizing Clauses Identify each group of italicized words as an *Independent Clause* or a *Subordinate Clause.* Then show how each subordinate clause functions by writing *Adjective, Adverb,* or *Noun.*

1. Before the Revolutionary War, *the most popular currency in the United States was the Spanish dollar.*
2. This silver dollar, *which was stamped with a large 8,* was known as a "piece of eight."

3. *The silver dollar was worth eight Spanish coins,* which were called "reals."
4. Eventually these pieces of eight were cut *so that coins of smaller denomination could be used.*
5. *The results were halves and quarters* called "bits."
6. Today, *"two bits" is an Americanism for a quarter.*
7. These bits also produced the colloquial expression "two bit," *which means cheap or inferior.*
8. *How Great Britain got the halfpenny* is not hard to guess.
9. A halfpenny was one piece of a penny *that had been cut in half.*
10. *When a penny was quartered,* it became a farthing.

D. Identifying Sentence Types Identify each sentence as *Simple, Compound, Complex,* or *Compound-Complex.*

1. One of the oldest forms of money is shells.
2. The most valuable shell is the cowry, and the rare white-toothed variety is the most valuable of all.
3. Historians know that Native Americans used shells called "wampum" as currency.
4. Bread was used as currency in ancient Egypt, and pictures of bakeries served as symbols of wealth in the occupant's tomb.
5. The Romans used salt as a form of money, and the word *salary* comes from *salarium,* which is the Latin word for "payments of salt" to the soldiers of Julius Caesar.
6. Because pepper was a highly valued spice during the Middle Ages, in some towns it could be used to pay taxes.
7. At one time, dried codfish served as money in Newfoundland, and sugar served as money in the West Indies.
8. Even tobacco, the mainstay of the economy of the southern colonies, was used as currency for a short time in Virginia.
9. In Iran, people use money, or they negotiate with fine carpets, which can be used as collateral.
10. In Australia, some groups still use bird feathers as currency!

E. Identifying Fragments Label each of the following groups of words *Phrase Fragment, Clause Fragment,* or *Complete Sentence.* Then expand each fragment into a complete sentence.

1. To destroy all damaged or old currency.
2. Seven denominations of U.S. paper money are in use today.
3. That no living person be portrayed on a denomination of U.S. paper money.
4. On the front of the dollar bill.
5. Which bears the signature of the Secretary of the Treasury.

Directions One or more of the underlined sections in the following sentences may contain errors of grammar, usage, punctuation, spelling, or capitalization. Write the letters of each incorrect section. Then rewrite the item correctly. If there is no error in an item, write E.

Example Reduced to the lowest possilbe price, the sales clerk
                                     A   **B**

put the shoes on display. No error
C   **D**   **E**

Answer A—The sales clerk put the shoes, reduced to the lowest possible price, on display.

---

1. Ethnocentrism is the tendency to believe that one's own group or culture is supe-
                                      A   **B**
   rior to that of other people, this is one explanation that is often given for the fre-
                              C   **D**
   quency of war. No error
                    E

2. An amoeba does not die the way a multicellular organism does; it simply splits in
              A   **B**
   two and becomes two juvenile organisms. No error
       C   **D**   **E**

3. Is it true that storms are often preceded by periods of calm, or is that just another
   A   **B**   **C**
   bit of meteorological folklore. No error
                          D   **E**

4. Covering an area of over sixty-four million square miles. The pacific is by far the
   A   **B**
   largest ocean on the earth. No error
   C   **D**   **E**

5. In 1769 Nicholas Cugnot invented a three-wheeled motor car; which he promptly ran
              A   **B**   **C**
   into a stone wall. No error
   D   **E**

6. Isaac Newton formulator of much of classical physics became increasingly interested
   A   **B**
   in mysticism and Religion in his old age. No error
                    C   **D**   **E**

7. The defense <u>attornies</u> argued that the <u>prosecutor's</u> case was <u>ilogical</u> because the
         A   **B**   **C**

   defendant <u>could not have been</u> in two places at the same time. <u>No error</u>
             D   **E**

8. <u>At the beginning</u> of <u>most published plays</u> is the *dramatis personae.* A list of
       A   **B**   **C**

   <u>characters</u> <u>appearing in the play.</u> <u>No error</u>
     C   **D**   **E**

9. <u>Stewed to her complete satisfaction,</u> grandmother <u>removed</u> the <u>tomatoes</u> from the
                 A   **B**   **C**

   stove and poured them <u>into a casserole dish.</u> <u>No error</u>
                      D   **E**

10. The <u>tour</u> guide <u>pointed out</u> <u>the many small islands</u> to the tourists <u>out in the bay.</u>
        A   **B**   **C**   **D**

    <u>No error</u>
     E

11. The <u>British</u> royal family had the <u>German</u> surname <u>Hanover.</u> Until strong anti-
        A   **B**   **C**

    German feeling forced them to change it to <u>Windsor</u> during World War I.
                                           D

    <u>No error</u>
     E

12. <u>Looking directly up,</u> thousands <u>of stars</u> were spread <u>across the sky,</u> like so many
         A   **B**   **C**

    lights on a <u>Christmas</u> tree. <u>No error</u>
            D   **E**

13. Scientists <u>have bred</u> a strange animal called a <u>geep,</u> it is a combination <u>of a goat</u>
            A   **B**   **C**

    and <u>an</u> angora sheep. <u>No error</u>
      D   **E**

14. <u>What</u> gave <u>director</u> <u>Alfred Hitchcock</u> the <u>idea?</u> To make a brief <u>appearance in more</u>
      A   **B**   **C**   **D**

    <u>than thirty of his own spine-chilling movies?</u> <u>No error</u>
                D   **E**

15. <u>Trapped in a well for more than a day,</u> the <u>child</u> came <u>close</u> to dying
                A   **B**   **C**

    before <u>she was finally rescued.</u> <u>No error</u>
             D   **E**

16. The surface <u>of Venus</u> reaches temperatures of over <u>900° Fahrenheit;</u> <u>moreover the</u>
             A   **B**   **C**

    atmosphere is <u>a thick soup of toxic gases.</u> <u>No error</u>
               D   **E**

17. The <u>Van Allen belts</u> <u>are</u> belts of <u>Radiation</u> circling the <u>earth.</u> <u>No error</u>
           A   **B**   **C**   **D**   **E**

18. By the late nineteenth century enough track <u>had been laid in the United States</u> to
                                                 A

reach around the globe two <u>times moreover,</u> trains <u>were bringing</u> thousands of
                            B   **C**

settlers into the <u>midwest and west.</u> <u>No error</u>
             D   **E**

19. <u>Wow.</u> Did you know that a neutrino <u>can travel</u> right through the earth as though
    A   **B**

<u>it</u> were traveling through a thin cake of <u>butter.</u> <u>No error</u>
 C   **D**   **E**

20. The color pictures <u>that</u> <u>one sees</u> printed in books and magazines <u>are made up</u> of
                 A   **B**   **C**

tiny dots of <u>cyan, magenta, yellow, and black.</u> <u>No error</u>
            D   **E**

21. <u>Cross-country skiing</u> <u>is</u> wonderful <u>exercise and allows</u> the skier <u>to view the</u>
                A   **B**   **C**   **D**

<u>countryside</u> close-up. <u>No error</u>
   D   **E**

22. Nearby <u>lived</u> the three <u>talented,</u> intelligent Bronte <u>sisters</u>—Charlotte, <u>Emily and</u>
        A   **B**   **C**   **D**

Anne. <u>No error</u>
     E

23. The <u>Medici family</u> were patrons of the <u>arts for</u> two centuries they made <u>Florence</u> a
      A   **B**   **C**

<u>golden city</u> of intellectual and artistic life. <u>No error</u>
  D   **E**

24. Scientists prior to the <u>nineteenth century</u> were <u>altogether</u> wrong in their <u>belief</u> that
                  A   **B**   **C**

empty <u>Space</u> was filled with ether. <u>No error</u>
     D   **E**

25. As soon as the <u>World Bank</u> lent <u>Brazil</u> the money for the <u>road thousands</u> of set-
           A   **B**   **C**

tlers began to pour into the rain forest, <u>bringing disease and death to the native</u>
                                          D

<u>Indians.</u> <u>No error</u>
  D   **E**

Verb Usage

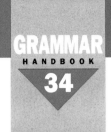
THE PRINCIPAL PARTS OF VERBS

A **verb** is a word that expresses an action, a condition, or a state of being. **Action verbs** describe physical or mental actions. **Linking verbs** do not describe actions; they link, or relate, the subject of a sentence with a word in the predicate that renames or modifies the subject. See Handbook 31, pages 552–554, for additional information about verbs.

Every verb has different forms. Speakers and writers construct these forms by using the four **principal parts** of the verb: the **present infinitive** (or **present**), the **present participle**, the **past**, and the **past participle**.

Present	Present Participle	Past	Past Participle
know	(is) knowing	knew	(have) known
steal	(is) stealing	stole	(have) stolen
jump	(is) jumping	jumped	(have) jumped
laugh	(is) laughing	laughed	(have) laughed

Note that forms of the auxiliary verbs *be* and *have* are given in parentheses before each present and past participle. Participles cannot be used alone as the main verb of a clause or sentence. They must always be used with auxiliary verbs.

The present participle of every verb is formed by adding the ending *-ing* to the present infinitive form. The past and the past participle, however, may be formed in a number of different ways. The ending of the past and the past participle of a verb determines whether a verb is classified as regular or irregular.

Regular Verbs

Most verbs in the English language are regular. The past and past participle of all regular verbs are formed by adding the ending *-d* or *-ed* to the present. However, the spelling of the present form of some regular verbs is changed before adding *-ing* or *-ed*. Study such spelling changes in the chart below.

Present	Present Participle	Past	Past Participle
smile	(is) smiling	smiled	(have) smiled
drop	(is) dropping	dropped	(have) dropped
carry	(is) carrying	carried	(have) carried
picnic	(is) picnicking	picnicked	(have) picnicked
cruise	(is) cruising	cruised	(have) cruised
hope	(is) hoping	hoped	(have) hoped

Practice Your Skills

DRAFTING SKILL

Verbs Make four columns, each headed with the name of a principal part, and write the principal parts of each verb below. Then use each verb in a sentence that relates to making a decision.

1. panic	2. tarry	3. debate	4. worry
5. plan	6. mimic	7. stir	8. vote

Irregular Verbs

The past and past participle forms of irregular verbs are not formed by adding *-d* or *-ed* to the present. The irregular forms of each of these verbs can be found in a dictionary entry for the present form of the verb. You may decide to memorize these forms, however, since irregular verbs occur frequently in reading and writing. Memorizing will be easier if you divide the verbs into the following five groups.

Group 1 The present, past, and past participles of the first group of irregular verbs have the same form.

Present	Present Participle	Past	Past Participle
burst	(is) bursting	burst	(have) burst
cost	(is) costing	cost	(have) cost
cut	(is) cutting	cut	(have) cut
hit	(is) hitting	hit	(have) hit
hurt	(is) hurting	hurt	(have) hurt
set	(is) setting	set	(have) set
shut	(is) shutting	shut	(have) shut

Group 2 The past and past participle of each verb in this group are spelled alike. Notice that *get* has a second past participle form, *gotten*. In American speech and writing, *gotten* is the preferred form.

Present	Present Participle	Past	Past Participle
bring	(is) bringing	brought	(have) brought
catch	(is) catching	caught	(have) caught
fight	(is) fighting	fought	(have) fought
flee	(is) fleeing	fled	(have) fled
fling	(is) flinging	flung	(have) flung
get	(is) getting	got	(have) got *or* gotten
lead	(is) leading	led	(have) led
lend	(is) lending	lent	(have) lent
lose	(is) losing	lost	(have) lost
say	(is) saying	said	(have) said
shine	(is) shining	shone	(have) shone
sit	(is) sitting	sat	(have) sat
sting	(is) stinging	stung	(have) stung
swing	(is) swinging	swung	(have) swung
teach	(is) teaching	taught	(have) taught

Practice Your Skills

A. CONCEPT CHECK

Verbs Write the past or past participle form of the verb indicated in parentheses.

Writing Theme
Overcoming
Handicaps

1. Louis Braille (bring) the gift of sight to many blind people.
2. At age three, a serious accident (cost) Louis his eyesight.
3. Later, while at the National Institute for the Blind in Paris, Louis learned of a dot code punched on cardboard that (lend) itself to use by the blind.
4. Captain Charles Barbier, a French military officer, had (teach) his soldiers to use such a dot code to send messages at night.
5. The idea (burst) on young Braille: the blind might be able to use a raised dot system to read by touch.
6. In 1829 Braille's own dot system (catch) the world's attention.
7. A light had suddenly (shine) in the darkness; the invention of braille provided hope for blind people everywhere.
8. Later in life, Braille adapted the code for musical notation; the sightless would no longer be (shut) out of the world of music.
9. Braille's inventiveness has since (lead) to the use of the dot system in mathematics, science, and computer technology.
10. Recently, medical science has (set) new standards in combating diseases of the eye.

11. Before, diabetics with retinopathy often (lose) their sight.
12. This disease often (hurt) the retina of the eye, and sometimes caused the retina to detach from the rest of the eye.
13. For many years doctors (fight) retinopathy with surgery.
14. Surgeons (cut) into the wall of the eye to reattach the retina.
15. By the early 1960's, the advent of the laser (bring) eye surgery to new levels of safety and success.

B. PROOFREADING SKILL

Verbs   Rewrite the following paragraphs, correcting errors in spelling, punctuation, capitalization, and verb forms.

Martine Kempf brang new mobility to many handicaped people with her creation of voice-activated computer technology in the early 1980's, at that time Kempf set up her Katalavox computer program on a home computer. She quikly adapted it to control wheelchairs, and she teached some armless teenagers to direct the chairs by using their voices. She was inspired to do this by her father, who had fought the efects of polio and had developed a busness customizing automobiles for hisself and other people with mobility problems.

Doctors have found that Kempf's Katalavox also lend itself to microsurgery. Using the voice-activated computer controler. Surgoens can move their delicate magnifying equipment simply by saying where they need it. With this procedure, they do not lose prescious time swinging the lenses around manually.

Group 3   To the past forms of the verbs in this group, add *-n* or *-en* to form the past participle. The one exception is the past participle of *bear*. Note also spelling changes in the past participle forms of *bite, swear, tear,* and *wear.*

Present	Present Participle	Past	Past Participle
bear	(is) bearing	bore	(have) borne
beat	(is) beating	beat	(have) beaten
bite	(is) biting	bit	(have) bitten
break	(is) breaking	broke	(have) broken
choose	(is) choosing	chose	(have) chosen
freeze	(is) freezing	froze	(have) frozen
speak	(is) speaking	spoke	(have) spoken
steal	(is) stealing	stole	(have) stolen
swear	(is) swearing	swore	(have) sworn
tear	(is) tearing	tore	(have) torn
wear	(is) wearing	wore	(have) worn

Practice Your Skills

A. CONCEPT CHECK

Verbs Write the past or the past participle form of the verb in parentheses.

1. For many centuries, troubadors and poets have (speak) of the legends of the Trojan War and the adventures of Odysseus.
2. In this epic poem, the great bard Homer (speak) of glory, danger, and pride.
3. In the *Iliad,* Aphrodite, the Greek goddess of love, had (swear) to the Trojan prince Paris that she would grant him whatever he wished if he judged her the fairest of the immortals.
4. Granted his wish, Paris had (choose) to marry the most beautiful mortal woman on earth.
5. When visiting the Greek city of Sparta, Paris met and fell in love with Helen, the wife of King Menelaus; and the prince (steal) away with her to Troy.
6. Menelaus (tear) his hair in grief when he discovered that his wife had left.
7. Paris had not only insulted him gravely, but he had also (break) the divinely sanctioned laws of hospitality.
8. Menelaus's brother, King Agamemnon of Mycenae, (raise) a great army to avenge the insult.
9. Two of the heroes of this army, Achilles and Ajax, (wear) glorious armor into battle against Troy.
10. After nearly ten years of fighting, the Greeks had won several battles, but the Trojans had (beat) them in others.
11. Complaining that they had nearly (freeze) to death in their tents, the Greeks eventually began to criticize their leaders.
12. Furthermore, the Greeks were upset because the great hero Achilles had (choose) to withdraw from battle.
13. The gods, however, (swear) to Achilles that he would achieve undying fame if he remained with the Greeks to fight at Troy.
14. Achilles finally returned to battle, and before long he had (beat) the Trojan champion Hector in a fierce contest.
15. In Virgil's *Aeneid* we learn that the clever hero Odysseus (speak) in council and recommended that the Greeks deceive the Trojans by pretending to sail home.
16. The Greeks left behind a wooden horse, which the Trojans foolishly (bear) into their city as an offering to the gods.
17. Then Odysseus and his troops, hiding inside the horse, suddenly (break) out and attacked the Trojan soldiers.
18. After they had (tear) open the gates of Troy, the Greeks proceeded to destroy the city of their enemies.

19. The sudden surprise had (freeze) many Trojans in fear, and they could not halt the attacking Greeks.
20. Helen, who had been (steal) away by Paris so many years before, returned to Greece and Menelaus.

B. PROOFREADING SKILL

Verbs Rewrite the following summary of Homer's epic poem, the *Odyssey*. Correct all errors in spelling, punctuation, capitalization, and verb forms.

After the Trojan War. The hero Odysseus and his companions chose to return to their native Ithaca. Homer's *Odyssey* recounts how two of the gods Poseidon and Helios sweared that they hated Odysseus. The sea god poseidon was angry because Odysseus had beat Poseidon's son, the man-eating monster Cyclops. The sun god Helios became furious when Odysseus' men breaked their leader's command. The sailors stealed the sun god's special oxen and then cooked and ate them. After Helios had destroyed the heroes companions in a storm Odysseus was borne on the waves, all alone, clinging to a single spar.

This spar, which had been tore from his sinking ship, probably saved Odysseus life. When he finally returned to Ithaca ten years after the end of the Trojan War, Odysseus prudently wore a disguise. When he discovered that some insolent young men in ithaca had been courting his wife, Penelope, and were hoping to depose him from power. He bit his tongue to keep from divulging his identity and spoiling his revenge. By his own wits and with the aid of his son Telemachus, however, Odysseus freezed the suitors in their tracks; his glorious homecoming has been spoke of for thousands of years.

C. APPLICATION IN WRITING

Myth The purpose of many ancient myths was to explain the origins of natural phenomena. For example, according to the myth of Phaëthon, the deserts of the world were formed when the sun god's mortal son, Phaëthon, took the reins of his father's fiery chariot and drove too close to the earth. Write your own myth, using either imaginary characters or ones from ancient mythology. In your myth, explain the origin of some natural phenomenon, such as bees, thistles, or pebbles at the bottoms of streams. Use at least four of the verbs from the Group 3 list on page 634.

Group 4 In this group of irregular verbs, the vowel *i* in the present changes to *a* in the past and *u* in the past participle. Notice the two past forms of *spring*. *Sprang* is the preferred form.

Present	Present Participle	Past	Past Participle
begin	(is) beginning	began	(have) begun
drink	(is) drinking	drank	(have) drunk
ring	(is) ringing	rang	(have) rung
shrink	(is) shrinking	shrank	(have) shrunk
sing	(is) singing	sang	(have) sung
sink	(is) sinking	sank	(have) sunk
spring	(is) springing	sprang *or* sprung	(have) sprung
swim	(is) swimming	swam	(have) swum

Practice Your Skills

A. CONCEPT CHECK

Verbs Write the past or the past participle form of the verb in parentheses to complete each sentence below. Then write the name of the principal part.

Writing Theme
Aquatic Pastimes

1. Pachio Lopez, a resident of San Ignacio Lagoon, had (begin) to worry.
2. The grey whales were late, and with each day's delay his hopes (sink) a little more.
3. As long as he could remember, each January they had come, had (swim), and had borne their young here in Baja, California.
4. Last year, one (swim) so close that Pachio could touch it.
5. He also recalled with sadness that the number that had come last year had (shrink) noticeably.
6. As he mused, the lonely cries of the gulls (ring) out around him.
7. All morning long the bell on the buoy at the mouth of the bay had (ring) mournfully, adding to his gloom.
8. Pachio tried to shake off the sadness as he waved to Miguel, who had just (begin) to repair his panga, a twenty-foot motorboat.
9. It had (spring) a leak and was useless for fishing.
10. Fortunately, Miguel had acted quickly when it happened or the boat might have (sink).
11. Watching Miguel, Pachio (sing) to himself to raise his spirits.
12. Then he (drink) some steaming coffee to ward off the dampness.
13. Suddenly a welcome sight (spring) into view.
14. First a spout, and then the whales' blowing (begin).
15. Pachio beamed with joy when a cow (swim) right in front of him, showing off her calf.

B. PROOFREADING SKILL

Verbs Rewrite the following passage, and correct errors in verb usage, spelling, punctuation, and capitalization.

On September 21, 1961, Antonio Abertondo begun an unprecedented feat. His challenge was to swim the English channel. Others before him had swam the twenty two miles from Dover to calais France; but he was going to accomplish a round trip, 44 miles, without rest. As he greased his body to protect himself from the icey water, the cry of a lonely gull rung out above him. his mind sprung back to a time a few years before when he swum 262 miles down the mississippi river.

The first half of his English Channel swim went well, and he made good time. When he reached shore, he paused only two minutes and drunk a hot bevrage. He plunged in for the return trip, but extreem weariness had began to take it's toll. Waves buffeted his face and stinged his eyes. He fought his way onward. After more than fourty three hours in the water and over a day since he had touched land, Abertondo stagered ashore and collapsed.

C. APPLICATION IN WRITING

A Historical Account Research one of the following water sports, and write a brief history telling when, where, and how the sport originated. Use at least three verbs from the Group 4 list on page 637.

jet skiing	scuba diving	snorkeling
surfing	water skiing	wind surfing

Group 5 These verbs are grouped together because the past participle is formed from the present rather than the past form.

Present	Present Participle	Past	Past Participle
blow	(is) blowing	blew	(have) blown
come	(is) coming	came	(have) come
do	(is) doing	did	(have) done
draw	(is) drawing	drew	(have) drawn
drive	(is) driving	drove	(have) driven
eat	(is) eating	ate	(have) eaten
fall	(is) falling	fell	(have) fallen
give	(is) giving	gave	(have) given
go	(is) going	went	(have) gone
grow	(is) growing	grew	(have) grown
know	(is) knowing	knew	(have) known
ride	(is) riding	rode	(have) ridden
rise	(is) rising	rose	(have) risen
run	(is) running	ran	(have) run
see	(is) seeing	saw	(have) seen
shake	(is) shaking	shook	(have) shaken
slay	(is) slaying	slew	(have) slain
take	(is) taking	took	(have) taken
throw	(is) throwing	threw	(have) thrown
write	(is) writing	wrote	(have) written

Practice Your Skills

A. CONCEPT CHECK

Verbs Write the past or the past participle form of the verb in parentheses.

Writing Theme
Volcanoes

1. In 1816 in the northeastern United States, the cold April weather (give) no hint of anything especially unusual.
2. By May, however, when the temperature still had not (rise), people became concerned.
3. The icy winds that had (blow) from January to April continued to lash the countryside.
4. A snowstorm in early June (drive) flocks of grazing sheep to take cover.
5. When twelve inches of snow (fall) in New York City on June 5, people suspected that something very strange was happening.
6. No crops (grow) that summer, as they had all been destroyed by the unusually cold weather.
7. On July and August mornings that year, people (shake) in temperatures that plunged to the low thirties.

8. Some scholars of the day (write) articles blaming the deceased Benjamin Franklin for the weird spell of weather.
9. According to their theories, lightning rods developed by Franklin had (draw) all the heat from the air, depriving the earth of summer!
10. If Franklin had been alive in 1816, he might actually have (know), or at least suspected, what was causing the phenomenon.
11. In 1784, Franklin had (come) to recognize a connection between volcanic eruptions and sudden changes in weather.
12. Franklin had (see) that volcanic dust could block out sunlight for months at a time.
13. In agreement, scientists now believe that the cause of the unusual weather in 1816 had (take) place the year before, in the faraway Dutch East Indies of the Pacific Ocean.
14. A huge volcanic eruption of Mount Tambora in that area had (throw) tremendous amounts of volcanic dust into the atmosphere, and that dust had encircled the earth blocking out the warmth of the sun.
15. The long-term damage that this eruption (do) was widespread, affecting European countries as well as the United States.

B. PROOFREADING SKILL

The Principal Parts of Verbs Rewrite the following passage, and correct errors in verb usage, spelling, punctuation, and capitalization.

Another terribly destructive volcanic eruption taken place on the Caribbean island of Martinique in 1902. On the morning of may 8, the residents of the beautiful port town of St. Pierre eaten their breakfasts as usual. The calm was broken, however. When Mount Pelée erupted violently. Ironically, the volcano had gave clear signals of an eruption for over a month. Nevertheless because of an important election scheduled for May 10 that year the government had urged people to remain in St. Pierre; the governor himself had went there to reassure them. The wife of the American consul, in fact, written to her family in Boston, assuring them that her city was in no danger. When the volcano finally done its damage, a fiery cloud of superheated gases raced directly toward the city, six miles away. When they saw it coming, the inhabitants of st. pierre ran for safety, but to no avail. The disaster slay about 30,000 people. Although the zone of destruction was less than ten square miles, the eruption of Mount Pelée remains one of the greatest disasters in the annals of volcanic eruption.

A News Story Use reference sources to research the destruction of Pompeii by the eruption of Mount Vesuvius in A.D. 73. Then write a newspaper account of the destruction as if it had just happened. Use at least four verbs from the Group 5 list on page 639.

VERB TENSES

A verb has different forms to show when an action occurs. These forms are called **tenses.** Every verb has three *simple tenses*—the present tense, the past tense, and the future tense—as well as three *perfect tenses*—the present perfect, the past perfect, and the future perfect. As you study this part of the handbook, you will learn how to form the tenses and when to use them.

Verb Conjugation

A **conjugation** is a presentation of all the tenses of a verb. The conjugation of the regular verb *pull* appears below.

Writing
TIP

Use proper verb tenses to show logical sequence in your writing.

Principal Parts

Present	Present Participle	Past	Past Participle
pull	(is) pulling	pulled	(have) pulled

Simple Tenses

	Singular	Plural
Present Tense		
First Person	I pull	we pull
Second Person	you pull	you pull
Third Person	he, she, it pulls	they pull
Past Tense		
First Person	I pulled	we pulled
Second Person	you pulled	you pulled
Third Person	he, she, it pulled	they pulled
Future Tense (*will* or *shall* + the present form)		
First Person	I will (shall) pull	we will (shall) pull
Second Person	you will pull	you will pull
Third Person	he, she, it will pull	they will pull

Perfect Tenses

Present Perfect Tense   (*has* or *have* + the past participle)

First Person	I have pulled	we have pulled
Second Person	you have pulled	you have pulled
Third Person	he, she, it	they have pulled
	has pulled	

Past Perfect Tense   (*had* + the past participle)

First Person	I had pulled	we had pulled
Second Person	you had pulled	you had pulled
Third Person	he, she, it	they had pulled
	had pulled	

Future Perfect Tense   (*will have* or *shall have* + the past participle)

First Person	I will (shall)	we will (shall)
	have pulled	have pulled
Second Person	you will have pulled	you will have pulled
Third Person	he, she, it will	they will have pulled
	have pulled	

Using the Simple Tenses

Rules for forming and using the three simple tenses and the three perfect tenses are presented on the next several pages. Review these rules so that you use tense correctly in your writing.

The Present Tense   Add *-s* or *-es* to the present—the first principal part—to form the third-person singular form of the present tense: he *wishes,* she *acts.* Use the unchanged present form for all other singular and plural forms of the present tense: I *wish,* you *act,* we *wish,* they *act.*

Use the present tense to express any of these actions: (1) a present action, (2) a regularly occurring action, or (3) a constant or generally true action.

Present Action	Although this apple *looks* ripe and juicy, it *tastes* quite sour.
Regular Action	The ticket office *opens* at nine each weekday morning.
Constant Action	Water *freezes* at zero degrees Celsius and thirty-two degrees Fahrenheit.

Use the **present historical tense** to express a past action as if it were happening now. This tense is also used frequently for writing about a piece of literature.

> General Pershing places a wreath on the tomb and says, "Lafayette, we are here."

> Juliet steps onto her balcony and proclaims her love to the night.

The Past Tense To form the past tense of a regular verb, add *-d* or *-ed* to the present: she *joked,* they *laughed,* they *pushed,* we *pulled.* The past tense of an irregular verb is the third principal part of the verb: it *sank,* I *swam.*

To express an action that began and ended in the past, use the past tense.

> In *Forgotten People,* George Sanchez *spoke* out against inadequate education for Mexican-American children.

The Future Tense To form the future tense, place the auxiliary verb *shall* or *will* before the present form of a verb: I *shall investigate,* you *will investigate,* they *will investigate.*

Use the future tense to express an action that will occur some time after this moment.

> We *shall visit* the ruins of Tikal.

> They *will tour* Guatemala City and the surrounding countryside before heading back to Mexico City.

Usage Note In formal writing many writers use the auxiliary verb *shall* for the first-person future and the auxiliary verb *will* for the second- and third-person future. In informal writing situations, however, *will* can be used with all subjects.

© DIGICON, INC.

You can also express a future action by using the **present tense** of a verb with an adverb or a group of words that indicates a future time.

> The awards dinner *starts* at 7:00 this evening. (The phrase *at 7:00 this evening* indicates a future time.)

Using the Perfect Tenses

Following are the rules for forming and using the **present perfect,** the **past perfect,** and the **future perfect** tenses.

The Present Perfect Tense   To form the present perfect tense, place the auxiliary verb *has* or *have* before the past participle of a verb: she *has arrived,* we *have seen* her. Use the present perfect tense to express (1) an action completed at an indefinite time in the past or (2) an action that started in the past and continues at the present time.

> The commercial jet *has made* the world a smaller place. (action completed at an indefinite time)

> These swift planes *have carried* passengers and cargo since the 1950's. (action continuing into the present)

The Past Perfect Tense   To form the past perfect tense, place the auxiliary verb *had* before the past participle of a verb: I *had shouted,* she *had heard.* Use the past perfect tense to express a past action that took place before another past action.

> Thomas Jefferson *had supported* the French Revolution until he heard of its excesses.

The Future Perfect Tense   To form the future perfect tense, place the auxiliary verbs *shall have* or *will have* before the past participle of a verb. Use the future perfect tense to express a future action that will take place before another future action.

> The play *will have run* for six years when it closes next week.

Problems in Using Tenses

Study the following guidelines to avoid special problems related to the use of tenses.

Special Uses of the Past Perfect   In some sentences, two verbs express actions that happened at different times: one action happened before the other. To express the action that happened first, use the past perfect tense. Use the simple past tense to express the other action.

Incorrect	In the 1970's, many airline pilots *reported* they *sighted* UFO's.
Correct	In the 1970's, many airline pilots *reported* they *had sighted* UFO's.

The incorrect sentence below tells about two past actions. The past action in the *if* clause occurred before the past action in the other clause. This error is corrected by omitting *would have* and using the past perfect of the verb in the *if* clause.

Incorrect	If the detectives *would have discovered* the fingerprints earlier, they might have apprehended the criminal responsible for the robbery sooner.
Correct	If the detectives *had discovered* the fingerprints earlier, they might have apprehended the criminal responsible for the robbery sooner.

Using *Having* with a Past Participle   To show that one action was completed before another, use *having* with the past participle in a participial phrase.

Incorrect	*Completing* the application, Todd mailed it to the admissions office.
Correct	*Having completed* the application, Todd mailed it to the admissions office.

Using Present and Perfect Infinitives   The present infinitive (*to sign*) and the perfect infinitive (*to have signed*) are used to express actions that take place at different times.

Use the present infinitive form to express an action that happens *after* another action.

Incorrect	The leaders of the two countries had hoped *to have signed* the treaty before the end of the year. (The perfect infinitive is incorrect. The action it is intended to express happened after the action expressed by *had hoped*.)
Correct	The leaders of the two countries had hoped *to sign* the treaty before the end of the year.

Use the perfect infinitive form to express an action that happens before another action.

> I am sorry *to have missed* your party last week. (The perfect infinitive is used correctly to express an action that happened *before* the action the verb *am* expresses.)

Practice Your Skills

A. CONCEPT CHECK

Verb Tenses   Write the verbs in the following sentences. Remember to include any auxiliary verbs. Then identify the tense of each verb.

1. For most of recorded history, people have measured time according to the phases of the moon.
2. Native Americans recorded the times of harvests and hunts by designating "moons" as units of time.
3. Muslims and Jews still use the lunar calendar as the basis for religious holidays.
4. Before the time of the Romans, many ancient peoples, including the Egyptians, the Babylonians, and the Greeks, had honored the moon as a goddess.
5. In a dictionary, you will find an etymological link between the word *moon* and Old English words for *month* and *Monday*.
6. The moon has also inspired musical compositions, including a sonata by Beethoven and the popular song "Moon River."
7. For centuries, astronomers had speculated about the moon's shape, size, and motion.
8. In 1609, Galileo observed the moon's surface for the first time through a crude telescope.
9. Galileo had identified dark patches on the moon as "seas" before the invention of more powerful telescopes.
10. Today, scientists describe these "seas" as dry, rocky lowlands on the near side of the moon.
11. Many science fiction writers have written about imaginary space flights to the moon.
12. Jules Verne, the author of *Twenty Thousand Leagues Under the Sea*, also wrote a story called *From the Earth to the Moon*.
13. In the early 1960's, President Kennedy challenged the country to make the ancient dream of space travel a reality.
14. Kennedy set up the National Aeronautics and Space Administration to direct America's space program.
15. On Christmas Eve, 1968, as the whole world watched on television, the *Apollo 8* spacecraft with Frank Borman, William Anders, and James Lovell orbited the moon.
16. On July 20, 1969, Neil Armstrong and Buzz Aldrin of the *Apollo 11* crew landed on the moon.
17. President Kennedy's dream of reaching the moon had become a reality at last.
18. Perhaps this marvelous achievement will seem ordinary to scientists of the future.

19. By that point in time, however, missions such as *Apollo 8* and *Apollo 11* will have provided volumes of invaluable information.
20. After the successful completion of a mission to the planet Mars early in the next century, our body of knowledge about the entire solar system will have become quite impressive.

B. REVISION SKILL

Verb Tenses   Revise the following paragraphs, correcting any errors in verb tenses to clarify the order of events. If the verb tense is correct, write *Correct*.

(1) Ideas are like a line of dominoes standing on end; their flow, or their toppling, continue until they reach an obstacle. (2) Such an obstacle stopped the flow of ideas for almost thirteen centuries. (3) Nicolaus Copernicus was the man who removed the obstacle and allows ideas to flow again.

(4) In the sixteenth century, Copernicus and others have become dissatisfied with the theory that Earth was the center of the universe. (5) Aristotle had devised this theory, and Ptolemy's models in the second century supports it. (6) For centuries this theory have helped philosophers and religious leaders to explain the importance of Earth and humanity in relation to the universe. (7) However, once astronomers learned to make more accurate observations, the theory no longer explains all observed phenomena.

(8) Copernicus looked for an alternative explanation. (9) He reads many works of ancient Greek writers and discovered that an alternative had already been proposed. (10) In fact, to this day, no one was sure why such early ideas were discarded. (11) Copernicus then made observations and performs many computations. (12) Gradually, he becomes convinced that the planets spin around the sun. (13) Had his friends not coaxed and nagged him, Copernicus might never have published his theory. (14) In fact, his pupil Georg Joachim Rhaticus undertook the task of having the manuscript printed. (15) The manuscript, *On the Revolutions of the Celestial Spheres,* starts the "Copernican Revolution" and unblocks a flow of ideas that will continue today.

C. APPLICATION IN WRITING

A Poem   Write a poem comparing the stages in a person's life to the phases of the moon. Experiment with line breaks and elements of sound such as rhyme and alliteration. When you have finished, write the verbs that you used and the tenses of these verbs.

In the preceding section, you learned that every English verb has six basic tenses. In this section, you will study and use other special forms of a verb—six progressive forms and two emphatic forms.

Using the Progressive Forms

The **progressive forms** of a verb are used to express progressive, or ongoing, actions. As you can see in the examples below, the six progressive forms are constructed by combining simple and perfect tenses of *be* with the present participle of a verb.

> I *am pulling* the weeds. (present progressive)
>
> I *was pulling* the weeds. (past progressive)
>
> I *shall be pulling* the weeds. (future progressive)
>
> I *have been pulling* the weeds. (present perfect progressive)
>
> I *had been pulling* the weeds. (past perfect progressive)
>
> I *shall have been pulling* the weeds. (future perfect progressive)

The **present progressive** form should be used to express an ongoing action that is happening at the present time.

> Soccer *is becoming* a popular sport with high schools all over the country.

When used with an adverb or with a group of words that indicates a future time, the **present progressive** form can also express a future action.

> The flight from Denver *is arriving* in one hour.

The **past progressive** form should be used to express an ongoing action that occurred in the past.

> In the late 1800's, the women's rights movement *was gaining* momentum in the United States.

The **future progressive** form should be used to express an ongoing action that will take place in the future.

> Halley's comet *will be rushing* through the solar system for millennia.

The **present perfect progressive** form should be used to express an ongoing action that began in the past and is continuing in the present.

> The fate of the dinosaurs *has been puzzling* scientists for years.

The **past perfect progressive** form should be used to express an ongoing past action that is interrupted by another past action.

> Maria Martinez *had been making* pottery in the old pueblo style for many years before she received the American Ceramic Society Award in 1969.

The **future perfect progressive** form should be used to express an ongoing future action that will have taken place by a designated future time.

> By the time your great-grandchildren are adults, people *will have been exploring* other planets for decades.

Using the Emphatic Forms

The **emphatic forms** of the present tense and past tense lend force and emphasis to verbs. To form the **present emphatic,** place the auxiliary *do* or *does* before the present tense of the verb. To form the **past emphatic,** place the auxiliary *did* before the present tense.

Present	The ozone layer above the South Pole *seems* to be disintegrating.
Present Emphatic	The ozone layer above the South Pole *does seem* to be disintegrating.
Past	Phillis Wheatley, the first important African-American poet, *impressed* both British and American readers.
Past Emphatic	Phillis Wheatley, the first important African-American poet, *did impress* both British and American readers.

The present emphatic and past emphatic often appear in questions and negative statements. In these cases, emphasis is ordinarily not intended.

> A rain shower usually *does*n't *last* long in the tropics.

> *Did* Euclid *create* a form of geometry?

Writing
TIP
Use emphatic forms to add force to your writing.

Practice Your Skills

Writing Theme
A Changing World

A. CONCEPT CHECK

Progressive and Emphatic Verbs   Rewrite each of the following sentences, adding the verb form named in parentheses.

1. In 1945, after the end of World War II, many European nations _____ how to pool their resources for more efficient trade and economic development. (*wonder*—Past Progressive)
2. In the early 1950's, in spite of national borders and loyalties, the desire for cooperation _____ strong. (*appear*—Past Emphatic)
3. Their different languages _____ not _____ these countries from entering negotiations. (*prevent*—Past Emphatic)
4. Two French statesmen, Robert Schuman and Jean Monnet, _____ plans for European economic development for some time. (*draft*—Past Perfect Progressive)
5. At the time, Schuman and Monnet _____ a united Europe. (*envision*—Past Progressive)
6. Although this dream may have seemed farfetched to some observers of the period, today economists and historians _____ these French leaders' farsightedness. (*recognize*—Present Progressive)
7. For nearly four decades, their original idea _____ first into the Common Market and then into the European Economic Community. (*expand*—Present Perfect Progressive)
8. The European Economic Community has been in existence since 1967; now as then, it _____ the gradual elimination of tariff and customs barriers. (*promote*—Present Emphatic)
9. The Community, currently numbering twelve European countries, _____ extremely successful. (*seems*—Present Emphatic)
10. Recently, nations such as Turkey have applied for membership, and no doubt more _____ the same. (*do*—Future Progressive)
11. The nations of the European Economic Community _____ together to create a single market of 325 million consumers. (*join*—Future Progressive)
12. To prepare for this change, many international companies _____ "Eurobrands" for their products. (*prepare*—Present Perfect Progressive)
13. Advertisers for these companies _____ national brands in an effort to create pan-European candy bars and sportswear. (*abandon*—Present Progressive)
14. These advertisers _____ messages that can be recognized throughout the European continent, regardless of language differences. (*create*—Present Progressive)
15. By the year 2000, the Community _____ the European way of life for almost a decade. (*affect*—Future Perfect Progressive)

B. DRAFTING SKILL

Progressive and Emphatic Verbs   Many areas of the world, such as Europe and Africa, have seen ongoing change in recent times. Write ten sentences using the verb forms indicated below to describe some of these changes.

1. expect (future progressive)
2. count (present progressive)
3. study (present perfect progressive)
4. watch (past perfect progressive)
5. live (future perfect progressive)
6. carry (past perfect progressive)
7. plan (past progressive)
8. report (past emphatic)
9. hope (present progressive)
10. know (present emphatic)

Improper Shifts in Tense and Form

Use the same tense to express two or more actions that occur at the same time.

Avoid a shift in tenses within a sentence or between consecutive sentences, except when a shift is needed to make the meaning clear. In most compound sentences and in sentences with a compound predicate, be sure that all the verbs are in the same tense.

Incorrect	Hamlet *feigns* insanity but *did* not *deceive* his father's murderer.
Correct	Hamlet *feigns* insanity but *does* not *deceive* his father's murderer.
Incorrect	Maria Cadilla de Martinez *worked* to preserve the literary and cultural traditions of Puerto Rico, and she *receives* many awards for her achievements.
Correct	Maria Cadilla de Martinez *worked* to preserve the literary and cultural traditions of Puerto Rico, and she *received* many awards for her achievements.

Sometimes a shift in tense is necessary to show a logical sequence of actions or the relationship of one action to another.

The Beatles *had performed* (past perfect) in small German clubs before they *rocketed* (past) to international fame.

By the time our team *wins* (present) a world championship, the Ice Age *will have returned* (future perfect).

Writing
―TIP―

Have a good reason for each change in tense you make. Be sure your reader can follow the change.

Verb Usage   **651**

Practice Your Skills

A. CONCEPT CHECK

Tenses Write each underlined verb in the following lines of poetry. Then identify its tense.

1. In Xanadu <u>did</u> Kubla Khan a stately pleasure dome <u>decree</u>
   Where Alph, the sacred river <u>ran</u>
     through caverns measureless to man
   Down to a sunless sea.   **Samuel Taylor Coleridge**

2. I <u>have desired</u> to go
   Where springs not <u>fail</u>,
   To fields where <u>flies</u> no sharp and sided hail
   And a few lilies <u>blow</u>.   **Gerard Manley Hopkins**

3. The first Day's Night <u>had come</u>—
   And, grateful that a thing
   So terrible <u>had been endured</u>,
   I <u>told</u> my soul to sing.   **Emily Dickinson**

4. O Captain! My Captain! our fearful trip is done,
   The ship has weather'd every rack, the prize we
     <u>sought</u> is won.   **Walt Whitman**

5. Carriages without horses <u>shall go</u>,
   And accidents fill the world with woe.
   Around the world thoughts <u>shall fly</u>
   In the twinkling of an eye.   **Martha "Mother" Shipton**

6. Shall I find comfort, travel-sore and weak?
     Of labour you <u>shall find</u> the sum.
   <u>Will</u> there <u>be</u> beds for me and all who seek?
     Yea, beds for all who come.   **Christina Rossetti**

B. REVISION SKILL

Shifts in Verb Tense and Form Rewrite each sentence to correct any error in the use of verb tenses. If the sentence is correct, write *Correct.*

1. In August 1909, paleontologist Earl Douglass found eight tail-bones of a brontosaurus that died in the arid hills of eastern Utah.
2. Since then, archaeologists have exhumed thousands of bones from the area and reconstructed entire dinosaur skeletons from them.
3. People who visit this interesting site today begin their tour in a skylit building that surrounded the quarry, the Dinosaur National Monument Visitor Center.

4. Many people end their visit there, but the entire monument covered a 320-square-mile area.

5. The triangle-shaped area, which includes two rivers and a considerable number of canyons, cliffs, valleys, ridges, and buttes, is best traversed by bicycle.

6. From a bicycle, visitors not only gain an unparalleled perspective on the monument's wildlife and foliage, but they will also get an excellent workout on its varied terrain.

7. Cyclists riding on thin tires may prefer the paved, thirty-one-mile ride from Monument Headquarters up to Harper's Corner Overlook, with views of a hundred miles and more most of the way.

8. Some mountain bike riders take the steep Echo Park route from Harper's Corner that wound around in the canyons for thirteen miles.

9. The dinosaurs represented in this park actually lived millions of years ago.

10. Now, however, bicycling explorers can wander the cliffs and canyons and visualize how those dinosaurs roam the arid countryside.

C. PROOFREADING SKILL

Verb Tenses and Forms   Rewrite the following paragraphs, correcting errors in verb usage, capitalization, punctuation, and spelling.

The destination of the lowly hedgehog is often, simply, the other side of the road. Until recently, however, hedgehogs in england, were loseing the battel of the roadways. For quite some time. Cars, trucks, and buses had been killing 100,000 of the spiny creatures each year, thousands more have been crippled by fast-moving moter vehicles. often the injured hedgehogs managed to drag themselves from the roads into the woods genrally, however, after a few days, the animals die of there injuries.

Things were looking less than hopeful for the prickly hedgehogs. Then along comes Sue and Les Stocker. Witnessing the slaughter on the highways over the years, the Stockers had long wanted to have done something about it. Eventually they did do something. They opened St. Tigglywinkle's, a hospital for hedgehogs. Most of the patients at St. Tigglywinkle's has been hurt in highway accidents. A few have lost scrapes with dogs and cats. One patient might never have saw the inside of the hedgehog hospital. If it would have stayed out of the rhino cage at the zoo. Not surprisingly, one of the rhinos stepped on the careless creature.

A. On a piece of paper, write four column headings with the names of the principal parts of verbs: *Present, Present Participle, Past,* and *Past Participle.* Write each of the italicized verbs below in the appropriate column.

1. Australia is the world's only island continent, and it *sits* between the Indian and Pacific oceans.
2. Scientists estimate that people were *beginning* to settle there forty thousand years ago.
3. Aborigines had *lived* in Australia long before the first Europeans set foot on the continent.
4. The word aborigine *comes* from a Latin phrase meaning "from the beginning."
5. Now, as before, Australian Aborigines *set* great value on family relationships.
6. For example, before they were influenced by European customs, Aborigines had *chosen* to live in tribal groups that were joined by marriage ties.
7. Although the tribes had no formal government, tribal elders *led* their people in matters of law and custom.
8. The elders *taught* the people the importance of cooperation in hunting and food collecting.
9. Because of the continent's warm climate, ancient Aborigines *wore* little clothing.
10. For food, Aborigines *slew* large sea animals with harpoons and land animals with boomerangs.
11. Scientists speculate that Aborigines also *ate* shellfish, fruits, vegetables, and turtle eggs.
12. The task of finding sufficient food and shelter probably *cost* the Aborigines much effort.
13. Gradually, the art of making stone tools *sprang* up among the tribes.
14. Before they moved to more modern types of housing, Aborigines had been *seeking* shelter in caves for decades.
15. Recently, the designs drawn by Aborigines on cave walls have been *drawing* attention.
16. Even after tens of thousands of years, freshness and vitality still *spring* forth from this cave art.
17. In recent years, the beauty and power of these paintings have *caught* the eye of the international art world.
18. Now, Aboriginal art is *becoming* better known in countries throughout the world.

19. At the same time, some Aborigines *have been taking* a public stand to promote interest in Aboriginal history.
20. They *speak* to others about the richness and dignity of the Aboriginal past.

B. Write the correct form of the two verbs in parentheses.

1. By the eighteenth century, the modern history of Australia had (began, begun).
2. By then, Portuguese, Spanish, and Dutch explorers had already (taken, took) their ships through the strait between New Guinea and Australia.
3. None of these sailors, however, knew that the land they had (saw, seen) was a huge continent.
4. In 1770, the British naval captain James Cook (came, come) to Australia's fertile east coast and claimed the region for Great Britain.
5. It was not until 1788, however, that British ships actually (brang, brought) the first settlers to the new land.
6. Until the American colonies (rose, risen) in rebellion against the British in 1776, England had been shipping many of its convicts to America.
7. People (knew, known) this policy as "transportation," and it had helped to relieve overcrowding in British jails.
8. Therefore, the British needed to find a new place to ship their convicts once America had declared its independence and had (broke, broken) its ties with England.
9. The British government finally (hit, hitted) upon the idea of a convict settlement in Australia.
10. In May 1787, Captain Arthur Phillip (set, sat) out from England with a convoy of eleven ships.
11. These vessels (bore, borne) about 470 male and 160 female convicts, as well as 200 British guards.
12. Under the severe laws of eighteenth-century England, some people were prisoners simply because they had (stole, stolen) a chicken or a few loaves of bread.
13. By the end of January 1788, all of Phillip's ships had (sail, sailed) into Botany Bay, near what is now Sydney.
14. In his book *The Fatal Shore,* Australian Robert Hughes (wrote, written) eloquently of the early settlers' hardships in trying to establish homes in the new land.
15. In 1988, two hundred years after its unique beginning, Australia proudly held its bicentennial, and bells (rang, rung) out in celebration.

C. Write the verb in parentheses in the tense indicated.

1. If questioned, most Australians (*speak*—Future) proudly about the distinctive animal life of their continent.
2. About 200 million years ago, the Australian landmass (*break*—Past) away from the other continents.
3. As a result, Australian animals (*grow*—Present Perfect) and developed differently from those in other areas of the world.
4. Within days of their arrival, most visitors (*see*—Future Perfect) examples of Australia's world-famous marsupials.
5. Australians (*know*—Present Perfect) for a long time that koalas, wallabies, wombats, and kangaroos draw tourists.
6. Observers are intrigued, for example, by the fact that kangaroos move in amazingly long hops when they (*hit*—Present) the ground and quickly spring forward.
7. Kangaroo babies are also an interesting sight as they (*ride*—Present) comfortably in a pouch on their mother's abdomen.
8. Not only are they an interesting sight, but these young that the kangaroos (*bear*—Present Perfect) are also well protected.
9. Another uniquely Australian animal, the koala, (*eat*—Future) up to two pounds of leaves from a eucalyptus tree on a typical day.
10. A visitor to Australia might look up into a tree in a hotel garden only to find that a cuddly looking koala (*swing*—Past Perfect) into a position directly above his or her head.

D. Write the form of the verb indicated in parentheses.

1. If you visit Australia in the summer, chances are that soon after your arrival you (*see*—Future Progressive) a cricket match.
2. Cricket, a game with British origins, (*grow*—Present Perfect Progressive) in popularity with the Australians for years.
3. Australian sports fans continually (*bring*—Present Progressive) one another up to date on the scores of the big matches.
4. Recently, Australia (*lead*—Past Progressive) New Zealand in an important test match.
5. When the game (*go*—Past Perfect Progressive) on for a while, however, New Zealand (*regain*—Past Emphatic) the lead with a surprise move.
6. "Doubtless," a visitor remarked to a fan, "this match (*end*—Future Progressive) in a few hours."
7. "Oh, no," chuckled the native. "By the time a cricket match is finally decided in Australia, normally the two sides (*fight*—Future Perfect Progressive) it out for several days!"
8. "My goodness," remarked the visitor, "you (*take*—Present Emphatic) your cricket seriously."

VOICE AND MOOD

Speakers and writers can choose from several tenses to express present, past, and future actions. They can also choose from among several progressive and emphatic forms. Verbs also have other more subtle forms that speakers and writers can use for special purposes.

Active and Passive Voice

The voice of a verb indicates whether its subject is the performer or the receiver of the action the verb expresses. When the subject is the performer of the action, the verb is in the **active voice.** When the subject is the receiver of the action, the verb is in the **passive voice.**

Active Voice	The quarterback *threw* the football past the rushing linemen. (The subject, *the quarterback,* is the performer of the action.
Passive Voice	The football *was thrown* past the rushing linemen by the quarterback. (The subject, *the football,* is the receiver of the action.)

The verb *threw* in the first sentence is transitive because it has a direct object. When this verb is changed to the passive voice, the direct object *football* becomes the subject. Only transitive verbs can be changed from active voice to passive voice.

Retained Objects   Verbs in the active voice can have indirect objects as well as direct objects. Either of the two objects can become the subject of the sentence when a transitive verb is changed from the active to the passive voice. The object that does not become the subject continues to function as an object and is called a **retained object**.

Active Voice	The citizens of France gave the American *people* the *Statue of Liberty.* (*People* is the indirect object; *Statue of Liberty* is the direct object.)
Passive	The American people were given the *Statue of Liberty* by the citizens of France. (*Statue of Liberty* is a retained object.)
Passive	The Statue of Liberty was given the American *people* by the citizens of France. (*People* is a retained object.)

If a retained object sounds overly formal, use a prepositional phrase instead: The Statue of Liberty was given *to the American people* by the citizens of France.

Using Voice in Writing

Active voice verbs are more forceful and direct than passive voice verbs. Avoid weak, wordy expressions by using the active voice rather than the passive voice. Also avoid using both active and passive voice verbs in the same sentence and in related consecutive sentences.

However, the passive voice need not always be avoided. It can be used effectively when a speaker or a writer wants to call attention to the person or thing receiving the action of a verb or does not know who or what is performing an action.

Arguments for and against nuclear power plants *are heard* frequently.

Many books and articles *have been written* on the subject.

Practice Your Skills

A. CONCEPT CHECK

Active and Passive Voice   Write the verbs in the following sentences. Identify each verb according to its voice: *Active* or *Passive*. Then, if a sentence can be made more direct by rewriting the verb in the active voice, do so.

1. On the morning of April 3, 1860, a journey of two thousand miles was started by a young horseback rider from St. Joseph, Missouri.
2. On the same day in Sacramento, California, another rider began a trip in the opposite direction.
3. These journeys marked the beginning of an American legend, the Pony Express.
4. Before the Pony Express, mail from coast to coast often was not delivered for six months.
5. The delivery period was reduced by the new system to ten days.
6. The Pony Express system included about eighty riders and between four hundred and five hundred horses.
7. Every twelve miles or so, the riders rested for two minutes at one of the relay stations.
8. Candidates for the Pony Express were given posters by employment recruiters that read: "Orphans preferred"!
9. The legend of the Pony Express has been dramatically exaggerated by Hollywood movies and television.
10. Despite the dangers, only one rider was actually killed, and his horse ran on to the next station with the mail intact!

B. REVISION SKILL

Using the Active Voice Rewrite the following passage, using the active voice where possible.

(1) On the night of September 13, 1814, the British bombardment of Fort McHenry was witnessed by a young American lawyer detained on a British ship. (2) The rockets that were fired by the British were the first ever seen in America. (3) These rockets had been designed by Sir William Congreve, the royal fire master, to streak across a range of two miles and to explode on impact. (4) The rockets were guided by polelike rudders; on impact, a shower of deadly shrapnel was thrown out by the rockets. (5) Francis Scott Key, the young lawyer, was inspired by the rockets' blazing trails to write the lines "And the rockets' red glare/The bombs bursting in air."

Understanding and Using Mood

Mood is a grammatical term that identifies the manner in which a verb expresses an idea. Verbs have three moods: the indicative, the imperative, and the subjunctive. Speakers and writers use the **indicative mood** most frequently. This mood states a fact or asks a question.

> *Did* Dorothea Dix *work* for proper treatment of the mentally ill in the mid-1800's?

> Environmental activists *work* to enact strict laws regulating pollution.

Use the **imperative mood** to give a command or make a request. Remember that verbs in this mood are always in the present tense and second person.

> *Participate* in conservation activities.
> Please *save* our planet from extinction.

Use the **subjunctive mood** (1) to express a wish or a condition that is contrary to fact or (2) to express a command or request after the word *that*.

> I wish I *were* a billionaire. (to express a wish)

> If I *were* that wealthy, I would help needy people. (to express a condition contrary to fact)

> I would order that the hungry *be* fed. (to express a command after the word *that*)

The indicative and subjunctive moods have exactly the same forms, except for the following.

1. The *-s* is omitted from verbs in the third-person singular.

    Indicative   The President *holds* a news conference frequently.

    Subjunctive   The networks asked that the President *hold* a news conference next week.

2. In the present subjunctive mood, the form of the verb *to be* is always *be.*

    Present Subjunctive   The President suggested that the news conference *be* on Tuesday.

3. In the past subjunctive mood, the form of the verb *to be* is always *were.*

    Past Subjunctive   If TV time *were* available, the President would hold a news conference every week.

Practice Your Skills

CONCEPT CHECK

Identifying Mood Read the following folk tale. Then write the mood of each italicized verb.

(1) Once upon a time, in a certain village in Nagaland, a wise old man *lived* with his grandson.
(2) "If I *were* you," the old man advised his fellow villagers, "I would spend all my time cultivating rice."
(3) Many of the villagers, however, suggested that the old man *be* ignored. (4) They therefore *continued* to gather wild yams and fruits, to hunt wild animals, and to fish in the streams.
(5) One day, the grandson said to the old man, "Please *allow* me to hunt and fish in the forest." (6) The old man refused, insisting that the boy *accompany* him every day to the rice fields.
(7) Soon afterward, the old man said to a friend of his grandson, "*Bring* me back a small fish, and *make* sure that it is still alive." (8) The boy *returned* later that day with a fish. (9) Then, to prove a point, the old man asked that his grandson *put* the fish into a wooden trough filled with water. (10) "Now, my boy, *catch* the fish and *give* it to me," he ordered.
(11) However, no matter how hard he *tried,* the boy was unable to catch the fish.

(12) The grandfather dryly told him, "If fishing *were* as easy as you had thought, you would grow up to be a rich man; let us tend to our rice cultivation instead!"

(13) When harvest time *came,* the old man and his grandson sold their plentiful harvest of rice for fish, game, yams, and fruits.

(14) "Do you *understand* now why rice is magic food?" the old man asked the child. (15) The villagers, impressed by the grandfather's wisdom, soon asked that he *consent* to be their chief.

COMMONLY CONFUSED VERBS

The verb pairs *lie* and *lay, rise* and *raise,* and *sit* and *set* can be confusing because the spelling and the meanings of the verbs in each pair are similar. Learn to use these verbs correctly.

Lie and Lay

Lie and *lay* are two different words. Here are the principal parts.

Present	Present Participle	Past	Past Participle
lie	(is) lying	lay	(have) lain
lay	(is) laying	laid	(have) laid

The meaning of the intransitive verb *lie* is "to rest in a flat position." *Lie* never takes a direct object.

> The Great Barrier Reef *lies* off the northeast coast of Queensland, Australia.

> The remains of the *Titanic* had *lain* on the floor of the Atlantic undisturbed until 1986.

Usage Note Do not mistake the verb *lie* for its homonym meaning "to tell an untruth." The principal parts of the homonym are *lie, lying, lied, lied.*

Lay is a transitive verb meaning "to place." Except when it is in the passive voice, it usually has a direct object.

Active Voice   A skillful worker can *lay* wall-to-wall carpeting in a short time.

Passive Voice   A carpet can be *laid* in a short time by a skillful worker.

Occasionally *lay* can be used as an intransitive verb.

> The hens *are laying* well this year.

Rise and Raise

Rise and *raise* are two different words. Here are their principal parts.

Present	Present Participle	Past	Past Participle
rise	(is) rising	rose	(have) risen
raise	(is) raising	raised	(have) raised

Rise is an intransitive verb meaning "to go upward." It never takes a direct object.

> Cream *rises* to the top of a container of milk that has not been homogenized.

> The water level of the world's oceans *rose* after the glaciers of the Ice Age melted.

The transitive verb *raise* means "to lift" or "to make something go up." *Raise* nearly always has a direct object; it does not have a direct object when it is in the passive voice.

Active Voice	The builders *will raise* the entire house and put a new foundation under it.
Passive Voice	The many flags in front of the United Nations headquarters *are raised* ceremoniously each day.

Sit and Set

Sit and *set* are two different words. Here are their principal parts.

Present	Present Participle	Past	Past Participle
sit	(is) sitting	sat	(have) sat
set	(is) setting	set	(have) set

The intransitive verb *sit* means "to occupy a seat." It usually does not take a direct object.

> Some airline passengers are so superstitious they *will* not *sit* in row 13.

> Queen Elizabeth II *sat* on the Stone of Scone during her coronation.

If *sit* is used to mean "position in a seat," it is transitive and can take a direct object.

> *Sit* the patient carefully in that chair.

> *Sit* the baby in the safety seat and strap her in.

Set is a transitive verb meaning "to place." It usually has a direct object.

> The Archbishop of Canterbury *set* the royal crown onto the new queen's head.

> Many science-fiction writers *have set* the action of their stories on distant planets.

In certain situations, *set* is intransitive, taking no object.

> The sun *sets* early in the winter.

Practice Your Skills

A. CONCEPT CHECK

Commonly Confused Verbs Write the correct verb form of the two verbs in parentheses.

Writing Theme
Extremes
in Nature

1. Deserts (lie, lay) across one seventh of the earth's land surface.
2. Daytime temperatures in a desert may (raise, rise) to over 120 degrees Fahrenheit.
3. Some plants, such as the saguaro cactus, can (sit, set) happily in the severe surroundings for a lifetime.
4. In fact, even with little water this plant can (raise, rise) to heights of fifty feet and live nearly two centuries.
5. The cactus (lies, lays) down a shallow, broad root system just beneath the surface of the soil.
6. This root network acts as a pump, rapidly absorbing rainwater and (raising, rising) the plant's water level.
7. Desert-dwelling people such as the Bedouins, however, usually (sit, set) their tents near an oasis.
8. They do not (rise, raise) crops but keep herds of animals.
9. Very sociable, they can often be seen (sitting, setting) in a village marketplace telling stories or reciting poems.
10. A few desert settlements, mostly mining areas, have (laid, lain) pipelines to get water, but this is difficult and costly.

B. PROOFREADING SKILL

Errors in Verb Usage Proofread the following paragraphs for errors in verb usage, spelling, punctuation, and capitalization. Then rewrite the paragraphs correctly.

> Scientists had known for centuries that some plants rise their temperatures as they mature. Then, in 1937, A. W. H. van Herk sat forth the idea that the flowers warmed them-

selves by releasing a chemical that he calls calorigen. Fifty years later, Botanists in the United States announced that they had discovered the chemical.

The voodoo lily is one plant that exhibits this chemical "magic." It produces salicylic acid—part of the compound that composes aspirin—as part of its reproduction process. That aspirin substance lowered the temperature of the human body, but it rises the temperature of the beautiful voodoo lily by as much as twenty-five degrees Farenheit.

The voodoo lily blooms immediately after it manufactured the salicylic acid. Then the interaction of the sun with the acid creates heat, and four-and-a-half hours later the temperature of the lily has raised to its peak.

Biologist Ilya Raskin explains that the carrion beetles that polinate the voodoo lily are attracted by the smell of the nitrogen compounds emitted as the lilys temperature rises. Once a beetle enters the lily's pollination chamber, it lays there as the lily goes through another warming phase. The beetle gathers sticky pollen on its feet, and then it moves to set on the next lily and unwittingly deposit its reproductive contribution.

CHECK POINT
PAGES 657–664

Writing Theme
The Vikings

A. Rewrite the following sentences, changing the verbs from the passive voice to the active voice.

1. More than a thousand years ago, present-day Scandinavia was dominated by the Vikings.
2. The word *viking* has been explained by historians as a form of *Vik,* the name of a pirate center in southern Norway.
3. The Scandinavians were called Norsemen or Northmen by other Europeans.
4. Although *to go a-viking* meant "to fight as a pirate," not all of the Vikings' activities were centered around warlike activities.
5. The occupation that was favored by most Vikings was farming.
6. A number of interesting discoveries about Viking customs have been made by archaeologists.
7. Each Viking community was ruled by a king or a chief.
8. Viking gods and battles were praised in song by the *skalds,* or royal poets.
9. Women were accorded considerable freedom by Viking tradition.
10. For example, married women were permitted by Viking communities to divorce their husbands whenever they wished.

B. Identify the mood of each italicized verb as *Indicative, Imperative,* or *Subjunctive.*

1. Viking warriors were especially *renowned* for their ferocity.
2. If a soldier *were* more fearsome than most, he might be called a "berserker."
3. This term *gave* the English language the word *berserk,* a descriptive term for someone who acts wildly.
4. Many Europeans were so terrified of the Vikings, they urged that special prayers *be* recited in churches.
5. The text of one prayer was as follows: "God, *deliver* us from the fury of the Northmen!"
6. Viking chiefs ordered that raids *be* launched to acquire food, cattle, horses, gold, and silver.
7. Ordinarily, Viking warfare was *waged* by small raiding parties.
8. Occasionally, however, Vikings *organized* fleets of several hundred warships to gain control of large territories.
9. In the year 886, for example, the King of France implored that a Danish Viking chieftain *end* his year-long siege of Paris.
10. "*Convince* me; *pay* me a huge treasure," the warrior might have retorted, "and I will command that my army *withdraw* from the city."

C. For each sentence, write the correct verb form of the two verbs in parentheses.

1. In the age of the Vikings, shipbuilding (rose, raised) to new heights of skill.
2. Shipbuilders improved vessels by (lying, laying) a keel.
3. By reducing the rolling motion of a ship underway, the keel helped the crews to (rise, raise) their speed.
4. The keel was also helpful to the steersman who (sat, set) at the helm.
5. It was easier to steer the ship and to maintain a consistent course that had been (sat, set) in advance.
6. Viking navigators used the (rising, raising) and (sitting, setting) of the sun and the stars to determine their ships' locations.
7. Sophisticated navigation charts helped them determine at any point the latitude where their ships (lay, laid).
8. The Viking chief Leif Ericson (raised, rose) an expedition for a voyage of discovery.
9. Ericson believed that a vast new territory (lay, laid) somewhere across the ocean to the west.
10. After a long voyage, Ericson and his crew finally (lay, laid) anchor in North America, which they called Vinland.

GRAMMAR
HANDBOOK
34

Writing Theme
Television

A. Using Verbs Correctly Write the correct verb form of the two given in parentheses.

1. Over the past half century, television has (grew, grown) into one of the most important communications media.
2. Experimental television broadcasts (taken, took) place in the 1930's.
3. In 1936, the Radio Corporation of America (led, lead) the way to widespread use by installing special receivers in 150 homes in New York City.
4. A New York City station (begun, began) transmitting programs to these homes.
5. The first program that home viewers (saw, seen) was a cartoon presentation of Felix the Cat.
6. World War II temporarily (drew, drawn) public attention away from television.
7. By 1950, however, the demand for television receivers had (set, sat) new records.
8. The number of television sets in the United States had (rose, risen) to about sixty million by 1960.
9. By today's standards, early TV shows (cost, costed) very little to produce, but fans loved them.
10. In those early days, some fans watched their favorite shows on neighbors' sets; the importance (lay, laid) in the viewing!
11. The first television entertainer who (caught, catched) the nation's attention was Milton Berle.
12. Berle's hilarious comedy routines (ran, run) on the *Texaco Star Theater* from 1948 to 1956.
13. Huge audiences (burst, bursted) into spontaneous laughter.
14. The immensely popular series *I Love Lucy* (gone, went) on the air in 1951.
15. Most viewers agreed that Lucille Ball (shone, shined) as the star of the show.
16. On Ed Sullivan's variety show, another audience hit, the Beatles (sang, sung) their first songs on television in the United States.
17. This appearance (brung, brought) the group wide exposure.
18. By 1960, it was clear that television had (sprang, sprung) into the political arena as a major force.
19. The presidential candidates John F. Kennedy and Richard M. Nixon (chose, chosen) to debate each other on TV.
20. It seemed that the clothing the candidates (wore, worn) and the way they looked were almost as important as the words they (spoke, spoken).

B. Verb Tenses and Forms Write the italicized verbs and identify the tense and/or the form of each verb.

1. By the mid-1950's, many technological improvements *were affecting* television.
2. For example, specialists *had added* the feature of color to television by the end of 1953.
3. The videotaping of programs gradually *replaced* live productions.
4. Unlike film, videotape *did* not *require* time to develop.
5. Videotape also *produces* good quality sound and pictures.
6. Since the 1970's, commercial communications satellites orbiting the earth *have been making* worldwide broadcasting possible.
7. For example, sports fans in Japan *will be watching* the coverage of the next Olympics as the events unfold thousands of miles away.
8. The popularity of videocassette recorders *has grown* enormously.
9. People *enjoy* taping their favorite shows on these machines.
10. By the end of this century, high-definition television (HDTV) *will have improved* picture and sound quality even more.

C. Understanding Verb Forms Rewrite each of the following sentences, changing the italicized verb to the form shown in parentheses. Rewrite the sentence if necessary.

1. Undoubtedly, television *exerted* a major impact on many aspects of life in the United States. (present perfect progressive)
2. Typical present-day adults *have spent* more time watching TV than on almost anything else. (present)
3. It is clear that TV *has* many beneficial effects on learning and on cultural enrichment. (present perfect)
4. Many home viewers *will have widened* their experience considerably by watching television. (present emphatic)
5. For example, the important acts of government officials *are presented* by the networks to vast audiences. (active voice)
6. Until the televised presentation in 1969, the public never *saw* a historic event like the moon landing before. (past perfect)
7. Experts, however, believe that viewers *had experienced* harmful effects from viewing certain kinds of programs. (future)
8. For example, some programs set up the expectation of a world that *will* always *seethe* with violence. (future progressive)
9. Another objection to TV viewing is that, by the end of an average week, viewers *will see* hundreds of commercial messages urging them to buy various products. (future perfect)
10. Some sociologists fear that, over the years, commercials *will be tending* to raise people's expectations unrealistically. (future)

Agreement of Subject and Verb

AGREEMENT IN NUMBER

In grammar, there are two numbers: **singular** when a word refers to one person or thing and **plural** if a word refers to more than one.

The subject and verb of a sentence must agree in number.

A singular verb is used with a singular subject; a plural verb is used with a plural subject. This is called **agreement.**

> This <u>calculation</u> (singular) accurately <u>demonstrates</u> (singular) the scientist's theory.

> These <u>equations</u> (plural) <u>demonstrate</u> (plural) the chemist's understanding of the substances.

Most verbs change form to show singular or plural only in the third-person present tense, where the singular form ends in *-s*. All verb forms are the same in the past tense.

Present Tense Verb Forms

Singular		Plural	
I	race	we	race
you	race	you	race
he, she, it, Juan	races	they, the joggers	race

Singular and Plural Forms of *Be* The box below presents all conjugations of the irregular verb *be.*

Forms of *Be*

	Present Tense		Past Tense	
	Singular	*Plural*	*Singular*	*Plural*
First Person	I am	we are	I was	we were
Second Person	you are	you are	you were	you were
Third Person	he, she, it is	they are	he, she, it was	they were

Usage Note The expressions *you was, we was,* and *they was* are nonstandard English and should be avoided in writing and speaking.

Writing
TIP

One exception to the use of non-standard forms involves dialogue. The use of such forms may add realism to a character's voice.

Words Between Subject and Verb

A verb agrees only with its subject.

Sometimes a word or phrase separates the subject from its verb. Such interruptions do not change the need for agreement between the verb and its subject.

> The <u>lawyers</u> in the public defender's office <u>have</u> excellent credentials. (*Lawyers,* not *office,* is the subject.)

> The <u>lawyer,</u> according to the newspapers, <u>has</u> questions for the witnesses. (*Lawyer,* not *newspapers,* is the subject.)

Beware of the prepositions *according to, along with, as well as, together with,* and *with.* The objects of such prepositions have no effect on the number of the verb. These prepositions may cause confusion since they appear to create a compound subject with which you would expect to use a plural verb.

Practice Your Skills

CONCEPT CHECK

Agreement in Number of Subject and Verb   Write the form of the verb that agrees in number with the subject of each of the following sentences. Then tell whether the verb form is *Singular* or *Plural.*

1. Unusual competitions around the United States (captures, capture) the public's imagination.
2. During summer, sand sculptors with their buckets of sand and water (vies, vie) to create compelling sculptures or castles.
3. Wood cutting, as well as pole climbing, (is, are) featured in annual contests of skill and daring for lumberjacks.
4. In contrast, a participant in hog-calling or yodeling contests (needs, need) more lung power than physical strength.
5. Young contestants from all over the country (competes, compete) in the International Rope Skipping Organization championships.
6. On the other hand, a frog, together with its owner, (wins, win) the Calaveras County Jumping Frog Jubilee held every year.
7. The most effective bird calls, according to a panel of judges, (is, are) given recognition in bird-calling contests.
8. Fairs in most rural areas (has, have) a variety of different tests of skill, including pie-eating and tractor-pulling contests.
9. A cash prize, along with ribbons or trophies, (is, are) usually presented to the most skilled contestants.
10. Indeed, people of all ages (enjoys, enjoy) trying to set records or to win awards.

Writing Theme
Contests and
Records

Use a plural verb with most compound subjects joined by the word *and*.

> <u>Oil</u> and <u>natural gas</u> <u>are</u> the most common heating fuels in the United States.

Use a singular verb with a compound subject joined by *and* that is habitually used to refer to a single thing.

> <u>Snow</u> and <u>ice</u> <u>creates</u> slippery roads.

Use a singular verb with any subject that is preceded by *each*, *every*, or *many a*.

> <u>Each</u> member and officer of the organization <u>gets</u> one vote.

> <u>Many a</u> writer at the beginning of a project <u>has needed</u> a source of inspiration.

When the words in a compound subject are joined by *or* or *nor*, the verb agrees with the subject nearer the verb.

> The editor or <u>proofreaders</u> <u>find</u> any errors in the final copy. (The plural verb *find* agrees with *proofreaders*, the subject nearer the verb.)

Practice Your Skills

A. CONCEPT CHECK

Writing Theme
What's in
a Name?

Agreement with Compound Subjects Rewrite these sentences, correcting all errors in subject-verb agreement. If a sentence is correct, write *Correct*.

1. Both creativity and dedication has inspired colorful epithets.
2. Neither wizardry nor magic tricks was the stock in trade of "the Wizard of Menlo Park."
3. Every scientist and amateur inventor considers Thomas Edison's laboratory at Menlo Park, which was staffed by assistants who helped Edison, the first industrial research facility.
4. The give and take of inventing by teamwork require the organization and skill of a genius such as Edison.
5. Skill and genius also marks the prolific writings of the "Bard of Avon."
6. Many a writer aspire to the greatness of William Shakespeare, who is credited with writing more than one hundred sonnets and thirty-seven plays.

7. Each byname and nickname describe the individual.
8. For example, her voice and appearance were so distinctive that Jenny Lind was called "the Swedish Nightingale."
9. Each modern nurse and doctor have probably heard of Florence Nightingale, called "the Lady with the Lamp" because she made nightly rounds of hospital wards.
10. Both the fans and the general public still refer to entertainer Elvis Presley as "the King."

B. PROOFREADING SKILL

Errors in Agreement   Rewrite the following paragraphs on your paper, correcting any errors. Be sure all subjects and verbs agree in number.

Many an essayist and novelist have published his or her writing under a pseudonym. Baroness Karen Blixen and Isak Dinesen, for example, is the same woman. Samuel Langhorne Clemens and Mark Twain are one man.

The aim and intent of writer's using other names have differed. In century's past, many a female novelist and poet were known to use a mans name to avoid public criticism of their feminine authorship. Currer Bell and Ellis Bell, who wrote the novels *Jane Eyre* and *Wuthering Heights* respectively, was actually two sisters. Neither the publisher nor the critics at the time was able to give Charlotte and Emily Brontë credit under her own names. Critics questioned whether both sensitivity and vigor was possible in a females work. Today each reader form his or her own standards based on the quality of the writing rather then the writer's gender.

Male novelists and essayists who wrote in more than one medium has sometimes used pen names as well. Charles Lamb and Charles Dickens was known by their *noms de plume*. Lamb published essays in *The London Magazine* under the name of Elia. Likewise, Dickens published sketches in the *Evening Chronicle* under the name Boz. Both Dickens and Lamb was recognized by thier true names when they wrote more serious novels and other works.

Agreement of
Subject and Verb   **671**

CHECKPOINT
PAGES 668–670

Writing Theme
Flora and Fauna
of the Sea

A. Write the form of the verb that agrees in number with the subject of each of the following sentences.

1. Probably every gourmet and connoisseur of Japanese cuisine (has, have) eaten dried seaweed fronds.
2. Surprisingly, many plants from the oceans of the world (contributes, contribute) to a variety of foods.
3. For example, kelp, along with other kinds of seaweed, (is, are) harvested and processed.
4. Both seaweed fronds and the stipe, or stem, (has, have) practical uses.
5. More importantly, giant kelp plants, growing to a length of 215 feet, (produces, produce) algin, a jellylike substance.
6. In addition, many seaweeds in the Pacific Ocean, such as red algae, (yields, yield) agar, a substance similar to gelatin.
7. Either algin or agar (is, are) usually added to foods such as ice cream and salad dressings to prevent crystallization, to make them smooth, or to help them retain moisture.
8. In the 1800's, kelp and other types of seaweed (was, were) an important source of the minerals potash and iodine.
9. The life and death of some food, cosmetics, and drug industries (depends, depend) on the harvesting of seaweeds.
10. Many a food product or medicine (uses, use) kelp and other forms of algae, an important yet little-known ingredient in the human diet.

B. Rewrite the following sentences, correcting all errors in subject-verb agreement. If a sentence contains no error, write *Correct.*

1. Wrapped in powerful tentacles, the drowning sailor, along with his rescuers, fight the monster octopus.
2. Many a science-fiction film and sea yarn have given cephalopods, or octopuses and squids, a bad reputation as vicious sea monsters.
3. In reality, the docile octopus, along with squids, are harmless to humans.
4. Neither the octopus, with its eight arms, nor the squid, with its ten arms, eats anything larger than crabs and lobsters.
5. Many a shy member of the cephalopod group change color to hide amid rocks and coral.
6. Both the octopus and the squid ejects an inky fluid.
7. This fluid, according to experts, acts as a protective screen.

8. These gentle creatures, together with the cuttlefish, is more likely to end up as the dinner rather than the diner.
9. The economic "bread and butter" of many restaurants rely on octopuses and their cousins.
10. Either octopus appetizers or a squid entrée is a special treat in the Mediterranean, the Orient, and other areas.

INDEFINITE PRONOUNS AS SUBJECTS

Indefinite pronouns vary in number: some are always singular, others are always plural. Yet others may be singular or plural, according to their particular use in a sentence.

Singular Indefinite Pronouns

another	either	neither	other
anybody	everybody	nobody	somebody
anyone	everyone	no one	someone
anything	everything	nothing	something
each	much	one	

Use a singular verb with a singular indefinite pronoun.

No one from the jury is allowed to go home.

Everything in the store costs less than twenty dollars.

Does anyone on the committee agree with the principal?

Plural Indefinite Pronouns

both	few	many	several

Use a plural verb with a plural indefinite pronoun.

Both of our class projects are due on the same day, and there is no compromise on either deadline.

Many of the students in our class do their research at the university library.

all	enough	most	plenty
any	more	none	some

These indefinite pronouns are singular when they refer to a quantity or a part of something. They are plural when they refer to a number of individual things. In some cases you may need to refer to an intervening prepositional phrase or a prior sentence to determine whether an indefinite pronoun is singular or plural.

> Some of the stolen money was retrieved. (quantity)
>
> Some of their trigonometry answers were wrong. (number)
>
> Mrs. Chang ordered several items from the catalog. Some were defective. (*Some* refers to items in the previous sentence.)
>
> Most of the mail was incorrectly addressed. (*Mail,* the object of the preposition, is singular.)
>
> Most of the informational brochures were about basketball camps. (*Brochures,* the object of the preposition, is plural.)

None and *any* may be either singular or plural depending on whether the writer intends to refer to one thing or to several. In such cases you need to examine the context of the sentence.

> None of the unused tickets was returned. (not one)
>
> None of the unused tickets were returned. (no tickets)
>
> Any of these interesting subjects has potential for further research. (any one)
>
> Any of these interesting subjects have potential for further research. (any subjects)

Practice Your Skills

CONCEPT CHECK

Agreement with Indefinite Pronouns Write the subject of each sentence. Then write the form of the verb that agrees with the subject.

1. Everybody in the United States (agrees, agree) that the country needs protection from tragic fires.
2. According to experts, many of the fire-prevention regulations today (is, are) based on intuition and guesswork.

Writing Theme
Fire Testing

3. One of the problems (lies, lie) in the lack of scientific knowledge about fire and how it spreads.
4. Much of the current testing (focuses, focus) on the dynamics of fire, such as what affects how quickly it ignites and spreads.
5. In one test at the National Bureau of Standards, several of the testers (watches, watch) as a match ignites a newspaper.
6. In one and a half minutes, plenty of thick smoke (spreads, spread) close to the floor.
7. In the same test, most of the objects in the room (has, have) caught fire within four minutes, and the temperature is 1,300° F.
8. Given the test results, few on the research team (questions, question) the need for educating the public about fire safety.
9. Everyone in the testing field (studies, study) computer models that re-create actual fires.
10. Nearly all of the existing fire codes (is, are) updated according to scientific knowledge gained from these tests.

OTHER AGREEMENT PROBLEMS

Although subject-verb agreement rules are simple, some situations often lead to errors. This section will help you avoid those errors.

Inverted Sentences

Agreement problems may occur in inverted sentences where the verb precedes the subject, as in some questions and in sentences beginning with *here* and *there*. To ensure agreement, think ahead and determine whether the verb should be singular or plural.

Incorrect   Near the smoldering wreck <u>stands</u> the dazed <u>victims</u>.

Correct   Near the smoldering wreck <u>stand</u> the dazed <u>victims</u>.

Incorrect   There <u>was</u> no bus <u>services</u> during the blizzard.

Correct   There <u>were</u> no bus <u>services</u> during the blizzard.

Incorrect   What<u>'s</u> the scientific <u>names</u> for these bacterial strains?

Correct   What <u>are</u> the scientific <u>names</u> for these bacterial strains?

Notice the misuse of the contraction *what's* in the last example above. Contractions such as *what's, here's, there's,* and *who's* contain the singular verb *is* and should be used only with singular subjects.

Sentences with Predicate Nominatives

Use a verb that agrees in number with the subject, not with the predicate nominative.

> Strong <u>muscles</u> <u>are</u> one sign of a fit body. (*Muscles* is the subject and takes a plural verb.)

> One <u>sign</u> of a fit body <u>is</u> strong muscles. (*Sign* is the subject and takes a singular verb.)

Sentences with *Don't* and *Doesn't*

Use *doesn't* with singular subjects and with the personal pronouns *he, she,* and *it*. Use *don't* with plural subjects and with the personal pronouns *I, we, you,* and *they*.

Singular   <u>Doesn't</u> the <u>governor</u> always have bodyguards?

 She <u>doesn't</u> always need protection.

Plural   <u>Don't</u> the <u>campers</u> need a ground cloth under their tent in case it rains?

 They <u>don't</u> want to sleep on the wet ground.

Practice Your Skills

A. CONCEPT CHECK

Other Agreement Problems   Write the form of the verb that agrees in number with the subject of each of the following sentences.

1. (Doesn't, Don't) everyone dream?
2. From modern sleep-research laboratories (comes, come) important information about dreams.
3. Recent events (is, are) one contributor to dreams—emotions, another.
4. However, (there's, there are) conflicting theories between the psychological and physiological sciences.
5. According to early twentieth-century psychoanalyst Sigmund Freud, dreams "(is, are) the royal road to the unconscious."
6. After all, (doesn't, don't) dreams often seem to reveal a person's problems, wishes, and anxieties?
7. On the other hand, physiological studies have shown that a dream (is, are) electrical impulses and chemical changes in the brain.
8. However, if each researcher (doesn't, don't) use accurate machines, then the findings are questionable.

9. Then (there's, there are) the careful physical measurements and the dreamer's oral report which make the data complete.
10. On some machines (is, are) recorded a subject's brain wave activity during sleep.
11. (There's, There are) also measurements of the dreamer's eye movement and muscle response.
12. The ultimate goal (remains, remain) the understanding of the content and the purpose of dreams.

B. PROOFREADING SKILL

Errors in Subject-Verb Agreement Rewrite the following paragraph to correct any errors in subject-verb agreement. Also correct errors in capitalization, punctuation, and spelling.

(1) In the writings of Homer are evidence of early beleifs about dreams. (2) There's dreams of prophesy in which zeus hands down instructions. (3) However, this gods instructions doesn't always seem clear to the dreamer. (4) Asclepius are an expert who interprets dreams. (5) Through his explanations come the method for destinguishing significant from ordinary dreams.

Collective Nouns as Subjects

A **collective** noun such as *band, committee,* or *bunch* takes a singular verb when the group acts as a single unit, and a plural verb when the members of the group act separately.

> The <u>flock</u> of sheep <u>is grazing</u> on the mountainside. (The whole flock is grazing.)

> The <u>flock</u> of sheep <u>are running</u> from the sheep dog. (Individual sheep are running.)

> Our <u>club</u> <u>ratifies</u> all of its rules and the fee structure annually. (The whole group ratifies rules and the fee structure.)

> Our <u>club</u> <u>voice</u> dissent and <u>disagree</u> on every item on the agenda. (The individual members of the club voice dissent and disagree.)

Usage Note Like other collective nouns, *number* is sometimes singular and sometimes plural. When *number* is preceded by *the* and followed by *of,* it is singular; when it is preceded by *a* and followed by *of,* it is plural.

> The <u>number</u> of blood donors from our school <u>is growing</u> each year.

> A <u>number</u> of blood donors <u>give</u> blood every month during the school year.

Singular Nouns with Plural Forms

Not every noun ending in *-s* is plural. A few nouns appear to be plural, but they are actually singular because they stand for only one thing. Examples are *molasses, measles,* and *news,* all of which take a singular verb.

> <u>Molasses</u> <u>is</u> a commodity that changed the pattern of world trade with the American colonies.

> Once <u>news</u> of the British duty <u>was known</u>, smugglers began to sell molasses.

A few nouns that end in *-s* refer to only one thing but still take a plural verb: *congratulations, eyeglasses, pliers, scissors, trousers.*

> <u>Scissors</u> <u>are</u> best <u>kept</u> out of the hands of small children.

> My <u>sunglasses</u> <u>fall</u> into the ocean every time I sail.
> <u>Congratulations</u> <u>were offered</u> to the finalists.

Nouns that end in -ics, such as *academics, aesthetics,* and *genetics,* can be either singular or plural. They are singular when they refer to a school subject, a science, or a general practice. In the plural form they usually follow a singular modifier or a possessive pronoun.

> Economics is more than just dollars and cents.

> World economics operate on a base of complicated relationships.

A geographic name or an organization ending in -s is singular even though it appears to be a plural form.

> The Philippines consists of thousands of islands and islets.

> The *Times* names all the contestants in the primary election.

Titles and Groups of Words as Subjects

Use a singular verb with a title.

The title of a book, play, story, poem, TV show, musical composition, painting, piece of architecture, or other work of art is singular and therefore requires a singular verb.

> *O Pioneers!* was written by Willa Cather, a great American novelist who captured the heroic, creative spirit that was so much a part of the nineteenth century.

> *The Four Seasons* represents Antonio Vivaldi in the repertoire of many chamber orchestras.

Any group of words referring to a single thing or thought is used with a singular verb.

> "Rose is a rose is a rose is a rose" is an often-quoted line from a poem that illustrates Gertrude Stein's use of repetition.

> How people will respond to a crisis depends on their experience and temperament.

Illustration by Robert Crawford

Agreement of
Subject and Verb   **679**

Words of Amount and Time as Subjects

Words stating amounts are usually singular.

Use a singular verb with subject words or phrases that express periods of time, weights, measurements, fractions, or amounts of money.

> Three hours *is* longer than anyone should have to wait to see a doctor.

> Fifty dollars *seems* like a lot to spend on a gift.

> Eight tons *is* the weight limit of many local streets and highways.

If the subject is a period of time or an amount that is thought of as a number of separate units, use a plural verb.

> Four companies of fire trucks *come* to every alarm at a hospital.

> Twenty-four players *stay* on the active roster during the football season.

Practice Your Skills

A. CONCEPT CHECK

Agreement Problems Write the form of the verb that agrees in number with its subject.

1. It is the turn of the century, and the Roaring Twenties (is, are) a golden age of dizzying prosperity.
2. The United States (enjoys, enjoy) great industrial growth, as seen in the automobile industry.
3. Thanks to mass production, three hundred dollars (is, are) enough to buy a Model T Ford.
4. "You can get a Model T in any color, so long as it is black" (becomes, become) a familiar witticism of the day.
5. In 1933 the President's Research Committee on Social Trends (reports, report) 150 ways the automobile has changed the American way of life.
6. With new mobility gained from the use of automobiles, the American family (moves, move) away from the city to create the suburbs.
7. During the Roaring Twenties, radio also comes of age; at this time, nearly one-half the homes in the United States (has, have) radio sets.

8. A group of broadcasters (airs, air) the first commercial radio program in 1920 at station KDKA in Pittsburgh.
9. Within six years, the number of radio stations in the United States (grows, grow) to 732.
10. In addition, the movie *The Jazz Singer* (makes, make) history as the first talking movie.
11. Unfortunately, this is also a time when America's ethics (is, are) questioned as people bemoan an apparent decline in moral standards.
12. A number of writers (describes, describe) the disillusionment and alienation of a society trying to learn a new and vastly different role in the machine age.
13. "A vast . . . herd of good-natured animals" (is, are) how writer H. L. Mencken characterizes society.
14. T. S. Eliot's poem "The Hollow Men" (predicts, predict) that everything civilization has accomplished will end "not with a bang but a whimper."
15. Indeed, for good or bad, the economics of the era (inspires, inspire) great changes in American life.

B. REVISION SKILL

Problems of Subject-Verb Agreement Rewrite the following sentences, correcting all errors in subject-verb agreement. If a sentence has no errors, write *Correct.*

(1) A few hours are enough time for readers to become entranced with the Jazz Age of the 1920's. (2) Through F. Scott Fitzgerald's short stories and his novel *The Great Gatsby,* wealthy society comes to life. (3) It is a time when almost three million copies of the popular magazine the *Saturday Evening Post* is sold each week. (4) A number of Fitzgerald's short stories first appears in the *Post* and other popular magazines of the time. (5) "Winter Dreams," published in *Metropolitan Magazine,* are among the pre-Gatsby short stories.

(6) In one scene of "Winter Dreams," the news of a boyfriend's penniless state upset a selfish but beautiful young woman. (7) Her family are very wealthy and belong to the country club where the hero formerly worked as a caddy. (8) Doing the laundry of the rich is how the hero, Dexter Green, now makes a living. (9) During his youth, the elite group of rich families fan his imagination. (10) How to acquire the trappings of the rich become his obsession. (11) Knickerbockers is the fashion on the golf course; elegant Pierce Arrows fill the parking lots. (12) Both Fitzgerald's Jay Gatsby and Dexter suffer years of disillusionment after trying to obtain the unattainable.

(13) The rich crowd are portrayed as selfish and superficial in another of Fitzgerald's short stories. (14) "Dice, Brass-knuckles & Guitar" explore the cultural differences that exist between the rich and the poor. (15) "You're better than all of them put together" are a line from this short story that forecasts a later line in *The Great Gatsby,* reassuring the hero of his worth despite what he sees as his shortcomings.

C. APPLICATION IN WRITING

Comparison and Contrast Think about the time in which you are living. In what ways do you think the 1920's and this decade are similar? How are they different? Think about what people owned, what they believed about getting rich, and what they bought during the 1920's. Then think about the same things as they apply to society today. Compare and contrast the two time periods. Be sure your subjects and verbs agree.

RELATIVE PRONOUNS AS SUBJECTS

When a relative pronoun is used as a subject, it may be either plural or singular, depending on the number of its antecedent.

A relative pronoun agrees with its antecedent in number. When a relative pronoun is used as the subject of an adjective clause (see page 608), the verb of the clause must agree in number with the antecedent of the relative pronoun.

Singular   Amelia Earhart was a famous aviator <u>who</u> <u>has</u> the distinction of being the first woman to fly solo across the Atlantic. (*Who* refers to the singular antecedent *famous aviator* and takes the singular verb *has*.)

Plural   It is Richard Byrd and Floyd Bennett, two Americans, <u>who</u> <u>rank</u> as the first aviators to fly over the North Pole. (*Who* refers to the plural antecedent *Richard Byrd and Floyd Bennett* and requires the plural verb *rank*.)

In some sentences, it may be difficult to determine whether the verb should take the singular or plural form because there seems to be more than one possible antecedent. Sentences with the expressions *one of the* or *one of those* often prove confusing, as illustrated by the following examples.

Incorrect   Susan Glaspell is one of those playwrights <u>who</u> <u>has</u> won the Pulitzer Prize for drama.

Correct   Susan Glaspell is one of those playwrights <u>who</u> <u>have</u> won the Pulitzer Prize for drama. (Other playwrights have won the award besides Glaspell. Therefore, *who* refers to the plural antecedent *playwrights*.)

When the expression *the only one of those* is used, the relative pronoun modifies *one* and is therefore singular.

Eugene O'Neill is the only one of those playwrights <u>who</u> <u>has</u> been awarded four Pulitzer Prizes for drama. (The other playwrights did not win four Pulitzer Prizes; only O'Neill did. *Who* refers to the singular antecedent *one*.)

Always consider the context of the sentence. Usually the context will allow you to determine the correct antecedent and ensure that subject-verb agreement is correct.

Practice Your Skills

A. CONCEPT CHECK

Agreement with Antecedents of Relative Pronouns   Write the form of the verb that agrees in number with the subject of the adjective clause.

1. Edwin Budding is one of those inventors who (remains, remain) unsung heroes of modern technology.
2. All the people who (mows, mow) lawns in the summer can thank him for making their job easier.
3. Picture a British textile mill in the 1800's and a rotary shearing machine that (trims, trim) the nap off cotton cloth.
4. Budding tinkers with the cutters that (rotates, rotate) around a fixed cutter.
5. It is this tinkering that (leads, lead) Budding to the idea for his invention, the push mower.
6. Budding was the only one of those inventors of his day who (was, were) to apply for a patent on a rolling mower.
7. Before Budding's invention, English gardeners used a scythe, which (is, are) a long sharp blade with a handle.
8. Today we use mowers that (is, are) gasoline-powered.
9. Edwin George, an American army colonel, was one of the tinkerers who (was, were) responsible for the gasoline mower.
10. One of those people who never (wastes, waste) things, George used an old washing machine motor to power his mower.

B. PROOFREADING SKILL

Agreement with Antecedents of Relative Pronouns   Rewrite this paragraph, correcting all agreement errors and all errors in capitalization, punctuation, and spelling.

> Elevators, which provides vertical transportation, have been around in some form for over 2,000 years. It is believed that Archimedes, who were an ancient greek mathematician, created one of the first elevators. By the 1840's anyone who were riding a steam-powered or hydraulic elevator would probably enjoy the convenience but might worry about safety. In a steam-powered elevator, when one of the ropes were broken, nothing could stop the elevator car from crashing. Fortunately, Elisha G. Otis was one of those people who sees a solution where others see only a problem It is his invention of the automatic safety devise that have made traveling in elevators the safest form of human transportation.

A. Select the form of the verb that agrees with its subject.

1. No one who (studies, study) English literature (denies, deny) the influence of the Bloomsbury Group.
2. In the inner borough of Camden north of the Thames (lies, lie) Bloomsbury, from which the group (takes, take) its name.
3. This group of noted writers, artists, and philosophers (was, were) known to hold spirited discussions.
4. Their aesthetics (is, are) still a significant influence on modern writers and thinkers.
5. (Who was, Who were) some of the group's members?
6. The noted author and frequent hostess of the Bloomsbury Group (was, were) Virginia Woolf.
7. Economist John Maynard Keynes, along with others, (is, are) one of the most illustrious guests who (was, were) invited.
8. Keynes's *The General Theory of Employment, Interest, and Money* (contains, contain) theories that (is, are) said to have influenced the policies of President Franklin D. Roosevelt.
9. Several in the group, such as E. M. Forster and Victoria Sackville-West, (was, were) prominent writers.
10. Three decades (seems, seem) a long time for a group to meet regularly, but meet it did from 1907 to 1930.

B. Rewrite the following paragraph to correct all errors in subject and verb agreement. If a sentence contains no errors, write *Correct.*

(1) There's very few artists whose interests were as diverse as Leonardo da Vinci's. (2) His versatility amazes those admirers of his genius who studies his work. (3) All of his life's energies was devoted to understanding the world around him. (4) Worthy of our praises are his research in mathematics, music, optics, aeronautics, and anatomy—a few of the fields that was to capture his curiosity. (5) Optics, for example, benefits from his inventiveness. (6) His *Code on the Eye* describe a water-filled tube sealed at the end with a flat lens, which were a precursor of the modern soft contact lens. (7) Twenty-one such manuscripts are his legacy to humanity. (8) Everyone who examine these detailed notebooks marvels at his notes and sketches. (9) In addition, his paintings, the *Virgin and Child with St. Anne,* for example, serve as models that inspires artists to this day. (10) Don't such a versatile and creative genius seem amazing?

Writing Theme
Creative Genius

These drawings by Leonardo da Vinci depict the workings of an automated spool-winding machine.

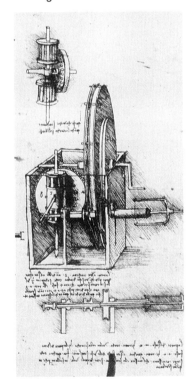

Agreement of Subject and Verb **685**

GRAMMAR
HANDBOOK
35

Writing Theme
Special Achievers

A. Making Subjects and Verbs Agree   Choose the correct form of the verb in parentheses.

1. It is the early twenties, and DeWitt Wallace, who (is, are) recovering from serious war wounds, (ponders, ponder) an idea for a magazine.
2. Three months in the hospital (produces, produce) a plan.
3. "(Doesn't, Don't) men and women in the Twenties have too much to do and too little time?" he wonders.
4. Plodding through many a long magazine article (takes, take) time; a digest that (condenses, condense) them would be helpful.
5. At home, Lila Bell Acheson (is, are) the only one of his acquaintances who (believes, believe) in his idea.
6. DeWitt is convinced that there (is, are) readers for such a digest.
7. However, none of the New York publishers (expresses, express) interest in publishing the magazine.
8. DeWitt, together with his bride Lila Bell, (publishes, publish) the magazine independently.
9. Out of a Greenwich Village basement, the *Reader's Digest* (sallies, sally) forth in February 1922.
10. Neither the general public nor the Wallaces (anticipates, anticipate) the overwhelming success of the magazine.

B. Solving Problems of Subject-Verb Agreement   Rewrite the following sentences to correct all problems of subject and verb agreement.

1. It is 1810, and a way of life and traditions is disappearing.
2. Neither cholera nor measles threaten native people as much as the American settlers' greed for land.
3. The increasing number of confrontations with settlers give rise to the leadership of Tecumseh of the Shawnee.
4. Most of his family have been killed by settlers and soldiers.
5. Certainly he is one who have reason to mistrust, yet he risks his life on behalf of white prisoners held by the Shawnee.
6. Tecumseh proves to be one of those leaders who strives to unite people under a single cause.
7. His strong convictions, as well as his eloquent oratory, convinces some of the tribal leaders to unite.
8. Yet few in the American government understands Tecumseh's defense of the land.
9. What he states in his arguments are that no one can own the air and water; likewise, no one can possess the land.
10. Tecumseh's rise and fall are a subject of interest to both his admirers and critics.

C. Correcting Errors in Agreement Read the passage and identify errors of subject-verb agreement. Write the correct verb for each sentence. If a sentence has no errors, write *Correct*.

(1) "You must do the thing you think you cannot do" are a famous saying of Eleanor Roosevelt's. (2) Few of the people who hear these words today realizes that they were spoken by a woman who had to surmount enormous fears. (3) As a young girl, Eleanor Roosevelt were painfully shy and frightened "of practically everything," as she later recalled. (4) She was one of those students who fears even the simple task of standing up at her desk and spelling a word aloud in front of one's classmates.

(5) None of her childhood fears, however, was as crippling as her fear of water. (6) When she was three, Eleanor and her parents were involved in a serious steamship accident while traveling to Europe. (7) As her father, along with other passengers, were standing in a lifeboat beneath, a crew member tried to throw the young girl overboard. (8) The terrified child clutched so fiercely that her fingers had to be pried loose before she were thrown to safety.

(9) Later in her childhood, Eleanor almost drowned again, but neither the traumatic steamship incident nor these ocean immersions was enough to defeat her.

(10) Though she realized that her anxieties could not be dispelled completely, she knew that she could overcome a portion of the fear that were gnawing at her self-esteem. (11) She decided to deal with her problem one step at a time. (12) First, she learned to sail; then she learned to swim; and finally, when she was fifty-six years old, she learned to dive.

(13) In these small acts of personal heroism reside the key to her life's achievement. (14) There's a lesson here that all of us can still profit from today. (15) As she herself wrote near the end of her life: "We do not have to become heroes overnight, just one step at a time, meeting each thing that comes up, seeing it is not as dreadful as it appeared, discovering we have the strength to stare it down."

On the Lightside

INFLUENTIAL MEDICAL TERMS

Medical terms are much more than labels. They can be keys to unlocking bits and pieces of medical history. *Flu*, for instance, is a shortened form of the term *influenza*, which doctors borrowed from the Italian *influenza*. *Influenza* came from the medieval Latin word *influentia*, meaning "inflowing" and refering to "ethereal power or fluid flowing from the stars and believed by astrologers to affect the characters and actions of people." Thus we can speculate that when doctors first identified the illness we now call the flu, they may have believed that it was caused by some astrological or occult influence.

Penicillin, too, is much more than just a label. The man who discovered this antibiotic, Alexander Fleming, gave it the name *penicillin* because he derived it from the mold *Penicillium notatum*. *Penicillium* got its name from the Latin word *penicillus*, meaning "paintbrush," because its spore-bearing structures are brushlike in appearance.

Finally, even the term *vaccine* provides a clue to its interesting origins. *Vaccine* comes from the Latin word *vacca* meaning "cow." The first preparation introduced into a body to prevent an illness was made from the cowpox virus and introduced into the body of a boy.

So, the next time you're scanning the rows of medicines at the local pharmacy, you might think twice about the names on those labels. Each one of those names just might have a fascinating story to tell.

influentia

vacca

penicillium

notatum

"Now this end is called the thagomizer...after the late Thag Simmons."

Sketchbook

Developments in transportation have dramatically changed the way people get around. Automobiles and airplanes are as common in this country now as horse-drawn carriages once were. Think about how you might have traveled from Boston to Seattle 150 years ago, how you would make the trip today, and how you might make the trip 150 years from now. Then write a three-paragraph essay describing each trip as you imagine it taking place. Be sure to use verb tenses correctly.

Additional Sketches

Suppose that you have been appointed principal of your school. A national news magazine has asked you to write an article about your new position, in which you would discuss the following: highlights of your school's history, your school's present status, and your plans for making improvements. Write the article, making sure you use appropriate verb tenses.

The senior class is trying to decide on an appropriate and memorable gift to give the school. Write a letter to the school newspaper in which you present an idea and attempt to persuade others to go along with it. Use compound subjects and correlative conjunctions in your letter whenever possible.

Directions One or more of the underlined sections in the following sentences may contain errors of grammar, usage, punctuation, spelling, or capitalization. Write the letters of each incorrect section. Then rewrite the item correctly. If there is no error in an item, write E.

> **Example** Late in the battle, the Huns, <u>retreating</u> <u>in haste,</u> <u>left</u>
>   **A**   **B**   **C**
> many of <u>their</u> prisoners go free. <u>No error</u>
>   **D**   **E**
> **Answer** C—let

1. Big Ben, <u>the bell in the tower of the British House of Parliament,</u> has <u>rang</u> out the
                   A   **B**
   <u>Time</u> of day <u>since 1859.</u> <u>No error</u>
    C   **D**   **E**

2. Al McReynolds <u>received</u> a <u>$250,000</u> prize when he <u>catched</u> a 78-pound <u>stripped</u>
                 A   **B**   **C**   **D**
   bass. <u>No error</u>
      E

3. At the age of <u>fourteen,</u> the <u>young Albert Einstein</u> asked <u>himself,</u> "How would the
              A   **B**   **C**
   world look if I <u>was</u> able to ride on a beam of light?" <u>No error</u>
             D   **E**

4. At <u>extremely</u> <u>high or low latitudes,</u> the sun never <u>sits</u> during <u>the summer.</u> <u>No error</u>
        A   **B**   **C**   **D**   **E**

5. The <u>length</u> of these articles <u>are</u> not a problem, but the <u>mispellings</u> in them are
        A   **B**   **C**
   another matter <u>altogether.</u> <u>No error</u>
             D   **E**

6. My family <u>subscribe</u> to two newspapers, but we <u>rarely</u> listen to <u>television news</u>
             A   **B**   **C**
   programs such as *Sixty Minutes* and *The MacNeil, Lehrer News Hour.* <u>No error</u>
                                       D   **E**

7. <u>Economics</u> <u>is</u> one of the most fascinating and practical of all the sciences <u>because</u>
    A   **B**   **C**
   it deals with <u>how people go about making a living.</u> <u>No error</u>
                 D   **E**

8. <u>Neither</u> the most important financial center <u>nor</u> the most productive industrial
     A   **B**
   center <u>are based</u> in the <u>nation's</u> capital. <u>No error</u>
          C   **D**   **E**

9. During <u>World War II,</u> the Nazis <u>stealed</u> the crown of <u>Charlemagne,</u> but American
           A   **B**   **C**
   soldiers <u>eventualy</u> recovered it. <u>No error</u>
          D   **E**

10. <u>Because</u> the <u>Greek Goddess</u> Persephone had <u>ate</u> some pomegranate <u>seeds,</u> she had
     A   **B**   **C**   **D**
    to spend half her time on earth and half in Hades. <u>No error</u>
                                       E

11. According to <u>some</u> geologists, <u>known</u> petroleum reserves <u>run</u> out sometime
               A   **B**   **C**
    <u>before the end of this century.</u> <u>No error</u>
             D   **E**

12. Born in 1910, <u>Colonel Harlan Sanders</u> <u>founds</u> the chain of restaurants and was
                 A   **B**
    very successful, leaving fried chicken restaurants all over the <u>United States</u> and the
                                                  C
    world <u>when he died.</u> <u>No error</u>
          D   **E**

13. Each of these poems by Robert Frost—<u>"Stopping by Woods on a Snowy Evening,"</u>
                                                 A
    in particular—<u>seem</u> simple <u>but</u> <u>are</u> actually quite sophisticated. <u>No error</u>
                B   **C** **D**   **E**

14. If Catherine Littlefield Green <u>would have got</u> the credit <u>she deserved</u> for helping
                             A   **B**
    Eli Whitney design the cotton <u>gin,</u> she might <u>have become</u> as famous as he.
                             C   **D**
    <u>No error</u>
     E

15. <u>Don't</u> stalactites grow up <u>from the floor,</u> and don't stalagmites <u>grow</u> down
     A   **B**   **C**
    <u>from the ceiling?</u> <u>No error</u>
         D   **E**

16. <u>Neither Lincoln nor his generals</u> <u>was</u> able <u>to come up with</u> an acceptable plan for
                A   **B**   **C**
    bringing a quick end to the <u>hostilities.</u> <u>No error</u>
                       D   **E**

17. In June of 1986, a woman told us that she sighted the Loch Ness monster
    A   B   C
    a month before. No error
    D   E

18. One can only imagine what life might be like today if the Nazis would have won
    A   B
    world war II in Europe. No error
    C   D   E

19. In the early 1960's President John F. Kennedy had promised to have sent American
    A   B   C
    astronauts to the moon by the end of the decade. No error
                          D   E

20. Did Werner von Braun really say, "I just build them. I'm not responsible for
    A   B   C
    where they come down?" No error
                    D   E

21. The speaker implied that most of the animals that apeared during the Cambrian
                A   B   C
    era became extinct. No error
        D   E

22. Early in the novel Huck fakes his own death and then slipped away down the river
                       A   B   C   D
    on a raft. No error
              E

23. Firefighters worked furiously after the great quake, but before they could put the
                        A   B
    flames out, most of the city were destroyed. No error
           C   D   E

24. The density of a human body and the density of water is almost exactly the same.
                 A   B   C   D
    No error
    E

25. Until the first debate, the candidate had hoped to have avoided the issue of higher
                       A   B   C   D
    taxes. No error
          E

Pronoun Usage

CASES OF PRONOUNS

A pronoun is a part of speech that may take the place of a noun. A pronoun changes form, or **case,** according to its function in the sentence.

The three cases in English are the **nominative case,** the **objective case,** and the **possessive case.** Nominative case pronouns act either as subjects or as predicate nominatives. Objective case pronouns act as objects of verbs or as objects of prepositions. Possessive case pronouns show ownership or possession.

Personal pronouns have the most varied forms of all the categories of pronouns (see Handbook 31 for the categories of pronouns). The forms of the personal pronouns are shown in the box below.

Singular Personal Pronouns

	Nominative	Objective	Possessive
First Person	I	me	my, mine
Second Person	you	you	your, yours
Third Person	he, she, it	him, her, it	his, her, hers, its

Plural Personal Pronouns

	Nominative	Objective	Possessive
First Person	we	us	our, ours
Second Person	you	you	your, yours
Third Person	they	them	their, theirs

Personal pronouns change form, not only according to case but also according to number, person, and gender. The possessive forms *my, your, his, her, its, our,* and *their* function as adjectives that modify nouns: *my* suggestion.

The forms for the pronouns *who* and *whoever* are shown by case below.

Nominative	Objective	Possessive
who	whom	whose
whoever	whomever	whosever

Most indefinite pronouns, such as *anyone* and *no one,* change form only in the possessive case. The possessive case form ends in *'s: someone's, no one's.* For a list of indefinite pronouns, see page 551.

The pronouns *this, that, these, those, which,* and *what* do not change form to indicate case.

Practice Your Skills

CONCEPT CHECK

The Cases of Pronouns In the following passage, identify each personal pronoun as *First, Second,* or *Third Person;* as *Singular* or *Plural;* and as *Nominative, Objective,* or *Possessive Case.* Also, identify the case of indefinite pronouns and forms of *who.* If the sentence does not contain a personal pronoun, write *No pronoun.*

(1) Occasionally Mother, whom we seldom saw in the house, had us meet her at Louie's. . . . (2) While we sat on the stiff wooden booths, Mother would dance alone in front of us to music from the Seeburg. (3) I loved her most at those times. (4) She was like a pretty kite that floated just above my head. . . .

(5) The Syrian brothers vied for her attention as she sang the heavy blues that Bailey and I almost understood. (6) They watched her, even when directing their conversation to other customers, and I knew they too were hypnotized by this beautiful lady who talked with her whole body and snapped her fingers louder than anyone in the whole world. (7) We learned the Time Step at Louie's. (8) It is from this basic step that most American Black dances are born. (9) It is a series of taps, jumps and rests, and demands careful listening, feeling and coordination. (10) We were brought before Mother's friends, . . . to show our artistry. (11) Bailey learned easily, and has always been the better dancer. (12) But I learned too. . . . (13) We were applauded, . . . but it was to be years later before I found the joy and freedom of dancing well.

Maya Angelou, *I Know Why the Caged Bird Sings*

Maya Angelou

PRONOUNS IN THE NOMINATIVE CASE

Pronouns, like nouns, may function as subjects or as predicate nominatives. Pronouns used in these ways are in the nominative case.

Pronouns as Subjects

The nominative form of the pronoun is used as the subject of a verb.

Choosing the proper case for pronouns used as subjects usually causes difficulty only in compounds. To decide which pronoun form to use, try each part of the compound by itself with the verb.

> Rena and (I, me) played a duet. (Rena played; I played, *not* me played. *I* is a nominative case pronoun used as part of a compound subject.)

The plural forms *we* and *they* often sound awkward in compound subjects. The problem can be eliminated by recasting the sentence.

Awkward   They and we waited in line for the ticket office to open.

Better   We all waited in line for the ticket office to open.

Pronouns as Predicate Nominatives

A predicate pronoun is linked to the subject by a form of the verb *be.*

The nominative form is used for a predicate pronoun.

The rule above also applies to verb phrases in which the main verb is a form of *be,* such as *could have been, can be,* and *should be.*

> It *was she* waving from the pier.

> The winners of the band contest *should have been they.*

Sometimes the use of the nominative case after the verb *be* sounds awkward. This awkwardness can be avoided by recasting the sentence.

Awkward   The acrobat at the top of the human pyramid was I.

Better   I was the acrobat at the top of the human pyramid.

Writing
—TIP—

Use the nominative case for predicate pronouns in all formal writing.

Practice Your Skills

CONCEPT CHECK

Nominative Case Pronouns   Write the correct form of the pronoun for each sentence. Choose from those given in parentheses.

1. Luisa and (I, me) are among 300 eager applicants to the clown training school in Venice, Florida.
2. The other applicants and (we, us) are enchanted with the colorful language used by circus people.
3. For starters, neither (she, her) nor (I, me) want to be "jossers."
4. Jossers are (they, them) who are not part of the circus business.
5. Of course, the clowns are best; in the words of P. T. Barnum (they, them) are "the pegs to hang the circus on."
6. The "Auguste" clown is (he or she, him or her) who gets a pie or seltzer water in the face.
7. The "Joeys" are the regular clowns; (they, them) are the main attractions for the "flatties," or spectators.
8. Of the two of us, it is (I, me) who most wants to become an Auguste.
9. The other applicants and (we, us) hope to graduate and then be chosen to receive a two-year contract with the circus.
10. Luisa and (I, me) hope that we will be the students most likely to join the graduate clowns.

PRONOUNS IN THE
OBJECTIVE CASE

Like nouns, pronouns can function as objects of verbs, as objects of prepositions, and as part of infinitive phrases.

Pronouns as Objects of Verbs

The objective pronoun form is used as a direct or indirect object.

When the object of the verb is a compound object consisting of a noun and pronoun, it is often difficult to decide which pronoun form to use. It is helpful to try each part of the object by itself.

Direct Object   Dennis joined Maria and (I, me) at the bandshell. (joined Maria; joined me, *not* joined I.)

Indirect Object   John gave the mayor and (she, her) a tour of his garden. (gave the mayor; gave her, *not* gave she)

Pronouns as Objects of Prepositions

The objective form of a pronoun is used as the object of a preposition.

Again, the dilemma of deciding which pronoun form to use as the object of a preposition occurs chiefly when an object is compound. To decide, try each pronoun separately in the sentence.

The note on the door was addressed to Katie and (I, me).
(to Katie; to me, *not* to I)

Usage Note In informal speech, people often incorrectly use nominative case pronouns as objects of prepositions. This misuse is particularly common with the preposition *between: between you and I.* Use only objective case pronouns for objects of prepositions. The correct form, then, is *between you and me.*

Pronouns with Infinitives

The infinitive is a verb that is preceded by *to.* See Handbook 33 for more information about infinitives.

The objective form of the pronoun is used as the subject, object, or predicate pronoun of an infinitive.

Subject of Infinitive	The clerk asked *me to complete* this form. (*Me* is the subject of *to complete.*)
	We helped *him find* his keys. (*Him* is the subject of *find,* an infinitive in which *to* is omitted.)
Object of Infinitive	Neil went *to meet them* at the airport. (*Them* is the object of *to meet.*)
Predicate Pronoun	We didn't expect the first guest *to be her.* (*Her* is the predicate pronoun after *to be.*)

Practice Your Skills

A. CONCEPT CHECK

Objective Case Pronouns Choose the pronoun that makes each of the following excerpts of poetry correct.

1. And the afternoon, the evening, sleeps so peacefully!/Smoothed by long fingers,/Asleep . . . tired . . . or it malingers,/. . . here beside you and (I, me). **T. S. Eliot**
2. In a field by the river my love and (I, me) did stand,/And on my leaning shoulder she laid her snow-white hand. **W. B. Yeats**

3. It was not (I, me) who began it./Turned out into draughty caves,/hungry so often, having to work for our bread,/hearing the children whining, I was nevertheless not unhappy.   **Judith Wright**

4. Well, I would like to make,/thinking some line still taut between (I, me) and (they, them),/poems direct as what the bird said,/ . . . mysterious as the silence when the tailor/would pause with his needle in the air.   **Denise Levertov**

5. Ah, love, let (we, us) be true/To one another! for the world, which seems/to lie before (we, us) like a land of dreams, . . ./Hath really neither joy, nor love, nor light. . .   **Matthew Arnold**

6. The instructor said,/*Go home and write/a page tonight./And let that page come out of you—/Then it will be true . . ./*It's not easy to know what is true for you or (I, me) at twenty-two, my age. But I guess I'm what I feel and see and hear, Harlem, I hear you. . . .   **Langston Hughes**

7. if i heard/a voice/coming from/a rock/i'd know/and her words/would flow inside (I, me)/like the light/of someone/stirring ashes/from a sleeping fire/at night.   **Ray Young Bear**

8. Self-reliant like the cat—/that takes its prey to privacy,/the mouse's limp tail hanging like a shoelace from its mouth—/(they, them) sometimes enjoy solitude, and can be robbed of speech/by speech which has delighted (they, them).   **Marianne Moore**

9. Each child seemed a child, like (I, me), on a loose perch,/Holding to childhood like some termless play.   **Hart Crane**

10. Great Nature has another thing to do/To you and (I, me); so take the lively air,/And, lovely, learn by going where to go.   **Theodore Roethke**

B. PROOFREADING SKILL

Objective Pronouns   Rewrite the following paragraph, correcting any errors in pronoun use, in spelling, or in mechanics.

Emily Dickinson was a quiet, somewhat shy young woman. Critics consider she to be one of the greatest of the Modern Poets. Her poems tell we and any future readers of her intense concern for the mysterys of life and death. Most of her works explore the relationship between she and the external world. Although Dickinson lived primarily in seclusion, she had a few close freinds. In general, she preferred to see only they and her family. Some sources link she and the Reverand Charles Wadsworth romantically. However she reguarded him only as "her dearest earthly friend." His move to san francisco ended any chance for he and her to have a future together which sugests one reason for her reclusive lifestyle.

C. APPLICATION IN WRITING

A Poem Write a diamond-shaped poem to compare and contrast two people: for example, two friends or two athletes. The top half of the diamond should describe the traits of one person, and the bottom half, the other person. Start the poem with a one-word line, continue with a second line of three words, a third of five words, and so on. The middle or longest line might be a summary or transitional statement about the people. The line lengths of the bottom half then begin to decrease. Use pronouns correctly.

C H E C K P O I N T
PAGES 693–697

Write the correct pronoun from those given in parentheses. Then tell the case of the pronoun you chose.

Writing Theme
Winston Churchill

1. We British and Americans were never closer as allies than (we, us) were during World War II.
2. At that time, Winston Churchill was Prime Minister, and it was (he, him) who united the British to fight Adolph Hitler.
3. Churchill and President Franklin D. Roosevelt formed a strong bond; Churchill asked (he, him) to aid Great Britain.
4. "Give (we, us) the tools and (we, us) will finish the job," he said.
5. Londoners were suffering nightly German bombing raids; for (they, them) life had become a nightmare.
6. Over a million women and children left London because the government strongly urged (they, them) to evacuate the city.
7. Churchill's walking tours of London to inspect damage and boost morale were, for (he, him), a fraction of his work.
8. It was (he, him) who inspired the people with his oratory.
9. Journalist C. L. Sulzberger wrote about (he, him): "(He, Him) fancied . . . oratory, at which (he, him) was magnificent."
10. In one of his most famous speeches, Churchill said, "(I, Me) have nothing to offer but blood, toil, tears, and sweat."
11. "(We, Us) have before (we, us) an ordeal of the most grievous kind," he continued.
12. The British sorely needed inspiring words; a much beleaguered people were (they, them) after the bombing started.
13. Roosevelt and Churchill remained in close contact; Roosevelt agreed to meet (he, him) off the coast of Newfoundland.
14. When the two leaders met, Roosevelt and (he, him) renewed their warm, personal, and official relationship.
15. The Atlantic Charter, issued jointly by (they, them), outlined policies on which (they, them) based hopes for a better future.

PRONOUNS IN THE POSSESSIVE CASE

Personal pronouns that show possession take the possessive case. The possessive pronouns *mine, yours, his, hers, its,* and *theirs* are used in place of nouns: The red towel is *mine. Yours* is striped.

My, our, your, his, her, its, and *their* are used as adjectives to modify nouns: *My* beach towel is red. *Your* beach towel is striped.

Possessive Pronouns Modifying Gerunds

The possessive pronoun is used when the pronoun immediately precedes a gerund.

> *His running for the train* told us that the hour was late. (*Running for the train* is a gerund phrase functioning as the subject. The possessive form *His* modifies the gerund phrase.)

Remember that present participles also end in *-ing*. However, the possessive case is not used for pronouns that precede participles.

> When we saw *him* running for the train, we knew it was late. (*Him* is the object of the verb. *Running for the train* is a participial phrase modifying *him*.)

If the *-ing* word is used as a noun, it is a gerund; used as a modifier, it is a participle. A gerund often functions as the subject or object in a sentence. Check to see how the *-ing* word is used.

> The neighbors objected to *their* playing the drums at midnight. (*Playing the drums at midnight* is a gerund phrase, the object of the preposition *to.* The possessive pronoun *their* should be used before the gerund. The act of playing is focused on.)

> The neighbors heard *them* playing the drums at midnight. (*Playing the drums* is a participial phrase modifying *them.* The persons playing the drums are focused on.)

In some sentences, either form of the pronoun can be used, depending on the meaning and the emphasis desired.

> Imagine *his ice-skating in the Olympics.* (emphasizes action)

> Imagine *him ice-skating in the Olympics.* (emphasizes person)

For more about gerunds and participles, see Handbook 33.

Writing **TIP**

Proofread your writing to be sure you have not used an apostrophe with a possessive pronoun.

Practice Your Skills

CONCEPT CHECK

Possessive Pronouns   Choose the correct pronoun in parentheses.

1. Sofia, a computer programmer, found that (she, her) researching the history of computers led her to a book about Charles Babbage.
2. She learned about (him, his) trying to eliminate errors in logarithmic tables during the early 1800's.
3. Babbage wanted to build a complicated machine to eliminate the necessity of (him, his) doing all calculations by hand.
4. Over the course of a long lifetime, Babbage devoted many hours to (him, his) working out the details of his marvelous machine.
5. Babbage's machine was an early attempt at a computer; (it's, its) parts could manipulate numbers to solve a variety of problems.
6. He approached the government and scientific societies for money; he promised (them, their) programming and calculating devices.
7. Babbage assured his sponsors that not only would his machine have a "memory," but (his, him) attaching the machine to a printer would result in (its, it's) printing answers.
8. His demonstration of the use of punch cards led to sponsors giving (them, their) support.
9. Babbage never did come up with anything that worked like (us, our) computing devices of today.
10. Nevertheless, (his, him) pioneering laid some of the groundwork for exciting computer developments that were to come later.

PROBLEMS IN PRONOUN USAGE

The most common problems in pronoun usage occur in deciding whether the nominative or the objective form is the correct one.

Who and Whom in Questions and Clauses

In choosing whether to use *who* or *whom* in a question, it is necessary to understand the function of the pronoun.

Who, the nominative form of the pronoun, is used as the subject of a verb or as a predicate pronoun. *Whom,* the objective form, is used as the direct object or as the object of a preposition.

> *Who* auditioned for the lead role? (*Who* is the subject of *auditioned.*)

> *Whom* did the director choose for the lead role? (*Whom* is the direct object of *did choose.*)

Pronoun Usage   **701**

Writing
─TIP─

In formal writing,
use *whom* when-
ever the objective
case of *who* is
needed.

The pronouns *who, whoever, whom, whomever,* and *whose* may be used in noun or adjective clauses. These pronouns have a function within the clause.

Who and *whoever* are nominative case forms and can act as subjects or predicate pronouns in a clause. *Whom* and *whomever* are objective forms and can be direct objects or objects of a preposition.

In determining which pronoun you should use, first isolate the subordinate clause. Next determine how the pronoun functions in that clause.

> The writer (who, whom) we just studied was Thomas Malory. (The adjective clause is *[who, whom] we just studied.* The pronoun functions as the direct object of *studied* in the clause. *Whom,* the objective case pronoun, is needed.)

> The Holy Grail would be found by (whoever, whomever) was the most worthy person. (The noun clause is *[whoever, whomever] was the most worthy.* The entire clause is the object of the preposition *by.* The pronoun acts as the subject of the verb *was* within the clause. The nominative case pronoun *whoever* is the correct choice.)

In determining whether to use *who* or *whom,* do not be misled by parenthetical expressions in the subordinate clause.

> In one version of the legend, it is Perceval who, *I think,* finds the Holy Grail. (*Who* is the subject of *finds* in the subordinate clause. *I think* is a parenthetical expression.)

The pronoun whose functions as a possessive pronoun.

> The knight *whose* destiny was to find the Holy Grail was Galahad. (*Whose* is a possessive pronoun modifying *destiny.*)

Practice Your Skills

A. CONCEPT CHECK

Who and Whom Choose the correct pronoun from those given in parentheses.

1. Rock-and-roll became familiar to the American public through Bill Haley and the Comets, (who, whom, whose) combined a heavy beat with a call to dance.
2. There were few teens of the fifties for (who, whom) the Comets' "Rock Around the Clock" was not a favorite.
3. It is Alan Freed, a Cleveland disc jockey, to (who, whom, whose) credit is given for popularizing the term *rock-and-roll.*

Writing Theme
History of
Rock-and-Roll

4. (Whoever, Whomever) listened carefully to early rock-and-roll recognized its origin in rhythm and blues.
5. There is one musician, Chuck Berry, (who, whom) critics consider important to the early history of this music.
6. Berry was a trailblazer (who, whom, whose) virtuoso electric guitar playing helped set the style of rock.
7. (Who, Whom) does not think of the name Elvis Presley when rock is mentioned?
8. There was no one before him (who, whom) mixed country with rhythm and blues to produce songs such as "Heartbreak Hotel."
9. (Who, Whom) do people think of when they hear "I Want to Hold Your Hand"?
10. The sixties brought the Beatles, (who, whom, whose) new harmonies and effective lyrics transformed rock.
11. This British group, (who, whom) American audiences flocked to hear, had its first US hit in 1964.
12. All of these artists (who, whom) helped shape rock-and-roll contributed to what has become a popular musical style in our culture.

B. DRAFTING SKILL

Sentence Combining   Rewrite the following paragraph by drafting combined sentences by using forms of *who, whom,* or *whose.*

(1) In the sixties, musicians helped form popular culture. Their music appealed to the youth of the decade. (2) P. F. Sloan was one of the songwriters. He stirred consciousness of social issues in the United States. (3) Barry McGuire was a singer. With him, Sloan worked on the song "Eve of Destruction." (4) Others sang of many other social issues and problems. To them music was meant to convey a message. (5) British bands, such as the Rolling Stones, were also among the groups. Their music and messages influenced the youth movement. (6) One member of the Rolling Stones was Mick Jagger. People are likely to recognize Mick Jagger today. (7) The Rolling Stones and the Doors were especially popular with young people. Some of the young people considered themselves part of the counterculture. (8) Other youths listened to the message music of Peter, Paul, and Mary and of Simon and Garfunkel. These youths were not necessarily part of the counterculture. (9) They were among the many groups. They sang thought-provoking songs with gentle rhythms. (10) Overall, the music of the sixties offered myriad messages set to various beats. Anyone would listen for its meaning.

A Biography Choose a famous figure from the history of rock-and-roll, such as Chuck Berry or Grace Slick. Do some research and write a biographical sketch of this person. Use *who* or *whom* to add clauses identifying the actions of influential persons in your subject's life.

Pronouns Used with and as Appositives

Appositives are words or phrases that immediately follow another word for the purpose of identifying that word. A pronoun can be the appositive, part of the appositive, or the word identified.

Pronouns Used with Appositives The pronouns *we* and *us* are often followed by appositives. To decide whether to use the nominative case *we* or the objective case *us,* read the sentence without the appositive.

> The usher told (we, us) Ranger fans to return to the stadium. (told us, *not* told we)

> (We, Us) Rangers trounced the Tigers in both games. (We trounced, *not* us trounced)

Pronouns as Appositives The correct form of a pronoun used as an appositive is determined by the use of the noun to which the pronoun is in apposition.

> The children, *Jerry and she,* were riding on the carousel. (*Jerry* and *she* are in apposition to *children,* which is the subject of *were riding.* The nominative form *she* is required.)

To determine which form of the pronoun to use in apposition, try the appositive by itself in the sentence.

> The usher guided the latecomers, Gina and (he, him), to their seats with a flashlight. (guided him, *not* guided he)

Practice Your Skills

CONCEPT CHECK

Appositives Choose the correct pronoun from those in parentheses.

1. (We, Us) reviewers do not often rave about performances.
2. Nevertheless, the production of Tchaikovsky's *Swan Lake* left the audience, ballet aficionados and (we, us), breathless.
3. Liv Ullman explained to (we, us) members of the audience that the ballet was a cooperative effort of the Soviet and U.S. citizens.

Writing Theme
Ballet

4. The producers, (they and we, them and us), combined the best in the ballet world.
5. The choreography was done by Konstantin Sergeyev; two brilliant minds, Natalia Dudinskaya and (he, him), staged the ballet.
6. The finest part of the production was the dancing of Nina Ananiashvili; Devon Carney and (she, her) danced the leads.
7. Needless to say, both dancers, (he and she, him and her), brilliantly portrayed the prince and the beautiful swan.
8. After the performance, (we, us) spellbound viewers loudly proclaimed, "Bravo! Brava!"
9. All the participants in this collaboration, both (we and they, us and them), were delighted with the response.
10. A hope held by many, including my fellow reviewers and (I, me), is that the future holds other Soviet–United States productions—*Sleeping Beauty,* perhaps?

Reflexive and Intensive Pronouns

A pronoun ending in *-self* or *-selves* can be used intensively for emphasis or reflexively to refer to a preceding noun or pronoun.

> I *myself* completed the one thousand piece jigsaw puzzle. (intensive)

> Richard locked *himself* out of his car. (reflexive—direct object)

Pronouns ending in *-self* or *-selves* cannot be used alone. Each must have an antecedent—the word to which it refers—in the same sentence.

Incorrect   Sara and myself are interested in robotics.(There is no antecedent for *myself.*)

Correct   Sara and I are interested in robotics.

The forms *hisself* and *theirselves* are nonstandard. Do not use them.

Practice Your Skills

CONCEPT CHECK

Reflexive and Intensive Pronouns   Write the correct pronoun from those given in parentheses.

1. The Irish pride (them, themselves) on their flair for highly imaginative storytelling.
2. An Irish storyteller, Lord Dunsany, provided (us, ourselves) with stories described as credible fantasy.
3. In one story, a young man dining at a restaurant has an animated conversation, seemingly with (him, himself).
4. The young man asks his "guest" if he has actually seen Helen of Troy (her, herself).
5. Between (them, themselves), the conversation ranges from Cheops to Cleopatra.
6. The reader senses that the guest (hisself, himself) knew them all personally.
7. One also wonders if the young man might be lovesick over a woman busy amusing (her, herself) elsewhere.
8. After dinner, the young man cryptically tells his guest, "I (me, myself) haven't taken (you, yourself) much out of your way."
9. With this the young man drinks the coffee he (him, himself) poisoned, and falls to the floor.
10. Discerning readers praise (them, themselves) for guessing that Death was the young man's guest.

Pronouns in Comparisons

A clause that begins with *than* or the sequence *as . . . as* can be used to establish a comparison.

> Marie is more musical *than* Lillian is.
> I did *as* many push-ups *as* Francisco.

The final clause in a comparison is sometimes elliptical; that is, some words are omitted. The omission of words makes it difficult to determine the correct pronoun.

> Marie is more musical than she.
> I did as many push-ups as he.

To decide which pronoun form to use in an elliptical clause, fill in the words that are not stated.

> The noise scared Phyllis more than (I, me). (The noise scared Phyllis more than it scared *me*.)

Sometimes either the nominative case or the objective case pronoun form may be correct, depending on the meaning.

> She writes her sister more often than he. (This means "She writes to her sister more often than he does.")

> She writes her sister more often than him. (This means "She writes to her sister more often than she writes to him.")

Practice Your Skills

A. CONCEPT CHECK

Pronouns in Comparisons Choose the correct pronoun from those given in parentheses.

Writing Theme
The Business
of Film

1. Mickey, Minnie, Donald, and Goofy—no characters in the world are as beloved as (they, them).
2. No fans have ever been more devoted than (we, us).
3. Their creator, Walt Disney, was a man of many talents; perhaps no one other than (he, him) could have built such an empire.
4. The success in 1928 of *Steamboat Willie* made Disney famous; audiences as well as (he, him) were enchanted with "talking films."
5. No one in the business worked harder than (he, him) and his brother Roy, who was the company's business manager.
6. Together they built a successful industry involving much more than short cartoons, which surprised their audiences as much as (they, them).
7. Moviegoers of the 30's were not as accustomed to products tied to movies as (we, us).
8. No one foresaw the possibilities of licensed products as well as (they, them), the founders of the Disney empire.
9. From cartoons to amusement parks, Disney has delighted fans in the past as much as (we, us) audiences today.
10. For a man who built an empire on fantasy, a realist more astute than (he, him) would be hard to find.

B. PROOFREADING SKILL

Pronouns Rewrite the following paragraph. Correct all errors in pronoun usage, as well as any errors in spelling, capitalization, and punctuation.

Us movie spectators see many special effects, from dog-fights in Space to poltergeists in houses. In one longstanding movie technique, a peace of film is superimposed over another. It was the film pioneer Georges Méliès whom first exploited this process in narritive films of the early 1900's. In the recent *Star wars* movies by George Lucas, his special-affect team and him advanced the technique. Computers were used to track two camaras so that, after shooting separate exposures could be put together into one final film. This method allowed himself and his team to produce such classic scenes as the flight through the forest in *return of the jedi,* where both the characters and the background move. In fact the computers worked so well that to he and his team the results seemed too perfect. Therefore, they introduced random movements into the computer program for variety.

C. APPLICATION IN WRITING

A Movie Review Think of a movie you have seen recently that included special effects. Describe the effects and compare them with similar effects you have seen in other movies. Think about the ways in which the effects were unique or fascinating and might be of special interest to other moviegoers. You might also want to speculate on how some of these effects were created. Use pronouns correctly as you write.

CHECK POINT

PAGES 700–708

Choose the correct pronoun of the two given in parentheses.

1. (We, Us) mystery fans know well the address 221B Baker Street, in London.
2. The person (who, whom) lived at this address was Sherlock Holmes, the most famous detective in all fiction.
3. Many mystery fans know that Sir Arthur Conan Doyle, (who, whom) created Holmes, based some of (his, him) writing on the actual life of Dr. Joseph Bell, a surgeon and teacher.
4. Bell was renowned for (his, him) careful analytic thinking.
5. Few were better at deductive reasoning than (he, him).
6. Another person (who, whom) Doyle used as a model for Holmes was a cricket-playing friend named Sherlock.
7. In addition, Doyle modeled after (him, himself) some aspects of the character, Holmes.
8. In the Sherlock Holmes stories, Holmes works for (whoever, whomever) comes to him with an interesting case.
9. At the famous Baker Street address, Dr. Watson and (he, himself) discuss many a crime.
10. Holmes is a smart, capable man, but Watson is more amiable and good-natured than (he, himself).
11. In case after case, Holmes and Watson prove (them, themselves) superior to their adversaries, the craftiest criminals of the day.
12. Watson is a loyal friend, and part of practically every story is devoted to (his, him) extolling Holmes's virtues or exclaiming over Holmes's powers of reasoning.
13. (Whoever, Whomever) reads the Sherlock Holmes stories will find that Watson serves as a foil for Holmes.
14. Watson is a foil because (his, him) plodding makes Holmes's brilliance seem even more spectacular by contrast.
15. The Sherlock Holmes stories have given (we, us) mystery readers untold pleasure for many years.
16. Some readers have even formed clubs that discuss the situations Holmes gets (hisself, himself) into.
17. The members of one such club in New York call (theirselves, themselves) the "The Baker Street Irregulars."
18. A similar group, (who, whom) meet in London, have a more traditional name: "The Sherlock Holmes Society."
19. Few writers have had more demanding fans than (he, him).
20. Tiring of his hero, the author wrote Holmes' death scene; however, the public would not stand for (his, him) killing Holmes off.

PRONOUN-ANTECEDENT AGREEMENT

An antecedent is the noun or pronoun to which a pronoun refers.

A pronoun must agree with its antecedent in number, gender, and person.

Agreement in Number   If the antecedent of a pronoun is singular, a singular pronoun is required. If the antecedent is plural, a plural pronoun is required.

The following indefinite pronouns are singular. When one of these is an antecedent, the second pronoun must be singular.

another	anything	everybody	neither	one
anybody	each	everyone	nobody	somebody
anyone	either	everything	no one	someone

Each (singular) of the violinists brought *his* (singular) violin. (*Each* is the antecedent of *his*.)

Everyone (singular) indicated *his or her* (singular) preferences in the marketing opinion survey.

Remember that a prepositional phrase following a singular indefinite pronoun does not affect the number of any other word in the sentence.

The following indefinite pronouns are plural and are referred to by the plural possessive pronouns *our, your, their.*

both	few	many	several

Both of the candidates had given *their* speeches by ten o'clock.

Many of us have taken all *our* required math courses.

The indefinite pronouns *all, some, any, most,* and *none* may be referred to by a singular or plural pronoun, depending on the meaning.

All of the play had *its* setting in a steam bath.

All of the networks are showing *their* best shows.

In the preceding examples, the indefinite pronouns are used as subjects. Note that the verb, as well as any pronouns referring to the subject, agrees in number with the subject.

Notice the other pronouns and the verbs in the following sentences that contain the indefinite pronoun *none*.

Incorrect   None of the debaters *has* made *their* rebuttal.

Correct   None of the debaters *has* made *his or her* rebuttal.

Correct   None of the debaters *have* made *their* rebuttals.

Two or more singular antecedents joined by *or* or *nor* are referred to by a singular pronoun. When any part of a compound antecedent joined by *or* or *nor* is plural, use the noun nearer the verb to determine whether the pronoun is singular or plural.

Either *Kate* or *Geraldine* will lend me *her* skis.

Neither *Marty* nor the *other gymnasts* have met *their* new coach.

Collective nouns may be referred to by either a singular or plural pronoun, depending on the meaning intended.

The committee has made *its* decision on the location of the new park. (The committee is thought of as a singular whole.)

The committee made *their* position speeches on the location of the new park. (The committee members are considered as individuals.)

Agreement in Gender   A pronoun must be of the same gender as the word to which it refers. *He, his,* and *him* are masculine pronouns. *She, her,* and *hers* are feminine pronouns. *It* and *its* are neuter.

When a singular pronoun refers to an antecedent that includes both males and females, the phrase *his or her* is acceptable. In fact, it is preferred to the use of *his* by many who want to avoid sexist language.

Correct   Each climber should bring *his* survival kit.

Correct   Each climber should bring *his or her* survival kit.

Agreement in Person   A personal pronoun must be in the same person as its antecedent. *One, everyone,* and *everybody* are in the third person. They should be referred to by the third-person pronouns.

Incorrect   Everyone should clean up your own lab area.

Correct   Everyone should clean up his or her own lab area.

Practice Your Skills

A. CONCEPT CHECK

Pronoun-Antecedent Agreement Find and correct the errors in agreement in these sentences. Write *Correct* if there is no error.

1. In medieval times, neither a knight nor his page was likely to be seen without one of their weapons—a lance, a dagger, or a spear.
2. In fact, most of the people judged his or her favorite knight by the type and number of his weapons.
3. When knights engaged in jousting, the combat between two horsemen, each rider carried a lance tucked under their arm.
4. Not everyone, however, was able to control both his horse and his heavy lance at the same time.
5. Each of the knights who jousted spent many hours of their day in careful training and practice.
6. Both of the combatants in a joust had to be ready to aim and thrust their lances as well as to deflect blows.
7. Despite all of this rigorous training, many of the knights who fought in actual combat did not use their lances at all.
8. Anyone who fought on foot knew their lance was too long.
9. All of the French knights who fought on foot shortened his lances.
10. Most of the knights also took off their foot-armor; that way, the army could handle their task of fighting on foot more efficiently.

B. PROOFREADING SKILL

Pronoun-Antecedent Agreement Rewrite the paragraph. Correct all errors in pronoun usage, spelling, capitalization, and punctuation.

One of the most romantic sports—fencing—have a long history. There is even an ancient egyptian carving of fencers. Unlike fencing in centuries past, none of the modern fencers try to wound his opponents? Both women and men are modern practitioners of the sport, which involves the skilful use of swords for attack and defence. Most maintains that fencing is more like a game of live chess. Each of the fencers tries to outwit their opponent. The object for a fencer is to touch their opponent with a foil—without being touched yourself. Since a fencer needs to strike quickly and know when to strike, both physical and psychological skills have its place in the sport. For the fencers protection, each of the foils has a blunted tip at the end of their blade. All of the equipment—a canvas jacket, a mesh mask, and the foil—is available for you to rent in fencing classes.

PRONOUN REFERENCE

A writer must be sure that pronouns have clear antecedents. If the pronoun reference is vague or ambiguous, the resulting sentence may be confusing to the reader. This section covers some of the common kinds of errors that occur with pronoun reference.

Unidentified and Indefinite Reference

To avoid any confusion for the reader, each personal pronoun should have a clear antecedent.

If no antecedent for the pronoun is present, or if the antecedent is vague or indefinite, the reader will be misled.

Unidentified Reference   The words *it, they, this, which,* and *that* can create problems because in some cases they appear without a referent. Often the problem can be solved by reworking the sentence.

Unidentified	It says in the introduction that the story is true.
Better	The introduction states that the story is true.
Unidentified	In New Guinea they used large stones as money.
Better	People in New Guinea once used large stones as money.

The pronoun *you* is sometimes used to refer to people in general, rather than to the person spoken to. Avoid this confusing use of *you.*

Weak	In pioneer days you had to travel on horseback, by covered wagon, or on foot.
Better	The pioneers had to travel on horseback, by covered wagon, or on foot.

Indefinite Reference   When the idea to which the pronoun refers is only weakly or vaguely expressed, a clear antecedent must be supplied. Sometimes the solution is to replace the pronoun with a noun.

Weak	Richard juggles at children's parties. It takes up much of his free time on weekends. (There is no clear antecedent for the pronoun *It.* The pronoun vaguely relates to the verb *juggles,* but a verb cannot be the antecedent for a noun.)
Better	Richard juggles at children's parties. Juggling takes up much of his free time on weekends.

Weak	Hiking is my favorite sport although I haven't been on one yet this summer. (There is no clear antecedent for *one;* the verbal *hiking* cannot be a replacement for *one.*)
Better	Hiking is my favorite sport although I haven't yet been on a single hike this summer.
Vague	Computers are used to give farmers data on prices. This helps them track the profitability of their operations. (There is no clear antecedent for *This.*)
Better	The use of computers to get data on prices helps farmers track the profitability of their operations.
Vague	We arrived at the theater twenty minutes early, which meant we had time to read the program. (There is no clear antecedent for *which.*)
Better	Because we arrived at the theater twenty minutes early, we had time to read the program.

Writing
—TIP—

When you proof-read your writing, make sure that each pronoun has a clear, specific antecedent pre-ceding it.

Writing Theme
Famous Animals

Ambiguous Reference

The word *ambiguous* means "having two or more possible meanings." The reference of a pronoun is ambiguous if the pronoun may refer to more than one word. This situation can arise when a noun or pronoun falls between the pronoun and its true antecedent, as shown in the following examples.

Ambiguous	Before putting the car in the garage, Beth cleaned it. (What did she clean? the car? the garage?)
Better	Beth cleaned the car before putting it in the garage.
Ambiguous	Barry told Kev that his camera was defective. (Whose camera? Barry's or Kev's?)
Better	Barry examined Kev's camera and told him it was defective.

Practice Your Skills

A. CONCEPT CHECK

Pronoun Reference   Rewrite the sentences to remove all indefinite or ambiguous pronoun references.

1. They tell a story about a famous Indian elephant that was brought to the United States in 1920.
2. It states in one source that the elephant was a present for a little girl.

3. The elephant was taken to its new home in a taxi, where it was deemed too difficult to handle.
4. From there, the elephant was given to a circus and entrusted to a trainer; he learned to do tricks.
5. The elephant, whose name was Ziggy, pleased the crowds by playing "Yes, Sir, That's My Baby" on the harmonica, and they loved it.
6. Nevertheless, you can lose your popularity at any time, and the day came when Ziggy was sent to the zoo.
7. The press reported that Ziggy and his keeper did not get along, and that he tried to kill him.
8. Ziggy spent the next thirty years in a cage apart from the other elephants; it was an isolation that aroused a great outcry of public sympathy.
9. Eventually, children raised enough money to "save" Ziggy. This enabled them to get a larger cage in a sunny location for the elephant.
10. By 1970 Ziggy was leading the good life again, romping with the other elephants. It filled the old elephant's time and seemed to bring him happiness.

B. REVISION SKILL

Revising to Correct Errors in Pronoun Usage   Revise the following paragraph, correcting any unidentified, indefinite, or ambiguous references. One sentence in the paragraph contains no error; label that sentence *Correct*.

(1) "I don't know which is more high strung, my horse Bucephalus or my son Alexander. I ought to have him destroyed," mused Philip II, leader of Macedonia, "especially since no one can ride him." (2) It says in legend that Philip had sought a horse for combat. (3) It described the high-spirited horse, Bucephalus, who was brought by a clever horse trader. (4) Philip immediately realized he was unusual. (5) In Bucephalus you found speed, daring, and beauty—and a horse that was afraid of its own shadow. (6) Alexander bet Philip that he could ride the horse. (7) Philip took the bet because it seemed certain that Alexander would not win. (8) However, Alexander had never ridden one he couldn't master. (9) This enabled him to discover a way to break the steed. (10) Alexander turned Bucephalus to face the sun so that the horse would not see its own shadow, jumped on its back, and galloped across the field, thus winning the bet.

Writing Theme
Georgia O'Keeffe

Rewrite the following sentences, correcting any errors in pronoun usage.

1. Each of the great artists can be said to have their own personal vision, and the American artist Georgia O'Keeffe found hers.
2. In an article about O'Keeffe, it says that she worked between realism and abstraction.
3. In O'Keeffe's paintings you find gigantic flowers and the haunting images of bleached bones against the dark earth and sky.
4. Her artistic talent was recognized in her early teens, and she knew she wanted to become one.
5. O'Keeffe's fame came almost by accident in 1916 when she sent to a friend some charcoal drawings which she liked.
6. Her friend showed the drawings to an art gallery director, and they were put on display, which first brought her work to public attention.
7. In the late 1920's O'Keeffe visited New Mexico, and this had a strong effect on her personal artistic vision.
8. Her later paintings has its inspiration in the New Mexican landscape.
9. Some of her cityscapes have large forms that occupy most of the canvas, and they make a strong impact on the viewer.
10. O'Keeffe stands as one of the great artists of the twentieth century, which is fitting for one who gave her individual expression to the American spirit.

New Mexican Landscape,
1930, Georgia O'Keeffe

GRAMMAR
HANDBOOK
36

A. Choosing Correct Pronouns Choose the correct pronoun from those given in parentheses.

1. When a person uses an automated teller machine, an ATM, (he or she, him or her) is involved in cryptology.
2. A personal identification number, or PIN, is issued to (whoever, whomever) is authorized to use the card.
3. The PIN is coded either on the card or in the bank's computer in (its, their) encrypted form.
4. Between (you, yourself) and (I, me, myself), few thieves are smart enough to figure out the special cipher (theirselves, themselves).
5. Clever criminals need the bank's key to the code and the customer's PIN in order for (they, them) to steal funds by computer.
6. Cryptologists, however, are more clever than (they, them).
7. By (them, their) devising this special coding, cryptologists have rendered the cardholder's code totally protected.
8. It is impossible for anyone (who, whom) breaks into the computer file to figure out the ciphered PIN, even if (he or she, they) knows the key.
9. Thus, the average cardholders, you and (I, me), are protected from computer hacks (who, whom, whose) designs are dishonest.
10. Likewise, phone signals from the automatic teller machines to the bank's central computer are encrypted; (they, them, their) transmitting of a transaction is completely secure.
11. (We, Us) would-be millionaires are also protected by codes from lottery-ticket forgers.
12. All of the lottery ticket numbers are printed on the cards in (its, their) encrypted forms.
13. People to (who, whom) the winning cards have been sold must turn in cards that have both the real and the encrypted numbers.
14. (Whoever, Whomever) has the equipment available can probably forge a card (hisself, himself, themselves).
15. However, if forgers do not include the correct cipher, the real losers will be (they, them).

B. Correcting Pronoun Errors Rewrite the sentences, eliminating pronoun errors. If there are no errors, write *Correct*.

1. The historian was interested in the early history of secret codes; it was either her or her assistants whom found *The Codebreakers*.
2. Whoever is an expert on codes knows that they are all based on two fundamental principles—transposition and substitution.
3. One of Julius Caesar's first military achievements was his creation of a substitution cipher, but he soon abandoned it.

Writing Theme
Codes and
Code-Breaking

4. He did not trust Cicero, with who he had shared the secret of the code.
5. Cicero hisself had his scribe, a man named Tyro, invent a form of secret writing.
6. Tyronian characters that looked like modern shorthand evolved; several of them are still familiar to we today.
7. Lysander of Sparta, whom was a famous Greek warrior, is also associated with a device for breaking codes.
8. Surrounded by traitors, Lysander knew that one false move could mean that Sparta and him were both lost.
9. He tested the truthfulness of whomever came before he.
10. When a traitor with a secret message entered Lysander's presence, he decoded the message through the use of a cylindrical staff known as a scytale.
11. Few generals were as distrustful and wary as him.
12. The art of cryptography faded for many centuries; the monks revived it during the Middle Ages.
13. Anyone living during the Middle Ages probably would not have recognized the Zodiac Alphabet as a code or deciphered it by themselves.
14. Centuries later, Giovanni Baptista della Porta devised the Porta Table; the Father of Modern Cryptography is said to be him.
15. A Frenchman named Vignère evolved a similar table; both of these men claimed that his cipher was indecipherable.

C. Proofreading for Pronoun Errors Rewrite the following paragraphs. Correct all errors in pronoun usage as well as any errors in spelling, capitalization, punctuation, or agreement.

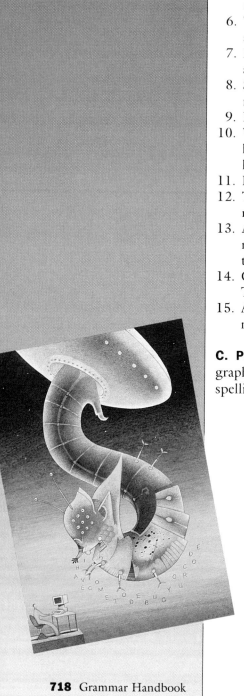

Each of the greats in the history of cryptanalysis—code breaking—have had their triumphs; but it is William Friedman who experts called the "harry Houdini" of code breakers. Interestingly, it was Shakespeare whom indirectly started Friedman on his career.

An eccentric millionair hired Friedman because he believed that all of Shakespeares plays had been written by another sixteenth-century writer, Francis Bacon. In fact, the millionaire thought that Bacon had left coded secret messages in them. Friedman set out to find and decipher the messages, and it became his career. He distinguished hisself during both World War I and World War II by applying statistical analysis to cryptanalysis and became the chief code breaker for the War Departmint. Moreover, the fact that Friedman's achievements occurred before the age of computers makes it even more surprising.

Adjective and Adverb Usage

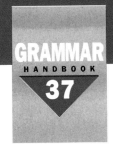

UNDERSTANDING MODIFIERS

Before examining the usage rules for modifiers, you may wish to review their basic definitions and functions. You will recall that an **adjective** is a modifier that describes or limits a noun or pronoun. An **adverb** is a modifier that describes a verb, adjective, or other adverb. A modifier can be identified as an adjective or an adverb by determining the part of speech of the word it modifies.

Adjective and Adverb Forms

Most adjectives have no identifying form or ending. Many adverbs, however, can be recognized by their *-ly* endings. These adverbs are formed by adding *-ly* to adjectives.

Adjective	Adverb
close	closely
fearless	fearlessly
respectful	respectfully
moody	moodily

A few adjectives and adverbs have identical forms.

Adjective	Adverb
a *rough* surface	play *rough*
the *first* act	arrive *first*
a *low* bush	threw *low*
your *left* hand	turn *left*

Most adjectives and adverbs that have only one syllable have the same form. Adjectives with more than one syllable usually add an *-ly* ending if they are to form an adverb.

The *violent* storm made us nervous.
The storm raged *violently* and made us nervous.

The lifeguard pulled the *hysterical* swimmer out of the powerful surf.
The swimmer shrieked *hysterically* as the lifeguard pulled her from the powerful surf.

Grammar Note Some adjectives end in *-ly*. For example, *lively, deadly, friendly, manly, costly,* and *beastly* are adjectives. Do not assume that all words that end in *-ly* are adverbs.

Writing
—**TIP**—

Use modifiers with economy. One precise modifier can often replace two general ones, as *minuscule* replaces *very small*.

Several adverbs have two forms, one with the *-ly* ending, the other without. Both forms are acceptable, but the longer form is used in formal writing. In a few instances, the two forms have completely different meanings and applications: for example, *late, lately; near, nearly.*

He always arrives *late.*	He hasn't come to any meetings *lately.*
Come *near.*	They ran *nearly* a mile.
Go *slow!*	He drove *slowly* on the snow-covered streets.
Reach down *deep.*	She appeared *deeply* troubled about the problem.

Modifiers That Follow Verbs

A word that modifies an action verb, an adjective, or another adverb is always an adverb.

Original thinkers experience ridicule *often.* (The adverb *often* modifies the action verb *experience.*)

Ridicule can be *terribly* demoralizing. (The adverb *terribly* modifies the adjective *demoralizing.*)

Original thinkers *very* definitely need self-confidence. (The adverb *very* modifies *definitely,* another adverb.)

Action verbs are frequently followed by adverbs. Modifiers that follow linking verbs are predicate adjectives. Choosing the correct modifier after a linking verb usually causes no problem when the linking verb is a form of *be.*

Remember, however, that most other linking verbs can also function as action verbs. If you are unsure whether to use the adjective or adverb form following a verb, determine whether the verb is linking or action.

Linking Verb	**Action Verb**
The man *looked* suspicious.	The detective *looked* suspiciously at the man.
The ship *appeared* damaged.	The ship *appeared* suddenly in the fog.
The crowd *sounds* angry.	The timekeeper *sounded* the buzzer to end the game.
You'll *feel* better if you exercise daily.	*Feel* the luxurious texture of this velvet cloth.

Practice Your Skills

A. CONCEPT CHECK

Adjectives and Adverbs Write the correct modifier of the two given in parentheses. Label it *Adjective* or *Adverb*. Then write the word or words it modifies.

1. Interest in late Medieval and early Renaissance music has increased (considerable, considerably) in the past few decades.
2. This increased interest is (large, largely) due to the efforts of one person—Christopher Hogwood.
3. Hogwood, who himself plays the harpsichord (beautiful, beautifully), founded the Academy of Ancient Music.
4. The Academy performs and records Medieval and Renaissance music on original instruments—ones that are (clear, clearly) museum pieces.
5. These recordings and performances sound (wonderful, wonderfully) because of the authenticity of the instruments.
6. Even in recent years, some of these ancient instruments have been in (common, commonly) use by musicians such as Wanda Landowska, who has performed and recorded extensively on the harpsichord.
7. Others, such as the cornet, the krummhorn, the sackbut, and the shawm, have become (rare, rarely).
8. The Academy members are known, not only for their use of restored or reconstructed ancient instruments, but also for the (authentic, authentically) manner of their playing.
9. A listener can almost imagine being in the court of a great duke or earl, watching an (elaborate, elaborately) staged performance.
10. The recordings made by the Academy are (brilliant, brilliantly) and well worth adding to any music collection.

Writing Theme
Medieval and Renaissance Music

Harmony,
Bartolomeo Bettera

B. REVISION SKILL

Adjectives and Adverbs   Rewrite the following sentences to correct all errors in the use of adjectives and adverbs. If a sentence contains no errors, write *Correct*.

1. Reproducing historical accurate musical instruments is a very demanding craft.
2. Musicians insist that the reproduced musical instruments appear and sound authentically.
3. Skilled artisans strive diligently to achieve the original look and feel of the instruments they reproduce.
4. Each step must be completed deliberate.
5. First, the artisan studies careful the musical instrument to be reproduced.
6. The original instrument may be made of a rare wood.
7. Finding wood that is appropriately may be very difficult.
8. One determined craftsman painstaking searched the South American rain forests for snakewood.
9. Such devotion to detail may seem foolishly, but it is crucial to the creation of a fine instrument.

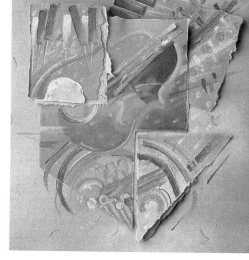

10. With their commitment, skill, and pride, these artisans have been steady opening a window to the music of the great composers of the past.

C. APPLICATION IN WRITING

Historical Fiction   Historical fiction helps people imagine what it would have been like to live in a different place and time. Some historical fiction is told by means of letters. Choose some real or imaginary historical event, such as a concert at the court of Elizabeth I of England, and write a letter to a friend describing the event from the point of view of someone who attended the event. In your letter, use at least three adjectives and two adverbs.

COMPARING ADJECTIVES AND ADVERBS

Adjectives and adverbs have three forms, or degrees. The first form, the **positive degree,** is used to describe people, places, things, actions, or groups. This form of the modifier is the one used as the entry word of a dictionary definition.

Positive   Umberto Boccioni is considered a *great* Italian sculptor.

The **comparative degree** of a modifier is used to compare the thing modified with something else.

Comparative   Umberto Boccioni is considered *greater* than any other Italian sculptor of the early twentieth century.

To decide whether to use the comparative degree of the modifier, watch for clues such as "the other one," "any other," "of the two," and "of the pair." These clues signal that two things are being compared.

The **superlative degree** of an adjective or adverb should be used to compare the thing modified with two or more other things.

Superlative   Umberto Boccioni is considered the *greatest* Italian sculptor of the early twentieth century.

Notice that the context of a superlative often does not contain a number clue, but it does imply that a comparison is being made among more than two things. In the first example below, Humphrey Bogart is compared to all other actors who have played gangster roles. In the second example, the air conditioner is compared to all other inventions of this century.

> Humphrey Bogart was one of the *most* popular gangster actors of all time.

> Perhaps the *best* invention of this century is the air conditioner.

Development of the Bottle in Space, Umberto Boccioni

Adjective and Adverb Usage

Regular Comparisons

Like verbs, adjectives and adverbs have both regular and irregular forms. However, most of these modifiers are regular, and their comparative and superlative degrees can be formed in one of these two ways.

1. **A one-syllable modifier forms the comparative and superlative by adding *-er* and *-est*. A few two-syllable modifiers also form the comparative and superlative in this way.**

Positive	Comparative	Superlative
straight	straighter	straightest
thin	thinner	thinnest
pale	paler	palest
wealthy	wealthier	wealthiest
pretty	prettier	prettiest
sleepy	sleepier	sleepiest
fast	faster	fastest
clear	clearer	clearest

Spelling Note Spelling changes must be made in the positive of some modifiers before adding the comparative and superlative endings. Such spelling changes are indicated in the dictionary under the positive form of the modifier.

2. **Most modifiers with two syllables and all modifiers with three or more syllables use *more* and *most* to form the comparative and the superlative.**

Positive	Comparative	Superlative
careless	more careless	most careless
powerful	more powerful	most powerful
hastily	more hastily	most hastily
ignorant	more ignorant	most ignorant
impressively	more impressively	most impressively
ambiguously	more ambiguously	most ambiguously

Negative comparisons of modifiers are formed by placing the words *less* and *least* before the positive form.

Positive	Comparative	Superlative
disastrous	less disastrous	least disastrous
precisely	less precisely	least precisely
fragrant	less fragrant	least fragrant
bravely	less bravely	least bravely
colorful	less colorful	least colorful
skillful	less skillful	least skillful

Irregular Comparisons

Some commonly used modifiers have irregular comparative and superlative forms. You may wish to memorize them.

Modifiers with Irregular Forms		
Positive	**Comparative**	**Superlative**
bad	worse	worst
far	farther *or* further	farthest *or* furthest
good	better	best
ill	worse	worst
late	later *or* latter	latest *or* last
little	less *or* lesser	least
many	more	most
much	more	most
well	better	best

Usage Note *Farther* and *farthest* compare distances; *further* and *furthest* compare times, amounts, and degrees: Boston is *farther* from San Francisco than Minneapolis is. We will discuss this matter *further* at a later time.

Practice Your Skills

A. CONCEPT CHECK

Comparative and Superlative Forms Write the correct comparative or superlative form of the modifier given in parentheses.

1. Swimming is one of the (old) of all sports.
2. An Egyptian hieroglyph for swimming, from 2500 B.C., shows a man doing a form of the crawl, considered by many to be the (efficient) stroke of all.
3. References to swimming mentioned in epic and legend include the Anglo-Saxon hero Beowulf's boast that he was (strong) than his foe and could swim better—even fully armed.
4. The (early) swimming competition in history took place in 36 B.C.
5. Later, during the Middle Ages, swimming became (little) popular because people feared that the bubonic plague could be spread through the water.
6. When swimming made its comeback in the 1700's, the crawl had been forgotten and (slow) styles were used—the side stroke and the breast stroke.

Writing
TIP

Look for opportunities to replace overused adjectives such as *nice, pretty, good, bad, big,* and *little* with fresh, lively modifiers.

Writing Theme
Sports History

7. In the late 1800's, the crawl was rediscovered when an Australian coach observed a twelve-year-old boy from a Pacific island who had a much (fast) style than the coach's swimmers.
8. Of all the strokes, the once-forgotten crawl again became the stroke (much) favored by racers.
9. Perhaps the (healthful) of all sports, swimming strengthens the muscles and develops the cardiovascular system.
10. Because the weight of the body is buoyed in the water, swimmers have a (good) chance of training without injury than do other athletes.

B. REVISION SKILL

Comparative Forms of Adjectives and Adverbs   Rewrite the following sentences to correct all errors in the use of comparative and superlative modifiers. If a sentence has no errors, write *Correct*.

1. Which is the most difficult game, lawn bowling or curling?
2. The games are similar, but curling, which is played on the ice, demands the greatest sense of balance.
3. Curling also requires more precise aim, because the player must grip a heavy stone or iron by its handle and cast it off by sliding it on the ice.
4. The stones or irons vary in weight, the most heaviest weighing forty-four pounds.
5. Both teams try to place their stones within a circle around a distant tee, and the team that places more stones in the circle wins.
6. Even in the 1500's curling was played in various regions of the British Isles, but Scotland promoted the game most actively.
7. Of all curling games played in America, the earlier ones were those played during the Revolutionary War by British soldiers stationed in Canada.
8. They played using flattened cannon balls—probably devising the less destructive use of cannonballs in history.
9. Today, Canada hosts the world's most large curling competition.
10. Even so, following World War II, women's curling associations increased most rapidly in the U.S. than in other countries.

C. APPLICATION IN WRITING

A Recommendation   Imagine that you are a talent scout for a sports team. You have found three potential superstars whom you want to recommend. Write a report describing and comparing your three prospects. Use various forms of adjectives and adverbs to compare their physical characteristics, personalities, and performances.

CHECK POINT
PAGES 719–725

PAGES 719–725

A. Choose the correct form of each modifier to restore the excerpt to the original. Label the modifier *Adjective* or *Adverb*.

1. She looks (younger, youngest) than I do, her eyebrows are (thicker, thickest), her lips (fuller, fullest). Her (natural, naturally) curly hair is parted on the left, one wisp tendrilling off to the right. She wears a scholar's white gown, and she is not thinking about her appearance. She stares (straight, straightly) ahead as if she could see past me to her grandchildren and her grandchildren's grandchildren.

   Maxine Hong Kingston

2. He went into the rickety barn and brought out a rope, and he walked the horse (agile, agilely) enough up the hill to catch the horse. When he was ready and mounted before the door . . . Mama brought out the round black hat with the tooled leather band and she reached up and knotted the green silk handkerchief about his neck. Pepe's blue denim coat was much (more darker, darker) than his jeans for it had been washed much (less, lesser) often. The black hat, covering the high pointed head and black thatched hair of Pepe, gave him dignity and age. He sat the rangy horse (good, well).

   John Steinbeck

3. We had a good week at camp. The bass were biting (well, good) and the sun shone (endless, endlessly), day after day. We would be tired at night and lie down in the accumulated heat of the little bedrooms after the long hot day and the breeze would stir almost (imperceptible, imperceptibly) outside and the smell of the swamp would drift in through the rusty screens. Sleep would come (easy, easily) and in the morning the red squirrel would be on the roof, tapping out his merry routine.

   E. B. White

4. Evenings were spent mainly on the back porches where screen doors slammed in the darkness with those (real, really) very special summertime sounds. And, sometimes, when the Chicago nights got too steamy, the whole family got into the car and went to the park and slept out in the open on blankets. Those were, of course, the (better, best) times of all because the grownups were (invariable, invariably) reminded of having been children in the South and told the (better, best) stories. And it was cool and sweet to be on the grass and there was (usual, usually) the scent of (fresh, freshly) cut lemons or melons in the air.

   Lorraine Hansberry

5. The country is lyric,—the town dramatic. When mingled they make the (most perfect, more perfect) musical drama.

   Henry Wadsworth Longfellow

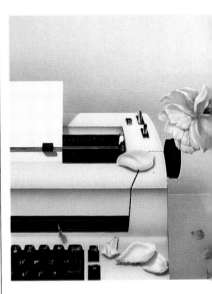

Writing Theme
Writers and
Their Craft

Adjective and
Adverb Usage

B. Write the correct form of the modifier given in parentheses. Then label the modifier as either an *Adjective* or an *Adverb*.

1. The writing profession is probably (less clearly, least clearly) understood than any other.
2. Robert Penn Warren thought of writing (primary, primarily) as a compulsion, like an itch that needs to be scratched.
3. This compulsion explains why James Michener kept very (odd, oddly) working hours when he wrote *Tales of the South Pacific.*
4. Writing was (easier, more easy) for him at night because he had another job during the day.
5. Now he writes almost (exclusive, exclusively) in the day.
6. Hortense Calisher, another writer, believes writers must feel (serious, seriously) about their work in order to succeed.
7. According to Calisher, she works (real, really) well in the morning.
8. By contrast, Eudora Welty (usual, usually) works whenever a story demands to be written.
9. Sometimes the (better, best) ideas come to her (sudden, suddenly) in the dead of night.
10. Instead of getting up to work, her (more practical, most practical) solution is to jot down the idea.

C. Rewrite each sentence to correct any error in the use of an adjective or adverb. If a sentence has no error, write *Correct.*

1. The two more famous awards for writing are the Nobel Prize in literature and the Pulitzer Prize.
2. The Nobel and the Pulitzer prizes were established by Alfred Nobel and Joseph Pulitzer, respective.
3. The lists of award winners appear very impressively.
4. Of the two, the Pulitzer offers the widest variety of awards: eight for journalism and six for literary works.
5. Some of the more famous writers in the world have received awards.
6. In 1950 after publishing *Annie Allen,* a collection of poems about an African-American woman growing up, Gwendolyn Brooks felt proudly to receive the Pulitzer Prize in poetry.
7. Brooks was the first African-American woman to receive this highly prestigious award.
8. Earliest in her career she had won awards at writer's conferences as well as grants of money called Guggenheim fellowships.
9. Although Brooks's poetry features ordinarily black people and their everyday lives, Richard Wright said "It is the honesty in her poems that makes them true for all people."
10. In particular, Wright praised Brooks for her ability to depict "the tiniest incidents that plague the lives of the desperately poor."

USING COMPARISONS CORRECTLY

Avoid making double comparisons and illogical comparisons by keeping the following guidelines in mind.

Avoid Double Comparisons

As you know, the comparative degree of a modifier is formed either by adding *-er* to the positive form or by placing *more* before the positive form. Using *-er* and *more* together is incorrect. Similarly, the superlative is made by adding either *-est* or *most*. Using both is incorrect.

Incorrect	The Cahow is a *more rarer* sea bird than the sea gull.
Correct	The Cahow is a *rarer* sea bird than the sea gull.

Incorrect	The Nile Valley is the *most fertilest* part of Egypt.
Correct	The Nile Valley is the *most fertile* part of Egypt.

Avoid Illogical Comparisons

An illogical or confusing comparison results if two unrelated things are compared or if something is compared with itself.

The word *other* or the word *else* should be used in a comparison of an individual member with the rest of the group.

Illogical	This band has won more competitions than any band in the state. (Is this band in the state?)
Clear	This band has won more competitions than any *other* band in the state.

Illogical	Julius Caesar was as brilliant as any general in the history of Rome. (Was Julius Caesar a Roman general?)
Clear	Julius Caesar was as brilliant as any *other* general in the history of Rome.

The word *than* or *as* is required after the first modifier in a compound comparison.

Illogical	Ian's grades are better or at least as good as Kim's.
Clear	Ian's grades are better *than*, or at least as good as, Kim's.

Illogical	Felicia scored as many goals if not more than Steve.
Clear	Felicia scored as many goals *as* Steve, if not more.

Certain modifiers cannot logically be used in the comparative or superlative forms because they are absolute.

Incorrect	*Twelfth Night* is a more perfect play than is *As You Like It*. (*Perfect* is absolute and cannot logically be compared.)
Correct	*Twelfth Night* is almost a perfect play, but *As You Like It* has many weaknesses.
Incorrect	The number of stars is more infinite than the number of grains of sand. (*Infinite* is absolute and cannot be logically compared.)
Correct	The number of stars and the number of grains of sand are infinite.
Incorrect	Calculus is more impossible than algebra. (*Impossible* is absolute and cannot be compared.)
Correct	Calculus is a more difficult form of math than is algebra.

Both parts of a comparison must be stated completely if there is any chance of its being misunderstood.

Unclear	I see Karen more often than Carla.
Clear	I see Karen more often than Carla *does*.
Clear	I see Karen more often than *I see* Carla.
Unclear	The Lakers beat the Celtics worse than the Knicks.
Clear	The Lakers beat the Celtics worse than the Knicks *did*.
Clear	The Lakers beat the Celtics worse than the Lakers *beat* the Knicks.

Practice Your Skills

A. CONCEPT CHECK

Double and Illogical Comparisons Find the errors in comparison in the following sentences. Rewrite the sentences correctly.

1. In 1922, the nation of Japan stated that it respected China's autonomy as much as any country did.
2. However, in 1931, in one of the most bloodiest takeovers in history, Japan invaded the Chinese province of Manchuria.
3. This act upset Europe as much if not more than the United States.
4. After Japan's all-out invasion of China in 1937, a peaceful solution to the problem seemed more impossible.
5. Japan needed land and resources more than anything to bolster its economy.

6. At the same time in Europe, Hitler's Germany was becoming as aggressive if not more than Japan.
7. The threat of war seemed much more greater in Europe.
8. However, during the Great Depression, America thought its own problems were more important than any country's.
9. Americans felt more sympathy for Europe than China.
10. The U.S. was in a most unique situation.
11. Americans' most fiercest debate was over isolation versus intervention.
12. On December 7, 1941, the Japanese proved that the United States was as vulnerable as any target.
13. Tiny Japan, in the most boldest attack imaginable, bombed the American naval base at Pearl Harbor.
14. The attack resolved the Americans' debate more quickly than any action could.
15. Likewise, Hitler's attacks on U.S. escort ships more finally resolved the issue: America would go to war.

Ready for take-off, World War II pilot-in-training Nancy Nesbit of Pomona, California, checks with the control tower for instructions, 1943

B. PROOFREADING SKILL

Double and Illogical Comparisons The following paragraph has errors in the use of comparisons, spelling, capitalization, and punctuation. Rewrite the paragraph, correcting all errors.

(1) World War II probably created more changes in our society than any event in History. (2) On the home front, factries produced war materials more than anything. (3) In fact, the most proudest time in many americans lives was during their "service" in the factories at home. (4) Victory depended on well-made goods as much as productive workers

(5) Some imported natural resources were as valuable if not more than many domestic resources. (6) Because of the war, imports of rubber, silk, and tin had stoped more completely. (7) Families suffered from the rationing of goods made from these materials as much as industry. (8) Among the most scarcest items were canned foods, shoes, and gasoline. (9) Candians rationed consumer goods as much as Americans. (10) Conservation of resources became a patriotic duty as important if not more than buying war bonds.

C. APPLICATION IN WRITING

A Biography Choose two figures from some period in American history and do some brief research about their lives. Write a paragraph comparing and contrasting these figures.

SPECIAL PROBLEMS WITH MODIFIERS

Certain adjectives and adverbs are often misused. Study the following information to avoid problems.

This and *These; That* and *Those*

This and *that* are adjectives that modify singular nouns and pronouns. Similarly, the adjectives *these* and *those* modify plural nouns and pronouns. *This* and *these* are used to refer to nearby things; *that* and *those* are used to refer to things at a distance. Notice how *kind* and *sort* signal that a singular adjective should be used.

Incorrect	*These* kind sold faster than *those* kind.
Correct	*This* kind sold faster than *that* kind.
Incorrect	*Those* sort of argument are a waste of time.
Correct	*That* sort of argument is a waste of time.

Them and *Those*

Those can act as either a pronoun or an adjective. However, *them* is always a pronoun, never an adjective.

Incorrect	Where did you get *them* sunglasses?
Correct	Where did you get *those* sunglasses? (adjective)
Correct	Where did you get them? (pronoun)
Correct	Those are fantastic sunglasses! (pronoun)

Bad and Badly

Bad is an adjective. It is used before nouns and after linking verbs in standard English. The word *badly* is an adverb. It can only modify action verbs, adjectives, and other adverbs—never a noun.

> Justin feels *bad* (not *badly*) about the disagreement. (adjective)
> Rhoda cut her knee *badly*. (adverb)
> The doctor treated the *badly* burned firefighters. (adverb)

Good and Well

The word *good* is always an adjective. It can modify only a noun or a pronoun.

> Barry has developed a *good* serve.

When *good* is used after a linking verb in a sentence, it functions as a predicate adjective that modifies the subject. As a predicate adjective, *good* can mean either "pleasant," "comfortable," or "in a happy state of mind."

> Barry's serve has become *good*.
> *He feels good* about it.
> He will be *good* at tennis some day.

Well can be used as an adverb to modify an action verb. Used as an adverb, *well* means that the action expressed by the verb is performed expertly or properly.

> Nikia writes *well* when she puts her mind to it.

Well can also be used as a predicate adjective after a linking verb. As a predicate adjective, *well* means "in good health."

> Although Danielle appeared *well*, she was really quite sick.

The Double Negative

If you add a negative word to a sentence that is already negative, the result will be an error known as a **double negative.**

Incorrect	He did*n't* tell me *nothing.*
Correct	He did*n't* tell me *anything.*
Correct	He told me *nothing.*

Incorrect	I did*n't* get *no* news from him.
Correct	I did*n't* get *any* news from him.
Correct	I got *no* news from him.

Using *hardly, barely,* or *scarcely* with a negative word is also incorrect.

Incorrect	There was*n't hardly* any juice in the pitcher.
Correct	There was *hardly* any juice in the pitcher.

Incorrect	The little juice that was left in the pitcher did*n't scarcely* wet my throat.
Correct	The little juice that was left in the pitcher *scarcely* wet my throat.

Certain expressions with the word *but* sometimes have the effect of creating a double negative. Study the examples below.

Incorrect	I *can't* help *but* feel sorry for him.
Correct	I *can't help feeling* sorry for him.

Incorrect	I have*n't but* one true friend.
Correct	I have *only* one true friend.

Incorrect	There are*n't* only *but* seven countries that don't allow women to vote.
Correct	There are *only* seven countries that don't allow women to vote.

Practice Your Skills

A. CONCEPT CHECK

Correct Use of Modifiers Choose the correct modifier from the two given in parentheses.

1. Vasari, an Italian Renaissance biographer, chronicles (good, well) an unusual side to Leonardo da Vinci.
2. It seems Leonardo liked (those, that) sort of activity characteristic of a mad scientist.

3. As a young man, he (didn't enjoy nothing better, enjoyed nothing better) than shutting himself up in a secret part of the house so that he could create a composite monster.
4. Leonardo didn't feel (bad, badly) about using bits and pieces of lizards and bats.
5. The biographer also tells us that he (didn't hardly notice, hardly noticed) the stench around him.
6. (One can't help but, One can hardly help) picturing a reptilian Frankenstein's monster.
7. In some ways, Leonardo's creative genius can be compared to the fertile imaginations of (them, those) people who write science fiction.
8. There (aren't but a few, are only a few) minds that could envision a submarine or a vehicle capable of flight years before such things were technically possible.
9. Both Leonardo and writer Jules Verne accomplished this feat (good, well).
10. Think about what someone with an imagination that worked that (good, well) could dream up in our time!

B. REVISION SKILL

Problems with Modifiers   Rewrite the following sentences to correct misused modifiers and double negatives.

1. Mary Cassatt, like many other nineteenth-century American artists, didn't want to study art nowhere but in Europe.
2. Her father, who was a very stern man, didn't hardly approve of her aspirations.
3. Cassatt had always been an obedient daughter, and she felt badly about opposing her father.
4. However, she wouldn't allow nobody's objections to discourage her.
5. While living in Europe, she couldn't help but be inspired by the exploding Impressionist movement in art.
6. The Impressionists were them painters who try to show what the eye sees at a glance about a scene or object.
7. In these type of painting, tiny splashes of primary colors placed on the canvas simulate the vibration of reflected light.
8. Cassatt's paintings of mothers and children demonstrate her talent and techniques good.
9. With those sort of subject, she used flat, delicate colors and strong, clear lines.
10. Edward Degas, another of them artists who mastered impressionism, became a close friend and mentor to Mary Cassatt.

C. PROOFREADING SKILL

Errors in Modifier Usage   Rewrite the paragraph to correct errors in capitalization, punctuation, and spelling.

Them paintings on the cieling of the Sistine chapel are the work of the Italian Renaissance artist, Michelangelo Buonarotti. There isn't scarcely a painter or sculptor of the human form whose work has not been influenced by Michelangelo. Interestingly, Michelangelo didn't hardly want to be a painter. In fact, he felt badly when he had to take time away from sculpting to paint. His statues show that he hadn't but one true love. Watching forms emerge from marble.

Michelangelo prefered sculpting those kind of heroic, larger-than-life work, typified by his *David.* If Pope julius hadn't comissioned him to do the Sistine chapel frescoes, Michelangelo might have continued to produce nothing but sculpture. Some sources indicated that in later years his hands became stiff and crippled bad. Yet, even when due to advanced age he wasn't feeling good, he produced the giant fresco, "The last Judgment."

CHECK POINT
PAGES 729–736

A. Write the correct word or phrase from the two in parentheses.

1. In 1974, the high school in Roseville, California, (had only, didn't have but) one girl on its track team—Evelyn Ashford.
2. This girl, destined to become the (faster, fastest) woman runner in the world, attracted recruiters from the University of California at Los Angeles, who offered her a track scholarship.

3. One track coach who thought her stopwatch had malfunctioned (couldn't hardly, couldn't) believe Ashford was capable of such speed.
4. In the years that followed, Ashford won several events in the World Cup Games, and she felt really (good, well) about breaking the world record for the 100-meter dash in both 1983 and 1984.
5. She did not reach her (ultimate, most ultimate) goal until the 1984 Olympics, when she won the gold medal for the 100-meter dash.

B. Rewrite each of the following sentences, correcting all errors in the use of modifiers.

1. Many people feel badly because they do not exercise.
2. They can't hardly force themselves to do the same old exercises every day.
3. Perhaps they should try joggling, one of the most unique new sports.
4. These kind of activity combines jogging and juggling.
5. In joggling, the ability to juggle is as important if not more than the ability to jog.
6. Learning to juggle is more complicated than some activities.
7. Good eye-hand coordination is required to keep them balls in the air without dropping them.
8. Top jugglers say that they can joggle as good as they can run.
9. Jogglers also say they can't help but improve their lower body muscles as well as their coordination.
10. However, the aerobic benefits of joggling can be greater than any benefits.
11. One joggler discovered that by juggling with heavier balls, he received a much more perfect workout.
12. The more heavier the balls he juggled, the more his heart rate increased.
13. Albert Lucas is one of them jogglers who love to compete.
14. In 1986, when he entered the Los Angeles Marathon as a joggler, no one there had never heard of joggling.
15. Representatives from the *Guinness Book of World Records* were as interested in the marathon as Lucas.
16. They wanted to be sure that the record for joggling would be recorded and verified good.
17. Lucas didn't do bad in 1986; he ran the 26.2 miles in 3 hours, 29 minutes, 17 seconds.
18. Even while joggling, he finished the race as fast if not faster than most of the other runners.
19. In 1988, he had a far more better finish, beating his old record.
20. Who knows? Someday, people may prefer joggling to any form of exercise.

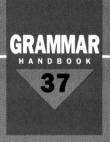

GRAMMAR
HANDBOOK
37

Writing Theme
Cities Lost
and Found

A. Using Modifiers Correctly Write the correct form of the two modifiers given in parentheses.

1. The provincial Roman city of Pompeii is perhaps more famous than (any, any other) ruin from ancient Rome.
2. The people of Pompeii lived (prosperous, prosperously) in their seaside community prior to A.D. 79.
3. Then, on August 24, A.D. 79, they suffered a disaster (as destructive as, as destructive), if not more destructive than, the wars that destroyed other ancient cities.
4. Nearby Mount Vesuvius erupted, burying the city in ash and leaving (scarcely any, scarcely no) survivors.
5. (Them, Those) ruins of Pompeii lay buried under ash for almost 1,700 years.
6. After the site was discovered, early excavations were done somewhat (careless, carelessly).
7. Johann Winckelmann studied the ruins of Pompeii (careful, carefully), sorting them out and making sense of them.
8. Modern archaeologists have gone (slow, slowly) in order to preserve and catalog the buried secrets.
9. Over the past two centuries, excavations at Pompeii have proceeded quite (good, well), yielding exciting results.
10. Today, tourists find the ruins of Pompeii (as popular, as popular as), if not more popular than, the Roman Forum.

B. Choosing the Correct Modifier Rewrite each of the following sentences, correcting any errors in the use of modifiers.

1. When he was only seven years old, Heinrich Schliemann looked regular at an illustrated book that was very special to him.
2. Young Heinrich couldn't hardly contain his excitement each time he looked at the book's picture of the city of Troy in flames.
3. When he grew up, this boy was destined to become more famous than any archaeologist in history.
4. Throughout his youth, Heinrich looked radiantly whenever the subject of Troy came up.
5. There was scarcely no aspect of the story of Troy that did not fascinate him.
6. The more famous of all the cities of the ancient world, Troy was the site of a great battle described by the Greek poet Homer in his epic work titled the *Iliad.*
7. Young Heinrich learned to read classical Greek really good so that he could study Homer's works in their original language.
8. He believed that Homer's poems, the *Iliad* and the *Odyssey,* were more beautiful and inspiring than any poems ever written.

9. He also believed something that hardly no one else at that time believed: that Homer's stories were true and Troy was real.
10. These sort of behaviors made many people consider Heinrich a bit eccentric.
11. Professional archaeologists scoffed: they had never heard of a more impossible theory.
12. Nevertheless, Heinrich persisted in his belief that them poems contained clues to the location of the ancient city.
13. Once he reached adulthood, Schliemann became enormous wealthy through activities as a merchant.
14. He married a Greek woman whom he thought more beautifuller than Helen of Troy herself.
15. Schliemann and his wife, along with a hundred hired workers, set out to find Troy, following them clues from Homer's poems.
16. It would be difficult to say who was most zealous about the attempt to find Troy, Schliemann or his new wife, Sophia.
17. There wasn't hardly a piece of evidence from the poems that they overlooked.
18. Surprisingly, Schliemann's literary approach to archaeology succeeded quite good, for in 1871 he found an ancient city on the Turkish coast.
19. At this site, Schliemann and later archaeologists dug up ten layered ancient cities; of these, the ninth from the top was considered the most likeliest site for the Troy of Homer's poem.
20. Doubtless, this discovery was the more exciting in the history of modern archaeological investigation.

C. Errors in Modifier Usage The following paragraph contains errors in the use of modifiers as well as errors in capitalization, spelling, and punctuation. Rewrite the paragraph to correct all of these errors.

By the mid-1500's, Pizzaro and his Spanish *conquistadores* thought there wasn't no city in the Incan Empire they had not conquered. However, the invaders from Spain were bad mistaken, there was one Incan city they didn't never find. This city was as grand if not more grander than any settlement built by the skillful incan artisans. The city straddles the 9,000-foot peek of Machu Picchu, a mountain in the Peruvian Andes. For hundreds of years after the Spanish conquest, the secret of the existance of Machu Picchu was kept good. However on July 24, 1911 the city was discovered by a young American explorer named Hiram Bingham. Today, the sight is one of the most popular tourist attractions in south America.

Directions　One or more of the underlined sections in the following sentences may contain errors of grammar, usage, punctuation, spelling, or capitalization. Write the letters of each incorrect section. Then rewrite the item correctly. If there is no error in an item, write E.

Example　<u>Them</u> postponing the vote <u>until</u> the next session of
　　　　　　　　A　　　　　　　　　　　　　**B**

the <u>legaslature</u> increases the likelihood of the <u>bill's</u> defeat.
　　　C　　　　　　　　　　　　　　　　　　　　　**D**

<u>No error</u>
　E

Answer　A—their, C—legislature

---

1. <u>Fats Waller</u> wrote the song "Ain't Misbehavin'"; <u>he</u> and Jelly Roll Morton <u>were</u>
　　A　　　　　　　　　　　　　　　　　　　　**B**　　　　　　　　　　　　　**C**
influential jazz <u>pianists</u> and composers. <u>No error</u>
　　　　　　　　D　　　　　　　　　　**E**

2. The <u>Flying Wallendas</u> were tightrope walkers <u>who created the first high-wire pyramid,</u>
　　　A　　　　　　　　　　　　　　　　**B**
and few performers <u>were</u> as daring as <u>them.</u> <u>No error</u>
　　　　　　　　　C　　　　　　　**D**　　**E**

3. The astronaut <u>claimed</u> that no one who has only seen the earth from the ground
　　　　　　　　A
<u>can feel</u> <u>like</u> an astronaut <u>does</u> about the beauty and fragility of our planet.
　B　　**C**　　　　　　　**D**
<u>No error</u>
　E

4. In Sophocles' play, when Creon <u>forbade</u> the burial of <u>Antigone's</u> brother,
　　　　　　　　　　　　　　　　A　　　　　　　　**B**
<u>him and her</u> <u>became antagonists.</u> <u>No error</u>
　C　　　　　**D**　　　　　**E**

5. Alexander Selkirk, on <u>who</u> Daniel Defoe <u>based</u> his character of Robinson Crusoe,
　　　　　　　　　　A　　　　　　　**B**
was a British sailor <u>whom</u> was actually shipwrecked <u>for several years.</u> <u>No error</u>
　　　　　　　　C　　　　　　　　　　**D**　　　　　　**E**

6. Although Socrates <u>is regarded</u> as the originator of Western <u>thought,</u> he <u>hisself</u> did
　　　　　　　　A　　　　　　　　　　　　　　　　**B**　　　**C**
not write down his <u>ideas;</u> they were written down by one of Socrates' famous pu-
　　　　　　　　D
pils, an aristocratic youth named Plato. <u>No error</u>
　　　　　　　　　　　　　　　　　　E

7. <u>His</u> discovering the more-than-two-thousand-year-old tomb of Tutankhamen
   A
   <u>in 1922</u> <u>made</u> Howard Carter a <u>worldwide celebrity.</u> <u>No error</u>
   B   **C**   **D**   **E**

8. In Maria Montessori's method of education for young <u>children,</u> each of the chil-
   A
   dren <u>are</u> treated <u>like an individual</u> <u>who</u> brings a great deal of talent and knowledge
   B   **C**   **D**
   to the learning situation. <u>No error</u>
                              E

9. The two <u>russian</u> dancers, Mikhail Baryshnikov and <u>him,</u> dance in a style <u>called</u>
   A   **B**   **C**
   bravura, with <u>brilliant,</u> daring moves. <u>No error</u>
   D   **E**

10. <u>Jacob Grimm and his brother Wilhelm</u> collaborated on writing fairy <u>tales,</u> and it
    A   **B**
    was <u>he</u> <u>who</u> also developed a basic law of linguistics. <u>No error</u>
    C **D**   **E**

11. The finch <u>is</u> a <u>spirited</u> bird that sings <u>beautiful</u> and <u>is often kept</u> as a pet. <u>No error</u>
    A   **B**   **C**   **D**   **E**

12. Of all the actresses <u>who</u> have played <u>Juliet,</u> Olivia Hussey <u>performed</u> the part <u>more</u>
    A   **B**   **C**   **D**
    sensitively. <u>No error</u>
                 E

13. <u>Queen Anne's</u> lace, <u>which is really a wild carrot,</u> is <u>as beautiful as or more beautiful</u>
    A   **B**   **C**
    <u>than</u> <u>any wild plant.</u> <u>No error</u>
    C   **D**   **E**

14. Michelangelo painted <u>so good</u> that he <u>was commissioned</u> by the <u>Pope</u> to paint the
    A   **B**   **C**
    <u>ceiling</u> of the Sistine Chapel. <u>No error</u>
    D   **E**

15. <u>Them</u> humorous, delicate, <u>exquisitely beautiful</u> paintings of monkeys on display
    A   **B**
    <u>at the De Young Museum</u> were painted <u>by a twelve year old girl.</u> <u>No error</u>
    C   **D**   **E**

16. The ancient <u>Romans,</u> <u>who</u> we respect for their <u>culture,</u> regularly practiced
    A   **B**   **C**
    <u>bribery and infanticide.</u> <u>No error</u>
    D   **E**

17. <u>All of</u> the locations proposed for <u>the disposal</u> of these nuclear wastes have <u>its</u>
      A   **B**   **C**
   <u>disadvantages.</u> <u>No error</u>
         D   **E**

18. Although it is a <u>one-celled</u> <u>animal,</u> the amoeba <u>can't barely</u> be seen
                         A   **B**   **C**
   <u>by the naked eye.</u> <u>No error</u>
         D   **E**

19. Between bites of his <u>hot dog,</u> Gene chatted with the players <u>who</u> <u>were waiting</u> for
                            A   **B**   **C**
   <u>their</u> turn at batting practice. <u>No error</u>
      D   **E**

20. Mark told Sara <u>that</u> Jane should take <u>her</u> sculpture <u>to the crafts fair</u> in
                      A   **B**   **C**
   <u>Peterborough New Hampshire.</u> <u>No error</u>
                D   **E**

21. The police pulled the car over <u>because</u> its driver looked <u>suspiciously,</u> and they
                                      A   **B**
   <u>found</u> that the driver was only <u>seven years old!</u> <u>No error</u>
      C   **D**   **E**

22. The <u>giant</u> octopuses along the <u>pacific coast</u> <u>are becoming</u> <u>more and more rarer</u> be-
          A   **B**   **C**   **D**
   cause of human disturbance of their habitat. <u>No error</u>
                                                   E

23. Jake feels <u>that</u> <u>"Macbeth"</u> is more suspenseful and dramatic than <u>any play</u> by
                 A   **B**   **C**
   <u>William Shakespeare.</u> <u>No error</u>
            D   **E**

24. One <u>principle</u> that is central to <u>American democracy</u> <u>is the notion</u> that there <u>is</u>
          A   **B**   **C**   **D**
   strength in diversity. <u>No error</u>
                             E

25. The <u>Department of Public Works</u> <u>announced</u> that the project <u>would be awarded</u> to
              A   **B**   **C**
   <u>whomever</u> was the lowest bidder. <u>No error.</u>
        D   **E**

Sketchbook

Satellite communications permit almost instantaneous transmission of news from one part of the world to another. A century ago, news could take months, or even years, to travel around the globe. The advantages of increased speed in the transmission of news are obvious. Have you ever thought, though, of some of the disadvantages? Write an essay in which you compare methods of news transmission used in the past with the super fast technologies used today. Use precise adjectives and adverbs in your essay.

Additional Sketches

Imagine that you are moving to another area, but that you will be able to take three of your favorite places with you, such as a particular room in your house, a local snack shop, or a park. Write three paragraphs in which you describe these places and why they are important to you. Use pronouns correctly.

To what groups do you belong? Write about one group, explaining the characteristics that members of the group have in common and how members differ from nonmembers. Use pronouns and comparative modifiers clearly and effectively.

Capitalization

PERSONAL NAMES AND TITLES, NATIONALITIES, AND RELIGIONS

A **common noun** is the name of a person, place, thing, or idea. A **proper noun** is the name of a particular person, place, thing, or idea. Proper nouns are capitalized. A **proper adjective** is also capitalized.

Common Noun	Proper Noun	Proper Adjective
philosopher	**S**ocrates	**S**ocratic method
city	**R**ome	**R**oman fountain

A prefix and a proper noun or adjective may form a hyphenated compound. Capitalize the prefix if the word falls at the beginning of a sentence or if it is part of a title.

pre-**N**ixon   anti-**C**ommunist   mid-**S**eptember   non-**E**uropean

Personal Names and Titles

Capitalize personal names and initials standing for names.

E. B. White   **G**ertrude **S**tein   **L**ydia **H. P**almer-**W**atson

Capitalization rules for particles in foreign names vary widely. If you are unsure about the spelling of a foreign name, consult a reference source. Accepted capitalization includes the following:

Daphne du **M**aurier   **F**lannery **O'C**onnor   **V**incent van **G**ogh

Capitalize a title or an abbreviation for a title when it immediately precedes a name or when it is used in direct address.

Cardinal Krol   **P**rofessor Rodriguez   **S**enator Simon

I think you will agree, **D**r. Ortega, that we must act soon.

Usage Note   Capitalize all words except *the* in a nickname.

the **G**reat **E**mancipator   **W**illiam "the **R**efrigerator" **P**erry

Capitalize the abbreviations *Jr., Sr., II,* or *III* after a person's name. The abbreviations *Jr.* and *Sr.* are preceded by a comma, and they are followed by a comma if they do not fall at the end of the sentence.

John Littleton, **J**r., performed a piano concert.

He was named Victor Garcia **III** after his father and grandfather.

Abbreviations for academic degrees, such as *Ph.D., M.S.,* and *B.A.,* are capitalized when used with or without a proper name.

It took him three years to earn his **M.S.**
Kay Monroe Smith, **Ph.D.**, will instruct the class next week.

In general, do not capitalize a title when it follows a name or when it is used alone.

Tamara Richards, the president, called the meeting to order.
Call the professor for an appointment.

Capitalize a title used alone only when it refers to a head of state or to a person in some other uniquely important position.

the **P**resident and **V**ice-**P**resident of the United States

the **Q**ueen of **E**ngland   the **S**ecretary of **S**tate
the **J**oint **C**hiefs of **S**taff   the **P**ope

Do not capitalize the prefix *ex-,* the suffix *-elect,* or the word *presiding* when it is part of a title.

ex-President Reagan   Governor-elect Sara Kole
presiding Judge Jones

Kinship Names

Capitalize kinship names when they are used before a proper name or when they are used in place of one.

We visited **A**unt Josie, my father's sister.
Will **G**randma meet us for lunch after she plays golf?

Do not capitalize kinship names when they are preceded by articles or by possessive nouns or adjectives.

Her aunt and my grandmother were both living in Detroit.
The mother of the boy was not available for comment.

Names of Races, Languages, Nationalities, Tribes, and Religions

Capitalize the names of races, languages, nationalities, tribes, and religions. Capitalize any nouns or adjectives that are derived from such names.

Aztec   **H**ispanics   **Y**iddish
Inuit   **M**ethodist   **L**atin
Greek alphabet   **P**arisian cafés   **A**ustralian banks

The Supreme Being, Other Deities, and Sacred Writings

Capitalize all words referring to God, the Holy Family, other deities, and religious scriptures.

Jesus	**B**ook of **M**ormon	**K**oran
Revelations	**V**irgin **M**ary	**Y**ahweh
Messiah	**H**oly **S**pirit	**A**llah

Capitalize the names of mythical deities.

Jupiter	**A**starte	**Z**eus
Gaia	**T**hor	**H**era

Do not capitalize the words *god* and *goddess* when they refer to mythological deities. Capitalize personal pronouns that refer to God as the supreme deity but not those that refer to mythological figures.

They pray to **G**od and ask **H**im to answer their prayers.
Diana was a Roman goddess, and women often worshiped her.

The Pronoun *I* and the Interjections *O* and *Oh*

Always capitalize the pronoun *I*.

When **I** reached safety, **I** heaved a sigh of relief.

Capitalize the interjection *O,* which often appears in poetry, the Bible, and prayers or petitions. Capitalize the interjection *oh* only when it is the first word in a sentence.

Help us, **O** mighty king!   My, oh my, what a mess!

Practice Your Skills

A. CONCEPT CHECK

Using Capital Letters   For each of the following sentences, rewrite the words that have capitalization errors, capitalizing or lower-casing as necessary.

1. At first the audience was disappointed that the vice-president of the United States was unable to attend.
2. Everyone in the crowded meeting room, including mayor chun, was delighted that the explorer, grover "the rover" burke, jr., had agreed to speak.
3. Burke, whose Grandfather had been a friend of president teddy roosevelt, held an m.a. and a ph.d. in anthropology.

4. "Today," he began, "the people of Easter Island speak the spanish language and are chilean citizens.
5. However, the Prehistoric wanderers who first arrived with their panoply of ancient Gods and Rituals were polynesian.
6. In 1722, a dutch Admiral, jacob roggeveen, was the first european to set foot on this remote Volcanic Island.
7. When i was a boy, grandfather burke told me about the mystery of Rapa Nui, the polynesian name for the island.
8. Questions concerning the Giant Stone Statues found on the Island still baffle Archaeologists.
9. One theory suggests that chief hotu matu's tribe made them; another, that people of a pre-incan peruvian culture did.
10. Archaeologist dr. w. mulloy believed that those who made them, whether polynesian or non-polynesian, were Masters of Masonry."

B. PROOFREADING SKILL

Capitalization Rewrite the following paragraphs, correcting errors in capitalization, punctuation, and spelling.

After Easter Island's initial exploration by the dutch, british adventurer James Cook visited the mysterious isle. On behalf of the king of England. In 1862, the Population was nearly wiped out by a peruvian Slave raid and a Smallpox epedemic. With the introduction of christianity in 1868, the population moved to the Village of Hanga Roa on the west coast.

At the time of the arrival of the dutch, the easter islanders ate primarily their own Fish and sweet potatoes now they depend on supplies brought by the chilean Navy. Visitors to this part of the South Pacific are drawn to the mystereous statues for which the island is famous. Carved from the rock of the volacano rana Roraka, these eyeless forms take the shape of heads fourty feet tall. Were they intended to honor some Diety as the parthanon honors athena. We can only guess.

C. APPLICATION IN WRITING

A Travel Brochure Do some research on one of the following islands or some other exotic destination. Put your findings in the form of copy for a travel brochure that might be sent out by the island's tourism bureau. Describe the people, language, culture, sights, and any other special features.

Aruba   Jamaica   Bermuda   Madagascar

Statues, Easter Island, Chile. These ancient statues, as well as other archaeological remains, are of unknown origin.

Capitalization   **747**

Place Names

Capitalize the names of parts of the world, political divisions, topographical names, and the names of structures and public places. Do not capitalize articles or prepositions of fewer than five letters in such names.

Parts of the World	Asia, South America, Antarctica, Africa, the Northern Hemisphere, the Orient, the New World
Political Divisions	Orange County, the Dominion of Canada, the Province of Quebec, Saudi Arabia
Topographical Names	Death Valley, Mount Ranier, Ohio River, Channel Islands, the Gobi Desert, the Grand Tetons
Structures and Public Places	Vietnam War Memorial, Blarney Castle, Magnificent Mile, Pennsylvania Turnpike, the Capitol

Usage Notes Such words as *lake, mountain,* and *river* are capitalized when they are part of an official or formal name but not when they stand alone or when they follow two or more proper names.

> Lake Michigan   the lake   Indian and Tupper lakes

In official documents, such as a constitution, words such as *city, state,* and *country* are capitalized when they are part of the name of a political unit.

> the City of Houston (official document)
> the city of Houston (regular usage)

Directions and Regions

Capitalize the names of regions of the country but not of directions of the compass.

> Driving to the East Coast will be expensive.
> During spring break many college students migrate south to enjoy the warm weather.

Capitalize proper adjectives derived from names of regions of the country. Do not capitalize adjectives derived from words denoting direction.

a **W**estern city   a **S**outheastern college
a northbound train   an easterly wind

Astronomical Terms

Capitalize the names of stars, planets, galaxies, constellations, and other heavenly bodies. Do not capitalize *sun* and *moon*.

Mars   eclipse of the sun   **A**lpha **C**entauri
Saturn   moon's orbit   **M**ilky **W**ay
Mercury   sunset   **U**rsa **M**inor

Usage Note   The word *earth* is capitalized only when it is used in context with other astronomical terms. *Earth* is never capitalized when it is preceded by the article *the*.

The earth is the fifth largest planet.

Mercury, **V**enus, and **E**arth are the planets nearest the sun.

Vehicles

Capitalize the names of ships, trains, automobiles, airplanes, and spacecraft.

Orient Express   *U.S.S. Enterprise*
Empress of Ireland   **E**dsel

Practice Your Skills

A. CONCEPT CHECK

Using Capitalization   Rewrite the following sentences, capitalizing words as necessary. Use the rules you have studied in this chapter.

1. On the atlantic coast of central florida, just east of the city of orlando, is a promontory known as cape canaveral.
2. Cape canaveral, one of the most famous places in the western hemisphere, is the location of the john f. kennedy space center.
3. This east coast space center is the primary launching site for missions of the american space program.
4. It was from this site that the *apollo 11* mission, the first manned mission to the moon, was launched.
5. The first flight of the space shuttle *columbia* took place in 1981 under the direction of commander john young.

Writing TIP

Underline the names of ships, trains, airplanes, and spacecraft (but not the names of automobiles) in a typed or handwritten manuscript. On a word processor, use italics.

Writing Theme
Space Exploration

6. The space shuttles have been used to launch, retrieve, and repair many satellites, including indonesia's *palapa b* communications satellite and Western Union Corporation's *westar* satellite.
7. Space shuttle missions have also carried devices used to study mars and other planets, the sun, the moon, and the stars.
8. The nile river in egypt and the great wall in the people's republic of china can be seen quite clearly from space at times.
9. During the *apollo 7* mission, the people of brisbane, australia, turned their lights on all at once as the spacecraft passed over.
10. Through space exploration, much can be learned about our galaxy and perhaps about galaxies beyond the milky way.

B. PROOFREADING SKILL

Correcting Errors in Capitalization Rewrite the following paragraph, correcting all errors in capitalization.

(1) In the summer of 1983, sally ride became the first american woman to lift off into space. (2) Ride and four other astronauts blasted off in the *challenger* from the launch pad at cape canaveral, florida, and orbited the earth for seven days before landing in california. (3) Traveling at five miles per second, circling the earth once every ninety minutes, ride and her fellow astronauts had magnificent views. (4) As they looked at north america, they could clearly see los angeles and, to the north, puget sound. (5) Within minutes, they would be admiring florida's distinctive coastline and the city of new york. (6) Their panoramic view included huge dust storms blowing over deserts in africa and smoke spewing from active volcanoes in hawaii. (7) The astronauts spotted enormous chunks of ice floating in antarctic waters and electrical storms raging over the atlantic. (8) Looking eastward toward wales and england, they saw the english channel, cardigan bay, and the bristol channel. (9) Natural and artificial wonders dazzled ride during her orbits around the earth. (10) Through books, talks, and television appearances, she has shared her excitement about space travel with people in all parts of the united states.

C. APPLICATION IN WRITING

Science Fiction If you could travel throughout the universe, where would you go? What might you see there? Let your imagination soar. Use existing facts, names, and theories, or create your own. Write a brief essay in which you describe your imaginary universe. Remember to use correct capitalization.

Other terms that are to be capitalized include the names of organizations and institutions, certain historical and cultural terms, and calendar and time designations.

Organizations and Institutions

Capitalize the names of organizations and institutions and their abbreviations.

Capitalize all the words in the name of an organization or institution with the exception of prepositions and conjunctions. Capitalize the abbreviations and acronyms for such names.

the **B**oard of **R**egents of the **U**niversity of **T**exas
Washington **N**ational **S**ymphony
American **S**tock **E**xchange
Bureau of **I**ndian **A**ffairs (**BIA**)
Home **B**ox **O**ffice (**HBO**)
First **B**aptist **C**hurch

Do not capitalize words such as *school, company, church, college,* and *hospital* unless they are part of a proper noun.

She finished high school and applied to **B**oston **C**ollege.

Historical Events, Periods, and Documents

Capitalize the names of historical events, periods, and documents.

Navigation **A**ct
Treaty of **V**ersailles
Boston **T**ea **P**arty

Black **F**riday
Civil **W**ar
the **D**ark **A**ges

A Visit from the Old Mistress, Winslow Homer, National Museum of American Art. Homer illustrated various aspects of the Civil War, including the living conditions of slaves.

Writing
—TIP—

Numbered centuries, such as the twentieth century, do not qualify as historical periods.

Capitalization   **751**

Months, Days, and Holidays

Capitalize the names of months, days, and holidays, but not the names of seasons.

> We always go to my uncle's house for **T**hanksgiving.
> In **O**ctober, autumn colors reach their peak in this area and by late **M**ay spring flowers appear.
> On the fourth **T**hursday in **J**une, we'll pick strawberries.

Time Abbreviations

Capitalize the abbreviations B.C., A.D., A.M., and P.M.

> The Roman historian Livy lived from 59 **B.C.** to **A.D.** 17.
> Football replays will be shown at 10:00 **A.M.** and 2:00 **P.M.**

Capitalize the abbreviations for time zones.

> **PDT** (Pacific Daylight Time)   **EST** (Eastern Standard Time)

Awards, Special Events, and Brand Names

Capitalize the names of awards and special events.

> **S**uperbowl   **G**rammy **A**wards   **H**eisman **T**rophy   **M**ardi **G**ras

Capitalize the brand name of a product but not a common noun following the brand name.

> **D**azzle nail polish   **D**are **T**o **B**e **D**ifferent ties and shirts

School Subjects and Names of School Years

Do not capitalize the general names of school subjects. Do capitalize the names of specific courses, including those designated by numbers. The name of a language course is always capitalized.

> history   **W**orld **H**istory II
> physical education   **E**nglish 101

Capitalize the words *freshman, sophomore, junior,* and *senior* when they are used as adjectives referring to specific classes (or class events). Also capitalize them when they are used as nouns in direct address.

> The **S**enior **C**lass excelled in raising money for a new gym.
> College recruiters hoped to impress the juniors and seniors.
> Now is the time, **S**eniors, to complete college applications and submit applications fees.

Practice Your Skills

A. CONCEPT CHECK

Capitalization   Rewrite the following sentences, capitalizing words as necessary. You may use a dictionary for guidance.

1. History can be cruel, as many a college freshman enrolled in engineering 100, introduction to engineering, has learned.
2. As if it were unimportant, history has lost the name of the remarkable Mesopotamian inventor who, about 3000 b.c., invented the chariot.
3. The thousands of New Yorkers who ride the subway on the fourth thursday of every november to macy's thanksgiving day parade give little thought to the engineers who created the underground train.
4. Few, if any of them, realize that tammany hall and "Boss" Tweed stifled a revolutionary subway system in 1866.
5. Alfred ely beach would surely have won an award titled inventor of the decade had his air-powered subway train not been scuttled.
6. From 6:00 p.m. to 12:00 a.m. for 58 days, Beach's men built the block-long model that was later legislated into oblivion.
7. In february, 1912, construction workers accidentally uncovered Beach's pneumatic subway train.
8. Who in San Francisco thanks the inventors of bart (bay area rapid transit) for the first completely automated transit system?
9. Did engineers earn an award during the civil war when their confederate submarine sank a union ship on february 17, 1864?
10. Perhaps the freshman class should research forgotten inventors from 2000 b.c. to a.d. 2000.

B. REVISION SKILL

Using Capitalization   Correctly write the words in each sentence that need capital letters.

(1) Several of the majestic automobiles built during the twenties and thirties, such as the american duesenberg, the english rolls-royce, and the french hispano-suiza and bugatti, are considered classic cars. (2) According to the classic car club of america, a classic is one that was made between 1925 and 1942, of a limited series, and with special technical features. (3) The only exceptions are the lincoln continentals of 1946–48, which are also considered classics. (4) The quality of the classic car engine is exemplified by the hispano-suiza that was driven 1,100 miles from paris to nice and back and then parked over white paper; not a trace of oil or water dropped from the engine.

Charles S. Rolls and Henry Royce produced the Rolls-Royce Silver Ghost, known by its distinctive grill, the double-R trademark, and the flying-lady radiator ornament.

(5) Ettore bugatti, an italian, built his famous cars in molsheim, a small town in eastern france. (6) the haughty bugatti, who liked to be called "*le patron*," once refused to sell a car to a king, the king of albania in fact, because he disapproved of the ruler's table manners.

(7) At the age of 40, henry royce built his first car because he was dissatisfied with the one he had just bought. (8) In 1904, royce began the manufacture of rolls-royces with a london car dealer, charles rolls. (9) Rolls-royce factories produced the classic silver ghost, the phantom I, and the phantom II.

(10) Sometimes mistakenly thought of as a german car, the duesenberg is a classic american-built car. (11) Racing duesenbergs won the indianapolis 500 in three different years —1924, 1925, and 1927. (12) The j cars, built primarily between 1930 and 1936, could only be afforded by the very rich. (13) The chassis alone cost as much as ten thousand depression-era dollars.

(14) Classic cars are on display at the following places: harrah's automobile collection in reno, nevada; briggs cunningham automotive museum in costa mesa, california; and the early american museum in silver springs, florida. (15) A number of other classic-car museums are scattered throughout the united states.

C. PROOFREADING SKILL

Capitalizing Correctly   Imagine that you are a reporter for a news magazine directed toward high-school students. You have written a story about a new sport—one of the many that have grown out of unusual modes of transportation—a sport called snowboarding. The following is your rough draft. Rewrite the draft, correcting all errors in spelling, punctuation, and capitalization.

Snowboarding, a fairly young Sport invented in the mid-1960's, is a great way for Hill Riders to hang ten when snow falls. From vermont to california, Snowboarders are traveling the slopes on a cross between a Surfboard and a Ski. It is a five-foot-long, ten-inch-wide piece of laminated Wood or Fiberglass, with fixed bindings that strap around any sturdy boot. No Poles are needed for this cousin sport to Surfing and Skateboarding. Boarders shoot down a slope in a surf-style sideways stance, boarders can ride on anything from a tiny hill in new england to a giant mountinside in the rocky Mountins.

CHECK POINT
PAGES 744–755

A. Rewrite the following sentences, capitalizing or lower-casing as necessary.

1. In 1498, the portuguese Explorer vasco da gama, who commanded the Ships the *berrio,* the *saint gabriel,* and the *saint raphael,* became one of the first europeans to visit the exotic Land of india.
2. The vast Subcontinent stretches from the hindu kush mountains in the north to cape comorin in the south.
3. In the Northern Region, the People depend heavily on the ganges, indus, and brahmaputra rivers, especially during the Monsoon Season from june to september.
4. The earliest indian civilization dates from about 2500 b.c.
5. Today, india is larger than any other Democracy in the western world.
6. The streets of new delhi are crowded at 3:00 p.m. or 3:00 a.m.
7. More than 200 languages are spoken, including telugu, tamil, and bengali; the official languages are hindi and english.
8. Historically, the two largest religious groups in india, the hindus and the moslems, have disagreed on many issues.
9. The islamic, or moslem, sects worship allah.
10. Hindus worship many Gods, two of whom are vishnu and shiva.
11. Mohandas karamchand gandhi—who was called mahatma, or "Great Soul"—made efforts to reconcile religious differences.
12. Gandhi led the indian national congress in a policy of non-cooperation with british rule.
13. He wrote: "i believe nonviolence is infinitely superior to violence."
14. In 1947, independence from britain resulted from the efforts of prime minister jawaharlal nehru, gandhi's follower.
15. Nehru's Daughter, indira gandhi, became prime minister in 1966.

B. Application In Literature Rewrite the following paragraph, re-storing capital letters or lower-casing where necessary.

> Anything is possible on a Train: a great Meal, a Binge, a Visit from card players, an Intrigue, a good night's Sleep, and strangers' Monologues framed like Russian Short Stories. It was my intention to board every Train that chugged into view from victoria station in London to tokyo central; to take the branch line to simla; then go through khyber pass and the line that links indian railways with those in ceylon; the *mandalay Express,* the malaysian *golden arrow,* the Locals in Vietnam, and the trains with bewitching names, the *orient express,* the *north star,* the *trans-siberian.*
>
> **Paul Theroux, *The Great Railway Bazaar***

Capitalize the first words of sentences, lines of poetry, and direct quotations.

Sentences and Poetry

Capitalize the first word of every sentence.

Graduation marks the beginning of new life choices.

In general, capitalize the first word of every line of poetry.

In the deserted moon-blanch'd street
How lonely rings the echo of my feet!

Matthew Arnold, "A Summer Night"

Quotations

Capitalize the first word of a direct quotation.

Rev. King said, "We have no alternative but to protest."

In a **divided quotation,** the first word of the second part of the quotation is capitalized only when it begins a new sentence.

"I like football," Vito said, "because it is action-packed."
"I like football," Vito said. "It's action-packed."

Parts of a Letter

Capitalize the first word in the greeting and complimentary close of a letter. Capitalize the title and name of the person addressed or words such as *Sir* and *Madam* that take the place of a name.

Dear Manager: Dear Ms. Macon,   Sincerely yours,

Outlines and Titles

Capitalize letters that introduce major subsections in an outline, and capitalize the first word of each item.

    I. Solar system
      A. Planets
        1. Mars
        2. Jupiter
      B. Moons

Writing
—TIP—

In modern poetry, first words are not always capitalized. When you write your own poetry, choose the style that suits your subject.

Capitalize the first, last, and all other important words in titles. Do not capitalize conjunctions, articles, or prepositions with fewer than five letters.

Book Title	*The Prince of Tides*
Newspaper	*Los Angeles Free Press*
Magazine	*Sports Illustrated*
Play	*King Lear*
Movie	*Sophie's Choice*
TV Series	*Nightline*
Long Musical Composition	*William Tell Overture*
Short Story	"The Sojourner"
Poem	"The People, Yes"
Magazine Article	"College Tuitions on the Rise"
Chapter	Chapter III: "Colonial America"
Cartoon	*Calvin and Hobbes*
Song	"Let It Be"
Work of Art	*Silence*

Capitalize the words *the* and *magazine* only when they are part of the title.

The Wall Street Journal   the *California Farmer*
Texas Homes Magazine   *Seventeen* magazine

Usage Note   Always capitalize the first element of a hyphenated compound used in titles. Capitalize the second element if it is a proper noun or if it has equal force with the first element. Do not capitalize the second part if it is a modifying participle.

Eighteenth-Century Art   Japanese-made Automobiles

Practice Your Skills

A. CONCEPT CHECK

Capitalization Errors   Rewrite the following items, capitalizing words as necessary. Underline the words that are italicized.

1. s. s. osgood's painting *poe* depicts a gentle young man.
2. tam mossman writes: "edgar allan poe's name is now synonymous with horror, mystery, and the macabre."
3. Few know that poe wrote tall tales, such as "the angel of the odd."
4. There is nothing sinister about his romantic poems, such as "to the river."
5. Poe even pokes fun at the literary magazines and writers of his day in "the literary life of thingum bob, esq., late editor of the *goosetherumfoodle*."

6. "He virtually created the detective story," writes critic robert regan. "he also produced some of the most influential literary criticism of his time."

7. In 1835, he was editor of the *southern literary messenger.*

8. The following stanza from "annabel lee" shows his romantic nature:

> it was many and many a year ago,
>   in a kingdom by the sea,
> that a maiden there lived whom you may know
>   by the name of annabel lee;
> and this maiden she lived with no other thought
>   than to love and be loved by me.

9. His poem "the raven" was so popular that he once apologized for not keeping a pet raven.

10. an encyclopedia might outline his biography as follows:

> I. poe's life
>   a. youth in virginia
>   b. work as writer and critic
>   c. problems in his adult life

B. PROOFREADING SKILL

Capitalization   Rewrite this letter, capitalizing words as necessary.

> 5050 west third street
> normal, illinois 61761
> october 19, 19—
>
> James rankin
> 555 north sycamore
> Joplin, Missouri 64802
>
> dear Mr. rankin:
>   please reserve for me the first-edition copies of poems by edgar a. poe and tales of the grotesque and arabesque advertised in bookbuyers' bulletin.
>
> sincerely yours,
>
> c.a. dupin

C. APPLICATION IN LITERATURE

Capitalization   Rewrite the following passage, capitalizing words as necessary.

> i am not a son of charleston. nor could i be if i wanted to. i am always a visitor, and my allegiance lies with other visitors, sons and daughters of accident and circumstance. edgar allan poe was a son by visitation. it was no surprise to me when i was a freshman at the institute to discover that poe was once stationed at fort moultrie and that he wrote "the gold bug" about one of the sea islands near charleston. . . . i like to think of the city shaping this agitated, misplaced soldier, keening his passion for shade, trimming the soft edges of his nightmare, harshening his poisons and his metaphors, deepening his intimacy with the sunless wastes that issued forth from his kingdom of nightmare in blazing islands, still inchoate and unformed, of the english language. whenever i go back to charleston, i think of poe.
>
> **Pat Conroy, *The Lords of Discipline***

D. APPLICATION IN WRITING

A Movie Review   Thrillers remain as popular today as they were in Poe's time. Moviemakers profit from this fact. Think about a spine-tingling movie you have recently seen. If you have not seen an exciting movie lately, invent your own idea for one. Write a brief review of the film. Include some quotations from your friends about the movie. You might wish to put your review in the form of a letter to a motion-picture studio. Use correct capitalization throughout.

C H E C K   P O I N T
PAGES 756–759

A. Rewrite the following sentences, capitalizing words as necessary.

1. The july 1990 issue of the magazine *rural new england* included a feature on an interesting book.
2. "each page," the magazine tells us, "contains a short poem of rhymed couplets and a freehand illustration."
3. subtitled *a manual of flornithology for beginners,* this little book on distinguishing birds from flowers is a masterpiece of pre-depression light verse and cartooning.
4. published in 1907 by paul elder and company of san francisco, the book was written and illustrated by robert williams wood.

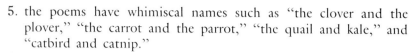

5. the poems have whimiscal names such as "the clover and the plover," "the carrot and the parrot," "the quail and kale," and "catbird and catnip."

6. one poem from the book, "the cowbird and the cowslip," goes as follows:

> growing in mires, in gold attired,
> the cowslip has been much admired,
> altho' its proper name, we're told,
> is really the marsh marigold:
> the cowbird picture, i suspect,
> is absolutely incorrect,
> we make such errors now and then,
> a sort of cowslip of the pen.

7. "wood's book of drawings and poems is important," says historian richard shenck. "for one thing, it is one of but a few examples of non-political cartooning produced before world war i."

8. Indeed, most nineteenth-century cartoons, such as those done by Thomas Nast for *harper's weekly,* were political.

9. One exception was one of the first cartoon strips, James Swinnerton's *the little bears* and *tigers*.

10. this strip appeared in the *san francisco examiner* in 1892.

B. For each numbered sentence, rewrite the words that need capitalization and those that are incorrectly capitalized.

(1) in gary larson's comic strip, *the far side,* animals act like Humans and humans act like animals. (2) the One-Panel Cartoon, run in Seven Hundred Daily Newspapers, is loaded with animals making fun of people, and people making fools of themselves.

(3) "*the far side* is a Collage of Charles addams and the politics of the Green Party," said peter richmond, a reporter for *the miami herald.* (4) "it's rod serling crashing at the ozzie nelson household, george romero produced by disney."

(5) in a Second-story Studio in seattle, washington, gary larson produces seven editions a week of *the far side.* (6) a former Music-Store Clerk, larson wanted to make people laugh and thought his cartooning might make him a living. (7) through Newspapers, Books, and other Media, larson's potential readership is eighty million people.

(8) "i'm a little worried that too many people appreciate the cartoon," larson said. (9) "when people don't get the strip, i like that. (10) i like that *the far side* can be confusing, because that means i'm still being experimental."

Gary Larson, American cartoonist and creator of *The Far Side*

A. Capitalization Rewrite the following sentences, capitalizing words as necessary.

1. sophocles, who lived from 497 to 406 b.c., was one of the great writers of greek tragedy.
2. only seven plays by sophocles remain; most of them are taught in either world literature or western civilization.
3. sophocles lived in athens, located in southeastern greece on a peninsula between the aegean and mediterranean seas.
4. he lived in athens during the golden age of greece.
5. records indicate that he was a general during the samian revolt and the peloponnesian war, and he was treasurer of the delian league in athens.
6. his plays were staged at the theater of dionysus; the building's remains can still be seen on the southern slope of the acropolis near the center of modern athens.
7. theater originated in greece as part of the springtime celebrations honoring dionysus, the god of wine and fertile crops; such festivities were held at about the time that christians celebrate easter.
8. each year in athens, a play-writing contest, which can be considered an olympics of drama, was held.
9. sophocles won this contest twenty-four times, with such plays as *antigone, oedipus rex, ajax,* and *electra.*
10. the play *antigone* tells of a woman torn between loyalty to her dead brother and the dictates of the state.
11. "the ideal condition," wrote sophocles in the play, "would be, i admit, that men should be right by instinct."
12. in the play *oedipus rex,* oedipus unknowingly kills his father, king laius, and marries his mother, queen jocasta.
13. the greek philosopher aristotle, writing in his *poetics,* praised *oedipus rex* as the ideal model for tragedy.
14. in *ajax,* a father says, "my son, may you be happier than your father."
15. however, ajax's pride leads him to his downfall, on a course as unerring as the orbit of the planet earth.
16. one might begin an outline on sophocles' life as follows:

    i. sophocles the man
       a. his youth in colonus
       b. his education
       c. his family

17. the plays of ancient greece greatly influenced the dramas written in the days of the roman empire, but they were unknown to most european scholars during the middle ages.

Writing Theme
Playwrights

18. interest in greek drama was revived throughout europe during the renaissance.
19. the birth of opera in the late sixteenth century resulted from the rediscovery of information that confirmed the importance of music in the performances of the ancient greeks.
20. today, people in the united states enjoy plays by aeschylus, sophocles, euripides, and aristophanes, writers who lived and worked in the fifth century b.c., more than 2,000 years before the founding of our nation.

B. Correct Capitalization After each sentence number, rewrite the words from the sentence that have errors in capitalization. Capitalize or lower-case each word as necessary.

(1) Eugene O'neill is one of america's greatest Playwrights. (2) He was born in 1888 in New York city and attended princeton university before deciding to strike out on his own as a Seaman.

(3) Traveling on Ships, o'neill visited Africa, south america, and many Islands. (4) His experiences at Sea and his observations of Islanders and crew are reflected in many of his works, including the Trilogy entitled *mourning becomes electra,* which is based on a greek trilogy by aeschylus. (5) O'neill used Greek forms, themes, and Characters, but set the drama in new england during the civil War.

(6) eugene o'neill suffered from tb (tuberculosis) early in life and parkinson's disease later on; nevertheless, he wrote forty-five plays during his lifetime. (7) These included One-Act plays, Full-Length plays, and Extended plays, such as his Trilogy. (8) Some of the playwright's Works, such as *the great god brown,* were experimental, but other plays were more traditional in form. (9) His play entitled *long day's journey into night* was Autobiographical.

(10) Most of o'neill's plays show compassion for the characters and at the same time demonstrate their faults. Walter f. Kerr, a writer for the *New York herald tribune,* once wrote that O'Neill wrote his play about his family as "An Act of Forgiveness." (11) O'neill himself once stated, "to me, the Tragic alone has that significant Beauty which is Truth."

(12) Although eugene o'neill died in 1953, he remains a vital part of American Culture. (13) He gave american Literature some of its greatest tragedies. (14) During his lifetime, He was honored with the nobel prize for literature and three Pulitzer prizes. (15) After his Death, his memory was honored with a fourth Pulitzer prize.

End Marks and Commas

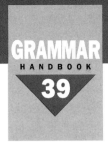

END MARKS

Using end marks correctly is an important skill for satisfactory communication. The first part of this handbook reviews the proper use of the period, the question mark, and the exclamation point.

The Period

Use a period at the end of all declarative sentences and most imperative sentences.

> The Food and Drug Administration has approved the use of irradiation as a safe method of keeping food fresh longer.

> Turn on the floodlight when it gets dark.

Use a period at the end of an indirect question.

An indirect question is repetition without the direct quotation of something asked or requested. (See page 807 for punctuation used with direct questions.)

> Mark asked whether Sylvia Plath was a poet or a novelist.

> Aunt Caterina requested that we arrive at her house early.

Use a period at the end of an abbreviation or initial.

Mr.	M.D.	Inc.	Jan. 16	7:30 A.M.
Ms.	Rev.	Sgt.	Fri.	100 B.C.

Do not use periods for abbreviations of metric measurements, acronyms, the initials of company or organization names, the abbreviations for some nations, or the two-letter abbreviations for states.

m	Kg	SADD	AT&T	US	TX

Use a period after each number or letter in an outline or a list.

Outline	List
I. Volcanoes	1. labels
A. Central-vent	2. manila folders
1. Shield	3. typing paper
2. Composite	4. typewriter ribbons
B. Fissure	5. eraser

Use a period with decimals.

> $32.75   7.135%   0.3334 second

Writing TIP

A polite request in a business letter may be followed by a period or a question mark.

The Question Mark

Use a question mark at the end of an interrogative sentence or fragment.

Did Han Suyin write *The Crippled Tree*?
The cat? It's asleep in the window as usual.

Use a question mark after a declarative sentence that is expressed as a question by being pronounced with rising inflection.

Rita scored ten points. (declarative, falling inflection)
Rita scored ten points? (interrogative, rising inflection)

The Exclamation Point

Use an exclamation point at the end of an exclamatory sentence. Use an exclamation point after a strong interjection or any other forceful expression.

This is wonderful!
No! Don't open the lion's cage!

Although an imperative sentence usually ends with a period, it can end with an exclamation point when strong emotion or excitement is expressed.

Grab onto that life preserver!
Watch out for that candle flame!

The sentence following an interjection may end with a period, a question mark, or an exclamation point.

Oof! Akim's fall knocked the wind out of him.
Wow! Is that for me?
Ouch! That really hurts!

Practice Your Skills

A. CONCEPT CHECK

End Marks   Rewrite the following sentences, adding periods, question marks, and exclamation points where needed.

1. It's a miracle
2. Reporters asked whether people could believe their eyes
3. What was the cause of their amazement The Berlin Wall was coming down
4. In 1948, Berlin was divided into two sectors, East Berlin and West Berlin

Writing
—TIP—

Check the end punctuation of sentences that begin with *what* or *how*. They may be exclamatory sentences.

Writing Theme
Historic Events

5. Work began in Aug 1961 on what would eventually become 850 miles of concrete and barbed wire

6. How tall was the Berlin Wall

7. Over a period of twenty years, it rose to about 10 ft, or 305 (three and five-hundredths) meters in height

8. What led to the dramatic changes on Nov 9, 1989

9. The following factors contributed to the historic event:

   a Mikhail Gorbachev, the leader of the Soviet Union, instituted widespread reform, called *perestroika*

   b Other East European countries were opening their borders

   c The May elections and demonstrations that followed in East Germany urgently called for reforms

10. After US President George Bush attended a NATO meeting in May, he encouraged East Germany to tear down the wall

11. Bush urged West Germany to be "partners in leadership" with us

12. Reporters at the scene exclaimed, "The atmosphere is one of great rejoicing and festivity It's incredible"

13. "I shall return to East Berlin," said one West Berliner, Mrs Schmidt She said that it was home for her.

14. Soon TV commercials sold pieces of history for less than fifty dollars, blaring, "Own a piece of the Berlin Wall for only $3995!"

15. What a happy day

B. PROOFREADING SKILL

Punctuation Errors   Rewrite the following passage, correcting errors in end marks, spelling, and capitalization.

> Didn't the war end imediately when Berlin was captured in World War II No In fact, the Nazi troops, under Grand Adm Karl Doenitz, fought for one week longer. Many Nazi soldiers didn't know that Hitler had taken his own life at 3:30 PM on May 1, 1945 The chaos in Berlin was horible Mr Claus Fuhrmann, a Berlin civilian, wrote that the 2-cm. antiair-craft guns were useless and people were desperate for supplies. Even two lbs of potatos was impossible to get? Russian planes would machine-gun people waiting in lines When the firing stopped on may 2 people cried, "At last" Berlin civilians were glad to see the Russian and US troops?

C. APPLICATION IN WRITING

An Eyewitness Report   Choose an exciting event from recent news reports. Write a brief news story as if you were an eyewitness to the event. Use end marks and punctuation with abbreviations correctly.

A comma is used to add clarity to a sentence and to enable a reader to understand the relation of its parts more quickly.

Commas in a Series

Use a comma to separate the elements in a series.

A series consists of three or more words, phrases, or clauses. When one or more of the elements contain a comma, semicolons instead of commas are used to separate the elements in a sentence. (See page 784.)

Words   The Japanese syllabic, the Chinese logographic, and the Korean alphabetic writing systems look similar.

Phrases   The Chinese language is pronounced differently in many provinces of the country, in Taiwan, and in Hong Kong.

Clauses   Some people believe that Japanese is difficult to pronounce, that its writing system is complicated, and that learning the language takes many years of study.

No commas are used in the series if all of the items are joined by *and, or,* or *nor.*

> The icy wind numbed the climber's face *and* feet *and* hands.

Use commas after the words *first, second,* and so on when these words introduce items in a series. (Note the use of semicolons in the example below.)

> The word *aborigine* refers to three groups of people: first, an ancient mythical people of Italy; second, the aboriginal tribes of Australia; and third, any original inhabitants of a country.

Use commas between coordinate adjectives that modify the same noun.

Coordinate adjectives are adjectives of equal rank. To determine whether adjectives are coordinate, try placing *and* between them. If *and* sounds natural, and if you can reverse the order of the adjectives without changing the meaning, then a comma is needed. Study the examples on the next page.

Writing
─TIP─

In journalistic style, the comma before the conjunction in a series is often omitted.

The cold, exhausted climbers returned to their camp. (*And* sounds natural between *cold* and *exhausted,* and the meaning is not changed by reversing their order. Therefore, a comma is needed.)

Many animals grow a thick winter coat. (*And* does not sound natural between *thick* and *winter,* and the adjectives cannot be reversed. No comma is necessary.)

Do not use a comma before the final adjective in a series if the adjective is thought of as part of the noun.

As the horns blared, the marchers formed a colorful, shimmering American flag. (*American flag* is considered one item. *Colorful* and *shimmering* modify *American flag,* not just *flag.* Thus, there is no comma between *shimmering* and *American.*)

If one word in a series modifies another word in the same series, no comma separates them.

Incorrect	A dark, brown coat was left in the closet.
Correct	A dark brown coat was left in the closet. (*Dark* modifies *brown,* telling what shade of brown. It does not modify the noun *coat.*)

In general, no comma is needed after numbers and after adjectives of size, shape, and age.

an old Italian custom   five small round windows

Practice Your Skills

A. CONCEPT CHECK

Commas   Write the word before each missing comma and place the comma correctly. If the sentence is correct, write *Correct.*

1. Natural habitats include such areas as wetlands deserts grasslands and deciduous forests.
2. A grassland is defined as a habitat in which most of the plants are grasses rather than woody shade-giving trees and shrubs.
3. Grasslands are known by various names: as prairies in North America as steppes in Asia and as savannas in tropical Africa.
4. The vast spectacular grasslands of South America are the pampas.
5. Australia's grasslands provide a home for such unusual animals as emus and dingoes and red kangaroos.
6. In North America, the symbol of the flat open prairie has long been the buffalo, or plains bison.

7. Scientists have described three types of North American prairie: first tall-grass prairie near the Mississippi River; second mixed-grass prairie somewhat farther west; and third short-grass prairie, farther west still.

8. Grasses on the African savannas develop a beautiful light golden color, and, the savannas abound with lions cheetahs and wildebeest.

9. It is not unusual to see three or four tall giraffes together there, munching the distinctive thorny leaves of the acacia tree.

10. Bird lovers are familiar with these facts: the ostrich is found on African savannas; the emu lives on Australian grasslands; and the habitat of the long-legged, swift-running rhea is the dry South American pampas.

B. REVISION SKILL

Sentence Combining Reduce the repetition in the paragraph below by combining sentences and eliminating unnecessary words. Use commas correctly.

The Snake Charmer (detail), Henri Rousseau

The tropical rain forests of the world are located in the Amazon region of South America. There are rain forests in central and western Africa. They also exist in southeast Asia. Rain forests are natural habitats containing many species of tall evergreen trees. The evergreen trees are shady. The treetops form an unbroken shield against the sunlight. There are several levels, or strata, of vegetation in the rain forest. The highest level, the canopy, provides a food supply of flowers. Fruits and nuts are also part of the food supply at this level for many animals. Below the canopy are several additional levels. The second level is the understory. The next level is called the shrub level. Then there is the forest floor.

C. APPLICATION IN WRITING

A Personal Essay The natural habitats of many species are being threatened or destroyed by residential and industrial development. Write a brief essay on this topic or another of your choice in which you express your opinions or offer a solution to a problem.

Commas with Introductory Elements

Use a comma after an introductory word, mild interjection, or adverb at the beginning of a sentence.

> Well, the meeting is about to start.

> Wait, I think I can access this encoded computer file.

> However, the suspect refused to answer Holmes's question.

Use a comma after a series of prepositional phrases at the beginning of a sentence.

> From his seat in the senate, the Emperor Augustus listened intently.

> Under a table by the window, our puppy curled up for a nap.

A single prepositional phrase at the beginning of a sentence need not be followed by a comma unless the comma is needed for clarity.

> On Saturday I work until noon.

> Before the new hit, *Grease* was the group's best production.

Use a comma after an introductory infinitive phrase or introductory participial phrase used as a modifier.

> To activate the system, pull the toggle switch.

> Erupting violently, Mount St. Helens spewed volcanic ash for miles.

Use a comma after an adverb clause at the beginning of a sentence.

> Although asparagus is used as a vegetable, it is actually a member of the lily family.

> Since Melody visited the museum, she has been interested in Asian art.

For more information on verbals and adverb clauses, see Handbook 33, pages 594–612.

Use a comma after a word or phrase that has been moved to the beginning of a sentence from its usual position.

> The crime was apparently committed at night. (usual order)

> Apparently, the crime was committed at night. (transposed order)

Commas with Interrupters

Use commas to set off nonessential appositives.

A **nonessential appositive** is a word or phrase that adds additional information to a sentence that is already complete.

> Mercury, a heavy metal, is also known as quicksilver.

> San Angel, a Mexico City suburb, has a colorful craft market.

An **essential appositive** qualifies or limits the word it modifies in such a way that it could not be omitted without affecting the meaning. Do not set off an essential appositive with commas.

> The opera *La Traviata* was written by the Italian composer Giuseppe Verdi.

> The sculptor Lois Nevelson works predominantly in wood.

Use commas to set off words of direct address.

> Nguyen, will you direct this year's holiday talent show?

> Ghosts, my gullible friend, have no basis in reality.

Use commas to set off parenthetical expressions.

A **parenthetical expression** is a word or phrase inserted in a sentence as a comment or exclamation. The sentence is complete without it, and it should always be set off with commas. The following expressions are often used parenthetically:

after all	by the way	for instance
of course	as a matter of fact	for example
on the other hand	I believe (hope, suppose)	however

> The train, after all, is over an hour late.

When these words and phrases are used as basic parts of the sentence, they are not set off by commas.

> The train was late after all our rushing to be on time.

When adverbs such as *however, therefore,* and *consequently* are used parenthetically in a sentence, they are set off with commas.

> His older brother, however, is a much better athlete than he.

When these same adverbs modify a word in a sentence, they are an essential part of the sentence and are not set off by commas.

> We must repair the broken generator however long it takes.

When these adverbs are used to join two independent clauses, they are called **conjunctive adverbs.** A conjunctive adverb is preceded by a semicolon and followed by a comma.

> The climate in Denmark is generally mild; however, some winters there have been bitterly cold.

Practice Your Skills

A. CONCEPT CHECK

Commas   Rewrite the following sentences, adding commas where needed. If no additional commas are needed, write *Correct.*

1. It's a cravat child and a beautiful one, as you say.
2. Humpty Dumpty Lewis Carroll's fictional character points out the importance of using just the right word.
3. Clearly vocabulary was very important to Carroll.
4. The book *Through the Looking-Glass* uses several invented words.
5. To describe words that are formed by telescoping two words into one Carroll coined the term *portmanteau.*
6. The term is the French name for a stiff leather suitcase.
7. Such a suitcase by the way opens into two compartments.
8. Thus Carroll derived the idea of blending two words into one.
9. Blending *chuckle* and *snort* for example resulted in *chortle.*
10. Such blending is not limited to Carroll's work *Through the Looking-Glass;* indeed several words in English—such as *smog, motel,* and *brunch*—were formed in this way.

B. APPLICATION IN LITERATURE

Using Commas   Some commas have been omitted from these passages. Write the word before each missing comma, and place the comma correctly. Use the rules you have learned in this chapter.

1. If it is any use to know it I always try to write on the principle of the iceberg. There is seven-eighths of it under water for every part that shows.   **Ernest Hemingway**
2. Biography like a game is one of the recognized forms of sport, and is as unfair as only a sport can be.   **Philip Guedalla**
3. I never told you mother that if I can ride my horse and *get there,* then I'm absolutely sure . . . Mother did I ever tell you? I am lucky!   **D. H. Lawrence**
4. [Dorothy Parker's] wit of course was delicate, clear, and sharp.   **Lillian Hellman**
5. Art it seems to me should simplify. That indeed is very nearly the whole of the higher artistic process. . . .   **Willa Cather**

6. And it is such a pleasure my dear such a very great pleasure when now and again I open the door and see someone standing there who is just *exactly* right.   **Roald Dahl**
7. In every man's writings the character of the writer must lie recorded.   **Johann Wolfgang von Goethe**
8. Money much as I enjoy it will never provide the drive to my life.   **Rita Mae Brown**
9. The secret Eliza is not having bad manners or good manners or any particular manners, but having the same manner for all human souls.   **George Bernard Shaw**
10. Until you understand a writer's ignorance presume yourself ignorant of his understandings.   **Samuel Taylor Coleridge**

C H E C K   P O I N T
PAGES 763–771

Rewrite the following sentences, adding periods, question marks, exclamation points, and commas as needed.

Writing Theme
Ireland

1. Ireland also called Eire gained its independence from Britain in Dec 1921 and became a republic in 1949
2. For all the charms of its island life it has the highest rate of emigration of any European country
3. Who could leave the idyllic emerald-green beauty of Ireland
4. The population as a matter of fact is declining
5. The major cities of Dublin Cork Limerick and Galway have long captured the imagination of visitors
6. Not all visitors have been welcome: first the Celts invaded about 300 BC; second the Vikings, about AD 795; and third the Angles and Normans, around AD 1169.
7. Overall the population is homogeneous
8. More than 94 percent are of Irish nationality, and 931 (ninety-three and one-tenth) percent are Roman Catholics
9. Tourist guides often ask whether visitors have heard how St Patrick banished the snakes from Ireland
10. What a rich artistic and literary history Ireland offers
11. Although anecdotes of Irish wit abound some of the choicest involve playwright George Bernard Shaw.
12. Yes Shaw was a crusty and idealistic and eccentric writer.
13. Inquiring solicitously a hostess once asked him, "Are you enjoying yourself Mr Shaw"
14. "Certainly There is nothing else here to enjoy," he replied.
15. This exchange is attributed to Shaw; however some claim it was the Irish-born author Oscar Wilde who said it

Use commas to set off a direct quotation from the rest of the sentence.

The clause that identifies the source of a quotation may appear at the beginning, in the middle, or at the end of the sentence. When it follows the quotation, the comma goes inside the quotation marks.

> Francis said, "The Atomic Energy Commission recently sold some californium-252 for $1,000 per microgram."
> "But," said Midori, "that's about $350 billion a pound!"
> "I guess we won't be using that element in our chemistry experiment," Akesha said with a laugh.

Do not use commas with indirect quotations.

> Francis said that the Atomic Energy Commission had recently sold some californium-252 for $1,000 per microgram.

Commas in Compound Sentences

Use a comma before the conjunction that joins the two independent clauses of a compound sentence.

> The famous Hope diamond is said to be cursed, and many of its owners have died suddenly or mysteriously.

> Vincent van Gogh threw away his masterpieces, but his brother Theo saved them for posterity.

A sentence with a compound predicate needs no comma.

> The pilot *radioed* the control tower and *received* instructions to change runways.

Do not use a comma if the independent clauses of a compound sentence are very short and are joined by the conjunction *and, but, so, or,* or *nor.*

> The snake hissed and I stood still.

However, a comma should separate clauses joined by *yet* or *for.*

> The snake slithered away, yet I remained motionless.

Writing TIP

Three or more independent clauses in a series are usually separated by semicolons. If the clauses are short, they may be separated by commas.

Practice Your Skills

A. CONCEPT CHECK

Using Commas Rewrite the following sentences, adding commas where needed. If no additional commas are needed, write *Correct*.

1. "I think; therefore I am" wrote the French philosopher René Descartes in the year 1637.
2. These famous words announced the beginning of the Enlightenment and ushered in the Age of Reason in Europe.
3. Enlightenment philosophers held that each person has a rational will and they believed that nature obeys universal, orderly laws.
4. Reason, balance, and order permeated and shaped politics, science, and literature.
5. "Nature" wrote the English poet Alexander Pope "is a mighty maze, but not without plan."
6. Newton's discoveries were controversial but the leaders of the Enlightenment used them to support their theories.
7. Writers emulated the classics so prose was orderly and clear.
8. Samuel Johnson thought that order should prevail in the English language.
9. As a result of the publication of his dictionary, some pronunciations were fixed and many spellings were standardized.
10. "The material world" said the French philosopher Montesquieu "has its laws the beasts, their laws, and Man, his laws."

B. APPLICATION IN LITERATURE

Comma Usage Rewrite the passage, adding eighteen missing commas. You will use several of the comma rules you have learned so far. Notice how the use of commas adds clarity and organization.

(1) During the Age of Reason in England Joseph Addison and Richard Steele attracted and amused a large reading public with their witty polished essays. (2) Addison and Steele had quite different personalities yet the two writers were friends from childhood. (3) Addison was quiet and reserved but Steele was warm open, and charming. (4) In the early years of the eighteenth century each author wrote and edited essays for London periodicals devoted to news poetry and town gossip. (5) The essays of Addison and Steele ranged along quite a broad spectrum of everyday life; consequently they became popular authors. (6) In the pages of Addison's paper *The Spectator* for example a reader of the time could recognize ordinary realistic situations in the lives of a cross-section of social types. (7) Addison wrote "I shall endeavor to enliven

morality with wit and to temper wit with morality. (8) There are none to whom this paper will be more useful" he continued "than to the female world." (9) One secret of Addison's popularity in fact was that *The Spectator* attracted a large readership of women. (10) Writing about his ambitious project to produce *The Spectator* on a daily basis Addison promised his readers to quit if he should ever be convicted of the sin of literary dullness.

C. Moulton, *Teaching English Literature*

Commas with Nonessential Clauses and Phrases

Use commas to set off nonessential clauses.

A **nonessential clause** adds additional information to a sentence and can be omitted without changing the meaning of the sentence. An **essential clause** adds information necessary to the meaning of the sentence and is not set off by commas.

Nonessential Clause	Vatican City, which is an independent state, encompasses 109 acres within Rome.
Essential Clause	The city that serves as the seat of the Roman Catholic Church is Vatican City.
Nonessential Clause	The painter Thomas Moran, who came from England, helped Americans see the beauty of their own country.
Essential Clause	The painter who helped Americans recognize the need for national parks was Thomas Moran.

Use commas to set off nonessential participial phrases.

A **nonessential participial phrase** adds detail to a sentence but does not change its meaning. An **essential participial phrase** is necessary to complete the meaning of a sentence. It is not set off by commas.

Nonessential Participial Phrase	The tourists, wishing to see a variety of European dwellings, visited both thatched cottages and castles. (The participial phrase can be dropped.)
Essential Participial Phrase	Tourists wishing to see a variety of European dwellings can visit thatched cottages and castles. (The phrase cannot be dropped.)

Writing
—**TIP**—

In formal writing, *which* introduces nonessential clauses, and *that* introduces essential clauses.

Practice Your Skills

CONCEPT CHECK

Commas Rewrite the following sentences, adding commas where needed. If no additional commas are needed, write *Correct*.

1. The name that many music lovers consider the greatest in the annals of Italian opera is Giuseppe Verdi.
2. Verdi who came from a poor family was born in 1813.
3. At that time students desiring a musical education generally applied to the Milan Conservatory.
4. Verdi who failed his entrance exams had to study privately.
5. The first opera that he produced at La Scala in Milan enjoyed a moderate success.
6. The young composer grieving for the sudden deaths of his wife and two children almost gave up opera altogether.
7. In the 1840's Italy which was then ruled by Austria experienced a wave of nationalism.
8. Hoping to inspire Verdi the manager of La Scala urged him to compose an opera about the Biblical King Nebuchadnezzar.
9. The opera's theme which centered on the king's oppression of captive Israelites furnished a political parallel to Italy's situation.
10. This work which Verdi entitled *Nabucco* was a huge success.
11. Loving both music and freedom Italians made Verdi their hero.
12. Verdi's career lasting over half a century yielded twenty-six operas.
13. Three Verdi operas that were based on works of Shakespeare are *Macbeth, Otello,* and *Falstaff.*
14. Verdi's supreme ambition was to involve the emotions of his audiences in the drama that was played out onstage.
15. At his funeral in 1901 the crowd saluted the composer whom they loved by spontaneously singing a chorus from *Nabucco.*

Interior of the Teatro Regio, one of Italy's many beautiful opera houses, by Domenico Oliviero

C OMMAS: OTHER USES

Below are other common situations in which commas are used.

Commas in Dates, Place Names, and Letters

In dates, use a comma between the day of the month and the year. When only the month and year are given, no comma is used.

June 5, 1932   September 1992

When a date falls within a sentence, use a comma after the year.

July 20, 1969, was the date of the first moon landing.

Use a comma between the name of a city or town and the name of its state or country.

San Antonio, Texas   Madrid, Spain   Sofia, Bulgaria

Use a comma after each item in an address or place name within a sentence. No comma separates the state and the ZIP code.

Mail sent to 210 Geneva Road, Enid, Oklahoma 12339, will reach me.

Managua, Nicaragua, has been the site of much suffering.

Use a comma after the salutation of a friendly letter. Use a comma after the closing of a friendly letter or a business letter.

Dear Janet,   Your friend,   Sincerely,

Commas with Titles and Numbers

A title following a personal name is set off with commas; business abbreviations such as *Inc.* or *Ltd.* following a company name are also set off with commas.

Rader, Inc., has promoted Olympia Stavros, CPA, to vice-president.

In numbers of more than three digits, use commas between groups of three digits counting from the right, with the exception of ZIP codes, phone numbers, years, and house numbers.

The diameter of the earth is 7,926 miles.

Commas to Avoid Confusion

Use a comma to separate words or phrases that might otherwise be misread.

One source of confusion occurs when the conjunctions *but* and *for* are mistaken for prepositions.

Confusing	Every council representative approved the resolution for the city's historic buildings were being destroyed.
Clear	Every council representative approved the resolution, for the city's historic buildings were being destroyed.

A noun following a verb or verbal can cause confusion.

Confusing	While cooking Derrick burned his hand.
Clear	While cooking, Derrick burned his hand.

Writing
—TIP—

Commas are used to add clarity to sentences. However, overuse of commas can make sentences less clear.

End Marks
and Commas   **777**

An adverb at the beginning of a sentence may be mistaken for a preposition.

Confusing   Below the girl searched the ship's hold.

Clear   Below, the girl searched the ship's hold.

Use a comma to indicate the words left out of parallel word groups.

Sometimes a writer prefers not to repeat the same verb or the same subject and verb in a compound sentence; in such a sentence a comma indicates the missing element or elements.

The corn was tall; the wheat, golden.

Maria's culinary specialty is dessert; Daniel's, soup.

Practice Your Skills

Writing Theme
Track and Field

A. CONCEPT CHECK

Commas   Rewrite the sentences, adding commas where needed.

1. Jim Thorpe was born on May 28 1888 near Prague Oklahoma.
2. Thorpe's background was well known for his great-grandfather was Black Hawk, a famous chief of the Sauk tribe.
3. Charles, Jim's twin brother, was described as sweet and gentle; Jim as boisterous and restless.
4. After his brother's death, Thorpe attended the Indian Industrial School in Carlisle Pennsylvania.
5. While studying Jim led the school to national fame in football.
6. Then a letter came:

    Dear Mr. Peairs

    Please send Jimmy home. His father is badly hurt. Hunting accident.

    Sincerely
    Charlotte Thorpe

7. When Thorpe returned home, he found his father was healing; his mother dying.
8. Despite this tragedy, Thorpe achieved success for his athletic ability led him to the 1912 Olympic games in Stockholm Sweden.
9. Until the 1912 Olympics, one athlete had always been champion of the pentathlon; another of the decathlon.
10. Before no single athlete had ever won both strenuous events.
11. Though they were demanding Big Jim Thorpe won both events with ease.
12. He scored 8412 out of a possible 10000 points in the decathlon!

13. In January 1913 the Amateur Athletic Union revoked his amateur status because he had earned a small salary playing baseball.

14. However, in 1973—twenty years after his death—the AAU restored his amateur standing; in 1982 his medals.

15. In 1949 before Thorpe was exonerated Warner Brothers Inc. produced the movie *Jim Thorpe, All American.*

B. REVISION SKILL

Comma Usage Rewrite the following friendly letter, adding commas where needed.

>   August 10 19--
>
> Dear Juanita
>   I'm writing now to remind you about our goal: to see each other at the starting line on November 29 at the Park Forest Annual Community 10K Race. I've been training hard all summer in the area surrounding Boulder Colorado but now I'm back home in Irvine California putting the finishing touches on my training.
>   My new coach this season Diana T. Riggio Ph.D. really seems to know her stuff. In addition to our weekly mileage she makes us log at least one hour a day in the weight room. I'll probably have lifted over 20000 pounds by Thanksgiving!
>   I'll be at a special training camp for the next two weeks, before my first road race on August 25. You can address letters to me at Camp High Mileage RFD 12 Upland California 47647.
>   I hope your training is going well. Here's your tip for the month: By mentally rehearsing your race beforehand you can really improve your performance. Keep working on your 10000-meter pace!
>   On the run
>   Mary Beth

C. APPLICATION IN WRITING

A Sports Story Attend a sporting event at school or watch one on television. Then write a newspaper report on the event. Read several sports columns first, to get an idea of the style you should use. Use commas correctly in dates, for place names, and for titles.

Rewrite the following sentences, adding commas where needed. If no additional commas are needed, write *Correct*.

1. Throughout the world, people wishing to be informed are turning increasingly to the television nightly news.
2. On June 24 1990 *The New York Times* published an interesting article about television news in various countries.
3. The writer of the article who analyzed the similarities and differences of these programs was a journalist named James Brooke.
4. Brooke asserted that news aired in such capital cities as Tel Aviv Israel and Paris France assumes the same format as our programs.
5. He wrote "Studio sets may not be the sleek extravaganzas they often are here but electronic paraphernalia is roughly equivalent."
6. According to Brooke, the anchor who delivers the news abroad is frequently well known; sometimes revered as a celebrity.
7. "But beyond the trappings" Brooke noted "lie deep differences."
8. "To begin with much of the coverage abroad comes from state-owned networks and stations" he wrote.
9. In such places as Beijing China and Pretoria South Africa the result has been outright control of the news.
10. On such broadcasts, the news is commonly a reflection of government policy; the anchor a mouthpiece for its leadership.
11. In America, of course, the Constitution protects news organizations, such as CBS Inc. and Time Inc. from governmental control.
12. Some countries such as West Germany have state-owned television stations yet the newscasts seem to be balanced and fair.
13. Brooke wrote that in the U. S., news organizations are basically spectators; overseas, news-gathering associations are political.
14. In Rio de Janeiro Brazil, for example, a candidate's ownership of a TV network was an influential factor in the election of a president.
15. In Israel viewership of "Mabat," the nightly news program, can be as high as 90 percent, or 4029000 out of a population of 4477000.
16. American television networks, such as NBC Inc. or ABC Inc. would surely be pleased with ratings like that!
17. "The Israelis are a nation of news hounds" Brooke wrote.
18. In Israel, according to Brooke, television news is serious and important; the broadcasts essentially neutral.
19. Elsewhere in Italy, for example, party bias is often evident on the part of state-owned stations.
20. Japanese television news tends to be respectful to authority yet some stations do air controversial issues—in the middle of the night!

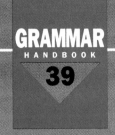

GRAMMAR
H A N D B O O K
39

A. Using Punctuation Correctly   Rewrite the following sentences, adding punctuation where necessary.

1. On Apr 15 1912 at 2:20 AM the British passenger ship *Titanic* sank to the floor of the Atlantic Ocean
2. The Titanic which experts considered unsinkable had collided with an iceberg about 2750 km northeast of New York City.
3. According to the US Senate Investigating Committee 1517 people lost their lives in the dark icy waters of the Atlantic.
4. Who could have predicted that oddly enough one of the most useful inventions of the twentieth century would be a product of this tragedy
5. The loss of the *Titanic* focused scientists' attention on how to detect underwater objects
6. L. F. Richardson a British meteorologist suggested using echoes as a means of iceberg detection.
7. A US radio pioneer Prof Reginald A Fessenden made the first successful experiments before World War I broke out in 1914.
8. Because they can determine the position size and depth of under-sea objects echo-sounding devices offer many applications in both war and peace.
9. The US Navy for example uses hydrosearch systems to detect hostile submarines.
10. Oil companies use echoes to survey sea-level pipelines and commercial fishing companies use them for finding fish.

Writing Theme
Inventions

B. Finding Punctuation Errors   For each item, identify where punctuation is missing. List any word that should be followed by an additional punctuation mark. Then place the mark correctly.

1. On May 12 1990 reporters in Ames Iowa interviewed a scientist for their *Iowa Today* program stressed science themes.
2. To discuss the transistor Dr Craig Jones Jr from Bell Telephone Laboratories Inc. was invited to the show.
3. "Tell us Dr. Jones about the transistor" said the moderator.
4. Jones asked what they would like to know
5. "Well tell us the basics: first who invented it; second what it is; and third how it is used" replied one interviewer.
6. Jones explained that John Bardeen Walter H Brattain and William B Shockley working together invented the transistor in 1947
7. "What is a transistor" asked a reporter on the panel
8. "A transistor you may recall is a device that amplifies controls and generates electrical signals" said Jones.
9. "For example transistors are used in radios television sets and hearing aids" he continued.

10. "Aha!" cried a reporter "When I was twelve I spent 999 (ninety-nine and nine-tenths) percent of my time listening to my transistor radio"

11. "Tell us please about its other applications" requested another reporter.

12. "The transistor" continued Jones "was critical in making computers smaller."

13. Before the transistor computers were enormous; afterward quite small indeed.

14. One early computer was 16 ft long 8 ft high and 4 ft deep; it contained 100000 soldered connections.

15. Bardeen Brattain and Shockley who shared the 1956 Nobel Prize for physics revolutionized the technology of electronics; however transistors were replaced by integrated circuits in the 1970's.

C. Errors in Comma Usage Rewrite the following passage, correcting errors in the use of end marks and commas.

Ethlie Ann Vare and Greg Ptacek authors of *Mothers of Invention* claim that in the case of Bette Nesmith Graham "necessity was the mother of invention." Bette worked as a secretary at Texas Bank and Trust. Bette was a poor typist but she had become adept at erasing her mistakes In a new job as executive secretary she was given an electric typewriter with a film ribbon and she quickly learned that mistakes no longer erased easily. Alas Bette was in trouble She was however also creative.

Bette had noticed something when decorating the bank windows for the holidays. "When lettering an artist never corrects by erasing but always paints over the error" she remembered. She decided to apply the technique to her typing errors. Bette explained "I put some tempera waterbase paint in a bottle and took my watercolor brush to the office." Her solution worked and she soon found herself mixing up batches of "Mistake Out" in her garage developing what would become a commercial formula for a quick-drying invisible correction fluid

By the end of 1957 Bette had named her product Liquid Paper and was selling about a hundred bottles a month. The business continued to grow and by the time she died in 1980 Bette Nesmith Graham was a wealthy woman

On the Lightside

REPUNCTUATION

How important is punctuation? Read these entries from a New York *magazine contest. Entrants were asked to alter the meaning of a famous phrase by using punctuation, italics, or capitalization.*

What's that on the road? A head?

I can get it. For *you*, wholesale.

What's for dinner—Mother?

How do! I love thee!
Let me count the ways.

R. Crusoe: "Thank God! It's *Friday*!"

Let *me* call YOU sweetheart.

What is this thing *called,* love?

Don't! Just stand there.

Look, before you leap . . .

Donald! *Duck!*

You're Rumple Stilt's kin.

A *Lice*? In *Wonder Land*?

Zip-a-dee-do-dah, zip-a-dee, Eh?

A horse? A *horse*? My kingdom for a HORSE?

"*I'm* a Yankee Doodle."
"Dandy."

Pop goes! The weasel.

Love is where? *You* find it!

Fly? ME? To the *moon*?

Take me out to the ball. Game?

I never promised *you* a rose garden.

Uncle, Sam wants you.

I remember you. Well?

First, *class* passengers only!

Half the world does not know how; the other half lives.

People who live in glass houses shouldn't. Throw stones!

Oh say, can *you* see by the dawn's early light?

Beware the fury of a patient, man.

What is so rare as a day in, June?

Do not *fold*: Spindle or Mutilate!

Rose's are red, *Violet's* are blue.

Rome, O Rome, O wherefore art thou?

"Simple," Simon says.

When I consider how, my life is spent.

What are you doing New Year's, Eve?

I love you for sentiment. AL REASONS.

"Jack Sprat could." "Eat?" "No!" "Fat, his wife, could." "Eat?" "No, lean!"

I *told* you. So?

Tom, Dick *and* Harry?

A. ROSEBY. Any other name would smell as sweet.

I love you. A. BUSHEL and A. PECK.

We have met. The enemy and the "Y" are ours.

The bear went over the mountain and what do you think? He saw!

Call me, Ishmael.

Mary Ann Madden, Ed.

Semicolons, Colons, and Other Punctuation

THE SEMICOLON

Semicolons, like commas, separate sentence elements. A semi-colon indicates a stronger break than a comma but not as strong a break as a period.

Semicolons Used with Commas

The independent clauses in a compound sentence are usually separated by a comma. However, if there are commas within the clauses, a semicolon is used to avoid confusion.

Use a semicolon between independent clauses joined by a conjunction if the first clause contains commas.

> Babe Didrikson Zaharias competed in swimming, tennis, and diving; but she won enduring fame as a result of her performance in golf and track.

> Kim, who had just learned to skate, had not yet learned how to stop; and she tumbled into the snowbank at the edge of the pond.

Use a semicolon between the parts of a series if there are commas within the parts.

> Three Connecticut patriots with the name Wolcott were Roger Wolcott, a colonial governor; Oliver Wolcott, a signer of the Declaration of Independence; and Oliver Wolcott, Jr., a secretary of the Treasury.

> New York's nickname is the Empire State; its motto, *Excelsior;* its flower, the rose; its bird, the bluebird.

Semicolons Between Main Clauses

The independent clauses in a compound sentence may be joined with a comma and a conjunction like *and* or *but,* or with just a semicolon.

> You may approve of the measure, *but* we do not.

> You may approve of the measure; we do not.

Use a semicolon to join the independent clauses of a compound sentence if no coordinating conjunction is used.

> Mikhail Gorbachev took the reins of Soviet government in 1985; he promptly initiated a series of bold reforms.

> Traveling medieval knights used a seal from their signet rings instead of cash; today travelers "pay" with credit cards.

In the sentences below, notice that the semicolon suggests a stronger relationship between the two ideas than a conjunction does.

> Watergate was one of the biggest political scandals in the history of the United States, *and* it resulted in the resignation of Richard M. Nixon as President.

> Watergate was one of the biggest political scandals in the history of the United States; it resulted in the resignation of Richard M. Nixon as President.

Do not use a semicolon to join unrelated clauses. A semicolon should be used only if the clauses are closely related.

Incorrect   Mary Cassatt was an American painter who became famous for her paintings of mothers and children; for many years she lived in France.

Correct   Mary Cassatt was an American painter who became famous for her paintings of mothers and children; she showed her subjects in everyday situations.

Semicolons and Conjunctive Adverbs

Use a semicolon before a conjunctive adverb or a parenthetical expression that joins the clauses of a compound sentence.

> Getting children to sit still is not easy; however, most photographers are prepared for that.

> All of us have special childhood memories; indeed, most family photo albums provide a record of such moments.

Note that conjunctive adverbs such as *however* and parenthetical expressions such as *indeed* are followed by a comma.

Mrs. Cassatt Reading to Her Grandchildren, 1880, Mary Cassatt

Practice Your Skills

A. CONCEPT CHECK

Semicolons Rewrite the following sentences, substituting semicolons wherever necessary.

1. In the fifth century A.D., the island of Britain was invaded by the Jutes and Angles from what is now known as Denmark, the Saxons, from what is now Germany, and the Frisians, from what is now Holland.
2. The native Celts were no match for the invaders, defeat was swift and complete.
3. These invasions from foreign lands continued for over a hundred years, the invaders who settled in Britain became collectively known as Anglo-Saxons.
4. Their culture became the basis for Angle-land, or English culture, and their guttural Germanic language became what is known today as Old English.
5. At first glance, Old English looks quite foreign, however, a modern reader can recognize a number of words.
6. These words include *hwaet,* which means *what, cyning,* which means *king,* and *meado,* which means *mead* and later, *meadow.*
7. To an Anglo-Saxon, life was a struggle to be endured, and evil and death were inescapable, fame was the only true immortality.
8. The Anglo-Saxons were largely illiterate, however, they had a rich oral tradition.
9. As they celebrated in great mead halls, the Anglo-Saxons vividly described victories and battles, as a result, they created epic tales of legendary deeds.
10. The most famous surviving work in Old English is the poem *Beowulf,* it is the earliest known long literary work in English.
11. The main character, Beowulf, is King of the Geats, he comes to the aid of the King of the Danes.
12. The monsters in the poem are the man-eating Grendel, which Beowulf kills, Grendel's mother, which Beowulf also kills, sea serpents, which Beowulf wrestles underwater, and a fire-eating dragon, which kills Beowulf.
13. The epic *Beowulf* is captivating to read, on the other hand, it also serves as an invaluable source of historical information.
14. In 1939 archaeologists uncovered an ancient burial mound at Sutton Hoo, and it contained more valuables dating from the Anglo-Saxon period than any other site yet unearthed.
15. A ship was discovered that dated from the seventh century A.D., this would have been about a century before *Beowulf* was first recorded.

B. REVISION SKILL

Semicolons Write the words before and after each missing semicolon in the following passage, and place the semicolon correctly.

(1) The history of English is usually divided into three periods: the Old English period, from A.D. 400 to A.D. 1100, the Middle English period, from A.D. 1100 to A.D. 1500, and the Modern English period, from A.D. 1500 to the present. (2) The cutoff dates for these periods are rough, arbitrary, and inexact, language changes continually. (3) In other words, one simply does not wake up one morning and find that the language has changed instead, such changes take place gradually.

(4) Sometimes, however, events occur that cause language to change more rapidly for example, the invasion and occupation of a country by people who speak a different language tends to result in rapid linguistic change as speakers of different languages borrow from one another. (5) The events that signal the cutoffs for major periods in the history of the English language are the Anglo-Saxon invasions of England, which started in the fifth century A.D., the conquest of England by the Norman French, which occurred in A.D. 1066, and the beginnings of English exploration and colonialism, which can be dated to roughly A.D. 1500.

THE COLON

The colon marks an important division in a sentence. It signals the reader that the material that follows is an explanation, an example, or a summation.

Use a colon to introduce a list of items.

Several parts of the sandal were leather: the upper sole, the strap, the vamp, and the midsole.

I had three chairs in my house: one for solitude, two for friendship, three for society.   **Henry David Thoreau**

In a sentence a colon often follows a word or phrase such as *these, the following,* or *as follows.*

Leading olive-growing countries include the following: Spain, Italy, Greece, Portugal, and Turkey.

Among the plays I have enjoyed are these: *Our Town, The Skin of Our Teeth, The Vegetable,* and *As You Like It.*

Do not use a colon immediately after a preposition or a verb (unless the verb introduces a formal quotation).

Incorrect	Two of my favorite Katharine Hepburn movies are: *The African Queen* and *On Golden Pond.*
Correct	Two of my favorite Katharine Hepburn movies are *The African Queen* and *On Golden Pond.*
Correct	Two of my favorite Katharine Hepburn movies are the following: *The African Queen* and *On Golden Pond.*
Incorrect	The country of New Zealand consists of: the North Island and the South Island.
Correct	The country of New Zealand consists of the North Island and the South Island.
Correct	The country of New Zealand consists of two islands: North Island and South Island.

Use a colon to introduce a quotation that lacks explanatory words such as *he said* or *she said*.

> Martha's answer was quiet but firm: "I'll stay here."

Use a colon to introduce a long or formal quotation.

> Winston Churchill once said: "We shall defend our island, whatever the cost may be, we shall fight on the beaches . . . and in the streets, we shall fight in the hills; we shall never surrender."

Use a colon between two independent clauses when the second explains the first.

> Mr. Jonas was in for a surprise: his car had a flat tire.

Other Uses of the Colon

A colon is conventionally used in the following ways: (1) after the salutation of a formal letter, (2) between the hour and minute figures of clock time, (3) between the chapter and verses in Biblical references, (4) between the title and subtitle of a book, (5) between the volume and number of a periodical or the volume and pages of periodicals, and (6) after labels that signal important ideas.

Dear Sir or Madam:	*Women's Labor History: In the Voices of the Women Who Lived It*
8:05 P.M.	*Time* 37:17–20 (volume and pages)
Job 3:2–4	Warning: High Voltage

Writing
═══**TIP**═══

The expression *such as* functions as a preposition and should not be followed by a colon: *Lily was talented in many fields, such as drama and sports.*

Practice Your Skills

A. CONCEPT CHECK

Colons and Semicolons   Copy the following items, adding colons and semicolons wherever necessary.

1. Hetty Robinson Green learned an important virtue early in life she learned the importance of thrift.
2. Green was raised in a prosperous New England family however, she failed to learn how to enjoy money.
3. At age thirty, in 1865, she received the following
4. Dear Miss Robinson

   We are writing to inform you that you are the beneficiary of two estates. The holdings include the balance of your father's estate, a sum of one million dollars one-half of your aunt's estate, another one million dollars and the interest that these funds have accrued. We have set an appointment for you at 900 Monday. Contact us if this is inconvenient.

   Sincerely,

   Barney and Brown Attorneys at Law
5. Later, in 1867, Hetty Robinson married Edward H. Green, who was also a millionaire yet she worked on to increase her wealth.
6. Green wisely put her funds into the following railroads, United States gold, bonds, and real estate.
7. The verse Ecclesiastes 11 1, about casting your bread upon the waters, certainly seemed true for her.
8. Her biographers noted an important aspect of her thrift "in the spending of money she might have been compared to an athlete who never broke training."
9. Green was afraid people would take advantage of her wealth therefore, she often pretended to be poor.
10. Her typical behavior included the following she dressed in rags, she denied herself a home by staying in cheap hotels, and she claimed she was a charity case.
11. On one memorable occasion, her son injured his knee Green refused to get him medical treatment.
12. Her stinginess certainly had dire consequences her son lost his leg from infection.
13. Green's excessive thrift brought results indeed, her family inherited over one hundred million dollars.
14. Green's son, who inherited a substantial portion of his mother's wealth, did not have his mother's problem he spent money readily.
15. His enjoyment of money was clear he bought yachts and diamonds, spending approximately three million dollars a year.

B. APPLICATION IN LITERATURE

Semicolons and Colons Semicolons and colons have been omitted from the following passages. Write the sentences correctly, restoring the punctuation marks.

1. Eat not to dullness drink not to elevation. **Benjamin Franklin**
2. Things were as she suspected she had been frank in her questions and Polly had been frank in her answers. **James Joyce**
3. Jade Snow had chosen it [sociology] without thought, simply to meet a requirement but that casual decision had completely revolutionized her thinking . . . **Jade Snow Wong**
4. Love must be learned, and learned again and again there is no end to it. Hate needs no instruction, but waits only to be provoked. **Katherine Ann Porter**
5. Humanity has but three great enemies fever, famine, and war. **Sir William Osler**
6. Four be the things I am wiser to know Idleness, sorrow, a friend, and a foe. **Dorothy Parker**
7. Nobody was smarter than anybody else nobody was better looking than anybody else nobody was stronger or quicker than anybody else. **Kurt Vonnegut, Jr.**
8. After a little, the plumber emerged from the earth first the light top of his head, then the burnt brow, and then the blue eyes fringed with whitest lash. **Kay Boyle**
9. No matter what time I start the column, I finish it at 600. It's kind of spooky. I've tried starting it at 800 in the morning I finish at 600. If I start at 500, I'll still finish at 600. **Harry Stein**
10. It was this way Pamela knew her sister had left a will in Woodville's favor. **Shirley Ann Grau**
11. Advice is seldom welcome those who want it the most always like it the least. **Lord Chesterfield**
12. It is a far, far better thing I do, than I have ever done it is a far, far better rest that I go to than I have ever known. **Charles Dickens**

THE DASH

Dashes are used to set off words that interrupt the main idea of a sentence. While commas set off material that is closely connected to the main idea, dashes indicate a looser connection. The words set off by dashes add extra information to an already complete thought. Dashes can also mean *in other words* or *that is* when they come before an explanation.

Use a dash to show an abrupt break in thought.

> The Morrises plan to see *Hamlet*—it's their favorite play—at the Shakespeare Festival in Stratford, Ontario.

> The trouble is—I suppose he knows it himself—he just can't get along with other people.

This use of the dash is especially appropriate in dialogue, where it adds a casual, conversational tone.

> "Did you know that Annie Oakley—her nickname was 'Little Sure Shot'—stood just five feet tall?"

> "Yes, and I know that the musical *Annie Get Your Gun*—have you seen it?—tells the story of her life."

> "Her husband, Frank Butler, allowed her to shoot a dime out of his hand—can you imagine such trust?"

Use a dash to set off a long explanatory statement that interrupts the main thought of the sentence.

> There was a feeling of curious anticipation—a feeling shared throughout the world—when Communist China first invited the President of the United States to visit Beijing.

> Tammany Hall—a powerful political machine in New York City during the late 1800's—was often attacked by cartoonists.

When an explanatory statement contains a number of commas, setting it off with dashes serves to clarify meaning and reduce confusion for the readers.

> Many prominent American poets—Elizabeth Bishop, Marianne Moore, and Robert Bly, to name just a few—have been published in that journal.

Punctuation Note Punctuation marks that belong to the material set off by dashes should be placed inside the dashes.

> I saw Sue—do you remember her?—when I visited my old school last week.

Use a dash to set off a summarizing statement from the rest of a sentence.

> Simplicity of operation, low cost, assembly-line production—these were the factors that Henry Ford introduced to revolutionize the manufacture of automobiles.

Writing
TIP

The overuse of dashes may confuse a reader or make your writing seem choppy.

Practice Your Skills

A. CONCEPT CHECK

Dashes   Dashes have been omitted from the literary quotations below. Rewrite these passages and return them to their original form by using dashes where they should occur. Notice how dashes serve as guides for the reader, clarifying the writer's train of thought.

1. Suddenly one of them it must have been Chino reached out, grabbed Godfrey's beard, and pulled hard. With his other hand, he snatched off Godfrey's dark glasses. There was no reaction from Godfrey.   **Nat Hentoff**
2. The apartment was bright with big rooms and the funny smell was stronger inside. I found out what it was gefilte fish.

    Louise Meriwether
3. Because of her creativity with flowers, even my memories of poverty are seen through a screen of blooms sunflowers, petunias, roses, dahlias, forsythia, spirea, delphiniums, verbena . . . and on and on.   **Alice Walker**
4. The Widow Wycherly if so fresh a damsel could be called a widow tripped up to the doctor's chair, with a mischievous merriment in her rosy face.   **Nathaniel Hawthorne**
5. One writes out of one thing only one's own experience.

    James Baldwin
6. At last, after what seemed a long time it might have been five seconds, I dare say he [the elephant] sank flabbily to his knees.

    George Orwell
7. From my fifteenth year save for a single interval I have lived about as solitary a life as a modern man can have.   **Thomas Wolfe**
8. The younger people, who grew up during the paper shortage, aren't used to filling the space. But that is journalism an ability to meet the challenge of filling the space.   **Rebecca West**
9. But today she passed the baker's by, climbed the stairs, went into the little dark room her room like a cupboard and sat down on the red eiderdown.   **Katherine Mansfield**
10. My well-fitted curriculum classes, homework, tennis, piano, editing was ordered with just one thought: to make room for the dance practice.   **Agnes De Mille**

B. APPLICATION IN WRITING

A Book Review   Think of a book that you read recently. What did you like about it? What were its weaknesses? Would you recommend it to a friend? Write a short book review, using semicolons, colons, and dashes correctly.

THE HYPHEN

Hyphens are sometimes used to combine words and word parts and sometimes used to separate them.

Use a hyphen in compound numbers from twenty-one through ninety-nine.

thirty-one   fifty-six   eighty-eight

Use hyphens in fractions.

She won the election by a two-thirds majority.

Three-fourths of the members voted for the measure.

Use a hyphen in a compound adjective before a noun. Usually no hyphen is used when a compound adjective follows a linking verb.

Before a Noun   Eleanor is a well-informed voter.

After a Linking Verb   Eleanor is well informed.

Use a hyphen in certain compound nouns.

sister-in-law   great-grandmother

Spelling Note Since the rules for hyphenation of compound nouns and modifiers are very complex, it is wise to consult a dictionary.

Use a hyphen with the prefixes *all-*, *ex-*, and *self-*; with the suffix *-elect*; and with all prefixes before a proper noun or proper adjective.

We invited the ex-senator to present a speech at the dedication of the new public library.

President-elect Bush was prepared for the reporter's questions.

The costume designer researched clothing worn in the post-Elizabethan period.

Use hyphens to prevent confusion and to avoid awkwardness.

For example, it is clearer to write *de-emphasis* rather than *deemphasis* in order to avoid a misreading of the word; similarly, it is clearer to write *co-chairperson* rather than *cochairperson*.

Use a hyphen if part of a word must be carried over from one line to the next.

Ed felt strongly about the issue, so he wrote his representative a long letter explaining his views.

Writing
—TIP—

Don't use a hyphen when a modifier includes a word ending in *-ly*: *newly painted fence*.

Try to observe the following rules when hyphenating words at the end of a line.

1. Separate words only between syllables.
2. Hyphenate a word only if it has two or more syllables.
3. Leave at least two letters of the hyphenated word on each line.

Practice Your Skills

CONCEPT CHECK

Hyphens If a line in the following paragraph contains words that need to be hyphenated, write the line number and the correctly hyphenated words after the number. If a line contains words that are incorrectly hyphenated, write the line number and the correct hyphenation after the number. If a line contains correct hyphenation, write *Correct*. You may wish to consult a dictionary.

Example 1 In the 1986 congressional race, two thirds of the
2 winners received over sixty-five percent of the vote.
3 In other words, people elected to the U.S. Congr-
4 ess these days tend to win by substantial margins.

Line 1 two-thirds
Line 2 Correct
Line 3 Con-gress

1 Many well informed political commentators have notic-
2 ed that congressional races in the United States tend to f-
3 avor returning, or incumbent, candidates. Consider the
4 following statistics: in 1863 fifty eight percent of those
5 entering office after an election were first term
6 members. By contrast, in 1981 only sixteen percent of
7 entering representatives were first termers. What has
8 happened? Why is Congress now, more often than not, a
9 lifelong career? Why is your representative elect most
10 likely *not* a new face? The answer lies in the enor-
11 mous power that an incumbent has to get his or her
12 message out to the people. Incumbent representatives
13 receive more press coverage than their opponents. They
14 also have better funded campaigns. Finally, they can
15 make use of free, taxpayer paid mailings. Of course,
16 members of Congress generally feel that it would be self
17 defeating for them to pass legislation to make
18 congressional elections fairer. However, several ex
19 representatives have called for major reform in
20 congressional election practices.

PARENTHESES, BRACKETS, ELLIPSES

Parentheses and brackets are used to enclose information that is separate from the main idea of the sentence.

Parentheses

Use parentheses to set off the supplementary or explanatory material that is either nonessential or loosely connected to the sentence.

> The Xhosa (kō′ sä) are a pastoral people who live in South Africa.

> Edna St. Vincent Millay's poem "Renascence" (written in 1912) was composed when she was just nineteen years old.

Use parentheses to identify a source of information, such as author and page number of a reference.

> "Things happened to young Walt Disney that he would recall with clarity in later years." **(Thomas 10)**

For more information on documenting sources of information, see Writer's Workshop 9, pages 283–284, and Writing Handbook 24, pages 486–487.

Use parentheses to enclose figures or letters that identify items in a series.

> The years after the turn of the century were years of change for the people of England: (1) in social conditions, (2) in government, and (3) in the expansion of their empire.

Use parentheses to set off certain numerical information.

> Call our toll-free number (800) 555-3211.

> William Penn (1644–1718) founded the colony of Pennsylvania.

Place punctuation marks inside the parentheses when they belong to the parenthetical material. When punctuation marks belong to the main part of the sentence, place them outside the parentheses.

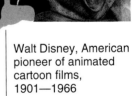

Walt Disney, American pioneer of animated cartoon films, 1901—1966

Brackets

Use brackets to enclose corrections or to insert additional information into material quoted from a source.

"On the 4th [5th] of March, Hayes took office." (correction)

The letter read: "We have him [Jordahl] at our mercy." (an explanatory word inserted by the editor)

Ellipses

Use ellipses points—three dots (. . .)—to indicate the omission of part of a quoted sentence. Use four dots—a period plus ellipses points—when the omission is between sentences or after a sentence.

"Dear Madam: I have been shown in the files of the War Department . . . that you are the mother of five sons who have died gloriously on the field of battle. . . ."

Abraham Lincoln

Practice Your Skills

CONCEPT CHECK

Writing Theme
Goethe

Parentheses and Brackets   Revise each sentence, inserting parentheses and brackets as needed.

1. Johann Wolfgang von Goethe 1749–1832 is believed by some to have been the most intelligent person who ever lived.
2. He made major contributions to many fields of endeavor: 1 to literature, 2 to the theory of optics, and 3 to botany and zoology.
3. One critic has written: "There is none to whom we can look more trustingly as the father of world literature than Goethe." Spender 56
4. Spender writes: "Poetry is not for him Goethe a refuge, a habitation, or a confessional; it is an occasion for a magnificent statement."
5. Literary scholar Jergen Kloss wrote: "Goethes' Goethe's most famous literary work is his *Faust,* an epic drama in verse."

CHECK POINT
PAGES 784—796

Rewrite the sentences, adding or changing punctuation as necessary. Use semicolons, colons, dashes, hyphens, and parentheses.

Writing Theme
Vincent van Gogh

1. Vincent van Gogh 1853–1890 sold only one painting in his lifetime nevertheless, he is considered a truly great artist.
2. The words of Proverbs 14,13 describe his personal life "Even in laughter the heart is sorrowful."

3. For roughly two thirds of his life, van Gogh his artistic career only lasted ten years tried several professions.
4. He worked for an art dealer in London, England, a bookseller in Dordrecht, Holland, and a church in Brussels, Belgium.
5. His work as a missionary with poverty stricken coal miners in Belgium certainly had an unfortunate end, he was fired.
6. In his letters to his brother Theo he explained how he channeled religious feeling into art "I want to paint . . . with that something of the eternal which the halo used to symbolize."
7. Van Gogh relied on his brother Theo was his lifeline for both moral and financial support.
8. In his letters to Theo, van Gogh also expressed his feelings on many subjects such as the following art, religion, and poetry.
9. Van Gogh's letters few can read them without being moved reveal a master of written as well as visual imagery.
10. Bold, brilliant, erratic, all describe the man and his art.
11. These artists influenced his work, giving him needed self confidence Jean-François Millet, Georges Seurat, Jean-Baptiste-Camille Corot.
12. He and artist Paul Gauguin were coworkers for two months however, their relationship was tempestuous.
13. Under great emotional strain, van Gogh cut off part of his left ear when he was thirty five years old.
14. He feared for his sanity from that point on, his mental anguish alternated with periods of artistic genius.
15. He produced works such as *Garden of the Asylum* and *Olive Trees,* and he experimented greatly with style and color.
16. Historian H.W. Janson wrote "Despairing of a cure, he committed suicide . . . art alone made his life worth living."
17. After his death the world acclaimed his genius thus, he is now one of the most well known artists of all time.
18. The book *Genius and Disaster The Ten Creative Years of Vincent van Gogh* gives us insight into a complex artist.
19. Impressively, van Gogh painted more than six hundred works of art how remarkable! in a ten year span.
20. Van Gogh did not become wealthy during his lifetime however, in the late 1980's, his painting *Irises* commanded one of the highest prices ever paid at auction for a piece of artwork $53.9 million.

The Garden of the Hospital at Arles, 1889, Vincent van Gogh

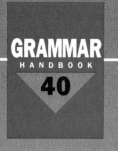
Writing Theme
Classification

A. Semicolons, Colons, and Other Punctuation   Notice that the following paragraph has only four sentences. Much information is packed into these sentences through the use of punctuation: parentheses, semicolons, and a colon. Read the passage carefully and then restore any missing parentheses, semicolons, and colons.

> Slavic falls into three main subdivisions East Slavic includes Great Russian (or just Russian), the common and literary language of Russia; Ruthenian or Ukrainian, spoken in the Ukraine and White Russian (or Byelorussian), spoken to the north of the Ukraine. West Slavic includes Polish, Czech, the highly similar Slovak, and Serbian or Wendish, a language spoken by a small group of people in East Germany these languages have lost many of the early forms preserved in East Slavic. The South Slavic languages are Bulgarian, Serbo-Croatian, and Slovenian. The oldest Slavic writing . . . is in Old Bulgarian, sometimes called Old Church Slavic or Old Church Slavonic, which remained a liturgical language long after it ceased to be generally spoken.

> **Thomas Pyle,**
> ***The Origins and Development of the English Language***

B. Punctuating Correctly   Rewrite the following sentences, punctuating them correctly.

1. At 725 A.M. every Monday, Wednesday, and Friday, bleary eyed students file into Biology 101.
2. For centuries, students have studied biology thus *Linnaeus* should be a household word, but it's not.
3. Carolus Linnaeus 1707–1778 was a Swedish botanist.
4. Linnaeus his family called him "the little botanist" was the son of a clergyman in Rashult, Sweden.
5. Perhaps Ecclesiastes 3 1 inspired him "To every thing there is a season, and a time to every purpose under heaven."
6. Linnaeus attended the university in Uppsala, northwest of Stockholm, Sweden, and he was appointed lecturer in botany there at the age of twenty three.
7. There, the botanist Olof Celsius not to be confused with Anders Celsius, who invented the temperature scale helped Linnaeus's career.
8. In 1732, Linnaeus led an expedition to Lapland as a result, he wrote *Flora Lapponica* 1737.
9. His contribution to science not just the discovery of some little known plant is the system of classifying living things.

10. The system, from highest to lowest rank, is as follows kingdom, phylum, class, order, family, genus, and species.
11. Professor Paul B. Weisz wrote "This . . . system of taxonomy has since become greatly elaborated and is now in universal use."
12. Consider the corn plant its phylum is *Tracheophyta,* class, *Angiospermae,* order, *Graminales,* and family, *Graminaceae.*
13. The system was useful in two ways 1 it gave scientists a method of classifying, or relating, flora and fauna; and 2 it set forth an order of taxonomies, or classifications.
14. One unappreciative student wrote this note "Thanks to you Lineus Linnaeus I'm playing with phyla and not the all star team!"
15. Linnaeus's manuscripts, herbarium, collections of insects and shells all are preserved by the Linnean Society in London.

C. More Correct Punctuation Rewrite the following passage, correcting errors in capitalization and spelling as well as errors in the use of punctuation.

A night person enjoys burning the midnight oil, watching the late movie, or trekking home at 600 A.M. from a party, but a morning person is up at the crack of dawn, ready to conquer the day. Are such concepts real or merely excuses for doing what we want when we want?

Sceintists have discovered that the body does function in accordance with rhythms moreover these all important rhythms vary from person to person. About one tenth of the population can be considered night people, and about one tenth morning people. The rest of us are in between. Body Temperture peaks later in night people and earlier in morning people. Did you know that our body temperature is not always 98.6 degrees Fahrenheit? Rather, it varies slightly over the course of the day in a predictible pattern, the rising and falling of body temperature is linked with cicles of activity and sleep.

Why is it important to understand our bodies rhythms? Over coming jet lag, adjusting to unusual work schedules, fighting diseases these are just a few possible applications of scientific research into biological rhythms.

On the Lightside

TALK ABOUT PARENTHESES

As you have learned, parentheses may be used to set off material that is nonessential or loosely connected to the sentence. The poem below is a humorous example of parentheses used to an extreme.

Of all the fleas that ever flew
(And flying fleas are rather few
((Because for proper flying you
(((Whether you are a flea or not)))
Need wings and things fleas have not got)))—

(I make the further point that fleas
Are thick as these parentheses
((An illustration (((you'll agree)))
Both apt and pleasing to a flea)))—

Now then where were we? Let me see—
Ah, yes—We said to fly you ought
(Whether you are a flea or not)
To have some wings (yes, at least two
((At least no less than two will do
(((And fleas have something less than one
((((One less, in fact (((((or, frankly, none,
Which ((((((as once more you will agree))))))
Limits the flying of a flea)))))))))))).

And let me add that fleas that fly
are known as Flears. (You can see why.)
All I have said thus far is true.
(If it's not clear, that's up to you.
((You'll have to learn sometime, my dear,
That what is true may not be clear
(((While what is clear may not be true
((((And you'll be wiser when you do.))))))))))

Saturday Review

Sketchbook

To find creative writers, an advertising agency held a contest in which participants were asked to complete a series of writing assignments. Here are some of the assignments:

Write a "Dialogue in a Dark Alley." (Not more than 200 words).

You are a writer for Walletsize Books. Describe the history of the United States in one hundred words or less.

A delegation of Martians has just landed in a local park. They do not understand any Earth languages—only very basic symbols. Prepare a short speech comprised of pictures and symbols to welcome them and to tell them just what kind of place this is.

How would you complete one of these assignments? Be sure to capitalize and punctuate accurately as you write.

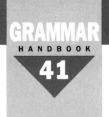

Apostrophes and Quotation Marks

APOSTROPHES

The apostrophe is used to show possession, to indicate omitted letters, and to form certain plurals, such as those of numbers.

Using Apostrophes to Show Possession

Use the apostrophe to form the possessive of singular and plural nouns.

To form the possessive of a singular noun, add an apostrophe and an -s even if the noun ends in -s.

 Emma's writer's city's
 Tess's   duchess's Joyce Carol Oates's

Punctuation Note The possessives of ancient classical names ending in -s and of names of more than one syllable with unaccented endings pronounced *-eez* are formed by adding just an apostrophe: *Demosthenes', R.S. Surtees', Ramses', Xerxes', Mars'.* The possessive of *Jesus* and *Moses* is formed the same way: *Jesus', Moses'.*

To form the possessive of a plural noun that ends in -s, add an apostrophe only.

 senators' churches' Johnsons' females'

To form the possessive of a plural noun that does not end in -s, add an apostrophe and -s.

 women's people's mice's

To form the possessive of a compound noun, add an apostrophe or an apostrophe and -s, depending on the form of the noun.

 mother-in-law's (singular) mothers-in-law's (plural)
 attorney general's (singular) attorneys general's (plural) *or*
             attorney generals' (plural)

To form the possessive of nouns such as *Secretary of State* and *President of the United States,* add an apostrophe and an *-s* to the last word.

 the Secretary of State's staff

Often it is preferable to use a prepositional phrase instead.

the staff of the Secretary of State

In cases of joint possession, only the last name mentioned takes the possessive form. Add an apostrophe or an apostrophe and -s, depending on the form of the last noun.

Gilbert and Sullivan's operettas
Felipe and Inez's grandmother
mothers and daughters' dinner

The rule for joint ownership also applies to the names of organizations and firms.

Boswell, Banks, and Chubbs's recruiters
Brown, Jackson, and Company's building

If possession is not joint, each name takes the possessive form.

Stephanie's and Masumi's desks
Van Dyke's and Rembrandt's use of light

If the possessive form is awkward, use a prepositional phrase instead.

the desks belonging to Stephanie and Masumi
the use of light by Van Dyke and Rembrandt

To form a possessive of an indefinite pronoun, add an apostrophe and an -s.

anyone's   everyone's   another's   everybody's

To form the possessive of a compound indefinite pronoun, add an apostrophe as an -s to the last word.

someone else's idea   no one else's grades

Do not use an apostrophe with a personal pronoun to show possession.

hers   his   its   ours   theirs   yours

That tennis racket is *hers*.
The finish on that car has lost *its* shine.

When used as adjectives, nouns expressing time or amount take the possessive form.

one day's pay   three days' pay
one month's delay   two months' delay
one dollar's worth   six dollars' worth

Writing
—TIP—
Careful writers
check for correct
apostrophe usage
as they proofread.

Using Apostrophes to Show Omissions

Use an apostrophe in contractions to show where letters have been omitted.

> hasn't = has not   he's = he is *or* he has

Use an apostrophe to indicate missing letters in dialect, poetry, or archaic speech.

> "I *s'pose* you know Lila's *leavin'*." (dialect)
> "Foul *whisp'rings* are abroad."   **William Shakespeare**

Use an apostrophe to show the omission of numbers

> the Chicago Bulls' first loss of '88
> the class of '92

Using Apostrophes to Form Certain Plurals

Use an apostrophe to show the plurals of letters, numerals, signs, and words referred to as words.

> Allan forgot to dot the *i's* on the poster.
> The 1970's saw the dawn of the microcomputer age.
> His *7's* look like *9's*.
> My writing has too many *and's* in it.

Usage Note   The last two rules are sometimes considered optional. Also, letters and words used as words are italicized in print and underlined in handwritten and typewritten work.

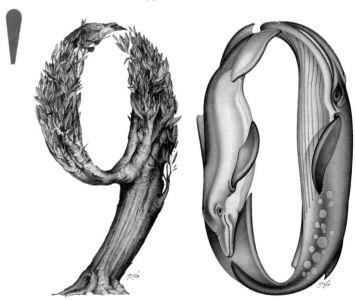

Practice Your Skills

A. CONCEPT CHECK

Apostrophes   For each of the following sentences, correctly rewrite each word containing an error in the use of apostrophes. If a sentence has no errors, write *Correct*.

Writing Theme
Technology
and Speed

1. There are no "ifs, and's, or buts" about it; human's throughout recorded history have been fascinated with achieving the goal of traveling at faster and faster speeds.
2. Perhaps the myth of the winged horse Pegasus' ascent to the skies inspired people to harness the horse's power and to dream of flight.
3. From the Roman's horse-drawn chariots to the American's sleek planes, technology has aided men and womens quest for moving at faster speeds.
4. As technology advanced, the three Rs of inventing—reading, writing, and rithmetic—changed rapidly.
5. Compared to the stagecoachs speed of nine miles' per hour, the inventors first cars seemed incredibly fast.
6. In the late 1800s, the twin brothers' Francis E. and Freelan O. Stanley built a steam-powered car that they called the Stanley Steamer.
7. Francis's and Freelan's car could travel at high speeds.
8. In 1906, the Stanley's car set a world's record at 127 miles per hour; no one elses' car at that time even came close to matching this amazing feat.
9. However, earthbound speeds did'nt satisfy humanitys thirst; it was flight that captured everyones' imagination.
10. Todays' high-technology airplanes are a far cry from Orville's and Wilbur's Wrights first inventions.
11. In airplane manufacturing companies, such as in Boeing and McDonnell Douglas's factories, every chief executive officers dream is attaining the fastest speeds in the safest ways' possible.
12. In the '50's, engineers' concerns focused on developing planes that traveled at the speed of sound (about 650 miles per hour at 35,000 feet).
13. Though planes soon filled people's ears with sonic booms, the quest for speedy travel did not end there.
14. In 69, Stafford's, Cernan's, and Young's flight set a record when *Apollo Xs* speed reached 24,791 miles per hour at an altitude of 400,000 feet.
15. What would the ancient Romans with their chariots think of tomorrows quest to travel at the speed of light (186,181 miles per second)?

Apostrophes and
Quotation Marks   **805**

B. PROOFREADING SKILL

Apostrophe Usage Rewrite the following paragraphs, correcting errors in spelling, capitalization, and punctuation. Pay close attention to the use of apostrophes.

No ones life has been unaffected by the quest for speed. Automatic teller machines dispense instant cash; Eyeglasses are made in an hours time; Letters are transmitted across a continent without a seconds delay. These are just a few of the inovations of the 1970s and 1980s that reflect Americas demand for speed. Think of the time-saving devices finding their way into Americans homes—for example, microwave ovens, remote controls, and food procesors. Many of the worlds time-saving services and products have originated in America, the credit for everything from fast-food restaurants to instantly-developed photographs is ours'.

Isnt our obsession with speed positive? Some people agree with the opinion expressed in Meyer Friedman's and Ray Roseman's recent book that to much emphasis on hurrying leads to unhealthful stress. However, in many sociologist's opinions, fast consumer services have become a necessity in todays world.

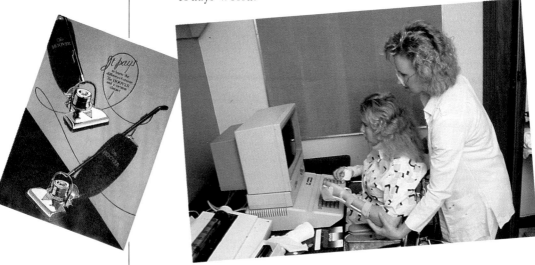

C. APPLICATION IN WRITING

Personal Opinion Essay What is your opinion about our culture's obsession with speed? Has technology done us a favor or not? Write a brief personal essay expressing and supporting your opinion. Use apostrophes correctly in your essay.

Quotation marks are used to set off direct quotations, titles, and words used in special ways.

Direct and Indirect Quotations

Use quotation marks to set off a direct quotation.

"Is there an intermission during the performance?" asked Carolyn.

An indirect quotation is the repetition without direct quotation of something said. An indirect quotation is expressed as a subordinate clause.

Do not use quotation marks to set off an indirect quotation.

Carolyn asked whether there was an intermission during the performance.

Punctuation of Direct Quotations

The following rules govern the use of punctuation and capitalization for direct quotations.

Use quotation marks to enclose the exact words of a speaker or writer. Capitalize the first word of the quotation.

"Portable phones are changing the way businesses operate," said Mrs. Collins.
Mrs. Collins said, "Portable phones are changing the way businesses operate."

A comma at the end of quoted material is always placed inside the quotation marks. When the sentence ends with the quotation, the period falls inside the quotation marks.

If the quotation is a question or an exclamation, put the question mark or exclamation point inside the quotation marks. Do not use a comma.

"Shouldn't we cancel the *Times*?" asked Laverne.
"Don't touch that!" she shouted.

Put a question mark or an exclamation point outside the quotation marks if it is not part of the quoted material.

Why did she say, "I'll see you later"?
I was shocked to hear her say, "I'm thinking of resigning"!

Writing
—TIP—
**In writing narra-
tives, use quota-
tion marks to set
off the exact
words of a char-
acter's thoughts.**
*Bob told himself,
"Think fast."*

"Punctuation"

A semicolon or a colon should always be placed outside the quotation mark.

These items were listed as "indispensable": laboratory tables, Bunsen burners, metal trays, and storage cabinets.

My boss told me, "You have just one week of vacation this year"; I guess I'll stay close to home.

Enclose both parts of a divided quotation within quotation marks. Capitalize the first word of the second part of the quotation only if it begins a new sentence.

"Take your time as you complete the test," said Mrs. Silva, "to avoid making errors due to haste."

In dialogue, a change in speaker is indicated by a new paragraph.

"Scientific research today is well organized," Mrs. Yee said. "Scientists work in teams, with each scientist investigating one aspect of a problem."

Gina asked politely, "Isn't it true that many inventions and discoveries are just a matter of luck?"

"Yes, indeed," answered Mrs. Yee, with a laugh. "We call it *serendipity*. You need a little luck in science, just as you do in other fields."

Use single quotation marks to set off a quotation within a quotation.

Diana reported, "When somebody told Churchill not to end sentences with prepositions, Sir Winston replied, 'That is the kind of nonsense up with which I will not put.'"

Sheila asked, "Was it Roosevelt who said, 'The only thing we have to fear is fear itself'?"

In quoting passages of more than one paragraph, use a quotation mark at the beginning of each paragraph and at the end of only the last paragraph.

When a quotation is a fragment and does not begin the sentence, do not capitalize the first word of the quotation.

In *Othello*, Shakespeare calls jealousy a "green-eyed monster."

Writing
─TIP─

In writing reports, you can set off a long quoted passage, an excerpt, without quotation marks. Double-space and indent all lines from the left.

Practice Your Skills

A. CONCEPT CHECK

Quotation Marks   Rewrite each of the following sentences, correcting all errors in punctuation and capitalization. If a sentence contains no errors, write *Correct.*

1. Welcome to this edition of *Art and Artists* said the announcer today we will discuss surrealism and Salvador Dalí.
2. Our guest she continued is our local art expert, Nora Freemont.
3. Welcome, Nora she said to begin, can you tell us when the surrealist movement was at its height.
4. Freemont replied the movement was at its height in Paris in the 1920's and 1930's.
5. She pointed to a chart of the surrealist "greats:" Salvador Dalí, Joan Miró, André Masson, and Max Ernst.
6. Of these artists, the most flamboyant was Dalí she said.
7. Oh, dear thought the announcer I hope she doesn't talk about some of Dalí's wild exploits.
8. Freemont explained that Dalí was known for his outrageous attire, spiky waxed mustache, and actions.
9. Pointing to a photograph of *The Persistence of Memory,* Freemont exclaimed his dreamy landscapes are remarkable!
10. A woman once asked Dalí if it was hard to paint a picture said Freemont.
11. Smiling, Ms. Freemont continued Dalí replied no. It's either easy or impossible.
12. Freemont stated that Dalí found inspiration in the Spanish town of Cadaqués.
13. The poet Federico García Lorca once said that Cadaqués was 'counterpoised between sea and hill;' however, Dalí's mental landscapes never matched reality.
14. His landscapes said Freemont were filled with images that had no rational explanation.
15. What a surprise it was when Freemont said, Dalí died a recluse with only his mental images for comfort!

B. APPLICATION IN LITERATURE

Punctuation   The following passage has been altered to include several <u>errors</u> in the use of punctuation, capitalization, and paragraphing. Rewrite the passage, returning it to its original form.

> I have visited a good deal of fine scenery before and since, but have found little that has pleased me more. . . . Far down the valley we could see Ravello and the sea, but that was the

Woman at the Window at Figueras, Salvador Dali

only sign of another world. Oh, what a perfectly lovely place said my daughter Rose. What a picture it would make! Yes, said Mr. Sandbach. Many a famous European gallery would be proud to have a landscape. . . . as beautiful as this upon its walls. On the contrary said Leyland, it would make a very poor picture. Indeed, it is not paintable at all. And why is that? said Rose, with far more deference than he deserved. Look, in the first place, he replied how intolerably straight against the sky is the line of the hill. It would need breaking up and diversifying. And where we are standing the whole thing is out of perspective. Besides all the colouring is monotonous and crude. I do not know anything about pictures I put in and I do not pretend to know: but I know what is beautiful when I see it, and I am thoroughly content with this. Indeed, who could help being contented! said Miss Robinson.

E. M. Forster, ''The Story of a Panic''

C. APPLICATION IN WRITING

Setting   Establish a setting for a science-fiction story or a Victorian Gothic mystery. Reveal the setting through the comments of two or three people. Combine narrative and dialogue to convey the details and mood of the setting.

Setting Off Titles

Use quotation marks to enclose chapter titles, part titles, and titles of short stories, poems, essays, articles, television episodes, songs, and short musical selections.

Chapter Title	Chapter 3: Women in Colonial America
Part Title	Part 3: Europe in the Twentieth Century
Short Story	Katherine Mansfield's The Garden Party
Poem	Emily Dickinson's I'm Nobody
Essay	Charles Lamb's A Dissertation upon Roast Pig
Article	What's New about New Age Music?
TV Episode	Thanksgiving on *The Cosby Show*
Song	Auld Lang Syne

The titles of books, magazines, newspapers, TV or radio series, plays, paintings, epic poems, or long musical compositions are underlined in writing or typing and italicized in print.

Setting Off Words Used in Special Ways

Use quotation marks to give special expression to words.

A writer may use quotation marks to show emphasis or irony or to set off words classified as slang.

> The "short paint job" my mother asked me to do took all day. (The phrase *short paint job* is being used ironically.)
>
> Mayor Richard J. Daley was known as the "Boss" of Chicago politics. (The word *Boss* is enclosed in quotation marks to show emphasis.)
>
> Two "far-out" fads of the 1970's were pet rocks and platform shoes. (The term *far-out* is enclosed in quotation marks because it is slang.)

Punctuation Note   Foreign words and words referred to as words are italicized or underlined. Phrases, however, are usually put in quotation marks. Also underline or italicize letters or figures referred to as such.

> The word *pantophobia* refers to the fear of everything.
>
> Blanca ordered *rajas,* strips of roasted, peeled chiles.
>
> Sabrina asked what the phrase "purple prose" meant.

Practice Your Skills

A. CONCEPT CHECK

Quotation Marks and Underlining   Rewrite the following sentences, adding quotation marks and underlining where necessary.

1. In the chapter The Home Fronts, C. L. Sulzberger describes civilian life during World War II.
2. In France, many civilians were part of la résistance, the resistance movement against the Nazis.
3. The British huddled together in bomb shelters, singing God Save the King and Roll out the Barrel as the Luftwaffe dropped bombs on their cities.
4. In the United States, the closest people came to the war was through movies such as Mrs. Miniver and Thirty Seconds over Tokyo.
5. During that time, girls wore huge sloppy Joe sweaters, saddle shoes, and short socks, dubbed bobbysox.
6. They swooned over Frank the Voice Sinatra and worked in munitions factories as W.O.W.'s, the acronym for Women Ordnance Workers.
7. People bought war bonds and planted small gardens, called victory gardens, to supplement their food rations.

Apostrophes and
Quotation Marks   **811**

8. The V for victory sign, made with the first two fingers to form the letter V, became a familiar gesture.
9. The war became real for everyone through Edward R. Murrow's many installments of his London After Dark radio program.
10. Likewise, songs such as This Is the Army, Mr. Jones let people know what life was like for the soldiers—or boys in fatigues.

B. PROOFREADING SKILL

Quotation Marks and Underlining Rewrite the following paragraphs, adding quotation marks and underlining as necessary. Also, correct errors in spelling, capitalization, and punctuation.

Many writers blossomed in the 1940s. Among them was Elizabeth Bowen, who's novel The Heat of the Day was set in wartime london. Americas first lady, Eleanor Roosevelt, wrote the essay Must We Hate to Fight? It was published in the Saturday Review magazine. Poets also expressed their feelings about war and reflected on the fact that World War I was the so-called 'war to end all wars.' Charles Causley's poem At the British War Cemetery, Bayeux is a work on this theme. Many poets' works may be found in the anthology Poems of This War, a collection of poetry about World War II.

Of course, not all Creative People were focusing on the war. Walt Disney, for example, produced the movies Fantasia and Pinocchio, which let moviegoers enjoy the technology of annimation. Noel Coward's play Blithe Spirit (1941) amused people in the theaters and, later, in the movie houses. J. B. Preistley, who was honored as one of the *living greats* in England when he received the Order of Merit, wrote the play An Inspector Calls. Also, his humorous essays, such as The Marx Brothers, Women and Clothes, and No School Report, were published in his collection titled Delight (1949.)

CHECK POINT
PAGES 802–812

A. Rewrite the following sentences, correcting errors in the use of apostrophes, quotation marks, and underlining.

Writing Theme
O. Henry

1. William Sydney Porter, whos better known as O. Henry, was, in his own words, born and raised in 'No th Ca lina.'
2. He learned the three Rs in his aunt Evelinas school.
3. Tom Tate, a schoolmate in the 1860s, wrote that, even as a boy, Porter had a 'Quaint dry humor.'

4. In Porters first comedy satire, his "dramatis personae" were characterized by the townfolks quirks and foibles.
5. It was some time before the young playwright was on speaking terms with some of his old friends said Tate.
6. Porter fondly recalled joining friends at Miss Ethels' or Miss Sallies' house and singing Swanee River.
7. An easygoing manner and joie de vivre were his', in spite of frequent 'bouts of ill health.
8. Porter once wrote that he was 'in the hands of a fine tyrant of a doctor;' nevertheless, he would complete a manuscript in two weeks time.
9. Later, in Texas, he served as the editor of a humor magazine "The Rolling Stone."
10. Porter even wrote poems for it, such as Nothing to Say.
11. The National Bank's of Austin accusation of embezzlement resulted in his serving what fellow inmates called a stint in the slammer.
12. Anyones assumption of his guilt, however, may be in error.
13. Many peoples opinion is that poor bookkeeping, not theft, was to blame.
14. Later, when Porter wrote as O. Henry, he lived in New York, which he nicknamed Bagdad-on-the-Subway.
15. No ones prose has stirred the heart so much as O. Henrys short story *The Gift of the Magi*.

B. APPLICATION IN LITERATURE

Punctuation   In the following passage, correct punctuation and paragraphing have been omitted. Rewrite the passage to return it to its original, correct form.

> Dont lie to me she [Hetty] said, calmly. What were you going to do with that onion? The young man suppressed a cough and faced her resolutely. . . . I was going to eat it said he with emphatic slowness just as I told you before. And you have nothing else to eat at home? Not a thing. What kind of work do you do? I am not working at anything just now. Then why said Hetty, with her voice set on its sharpest edge do you lean out of a window and give orders to chauffeurs in green automobiles in the street below? Because madam said he in *accelerando* tones I pay the chauffeurs wages and I own the automobile—and also this onion—this onion, madam. He flourished the onion within an inch of Hettys nose. . . . Then why pursued Hetty, inflexibly were you going to eat a raw onion? My mother said the young man always made me eat one for a cold.   **O. Henry, "The Third Ingredient"**

GRAMMAR
H A N D B O O K
41

Writing Theme
American
Humorists

A. Apostrophes and Quotation Marks Rewrite the following sentences, correcting any errors in the use of apostrophes, quotation marks, and underlining.

1. Dotting the is and crossing the ts didnt interest Samuel Clemens, better known as Mark Twain.
2. In fact, the colloquial phrase to tickle their funny bones might describe what Twain wished to do for his readers.
3. In his short story, Extracts from Adam's Diary, Twain has Adam write, 'The new creature says it's name is Eve'.
4. One critic said "Twains 'version of the folk tale "Jim Smiley and His Jumping Frog", has established his reputation as a humorist."
5. With this story 'Washoe Giant, the wild humorist of the Sage Brush Hills' as Twain had been known in California was now known in the East.
6. According to biographer Justin Kaplan, Twains "variety of interests mirrored his country and his times:" drama, storytelling, billiard playing, and inventing.
7. In 1906, A. B. Paine, a childrens' book author, said that he was honored to work on Samuel Clemens biography.
8. Ernest Hemingway once said, "all modern American literature comes from one book by Mark Twain called 'Huckleberry Finn.'"
9. Kurt Vonnegut compared Hemingway and Twain's writing.
10. He concluded that Hemingway has no ear for dialect and "he cant tell jokes;" thus, Twain remains the master.

B. Using Punctuation Correctly Rewrite the following sentences, correcting any errors in the use of apostrophes, quotation marks, and underlining.

1. One of Americas foremost humorists in the 1940s was James Thurber.
2. No one elses witty sophistication matches that of Thurber.
3. The results of a lifetimes study of human nature can be found in Thurbers works.
4. Most writers, said E. B. White would be glad to settle for any one of. . . . Thurbers accomplishments.
5. Yet in 38, Thurber wrote the essay E. B. W. that poked fun at E. B. Whites exaggerated avoidance of people.
6. His story The Catbird Seat is a further example of his wit.
7. It was first published in The New Yorker in 42.
8. In this story the protagonist, Mr. Martin, decides to rub out his co-worker, Mrs. Ulgine Barrows.
9. The term rub out, in the words of the story, suggests nothing more than a correction of an error.

10. X. J. Kennedy's and Dorothy M. Kennedy's analysis of this work makes an interesting point.
11. One of the storys most delectable ironies they say occurs when Martin tells Barrows "Im sitting in the catbird seat'.
12. The complete story can be found in The Thurber Carnival.
13. The Catbird Seat should be recommended for everyones daily humor requirement.
14. Marc Connelly, author of the book Green Pastures, praised the work of Thurber.
15. He said, Thurber had a sense of laughter that was a cleansing thing.

C. Application in Literature   The following passage includes errors in the use of apostrophes and quotation marks. Rewrite the passage using the correct punctuation. Also, although Thurber wrote the dialogue in two continuous paragraphs, follow the rules for paragraphing in rewriting it.

Mr. Martin got to the office at eight-thirty the next morning as usual. At a quarter to nine, Ulgine Barrows, who had never arrived at work before ten, swept into his office. Im reporting to Mr. Fitweiler now! she shouted. If he turns you over to the police, its no more than you deserve. Mr. Martin gave her a look of shocked surprise. I beg your pardon? he said. Mrs. Barrows snorted and bounced out of the room. . . .

Forty-five minutes later, Mrs. Barrows left the presidents office and. . . . Mr. Fitweiler sent for Mr. Martin. The head of the filing department, neat, quiet, attentive, stood in front of the old mans desk. Mr. Fitweiler was pale and nervous. . . . Martin, he said, you have been with us more than twenty years'. Twenty-two, sir, said Mr. Martin. In that time, pursued the president, your work and your—uh—manner have been exemplary. I trust so, sir, said Mr. Martin. I have understood, Martin, said Mr. Fitweiler, that you have never taken a drink or smoked. That is correct, sir, said Mr. Martin. Ah, yes. Mr. Fitweiler polished his glasses. . . . Mrs. Barrows, he said finally, Mrs. Barrows has worked hard, Martin, very hard. It grieves me to report that she has suffered a severe breakdown.

James Thurber, "The Catbird Seat"

Directions   One or more of the underlined sections in the following sentences may contain errors of grammar, usage, punctuation, spelling, or capitalization. Write the letters of each incorrect section. Then rewrite the item correctly. If there is no error in an item, write E.

Example   Novels <u>such as</u> <u>"Heidi" and "Little Women"</u> have long
               A   B

been considered <u>to be</u> classics of <u>childrens'</u> literature. <u>No error</u>
                 C   D   E

Answer   B—*Heidi* and *Little Women*, D—children's

---

1. Gustave Flaubert's book <u>"Three Tales"</u> consists of three stories, each illustrating a
                      A
   different <u>style</u> "The Legend of St. Julian the Hospitaller," a medieval <u>style;</u> "A
       B   C
   Simple Heart," a realistic <u>style; and</u> "Herodias," a Biblical style. <u>No error</u>
                           D   E

2. The original <u>declaration of independence</u> <u>is preserved</u> in the
                A   B
   <u>National Archives Building</u> in <u>Washington, D.C.</u> <u>No error</u>
        C   D   E

3. In the <u>U.S.S.R.</u> most <u>rivers, such as</u> the <u>ob and the lena,</u> flow <u>north.</u> <u>No error</u>
        A   B   C   D   E

4. Aspirin <u>should not be taken</u> by people <u>who must use</u> anticoagulants, blood
              A   B
   <u>thinners or</u> certain drugs <u>that treat</u> diabetes. <u>No error</u>
    C   D   E

5. <u>Jerry Siegel's and Joe Schuster's</u> cartoon character <u>Superman</u> made his first
               A   B
   <u>apearance</u> in the <u>1930's.</u> <u>No error</u>
    C   D   E

6. Of all the <u>creatures</u> on the <u>earth,</u> the clam <u>has</u> the <u>slowest</u> heart rate. <u>No error</u>
            A   B   C   D   E

7. Almost <u>two thousand</u> years ago Epictetus <u>said</u> "If you <u>wish to be</u> a <u>good</u> writer,
        A   B   C   D
   write." <u>No error</u>
      E

8. Thoreau <u>wrote, "the youth</u> gets together his materials to build a bridge to the
   A
   <u>moon</u> or perchance a palace or temple on the <u>earth,</u> and at length the
   B C
   <u>middle-aged man</u> concludes to build a wood-shed with them." <u>No error</u>
   D E

9. At the age of <u>seventy one,</u> <u>actress Sarah Bernhardt</u> had her leg amputated, but
   A B
   despite this operation and her advanced <u>age,</u> she continued <u>to preform.</u> <u>No error</u>
   C D E

10. The work of <u>political cartoonist</u> Thomas Nast <u>1840-1902</u> helped to send the
    A B
    <u>infamous</u> Boss Tweed to <u>prison.</u> <u>No error</u>
    C D E

11. Andy Warhol <u>was best known</u> for his paintings of commercial <u>products,</u> however,
    A B
    he <u>also</u> used silk-screen printing to reproduce pictures <u>from newspaper photographs.</u>
    C D
    <u>No error</u>
    E

12. Mercury and <u>Venus,</u> because they are between <u>earth</u> and the <u>Sun,</u> show phases very
    A B C
    much <u>like</u> those of the moon. <u>No error</u>
    D E

13. "A little <u>learning, wrote</u> Alexander Pope in one of <u>his</u> long <u>poems,</u> "is a dangerous
    A B C
    <u>thing."</u> <u>No error</u>
    D E

14. <u>N.A.S.A.</u> is the <u>Federal Agency</u> charged with the <u>responsibility</u> for managing the
    A B C
    <u>nation's</u> space program. <u>No error</u>
    D E

15. <u>El Dorado,</u> the legendary city of <u>gold,</u> was avidly sought by a multitude of <u>Spanish</u>
    A B C
    conquistadors during the <u>eighteenth</u> century. <u>No error</u>
    D E

16. On <u>August 2, 1943,</u> the <u>"Amigiri,"</u> <u>a Japanese ship,</u> rammed and sank PT-109, a
    A B C
    boat <u>commanded</u> by Lieutenant John F. Kennedy. <u>No error</u>
    D E

17. "Help. I'm trapped under hear," yelled the motorist from beneath the collapsed
     A   **B**   **C**   **D**
     freeway. No error
     D   **E**

18. Saber-toothed tigers which are extinct opened their jaws at a ninety-degree angle.
     A   **B**   **C**   **D**
     No error
     E

19. Henry Clay, a Whig politician of the early 1800s, was called "the Great
               A   **B**
     Compromiser;" somehow that doesn't sound complimentary. No error
     C   **D**   **E**

20. For three weeks the Morrison's sailed there small boat around the Caribbean,
           A   **B**   **C**
     stopping at a different port every evening. No error
                   D   **E**

21. "Is it true that three-fourths of the human body is made up of water?" Inez asked
     A   **B**   **C**
     the health teacher. No error
        D   **E**

22. The English word *reptile* comes from the Latin *repere,* meaning "to creep."
       A   **B**   **C**   **D**
     No error
     E

23. The *Washington Post* is one of the two most influential newspapers in the United
                 A
     States; it's editorials help shape public opinion. No error
     B   **C**   **D**   **E**

24. Orson Welles is known for his film "Citizen Kane" and for his radio adaptation of
               A   **B**
     H. G. Wells's novel *The War of the Worlds.* No error
     C   **D**   **E**

25. The poet William Butler Yeats married late in life and then moved
     A   **B**
     into an old Norman castle called Thor Ballylee. No error
               C   **D**   **E**

Sketchbook

Imagine that you are designing your "dream room." Although you can hire people to do all the work, you have to tell them exactly how you want the room to look. Write instructions that will enable the various workers to turn your dream into reality. Tell where the room will be located. Explain the floor plan—the location of the windows, doors, and so forth—and describe in detail how the room should be decorated and furnished. Use correct punctuation in your instructions.

Additional Sketches

Write a fantasy dialogue between two living things or two inanimate objects in which each "character" tries to convince the other of its superiority. Make sure that you correctly capitalize and punctuate your dialogue.

A magazine publisher has asked you to create a new magazine for readers your own age. Write a proposal in which you suggest several different names for the magazine and titles for five or more possible articles for the premiere issue. Use quotation marks, apostrophes, and underlining properly.

Directions One or more of the underlined sections in the following sentences may contain errors of grammar, usage, punctuation, spelling, or capitalization. Write the letters of each incorrect section. Then rewrite the item correctly. If there is no error in an item, write E.

Example The <u>leading roles</u> in the film *Driving Miss Daisy*
                              A   **B**
<u>were played</u> by Jessica Tandy and <u>he.</u> <u>No error</u>
        C   **D**   **E**

Answer D—him

---

1. The <u>Latin</u> expression <u>"Labor Omnia Vincit"</u> means "Labor Conquers <u>All"</u> it is
        A   **B**   **C**
   <u>Oklahoma's</u> state motto. <u>No error</u>
        D   **E**

2. Many species of animals became <u>extinct</u> before <u>conservationists</u> <u>had taken</u> <u>efective</u>
                                      A   **B**   **C**   **D**
   action. <u>No error</u>
              E

3. <u>Known only from hairs found in its leafy "bed" and from isolated sightings,</u> many
                                      A
   professional naturalists <u>are sure</u> that the so-called "wild man" of <u>China</u> actually
                                B   **C**
   <u>exists.</u> <u>No error</u>
      D   **E**

4. At the sight of <u>Patroclus</u> in the armor of <u>Achilles,</u> the fearful Trojans <u>fleed from</u>
                      A   **B**   **C**
   the <u>battlefield.</u> <u>No error</u>
          D   **E**

5. <u>Who</u> <u>exports</u> the <u>highest</u> volume of goods, <u>china or japan?</u> <u>No error</u>
     A   **B**   **C**   **D**   **E**

6. Just between you and <u>I,</u> I think that <u>T. S. Eliot's</u> *The Waste Land* <u>is</u> too obscure
                            A   **B**   **C**
   and fragmentary <u>to be considered</u> a finished work of art. <u>No error</u>
                        D   **E**

7. <u>The lute</u> <u>is</u> a <u>Medieval</u> stringed <u>instrument. Related to the guitar.</u> <u>No error</u>
        A   **B**   **C**   **D**   **E**

8. By the third chapter in the mystery <u>novel,</u> Marilyn had figured out <u>whom</u> the
   A   **B**
   murderer was and was no longer <u>anxious</u> to finish reading <u>it.</u> <u>No error</u>
                                   C   **D**   **E**

9. Everyone <u>should wear</u> <u>their</u> <u>most comfortable</u> pair of shoes for the hunger
            A   **B**   **C**
   <u>Walkathon.</u> <u>No error</u>
   D   **E**

10. The <u>Bostonians</u> claimed <u>that</u> they <u>didn't know nothing</u> about the <u>dumping</u> of the
        A   **B**   **C**   **D**
    tea into the harbor. <u>No error</u>
                         E

11. By the time this summer <u>ends;</u> the temperature <u>soars</u> above 100 degrees Fahrenheit
                            A   **B**
    many times, but <u>no one</u> really <u>knows</u> whether the high temperatures are due to the
                    C   **D**
    greenhouse effect. <u>No error</u>
                       E

12. The biologist felt <u>badly</u> about the cancelled trip to <u>Horicon Marsh</u> in Wisconsin
                       A   **B**
    because she had hoped to observe the <u>waterfoul</u> during their <u>fall</u> migration.
                                         C   **D**
    <u>No error</u>
    E

13. <u>One</u> of the <u>most enjoyable</u> parts of a vacation in the <u>greek</u> isles <u>are</u> the delicious
    A   **B**   **C**   **D**
    food. <u>No error</u>
          E

14. Tom Thumb, of the <u>Ringling Brothers and Barnum and Bailey Circus,</u> <u>was</u> tinier
                      A   **B**
    <u>than any</u> performer in the history <u>of show business.</u> <u>No error</u>
    C   **D**   **E**

15. "Nothing endures but <u>change</u>," wrote <u>the philosopher Heraclitus,</u> and students of
                         A   **B**
    geology <u>attest to</u> the truth of <u>this</u> statement. <u>No error</u>
            C   **D**   **E**

16. While in prison, <u>O. Henry</u> <u>wrote</u> *The Gift of the Magi* and <u>many other short stories.</u>
                     A   **B**   **C**   **D**
    <u>No error</u>
    E

17. The producer of the talk show decided that the segment <u>about the dancing snakes</u>
                                                                            A

    was just <u>to</u> <u>wierd</u> <u>to be shown</u> on the air. <u>No error</u>
           B   **C**   **D**   **E**

18. When John Steinbeck lived <u>in Monterey, California,</u> there was a great sardine fish-
                                           A

    ery in <u>Monterey Bay,</u> but now all the sardines have been killed by <u>overfishing, and</u>
          B   **C**

    the great canneries have <u>disappeared.</u> <u>No error</u>
                      D   **E**

19. We <u>saw</u> many <u>posters</u> and signs <u>advertizing</u> the concert, <u>walking through the school.</u>
         A   **B**   **C**   **D**

    <u>No error</u>
    E

20. Haydn <u>learned</u> Mozart <u>much</u> of what <u>he</u> knew <u>about writing symphonic music.</u>
            A   **B**   **C**   **D**

    <u>No error</u>
    E

21. <u>Us</u> science fiction buffs know that <u>todays</u> science fiction is <u>tomorrow's</u>
    A   **B**   **C**

    <u>ordinary daily reality.</u> <u>No error</u>
           D   **E**

22. <u>Deserts</u> are among the <u>most barrenest</u> places on the <u>earth, yet</u> even <u>their</u> life exists.
    A   **B**   **C**   **D**

    <u>No error</u>
    E

23. The designer of the <u>vietnam war memorial</u> originally planned that <u>it</u>
                    A   **B**

    <u>would represent</u> <u>all who fought</u> in the war. <u>No error</u>
         C   **D**   **E**

24. <u>Each</u> <u>of these</u> <u>elements</u>—nobelium, iodine, radium, and europium—<u>appears</u> in the
    A   **B**   **C**   **D**

    table. <u>No error</u>
         E

25. One of the <u>world's</u> <u>most famous universities,</u> the <u>Sorbonne was</u> founded in the
               A   **B**   **C**

    <u>1200's.</u> <u>No error</u>
     D   **E**

ACCESS GUIDE

IDEAS FOR WRITING

Writing ideas can come from just about any situation or experience. To stimulate your thinking, study the following lists. Then use your own discovery techniques to narrow your topic and organize it effectively.

Narrative
a bike race
a surprise ending
mending a relationship
leaving
no way out
the lesser of two evils
sudden good fortune
something from nothing
an unsolved mystery
a comic experience
a piano lesson
an unexpected encounter
making the news
a protest march

Descriptive
a December morning
sounds of a warm summer
    night
the circus
a favorite relative
an eccentric friend
a nonstop talker
a snowstorm
an airport at midnight
the coach's office
a famous place
electronic music
a snake
a courtroom
mosquitoes in paradise
an ocean beach
a science experiment
an empty stadium

Literary
an encounter with an
    intelligent being from
    another planet
a poem about someone you
    care for
a frightening experience
the Salem witches
gold mining in Alaska
a mysterious package
grappling with technology
    in everyday life
a medical discovery
a tall tale

Informative Exposition
What are "natural
    ingredients"?
Define selfishness.
What is jealousy?
Define one's "turf."
What does "cultural
    pluralism" mean?
What makes a good
    neighbor?
What is a stereotype?
What is the effect on society
    of good public schools?
What are the effects of
    television violence on
    children?
What causes a recession?
How have television news
    reports changed in the
    last 10 years?

How would you solve a
    currently important social
    issue?
What is the best way to raise
    money for a good cause?
Explain how to win a
    political campaign.
How can prime-time
    television be improved?

Persuasive
Should the government
    provide housing for
    homeless people?
What is a fair tax rate?
Should the United States
    convert to the metric
    system?
Should extremist groups be
    tolerated under the First
    Amendment?
Should drug tests be
    required of student
    athletes?
Should college admission be
    based solely on academic
    achievement?
Should anyone be allowed to
    censor art?
Should advertisers be
    allowed to use subliminal
    messages?
Should the federal
    government pay for all
    medical care?

Ideas for Writing in Subject Areas

The Arts
multimedia events and
  installations
realism in literature
How did jazz originate?
earth sculpture
Pennsylvania folk art
living museums
rock concerts in the 90's
Samuel Beckett
Shakespeare's plays with
  modern settings
the music of Duke Ellington
classical piano competitions
jazz dance
art censorship
Mozart's genius
John Huston's films

Science
acupuncture
songs of whales
causes/effects of ozone-
  layer thinning
how a CD player works
breaking an addiction
calculating the orbits of
  planets
magnetic resonance
  imaging
cancer research
laser technology
chemical warfare
predicting tornadoes
how radar works
space exploration
genome mapping

Social Science
the conference at Yalta
What motivated the early
  explorers?
the Children's Crusade
the worldwide economic
  depression of the 1930's
compare and contrast
  Europe after WWI and
  WWII.
the Industrial Revolution in
  Europe
the civil rights movement
laying the first trans-Atlantic
  cable
the statues at Easter Island
the beginnings of radio
the Magna Carta

Term Paper Topics

The Arts
cartoons that reflect society
Jane Austen's world
yellow journalism
Theater of the Absurd
protest songs
Indian pottery of the
  Southwest
the rise of female detectives
great landscape painters
music videos
how computer technology
  can alter photographs
history of science fiction
outdoor sculpture gardens
the life of Beethoven
designs of Helmut Jahn
Impressionism

Science
controlling viruses
carcinogens in food
  preservatives
insect communication
  systems
the Bermuda triangle
toxic waste control
aerospace medicine
What causes smog?
Why do people acquire
  habits?
What are the effects on
  people of continuous
  noise?
How is weather predicted?
What is a radio telescope?
industrial uses of lasers

Social Science
inside the Supreme Court
techniques of behavior
  modification
the Battle of Waterloo
the settlement of Alaska
ancient Japanese culture
Roman ruins in England
the Oregon Trail
the purpose of Stonehenge
the New Deal
the rise of Mao Zedong in
  China
demographic changes in the
  U.S.
the fall of the Berlin Wall
political importance of
  natural resources

OUTLINE FORM

When you make an outline, you organize information and ideas in a concise and logical way. Working from an outline as you write frees you to concentrate on expressing your ideas in a clear and interesting way.

Methods of Outlining

Outlines can be either informal or formal. An **informal outline** can be a simple list of ideas or details in the order in which the writer will present them. A **formal outline** is much more detailed. In a formal outline, Roman numerals identify the headings, the main points or divisions of a topic; letters and Arabic numerals mark the subheadings, the subtopics and details the paper will include.

There are two types of formal outlines: sentence outlines and topic outlines. In a **sentence outline,** all entries are presented as complete sentences. In a topic outline, they are presented as phrases.

Here is the first part of a sentence outline for an essay on the Colorado River. Note that just as an outline may begin with an introductory statement—a version of the thesis—an outline may end with a concluding restatement of the main point.

The Colorado River: Lifeblood of the Southwest

Introduction—The American Southwest depends on the resources of the Colorado River.

I. The Colorado River irrigates three million acres.
   A. The river is 1,450 miles long.
   B. It irrigates farmland in seven states and Mexico.
II. The Colorado River Compact regulates use of the water.
   A. In 1922, the seven basin states signed an agreement to regulate the use of the river's water.
   B. The compact covers new uses of the water.
      1. Hydroelectric power is supplied to southern Nevada and southern California for industries and homes.
      2. Drinking water is supplied to southern California and Arizona.

A topic outline, shown below, uses short phrases throughout.

How Streets Are Named

Introduction—the various ways in which streets get their names

  I. Geographical features
    A. Terrain
      1. Prairie Street
      2. Cliff Drive
    B. Bodies of Water
      1. Ocean Parkway
      2. Riverside Drive
 II. States
    A. Michigan Avenue
    B. Massachusetts Avenue
III. People
    A. Presidents
      1. Washington Street
      2. Adams Boulevard
    B. Influential citizens
      1. Martin Luther King Drive
      2. Rosa Parks Boulevard

Standard Outline Form Follow these outlining guidelines.

1. Center the title at the top of the page. Below it, write your thesis statement, or a shortened version of it.
2. Use the arrangement of numerals and letters that you see in the two models.
3. When a heading is a subpoint of the previous heading, indent its letter or numeral, placing it directly underneath the first letter in the first word of the previous heading.
4. Either use two or more subheadings or details under a heading or subheading, or don't use any at all. In other words, for every *A* there should be a *B*, and for every 1, a 2.
5. Entries of the same rank in a topic outline should be parallel. That is, if A is a noun, then B should also be a noun. Subtopics and main topics, however, do not need to be parallel.
6. Capitalize the first word in each entry. Do not use end punctuation in topic outlines.

BUSINESS LETTERS

When you use the correct form for your business letter, you make a positive impression on your reader. Following are explanations of the parts of a business letter and examples of two correct business letter forms.

Block Form and Modified Block Form

Use plain, white, 8½″ x 11″ paper for all business letters, whether you handwrite or type them. In **block form,** all parts begin at the left margin. Use this form only when you type the letter. In **modified block form,** the heading, closing, and signature are aligned near the right margin; the other parts begin at the left margin.

Block Form

```
_____    Heading
_____
_____    Date

_____    Inside
_____    Address
_____

_____:   Salutation

_____
_____
_____ Body
_____

_____,   Closing
              Signature
```

Modified Block Form

```
              Heading   _____
                        _____
              Date      _____

_____    Inside
_____    Address
_____

_____:   Salutation

_____
_____
_____ Body
_____

              Closing   _____,
              Signature
```

Heading The heading is written at the top of the page. The first line contains your street address; the second line contains your town or city, state, and ZIP code. Separate the city and state with a comma and write out the name of the state. The third line gives the date of the letter. Place the heading at the left or the right margin, depending on whether you use the block form or the modified block form.

Inside Address The inside address tells to whom the letter is being sent. Place the inside address at the left margin at least four lines below the heading. On the first line you should place the name of the receiver. If there is room, place the person's title on the same line, separated from the name by a comma. Otherwise, place the title on the next line. If you do not know the name of the person who will receive your letter, use the person's title or the name of the department. On the succeeding lines, place the company name and address, including the city, state, and ZIP code.

The inside address is important because occasionally a letter is opened by someone other than the addressee, and the envelope is discarded. If this happens, the name and address of the receiver can still be found in the inside address. Following are two typical inside addresses.

Ms. Deborah Aktar   Water Department
Gaia Computers, Inc.   City of Austin
1132 Falls Road   206 East Ninth Street
Coloma, Michigan 49038   Austin, Texas 78701

Salutation Position the salutation two lines below the inside address. Begin with the word *Dear*, follow it by the name of the person to whom you are writing, and end with a colon. Use only the person's last name, preceded by a title such as *Mr., Mrs., Ms., Dr.,* or *Professor*. If you do not know the person's name, use a general salutation such as *Ladies and Gentlemen*. Another alternative is to write to a department or to a position within a company. The following forms are acceptable:

Dear Mr. Sanders: Dear Sir or Madam:
Dear Ms. Joyce: Dear Product Information Department:
Dear Mrs. Alegria: Dear Executive Director:

Body The body, the main part of the letter in which you write your message, begins two spaces below the salutation. The body may contain a single paragraph or several paragraphs. Leave a space between each paragraph.

Closing The closing is placed two lines below the body, in line with the heading. Closings commonly used for business letters include *Sincerely, Sincerely yours,* and *Very truly yours.* Note that only the first word is capitalized and that the closing ends with a comma.

Signature Type or print your name four spaces below the closing, and sign your name in the space between.

Because word processors are widely used in business, knowing word processing may increase your employment opportunities. Following are some techniques to help you use a word processor effectively.

Goal	Technique	Comment
Create a record of observations, ideas, and experiences that especially interest you.	Create a file that functions like an expandable notebook.	Your electronic notebook can become an efficient way to retrieve ideas quickly and expand on them freely.
Exchange ideas with other students.	Use a disk of class ideas, available to anyone in the class.	Each class member might have a file on this disk. By opening your own file, you can add an idea or read others' responses to your ideas.
Experiment with language and style.	Express the same idea in a number of different ways. Separate alternatives using slashes (/).	Later, use the search command to find the slashes. Choose the best alternative and delete the others.
Add, replace, or reorder text.	Use the insert, delete, replace, move, cut, and paste commands.	A word processor encourages revision and experimentation because changes are simple and easy to make.

Goal	Technique	Comment
Quickly input revisions you've marked on a printout.	Use the search command to locate each word or phrase you wish to change.	Using search enables you to move quickly through your paper as you make changes and corrections.
Check your spelling.	Activate the "spelling" command if your program has one. In addition, always proofread carefully.	The program will highlight misspellings, many typing errors, and most proper nouns. Proofread for errors the program cannot catch, such as incorrect words.
Simplify business communications.	Set up attractive formats for different types of business communications, such as letters and memos. Save time by using a small number of basic formats.	A word processor can help you send copies of a similar letter to many people or organizations. For each copy, keep the heading, body, and closing the same; change the date, inside address, and salutation.
Create the right format for your document.	Experiment with type sizes and styles. You may even want to try a page layout program and a high quality printer.	Using a desktop publishing program even allows you to integrate text and graphics. Perhaps you will decide to publish a newsletter for your organization.

TECHNIQUES FOR PEER RESPONSE

The following response techniques can help you give and receive useful responses as you share your writing with others. These techniques can also help you as the writer to be in charge of the feedback process and to find out what kinds of responses are most useful to you.

How to Use	When to Use
Sharing	
Read your words out loud to a peer. Your purpose is simply to share and to hear how your words sound. Your listeners may ask you to slow down or to read your piece again, but they offer no feedback or criticism of any kind.	Do this when you are just exploring and you don't want criticism. Reading to a peer is also useful when your writing is finished and you want to celebrate by sharing it with another person.
Saying Back or Restating	
Ask readers, "What do you hear me saying?" As readers say back what they hear, they are inviting you to figure out better what you really want to say.	Use this type of feedback when you are still exploring and when you want to find ways to change and develop your ideas.
Pointing	
Ask readers to tell you what they like best in your writing. Tell them to pick specific parts of the writing and to avoid simply saying, "I liked it."	Use this technique when you want to know what is getting through to readers or when you want some encouragement and support.

How to Use	*When to Use*
Summarizing	
Ask readers to tell you what they hear as the main meaning or message in your writing. Make clear that you don't want evaluation of the writing at this time.	Use this technique when you want to know what is getting through to readers.
Responding to Specific Features	
Ask for feedback on specific features of the writing such as the organization, or the persuasive power, or the spelling and punctuation. Ask readers to respond to specific questions, such as, "Are the ideas supported with enough examples?" "Did I persuade you?" "Is the organization clear enough so you could follow the ideas easily?"	Use when you want a quick overview of the strengths and weaknesses of your piece.
Replying	
Discuss the ideas in your writing with your readers. Ask readers to give you their ideas on the topic. Be sure to talk with your peer readers about *what* you have said, not *how* you have said it.	Use this strategy when you want to make your writing richer by using new ideas.
Playing Movies of the Reader's Mind	
Invite readers to tell you what happens inside their heads as they read your writing. Interrupt the reading and ask readers to tell you what they are thinking at the moment of interruption.	This technique is useful at any stage of the writing. Because it can lead to blunt criticism, use this peer response method only when you have a relationship of trust and support with your reader.

Adapted from *Sharing and Responding* by Peter Elbow and Pat Belanoff.

SENTENCE DIAGRAMING

A sentence diagram is a drawing that helps you understand how the parts of a sentence are related. In addition, diagraming sharpens your critical thinking skills by requiring you to analyze sentences, classify their parts, and determine relationships among those parts.

The base for a sentence diagram is made up of a horizontal main line crossed by a short vertical line.

Subjects and Verbs

Place the simple subject on the horizontal main line to the left of the vertical line. Place the simple predicate, or verb, to the right. Capitalize only those words that are capitalized in the sentence. Do not use punctuation except for abbreviations.

Stars twinkle.

Stars	twinkle

Construction has begun.

Construction	has begun

Interrogative Sentences

In an interrogative sentence, the subject often comes after the verb or after part of the verb phrase. In diagraming, remember to place the subject before the verb to the left of the vertical line.

Is anyone studying?

anyone	Is studying

Do animals dream?

animals	Do dream

Imperative Sentences

In an imperative sentence, the subject is usually not stated. Since commands are given to the person spoken to, the subject is understood to be *you*. To diagram an imperative sentence, place the understood subject *you* to the left of the vertical line. Then enclose *you* in parentheses. Place the verb to the right of the vertical line.

Go!

(you)	Go

Rush!

(you)	Rush

Modifiers

Diagram adjectives and adverbs on slanted lines below the words they modify. If an adverb modifies an adjective or another adverb, write the adverb on an L–shaped line connected to the adjective or adverb that it modifies. Keep in mind that words like *not* and *never* are adverbs.

The old car would not start quickly enough.

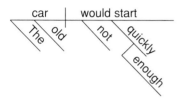

When two or more modifiers are connected by a conjunction, place the modifiers on slanted lines below the words they modify. Connect the slanted lines with a broken line and write the conjunction on it.

The untrained but eager staff worked quite competently.

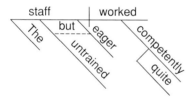

Direct and Indirect Objects

In a diagram, place the direct object on the main line after the verb. Separate the direct object from the verb with a vertical line that does not extend below the main line. Place indirect objects below the verb on lines parallel to the main line and connected to the main line by slanted lines, as you see here.

Bret was telling Sarah a long and implausible story.

Subject Complements

Place a predicate nominative or a predicate adjective on the main line after the verb. Separate the subject complement from the verb with a slanted line that extends in the direction of the subject.

Rosa is the nominee.
(*Predicate nominative*)

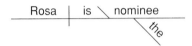

The foreman looked extremely proud.
(*Predicate adjective*)

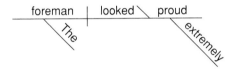

Sentences with Compound Parts

To diagram compound parts, place the parts on parallel horizontal lines as shown below. Then connect the parallel lines with a broken line. On the broken line, write the conjunction that connects the compound parts. Attach the compound parts to the main line with solid diagonal lines. The sentence below has a compound subject and a compound verb.

James Joyce and Elizabeth Bowen left Ireland and wrote important novels.

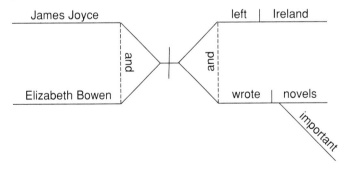

Compound Direct Objects and Indirect Objects To diagram compound direct objects or indirect objects, place the objects on parallel horizontal lines connected with a broken line. Write the conjunction on the broken line. Attach the compound parts to the main line as shown below.

The director gave Susan and me our scripts and costumes.

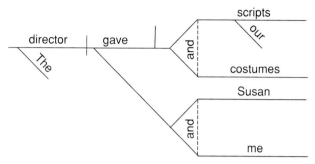

Prepositional Phrases

Draw a slanted line below the word the phrase modifies. From the slanted line, draw a line parallel to the main line. Place the preposition on the slanted line and the object of the preposition on the parallel line. Words that modify the object of the preposition are placed on slanted lines below the object.

Dom ordered a copy of the book.

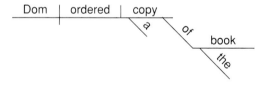

Under the house lived a fat raccoon.

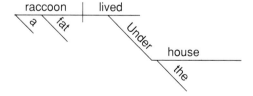

Gerunds and Gerund Phrases

To diagram a gerund, place it on a line drawn as a step ($\neg\!\llcorner$). Put the step on a forked line ($\wedge$) that stands on the main line. The placement of the forked line varies and is determined by how the gerund or gerund phrase is used.

We like trying foods from different countries. (*Gerund phrase used as direct object*)

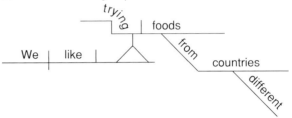

After arriving, the team gave a cheer. (*Gerund phrase used as the object of a preposition.*)

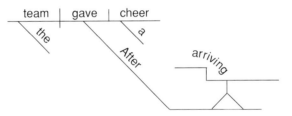

Participles and Participial Phrases

To diagram a participle, place the participle on an angled line below the word it modifies. If the participial phrase includes a direct object, separate the object and the participle with a vertical line. Place modifiers on slanted lines below words they modify.

Quickly calculating the risk, she scaled the wall.

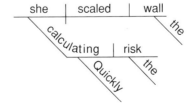

Infinitives and Infinitive Phrases

To diagram an infinitive, place the infinitive on an angled line. Write the word *to* on the slanted part and write the verb on the horizontal part of the angled line. Put the angled line on a forked line that stands on the main line. The placement shows how the infinitive or infinitive phrase is used in the sentence. In the sentences below, the infinitive is used first as a direct object and then as a subject.

Millie hoped to see a good play soon.

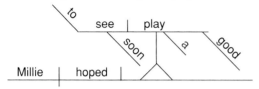

To exercise regularly was her plan.

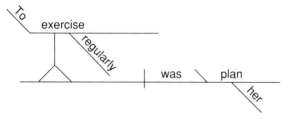

Appositives and Appositive Phrases

To diagram an appositive, place the appositive in parentheses after the word it identifies or explains. Place modifiers on slanted lines below the appositive.

The author, a dynamic speaker, lectured about UFO's.

Adjective Clauses

To diagram an adjective clause, place the clause on its own horizontal line below the main line and diagram it as if it were a sentence. Use a broken line to connect the relative pronoun in the adjective clause to the word that the clause modifies.

The car that I borrowed belongs to Tammy.

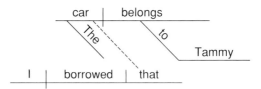

Adverb Clauses

To diagram an adverb clause, place the clause on its own horizontal line below the main line, and diagram the clause as if it were a sentence. Use a broken line to connect the adverb clause to the word it modifies. Write the subordinating conjunction on the broken line.

When his friend whistled, we dashed outside.

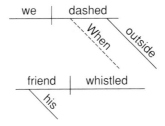

Noun Clauses

To diagram a noun clause, place the clause on a separate line that is attached to the main line with a forked line. The placement of the forked line in the diagram shows how the noun clause is used in the sentence. Diagram the word introducing the noun clause according to its function in the clause.

Whoever requested it got help. (*Noun clause used as subject*)

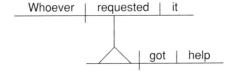

Compound Sentences

To diagram a compound sentence, place the independent clauses on parallel horizontal lines. Use a broken line with a step to connect the verb in one clause to the verb in the other clause. Write the conjunction on the step. If the clauses are joined by a semicolon, leave the step blank.

They accepted my story, but the editor delayed publication.

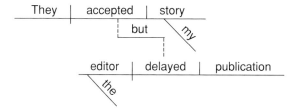

Complex Sentences

To diagram a complex sentence, decide whether the subordinate clause is an adjective clause, an adverb clause, or a noun clause. Then follow the rule for diagraming that kind of clause.

Compound-Complex Sentences

To diagram a compound-complex sentence, diagram the independent clauses first. Then attach the subordinate clause or clauses to the words they modify. Leave enough room to attach a subordinate clause where it belongs. For noun clauses, decide how the clause is used in the independent clause and place it accordingly.

The baseball bats were packed, but the helmets that the team needed were missing.

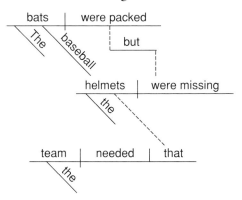

ALLEGORY a story in which the major events and characters have hidden or symbolic meanings; a quarrel between friends, for example, might represent a conflict between their native cultures.

ALLITERATION repetition of beginning sounds of words in poetry or prose; for example, the "c" sound in "creeping cat."

ALLUSION a reference to a historical or literary person, place, event, or aspect of culture.

ANALOGY a comparison used to explain an idea or support an argument. An analogy for strengthening a person's own values might be created by comparing that process with tending a garden.

ANALYSIS a way of thinking that involves taking apart, examining, and explaining a subject or idea.

ANECDOTE a brief story, told as an example to illustrate a point.

ARGUMENT speaking or writing that takes a position or states an opinion and provides the evidence or reasons to support it—often in a context of opposing points of view.

AUDIENCE the readers or listeners to whom any discourse is directed.

AUTOBIOGRAPHY a biography (life story) told by the person whose life it is.

BIAS to have a bias or be biased is to lean toward one side in an argument or contest; to be *unbiased* is to be neutral.

BRAINSTORMING a way of gathering many ideas by quickly listing them as they occur, without judging their usefulness.

CAUSE AND EFFECT a strategy for analyzing a subject by examining the reasons for specific actions or events or the consequences or results of certain causes.

CHARACTERIZATION the way people (the *characters*) are portrayed in a narrative work.

CLASSIFICATION a type of writing that involves systematically grouping items by some system or principle; frequently involves defining or comparing and contrasting items or groups of items.

CLICHÉ   a phrase, figure of speech, or idea used so often that it is predictable, showing little imagination or thought, as in "Rain came down in buckets."

CLUSTERING   a brainstorming technique that shows how ideas are connected to one another; gives a quick map of thoughts about a topic.

COHERENCE   connectedness, a sense that parts hold together; an essay is coherent when its parts fit together logically and are linked by connecting words and phrases.

COLLABORATION   working with other people; giving others support and advice; helping others solve problems.

COLLOQUIAL   conversational, linguistically informal; the way people ordinarily speak in conversation.

COMPARISON AND CONTRAST   a strategy for thinking or writing that involves explaining, defining, or evaluating subjects by showing how they resemble and differ from each other or from some standard for evaluation.

CONNOTATION   the attitudes and feelings associated with a word or idea as opposed to its dictionary definition. The word "cheap" differs from "inexpensive" in its connotations.

CONTEXT   the setting or situation in which something happens, particularly in which words or sentences are uttered or written.

CONTROVERSY   a disagreement, often one that has attracted public interest.

COUNTERARGUMENT   a refutation, an argument made to oppose (counter) another argument.

CRITICISM   discourse (usually an essay) that analyzes something (usually a literary or artistic work) in order to evaluate how it does or does not succeed in communicating its meaning or achieving its purposes.

CUBING   a method for discovering ideas about a topic by using six strategies (in any order) to investigate it: describe it, compare it, associate it, analyze it, apply it, argue for or against it.

DEDUCTIVE REASONING   deriving a specific conclusion by reasoning from a general premise.

DENOTATION the literal meaning of a word, without its *connotations*.

DESCRIPTION an account, usually giving a dominant impression and emphasizing sensory detail, of what it is like to experience some object, scene, or person.

DIALECT a form of language (usually regional) differing from the standard language in pronunciation, word choice, and syntax. Southern American English or New England English or Australian English are dialects of English.

DIALOGUE the spoken conversation of fictional characters or actual persons as it is presented in a novel, story, poem, play, or essay.

DOCUMENTATION naming the documents or other sources used to provide the information reported in an essay or other discourse: usually cited in footnotes or in parentheses.

ELABORATION the development of an argument, description, narration, or explanation with details, evidence, and other support.

EXPOSITION writing whose purpose is to explain an idea or teach a process rather than to tell a story, describe something, or argue for a point of view.

FICTION made-up or imaginary happenings, as opposed to statements of fact or nonfiction. Short stories and novels are fiction, even though they may be based on real events. Essays, scientific articles, biographies, news stories are nonfiction.

FIGURATIVE LANGUAGE language that uses such figures of speech as similes, metaphors, and personification to show one thing as if it were something else.

FREEWRITING a way of discovering what you know or think or feel by writing rapidly, without stopping, without editing, and without looking back (until you finish) at what you've written.

GENERALIZATION a statement expressing a principle or drawing a conclusion based on examples or instances.

GLEANING a method of picking up ideas by observing events and by scanning through newspapers, magazines, and books and talking to others in order to find material to write about or to use in writing.

GRAPHIC ORGANIZER a method for visually organizing a complex body of information; includes charts, graphs, outlines, clusters, and tree diagrams.

IMAGERY   figurative language and descriptions as the means of vividly rendering experience in language.

INDUCTIVE REASONING   a method of thinking or organizing a discourse so that a series of instances or pieces of evidence lead to a conclusion or generalization.

INFERENCE   a conclusion derived by reasoning from facts.

INTERPRETATION   to explain the meaning of any text, set of facts, object, gesture, or event.

INVISIBLE WRITING   typing with a dimmed computer screen or writing with an empty ball point pen on a paper that covers a piece of carbon paper and a clean bottom sheet.

IRONY   a figure of speech in which the intended meaning is the opposite of the stated meaning—saying one thing and meaning another.

JARGON   the special language and terminology used by people in the same profession or who share specialized interests.

KNOWLEDGE INVENTORY   a list of statements or phrases representing what a writer knows about a topic, including questions to direct further research.

LEARNING LOG   a journal or notebook used in connection with the study of a particular subject where a student records questions, problems, and state of understanding about the subject as it is studied and learned.

LOOPING   a process for discovering ideas by freewriting on a topic, stopping to find promising ideas, then producing another freewrite on that subject, repeating the loop several times.

MEMOIR   an account of true events told by a narrator who witnessed or participated in the events; usually focusing on the personalities and actions of persons other than the writer.

METAPHOR   a figure of speech describing something by speaking of it as if it were something else, without using such terms as "like" or "as" to signal the relationship. To say "the dinner was a symphony of flavors" is to speak *metaphorically*.

MONOLOGUE   a speech by one person without interruption by other voices. A *dramatic monologue* reveals the personality and experience of a person through a long speech.

MOOD feeling about a scene or subject created for a reader by a writer's selection of words and details; the mood of a piece of writing may be suspenseful, mysterious, peaceful, fearful, and so on.

NARRATION discourse that tells a story—either made up or true. Some common types of narrative are biographies, short stories, and novels.

NONSEXIST LANGUAGE language free from gender bias, representing the equality of men and women and showing them in both traditional and nontraditional roles.

ONOMATOPOEIA the use of words (usually in poetry) to suggest sounds; the *clinking* of knives and forks, the *trilling* of a flute.

PARENTHETICAL DOCUMENTATION the placement of citations or other documentation within the text and in parentheses.

PEER RESPONSE response to one's writing provided by writers who are peers or classmates rather than teachers or other editors.

PERSONIFICATION a figure of speech in which objects, events, abstract ideas, or animals are given human characteristics. "The crying of the wind" and "the trees danced" are examples of personification.

PERSUASION discourse focused on influencing a listener or reader to support a point of view or take an action. Examples of persuasive discourse would include political speeches, advertisements, position papers, editorials, and courtroom speeches by lawyers.

PLAGIARISM presenting the ideas or words of another as if they were one's own. Writers who use the ideas of others can avoid plagiarism by acknowledging their sources.

POINT OF VIEW the viewpoint or perspective through which the reader views the events in a story; defines what a narrator can know and tell about.

PORTFOLIO a place (usually a large folder) where writing is stored for future reference and review or to present for evaluation.

PRECIS a short summary of an essay, story, or speech, capturing only the essential elements.

PROOFREADING usually the last stage of the revising or editing process, when a writer checks work to discover typographical and other errors.

PROPAGANDA   discourse aimed entirely at persuading an audience, often containing distortions of truth.

SATIRE   a literary form that ridicules or mocks the social practices or values of a society, a group, or an important individual. To *satirize* something is to portray it in a way that shows it to be foolish.

SIMILE   a figure of speech comparing two things that are essentially unlike, signaling the comparison with a word such as *like* or *as*.

SPATIAL ORDER   a pattern of organization, used in descriptive writing, that is based on relationships in space; for example, a scene may be described from foreground to background, from left to right, or from top to bottom.

STYLE   the features of a discourse or work of art that are characteristic of a particular individual, type, period, or artistic philosophy.

SYMBOL   a word, object, or action that suggests something other than itself—as a sword can stand for war, or the desert might represent loneliness or solitude.

SYNTHESIS   the putting together of ideas or information to reach a conclusion, achieve an insight, or find a solution to a problem.

THESIS   the main point of an essay or other discourse. Often written in a sentence or two, a thesis statement may suggest a pattern of organization and reveal the tone of the essay.

TONE   the writer's attitude toward a subject—for example, detached, ironic, serious, or angry.

TOPIC SENTENCE   a statement expressing the main point of a paragraph; the idea (stated or unstated) around which a paragraph is organized.

TREE DIAGRAM   a visualized plan for an essay, also known as a "branching tree diagram" for the way it shows main and subordinate points as the trunk and main and minor branches of a tree.

TRITE PHRASE   a phrase used so commonly that it lacks precise meaning and suggests a lack of imagination, thought, or originality.

UNITY   oneness; the concept that in a written work all the parts must form a single whole, held together by a central theme or idea.

VENN DIAGRAM   a way of representing the relationship between two items that are distinct but have common or overlapping elements.

VOICE   the distinct sound and rhythm of a writer's language.

ACCESS GUIDE
WORKPLACE SKILLS

Workplace Know-how

What will the workplace of the future be like? What can you as a high school student do to prepare yourself to get a good job? A group of leaders in business, industry, and education, under the direction of the Secretary of the Department of Labor, explored these issues and published a report entitled *What Work Requires of Schools: A SCANS Report for America 2000.* (SCANS stands for the Secretary's Commission on Achieving Necessary Skills.) The SCANS study identified five competencies, or abilities, and a three-part foundation of skills and personal qualities that contribute to high-quality job performance.

Moreover, the study stressed that all students—not only those entering the workforce but the college-bound and those enlisting in the military—should acquire these competencies, skills, and personal qualities while in high school. Once you are in the workforce, you will continue to develop the know-how you have acquired in school.

The following guide summarizes the key points of the SCANS report. As you read, assess where you stand and what you need to do. Which competencies and skills are strong already? Which ones do you need to work on? What are the most effective ways to do so? Ask your teachers, counselors, and parents for suggestions. Think of your high school education as your passport to the world of work. Get yourself ready for the high-performance workplace of the 21st century.

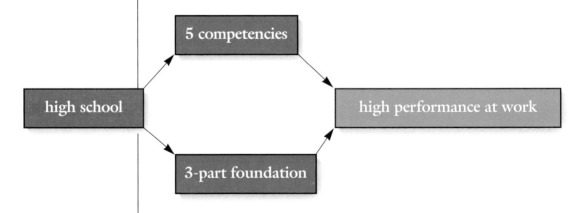

Effective workers make use of competencies in five key areas for high achievement.

Resources They effectively manage resources like the following:

- **Time**—selecting activities relevant to a goal and prioritizing them, allocating time, preparing and following schedules
- **Money**—using or preparing budgets, making forecasts, keeping records, and making adjustments to meet goals
- **Material and facilities**—acquiring, storing, allocating, and using materials and space efficiently
- **Human resources**—assessing skills of others and distributing work accordingly, evaluating performance, and providing feedback

Interpersonal Skills They work well with others in these ways:

- **Participating as a member of a team**—contributing to group effort to complete a project successfully
- **Teaching others new skills**—sharing knowledge with others
- **Serving clients or customers**—working to satisfy clients' or customers' expectations
- **Exercising leadership**—communicating ideas clearly, persuading and motivating others, responsibly challenging existing procedures
- **Negotiating**—working toward agreement, resolving conflicts
- **Working with diversity**—working comfortably with men and women from different age groups and different racial or cultural backgrounds

Information They handle information efficiently using these skills:

- **Acquiring and evaluating information**—identifying the need for data, obtaining them, and evaluating their importance and accuracy
- **Organizing and maintaining information**—understanding, sorting, and classifying information
- **Interpreting and communicating information**—analyzing information and using oral, written, graphic, pictorial, or multimedia methods to convey it to others
- **Using computers to process information**—entering, modifying, retrieving, storing, and verifying information electronically

Systems They know how the parts of a system work together and are skilled at:

- **Understanding systems**—knowing how social, organizational, and technological systems work; for example, knowing the right people to ask for information
- **Monitoring and correcting performance**—looking for trends, predicting their impact, and making changes to improve a product or service
- **Improving or designing systems**—suggesting modifications to systems and developing new or alternative ways to improve performance

Technology They use appropriate technology to work more efficiently, including:

- **Selecting technology**—choosing the best procedures, tools, or equipment, including computers and related technology
- **Applying technology to a task**—understanding the overall goal of a project and the procedures for setting up and operating equipment
- **Maintaining and troubleshooting equipment**—preventing, identifying, or solving problems with equipment, including computers and other technologies

THE FOUNDATION

The five competencies just discussed are supported by basic skills and one's own personal qualities.

Basic Skills

- **Reading**—knowing how to locate, understand, and interpret written information, including manuals, graphs, and schedules

- **Writing**—communicating ideas, information, and messages in writing; creating documents such as memos, letters, directions, manuals, reports, graphs, and flow charts
- **Arithmetic/mathematics**—performing basic computations and using a variety of mathematical techniques to solve practical problems
- **Listening**—receiving, attending to, interpreting, and responding to verbal messages and other cues
- **Speaking**—organizing ideas and communicating orally

Thinking Skills

- **Creative thinking**—generating new ideas; finding new solutions to problems; viewing situations from different perspectives
- **Decision making**—identifying goals, generating alternatives, considering risks, and evaluating and choosing the best alternative
- **Problem solving**—recognizing problems and devising and implementing plans of action
- **Visualizing**—creating flow charts and processing symbols, pictures, graphs, objects, and other visuals
- **Knowing how to learn**—using efficient learning techniques to acquire and apply new knowledge and skills; knowing where and how to obtain the necessary information to solve problems
- **Reasoning**—discovering the principle underlying the relationship between objects and applying it when solving a problem

Personal Qualities

- **Responsibility**—exerting a high level of effort toward attaining a goal; setting high standards; paying attention to details
- **Self-esteem**—believing in yourself and maintaining a good self-image
- **Sociability**—demonstrating understanding, friendliness, adaptability, and empathy
- **Self-management**—being a "self-starter"; assessing your job performance accurately, setting realistic personal goals, monitoring your progress, and exhibiting self-control
- **Integrity/honesty**—choosing ethical courses of action

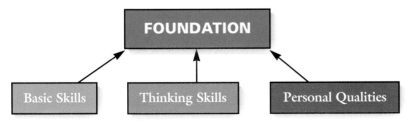

Writing Résumés

As you learned in Writing Handbook 28, your résumé is like an ad for yourself, highlighting your skills and accomplishments, your experience and responsibilities. A well-written résumé can help you obtain a part-time or full-time job, an internship, or admission to the college of your choice. The two sample résumés that follow are models you can use to write your own résumé. Of course, your résumé will look different depending on your purpose and where you choose to submit it.

Sample Résumé
for a Full-time Job Applicant

State your purpose or goal at the outset

Use reverse chronological order to list work experiences.

List activities or hobbies (especially if they are relevant to the job)

Charles Payone
5842 Hill Road
Jackson, MA 02111
(555) 555-1212

JOB OBJECTIVE
A full-time position as a mechanic with an automobile dealership

QUALIFICATIONS
Outstanding people skills
Interest in and knowledge about automobiles
Willingness to work hard

WORK EXPERIENCE
June through September, 1997: Peter's Service Station, Jackson, MA *Scheduled and coordinated car repairs; discussed problems with customers; assisted with record keeping and billing*
June through September, 1996: Peter's Service Station, Jackson, MA *Pumped gas, changed oil, and did minor car repairs*
Volunteer work: *Delivered lunches to homeless shelter, 1996*

EDUCATION
Jackson High School, Class of 1998
Honor Roll
Four years of Auto Mechanics

EXTRACURRICULAR ACTIVITIES
Baseball, Football, earned varsity letter, 1997
Senior Class Play

HOBBIES
Repairing and showing antique cars, golf

REFERENCES
Available upon request

Ariba el-Haffa
1743 Lancaster
Hoffman, Texas 80765
(407) 555-1213

Education Houston High School, Hoffman, Texas
4.6/5.0 average

Successfully completed advanced
placement courses in English and History

Earned 4 hours of college credit in calculus
at King Community College

Extracurricular Activities Flautist, Houston High School Marching
Band, 1993–1997

Treasurer, school newspaper

Awards National Merit Scholarship Winner, 1997
Dean's List, 8 semesters
Earned Honorable Mention in American
Legion Essay Contest for essay,
"Challenges Facing America in the 21st
Century"

Work Experience June 1996 to May 1997. Hampton Finer
Foods, Hoffman, Texas. *Cashier and
assistant at the sevice counter.*

June 1995 to September 1995. The Office
Depot, Hoffman, Texas. *Salesperson, waiting
on customers for an office-supply company.*

Community Activities June 1994 to May 1997. Volunteer reader at
Hoffman Rest Home. *Read to patients and
transcribed letters for them.*

Hobbies Cycling, figure-skating

References Available on request

**When submitting your
résumé to a particular
college, the "Education"
section appears in the most
prominent position.**

**Extracurricular activities
present a well-rounded
individual as well as a
successful student.**

**Remember to include
volunteer activities. They
show that you have a
sense of responsibility and
a sensitivity to the needs
of others.**

Small details can make a positive impression on the person who reads
your résumé. That's why it's important to check your résumé carefully
for accuracy and for correct grammar, usage, and spelling. You might
include a draft of your résumé in your writing portfolio and update it
as your skills, education, and experiences increase through high school.
Save a copy of your résumé on your computer or on a disk for
easy updating.

Using Electronic Resources

LIBRARY COMPUTER SERVICES

Electronic resources provide you with a convenient and efficient way to gather information. Many libraries offer computerized catalogs and a variety of other electronic resources.

Computerized Catalogs

You can search for a book in a library by typing the title, author, or subject into a computer. Most libraries also have software programs that allow you to search by typing in "keywords," that is, any word or combination of words found in the title, the subject, or the author's or publisher's name. When a book is not available, a librarian usually can search the catalogs of other libraries to locate another copy.

Other Electronic Resources

Many libraries offer a variety of electronic indexes. A newspaper index allows you to search the files of a particular newspaper, such as the *Chicago Tribune*, for recent articles on a chosen topic. *InfoTrac* provides a magazine index that lets you type in the subject you are interested in. The screen then displays a list of articles from several magazines that deal with that subject, with the most recent articles listed first. For each article, the index provides either an abstract (a kind of summary) or an extended citation that you can print directly from the screen. Another useful index, called *SIRS*, lists magazine and newspaper articles that concern social issues.

CD-ROM

A CD-ROM (compact disc–read-only memory) stores data that may include text, sound, photographs, and video. Almost any kind of information can be found on CD-ROMs, including

- encyclopedias, other reference books, and indexes
- news reports from newspapers, magazines, television, or radio
- literature and art collections
- back issues of magazines

ON-LINE RESOURCES

When you use your computer to communicate with another computer, you are working "on-line." On-line resources include commercial information services and Internet resources.

Commercial Information Services

Computer users can subscribe to various services that offer access to the following:

- up-to-date news, weather, and sports reports
- encyclopedias, magazines, newspapers, dictionaries, almanacs, and databases (collections of information)
- electronic mail (e-mail) to and from other users
- forums, or ongoing electronic conversations among users interested in particular topics
- the Internet

Internet

The **Internet**, a vast network of computers, allows computer users to exchange information with millions of other computer users throughout the world. News services, libraries, universities, researchers, organizations, government agencies, schools, and individuals use the Internet to communicate with people worldwide.

Finding and Exploring Sites The **World Wide Web**, one of the most popular resources on the Internet, connects pages of text and graphics stored on computers throughout the world. Each Web site has a specific location—somewhat like a postal address—known as its **URL**, short for Universal Resource Locator. When you type in a URL address in the Location field of a browser, your computer displays the corresponding site on your computer screen.

Following Links A Web site contains icons, pictures, or underlined and colored words and phrases called **links**. By clicking on a link, you immediately go to another site that contains related information. These links provide options, allowing you to explore subjects in more detail and to visit Web sites in the order you choose.

Using a Search Engine To find Web sites of interest to you, try using a **search engine**, or a navigational tool. Somewhat like an electronic card catalog, a search engine lets you search for sites by typing in a topic or key words.

COMPUSERVE

As you explore the Web, you can keep track of sites you have visited and may wish to revisit later. The browser that gives you access to the Internet probably contains a feature that lets you list visited sites for immediate access.

Yahoo, a popular search engine, offers an excellent menu of topic headings. Each time you click on a link, *Yahoo* scans thousands of databases to display the results on your computer screen.

Finding Newsgroups On the Internet you can visit thousands of "newsgroups" that contain articles about common areas of interest as well as postings from other computer users. You might even choose to add a posting of your own and chat electronically with others. Since computer users worldwide can access newsgroups, do not provide personal information if you decide to post something.

Exploring Other Areas of the Internet Tools such as Gopher and FTP (File Transfer Protocol) let you access other kinds of Internet documents. Available before the World Wide Web was created, Gopher and FTP contain pages of text without graphics or links. Gopher pages, which are run by colleges and universities, provide menus to conduct your searches. FTP servers store files such as transcripts of White House speeches. Even if your computer is connected to the Web, you might want to use Gopher and FTP to find information currently not available on the Web.

Using Information from the Internet

As you explore the Internet, you can print files or **download** them, that is, make an electronic copy to store on a computer. Be very careful when evaluating electronic information. Since computer users worldwide can put information on the Internet, the quality of the information varies greatly. Some information is excellent; other information, however, may be misleading, out of context, or even inaccurate. Consider the source of a piece of information carefully. National research centers such as the Library of Congress are highly reputable. Home pages created by individuals, however, usually are less reliable. Of course, it is important to check and then double check all information from electronic sources.

As when working with information from printed sources, avoid plagiarism, or appropriating someone else's words or ideas. Get into the habit of paraphrasing ideas—that is, stating them in your own words—and then crediting the source and listing the access date.

Follow these models to credit electronic sources in a list of works cited:

- **CD ROM**
  <u>The CIA World Factbook</u>. CD-ROM. Minneapolis: Quanta, 1992.
- **On-line Service**
  "Middle Ages." <u>Academic American Encyclopedia</u>. Online. Prodigy. 30 Mar. 1992.
- **An Electronic Text On-line**
  Shakespeare, William. <u>Hamlet</u>. <u>The Works of William Shakespeare</u>. Ed. Arthur H. Bullen. Stratford Town ED. Stratford-on-Avon: Shakespeare Head, 1911. Online. Dartmouth Coll. Lib. Internet. 26 Dec. 1992.

Publishing on the Internet

Why not consider publishing your own work on the Internet? If your school has a home page on the Web, you might publish your writing or a multimedia presentation on this site. You may also choose to send completed pieces electronically to an Internet site that showcases student writing, such as the McDougal Littell home page, at the following address.

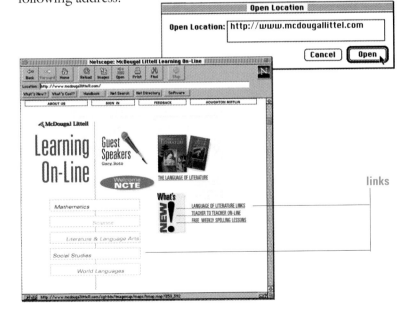

links

Writing with Computers

Word-processing programs provide tools for drafting, revising, and editing your writing. The techniques on pages 830–831 will help you incorporate technology into your writing process. This section will give you tips for creating visuals and for peer editing. Computers can help clarify and enhance your writing and also make it easy to share your writing with others.

USING VISUALS

Many computer programs include tools for creating graphics. Charts, graphs, diagrams, and pictures can enhance your writing by illustrating complex concepts, clarifying the steps in a process, or graphically summarizing statistical information. They can also make a page look more appealing. The visuals you choose will depend on the type of information you want to convey.

Kinds of Visuals

Combining words with pictures or graphics can increase a reader's understanding and enjoyment of your writing. Many computer programs enable you to create and insert graphs, tables, time lines, diagrams, and flow charts into your document. Some also allow you to import graphics and clip art into your document.

Tables Tables allow you to arrange facts or numbers into rows and columns so that your reader can compare information more easily. In many word-processing programs, you can create a table by choosing the number of vertical columns and horizontal rows you need and then entering information in each cell, as the illustration shows. A spreadsheet program provides you with a preset table that you can adapt to fit your data. Spreadsheet programs also perform mathematical functions for you.

Overview of Dance Budget

	A	B	C	D	E	F	G
1		1997	1997	1998	1998	1999	1999
2		Estimate	Actual	Estimate	Actual	Estimate	Actual
3	Decorations	$75.00	$98.00	$100.00	$112.28	$115.00	
4	Advertisements	$50.00	$45.50	$52.00	$56.72	$65.00	
5	Refreshments	$75.00	$100.00	$85.00	$92.50	$110.00	
6	Music	$200.00	$200.00	$150.00	$175.00	$175.00	
7	Souvenirs	$25.00	$25.00	$35.00	$35.00	$50.00	
8	TOTALS	$425.00	$468.50	$422.00	$471.50	$515.00	

Graphs and Charts A graph or chart allows you to present complex information in a single image. For example, you could use a line graph to show how a trend changes over time, a bar graph to compare statistics, or a pie chart to compare percentages. You might want to explore ways of displaying data in more than one visual format before deciding which will work best for you.

Other Visuals Art and design programs enable you to create visuals for your writing. Many programs include the following features:

- drawing tools that allow you to draw, color, and shade pictures you create and to import them into your text
- clip art that you can copy or change with drawing tools
- page borders that you can use to decorate title pages, invitations, or brochures
- text options that allow you to combine words with your illustrations
- tools for making geometric shapes in flow charts, time lines, and process diagrams
- tools that allow you to import your own photographic images to create slide shows or other multimedia presentations
- tools that allow you to animate your visuals

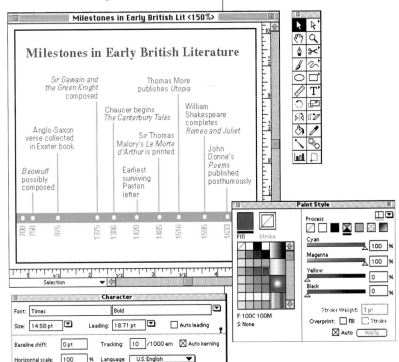

PEER EDITING YOUR WRITING

Improving your writing becomes easier when you use a word-processing program to elicit responses from your peers.

Peer Editing on a Computer The writer and the reader can both benefit from the convenience of peer editing "on screen." To use this method, be sure to first save your current draft and then make a copy of it for each of your peer readers. If your word-processing program has a

COMPUTER TIP

To help your readers easily understand the different parts of a pie chart or bar graph, use a different color or shade of gray for each section.

Technology **859**

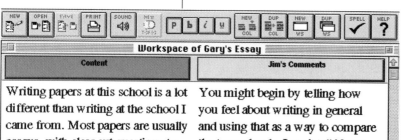

split-screen function, like Writing Coach, be sure to allow space in the side column so that your peer reader can write comments or questions. As an alternative, have your readers enter their comments within your text. In this case, have them use a different color, typeface, or type style from the one you used for your document.

Send a copy of your work to someone via e-mail or put it in someone's drop box if your computer is linked to others on a network. Ask each reader to include his or her initials in the file name. Then use the feedback of your peers to help you revise your writing. If your peer readers prefer to respond to a draft on paper rather than on the computer, remember to double-space or triple-space your document and leave wide margins so that your peer editors have space to ask questions, note their reactions, and make suggestions.

COMPUTER
TIP

Some progams include templates and stylesheet functions that make it easy to format your docmments.

EDITING AND FORMATTING

Once your readers have commented on your writing, you can use electronic editing tools to recheck your spelling and grammar and to address your readers comments. Consider each suggestion carefully before making a change. With spell-checking and grammar-checking software, in particular, you may often decide against a suggested change. And even with spell-checking software, you must be sure to proofread your work. The computer will not recognize that you may have used *lead* when you meant to use *led*. You can also use an electronic thesaurus to find synonyms for words you want to replace.

When you are satisfied with the content and the style of your writing, consider the format—the layout and appearance—of your work. Options such as type size and position of the text can help you distinguish the levels of headings or call attention to important inform-ation. The guidelines of your assignment or your plans for publishing your writing may affect the formats you choose. Keep your format simple. Your goal is to create an attractive, easy-to-read document.

Creating a Multimedia Presentation

A multimedia presentation is a combination of text, sound, and visuals such as photographs, videos, and animation. You can combine these elements in an interactive presentation—one in which the user chooses a path to follow in exploring the information.

LEARNING ABOUT MULTIMEDIA

To start planning a multimedia presentation, you need to know the options available to you. Ask your school's technology adviser which of the following elements you could include.

Sound

Including sound in your presentation can help your audience understand information in your written text. For example, the user may be able to listen to and learn from

- the pronunciation of an unfamiliar or foreign word
- a speech
- a recorded news interview
- a musical selection
- a dramatic reading of a work of literature

Photos and Videos

Photographs and live-action video clips can make your subject come alive. Here are some examples of visuals that can be downloaded or scanned in:

- video of news coverage of a historical event
- video of music, dance, or theater performances
- photos of an artist's work
- photos or video of a setting that is important to the text

Animation

Many graphics programs allow you to add animation, or movement, to the visuals in your presentation. Animated figures add to the user's enjoyment and understanding of what you present. You can use animation to illustrate

- the steps in a process
- changes in a chart, graph, or diagram
- ways your user can explore information in your presentation

PLANNING YOUR PRESENTATION

To plan a multimedia presentation, first choose your topic and decide what you want to include. For example, instead of writing a research report (see pages 270–300), Michele might want to create a multimedia presentation about King Arthur. She could include the following items:

- introductory text about King Arthur
- an excerpt from Geoffrey of Monmouth's version, with written commentary
- a videotaped classroom discussion about the versions written by Wace of Jersey and Chrétien de Troyes
- a dramatic reading from Malory's *Le Morte d'Arthur*
- a chronological gallery of works of art portraying Arthurian legend
- a text account of the real Arthur
- a time line setting the real Arthur in historical context

Next plan how you want your user to move through your presentation. You can choose one of the following ways to organize your presentation:

- step by step with only one path, or order, in which the user can see and hear the information
- a branching path that allows users to make some choices about what they will see and hear, and in what order

If you choose the second way—an interactive presentation—you need to map out your presentation in a flow chart, or navigation map. This will help you figure out the paths a user can take through your presentation. Each box in the navigation map on the following page represents a screen in Michele's presentation.

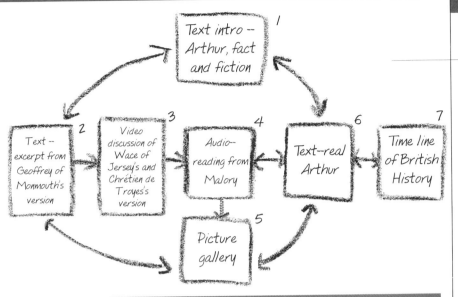

The writer has chosen to make part of the presentation linear. The user must follow screens 2–4—on early literary versions of the legend—in a fixed sequence. In other parts the user has more freedom to choose.

The diagram shows boxes labeled:

1. Text intro -- Arthur, fact and fiction
2. Text -- excerpt from Geoffrey of Monmouth's version
3. Video discussion of Wace of Jersey's and Chrétien de Troyes's version
4. Audio-- reading from Malory
5. Picture gallery
6. Text--real Arthur
7. Time line of British History

CREATING YOUR PRESENTATION

As you create your multimedia presentation, use the navigation map as a guide.

When you have decided on the content of a screen, it is helpful to sketch the screen out. Remember to include in your sketch the links you will create to other screens in the presentation. Refer to the navigation map to see what links you need to add to each screen.

The example below shows screen 5 from the navigation map above.

gallery. screen 5

Fact: the "real"Arthur   Literature: Geoffrey of Monmouth's retelling

PICTURE GALLERY OF KING ARTHUR   ● BACK TO START ◄►

Through the centuries there have been many artistic respresentations of King Arthur.

100%   Page 1

The user clicks on links to move to a different screen.

Navigational buttons can take the user back and forth, one screen at a time.

This screen contains works of art that have been scanned in.

and pronoun-antecedent agreement, 710–11
of pronouns, 549
subject-verb agreement in, 668
Numbers
apostrophes to show omission of, 804
commas with, 777
compound, 793
hyphens in, 793
plurals of, 804
use of, as numbers, 811
Numerical information, setting off, 795

O

O, Oh, capitalization of, 746
Objective case, 550, 693, 696–97
Objective complements, 576
Object of preposition, 561, 591
pronouns as, 697
subordinate clause as, 619
Object of verbs
complements, 573
direct objects, 574, 619, 696
indirect objects, 574–75, 696
pronouns as, 696
Observation and description
journalistic narrative, 54–65
personality profile, 66–69
video, 70–74
Observation charts, 341
Observations, 57
elaborating on, 333–36
Occupational interests and career choices
career search, 301–2
evaluating options, 507–9
investigating colleges, 511–15
investigating job opportunities, 509–10
Omissions, apostrophes to show, 804
On-line resources, 855–57
On the Lightside, 43, 108, 167, 197, 223, 259, 445, 490, 568, 590, 688, 783, 800
Onomatopoeia, 438, 846
Opinions, 380–81
unsupported, 402
or
in compound sentence, 773
compound subjects joined by, 670
and pronoun-antecedent agreement, 711
in series, 766
Oral presentation, 198–202
drafting, 201–2
planning, 200–1
publishing and presenting, 202
reviewing, 202

Organizing strategies. *See also* Graphic devices; Outlines
analysis, 123
cause-and-effect, 355–56
chronological, 29, 350
classification, 123, 352–53
comparison-and-contrast, 122, 352, 682
deductive, 356–57, 475
degree, 353–54
dialectic, 356
division, 352–53
feature analysis, 398
flashbacks, 29
general-to-specific order, 123
inductive, 356–57, 475
in medias res, 29, 371
inverted pyramid, 354
main idea and supporting details, 349
narration, 124
spatial, 350–52
Organizations, capitalization of, 751
Outlines, 826–27
in building argument, 504
capitalization in, 756
for debate speeches, 231–32
for literary analysis, 246
for oral presentation, 201
for research report, 282
periods in, 763
Overgeneralization, 477
Overloaded sentences, reducing, 403–6
Oxford Companion to English Literature, 498

P

P.M., 752
Panel discussion, 218
Paragraphs
coherence within, 384–88
unity within, 382–83
Parallelism, 410, 424
Parallel word groups, commas to indicate words left out, 778
Paraphrasing, 279, 483–84
Parentheses, 158, 795
in parenthetical definitions, 158
Parenthetical definitions, punctuating, 158
Parenthetical documentation, 486–88, 846
guidelines for, 284
Parenthetical expression, 770
commas to set off words of, 770, 785
Participial phrases, 598–600
essential/nonessential, 775

Photographer; **57:** © Marc Romanelli, The Image Bank, Chicago; **63:** © Kerry T. Givens, Bruce Coleman, Inc.; **66-67:** © Carl Sissac; **70-71:** *center* © H. Armstrong Roberts; **71:** *r* William Burlingham; **73:** Mick Wiggins; **79:** *l* The Bridgeman Art Library, *br* Wendell Minor; **80-81:** The Bridgeman Art Library; **84:** © 1984 Nancy Pendelton; **89:** Mary Lynn Blasutta; **93:** Stanislaw Fernandes; **96:** David Schleinkofer; **101:** Kurt Ritta; **102:** Guy Billout; **104-105:** © SuperStock; **105:** *r* Wendell Minor; **113:** *tr* Copyright Boeringer Ingelheim International GmbH, photo Lennart Nilsson;, *br* Rafal Olbinski; **117:** COPYRIGHT 1991 ARS NY/ADAGP; **118:** William Teason; **121:** Jeff Seaver; **123:** © Comstock, Inc.; **125:** Courtesy of Amoco Chemical Company; **126, 128, 129, 130:** © Comstock, Inc.; **132-133:** Copyright Boeringer Ingelheim International GmbH, photo Lennart Nilsson; **134:** © Lou Jones, The Image Bank, Chicago; **135:** Scott Harris; **137:** *t* © Comstock, Inc., *b* © Don Klumpf, The Image Bank, Chicago; **138-139:** Rafal Olbinski; **141:** David Wilcox; **146:** © Kobal Collection/SuperStock; **152:** Scot Stewart; **155:** John Rush; **159:** Scot Stewart; **167:** Steven Guarnaccia; **177:** *br* © Gary Irving, Tony Stone Worldwide; **185:** Drawing by Roland B. Wilson, © 1964 The New Yorker Magazine, Inc.; **189:** Evanston Township High School; **195:** Henrik Drescher; **198-199:** © Gary Irving, Tony Stone Worldwide; **202:** BASS & GOLDMAN, INC.; **206:** CALVIN AND HOBBES COPYRIGHT 1990 UNIVERSAL PRESS SYNDICATE. Reprinted with permission. All rights reserved; **207:** *l* © 1988 Doug Plummer, AllStock; **208:** *l* © 1988 Doug Plummer, AllStock; **208-209:** © Tony Stone Worldwide; **211:** Illustration © 1989 Farallon Computing, Inc. All rights reserved; **215:** Mark Frueh; **218:** Mark Chickinelli; **220:** Robert Neubecker; **236:** © 1980 Al Hirschfeld. Drawing reproduced by special arrangement with HirschfeldÚs exclusive representative, The Margo Feiden Galleries, Ltd., New York; **237:** *l* © Wendy Stone, Bruce Coleman, Inc., *tr* Penguin USA; **238-239:** © Wendy Stone, Bruce Coleman, Inc.; **239:** *br* © Robert P. Carr, Bruce Coleman, Inc.; **240:** © Wendy Stone, Bruce Coleman, Inc.; **240:** *b* © Robert P. Carr, Bruce Coleman, Inc.; **242:** "Born Free", by Edwin Salomon (Publisher: Jacques Soussana Graphics, Jerusalem); **247:** © Hervy, Robert Harding Picture Library; **253:** © UPI/Bettmann; **254-255:** *Because of Lozo Brown* by Larry L. King, illustrated by Amy Schwartz. Illustrations copyright © 1988 by Amy Schwartz. Reprinted by permission of the publisher, Viking Penguin, a division of Penguin Books USA, Inc.; **258:** CALVIN AND HOBBES COPYRIGHT UNIVERSAL PRESS SYNDICATE. Reprinted with permission. All rights reserved; **259:** Alabama Shakespeare Festival, photo by Overton; **263:** Charles White III; **268:** Bill Everitt, © Tom Stack and Associates; **271:** Mark Chickinelli; **274:** © Kobal Collection/SuperStock; **281:** © Robert Harding Picture Library; **281-284:** The Granger Collection, New York; **287:** credit unknown; **298:** The Bridgeman Art Library; **302:** © H. Armstrong Roberts; **308:** Spadem/Art Resource; **309, 310:** The Pierpont Morgan Library; **311:** *b* © Eric Meola, The Image Bank, Chicago; **312:** *b* © Michael Melford, The Image Bank, Chicago; **314:** Anthony Russo; **319:** Giraudon/Art Resource; **321:** Mark Stearney; **324:** Alan Nils Adler; **326:** The Bridgeman Art Library; **328:** Jeff Jackson; **330:** THE FAR SIDE COPYRIGHT 1987 & 1988 UNIVERSAL PRESS SYNDICATE. Reprinted with permission. All rights reserved; **334:** Sandy Skoglund; **351:** *l, r* © Photofest; **355:** *l* © Jeff Foott, Bruce Coleman, Inc., *r* © John E. Swedberg, Bruce Coleman, Inc., *b* © UPI/Bettmann; **369:** © Byron Gin, Stockworks; **383:** © Michael Fogden, Bruce Coleman, Inc.; **389:** Ed Lindlof; **390:** National Gallery of Art, Washington D.C.; **393:** *c* William Jordan; **396:** William McComb; **399:** Steven Pietzsch; **401:** The Far Side Cartoons by Gary Larson are reprinted by permission of Chronicle Features, San Francisco, CA; **402:** Henrik Drescher; **410:** Tim Lewis; **415:** Jeff Jackson; **416:** The Far Side Cartoons by Gary Larson are reprinted by permission of Chronicle Features, San Francisco, CA.; **418, 419:** Mirko Ilic; **421:** *r* © Stephen Marks, The Image Bank, Chicago/Stockphotos, Inc.; **426:** Reproduced from "A Study in Scarlet - The Hound of the Baskervilles" (1986), *World's Best Reading Series,* The Reader's Digest Association, Inc. Used by permission; **428:** © Comstock, Inc.; **431:** Warren Gebert; **437:** Katherine Mahoney; **440:** Jeff Seaver; **445:** Ralph J. Brunke; **451:** C.F. Payne; **455:** © BURK UZZLE/Lee Gross Associates; **466, 467:** © H. Armstrong Roberts; **469:** Barbara Maslen; **472:** John S. Dykes; **477:** The Far Side Cartoons by Gary Larson are reprinted by permission of Chronicle Features, San Francisco, CA.; **484:** © H. Armstrong Roberts; **485:** © W. Metzen, H. Armstrong Roberts; **488:** Larry Ross, The Image Bank; **492:** *l* © The Granger Collection; **501:** © Liberty Collection/The Image Bank, Chicago; **505:** Steven Guarnaccia; **511:** Bob Radigan; **524:** *t* © Dennis Hallinan 1990, FPG International, Corp., *b* Christopher Rory; **531:** Bill Bruning; **535:** *t* © Dennis Brack, Black Star, *b* © Jeff Smith, The Image Bank, Chicago; **537:** Elwood H. Smith; **540:** Tate Gallery, London/Art Resource; **548:** Courtesy of the Chicago Maritime Museum after a painting by Charles Vickery; **552:** Chris Moore; **557:** Edward W. Acuna; **558:** Scala/Art Resource; **560:** THE FAR SIDE COPYRIGHT 1986 UNIVERSAL PRESS SYNDICATE. Reprinted with permission. All rights reserved; **564:** David McCall Johnston; **568:** Deb Linc; **570:** © The Kobal Collection/SuperStock; **573:** © Kerry T. Givens, Bruce Coleman, Inc.; **577:** Bob Ziering; **578:** Giraudon/Art Resource; **585:** David Tamura; **587:** © Adobe Systems Incorporated. All rights reserved; **591:** Photographic Collection, Museum of Modern Art, New York; **597:** David Wilcox; **600:** Library of Congress; **604:** *l* Don Doll, S.J., *r* © John Shaw, Bruce Coleman, Inc.; **605:** Mark English; **607:** David Montiel; **610:** *b* © Wardene Weisser, Bruce Coleman, Inc., *t* © William Amos, Bruce Coleman, Inc.; **613:** The Bridgeman Art Library; **617:** Karen Barbour; **618:** Steve Johnson; **619:** *t* © SuperStock, *b* © Photofest; **623:** © Design Photographers International, Inc.; **636:** John Rush; **638:** *bl* © Edwin Santos, Bruce Coleman, Inc., *br* © Frink Waterhouse, H. Armstrong

Sally Wern Comport; **653:** Guy Billout; **662:** © B. Taylor, H. Armstrong Roberts; **672:** © O. Rebbot, Stock Boston; **677:** Barron Storey; **679:** Robert Crawford; **681:** Doug Johnson; **688:** c The Far Side Cartoons by Gary Larson are reprinted by permission of Chronicle Features, San Francisco, CA; **694:** t left Kurt Hansen, b © UPI/Bettmann; **698:** Greg Spalenka; **703:** Courtesy of Graceland; **705:** Giraudon/Art Resource; **707:** © Ellen Schuster, The Image Bank, Chicago; **708:** Gary Kurtz, © 1983 Lucas Film, Ltd.; **712:** Produced with permission of the U.S.P.S., illustration by Bob Peak; **716:** Museum of Fine Arts, Springfield, MA; **718:** James Endicott; **721:** Bartolomeo Bettera, Harmony; **722:** Liz Kathman-Grubow; **723:** Bridgeman Art Library; **727:** Dickran Palulian; **731:** Peter Stackpole, Life Magazine © Time Warner, Inc.; **736:** Scala/Art Resource; **747:** © H. Armstrong Roberts, Inc.; **751:** National Museum of American Art/Art Resource; **753:** © Al Gardner, Tony Stone Worldwide; **758:** Alan James Robinson; **760:** Gary Larson, Universal Press Syndicate; **765:** © Anthony Suau, Black Star; **768:** Musee d'Orsay/Art Resource; **776:** Scala/Art Resource; **779:** © Spencer Jones, Bruce Coleman, Inc.; **780:** Bob Conge; **785:** Bridgeman Art Library; **790:** Christine Bunn; **795:** t © Wide World Photos, Inc.; **797:** The Bridgeman Art Library; **804:** Jozef Sumichrast; **806:** l © The Granger Collection, r © The Image Bank, Chicago; **809:** Giraudon/Art Resource; **811:** © The Granger Collection; **819:** © Kaz Mori, The Image Bank, Chicago; **823:** Eugene Mihaesco; **855:** top Prodigy Internet and the Prodigy Internet logo are trademarks of Prodigy Services Corporation. For subscription information, call 1-800-PRODIGY or visit our Web Site at www.prodigy.com; center Copyright © 1997 America On Line. Used by permission; bottom CompuServe logo courtesy of CompuServe, Incorporated; **856, 857:** Copyright © 1996 Netscape Communications Corp. All rights reserved. This page may not be reprinted or copied without the express written permission of Netscape. Netscape Communication Corporation has not authorized, sponsored, or endorsed, or approved this publication and is not responsible for its content. Netscape and the Netscape Corporate logos are trademarks of their respective owners. **859:** Adobe and Adobe Illustrator are trademarks of Adobe Systems Incorporated; **861, 863:** computer screen Used with permission of Hewlett Packard; **861, 863** left: inset Detail of King Arthur from the Nine Worthies (about 1490), artist unknown. Tapestry, Historiches Museum, Basel (Switzerland)/Art Resource, New York; **863:** inset, right The Granger Collection, New York.

Cover Photography: Ryan Roessler